INVESTMENTS
An Introduction to Analysis and Management

PRENTICE-HALL INTERNATIONAL INC., London
PRENTICE-HALL OF AUSTRALIA PTY. LTD., Sydney
PRENTICE-HALL OF CANADA, LTD., Toronto
PRENTICE-HALL OF INDIA PRIVATE LTD., New Delhi
PRENTICE-HALL OF JAPAN, INC., Tokyo

SECOND EDITION

INVESTMENTS

An Introduction to
Analysis and Management

Frederick Amling
Professor of Finance, The George Washington University

Prentice-Hall, Inc., *Englewood Cliffs, New Jersey*

To Gwen, Jeff, Scott, and Terry

13–504258–5
Library of Congress Catalog Card Number 75–98679

Current printing (last digit)
10 9 8 7 6 5 4 3 2 1

Printed in the United States of America

PREFACE

This book covers the investment function with breadth and flexibility. It is basically descriptive and illustrative, yet it calls for an analytical approach, particularly in investment analysis and portfolio management decisions. The chapter material represents only a portion of the complete text; it is supplemented by problems at the end of each chapter. The most efficient allocation of time would be to read and understand each chapter, answer the discussion questions, and complete the problems, which highlight the principal points of the text and focus attention on the major analytical concepts presented.

  Investments is directed to those who must make decisions about their own funds or about funds they manage for institutional or eleemosynary investors. In our growing industrial society, more and more people are achieving the financial affluence that requires sophisticated financial decisions. As an individual's total income goes up, his discretionary income increases at a faster relative rate; thus dollars are made available for the purchase of investment securities and other financial obligations. The individual must make the best possible decision about the allocation of his investible funds. This book should provide a frame of reference in which better investment decisions can be reached. Account executives, analysts, counselors, or portfolio managers, those who are also called upon to manage the investment accounts of other people, must understand the needs and motivations of their clients; the text offers a background for the individual who will invest for others. Many people who achieve financial status and recognition are called upon to serve institutional investors —for example, colleges and universities—and the book familiarizes these individuals with the policies and objectives to help them solve the investment problems of these institutions. The approach, therefore, is oriented both to the person about to embark on an investments career and to the decision-making individual who is acting for himself and for others.

In many aspects this is a methodological book. It discusses investment functions, explaining the *how* of the decision-making process as well as the *why*. Answering questions like "Why is this a good company?" or "Why did you decide to buy *B* company and sell *S* company?" is often difficult unless one demonstrates how the decision was reached. The investor needs a frame of reference in which to make a value judgment based upon the risks and rewards of investment. His field of reference will widen and develop with experience. As his knowledge broadens, he will become a better and more sophisticated judge of investment values, and, it is hoped, a more successful investor.

The text presentation is designed to bring realism to the decision-making process, particularly in the areas of company analysis and portfolio management. Each chapter in these two areas first discusses the principles involved; second, the principles are demonstrated by practical cases providing an analysis that allows a tentative decision to be reached; third, problems based on the principles and descriptive material are raised at the end of each chapter, allowing the reader to apply what he has learned and to exercise his decision-making ability. It is not enough to tell the beginning investor what to do. He must be shown one alternative method of decision making, experience the method, and thus learn its good and bad points.

The book is divided into eight parts, arranged to follow closely the investment function and the investment decision-making process in practice and theory.

Part 1 provides a discussion of the concept of risk associated with securities investment, and attempts to provide measures of risk that can be used to make investment decisions relating to risk and rewards. It also explains the investment function; presents an array of securities for investment, ranked and identified by specific risk; provides an indication of range of yields; and indicates the sources of saving for investment. These are related to the financial position of the investor and his ability to assume risk.

Part 2 describes the various types of securities available to meet the needs of the investor. Fixed-income securities (including government, municipal, and corporate bonds) are examined first, then preferred stock and common stock; the advantages and disadvantages of each type are discussed in terms of the risk associated with each, the place they might have in the investor's portfolio, and the reward they might offer. Sources of investment information and the ratings of various securities are introduced in the discussion.

Part 3 deals with the valuation of common stocks. Emphasis is placed upon the present-value method for determining whether a common stock will provide the investor with a satisfactory return based upon future flows of income and capital. There is some discussion of the theory of valuation, and up-to-date literature on the subject is cited. A computer program is presented to aid the analyst or investor in obtaining valuation information and help in the decision-making process.

Part 4 describes the environment or the mechanics of investment; it tells where securities are purchased, who provides the selling and buying service, how the investor is protected, and what it costs to buy or sell securities. Criteria for selecting a broker, from both the individual and institutional points of view, are discussed. Regulation of the security market through the New York Stock Exchange and the SEC is discussed to indicate the amount of regulation going on in the industry and the ethics involved.

Part 5 examines the growth of the national economy and the industries included in the economy. Forecasts established by the National Bureau of Economic Research, McGraw-Hill, and others are presented along with current information published in *Business Cycle Developments*. The growth cycle of industry is presented in the belief that it is wise to invest in expanding industries in a national economy that is growing at present and in all likelihood continuing to grow in the future, although perhaps not steadily.

Part 6 provides a method of investment analysis for companies, with emphasis on (a) competitive position or growth characteristics, (b) earnings and profitability, (c) operating efficiency, (d) long-term financial analysis, (e) management analysis—with professional comments about personal interviews with management, and (f) stock price, price-earnings ratio, yield, and the investment decision. All these factors relate to and affect the price that must be paid for future earnings. Attention is focused upon the prospect for future earnings and whether the present price (when related to the amount and stability of future earnings) will provide a satisfactory yield commensurate with the risk involved. This type of analysis should lead to intelligent investment decisions. A complete case study of the electronics and the electronic products industry is presented, with the entire method of analysis described in the text brought to bear, to illustrate how one would reach a decision on whether to invest.

Part 7 presents a discussion of stock market forecasting, the independence of the stock market, and the part market analysis plays in the investment decision-making process. Point-and-figure charting and other more common methods of technical forecasting are presented. Psychological aspects of the market are mentioned.

Part 8 directs attention to the problems of portfolio management, in both theory and practice. A brief introduction is given to investment theory and what is being attempted in the process of managing a portfolio. Alternative solutions to the problem of management and the timing of the purchase and sale of securities are presented. Several authentic cases that portray the problems of the income and growth investor are included. The portfolio policies of the major institutional investors in the United States are discussed. Using the criteria of performance established earlier in the text, several portfolios are examined and yield measured to determine how well they would have performed in the interval between the first and second editions of this book. It is interesting to note that the decisions made in the past were not far off their mark with no interim management of the portfolios.

The second edition of *Investments* is based on many years of experience in teaching investments, both at the University of Pennsylvania and at Miami University, Oxford, Ohio, and on the author's practical experience as an investment advisor in putting to work the theory of investment analysis and portfolio management.

Many have given invaluable assistance in the book's preparation. The author wishes to acknowledge the late Jackson Belden Dennison, Professor of Finance, Miami University, and the late Professor Julius Grodinsky of the Wharton School, for their excellence in teaching and research, which provided me with a deep interest in investments. My sincere thanks to Dr. Jacob O. Kamm who, by his example of stimulating teaching and productive scholarship while at Baldwin-Wallace College, provided me with the initial inspiration to enter the field of finance. Appreciation must be expressed to Dean Willis Winn of the Wharton School for his continued interest in my career, to Dr. Bruce Ricks of the University of California at Los Angeles, and to Dr. Charles Linke of the University of Illinois, for their invaluable editorial and conceptual help in reading the manuscript to improve the product. My sincere thanks to Professor Harold G. Fraine, Graduate School of Business, University of Wisconsin; Professor Frederick G. Stubbs, Jr., University of Illinois–Chicago Circle; Professor James F. Volk, Mary College; and Dr. Alan J. Zakon, Vice-President, Boston Consulting Group, for their excellent and helpful reviews.

Many of my colleagues have provided me with valuable information over the years. I would like to mention particularly Gilbert Davis, William D. Gradison, and Jim Hutton of W. E. Hutton & Co., Al White and Al Carlotti of A. J. White and Carlotti, Inc., Dr. Robert H. Parks of Francis I. DuPont, James F. O'Neill of Boyd and Company, and William Craig and Elliot Fried, partners in Eastman Dillon, Union Securities & Co. To Joe Marcum of the Ohio Casualty Company and Henry Blohm of the Provident Mutual Life Insurance Company go thanks for their helpful comments on insurance, and to Dr. George Ellis, President, Keystone Custodian Funds, Inc., for the opportunity to participate in the formation of a new fund. I would like to express my gratitude to Fred Easter, Charles Briqueleur, and Jim Bacci, editors with Prentice-Hall, for their help in bringing this manuscript to completion, and to Betty Neville and Rita DeVries for their excellent editorial assistance.

Appreciation must be given to Mrs. Hugh Clawson, Mrs. Sarah Verges, Mrs. Barbara Loy and Mrs. Shirley Rowe for their assistance in typing the manuscript.

Above all, I wish to give special thanks to my wife for her help, encouragement, and patience during the writing of the book, and her continued assistance through the difficult process of revision.

FREDERICK AMLING

CONTENTS

I

RISK, THE INVESTMENT PROCESS, AND SAVINGS

II

THE ALTERNATIVE INVESTMENT OUTLETS FOR FUNDS

V

AN APPRAISAL
OF THE NATIONAL ECONOMY AND INDUSTRY—
PAST, PRESENT, AND FUTURE

VI

COMPANY ANALYSIS, YIELD, AND THE INVESTMENT DECISION

I

RISK,
THE INVESTMENT
PROCESS,
AND SAVINGS

1

INVESTMENT AND RISK

The Investment Process and Risk

The American economy has grown from its revolutionary beginnings almost two hundred years ago to become the most productive in the world. The productive capacity created in the process of this growth has allowed the citizens of the United States to enjoy a continually rising standard of living. In no small measure, the economic success of our country can be attributed to a people who in their private lives and in their commerce have acted freely and with a minimum of government control. The capitalistic system as it manifests itself in our country has provided a framework of economic and financial stability that has allowed individuals, institutions, and businesses opportunities to invest their capital profitably. This economic stability, coupled with the political stability of our federal and state governments, has resulted in the growth of large-scale productive enterprises and financial institutions. The growth of the corporate form of organization with its inherent basis of private property ownership has provided a vehicle for raising capital to meet corporate growth, and at the same time has provided outlets for the savings of millions of Americans. Few countries compare with the United States in providing their citizens with such well-developed outlets for their savings and investments; their economic structures do not offer as many financial instruments with such varying degrees of risks and rewards to meet different individual and institutional needs as we have in the United States.

Our economic structure is changing. The large multinational corporation dominates the economics of our culture, and corporate planning is changing the market system as it has been developed in the United States.[1] The capital for growth is being generated internally by the largest corporations and financial institutions. There is less dependence on the capital markets for funds than in prior years. The trend of change in society will continue in the future. Our society will undoubtedly retain private property ownership and all that it implies as its basic foundation; capital will be transferred through existing security markets; new capital will be raised in the investment banking process. These institutions will continue to function and grow. The implication is present, however, that if our growth as a capitalistic nation in a competitive world society is to continue, it must depend upon a people who are educated and knowledgeable about investment opportunities, who are willing to accept the risks of our economic system as well as the rewards, and who are willing to save and invest their funds to insure the future prosperity and world position of our society. The study and understanding of the subject of investments is worthwhile, for it enables individuals acting for themselves or for the institutions for which they are employed to benefit themselves, their fellowmen, and society as a whole.

The Meanings of Investment

This book is about securities investment in new and existing corporations. The word *investment*, however, has many meanings. In the academic community, one must be careful to differentiate between investment in the economic or business sense and investment in the financial or securities sense. There is no question about the meaning of investment to a member of the brokerage community. But even here, the concept of investment means one thing to one broker and something else to another. The shades of meaning may be slight; nonetheless, the difference in definitions might lead to misunderstanding.

If we leave the sophisticated area of the financial and academic community, we find an even wider difference in the meanings of the word. Many times laymen, who are part of the 24 million investors in the United States, misuse the term. Investment is often confused with the purchase of durable consumer items that have little to do with financial or business investment. It is necessary to differentiate between the concepts of investment so that we may clearly understand what it is we are talking about. The discussion will focus on three current uses of the word *investment*: consumer investment, business or economic investment, and financial or securities investment.

1 John Kenneth Galbraith, *The New Industrial State* (Boston: Houghton Mifflin Company, 1967), Chap. 1.

Consumer Investment

Consumer investment is really not a form of investment at all. The label is attached because consumers use the term; it is often used as a defense or rationalization for what the consumer has purchased. The term actually relates to the purchase of durable goods by consumers. Many individuals, for example, consider the purchase of an automobile an investment. Still others speak of the purchase of a vacuum cleaner or an automatic washing machine as an investment. The favorite expression used to describe this area of investment is, "I bought a new car. It was expensive but it will be a good investment." The correct use of the word *investment* precludes the consumer definition, since no rate of return is involved, nor is a financial return or capital growth expected.

Consumers do purchase houses and there is an investment aspect of home ownership. The purchase of a house is a way of saving money; that is, the mortgage is paid off over a period of time, allowing the owner to build up equity. The mortgage payments represent a form of forced savings. This is not investing one's funds, but it is a saving process. One very real reason why the purchase can be considered an investment is that it might earn a profit in the form of dollar income or appreciation in value. If an individual purchased a house as a residence and it increased in value sharply because of an increase in demand, it would also become a profitable investment, which would lead to the conclusion that it was a good "investment," or possibly a good "speculation," depending upon the circumstances.

Real estate may be purchased for investment or income purposes as a long-term hedge against inflation. No securities are involved. The owner either manages the property himself or hires a manager to undertake the chores of renting the premises, collecting the rents, and generally maintaining the property; however, this is not consumer investment but falls into the classification of a business or economic investment. Care and analysis are required in making investments of this type. They are usually discussed under the subject of real estate or real estate finance; however, although an important outlet for capital, they will not be discussed in this book.

Business or Economic Investment

A business or economic investment refers to a situation in which money is used to purchase business assets to produce income that is adequate compensation for the risks involved in the venture. Obviously, the profit motive is the initiating force in the transaction. The businessman is thoroughly willing to purchase productive assets to earn a profit and is aware of the risks involved. The business or economic concept of investment assumes that new productive facilities will emerge in the process of seeking a profit. A businessman who leases a store and invests in furniture, fixtures, and inventory is investing in the business or economic sense. He hopes that these assets will be productive, and when he combines his managerial talents with labor that he hires, he will be able to sell his product and earn a profit on his investment.

The large paper company that buys a new paper-making machine and purchases land and raw materials to be used with the machine is said to be investing. The company is investing in the real and economic sense of the word. The creation of the new plant and equipment has brought into being a new productive facility that it is hoped will return a profit. Possibly, additional securities will be sold by the company to finance the project. This represents the source of the money for the project but does not change the character of the investment.

Economic or business investment, therefore, is any investment in real assets that brings about the production of goods and services for the purpose of a profit commensurate with the risks involved. In all these situations a thorough economic and financial analysis is made about each project to determine the likelihood of success.

Financial or Securities Investment

Financial investment is a term often used by investors to differentiate between the pseudo-investment concept of the consumer and the real investment of the businessman or the economist. Financial investment refers to the purchase of an asset in the form of securities that will produce a profit for the investor. The investor assumes all the risks involved in such a purchase but attempts to keep these risks to a minimum and at the same time to maximize profits. Unlike the businessman, the securities investor has no direct control of the real assets. He must rely upon the talents of others to manage the assets for him. No new productive assets are created as a result of financial investment as is the case in business or economic investment. In fact, the investor usually purchases the existing securities from another owner. Sometimes, of course, the individual does buy securities from the company that wishes to raise money to build a new manufacturing plant. This results in investment in the economic and business sense and also represents investment in the financial sense. However, this is the exception rather than the general rule. The individual who buys the security gives up his claim on dollars for a claim on future income and profits, but no new productive assets are necessarily created in the process. It is simply a case of two individuals exchanging a claim on one asset for a claim on another. It is assumed that the investor, in the process of selecting securities for investment, does make a thorough analysis before making a decision based upon established standards of appraisal.

A Definition of Investment

Financial or securities investment is the focal point of this book. There-fore, the definition will be couched in these terms. The discussion sug-gests that *investment* is the purchase of a security or securities that upon an appropriate analysis offer safety of principal and a satisfactory yield, commensurate with the risks assumed over a long period of time.

A closer examination of the definition of investment makes it clear that we are investing in the existing securities of the corporation— common stock, preferred stock, and various types of bonds. The defini-tion further assumes that through a rational process of investment analy-sis, securities will be selected by the use of qualitative and quantitative methods that will result in better decisions being made than by any other system. The analysis of all pertinent information allows us to determine for a specific security the degree of safety of principal, the degree of risk involved, and whether the rate of return expected is satis-factory. All these factors are subject to judgment. The investor in the analysis process will compare one security with other securities based on standards imposed by sound financial practice. The analyst considers the basic and important variables, such as the appropriate price in rela-tion to future earnings expected from the company, and the degree of risk and the possibility of loss that might result.

Safety of principal varies with the type of security that is being analyzed. A bond is secure if its maturity value and interest are ade-quately covered by assets and income of a business. A common stock is secure if the price at which it is purchased is realistic in terms of future expectations of earnings and dividends. A satisfactory yield in-cludes both current income in the form of interest and dividends over a period of time, and capital gains brought about by the appreciation of value of a security. What is a satisfactory yield is dependent upon who the investor is and the risks involved, and must be defined as satis-factory by the individual or institution doing the investing. One book defines a satisfactory return as "any rate or amount of return, however low, which the investor is willing to accept, provided he acts with reason-able intelligence."[2] By this concept one investor might earn a yield of 4 percent and consider it a satisfactory yield. A second investor might earn a yield of 7 percent and have an unsatisfactory investment simply because he expected a 10 percent yield.

In our discussion, we assume that we wish to keep risk to a mini-mum and to maintain a fair degree of safety and security. We do not

2 Benjamin Graham, David L. Dodd, and Sidney Cottle, *Security Analysis*, 4th
  ed. (New York: McGraw-Hill Book Company, 1962), p. 50.

care to accept undue risk of loss of our principal investment. We might, as investors, desire to accept the risks involved with the purchase of speculative securities, providing we are certain the rewards that we can expect in the future adequately compensate for the risks involved. Securities may be classified according to the risk that they possess. This is a value judgment made on the basis of the observation and experience of past performance. Such things as the stability of earnings, of price, and of yield become important factors in determining risk. Past performance of securities is not a perfect measure. It is not highly scientific nor mathematical. Nonetheless, it is one guide we may use in making investment decisions. The risks we assume are caused by our inability to forecast or foresee the future perfectly. Financial success in the last analysis will come to those investors who have the ability of accurately judging future events. Our major concern, then, is the future success of our present decisions in a risk-laden and uncertain world.

The classification of investment securities by types of risk is an area that is now being explored by academic theoreticians and financial practitioners. The definition of a satisfactory investment provided by Graham, Dodd, and Cottle[3] does not suggest that anyone can establish a relationship between risk and reward and what is satisfactory. A value judgment is being made, for example, when a man says, "I'm willing to accept a 4 percent yield as satisfactory." The evidence suggests that in actual practice he should accept a greater risk with greater rewards. Since there are broad classifications of risk and of securities, the knowledge of the amount of risk present and the proper classification and identification of risk by security will enable the investor to make a better decision as to what is satisfactory for him.

The time period of investment is an important and integral part of the definition of investment. The time period helps, too, to distinguish speculation from investment. Investment is essentially long term, with the range in time from three to five years and as long as twenty years. An optimum time period for investment in our technological society would be five years. This period is long enough to eliminate the effects of the business cycle and the market cycle on security prices and yet is short enough to achieve economic results from new products, new developments, and new ideas. Often, a proper orientation to time helps the investor to achieve a satisfactory yield simply because his philosophy of being long term allows him to ignore the stock market cycles and hold for economic growth. The time period alone is not sufficient in the last analysis to differentiate investment from speculation. Long-term speculators, buying little-known companies in the hope that they will grow up over the next five years, are certainly speculating. In this par-

3 Graham, Dodd, and Cottle, *Security Analysis*, p. 50.

ticular case, we must rely upon the degree of risk rather than upon the time period for the final determination of investment or speculation.

Investment and Speculation Distinguished

The distinction between investment and speculation must be made clear, even though it is easier to state what an investment is and what a speculation is than to distinguish one from the other. At times it is impossible to distinguish between investment and speculation. Two individuals might buy the same security at the same time, yet one person is investing his money and the other is speculating with his. Assume, for example, that two individuals each bought 100 shares of IBM. One person makes a thorough analysis of the company and reaches the conclusion that IBM will provide a yield of 12 percent over the next five years. The yield includes both income and capital gains and is a satisfactory yield considering the risk and uncertainty involved. At the same time the second individual buys IBM and assumes that the price will increase 10 percent in the next thirty days. The second person has also made a thorough analysis. Which then is the speculation and which is the investment? We would have to conclude that the first alternative was the investment and the second was the speculation for three basic reasons. First, a greater degree of risk is involved in the second transaction than in the first. Hence, there is less security of principal. For some unexpected reason the stock may drop in the next thirty days, which would result in a loss to the speculator rather than a gain. This is a judgment in probability. Given a projected growth rate of earnings and price, there is a smaller probability that the price for IBM will be higher in the short term than in the long run. A second distinction is that the purchaser who buys IBM with the expectation of capital gain is not interested in moderate yield over a period of time nor is he interested in current income. He is interested in buying low and selling high, making a large capital gain and moving on to another security; therefore, he is speculating. No moral judgment is being made of this activity. We are interested only in what the speculator is doing in the securities market. A third difference is the time period of the investor versus the speculator. The longer time period orientation of the investor, as mentioned before, automatically places him in the category of our definition of investment.

Some people will argue that the first investor might also suffer a loss over time and might not earn a yield of 12 percent. This, therefore, makes him a speculator. Again, these critics may be right. The individual might be a speculator, but the speculation is for a longer period of time. Or he may have erred in his investment judgment.

We can distinguish a speculation from an investment in other ways. First, there is a greater emphasis upon conservatism in the investment transaction than in the speculative one. Therefore there is a greater interest in safety of principal. Second, and perhaps more important, the investor is interested in the internal condition of the company and its earning power. The speculator, on the other hand, is usually interested in trading in securities; he ignores dividends, accepts more risk, and is interested in the technical market position and the technical position of the stock, which includes such things as a study of the price movement, the pattern of prices, and the volume of shares traded.

One of the best-known exponents of market trading rather than fundamental investing is Gerald M. Loeb of E. F. Hutton & Company, a well-known Wall Street brokerage firm. Mr. Loeb has set forth his trading concepts in several articles in various journals and in particular in his book, *The Battle for Investment Survival*.[4] The best-known work in the field of traditional security analysis that follows the fundamental approach is *Security Analysis*.[5] Interestingly, each approach has been successful in the application of its principles. Both demand intelligence and a great deal of investigation. The Loeb approach is that of the intelligent speculator and the *Security Analysis* approach that of the intelligent investor. The plan of this book is to follow primarily the latter. There is no room, however, in either approach for unintelligent and unknowledgeable investment or speculation.

The Investment Process

When we defined the word *investment*, we were actually summarizing a whole series of activities that result in the purchase of securities providing the investor with a satisfactory yield commensurate with risk. It is much easier to define an investment than to make a satisfactory investment, even though the definition has its weaknesses and investment and speculative activities are difficult to differentiate. We must devote our attention not to what an investment is but to how we can investigate, analyze, and then select the securities that will allow us to make a satisfactory investment. In order to accomplish this end, we should be aware of the ingredients in the process of making a satisfactory investment and of what constitutes the investment function.

As an individual or institutional investor, we require substantial knowledge in order to do an intelligent job of investment. Basic information required includes the following topics presented in order of im-

---

4 G. M. Loeb, *The Battle for Investment Survival* (New York: Simon and Schuster, Inc., 1957). Other proponents of technical trading in the stock market are Joseph E. Granville, *A Strategy of Daily Stock Market Timing for Maximum Profit* (Englewood Cliffs, N.J.: Prentice-Hall, Inc., 1960), and R.O. Edwards and John Magee, Jr., *Technical Analysis of Stock Trends*, 4th ed. (Springfield, Mass.: Stock Trend Service, 1958).

5 Graham, Dodd, and Cottle, *Security Analysis*.

pact and logic, not necessarily in order of occurrence. If we were to follow events from the practical point of view of the individual investor, we would begin the analysis with the subject, "Where Can I Invest My Money?" or with an even more fundamental question, "Where Can I Get Some Money To Invest?" Needless to say, this cannot be solved easily. The subject will be covered in a discussion of portfolio management and its relation to risk, after we have covered some of the basic fundamentals of security analysis and the stock market. The first practical area we must understand is the nature and prevalence of risk associated with investment in securities. This includes an understanding of the behavioral characteristics of investors and how they react to risk. We must also understand the relationship of the risk associated with our nonsecurity assets and the impact that they might have on our ability to assume risk. Certainly, we must identify the variety of risks associated with each of the individual securities available to us for investment and the risk associated with our other financial assets.

Second, we must assume that money is available for investment. One of the problems of investments, however, is the source of investment funds and its impact upon risk. Many investors today are turning to money sources for investment that would not have been considered in past years because of financial conservatism. Our personal financial position goes a long way toward determining what kind of investor we will be and where we will invest our funds. Institutional investors obviously do not have a problem of the availablity of funds. However, the institutional and fiduciary relationship with owners and customers determines the nature of the investment program and degree of risk that they are willing to accept.

Third, we must obtain a thorough knowledge of the individual securities available for investment that will result in an optimum solution to our investment problem. This encompasses a broad spectrum of securities, from ownership instruments such as common stock to creditorship securities such as mortgage bonds and general credit bonds. In our information system, we must have specific information about the expectation of yield or return on investments. We must also have knowledge of the risks and rewards associated with nonsecurity investment as a part of our total financial plan. Without the specifics of risks and rewards, we cannot do an intelligent job of making the best investment decisions.

Fourth, we must have a method of economic and security analysis that will allow us to make the best possible selection of securities to meet our investment objectives. This automatically suggests an analysis of the national economy and the industries within the economy, and an analysis of a company in the economic environment with emphasis placed upon the analysis of the company's securities. The focal point for the analysis of the individual security relates to a forecast of the future earnings potential of the company and the degree of risk associated with these estimates—that is, the certainty or probability that the earnings pattern in the future is likely to occur or recur. It includes an analysis of what the investor will receive based upon the price and price-earnings relationship at the time of investment. This is the part of the investment referred to as the valuation appraisal. This coupled with portfolio management is the heart of investment.

Every decision that is made in the investment process by the investor should be based on an analysis of expected future events. Investment success is predicated on the ability to adequately and accurately forecast a pattern of future events based on observations of the past and present, and predictions and statements about the future. In a nutshell, it is the fundamental question of what we pay, what we receive, and how secure and accurate will be the results when we put money into the purchase of securities. Needless to say, the whole area of decision making is charged with emotion. This in itself is a special study that is required for success in the investment arena.

Fifth, it is imperative that we have an information system that allows us to keep up to date with the securities in which we invest and with those in which we would like to invest. This might mean for an individual complete reliance on the *Wall Street Journal*, annual reports of the company, materials in the library, and information obtained from the research department of a brokerage house. The professional analyst would rely upon a careful study of the management of the companies under analysis. The professional would use advanced computer technology to assist in the analysis of the economic and financial variables. It is my intent to develop the information system along with the discussion of the investment process, rather than to devote a separate chapter to sources of information. Included in this subject is an understanding of the mechanics of the securities market and the behavioral relationships in the industry, including the relationship of the broker to the investor.

Sixth, in understanding the investment process, we must understand the behavior of the stock market itself. The stock market might or might not behave as we would expect based on a fundamental analysis. The short-term orientation of the brokerage community makes the stock market susceptible to extreme variations based on the events of the moment. Some brokers consider the short term the totality of the securities business; speculation is their activity. Many technical traders attempt to make decisions based upon the short-term technical position of the market itself. Certainly, the psychology of the market and its expectations have an important bearing on the timing of our investments. As far as possible we must understand the stock market and its direction.

Seventh, once we have developed an understanding of the risks and rewards in investment based upon the method of analysis of a changing securities market, we must put our knowledge together and solve the investment problem of individual and institutional investors. It is therefore imperative that we understand what is referred to as portfolio management, which is the practice that allows investors to achieve their investment goals. This requires an understanding of the financial, personal, and psychological characteristics and motives of the investor. We must select from among all alternatives those that will give us an optimum combination of risk and reward. We must continue this process in the future by reacting to changes in individual securities that optimize the investor's investment program. These steps simultaneously represent the investment process. We will begin by examining the nature of risk.

Investment Risks

Understanding and measuring risk is fundamental to the investment process. Frequently, the problems of risk associated with security investment are ignored and only the rewards are emphasized. It is appropriate, therefore, to begin our study with the nature of investment risks. Not only will this increase our awareness of the investment problem, but it will serve to unite the investment process into a logical whole until we reach the point in our discussion where we consider portfolio management and risk.

When we consider investing our money, we are immediately aware of the conflict between our desire for the safety of principal and the amount of future yield we want to achieve. Virtually all our decisions revolve around this notion of risk versus reward. Certainly, we want to achieve a substantial yield from our investment, but we are not always willing to accept the risk associated with the high yields we anticipate. We often ask ourselves, "What is the possibility that we will lose all our money in an investment?" Usually we can satisfy ourselves that we will not lose *all* our money, but under certain circumstances we might be willing to accept the risk associated with a high probability that we will lose our entire investment. Speculative investments of this type should be limited to a small portion of total investment to limit risk. We next ask, "What is the probability that we will lose 30 percent of our investment?" We might answer this question with full knowledge that the price might drop 30 percent within the next few months because of uncertain market conditions. If we are not speculating and we do not have to sell even if the stock does drop, then we do not suffer the market risk. If we can invest for one, two, or three years, then economic growth of the company with an upward trend of earnings will reduce or overcome the market risk. With earnings moving up, prices of common stock usually reflect the expected growth of earnings. It is possible in extreme circumstances to have a market drop of 30 percent. Nobody in his right mind would invest in the stock market if he knew that tomorrow's stocks were going down 30 percent in price. However, we do not always know what's going to happen tomorrow. Therefore, we must be prepared for the worst, expect the worst, and also anticipate that we will achieve the economic growth possible from a given investment to overcome these short-term fluctuations.

In the day-to-day work of investing, the question is repeatedly asked before a stock is purchased, "What is the down-side risk associated with this stock?" The question is asked because timing is so important to investment success. We want to know the immediate risks, the quantity of risks (to the extent that we can measure them), and the variety of all the risks we face. Facing uncertainty and risk minimizes investment error. Living with uncertainty is the lot of the investor. Those who can predict an uncertain future will be the victors in the investment battle. Those who cannot live under these conditions are better off placing their funds in less risky and less profitable ventures.

Table 1–1 was constructed to indicate the broad spectrum of security investments and savings outlets available to the investor. In Table 1–1 the investments are ranked according to risk, reward, and the amount of management decision-making ability required from the investor. We will discuss the nature of the various risks and the analysis of various types of securities later on in the text. However, an array covering risk and reward of the majority of investment and speculative securities is appropriate. It is apparent that the more speculative securities provide the highest rate of return, but the risk is correspondingly high. The amount of risk and the amount of reward cannot be equated precisely. It is possible to buy a growth common stock that offers the expectation of a 10 percent yield and yet might have a much higher degree of risk than a speculative common stock that offers a 15 percent yield. The amount of risk is more difficult to measure than the expected yield, but it is desirable to come up with a precise measure of risk. It is also apparent that some securities offer a higher yield with moderate risks than others with a lower yield and a higher degree of risk, even though they are in the same investment category. Hence, there is great need for constant analysis and management of expected risk and expected yield.

The money we place in the bank account or the mattress or the cash box is highly susceptible to the purchasing-power risk. If we are faced with inflation as we were in 1968, then we should de-emphasize savings or fixed-income obligations. On the other hand, if we are facing a recession, the best places we can have our money would be in a savings bank or in government bonds. It is also apparent that some of the savings vehicles offer higher rates of return than do securities. The

TABLE 1–1

*Risk, rewards, and management sophistication
of securities and savings outlets*

			Ownership Risks		Creditorship Risks	
MANAGEMENT DECISION REQUIRED	SECURITY OR SAVINGS	REWARD: APPROXIMATE YIELD (%)	MARKET	BUSINESS OR CREDIT	INTEREST OR MONEY RATE	PURCHASING POWER OR INFLATION
	(Security)					
H	Speculative common stock	15-20	H	H	L	L
H	Speculative mutual funds	12-15	H	H	L	L
H	Growth common stock	10-12	H	H	L	L
M	High-quality common stock (blue chip)	8-10	M	M	L	L
M	Investment mutual funds	8-10	M	M	L	L
M	Income common stock	7-8	M-L	M-L	M	M
M	Balanced mutual funds	7-8	M-L	M-L	M	M
M	Convertible preferred stock	6-10	M-H	M-H	L	L
M	Convertible bonds	5-10	M-H	M-H	L	L
L	Corporate bonds, AAA	5-6	L	L	H	H
L	Corporate bonds, below BAA	6-8	M	M	M	H
L	Municipal bonds, tax-free	4-5	L	L	H	M
L	Government bonds	4-6	L	L	H	H
L	Short-term government rates	5-6	L	L	L	H
	(Savings)					
L	Variable annuity	7	L	L	L	M
L	Credit union	4-6	L	L	L	H
L	Savings and loan associations	4-6	L	L	L	H
0	Life insurance savings	4-5	L	L	L	H
0	Mutual savings banks	5	L	L	L	H
0	Commercial banks	5	L	L	L	H
L	Swiss bank account	0	L	L	L	H
0	Cash box	0	L	L	L	H
0	Mattress, drawer, desk	0	L	L	L	H

H = High
M = Moderate
L = Low
0 = Zero

yield figures in Table 1–1 are approximate, of course. At any given moment of time, the array might vary. However, the relationships among the securities, when we examine risks and rewards and the need for management, are significant points to remember as we move into a discussion of the specific securities we might purchase for investment. Our area of study will be where the greatest amount of management decisions and sophistication are required. It is therefore appropriate that we examine more closely the major risks associated with the purchase of securities. Two types of risk are associated with ownership securities, namely, the market risk and the business risk. Two types of risk are associated with debt securities, namely, the purchasing-power or inflation risk and the money rate or interest-rate risk.

The Market Risk

The market risk is the loss of capital associated with changes in common-stock prices, and has nothing to do with the fundamental economics of the company. The market risk is usually associated with changes in expectation by investors about the prospect of a company. Essentially, understanding market risk is understanding price behavior. Once the stock has developed a particular price pattern, it does not change this pattern quickly. The causes of changes in market price are usually beyond the control of the corporation. A surprise war, an election year, political activity, illness or death of a president, speculative activity in the market, the outflow of gold, or the cessation of hostilities in the Vietnam War are tremendous psychological factors in the market. Whatever the reason, the prices of common stocks change frequently, and the conclusion we reach is that there is no one price at which a stock is traded. Prices change daily and weekly. Some theorists suggest that stock prices act in a fashion comparable to a random walk by a sober or not-so-sober man. As a result of these changes, whatever the cause, an investor can lose money in the process if he is not careful about his timing. Assume, for example, that we had bought 100 shares of stock at $40 a share just before a sharp drop in the stock market. The stock now sells at $25 a share. If we were forced to sell the stock, we would have a capital loss of $15 per share. A complete analysis prior to purchase indicated that the stock was a good investment. Nothing in the forecasted earnings has changed from the time the stock was purchased until the market dropped. Whatever the reason, the drop in the market is temporary. The cyclical swing caused a temporary drop in the price of the stock. If we had to sell, we would have a substantial loss. Obviously, we try to avoid selling by being in a position to weather the storm of financial adversity until prices come back and favorable economic factors are given time to bear fruit.

It is appropriate that we examine the behavior of stock prices and the various types of securities to learn something of what we may expect in the future. The price movements of selected stock market indexes appear in Figure 1-1. It is apparent that common stock prices over a long period of time would have a substantial growth rate with fluctuations around the trend. The Dow Jones Industrial Average (DJIA), for

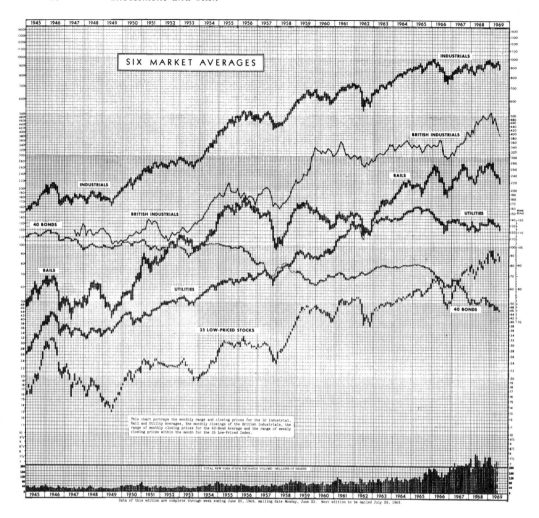

FIGURE 1–1

Price movements of Dow Jones industrial, rail, and utility averages, British industrials, 40 Bonds, and 35 Low-Priced Stocks

SOURCE *3-Trend Security Charts*, Securities Research Co., 208 Newbury Street, Boston, Mass. 02116, July, 1969, p. 1

example, has had a substantial growth. In any given year, however, there was a range in prices with a substantial market risk even for the high-quality companies. We see that the market price fluctuation of the 35 Low-Priced Stocks is substantial. The range of price movement is substantially greater than that of the DJIA, which indicates a much higher degree of market risk. In fact, if we fitted a curve to the data and then found the standard error of the estimate by using statistical techniques, we would find the standard error of the estimate in the case of low-priced stocks to be higher than for the DJIA over time. (A review of a basic statistics book describing the technique of estimating the standard error of the estimate might be appropriate.) The rhythmic pattern of stock price movements is not of the same magnitude. A drop in price, on the average, is usually followed by an increase, since the trend of stock prices has been upward for a substantial period of time. Because price stability is a very good measure of market risk, the standard error of the estimate around the trend line seems to be a good way of determining the degree of risk. If price movements are within statistical limits, we can consider them normal. If they go beyond these limits, prices are unstable and market risk is high. The greater the standard error relative to the absolute price level, the greater the market risk. The stability of earnings and of yield, as we shall discuss later, may also be used as indicators of risk.

Figure 1–2 (a–d), appearing on pages 20 and 21, shows examples of the price behavior of the various classes of common stock that exist in the market at any one time. We see examples of a recessive stock, a growth stock, an income stock, and a cyclical stock. These examples cover a wide range of the stocks in the securities market. The growth company is a successful company that relies upon earnings growth and increased market price. Its performance has been better than the market generally. But even so, prices move around a trend line rather than in a straight line. Even the growth stock has a cyclical pattern.

The cyclical stock by its very nature is influenced more by the business cycle. Usually the price movement is related to the earnings of the company and the expectation of those earnings. This type of company benefits greatly from economic boom and suffers from economic recession, making the market risk substantial. We cannot buy these companies and hold them for maximum gains. We must expect to trade to obtain the best benefits; we become more aware of the market risks in the process.

The income stock looks more like the Dow Jones Industrial Average than the other patterns. It offers modest growth, substantial dividend income, and movement around the norm so that one is aware of the market risks involved. These stocks are not completely vulnerable to cyclical changes but, on the other hand, they are vulnerable to the money-rate risk. As interest rate goes down, these stocks tend to increase in price, and vice versa.

Recessive stock is one that is declining. Earnings are usually going down and dividends are dropping. This might reflect a declining industry, poor management, or poor products, resulting in a basic decline. Not much interest is shown in this type of company, except by those people who think that it might be taken over by a stronger management and improved. In a "turn-around" situation, in which the new management turns a loss into a gain, the profits in price appreciation can be substantial. It would be possible to trade in this type of stock, if we were completely aware of the market risks involved. We see immediately that the prices move about a trend line downward, that the price variation from month to month is substantial, and that this type of stock should not be held for the long term.

The best quality stocks are susceptible to the market risk. General Motors, AT&T, Minnesota Mining & Manufacturing, Du Pont, Eastman Kodak, all excellent companies, move in a rather wide price pattern. In fact, a 10 percent price movement might be considered normal for many companies. Under conditions of severe stress, such as occurred in 1962, 1966, and again in 1968, we could expect market price movements to be substantially higher. However, we can be more precise in our knowledge of market risk by simply using some statistical estimates and a visual reference to come up with the range of prices that is going to occur over time for a particular stock. In Figure 1–2c a trend line fitted to the data for General Motors visually (this is a very unsophisticated way to measure) provides a range around the trend line of plus or minus fifteen points. This indicates a substantial market risk.

How can we compensate for the market risk? There are several ways in which this can be done. First, we must carefully examine each security to understand its price behavior. Stocks that have demonstrated a cyclical pattern in the past will be likely to continue this pattern in the future. Stocks that have demonstrated a growth pattern in the past will continue to do so in the future unless there is some drastic change in the expectations of the company. There are those people who say that history will not repeat itself. However, evidence suggests that the behavioral characteristics of stocks in the past will be carried into the future—not perfectly, but nonetheless, the characteristics will persist.

Secondly, as a result of our analysis, we might choose those stocks that have the lowest amount of market risk. Common stocks that are growth stocks or that offer a combination of growth and income usually do not have the same degree of market risk possessed by the recessive and the cyclical stock. Therefore, we can analyze the market behavior and select stocks that offer us growth or a combination of income and growth but do not offer the risks and penalties associated with the cyclical and recessive types of stocks.

Thirdly, we can reduce the market risk by being extremely careful in the timing of purchase or sale of common stock. If we used the standard error of the estimate as a gauge, we might find that we would buy

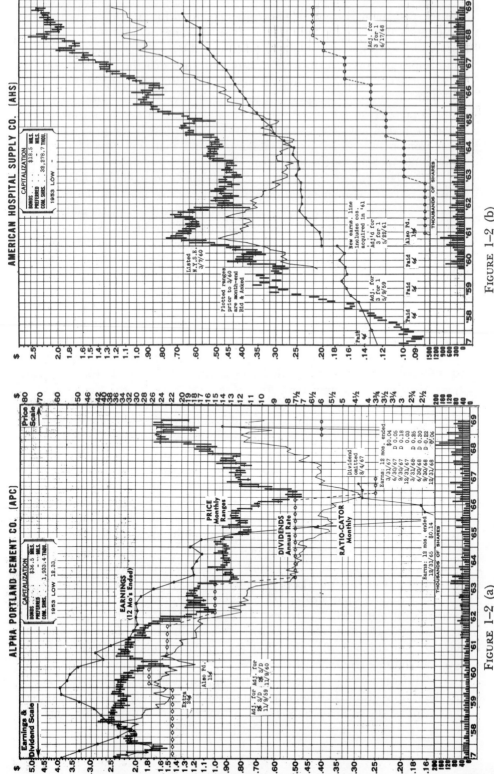

FIGURE 1-2 (a)

Example of price behavior for recessive stock

FIGURE 1-2 (b)

Example of price behavior for
growth stock

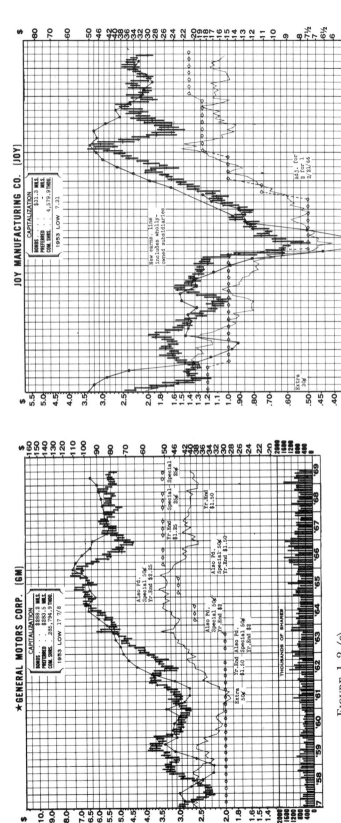

FIGURE 1-2 (c)

Example of price behavior for in-come stock

FIGURE 1-2 (d)

Example of price behavior for cy-clical stock

SOURCE *3-Trend Security Charts*, Securities Research Co., 208 Newbury Street, Boston, Mass. 02116, July, 1969, pp. 5, 7, 43, and 56

stocks when they are below the limits of one standard error of the estimate, and sell stocks if they went beyond this. Again, this is a statistical technique that is not perfect. On the other hand, over long periods of time, we would be better investors if we were somewhat more mathematical in our analysis. Many analysts now use sophisticated point and figure charts for determining the timing of purchases and sales. We will discuss them under the subject of portfolio management.

Fourth and last, we must be prepared to invest for a period of time that will allow us to benefit from the rising trend of market prices and avoid the cyclical activity of the market in its daily and monthly price movements. This is consistent with our definition of investment and in the process we minimize exposure to investment risk. We find in Figure 1–3 that if we buy at "A" and expect to obtain the rewards of our endeavors over time, we must hold for at least two years before we have a chance of getting our money back. This example is not far from reality. In fact, if we bought at point "A" and held until point "C," we would break even on our investment. It is not until we reach "D" three years after purchase that we have made money. It would have been better for us to have purchased at "B." Therefore, a simple statistical tool can be of help to us in our investment decision. If we pay too high a price for a stock, we must wait a substantial number of years to have any hopes of obtaining a satisfactory rate of return. The willingness to hold certainly does not preclude our attitude toward the timing of our purchase. We must simply combine timing with patience to obtain maximum investment rewards.

The Business Risk

Changes in the earning power of a company may result in a loss in income or capital to the investor. This inability of a company to maintain its competitive position and to maintain its earnings growth or stability of earnings is referred to as the business risk. Common stock, the lower rated preferred stocks, and bonds possess the business risk. Essentially, it is the condition in which the company cannot earn money or cannot earn as much as it had anticipated. The loss that results is either temporary or permanent. The various gradations of business risk might be put into the following categories: First, the growth company that expected to increase its earnings at the rate of 20 percent per year, but now only expects to increase its earnings growth rate at 10 percent per year because of a reversal in its competitive position in the industry. This results in a reassessment of the earning capacity of the company and can result in a substantial price decline and a resultant loss to the investor. Second, a company that has had stable earnings although it was

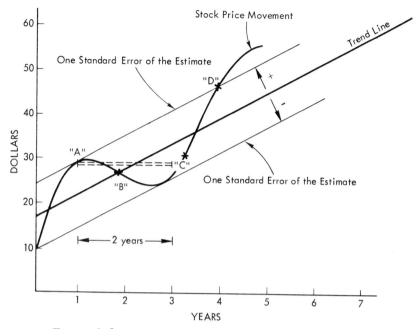

FIGURE 1–3

*Two years—a realistic time period
for market risk compensation for a
growth stock*

not growing very rapidly, but now finds that because of business reversals it cannot maintain its earnings, which begin to decline. This might be the recessive type of company that we mentioned earlier. There is a third class of company that has sustained a period of deficits because of its poor financial position, and its earnings are declining; there is a serious question as to whether the company will be able to remain in business.

Litton Industries is a good example of the company in the first classification. Litton in 1967 anticipated a substantial growth in earnings, but experienced a temporary loss in earnings in 1968 because several divisions were not as profitable as expected. This resulted in a drop in price and a potential loss to investors. General Motors is a company whose earnings have diminished somewhat, and the price of the stock has dropped to relate more closely to earnings. This is a case of a quality company experiencing a drop in earnings that results in a price drop. Presumably, this will be temporary in nature, but nonetheless, the price of the stock reflects a change in business conditions. Brunswick Corporation in 1962 was another example of a company that not only reduced its growth rate but actually sustained substantial losses in earnings. In order to survive, Brunswick had to improve its relative position in the market by improving its earnings. When its earnings finally turned around in 1968, the price began to move up. Many investors who had bought for the long term experienced substantial losses between 1962 and 1968. There are other examples of companies that have gone into receivership, and have been managed by court-appointed trustees to make certain that their assets would not be dissipated. The New York, New Haven, and Hartford Railroad was one of these. The stock of the company became worthless and the 4 percent bonds maturing in 2007 sold for less than twenty cents on the dollar. This company has actually suffered a permanent loss of its earning power. Any investor who had purchased the common stock or the bonds of the New Haven would have lost virtually all his capital. He would have lost because the railroad was unable to earn a profit, in spite of a subsequent merger.

Some indication of the extent of the business risk is found in the number of company failures that occur each year in the United States. The majority of these failures are small companies that close their business doors because they are unable to earn a profit. A few, of course, are large companies. The majority of investors are probably not aware of these companies because of their size and their legal form, but they do mirror the competitive characteristic of our business world.

The number of failures varies each year, but for an average year over 15,000 business firms fail. In fact, it has become fashionable for the smaller business to go into bankruptcy. Its claims are usually forgiven and the owners can go back into business again with a clean slate.

This should provide us with some insight into the risk associated with business activity of all companies and will help us realize the forces that have caused even large businesses to fail in the past. The causes of failure operate in the larger corporations in which we might invest our funds as well as in small companies.

The fluctuation in business activity or the business cycle is also an indication of the business risk. A recession in industrial output will lead to a drop in profits for some companies. The effect of the decline in sales varies from company to company. Some companies might be forced to close their doors to the public because of the losses sustained. For others, it will simply mean a drop in earnings or a slowing down of their growth. These changes in earnings will be reflected in the price of the shares in the market. The results are the same as those mentioned above. The Federal Reserve Board Index of Production can be used as an indicator of business health and business risk. Figure 1–4 indicates the variation in business activity between 1944 and the first seven months of 1967. The periods 1945–46, 1948–50, 1952–54, 1957–58, and 1960–61 were recession years, particularly for those durable manufactures in

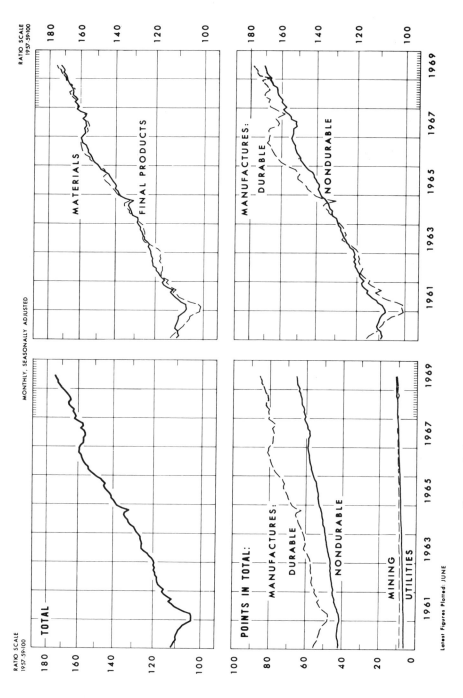

FIGURE 1–4

Industrial production

SOURCE *Federal Reserve Monthly Chart Book*, July, 1969, p. 58

which many firms lost money, with a resulting decline in the value of their shares. The utilities and nondurable manufactures have not been hampered to the same degree by the business cycle.

The instability in business activity is carried through to the instability of corporate profits presented in Figure 1–5. We see that corporate profits before and after taxes have continued to rise after the recession of 1961. This rise has been punctuated by the periodic climbs in profitability. The decline in profits after taxes indicates the risk involved in securities investment. Certainly, greater stability in profits would lead to greater stability in the amount of the business risk assumed by the investor.

One measure of the business risk is found by measuring the stability of earnings and the stability of the growth rate of earnings. The company having the greatest stability in its growth rate of earnings and the greatest stability of earnings would have less business risk than a company that had widely fluctuating earnings. In essence, an investor would

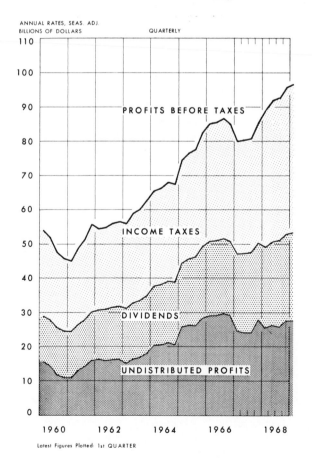

ANNUAL RATES, SEAS. ADJ.
BILLIONS OF DOLLARS   QUARTERLY

PROFITS BEFORE TAXES

INCOME TAXES

DIVIDENDS

UNDISTRIBUTED PROFITS

1960   1962   1964   1966   1968

Latest Figures Plotted: 1st QUARTER

Figure 1–5

Corporate profits, taxes, and dividends (Department of Commerce)

SOURCE *Federal Reserve Monthly Chart Book,* July, 1969, p. 42.

certainly be willing to pay more for the company with the stable growth earnings than for a company that had cyclical or widely fluctuating earnings. The author has used the stability of earnings as a basis for determining the risks involved in an investment. An estimate of earnings stability can be found by fitting a curve to the earnings per share of a company and finding the standard error of the estimate around those earnings. The company with the greatest stability of earnings and the lowest relative standard error of the estimate would have the lowest business risk. A mathematical analysis would show precisely these limits. However, visual inspection of the growth of earnings, particularly when the growth rate is analyzed, will give some idea of the stability of earnings and growth rate and the amount of risk involved. Certainly, before an investor makes an investment in a company, he should examine the trend of earnings to make certain that they are stable and therefore possess less business risk than those of a company with basically unstable earnings.

One study[6] suggests that risk be measured by the stability of yield from the common stock. Yield includes both income and capital gain or loss. The greater the stability of yield, the smaller the risk, and vice versa. Professor Pratt used quarterly yields on common stock as the basis for comparison and covered the period 1929 to 1965. The stocks with the most stable yields were placed in the grade A class, having the least risk. The stocks with the most unstable yield were placed in grade E class, having the highest risk. It was found that the yields increased as risk increased, but that the highest risk group was not fully compensated for risk and obtained diminishing returns. The study supports the thesis that the higher the risk, the higher the yield, but only up to a limit. Obtaining the most risky investments would not be wise investment policy, and would not compensate for the risk involved. Analysis would be required to eliminate the most risky stocks from investment consideration.

The question we as investors must answer is, How can we provide against the risk of loss associated with the failure—either partial or complete—of a business firm? There are several appropriate solutions to this problem. First, we can make a thorough analysis of the competitive position of the company and its future expectation for profitability. This requires a detailed analysis of the past profit performance of the company. Careful examination of the trends and stability of the profits will indicate the degree of risk involved. The stability index about a normal trend of profits will give us an indication of the relative risk. We must understand the behavioral characteristics of earnings and plan

6 Shannon T. Pratt, "Relationships Between Risk and the Rate of Return for Common Stock" (Unpublished dissertation, Graduate School of Business, Indiana University, 1966).

accordingly. We could avoid the common stocks of companies by purchasing fixed-income securities, such as preferred stocks and bonds. However, these still share in the business risks to a minor degree, even though these instruments have a prior claim upon the earnings and assets of a company. The company's having been able to withstand the financial strain of the business cycle and competition within the industry will tend to minimize the business risk. Second, we can attempt to purchase common stock when it offers an attractive yield on our investment in spite of the changes in the profitability. In short, we guard against the business risk by selecting securities carefully.

The Money Rate Risk—A Creditorship Risk

Many investors consider high-quality bonds or other fixed-income securities as the only safe way to solve the problems of investment risk. Some institutional investors must limit their investment primarily to mortgages and investment-quality bonds. These securities, however, possess two major risks. One is the purchasing-power risk, and the second is the money rate risk that we shall consider here.

The money rate risk is the risk of loss of principal brought about by changes in the money rates paid on new securities that are currently being issued. An example of how a change in money rates will result in a loss to the investor will clarify this risk that the bond or fixed income investor must face. Assume that a bond is purchased at par for $1,000 (quoted as 100) with an interest rate of 5 percent per year payable semiannually. The bond matures in twenty-five years, and the company promises to repay the $1,000 investment at maturity. The yield to maturity is 5 percent.[7] Now, let us suppose that interest rates rise because of a new supply-and-demand relationship for funds in the capital markets. Money is said to be tight. A tight money policy might be followed because of the government's attempt to prevent inflation in the domestic economy and to improve the international balance of payments problem such as occurred in 1968 and 1969 in the United States. As a result, yields are 7 percent on the new bonds of equal quality that are now being issued. What then happens to the bonds that were issued at 5 percent? The price of the 5 percent bonds must drop, and the 5 percent interest payment will actually result in a yield to maturity of 7 percent, which is just equal to the new 7 percent bonds that are being issued. The problem, however, is serious because a $1,000 bond now has a market

7 This will be discussed more thoroughly under "Bond Investment." Briefly, yield to maturity is the compound rate of interest earned from an investment over its lifetime. It includes both the interest income and the capital gains or losses. A simple way of approximating yield to maturity is by dividing average investment into average annual income, which includes both interest income and annual capital gains or losses. The word *yield* in this book refers to the compound rate of return.

value of $885, well below par. If the bond were sold, we would sustain a loss. If, on the other hand, we had assumed that the market yields declined from 5 to 4 percent, then our bond would increase in price, and we would have a capital gain instead of a loss. The significant point for us to note is that there was a change in price and yield independent of the quality of the bond, brought about by external money market conditions over which we had no control.

Another risk is assumed by investors if they purchase bonds with a higher rate of interest. If bond yields fall, these prices move to a premium, and there is a tendency on the part of the corporation issuing the bonds to call them and refinance at a lower rate of interest. This puts bondholders in a position where they might lose money not only through inflation in prosperous times but also in deflationary times when yields drop and bond prices increase, but the investor does not realize the gain because the company calls the bonds at a price lower than the market price.

Table 1–2 indicates how the yields on United States long-term marketable Treasury bonds have changed. These changes reflect the changes in the prices of the bonds. From 1941 to 1967 the trend of interest rates has been upward, which has meant a decline in the price of bonds issued between 1942 and 1955 as compared with bonds issued by the Treasury in 1968 and later.

The rising cost of money was brought about because of an expanding economy and the deficit that resulted because of the Vietnam War. As long as this expansion continues, the demand for funds remains high, and the trend of interest rates will continue upward.

TABLE 1–2

Yields on long-term United States Treasury bonds indicating long-term changes in money rates

Year	Treasury Bond Yields (%)	Year	Treasury Bond Yields (%)
1967	5.39	1954	2.52
1966	4.66	1953	2.90
1965	4.23	1952	2.68
1964	4.17	1951	2.60
1963	4.02	1950	2.32
1962	3.95	1949	2.28
1961	3.90	1948	2.43
1960	4.01	1947	2.24
1959	4.10	1946	2.19
1958	3.23	1945	2.34
1957	3.47	1944	2.38
1956	3.06	1943	2.29
1955	2.80	1942	2.27

SOURCES: Standard & Poor's *Trade and Securities Statistics, Security Price Index Record,* December, 1967, p. 210; and *Federal Reserve Bulletin,* December, 1967, p. 2103.

The investor must be realistic in solving the problem of a possible loss associated with changes in the money rates. One solution is to hold the investment to maturity. Thus, if we purchased a debt security, we would plan to hold it until it matured so that we would not lose capital because of money rate changes. Second, we might buy bonds with only a few years to go to maturity and avoid the problem of changes in long-term yields. Third, we might be able to sell the bond and take a loss, which is deductible, and then invest in the higher-yield bonds, which might improve our yield to maturity, particularly if we are in a high tax bracket. The best solution for most of us would be to space the maturity dates of our bond investments so that we do not have all our money in one issue. As the bonds mature, the proceeds can be reinvested at the new and higher yields if the trend of yields continues to move up. We should also shorten the time to maturity.

We could select, from all the bonds that are available to us in a particular class, those that are selling at a discount. These would sell at higher prices from the discount rate because of the lower coupon rates and give us a hedge should interest rates fall later on. It is not likely that these would be called. We would not lose in interest rate growth, we would gain. We would have the added advantage of having a taxable capital gain on bonds. Lastly, we must realize in our analysis of money market changes that there is a certain degree of instability in bond yields. Bond yields do fluctuate from time to time.

The Purchasing-Power Risk—A Creditorship Risk

Whether we buy securities or hold our surplus funds in a safety deposit box, we suffer from the purchasing-power risk. The risk of loss of income and principal because of the decreased purchasing power of the dollar is known as the purchasing-power risk. It is a problem that has been with us for some time, and it is likely to be one in the future. Table 1–3 gives evidence of what has happened to consumer and wholesale prices between 1941 and 1967. The significance of the data is apparent. We in the United States have experienced an increasing consumer price level since 1941. At times the increase has been acute, as was the case in 1966 and 1967. The wholesale price index has also increased but not as rapidly as the consumer price index. Further, this increase has continued into 1968, and we must probably expect a continuing gradual increase in prices in the future.

We must conclude that beginning in the mid-1940's we have experienced a constant decrease in the purchasing power of the dollar and that this trend is likely to continue. A dollar today, for example, will purchase less than half of what it could purchase twenty years ago. A ten-cent *Life* magazine of twenty years ago now costs forty cents on the stand. Some product improvement over the period has also increased

TABLE 1–3

Consumer and wholesale prices
(Bureau of Labor Statistics Indexes,
1957–1959 = 100)

YEAR	CONSUMER PRICES	WHOLESALE PRICES
1967	116.3	106.1
1966	113.1	105.9
1965	109.9	102.5
1964	108.1	100.5
1963	106.7	100.3
1962	105.4	100.6
1961	104.2	100.3
1960	103.1	100.7
1959	101.5	100.6
1958	100.7	100.4
1957	98.0	99.0
1956	94.7	96.2
1955	93.3	93.2
1954	93.6	92.9
1941	51.3	47.8

SOURCE: *Federal Reserve Bulletin*, December, 1967, p. 2130; December, 1968, p. A–64.

prices. A 1950 automobile might have cost only one-third of the price of a 1969 auto, but some people will say that a 1969 auto is three times as good as a 1950 auto, so we might not be too badly off with some products, in real terms, after all. However, college costs have soared. Medical costs have risen rapidly. At the present time, it costs forty dollars a day to keep a patient in the average hospital, and forecasts for ten years hence suggest costs of one hundred dollars a day. Housing costs have moved up substantially within the last few years. These are the real aspects of inflation. We can look at composite indexes all we wish, but when we get down to the category of the things that we buy and use every day, we find that inflation constitutes a real threat to our money and its purchasing power. We as investors must compensate for this inflation when we study the subject of investment and put our money to work in investment programs.

How can we solve the problem of inflation in our investment securities? Fixed-income securities do not solve the problem because they do not increase in value to compensate for the rising cost of living. Ownership securities in the form of common stock are the only securities that can provide against the purchasing-power risk because they will increase in price as purchasing power declines. The correlation between increasing stock prices and the consumer price index is not perfect. Stock prices tend to be more cyclical in character than consumer prices. But the trend of stock prices tends to compensate for the trend of increasing consumer prices. Except for real estate, real goods, precious metals, objects of art, and other valuable commodities, common stock is the best way in which an investor can compensate for this type of risk. The extent to which inflation governs the individual and institutional investment policy will determine where funds will be invested. Should inflationary conditions prevail, we would be wise to invest primarily in equity securities and to use fixed-income securities only to the extent that they fulfill the needs of conservative financial management or to the extent that income tax considerations demand that some form of tax-exempt bonds be used.

As investors, we must be aware of these risks of investment, and we must plan carefully to eliminate them as much as possible, based upon our own investment needs.

Summary

Investment, as used in this book, is the purchase of a security or securities that upon a thorough analysis offer safety of principal and a satisfactory yield with a minimum of risk. In order to understand the definition fully we must understand the investment decision-making process. Essentially, it is a process of balancing risks against rewards. The process includes: (1) a knowledge of the risks associated with investment and the behavioral characteristics of recessive, cyclical, growth, and income stocks; (2) a knowledge of the individual securities in which we can invest our surplus money, and their risks and yields; (3) a method of analysis that will allow the intelligent selection of quality companies with a future earning power that is attractive; (4) an awareness and use of an information system and an understanding of the behavior of the stock market; and (5) a knowledge of the fundamentals of portfolio management to meet the needs of an investor, both real and psychological.

Risks and rewards go together. The higher the past yield, the higher the risk, and the greater the reward. The top category of risk securities does not offer a corresponding yield. Risk securities require greater sophistication and managerial talent from the investor in his decision making. Securities offering the highest rewards and risks and requiring the greatest analytical and decision-making ability are speculative stocks, mutual stock funds, blue chip stocks, corporate stocks, bonds, and diversified mutual funds. Substantial risks are associated with the purchase of securities that might cause a loss of income or principal or both. These risks are the market risk and the business risk associated with common stock and the money rate risk and purchasing-power risk associated with bonds. We must recognize these risks when we begin an investment program, and we must make adequate compensation for them.

Each type of common stock possesses varying degrees of market risk as measured by the standard error of the estimate around the trend of prices. The business risk is substantial in common-stock investment and can be measured by the variation in stability of earnings. It has been suggested that the stability of quarterly yields reflects the amount of risk associated with common-stock investment. The money rate risk and the purchasing-power risk are most closely associated with fixed-income securities. High-quality common stocks are affected by money rate risk, particularly income equities. Some lower-quality bonds possess the market risk. Equities provide protection for the purchasing-power risk somewhat imperfectly. Analysis and understanding of the behavior of stock prices protect the investor against the business and market risks. Timing and perseverance also help, particularly in the case of long-term investors.

Review Questions

1. Explain the difference between consumer investment, business or economic investment, and financial investment.
2. Explain what is meant by the statement: "Investment is the purchase of a security or securities that upon a thorough analysis offer safety of principal and a satisfactory yield with a minimum of risk."
3. Distinguish between investment and speculation.
4. How can a security that yields 5 percent be a satisfactory investment for one investor but another security that offers an 8 percent yield be unattractive and unsatisfactory for another investor? Explain.
5. Discuss in detail the steps involved in the investment process.
6. What are the basic risks we face in the purchase of investment securities? Be certain to differentiate each carefully.
7. What is the relationship between risk and reward? Explain and give some examples of the relationship. How are each of these risks measured?
8. Explain or define the following words: greed, fear, loss, worry. What relationship do they have to investment?

Problems

1. (a) Assume that we bought a $1,000 face value United States Savings bond, Series E, in January, 1969, and will hold it until it matures. What rate of interest will we earn over the life of the bond?
   (b) What will be the approximate purchasing power of the money when the bond matures?
2. Assume that we bought $750 worth of General Motors common stock in January, 1969. How much should we expect GM stock to be worth at the same time the Series E bond matures? Spend all the cash dividends from the stock but keep all stock dividends received.
   (a) What would be the value and purchasing power of the General Motors stock at the end of the period?

    (b) How would this compare with the purchasing power of the savings bond?

    (c) What is the significance of this relationship?

3. Assume you bought 100 shares of Du Pont, January 2, 1968, and sold them June 21, 1968.

    (a) Would you have lost money on the purchase and sale?

    (b) What risk is demonstrated by this transaction?

4. Measure the market risk and business risk for AT&T, Eastman Kodak, Litton Industries, and Syntex for the past ten years. Compare the measurable risks with the measurable yields. Which stock is best?

Sources of Investment Information

Barron's
Federal Reserve Bulletin
Moody's Industrial Manual
New York Times
Wall Street Journal

Selected Readings

Latane, Henry A., and Donald L. Tuttle, "Probability in Industry Analysis," *Financial Analysts Journal* (July-August, 1968), p. 51.

Treynor, J. L., W.W. Priest, Jr., Lawrence Fisher, and C.A. Higgins "Risk Estimates," *Financial Analysts Journal* (September-October, 1968), p. 93.

West, David A., "Risk Analysis in the 1960's," *Financial Analysts Journal* (November-December, 1967), p. 124.

2

SAVINGS AND THE FINANCIAL PREREQUISITES FOR INVESTMENT

Conservative financial management dictates that an individual or an institution be in a strong financial position before an investment program is established. Financial strength permits the investor to accept more readily the risks associated with investment in securities. We assume that the majority of financial institutions possess this strength, since they must invest the funds they receive for the benefit of their customers or owners. We, as individuals, may not be in as strong a financial position to invest, and we should be aware of and able to fulfill the financial prerequisites to investment. We must also have funds that we can use to purchase securities for investment. On the other hand, we may be fortunate enough to have a rapidly rising income, adequate financial protection, and a need for developing the most effective program for keeping as much of our income as possible. However rapidly or slowly savings accumulate, the usual source of money for investment is savings from current income or funds that we have accumulated in the past. Institutions, too, invest current funds and those that have been received in the past. We, as individuals, can use borrowed money as a source of investment funds. However, we usually assume that individuals will not borrow money to invest but will buy securities only from savings. We do not recommend a "borrow and buy" program for security investment even though some investors are being encouraged to borrow the cash surrender value of their life insurance policies. This should be done with care and caution, with full recognition of the risks involved.

In this chapter we will examine the sources of funds that might be used by individuals and institutions to purchase securities. We will examine the savings of individuals on an aggregate and individual basis to gain some insight into their savings habits. We will examine the traditional financial prerequisites for investment and provide some ground rules to help us decide when we should be able to begin an investment program. This information should be helpful to us as individuals and as analysts or investment counselors. We will also examine some of the modern developments in the investment and financial community that might allow an individual to begin an investment program with only a small amount of money.

Most of us are in the financial position of trying to build up a fund for investment, and we soon learn that capital accumulation is a difficult and time-consuming process. Those who have achieved financial success also know that it is difficult to maintain it, because of high federal income taxes. We may be fortunate enough to have already accumulated a sum of money by past saving, or we may have inherited a large sum of money that allows us to begin an investment program. Whatever the source of funds, we find that the investment process is intimately associated with the savings of individuals and their personal financial positions. We will examine now the concept of savings, exploring some of the characteristics of savers as individuals and what determines the amount of money saved. We will examine the potential amount of money available from previously accumulated deposits, the sale of other types of investment securities, and borrowed funds used for investment in securities.

Savings from Current Income

The simplest definition of savings that we can use in our discussion is one that considers *savings* as money income that is not spent for consumption. If we do not spend our income for consumption goods, we save it. The money that remains may be "spent" by the individual, but this part of the total expenditure would be considered a saving. Purchases of durable consumer goods are usually considered consumption expenditures even though a portion could be considered savings. On the other hand, repayment of debts and purchases of real estate are considered savings. Deposits in savings institutions and savings deposits in commercial banks represent savings if they are built up from current income. Money from current income given to non-deposit-type institutions such as life insurance companies, pension funds, and investment companies represents savings. There is an element of investment in savings accounts and life insurance reserves; however, they are usually considered savings media and not investment media. Our definition of savings would also include money used by the individual to purchase securities directly. A person buying securities would be saving and investing, in the financial sense, in the same transaction.

Not all savings from current income are available for the purchase of securities by the individuals themselves. In fact, the major portion of annual savings goes to such financial intermediaries as pension funds, life insurance companies, deposits at savings institutions, and for debt repayment. The institutions will purchase securities and invest. Some of these activities result indirectly in investment in securities for the individual. Few transactions result in direct investment requiring the individual's decision.

The flow of funds/saving data now being presented in the monthly *Federal Reserve Bulletin* provides some idea of the sources and the uses of funds among the various individuals and institutions in our society. Table 2–1, for example, summarizes one segment of the principal financial transactions in the United States. In this category we find the equity

TABLE 2–1

Principal financial transactions—other securities
sector of total United States financial
transactions (billions of dollars)

Who Sold the Securities (Net):[a]	1962	1966	1967 2nd Qtr.
State and local governments	5.0	5.9	12.1
Nonfinancial corporations	5.1	11.4	15.3
Commercial banks	0.1	0.1	0.1
Finance companies	0.3	0.8	(—0.5)
Rest of world	1.0	0.4	1.0
Total	11.5	18.6	27.9[b]

Who Provided the Money to Purchase the Securities (Net):			
Households	(—1.7)	3.1	(—6.3)
Nonfinancial corporations	(—0.4)	0.8	0.7
State and local governments	2.0	5.2	7.8
Commercial banks	4.4	1.7	12.1
Insurance and pension funds	7.5	9.5	10.3
Finance, not elsewhere counted	(—0.3)	(—2.8)	(—1.0)
Security brokers and dealers	0.4	(—0.4)	(—0.8)
Investment companies net[c]	(—0.8)	(—2.5)	(—0.2)
Rest of world	0.1	0.9	1.1
Total	11.5	18.6[b]	27.9[b]

[a] The other transaction categories are demand deposits and currency, time and savings accounts, U.S. Government securities, mortgages, and bank loans.

[b] Does not add up because of statistical discrepancy.

[c] Investment companies buy and sell securities in which they have invested. If they sell a greater value of securities than they buy, the net value of the transaction is negative.

SOURCE: *Federal Reserve Bulletin*, December, 1967, p. 2139.

securities issued by corporations, that is, nonfinancial corporations. We find here, too, an approximation of the amount of ownership securities purchased directly by consumers and nonprofit corporations. Unfortunately, individuals' purchases are not separated from those of nonprofit organizations. As we look at the figures representing the transaction in this sector, we realize that individuals supply a relatively small amout of money directly to the sellers of securities. The greatest source of funds for the purchase of other securities came from insurance and pension funds both in 1962 and in 1966. In 1967, commercial banks purchased a substantial amount of these securities and were more important than the insurance companies and pension funds. Institutional investors were much more important as net purchasers of other securities, in the aggregate, than were individuals. This is true in other transaction categories except for time and savings accounts. In this category the individual is most important. We should also be impressed by the substantial income in securities sold and money provided by the financial institutions between 1962 and 1967. A growth of almost 150 percent occurred between those years.

The figures in Table 2–1 should not be confused with real savings presented in the national income accounts. The main conclusion from these financial transactions is that the individual who purchases securities for investment directly is in the minority. The financial institution however invests funds indirectly for individuals, and accomplishes this primarily through the purchase of debt securities.

Accumulated Savings of Individuals

Money for the purchase of investment securities is available from the past savings of individuals that have been built up in savings and loan accounts, mutual savings banks, savings accounts with commercial banks, credit union balances, and demand deposits with commercial banks. This money is available to the individual for direct investment in bonds or stocks of American corporations. Usually the money held on deposit by these institutions has already been used to purchase securities—predominantly debt securities. The funds deposited in the savings and loan companies are usually invested in residential mortgages and partially in government securities. Mutual savings banks also make mortgage loans and invest in government securities; they also buy private corporate debt and other debt instruments. The credit union, which is primarily in business to make loans to its members, also invests in short-term government securities, but it does not invest in equity securities. In fact, most of these financial institutions—including the credit union— do not invest in common stock. Pension funds, mutual funds, and life insurance companies do invest in common stock, and the amount has increased in recent years. If the individual chooses, he may draw on these balances for the purchase of securities directly. As we shall see, this is only one of the possible uses for these funds.

Pension funds and life insurance reserves are an important method by which individuals save a portion of their income each year. Over a long period of time these funds build up to large amounts of money that are available eventually for individuals to purchase securities directly if they wish to do so. The funds in the pension fund and in life insurance are, of course, invested in securities for the individual even if he does not elect to invest directly with the accumulated funds. Ordinarily we do not look upon pension funds or life insurance reserves as a source of funds for investment. If we did attempt to use these funds, we would be giving up some, although not all, of the benefits of the pension program or the life insurance. We cannot use pension funds until we retire, at which time the proceeds of the fund will usually be taken in the form of income rather than in a lump sum payment, although some pension funds do provide lump sum payments that can then be invested directly. Usually, money cannot be borrowed from the pension fund, and hence it is unavailable to us for investment as it is being built up. Life insurance reserves can be borrowed or pledged for a loan by the individual, and, as we shall see later, we do consider this a source of investment funds; but it is not necessarily a source for everyone, nor is it a recommended policy to borrow to invest. Again, most of us consider this a fund for retirement or for emergency loan purposes rather than for investment, and the money is not usually borrowed for direct investment.

The important point to remember about balances held with financial institutions, including insurance companies, is that they are available for the purchase of securities if we should desire to invest the funds ourselves. Table 2–2 provides figures on the growth of the total assets and time deposits of the leading savings institutions that would provide investment funds from previously accumulated balances. The data reveal a dramatic growth in our savings institutions since 1957 and show that we own large sums of money that could be invested directly into the stock market. We shall see in a moment that ordinarily these funds will not move into the direct ownership of securities because we have more than one alternative use for funds. We usually have a purpose in saving, and not all savings are available for common-stock ownership.

Other segments of the national economy also save and invest. Business units invest their surplus funds in government securities. They invest mainly in short-term securities to maintain liquidity. Government units themselves follow the same pattern as corporate investors. Foreign investors also provide funds from savings for investment; they usually invest in debt securities, and they represent a source of savings for investment in the United States.

TABLE 2-2

Total assets and time and savings deposits held in commercial banks, mutual savings banks, and savings and loan associations, by individuals, partnerships, and corporations; policy loans and total assets of life insurance companies; and savings in credit unions (millions of dollars)

	Commercial Banks		Mutual Savings Banks		Savings & Loan Associations		Life Insurance Companies		U.S. Credit Unions
YEAR	TOTAL LOANS & INVESTMENTS	TIME DEPOSITS (IPC)*	TOTAL ASSETS	DEPOSITS	TOTAL ASSETS	SAVINGS CAPITAL	POLICY LOANS	TOTAL ASSETS	SAVINGS ACCOUNTS
1967	336,129[a]	159,170[a]	65,696[b]	59,257[b]	141,796[b]	122,366[b]	9,875[c]	174,664[c]	---
1966	323,885	146,329	60,982	55,006	133,997	114,010	9,136	166,942	---
1965	306,060	134,247	58,232	52,443	129,580	110,385	7,679	158,884	---
1964	277,376	116,635	54,238	48,849	119,355	101,887	7,140	149,470	---
1963	254,162	102,886	49,702	44,606	107,559	91,308	6,655	141,121	---
1962	235,839	90,991	46,121	41,336	93,605	80,236	6,234	133,291	---
1961	215,441	76,680	42,829	38,277	82,135	70,885	5,733	126,816	5,577
1960	199,509	66,836	40,571	36,343	71,476	62,142	5,231	119,576	4,970
1959	190,270	62,718	38,945	34,977	63,530	54,583	4,618	113,650	4,436
1958	185,165	59,590	37,784	34,031	55,139	47,976	4,188	107,580	3,870
1957	170,068	53,366	35,215	31,683	48,138	41,912	3,869	101,309	3,382

SOURCE: *Federal Reserve Bulletin*, December issues, 1959–1967; and *Credit Union Yearbook*, 1962, p. 49.

* Individuals, partnerships, and corporations.

[a] June 30, 1967.

[b] October, 1967.

[c] September, 1967.

Savings and the Individual

Individuals contribute greatly to the aggregate savings of the national economy. The amount of money we save as individuals is directly dependent upon the amount of our income, how long we have earned our income, our expectations for future income, the stability or instability of our income, our attitude toward saving and thrift, and how people around us spend their income. We are interested in how the individual saves his money, since he will be able to invest when income and savings reach an adequate level. The fact that our nation aggregates large amounts of savings each year does not mean that a specific individual will be able to accumulate large enough liquid balances in a savings account to allow him to invest in securities. Saving to purchase securities requires not only a relatively large income but a desire to invest as a motive, as well as the desire to save.

The Amount of Income and Savings

As our incomes increase, we tend to save a greater portion, and we have more money available for the direct purchase of securities. This is particularly true when we experience a sharp increase in income.

The schedules of savings for various levels of income are provided in Table 2–3. The schedule indicates that at $7,000 of disposable income after taxes, $400 or 5.7 percent of income is saved. At the $11,000 level, $2,150 or 19.5 percent is saved. The family at the average income level finds it difficult to save, judging from figures on the consumption and saving pattern of family units in the United States. Only when we arrive at the income levels above $8,000, after federal income taxes, can we expect to be able to purchase securities as direct investments.

TABLE 2–3

Consumption expenditure and saving—
behavior at various levels of income

DISPOSABLE INCOME (AFTER TAXES)	CONSUMPTION EXPENDITURE	NET SAVING
$ 4,000	$4,110	$(—110)
5,000	5,000	0
6,000	5,850	150
7,000	6,600	400
8,000	7,240	760
9,000	7,830	1,170
10,000	8,360	1,640
11,000	8,850	2,150

SOURCE: Paul Samuelson, *Economics: An Introductory Analysis,* 6th ed. (New York: McGraw-Hill Book Company, 1964), p. 212.

What we are really saying is that the upper income groups do most of the saving and we would expect that they could purchase securities directly. The families in the middle income group will have larger accumulated savings if they are older and have earned their income for a number of years. Some individuals, particularly physicians and professional people, will have a sharp increase in income after a long period of little or no income. They will find that their personal expenditures and income taxes will be high, and it will be difficult for them to save. They will undoubtedly seek tax shelter in a financial plan that will reduce taxes and increase net income as a percentage of their total personal income. Ordinarily, people who expect their income to go up will save less from present income and will try to save more from future income. The physician wants to spend more and try to keep more, after a long period of fiscal restraint imposed by high medical school costs.

Social Competition and Age Factors

Even the upper income groups have difficulty saving and investing. Careful study of budget statistics shows that the difference between the consumption pattern of additional sums of money received by the rich and poor is not as great as we would imagine if we have accepted the idea that the upper income groups do all the saving and the lower income groups do very little. The upper income groups do pay more in federal income taxes, but they also spend more of their income for housing, travel, and education, which may increase the difficulty for them to save and invest directly. Social emulation may take hold of an individual in the higher income groups, and his attempt to keep up with the Joneses also limits his saving and investing. Professor Duesenberry believes that the people in any income group tend to compete with the people in the income group above them rather than with their own group.[1] This competition makes it difficult for the upper income groups to invest directly in the securities market.

The age pattern of the income group is also a factor in the ability of an individual in the upper income group to invest. The older people in the upper income group will have had a chance to accumulate savings and funds for investment. A younger person in the same income group might not be able to invest because of the demands on his income and because of the short period of time that he has been earning a high income. We are experiencing this phenomenon in the United States at the present time. More and more individuals and households are earning $10,000 and above, and this trend is expected to continue. Many, however, have just entered this income level and find it most difficult to save and invest. They have to wait until they have sufficient funds to

[1] James S. Duesenberry, *Income, Saving, and the Theory of Consumer Behavior* (Cambridge: Harvard University Press, 1949).

begin a direct investment program just like the physician who enters into a new and prosperous practice.

Attitude Toward Savings and Investment

The amount of money that we actually save for investment will be determined by out attitude toward thrift, in general, and the specific goals we have established for ourselves and our families.

When we do save we usually do so with a particular purpose or goal in mind. We save to purchase a major consumer good, to provide an education for our children, to provide additional income for our retirement years, or to buy a second home, a second car, a vacation hideaway, or a mink coat. Some of us save, of course, for the specific purpose of buying securities, which will in turn help us reach our financial goals. Few of us today save for the sake of saving. A study conducted by Dr. Ernest Dichter with the Institute for Motivational Research delved into the attitudes of Americans toward money and thrift. Dr. Leon Kendall of the United States Savings and Loan League commented upon two pertinent conclusions that resulted from the study:

> [1.] People still talk about savings goals and feelings toward money as if they were living in past eras. Emergencies and a rainy-day rationale are quite normal. The motivation folks say people do not mean what they say. Their actions, behavior and deeper explorations of their attitudes reveal contradictions and the emergence of new real values. Acceptance of cradle-to-grave security is a reality, even though there is much lip service paid to the necessity of saving for emergencies and security. Most Americans are convinced that the bare necessities of life will be provided even in emergencies. The Institute maintained that Americans really were saving for the extras —for the surplus over bare necessities of life. The good and leisurely retirement, a second home, a boat, travel to foreign lands, vacations —these have become the real reasons for savings.
>
> [2.] The financial age of Americans is rising. There is increasing acceptance among all socio-economic groups that money is itself a source of income. Money can work for its owner. One reason why savings and loans have been so successful is that they have introduced the American saver and investor to the world of investments. For the new investor they were the bridge leading from simple deposit-type institutions to the investment world. Americans continue to grow in financial sophistication ... So say the motivation research folks.[2]

These comments lead us to conclude that only a small amount of savings is nonpurposeful. Most savings are the result of a conscious

2 Leon T. Kendall, "Savings in the American Economy," Conference on Savings and Residential Financing, 1961, *Proceedings* (Chicago, May 11 and 12, 1961), pp. 76–77.

effort on the part of the individual to save for a specific purpose, and this often means investment. Other evidence exists of saving for the purpose of investment. One study[3] of large withdrawals and deposits from the savings and loan companies attempted to find out where the money deposited came from and how the withdrawals were used. The study involved people throughout the United States who withdrew or added $1,000 to their savings accounts during January, 1961. Of the total savers, 72.6 percent added to their accounts, and 56.3 percent withdrew; some both added and withdrew. The greatest percentage of people added to their savings accounts from current income or a bonus received at that period of time. Some added to their accounts because of stock or bond transactions. The most important reason for taking large amounts of money from the savings account was to buy stocks and bonds. Almost all the withdrawals were made for specific purposes, which supports the thesis that we save for the purchase of goods and services and we think of savings as a way to increase our standard of living and provide the luxuries in life.

Borrowed Funds as a Source of Investment Funds

Money for the purchase of securities may be obtained from borrowed money as well as from savings previously accumulated or from current income. The majority of professional investors would not recommend that money be borrowed to buy securities. We assume here that the investor will provide investment funds from savings. Some investors, however, consider it wise to borrow money to buy securities since they reason that they can earn a higher rate of return from securities investment than it costs to borrow the funds. This might be a satisfactory arrangement for some investors, but it adds extra risk to investment. The usual sources of funds borrowed to buy securities are: (1) margin loans from brokers, (2) security loans from commercial banks, and (3) life insurance loans.

Purchasing Stock on Margin

Securities may be purchased on margin through the securities broker. Before a margin account is opened, the broker must satisfy himself that the customer is reputable. The term *margin* refers to the amount of ownership that we must have in each share of stock that we purchase. A 70 percent margin means that we own 70 percent of the stock and that we can borrow 30 percent from our broker. If a stock is selling at 50 and the margin is 70 percent, we could borrow $15 per share and would need

3 Kendall, "Savings in the American Economy," p. 77.

$35 of our own money to complete the transaction. The margin requirement is determined by the Federal Reserve Board of Governors, who were given this power under the Securities Exchange Act of 1934. They have the authority to change the margin requirement as monetary policy dictates. During World War II and in times of inflation, the margin requirement has been 100 percent. In February, 1963, the margin requirement was 50 percent, indicating a somewhat easy credit policy in the securities market. It was increased to 70 percent in November, 1963, because of the sharp increase of stock market prices late in 1963 and continued in force through 1969. The margin requirement applies to all margin transactions in securities on registered security exchanges and also to bank loans that are made for the purpose of carrying any security traded on such exchanges.

The major advantage of purchasing stock on margin is the increased amount of stock that can be purchased with the same amount of money. If we have $1,000, we will be able to buy 100 shares at $10 per share on a straight cash basis. If the margin is 50 percent, we would be able to borrow, in effect, $1,000, and we would then be able to buy 200 shares of the same $10 stock. If the stock should increase in value, we will earn a profit on twice as many shares. On the other hand, if the price of the stock should decline, we will lose more; and we will be required to put up more margin or equity as the price falls. If we have no liquid assets or have borrowed so much that we cannot provide more margin, the broker can sell the shares and use the proceeds to return the money he loaned. Speculative situations such as these, in the past, have been disastrous for purchasers of securities.

Table 2–4 provides figures on the total amount of stock market credit outstanding for recent years and shows the amount of credit that was secured by government securities and by other securities. The total amount of money loaned against both customers' and broker and dealers' securities increased from 1958 to October of 1967, with the sharpest increases in 1962–1963 and 1966–1967. During this period the majority of the loans were made to carry securities other than United States Government securities. Customer credit by banks and stock exchange firms represent the bulk of the nongovernment borrowing. The amount of borrowing for the purchase of securities is variable. The dollar amounts involved appear to be large although they represent a small portion of the total value of securities traded and owned by individuals and institutions in the United States.

Security loans outstanding at any one time can be an unstabilizing influence in the securities market. When there is a great deal of stock market credit, the prices of securities are forced up by the additional demand for stock purchased with the proceeds of the loans. This was the situation in October, 1967 (Table 2–4). Under these conditions a

TABLE 2-4

Stock market credit
December, 1958–October, 1967
(millions of dollars)

		Customer Credit				Broker and Dealer Credit		
		Net debit balances with N.Y. Stock Exchange firms secured by:		Bank loans to others than brokers and dealers for purchasing and carrying:		Money borrowed on:		
DATE	TOTAL SECURITIES OTHER THAN U.S. GOVT. SECURITIES	U.S. GOVT. SECURITIES	OTHER SECURITIES	U.S. GOVT. SECURITIES	OTHER SECURITIES	U.S. GOVT. SECURITIES	OTHER SECURITIES	CUSTOMERS' NET FREE CREDIT BALANCES[b]
Oct. 1967	9,432	101	7,009	77	2,433	NA[c]	NA[c]	2,513
Dec. 1966	7,443	58	5,329	76	2,114	240	3,472	1,637
Dec. 1965	7,705	22	5,521	101	2,184	130	3,576	1,666
Dec. 1964	7,053	21	4,079	72	1,974	222	3,910	1,637
Nov. 1963	7,242	26	5,515	140	1,727	32	4,449	1,210
Dec. 1962	5,494	24	4,125	97	1,369	35	2,785	1,216
Dec. 1961	5,602	35	4,259	125	1,343	48	2,954	1,219
Dec. 1960	4,415	95	3,222	134	1,193	142	2,133	1,135
Dec. 1959	4,461	150	3,280	164	1,181	221	2,362	996
Dec. 1958	4,537	146	3,285	63	1,252	234	2,071	1,159

NOTE—Data in the first three columns and last column are for end of month, in other columns for the last Wednesday. NET DEBIT BALANCES AND BROKER DEALER CREDIT: Ledger balances of member firms of the New York Stock Exchange carrying margin accounts, as reported to the Exchange. Customers' debit and free credit balances exclude balances maintained with the reporting firm by other member firms of national securities exchanges and balances of the reporting firm and of general partners of the reporting firm. Balances are net for each customer—i.e., all accounts of one customer are consolidated. Money borrowed includes borrowings from banks and from other lenders except member firms of national securities exchanges. BANK LOANS TO OTHERS THAN BROKERS AND DEALERS: Figures are for weekly reporting member banks. Before July, 1959, loans for purchasing or carrying U.S. Government securities were reported separately only by New York and Chicago banks. Accordingly, for that period the fifth column includes any loans for purchasing or carrying such securities as other reporting banks. Composition of series also changed beginning with July, 1959; revised data for the new reporting series (but not for the breakdown of loans by purpose) are available back through July, 1958, and have been incorporated.

[a] May be looked upon simply as money borrowed to purchase securities.

[b] Considered to be money left on account at brokerage firm by customer and may be used immediately to buy securities.

[c] Not available.

SOURCE: *Federal Reserve Bulletin*, December, 1963, p. 1685; and December, 1967, p. 2104.

drop in prices may precipitate a demand for liquidity, securities may be sold, and prices may be forced down. By the same token, if money is borrowed to finance short sales, a stability may result. A short seller thinks the price of stock is going down. He sells stock that he borrows from or through his broker and sells the stock on the market. This adds to the supply of stocks and tends to depress the price. As the price of the stock declines, the short seller will buy stock in the market to repay the stock that he has borrowed. Since he sold at a higher price, he makes a profit. The act of buying adds to the demand for the stock and tends to support the price. Short sales are usually made on margin by speculators in the stock market. In the act of borrowing to finance his short sales, the market trader performs a stabilizing function. He adds to the supply of securities by borrowing stock from other owners when the market price of the stock is high. This tends to keep the price of stock from going higher. If and when the market price of the stock drops, the short seller buys stock in the market, which tends to support the price. If the majority of individuals bought securities with borrowed money, the impact on the securities market would, however, be unstabilizing, since there would be little market support if the market should begin to drop.

Commercial Bank Loans

Commercial banks lend money directly to purchase securities. When the securities are listed on a registered exchange, the amount of the loan is governed by the margin requirements established by the Federal Reserve Board. If the securities are traded in the over-the-counter market, the loan will be determined by the lender who must meet competition from other lenders. On high-quality debt securities of private corporations, the commercial banks will usually loan from 85 to 90 percent of market value. Loans on unlisted common stocks tend to follow the margin requirements of stocks traded on registered exchanges even though the banks vary the amount of the loan based on the quality of the stock. Security loans are short-term or term loans, and some provision is usually made for the gradual retirement of the loan.

Life Insurance Loans

Some people look upon life insurance as a source of funds for investment. The great majority of policy owners consider life insurance a part of their retirement program and would not borrow the money for the purchase of securities. Nevertheless, the cash surrender value of life insurance may be borrowed, and the money could be used to purchase securities. Because the rate of interest charged by life insurance companies is low, it is an economical way to borrow money. National Service Life Insurance, the federal government life insurance company, charges only 4 percent annually for the money borrowed against reserves and requires that the interest be paid annually. Monthly installments are not required to retire the debt. Commercial life insurance companies charge 5 percent interest, and no formal repayment plan is necessary. Since the borrower has the use of the funds for a full year, the effective rate of interest is low, and life insurance borrowing is one of the lowest-cost methods of obtaining short-term and long-term funds for the individual for whatever purpose he may have. Usually the interest for the first year is deducted in advance. If the loan is not paid off and the borrower dies, the amount of the loan is deducted from the value of the life insurance policy.

As a matter of financial conservatism, life insurance loans should be used to purchase securities, particularly common stock, only with the utmost care and knowledge of the risks and rewards involved. Actually, life insurance reserves should be earmarked for a specific purpose such as a retirement supplement, or for unexpected events. The market risk is real, and not all one's money should be invested in one outlet. In cases of financial emergencies life insurance cash values can be used as a low-cost, convenient source of funds. Table 2–2, referred to previously, shows the amount of life insurance loans in force. The amount of such loans has increased in recent years, and there have been increased efforts by mutual funds salesmen and some investment advisers to encourage life insurance policy owners to borrow the cash surrender value of their policies. The money would then be invested in mutual fund shares or managed by the investment advisers. Surely asset management by individuals is to be encouraged, but there are certain obvious weaknesses of such a program. If all policy owners borrowed and invested their cash surrender values, the first effect would be to raise equity prices; the second, to increase interest rates on policy loans; and the third, possibly to create instability in the capital markets.

Financial Prerequisites for Investment

Since an individual even in the higher income groups has difficulty accumulating savings or money to invest, and since investment is a function of the financial position of the individual, we will consider the financial prerequisites that the individual investor should meet before he undertakes investment in ownership securities. The usual and traditional financial prerequisites of investment are: (1) adequate life insurance, (2) substantial equity in a home, (3) a small amount of consumer debt, (4) an ample balance in the checking account, (5) savings for emergencies, and (6) money for the purchase of securities. In brief, the individual must be in a sound financial position before he can begin an investment program because it requires the acceptance of risk. Let us take a closer look at each of these prerequisites.

Adequate Life Insurance

One of the first financial prerequisites of investment for the individual is an adequate amount of life insurance. Just what is considered adequate will depend upon many variables, including annual income, amount of assets owned, age, occupation, health, and the awareness of a financial responsibility. The purpose of life insurance is to replace income that would be lost if the insured should die. At the same time, it provides funds to cover the immediate expenses incurred by the death of the insured, which can be substantial. Money is also provided for the settlement of the estate and prevents the sale of unmarketable assets that otherwise would force the estate to lose a substantial sum of money as a result of the forced sale. It provides an adjustment fund that allows the insured family to make the necessary transitional adjustments in their lives without financial hardship or sacrifice. Many families have been blessed with adequate funds upon the death of the breadwinner. What is a tragic period for any family might become a catastrophe without some financial reserves.

Ideally, we should have enough life insurance to provide the same amount of income that we would earn if we were alive. If a married man 25 years of age, for example, is earning $12,000 a year before taxes,[4] what would be an adequate amount of life insurance for him to carry? Based on the criterion of replacing income, he would need approximately $226,000 of life insurance or, because Social Security benefits are paid for surviving minor children, a lesser amount if he has children.[5] We assume, in this case, that the young man selects a settlement option whereby his wife will receive a life income of $3.24 per month per $1,000 of insurance with 240 months certain if he should die.

Our young man has other alternatives. His widow could invest the proceeds of the insurance and receive the interest, which would provide a steady income and keep the principal intact. Invested wisely, the insurance proceeds would provide enough interest to maintain the widow's present living standards. Another alternative would be for the widow to receive a large income per month for a specified number of years, but at the end of the period, probably a shorter period than the life of the

---

4 He's a young Ph.D. from Harvard in the Management Department at the University.

5 This was computed by first deducting the personal expenses of the father, income taxes, and life insurance premiums from the $12,000 income. These expenses amounted to $3,000. We must replace $9,000 of net income. The present value of $9,000 for 40 years, the man's working life span, at 2 1/2 percent is $225,920 or $226,000. If the man had children, his insurance needs would be lower. Social Security benefits would be paid until the children reached 18. We ignore the wife's benefits at age 62. The present value of Social Security income for two surviving children ages one and three is approximately $44,000, which reduces the amount of insurance needed to approximately $182,000.

widow, no income would be received. Another alternative would be to have the proceeds paid in equal monthly installments until the amount is used up. This is a life insurance settlement that offers—to the wife and then to the children if she should die—the benefit of a large income for a short period of time.

The only problem that our friend has is to pay for $226,000 (or $182,000 in the case of two children ages one and three) of life insurance on a gross income of $1,000 per month. If he decides to buy ordinary life insurance, which would provide him with protection for his life and also with savings in future years, ignoring dividends, his first annual premium will be $3,679.46, or $2,963.11 for the smaller amount.[6] Even if he purchases term insurance, which has the lowest annual premium, it will still be costly and will not provide future savings. A term policy to age 65, for $226,000 of insurance, would have a premium cost of $2,232.72. The young man could possibly buy the term insurance from current income at these rates, but more than 10 percent of his before-tax income would be spent on insurance, which would be out of balance with his other financial commitments. The ordinary life insurance would clearly be out of the question.

The solution to our young man's dilemma is to reduce the amount of insurance consistent with his income level and his life expectancy. Our man of 25 is quite fortunate. Out of 100 people 25 years of age now living, 76 will be alive at age 65. Our young man will probably be alive at 65, and his insurance needs will be less than we originally estimated. If he should die at an early age, his wife would be able to work, and this would help to reduce the annual income required from insurance. How much life insurance is purchased now depends upon how much the young man can put aside out of his income for insurance and how much he will actually need to provide protection. As a beginning, a $10,000 ordinary life insurance policy would be an acceptable minimum and would require only a modest portion of his $12,000 income. The premium on such a policy would be $188.10 per year, which is 1.6 percent of his gross income; he could easily afford three times as much life insurance and would be encouraged to take out this larger amount. The attractive feature of ordinary life is its savings feature as well as its protection. Without considering the dividends that will be paid over the life of the $10,000 policy, it will have a cash value at age 65 of $6,040. This money can be used by the insured, choosing any settlement option that he wishes.

As income increases and family situations change, additional insurance can be added to meet changing needs. When children come along, a house is purchased, or retirement is contemplated, insurance

6 *Underwriters Manual* (Philadelphia: Provident Mutual Life Insurance Company of Philadelphia, 1964), p. B57.

protection can be increased. As a standard, we might consider additional ordinary life insurance of between $5,000 and $10,000 per child as a minimum. When a house is purchased, our young man should consider additional ordinary life insurance or term insurance to cover the amount of the mortgage. The husband in a family with three children, a $15,000 mortgage, and $10,000 of income might have $55,000 of life insurance in force on his life, of which $40,000 might be ordinary life insurance—$10,000 for each child, and for the mother and the husband—and $15,000 in term insurance to cover the mortgage. If financial commitments made it impossible to meet the premiums on this much ordinary life insurance, then term insurance could be substituted. The advantage of ordinary life insurance is the flexibility it has not only for income and protection but for savings and retirement benefits. No savings are involved with term insurance. If $40,000 of ordinary life were taken out at age 25, this would provide a cash value of approximately $24,160 at age 65, which would provide substantial income benefits for retirement. In addition to these minimum needs, additional insurance could be purchased to provide a college fund or wedding fund for the children or to provide for the settlement of the estate. The amount of insurance purchased will depend on the income and desires of the insured. We have established no absolute minimum or maximum amount of insurance that our young man should keep in force. We simply suggest a workable minimum amount of insurance based on his changing needs and his income level. A wealthy man in a high tax bracket needing protection can buy substantial amounts of life insurance by borrowing the cash surrender value to pay the premiums. Eventually, interest that is tax deductible replaces the premium. Interest is deductible, but the premium payment is not; therefore, the after-tax cost to the purchaser is low if he is in a 40 percent tax bracket or higher.

Two other ways exist to establish an amount of insurance that is adequate. One way of determining the amount of insurance we need is to ask ourselves how much money would be needed if we should die. An amount for final expenses, including burial expenses, medical expenses, and legal fees will have to be paid from the estate. Second, any existing mortgage and installment loans must be paid off. Many consumer loans, however, have life insurance coverage, and if we should die, the loan would automatically be paid off. We should have enough insurance to provide income for our family during the various phases of their lives. We would want to support our widow if she had young children, and we would wish to provide for her if she were older and not able to work. We would probably wish to provide a college fund for our children, and if we should live to age 65, we would like to have a start toward a retirement fund. These requirements when added up would allow us to meet our insurance needs adequately.

The second approach is to set aside a fixed proportion of our income for insurance and thus increase our insurance as our income increases. A usual figure is 5 percent of gross income. Our young man earning $12,000 could spend up to $600 for insurance. As his income increased, the 5 percent allotted for insurance would provide more insurance to meet his greater need.

Substantial Equity in a Home

A second financial prerequisite to investment is a substantial amount of ownership in a home. More than 50 percent of American families own their own homes—which really means that they are buying their own homes. Only 10 percent of the home buyers pay cash for their homes; the remaining 90 percent borrow a portion or most of the money to pay for the house. In some local real estate markets, an individual can buy a small house for almost nothing down and pay off the loan in 360—or more—easy, equal installments. This is a hazardous situation for the marginal homeowner—the person who can just meet the monthly interest and principal payment and that is all. This person is in danger of losing his house should he be temporarily unemployed because of strike or illness or face a period of unforeseen extra expenses. Conservative financial standards suggest that a person put down as large a down payment as possible—a minimum of 10 percent. This is recommended on houses selling in the middle price bracket. On homes selling for higher prices the down payment should be greater. A house in the $25,000 price class should have at least a 20 percent equity, and a house selling for $35,000 at least 33 percent. (In many parts of the country, the standards for down payments are rather lower than these conservative ones.) A small mortgage in relation to the price of the house provides the owner with lower monthly rental payments, lower total interest costs, and greater ease of refinancing should the owner become ill and unable to pay the present mortgage. There is also financial security with a small mortgage in relation to a large equity in a house.

On the other hand, many people think it wise to have a large mortgage on a house. They reason that they will be able to sell a house more easily with a large mortgage than a small one, particularly if the rate on the existing mortgage is lower than the existing mortgage rate at the local savings and loan association. The large mortgage frees money for investment in common stock at higher rates of return. Assume, for example, that a person has a 5 percent mortgage for 80 percent of the value of the house. It would be unwise for him to reduce his mortgage to 50 percent of the value of the house if he could invest the money elsewhere at 10 percent. If his alternative were to invest elsewhere at a 4 percent rate, then he would be wise to pay off the mortgage. The subject comes up frequently among investors who want to know if they should pay off their 4½ percent G.I. loan. If we are in an inflationary economy, we would be wise not to be too anxious to pay off the mortgage, but to put our money to work at higher yields.

What is considered a substantial equity in a house? Each of us must answer this question for himself. Basically, we must have sufficient equity in a house when we purchase it to meet the requirement of the lending institutions. Once this is accomplished we are free to invest whatever money remains. We might even decide not to buy a house. Maybe we would rather live in a Park Avenue pad and invest the rest of our money—if any remains—in the stock market. It was once thought desirable not to have a mortgage. Today this concept is no longer true, because first, whether we have a mortgage-free house, a mortgage, or rent to pay, the cost of living in a house remains. Second, because of higher alternatives it might be better to put our money to work elsewhere. With these reasons in mind we must work out our own solution to the "equity, no equity–own a house, rent a house" syndrome, based upon the risks our financial sophistication allows us to accept and the rewards we wish to obtain.

A Minimum of Installment Debt

The installment debt that we owe should be modest in relation to our income. Where possible we should pay cash for items purchased. It is poor financial practice to borrow money at 6 percent interest, which leads to an 11 to 12 percent effective[7] rate of interest. Earning as high a rate of return on common stock is difficult, and in view of the added risk of stock ownership, it would be better to postpone investment and reduce the amount of installment loans. Certainly, the truth-in-lending laws will point up the high cost of borrowing money.

Those people in a high income tax bracket might find that the cost of borrowing is far less than the alternative yield obtainable from common stock. A person in the 50 percent tax bracket pays only 3 percent after taxes on a straight 6 percent note, or 5.54 percent effective rate on an installment loan. In this case we have a paradox: it is cheaper and wiser for a rich man to borrow who has the money than for a poor man to borrow who does not.

---

7 The formula for determining the effective rate of interest is:

$$i = \frac{2mD}{P(n+1)}$$

where i equals the annual rate of charge; m, the number of payments in one year (usually 12); D, the interest charge in dollars; P, the principal or cash advance; and n, the total number of payments. Assume a person borrows $1,200 for one year with the interest at 6% added on to the principal and then paid back in 12 equal installments of $106 per month. The interest cost is $72, there are 12 payments in one year, and the principal advanced is $1,200. Substituting in the formula, we find:

$$i = \frac{2 \times 12 \times 72}{1200 \ (12 + 1)} = 11.08\%$$

When individuals do borrow money for the purchase of durable consumer goods, the time period of the loan and the amount of installment debt should be limited. Three rules serve as a guide to the limits of installment debt. First, debt should not exceed one-third of discretionary income—the income remaining after all living expenses have been met. Second, debt should not exceed 20 percent of net annual income after taxes. Third, debt installments should not exceed 10 percent of monthly net income. If our net income is $500 per month, we can spend $50 per month for installment debt. The time period should be no longer than twenty-four months. Certainly installment debt should not exceed these amounts when applied to individual income. It is economical and conservative financial practice not to borrow money for installment purchases if a choice exists between investment and retiring consumer debt.

An Ample Checking Deposit

Another prerequisite for investment is to have an adequate amount of money in a checking account for transaction purposes. The amount on deposit should be sufficient to meet our monthly expenses with ease and flexibility and yet reasonably small to allow us to earn the maximum income on our accumulated savings. One month's salary after taxes would be considered adequate to meet our needs. If our net monthly income is $1,000, then the average balance in our commercial bank account should be $1,000. This might seem like a large average balance, but one-half of the requirement is met by having our monthly paycheck deposited in the bank. We need deposit only one half-month's income to meet our checking requirements. This amount, however, will vary depending on the nature and amount of individual transactions and the pattern of our income. If expenses are seasonal or annual rather than monthly or weekly, we will need a greater amount of money in our checking account. Our financial demands for cash vary from time to time, and liquidity needs are just as important to us as they are to the commercial bank manager or the financial manager of an industrial corporation. Just as these people need money to conduct their business, we as individuals need money to manage our financial activities. We must provide sufficient funds to pay our bills as they come due, and yet we do not want abundant balances in our account because we will lose income. Commercial bank deposits provide convenience, safety, and liquidity, but they do not create income.

Savings as an Emergency Fund

A fifth prerequisite for our investment program is a savings fund that can serve as an emergency fund for sickness or financial problems that develop beyond our capacity to pay out of current income. At one time investment advisers recommended six months' salary for the emergency fund. This was before Blue Cross, Blue Shield, Old Age Survivor Benefits, Social Security, major medical, accident and sickness policies, Medicare, Mutual of Omaha, and bank credit cards. With the protection plans available to and used by most of us, the old rule of thumb for an emergency fund is archaic. It is a good idea, however, to have some money readily available to meet emergencies, whether it be a visit from your mother-in-law or an unexpected business or vacation trip. Even this is not needed if you have developed a good credit relationship with your banker.

Whatever amount we decide to place in an emergency fund should be made to work for us. It is important that we select a deposit account at a savings institution or other savings medium that provides us with the highest rate of return consistent with safety, convenience, and liquidity. Liquidity is the ability to convert the asset into cash without a loss of principal or interest. There are several acceptable and safe depositories for our savings.

SAVINGS ACCOUNT AT THE COMMERCIAL BANK

Commercial banks offer many services to their customers beyond the deposit function and have been referred to as "department store banks" because of the wide variety of services they perform. The commercial bank does offer savings account services to its customers. Historically, the rate of interest paid on commercial bank savings accounts has been low. In the late 1950's, the maximum rate paid on savings deposits was 3 percent, and many commercial banks paid only 1 or 1 1/2 percent on these accounts. The Board of Governors of the Federal Reserve System and the Federal Deposit Insurance Corporation establish the maximum permissible rate of interest payable by member and insured nonmember commercial banks under Regulation Q. Effective September 26, 1966, commercial banks were permitted to pay up to 4 percent on savings deposits and on time deposits and marketable certificates of deposit of less than 90 days. They may pay up to 5 percent on time deposits and multiple maturity certificates of deposit with 90-day maturity or longer and on single maturity certificates of deposit of less than $100,000; and up to 5 1/2 percent for single maturity certificates of deposit on time deposits of $100,000 or more. The savings deposits of commercial banks have grown substantially in recent years, particularly with the increased rates, so that commercial banks have become much more competitive in the savings deposit and time deposit area and are now competitive with the savings and loan industry.

A commercial bank offers two methods of saving. One is a savings account where ownership is represented by a passbook. Deposits and withdrawals can be made freely by the depositor. The bank reserves the right to require 30 days' notice when a withdrawal is to be made, but this is very seldom enforced. Interest is paid in several different ways. The usual method requires the payment of interest every six months, but more and more banks are offering "instant" interest, paid beginning on the day the money is deposited. This method has attracted additional deposits to the commercial banks that use it. A typical rate of interest was 4 percent per annum on these accounts in January, 1968.

The savings account at a commercial bank is protected by the Federal Deposit Insurance Corporation, if the bank is a member, up to $15,000 for each account. Nonmember banks have comparable protection so that accounts of this type are safe; since they may be held in the bank where we have our checking account, they are convenient; and they offer liquidity, too, as they are usually available at the discretion of the saver.

Savings certificates or time savings certificates (CD's) offer a second means of saving at the commercial bank. Savings certificates can be issued for varying amounts, with typical denominations of $100, $500, and $1,000. Interest is paid every six months by check. Some banks require that these certificates be renewed every six months, and others renew annually but pay interest every six months. The interest is not compounded since it is not added to the account on balance. The rate on six-month and one-year certificates under the 1966 Federal Reserve regulation can be as high as 5 percent. The certificates offer the saver the possibility of a higher rate of return than does the savings deposit, but liquidity is sacrificed. Some banks have overcome the liquidity aspect by issuing marketable certificates of deposit. The dollar amount of savings certificates purchased is small in comparison to the total dollar amount of savings.

MUTUAL SAVINGS BANKS

If we live in an Eastern city in the United States, we might place our savings in a mutual savings bank. In such a case, our deposits are evidenced by a passbook, and we receive income on our deposits in the form of dividends. Depositors are the mutual owners of the association and receive all the benefits of ownership. We can withdraw our money at any time, although the banks can require from 30 to 90 days' notice of withdrawal. This rule is very seldom enforced, but if it were used in an emergency, we would be in a difficult position financially. Our savings account is protected by careful management and financial reserves. More than half of the mutual savings banks are insured by the FDIC up to $15,000 for each account. A savings account in a mutual savings bank would be as safe, as liquid, and as profitable as an account with a commercial bank. It might not, however, have the same convenience.

SAVINGS AND LOAN ASSOCIATIONS

Savings and loan associations have become more competitive in recent years for the savings dollar. Their growth has been extremely rapid in comparison to other savings institutions and commercial banks. Most of the associations are mutually owned, although some have deposit accounts and share accounts that distinguish depositors from owners. Both types of account pay the same rate of interest. Some savings and loan associations use the holding-company device to bring together several businesses under one roof. Some of the associations are state chartered and some are federally chartered. All federal associations must be members of the Federal Home Loan Bank System and the Federal Savings and Loan Insurance Corporation. The FSLIC insures deposits to $15,000 just as the FDIC does for commercial bank deposits.

The savings account with the savings and loan company is the same as one with the commercial bank or the mutual savings bank. Savings and loan companies are not required to pay depositors on demand, but for ordinary requests for money they will do so. In emergencies they would require from 30 to 90 days' notice. They are not required to pay the full amount even at the end of the notice period. In times of stress only a portion would be paid, to insure the continued operation of the savings and loan company.

Somewhat more risk is involved with savings accounts at the savings and loan company, but this risk is partially compensated for by the higher rate of dividends paid on these savings. Liquidity could be less than with other savings, particularly under the adverse economic conditions that persisted in the mid and late 1960's. The protection afforded depositors is the same as at other savings institutions, but the convenience of a savings and loan savings account is less than an account at the commercial bank. Where liquidity can be sacrificed, savings at the savings and loan association offers an attractive outlet for funds. These banks are more numerous than mutual savings banks.

UNITED STATES SAVINGS BONDS

Few Americans who lived through World War II or the Korean conflict do not know about United States Savings bonds. Many people who bought savings bonds during these wars had never saved before. They now found that it was an easy way to accumulate a savings fund, particularly with the device of payroll deduction plans. These funds were eventually used to buy houses, cars, and education, and even to provide a strong financial reserve for the future purchase of common stock. Some people were disappointed in savings bonds when inflation reduced the purchasing power of the dollar and many savers had less purchasing power when the bond matured than when it was purchased. Today, savings bonds are a desirable outlet for savings that serve as an emergency fund for the investor.

Many different series of savings bonds have been available since their first offering in March, 1935. Today, however, only three series are of importance for the saver: Series E and Series H United States Savings bonds, and Freedom Shares.

Series E Savings Bonds. The Series E bonds are part of the non-marketable debt of the United States Government. These bonds took the place of Postal Savings bonds and are typically purchased from banks, through payroll deduction plans, or through other agencies of the federal government. They are available in denominations of $25, $50, $100, $200, $500, $1,000, $10,000 and $100,000, with respective purchase prices of $18.75, $37.50, $75.00, $150, $375, $750, $7,500 and $75,000. The bonds increase in value over time. The longer the bonds are held, the greater their value, until they reach their maximum value at maturity. In May, 1968, the yield to maturity was $4\frac{1}{4}$ percent over the life of the bond, which was seven years. The bonds do not pay current interest by check, but a certain amount of interest is credited to the bond each year: for this reason, they are referred to as discount savings bonds. The interest added annually to the initial purchase price may be declared as income each year even though it is not received, or it may be declared as income when the bond matures. The interest rate is a compound rate over the life of the bonds, and the purchaser receives a greater interest rate in later years than in the earlier years. The bonds are available to individuals, who are limited annually to the purchase of $7,500 of bonds at the purchase price or $10,000 maturity value. Only trustees of employee savings plans may buy the $100,000 bonds.

The bonds are redeemable 60 days from the date of purchase. Once the initial waiting period has passed, the bonds may be presented for payment at any financial institution that is a paying agent of the U. S. Treasury—a commercial bank, a Federal Reserve Bank or branch, or the office of the Treasurer of the United States. If we had purchased Series E savings bonds and had to cash in some of them to provide funds for an emergency, we would be wise to cash in the bonds with the later maturities, since they receive a lower dollar amount of interest compared to bonds that are closer to maturity. Savings bonds are registered, and if the certificate is lost, it may be replaced upon proof of loss and presentation of the serial number of the bond to the Bureau of Public Debt. The bonds are automatically renewed at maturity at the existing rate of interest should the purchaser fail to present them for payment. The bonds represent a safe convenient method of saving, and after 60 days they are completely liquid. The rate of interest, however, is not competitive with savings and loan associations.

Series H Savings Bonds. The Series H bond is also a part of the nonmarketable debt of the United States. It is a current-income bond in contrast to the Series E appreciation bond; that is, the interest is paid by check rather than accumulated. The bonds may be purchased only by individuals, and the interest is paid semiannually, beginning six months from date of purchase. The purchase price and the maturity price are the same, and the bonds may be purchased in denominations of $500, $1,000, $5,000, and $10,000. The yield over the life of the bond is the same as the Series E bond, but it must be held 10 years to earn the same rate of interest. Series H bonds may be redeemed at face value any time after six months from issue date. One month's notice must be given for redemption. The bonds may be purchased at any Federal Reserve Bank or branch and at the office of the Treasurer of the United States. Purchase can be arranged through commercial banks and other financial institutions. Series H bonds have the same registration provisions as Series E bonds, they are nontransferable, income tax must be paid annually on interest received, and if the certificate is lost, it may be replaced by notifying the Bureau of Public Debt. If we purchase savings bonds, we should record the serial number elsewhere so that if the bond certificate is lost it may be properly identified.

Freedom Shares. Freedom Shares are actually short-term notes sold to members of bond-a-month plans. They have a yield of 5 percent when held to maturity of four and a half years. In order to buy Freedom Shares a person must buy an equal amount of Series E or H bonds. This lowers the effective yield on the combination purchase to 4 5/8 percent, which is still higher than the 4 1/4 percent paid on Series E or H bonds.

The Series E and H bonds are of high quality although the current level of yields is lower than in some forms of savings. Freedom Shares are more competitive with other savings outlets. The Series E bond and the Freedom Share possess a greater degree of liquidity than does the Series H bond and for emergency purposes would be more suitable than the Series H because of this feature. Both bonds must be held to maturity to earn the rate of interest that is guaranteed. Savers are penalized when they hold these securities only a short time. The lowest denomination of the H bond is $500, making it somewhat unattractive for the small saver. Series E bonds have the advantage of convenience of purchase, since they can be bought through the payroll deduction plan.

The Investment Fund

The final financial prerequisite of investment is an amount of money that can be used for the purchase of investment securities including stocks and bonds. Obviously, there is no limit to this amount—the larger the better. Investment can begin with $500, $1,000, $10,000, or $100,000. Investment might even begin with the monthly or quarterly purchase of common stock through a thrift plan in the company where we work. Most plans of this type offer us the opportunity to put a small amount of our salary into the common stock of the company or into selected investment companies. These small amounts, regularly contributed, can eventually lead to a sizable investment fund.

MONTHLY INVESTMENT PLAN

A person might also subscribe to a monthly investment plan (MIP) through a brokerage firm that conducts business on the New York Stock Exchange. Under this plan, we can buy shares of stock in one company or in an investment company. The investment company invests in the shares of other corporations, and trained managers provide continuous supervision and management of the funds. Usually we need a minimum amount of money to begin the program. In the case of one investment company, the minimum is $500. Then we would be required to pay monthly or quarterly amounts of at least $25, which is invested in additional shares. This type of program offers the advantage of buying stock in small amounts and eventually accumulating a rather large sum of money in investment securities if continued for a long period of time. The individual has the added advantage of being able to buy stock at various prices, thus taking advantage of both higher and lower prices to keep his average investment at a realistic price. This program provides one solution to the problem of timing investment purchases.

Under the MIP program, begun in 1953, more than 90 percent of the plans provide for the reinvestment of dividends. Under the New York Stock Exchange program, as little as $40 per quarter and up to $1,000 per month can be invested with ordinary commissions being charged. The major advantage of the MIP program is dollar averaging and the accumulation of principal through a regular savings program. Unfortunately, it is an expensive way to purchase common stock, since the dollar amounts are small and regular commissions are paid on these amounts at the highest rate, 6 percent.

ANNUAL INVESTMENT PLAN (AIP)

A better way to invest small amounts is to accumulate money on a regular basis and then to invest annually in common stock. One way to accomplish this would be to have monthly salary deductions for the purchase of Series E savings bonds. When the cash value of the bonds reached $500 or above they could be cashed in and the money used to buy common stock. There is economy involved in buying $500 worth of stock rather than 10 purchases of $50 each, as the savings in brokerage commissions over time can be substantial. We also achieve the same benefits of dollar averaging. Over long periods of time, it is just as advantageous to buy stock once a year as it is to buy once a month.[8] There is nothing magical about monthly stock purchase except that it is forced and becomes a habit. If we can invest larger amounts regularly and more cheaply, it is to our advantage to do so. The AIP program has greater merit than the MIP method.

INVESTMENT CLUB

Another alternative is to begin an investment fund in a small way by joining an investment club. In 1968, the National Association of Investment Clubs included over 9,400 clubs with more than 150,000 members. The number of members in a club varies from ten to twenty-five. The members pool their funds and decide which stock or stocks to purchase. Typically, $10 is invested by each member each month. The purpose of the investment club is not only to invest but to learn something about investment and our economic and financial system. It also allows us to invest small sums of money and purchase securities cheaply. It would be costly for one individual to buy such a small dollar amount by himself. The purchase of shares in quality companies over a long period of time can lead to a sizable investment fund.

The National Association of Investment Clubs has taken an active role in encouraging the growth of these clubs. Their annual and regional meetings are excellent. The information they distribute is extremely helpful for the "little investor."[9] However, the investment club idea is not confined to the small investor with $10 a month; several clubs of professional analysts require an initial investment of $500 and a $100 monthly contribution.

We assume in this text that the typical investment fund will be greater than a few hundred dollars. A better concept of the size of the fund for management would be close to $50,000. The principles of analysis and investment management, of course, apply to a small fund as well as to a large one. Indeed, it is often more difficult to manage a small fund because it is difficult to achieve diversification, which is easily obtained in the larger fund. It might seem logical at this point to discuss portfolio management principles for the individual investor or for individuals who will manage portfolios for other individual investors, mutual funds, pension funds, or college endowment funds. The plan, however, is first to obtain knowledge of the various investment alternatives available, establish a method of analysis, and study the behavior of the stock market before discussing portfolio management theory and subsequently the practical solution to investors' problems. The specific objectives and motives surrounding investors, the securities they

8 Frederick Amling, "Is There an Optimum Time Period for Dollar Averaging?" *Commercial and Financial Chronicle*, April 8, 1965, p. 10.

9 *Better Investing*, National Association of Investment Clubs, Detroit, Michigan.

choose, and the portfolio policies they follow will be discussed under portfolio management in later chapters.

A Personal Financial Statement

Many of us don't really know our own financial strength. One way of finding out is to take stock of what we have—to set up a statement of our financial position in the form of a balance sheet, just like the men who plan the financial affairs of billion-dollar multinational corporations. Table 2–5 presents such a financial statement for John and Mary at the end of the year. John, age 40, and Mary, age 36, have been married for 20 years. They have two children, ages 10 and 15. John earns $15,000 per year, but has just written a short story that makes his financial future much brighter. The financial position of John and Mary is excellent and demonstrates financial conservatism. Their checking balance is adequate, savings level good with some money available for investment—the $3,000 accounts receivable. The loan value of life insurance can be used for emergencies and a portion could be used for investment in the securities market, given John and Mary's financial position. They have adequate equity in their houses (one inherited) and modest loan commitments. They are ready now to assume the risks of security investment.

TABLE 2–5

Financial statement, December 31,
John and Mary

CURRENT ASSETS			CURRENT LIABILITIES		
Checking account	$ 1,000		Notes to banks (6%)	$2,000	
Savings account	3,000		Notes to friends	0	
Accounts receivable			Accounts payable	400	
(royalties)	3,000		Federal income taxes	300	
TOTAL		$ 7,000	TOTAL		$ 2,700
FIXED ASSETS			**FIXED LIABILITIES**		
Automobiles owned	$ 2,500		Life insurance loans (5%)	$ 2,250	
Stocks & bonds	3,000		Mortgages on real estate		
Mortgages owned	0		(5 1/2%)	18,500	
Life insurance (cash value)	5,800		Summer house (6%)	6,000	
Furniture and fixtures	10,000		TOTAL		28,250
Other personal property					
(boat)	500		Mortgages on autos (11%)	1,500	
Real estate owned					
(residence)	25,000				
Summer house	15,000				
		61,800	Net worth (ownership)		37,850
TOTAL		$68,800	TOTAL		$68,800

Postscript on Financial Prerequisites

The financial prerequisites for investment might seem stringent for individuals who are close to the median income level in the United States. Unfortunately, the observation is correct. Many people are not in a financial position to consider investment in ownership securities. They have funds to invest, but other demands upon their income preclude the assumption of risk. There are literally thousands of individuals, on the other hand, who are in a financial position to own, directly, securities in American industry. They meet the financial prerequisites on all counts, and yet for personal reasons and financial conservatism they choose not to buy stock. Those who can assume the risk are needed to supply capital to a growing economy. The new investment dollars will allow us to achieve our national economic goals. If all these financial prerequisites are met and adhered to by the individual investor or the professional adviser, then many of the investment risks are eliminated and the probability of success is much greater. It has been my experience that investors lose substantial sums of money simply because they violate the simple tenet of sound personal finance that everyone knows about.

Summary

Savings from current income represent one of the most important sources of funds for investment. Individuals save substantial sums of money each year, in many forms including contribution to pension funds, purchase of life insurance, addition to savings, and even the purchase of securities directly. Most of the saving of individuals is purpose saving, and one of the important purposes is to purchase investment securities. Previously accumulated savings that have been built up by individuals represent an important source of funds for the direct purchase of securities. Borrowed funds are also a source of money for the purchase of securities, although it is not recommended that the average investor borrow money to buy stock. Some funds, however, are borrowed to purchase securities, and they sometimes add substantially to the amount of funds in the market. Many loans are made through brokers or commercial banks. These loans are regulated by the Federal Reserve Board of Governors, who determine the amount of the margin. In January, 1964, the margin requirement became 70 percent. The customers of brokers and bankers themselves borrow money for the purchase of stock. Banks also provide loans on securities not regulated by the Federal Reserve Board of Governors.

Savings for investment depends upon the income level of the individual and his motivation. In our industrial society it is difficult for most families to accumulate savings. We would expect individuals in the upper income groups to add to security holdings, but even for these individuals savings and investment are difficult. The desire to spend the extra dollar of income is just as strong for the higher income groups as it is for the lower. The investment of funds in risk securities requires that the investor meet certain financial prerequisites. As investors we must have: (1) adequate life insurance, (2) adequate equity in a home, (3) a conservative amount of consumer debt in relation to income, (4) an adequate checking-account balance, (5) an emergency fund, and (6) money for the purchase of securities. Savings for investment may be put to work in savings accounts at the commercial bank, mutual savings bank, savings and loan association, or in United States savings bonds; and the investment fund may be set up through the MIP, AIP, or an investment club. These prerequisites make an investment program difficult to begin for many investors. Other people who can afford the risk of common-stock ownership do not accept it. Since this is such a fundamental part of our economic system, they should be encouraged, if possible, to accept this risk. Once the prerequisites have been met, the individual is free to invest in relation to his needs, his motives, and his portfolio objectives. Adherence to these simple financial prerequisites can go a long way in helping investors achieve success.

Review Questions

1. What is meant by the term *savings*, and why are savings so important to the investment process?
2. If an individual purchased common stock from current income, would saving or investment, in the financial sense, take place?
3. Individuals most frequently make their direct purchases of investment securities from previously accumulated savings. Comment.
4. Do private business corporations save money that can be used for investment?
5. Would the following financial transactions be considered as savings or investment in the financial sense:
   (a) contributions to a pension?
   (b) Social Security contributions?
   (c) deposits in a savings account?
   (d) the payment of life insurance premiums?
   (e) repayment of an auto loan?
   (f) mortgage payments on a home?
6. What determines the amount of money an individual will save from his annual income?
7. Does the wealthy young doctor have a savings problem?
8. What other sources of funds do we have for investment other than current or previously accumulated savings?

9. Should we borrow money to purchase investment securities?

10. What are the risks involved in borrowing money to purchase securities?

11. Where could we obtain security loans? Explain.

12. How are security loans regulated?

13. A mutual fund salesman suggests that you borrow the cash surrender value of your life insurance and buy his mutual fund. What would be your answer?

14. How are the financial prerequisites for investment related to risk and investment success?

15. Where can we put our savings to work?

16. What type of United States Government securities will enable us to save money with security and safety?

17. How large must the investment fund be before investment takes place, after the financial prerequisites have been met?

18. What are the advantages and disadvantages of the AIP?

Problems

1. What is the current rate of interest we would earn if we placed our money in:
   (a) a savings account at a commercial bank?
   (b) a savings account with a savings and loan association?
   (c) certificates of deposit at a commercial bank?
   (d) Series E savings bonds?
   (e) guaranteed rate on life insurance reserves excluding dividends?

2. If we decided to borrow money to buy securities, what rate of interest would we be required to pay if we borrowed money from:
   (a) the commercial bank?
   (b) the broker on margin?
   (c) a life insurance company as a policy loan?

3. (a) If we earned $10,000 per year, how much could we be expected to save?
   (b) How much would we have available for the purchase of securities directly from our savings at this income level?
   (c) What would be the financial prerequisites necessary at this income level? What should be one's savings, checking, and housing requirements, and the like?
   (d) If we assume that we are married and have three children, what would be our insurance requirements at the $7,500 income level?
   (e) If we owned our own home, would our life insurance requirements change? Explain.

4. Draw up a realistic balance sheet for yourself or for an investment client. Have the financial prerequisites for investment been met?

5. Assume that we have $1,000 in the local savings and loan association over and above our basic savings needs. We wish to buy an automobile that will cost us $1,000 plus our old car. The local bank will

loan us the $1,000 at 6 percent per annum and will give us two years to pay off the loan. The bank adds the interest on at the beginning and then we repay the total in 24 installments. The savings bank is currently paying 4 1/2 percent interest on deposits.

(a) Should we borrow the money and repay over a 24-month period, or should we use our savings? Explain.

(b) Should we borrow the money from the bank and then withdraw the savings and invest in common stock? Discuss.

6. A young couple earns $7,000 per year and is interested in starting an investment program. Specifically, what would be their financial requirements before they begin such a program? They have Blue Cross and Blue Shield, are in good heatlh, and do not own a house or have life insurance. They are in their early twenties. What would you advise them?

7. A doctor, age 33, earned $30,000 last year, his first year of practice. What would you tell him about the financial prerequisites to investment? What is his biggest financial problem?

Sources of Investment Information

Credit Union Yearbook
Federal Reserve Bulletin
Life Insurance Fact Book
Local: (a) Commercial banks
      (b) Credit unions
      (c) Employers with payroll deduction plans
      (d) Mutual savings banks
      (e) Savings and loan associations
      (f) Life insurance companies
Savings and Loan Fact Book
Survey of Current Business
National Association of Investment Clubs
New York Stock Exchange Fact Book

Selected Readings

Cock, Albert H., Jr., "Regulation of Interest on Deposits: An Historical Review," *The Journal of Finance* (May, 1967), pp. 274–99, including discussions by Charles Linke.

Crawford, Peter H., "Money and Household Liquidity," *Financial Analysts Journal* (January-February, 1967), p. 13.

Gaines, Tilford C., "A New Look at Certificates of Deposit," *Financial Analysts Journal* (March-April, 1967), p. 117.

Klaman, Saul B., "The Plenitude of Scarcity," *Financial Analysts Journal* (July-August, 1967), p. 59.

Korsvik, William J., "Consumer Installment Credit (A Review)," *Financial Analysts Journal* (July-August, 1966), p. 25.

Miller, Donald C., "Financial Markets Understressed," *Financial Analysts Journal* (January-February, 1968), p. 81.

Motley, Byran, "A Demand-for-Money Function for the Household Sector: Some Preliminary Findings," *The Journal of Finance* (September, 1967), p. 405.

Mueller, Eva, and Jane Lean, "The Savings Account as a Source of Financing for Large Expenditures," *The Journal of Finance* (September, 1967), pp. 467–70.

Neil, Herbert E., Jr., "The Consumer's Tomorrow's Buying," *Financial Analysts Journal* (May-June, 1967), p. 18.

Nicholson, G.A., Jr., and T.E. O'Hara, "Investment Clubs," *Financial Analysts Journal* (May-June, 1968), p. 141.

Packer, Stephen B., "Highest Interest Rates Forever?" *Financial Analysts Journal* (January-February, 1968), p. 84.

Ritter, Lucy E., "A Sense of Values," *Financial Analysts Journal* (January-February, 1967), p. 98.

II

THE ALTERNATIVE INVESTMENT OUTLETS FOR FUNDS

3

GOVERNMENT SECURITIES

Once we have reached a financial level at which we can begin an investment program, we are faced with the problem of selecting securities that will meet our investment needs. No one type of security will provide us with a solution to our investment problem. If we seek stability of income, we usually give up the possibility of growth. If we try to provide greater current income or greater capital appreciation, then we are forced to accept a greater degree of risk. The final decision we make in the selection of securities will be a delicate balance between risk and reward. As individual investors, we might wish to invest in an electronics company with a high growth rate that offers the hope of financial independence, but we are not certain that we want to accept the risks associated with a stock that is priced high in relation to its current earnings because of the competitive business risks involved.

We must also decide how much of our total funds should be devoted to assets that are liquid, or easily converted to money, and how much to assets that will be invested more or less permanently. There is an associated problem. If we have a sum of money now available for investment, should we put all our funds to work now, or should we wait and invest funds at a later time? Here we must balance liquidity with profitability, just as the financial manager of a large industrial corporation does. We should attempt to maximize profits from our investment portfolio consistent with the risks we are willing to assume. To do this, we must be thoroughly familiar with the types of investment securities from which we can select.

In this section we will discuss the various security investments available to us. They will be discussed in the order of their safety, stability, and risks, the safest and most stable securities first, beginning with marketable government bonds. In this chapter we will examine the long- and short-term debt securities of the United States Government and then securities issued by state and municipal governments. The relative investment merits of these securities and where they might fit in our investor's portfolio will be presented. In subsequent chapters, private corporate bonds, corporate preferred stock, common stock, and convertible securities will be examined. Ordinarily, each of these securities possesses more risk and less stabiliity than do government bonds. It is in these areas where risks and rewards are greater that we must undertake to develop more sophisticated financial judgment.

United States Government Securities

Money for an ever-growing federal government has provided institutional investors with an ample supply of quality securities in which to invest their funds. The magnitude of the United States federal debt is shown in Table 3–1, by type of security. Federal debt has kept pace with our expanding government activities. Historically, debt has surged forward because of war expenditures. In more recent years, debt has increased because of our defense efforts to maintain the peace and to fight an undeclared war in Vietnam. In Table 3–1 we see the rise in debt from 1941 to 1947, primarily because of World War II, and then the continued growth because of record federal spending from 1957 to the present. In only one year, 1960, was the total amount of federal debt reduced; otherwise, there has been some increase each year. In spite of this growth in debt, the credit position of our government is unquestioned. The United States has not defaulted or repudiated a bond issue, and the amount of debt and debt interest is modest compared with our national wealth and national income.

The ownership of United States debt is concentrated in the hands of institutional investors. Individuals, as a group, do not own a very large portion of marketable United States Government securities. This is demonstrated by the figures in Table 3–2, which show the ownership of our national debt. Individuals owned about 10 percent of the marketable United States Government securities in December, 1967. However, individuals owned almost 24 percent of the publicly held debt in the form of savings bonds. The bulk of the marketable debt is held by financial institutions, with the concentration of ownership at commercial banks. Commercial bank ownership is concentrated in short-term securities for more than 48 percent of the publicly held debt. Despite the lack of direct ownership of United States securities by individuals, these securi-

TABLE 3–1

Public issues[a] *of United States Government securities—by type (billions of dollars)*

YEAR	TOTAL ISSUES	Marketable Securities						Nonmarketable Securities	
		TOTAL	BILLS	CERTIFICATES	NOTES	BONDS	CONVERTIBLE BONDS[b]	TOTAL[c]	SAVINGS BONDS
1967	284.2	226.1	69.5	5.6	61.4	95.3	2.6	55.6	51.7
1966	273.0	218.0	64.7	5.9	48.3	99.2	2.7	52.3	50.8
1965	270.3	214.6	60.2	—	50.2	104.2	2.8	52.9	50.3
1964	267.5	212.5	56.5	—	59.0	97.0	3.0	52.0	49.7
1963	261.6	207.6	51.5	10.9	58.7	86.4	3.2	50.7	48.8
1962	255.8	203.0	48.3	22.7	53.7	78.3	4.0	48.8	47.5
1961	249.2	196.0	43.0	5.5	71.5	76.0	4.6	48.6	47.5
1960	242.5	189.0	39.4	18.4	51.3	79.9	5.7	47.8	47.2
1959	244.3	188.3	39.6	19.7	44.2	84.8	7.1	48.9	48.2
1958	236.0	175.6	29.7	36.4	26.1	83.4	8.3	52.1	51.2
1957	227.1	164.2	26.9	34.6	20.7	82.0	9.5	53.4	52.5
1947	225.3	165.8	15.1	21.2	11.4	118.1	—	59.5	52.1
1941	50.5	41.6	2.0	—	6.0	33.6	—	8.9	6.1

[a] Includes amounts held by U.S. Government agencies and trust funds, which totaled $13,943 million on October 31, 1963, and are considered part of publicly held debt.

[b] Includes Treasury bonds and minor amounts of Panama Canal and Postal Savings bonds.

[c] Includes Series A investment bonds, depository bank bonds, armed forces leave bonds, adjusted service bonds, certificates of indebtedness—foreign series, Rural Electrification Administration bonds, and, before 1956, tax and savings notes, not shown separately.

SOURCE: *Federal Reserve Bulletin*, December, 1967, p. 2110.

ties play an extremely important part in our financial system. Most of our financial institutions are dependent upon government securities for investment outlets; a few invest in government securities to the exclusion of all other securities. Some individuals purchase short-term marketable government securities to meet specific and temporary portfolio needs. Short-term Treasury bills are a haven for investors who want to keep their money working for them until favorable long-term investments are available among common stocks.

Government securities are classified into several groups. The two main groups are marketable and nonmarketable securities; convertible bonds are a smaller group representing one series of bonds. Marketable securities, which include Treasury bills, Treasury certificates of indebtedness, Treasury notes, and Treasury bonds, represent the largest portion of federal debt. Nonmarketable issues represent a large portion of the public debt; the most important security is United States Savings bonds and noninterest-bearing savings stamps. Treasury tax notes and savings notes are also included in this group. Another category of bonds closely related to the direct obligations of the government are the debt issues of government corporations and agencies that are not direct obligations of the United States. The specific securities included in this category are issues of the Federal Land Bank, Federal Home Loan Bank For Co-ops, Federal Intermediate Credit Bank, Federal National Mortgage Association, and The World Bank.

The marketable securities issued by the federal government are divided into short-term, intermediate-term, and long-term issues. Each has certain advantages and disadvantages for the individual investor. The demarcation between time classes is arbitrary. The majority of government securities in the short-term group have maturity dates of less than one year (Treasury bills); intermediate-term securities, from three to five years (Treasury notes); and long-term (Treasury bonds), with maturities of greater than five years. Prices for direct government obligations and agency bonds are quoted daily in the Wall Street Journal. Let us take a closer look at each of the marketable securities of the agencies of the federal government to learn how they can be used by us.

Treasury Bills

Treasury bills are short-term securities sold by the Treasury of the United States as a direct obligation. Most of these securities have a maturity of 91 days and are sold at a discount and redeemed at par at maturity. The bills are issued in bearer form in denominations ranging from $1,000 to $1,000,000. Individuals do not purchase the bonds directly from the Treasury: the Treasury advertises the bills by public notice and invites tenders for a stated amount of bills under competitive bidding. Dealers in government securities, commercial banks, and other

TABLE 3-2

United States Government securities held by the public—by type of holder[a]
(par value in billions of dollars)

END OF PERIOD (DEC.)	TOTAL	COMMERCIAL BANKS[b]	MUTUAL SAVINGS BANKS	INSURANCE COMPANIES	OTHER CORPORATIONS	STATE AND LOCAL GOVERNMENTS	*Individuals* SAVINGS BONDS	*Individuals* OTHER SECURITIES	FOREIGN AND INTERNATIONAL INVESTORS[c]	OTHER MISCELLANEOUS INVESTORS[d]
1967	220.1	63.9	4.2	8.8	12.5	25.0	51.1	22.9	15.7	16.3
1966	216.7	57.5	4.7	9.6	14.7	23.8	50.2	25.4	14.5	16.4
1965	218.7	60.8	5.4	10.4	15.5	22.9	49.6	22.7	16.7	14.7
1964	221.1	64.0	5.7	11.1	17.9	21.2	48.9	22.1	16.7	14.5
1963	218.5	64.3	5.8	11.3	18.7	21.1	48.1	20.1	15.9	13.3
1962	217.5	66.5	6.1	11.5	20.0	19.5	46.9	19.0	15.3	12.7
1961	213.0	67.2	6.1	11.4	19.4	18.7	46.4	18.8	13.4	11.6
1960	207.9	62.1	6.3	11.9	19.7	18.7	45.7	19.3	13.0	11.2
1959	210.6	60.3	6.9	12.5	22.6	18.0	45.9	22.3	12.0	10.1
1958	202.4	67.5	7.3	12.7	18.8	16.5	47.7	15.3	7.7	8.9
1957	195.4	59.5	7.6	12.5	18.6	16.6	48.2	15.8	7.6	9.0
1947	200.0	68.7	12.0	23.9	14.1	7.3	46.2	19.4	2.7	5.7
1941	57.0	21.4	8.2	8.2	4.0	0.7	5.4	8.2	0.4	0.5

[a] Excludes debt held by United States Government agencies and trust funds and Federal Reserve Banks.

[b] Includes banks in territories and insular possessions.

[c] Includes investments of foreign balances and international accounts with United States.

[d] Includes savings and loan associations, dealers and brokers, nonprofit institutions, and corporate pension funds.

SOURCE: *Federal Reserve Bulletin*, February, 1967, p. A-36.

financial institutions are the usual bidders. An individual would buy Treasury bills from a commercial bank or arrange the purchase through a brokerage firm.

The yields on Treasury bills are usually lower than they are for the longer maturity of Treasury bonds, but there have been exceptions to this pattern. In the last quarter of 1959, and again in 1966 and the first quarter of 1967, the yields on Treasury bills rose above the yields on long-term government bonds. The primary reason for this unusual phenomenon was a financing policy followed by the Treasury with short-term obligations. The resulting demand for short-term funds increased the interest rate on the short-term bills. In 1959, short-term rates rose because of an attempt on the part of the Federal Reserve Banks to restrict the inflationary growth of the economy and to prevent stock market speculation. In 1966 and 1968, short-term rates were high to prevent inflation and to stop the outflow of gold. William McChesney Martin, Jr., Chairman of the Board of the Federal Reserve Banks, announced that the discount rate was raised because of inflationary conditions in the economy brought about by the government's fiscal programs stemming from the Vietnam War. The yield on Treasury bills had been as low as $\frac{3}{4}$ of 1 percent during World War II, when the yield on bonds was supported by the open-market operations of the Federal Reserve Banks to keep the cost of Treasury financing low. In the fall of 1966, the yields on Treasury bills had risen above 6 percent. The Federal Reserve Banks were following a tight money policy on short-term funds to prevent the outflow of gold and to restore stability in the economy. The pattern of yields on Treasury bills from 1959 through March 1, 1968, is seen in Chart 3-1.

U.S. Treasury Certificates of Indebtedness

Certificates of indebtedness are direct obligations of the Treasury that are issued to cover Treasury expenditures. They usually have a longer maturity than Treasury bills and tend to sell at yields comparable to or slightly higher than Treasury bills. The yields on these obligations appear in Chart 3-1. This yield pattern is comparable to the Treasury bill pattern. The certificates are sold at the issuance price plus accrued interest, and later traded in the market where the price and yield can change. The amount of certificates outstanding is small in relation to other forms of federal debt, and they declined in relative importance. The yields on all government securities, including certificates of indebtedness, have moved up substantially in recent years because of the record demands for funds by the federal, state, and local governments and by private corporations. As of 1968, it was likely that the rates would continue high for the future.

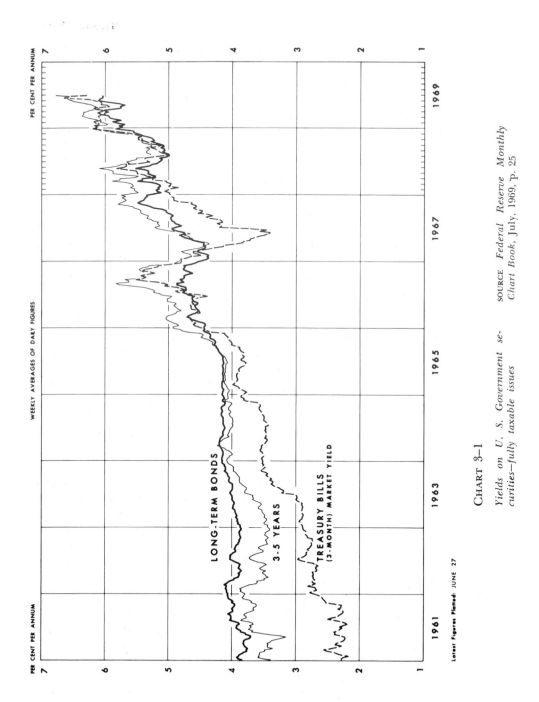

CHART 3–1

Yields on U. S. Government securities—fully taxable issues

SOURCE *Federal Reserve Monthly Chart Book*, July, 1969, p. 25

Treasury Notes

Treasury notes are really term loans made by the Treasury and are typically issued for from three to five years, although they can be issued with maturities of from one to five years. Once the securities are issued, they can be bought and sold freely in the money market. They assume the pattern of yields of other marketable securities having the same maturities. The yield pattern is shown in Chart 3–1. Treasury notes have become, in recent years, an important source of funds for the United States Treasury. Treasury notes give both the Treasury and the investor flexibility in their financial requirements. These bonds are short enough in maturity to offer some freedom from changes in money rates and yet long enough to afford somewhat higher yields to the investor than are offered by Treasury bills or certificates. Yields on intermediate-term bonds were higher than were those on bills and long-term bonds in 1959, in the first half of 1960, and from 1965 to the first half of 1968. The 3- to 5-year notes have been attractive to investors who want this type of investment.

Treasury Bonds

Treasury bonds are long-term interest-bearing debt of the United States and represent the largest portion of publicly held marketable debt. The maturities range from six months to thirty-five years with the concentration in the longer maturities. Yields on long-term bonds are provided in Chart 3–1. The long-term bonds offered yields somewhat higher than bills but lower than notes in early 1968. A greater degree of risk is assumed when these long-term bonds are purchased because of the potential loss through the fluctuation of money rates and because of the purchasing-power risk.

Treasury bonds are purchased primarily by institutional investors and others who desire a long-term, fixed-income investment with a high degree of safety and stability of income. We might consider government securities if we need stability of revenue and are willing to give up income for quality. However, there has been a substantial price variation in long-term bonds recently, along with an upward trend in interest rates and a generally declining trend in prices of existing long-term bonds. A commercial bank investment fund cannot buy common stock, but it can trade in bonds, and an astute money manager can buy low and sell high in bonds, just as he can in common stock. Aggressive money managers have improved yields substantially by trading in long-term government bonds and playing the pattern of the interest-rate curve. If we buy a long-term, 3 percent bond to yield 5 percent, we are buying it at a discount. We hold it until one year before maturity when, let us assume, we find short-term bill rates at 4 percent. The bond has increased in price and we have a capital gain. By selling the bond at a profit, we can reinvest the proceeds in higher-yield long-term bonds. Thus we receive a yield above 5 percent on our last year of investment, by trading out of the short end of the yield curve to the long end. The results are not spectacular, but when hundreds of millions of dollars are being invested, the amount of savings and profits can be substantial for a bank, private company, or other financial institution.

Bonds of Government Corporations and Agencies

The bonds of government corporations and agencies offer investment outlets for funds of individuals and of institutions. The debt sold by these corporations is long term, and the wide range of maturities offered would fit the portfolio requirements of most institutional investors and individuals. We are all familiar with some of the government corporations that have been established to help certain groups in our society or to provide for assistance in our world responsibilities. The major issues are discussed in the following sections. These bonds are not guaranteed by the United States Government.

FEDERAL LAND BANK OBLIGATIONS

The Federal Land Bank system was established by the Federal Farm Loan Act of 1916. Twelve banks were established to make long-term capital loans to farmers in the form of mortgages. These loans were to be made available through the joint efforts of the government and individuals, through National Farm Loan Associations. Money was raised in the form of debt securities from private investors. Hence Federal Land Bank bonds offer the investor an outlet for his loanable funds at rates consistent with other federal obligations. The long-term financing through the Federal Land Banks provided a great deal of help to the American farmer during the 1930's and later.

FEDERAL INTERMEDIATE CREDIT BANK SECURITIES

Federal Intermediate Credit Banks were established in 1923 in order to provide further aid to farmers by providing a source of intermediate credit loans. The loans are not made directly to the individuals but through twelve intermediate banks much like the Federal Land Banks. The banks are authorized to discount the notes given by farmers to local production credit associations and other agricultural credit associations. The money for purchasing the notes is obtained by selling bonds to the public. This is another debt instrument that we can purchase for the investment of funds. The yields on these are modest, and the period of the investment is short.

BANKS FOR COOPERATIVES

Twelve district banks were established in 1933 under the provisions of the Farm Credit Act to aid cooperatives that are helping farmers. Cooperatives have existed for almost 150 years. Strong cooperatives help farmers achieve purchasing and marketing economies. The Banks for Cooperatives make commodity loans, operating-capital loans, and facility loans. The banks may issue debentures to finance their needs, and this is where individuals and institutions supply capital. The debentures are relatively short term and bear a low interest rate.

FEDERAL HOME LOAN BANK BONDS

The Federal Home Loan Banks were established in 1932 to assure a steady flow of savings into banking institutions that are organized to provide mortgage funds. The system was patterned after the Federal Reserve Banking system. The banks will lend money to member institutions accepting mortgages as collateral. The banks, to obtain capital for their operations, borrow money from investors. The obligations that are sold tend to bear low rates and are short-term obligations.

FEDERAL NATIONAL MORTGAGE ASSOCIATION BONDS

The Federal National Mortgage Association (FNMA) was created in 1938 to provide a secondary mortgage market that would stimulate construction and create a market for government-insured FHA mortgages. In addition to providing a market for mortgages, the association makes mortgage loans on large-scale rental projects. The funds for these activities come from the sale of notes and debentures to investors. These securities are referred to in the trade as "Fannie Mae's." The maturities range from short term to long term, and yield rates are comparable to Federal Land Bank bonds and short- and long-term Treasury bonds. The assocation has been successful in meeting its objectives and provides a secure investment for investors.

WORLD BANK BONDS

The World Bank for Reconstruction and Development was established through the Bretton Woods Agreement of 1944. The basic purpose of the Bank is to make or guarantee, in whole or in part, loans that will be used for the reconstruction of development of countries. All members of the Bank must be members of the International Monetary Fund, and they contribute capital to the Bank in varying amounts. The United States has contributed over $6.35 billion. The World Bank lends money and may also borrow money for the purpose of helping countries that are trying to develop their resources. The yields on World Bank bonds are somewhat higher than on other agencies' securities. World Bank bonds are not issued by a federal agency, and the higher yield reflects the greater risks in the securities compared to those of federal agency bonds discussed above.

Advantages and Disadvantages of United States Government Securities

The advantages of United States Government securities as an investment are already apparent in the minds of most people. In spite of a large and increasing debt, our government enjoys an excellent credit position with domestic and foreign lenders. Most bond-rating agencies give government bonds the highest rating. The first advantage of government securities is the obvious quality of the investment and the security that it affords the investor. A second advantage is the stability of income they provide, particularly the long-term government securities. A third is the great degree of marketability that they possess. There is a broad and ready market for government securities, particularly among institutional investors. Those who invest in government bonds can sell them quickly and easily in the bond market when funds are needed immediately. Government bonds eliminate the market risk and the business risk because of their security of principal and stability of income. A fourth advantage is centered in their ability to meet the investment needs of financial institutions and institutional investors. A sophisticated financial manager can improve yields substantially by trading and by playing the pattern of rates when possible.

There are several disadvantages that we should associate with investment in government securities. There is little possiblity of capital appreciation without trading in the securities. Government securities are debt instruments: the government simply guarantees to repay principal at maturity. This is a secure and favorable pledge, but it does not provide us with capital growth. Unless the investor buys government bonds that are selling below par, there is no capital gain. The income is stable and secure but offers no chance for increases in the future, as the interest rate is established by contract and will not be changed over the life of the bond. The fixed income and fixed principal lead to two major disadvantages of government bonds: (1) their inability to guard against the risks of inflation, and (2) their susceptibility to changes in money rate. Bonds do not provide a hedge against inflation because income and maturity values are fixed. If the purchasing power of the dollar declines, so does the purchasing power of the bond, and there is no way to compensate for this loss.

If yields in the market should increase, as they did in recent years, the price of the bond existing in the marketplace will decline, and the investor will lose if the bond must be sold. Even if the investor can hold to maturity, he will lose the difference between the low rate of interest paid on the existing bond and the rates on new bonds. This risk of loss is brought about because of changes in money rates. If a person can invest in the bonds at a high rate of interest, this risk of loss is minimized. In this situation, if yields decline, the price of the bond will go up and the investor will gain, owing to the inverse relationship between bond prices and bond yields.

Short-term government securities are not subject to the risk of loss because of changes in money rates, owing to their short maturities. However, if an investor continually invested and reinvested in Treasury bills, he would solve the risk of changes in the money rate, but he would assume the purchasing-power risk. Investment in short-term government securities is no way to provide against the loss of purchasing power brought about by inflation.

Calculation of Bond Yields

If we understand how to calculate bond yields, we will understand the inverse relationship between bond prices and yields. The fulcrum around which yields vary is the interest rate, which is fixed in amount over the life of the bond. It is usually stated as a percentage of the par value of a bond. Thus, a 4 percent interest rate on a $1,000 bond is $40. This is the nominal rate, as we shall see later under the discussion of corporate bonds. If the market price of the bond drops to $900, the yield to maturity, or yield, goes up. If the market price of the bond goes up, the yield goes down. Changes in the level of current interest rates, however, provide for the change in yields. Therefore, if current interest rates move up, the market price of existing bonds or comparable bonds must go down to equate the yield of the existing bond with the yield on the new bond being issued at a higher interest rate. The interest rate on the new bond coming out at par is equal to the yield to maturity; but bonds are not always sold at par, and the yield will vary from the coupon or nominal rate, depending upon price.

The yields are calculated for the investor and reported in the *Wall Street Journal*. However, if we know the current market price and interest rate of the bond, we can calculate yield in one of two ways: by the approximate method or by the discount method. Yields may also be found from bond yield tables, but they are not always readily available for use by the investor.

APPROXIMATE METHOD

The approximate method of computing yield to maturity is accomplished by dividing average investment into average income for the life of the bond. The following formula can be used to make this calculation:

$$\text{Yield to maturity (YTM)} = \frac{i + \dfrac{P_m - P_p}{Y}}{\dfrac{P_p + P_m}{2}}$$

where i is the interest in dollars, P_m is the price at maturity or call, P_p is the purchase price, and Y is the number of years to maturity. Assume for example that we purchased a Treasury bond in January of 1969 that was to mature in January, 1986. It paid interest at the rate of 5 percent. We could buy it at 94.2, or 94 and 20/32. (Government bonds are quoted in 32nds of a point.) What would be the yield to maturity on the bond? Substituting in the equation, we would have the following:

$$\text{Yield to maturity} = \frac{50 + \dfrac{1{,}000 - 946.25}{17}}{\dfrac{946.25 + 1{,}000}{2}}$$

$$= \frac{50 + 3.16}{973.13}$$

$$= \frac{53.16}{973.13}$$

$$= .0546$$

$$= 5.46 \text{ percent}$$

The yield from the bond is approximately 5.46 percent, according to our calculations. This method of calculating yield can be used for any type of investment, including common stock. We may also use the formula to determine the yield of an investment for the time we held it.

YIELD BY USE OF THE PRESENT VALUE TABLE

Yield can also be approximated by use of present value tables, as in Tables 3–3 and 3–4. Anyone who has had experience with corporate capital budgeting in business finance will recognize the applications of this technique immediately. In using the present value tables, we equate the present value of the future interest payments and capital repayments to the purchase price of the bond. The discount rate that equates these two amounts is the yield to maturity. The yield is found by trial and error. An example can be derived by using the figures from the approximate method demonstrated above. From Table 3–4, we find the present value of the stream of income for 4 and 6 percent as follows:

	4%	6%	
Present value of $50 per year for 17 years ($50 × 12.166)	$ 608.30	$523.85	($50 × 10.477)
Present value of $1,000 face value due at maturity in 1986 (17 years) ($1,000 × 0.513) (Table 3–3)	513.00	371.00	($1,000 × 0.371)
Total present value	$1,121.30	$894.85	
Market price of bond		$946.25	

TABLE 3–3

Present value of $1 received at the end of year

Years Hence	1%	2%	4%	6%	8%	10%	12%	14%	15%	16%	18%	20%	22%	24%	25%	26%	28%	30%	35%	40%	45%	50%
1	0.990	0.980	0.962	0.943	0.926	0.909	0.893	0.877	0.870	0.862	0.847	0.833	0.820	0.806	0.800	0.794	0.781	0.769	0.741	0.714	0.690	0.667
2	0.980	0.961	0.925	0.890	0.857	0.826	0.797	0.769	0.756	0.743	0.718	0.694	0.672	0.650	0.640	0.630	0.610	0.592	0.549	0.510	0.476	0.444
3	0.971	0.942	0.889	0.840	0.794	0.751	0.712	0.675	0.658	0.641	0.609	0.579	0.551	0.524	0.512	0.500	0.477	0.455	0.406	0.364	0.328	0.296
4	0.961	0.924	0.855	0.792	0.735	0.683	0.630	0.592	0.572	0.552	0.516	0.482	0.451	0.423	0.410	0.397	0.373	0.350	0.301	0.260	0.226	0.198
5	0.951	0.906	0.822	0.747	0.681	0.621	0.567	0.519	0.497	0.476	0.437	0.402	0.370	0.341	0.328	0.315	0.291	0.269	0.223	0.186	0.156	0.132
6	0.942	0.888	0.790	0.705	0.630	0.564	0.507	0.456	0.432	0.410	0.370	0.335	0.303	0.275	0.262	0.250	0.227	0.207	0.165	0.133	0.108	0.088
7	0.933	0.871	0.760	0.665	0.583	0.513	0.452	0.400	0.376	0.354	0.314	0.279	0.249	0.222	0.210	0.198	0.178	0.159	0.122	0.095	0.074	0.059
8	0.923	0.853	0.731	0.627	0.540	0.467	0.404	0.351	0.327	0.305	0.266	0.233	0.204	0.179	0.168	0.157	0.139	0.123	0.091	0.068	0.051	0.039
9	0.914	0.837	0.703	0.592	0.500	0.424	0.361	0.308	0.284	0.263	0.225	0.194	0.167	0.144	0.134	0.125	0.108	0.094	0.067	0.048	0.035	0.026
10	0.905	0.820	0.676	0.558	0.463	0.386	0.322	0.270	0.247	0.227	0.191	0.162	0.137	0.116	0.107	0.099	0.085	0.073	0.050	0.035	0.024	0.017
11	0.896	0.804	0.650	0.527	0.429	0.350	0.287	0.237	0.215	0.195	0.162	0.135	0.112	0.094	0.086	0.079	0.066	0.056	0.037	0.025	0.017	0.012
12	0.887	0.788	0.625	0.497	0.397	0.319	0.257	0.208	0.187	0.168	0.137	0.112	0.092	0.076	0.069	0.062	0.052	0.043	0.027	0.018	0.012	0.008
13	0.879	0.773	0.601	0.469	0.368	0.290	0.229	0.182	0.163	0.145	0.116	0.093	0.075	0.061	0.055	0.050	0.040	0.033	0.020	0.013	0.008	0.005
14	0.870	0.758	0.577	0.442	0.340	0.263	0.205	0.160	0.141	0.125	0.099	0.078	0.062	0.049	0.044	0.039	0.032	0.025	0.015	0.009	0.006	0.003
15	0.861	0.743	0.555	0.417	0.315	0.239	0.183	0.140	0.123	0.108	0.084	0.065	0.051	0.040	0.035	0.031	0.025	0.020	0.011	0.006	0.004	0.002
16	0.853	0.728	0.534	0.394	0.292	0.218	0.163	0.123	0.107	0.093	0.071	0.054	0.042	0.032	0.028	0.025	0.019	0.015	0.008	0.005	0.003	0.002
17	0.844	0.714	0.513	0.371	0.270	0.198	0.146	0.108	0.093	0.080	0.060	0.045	0.034	0.026	0.023	0.020	0.015	0.012	0.006	0.003	0.002	0.001
18	0.836	0.700	0.494	0.350	0.250	0.180	0.130	0.095	0.081	0.069	0.051	0.038	0.028	0.021	0.018	0.016	0.012	0.009	0.005	0.002	0.001	0.001
19	0.828	0.686	0.475	0.331	0.232	0.164	0.116	0.083	0.070	0.060	0.043	0.031	0.023	0.017	0.014	0.012	0.009	0.007	0.003	0.002	0.001	
20	0.820	0.673	0.456	0.312	0.215	0.149	0.104	0.073	0.061	0.051	0.037	0.026	0.019	0.014	0.012	0.010	0.007	0.005	0.002	0.001	0.001	
21	0.811	0.660	0.439	0.294	0.199	0.135	0.093	0.064	0.053	0.044	0.031	0.022	0.015	0.011	0.009	0.008	0.006	0.004	0.002	0.001		
22	0.803	0.647	0.422	0.278	0.184	0.123	0.083	0.056	0.046	0.038	0.026	0.018	0.013	0.009	0.007	0.006	0.004	0.003	0.001	0.001		
23	0.795	0.634	0.406	0.262	0.170	0.112	0.074	0.049	0.040	0.033	0.022	0.015	0.010	0.007	0.006	0.005	0.003	0.002	0.001			
24	0.788	0.622	0.390	0.247	0.158	0.102	0.066	0.043	0.035	0.028	0.019	0.013	0.008	0.006	0.005	0.004	0.003	0.002	0.001			
25	0.780	0.610	0.375	0.233	0.146	0.092	0.059	0.038	0.030	0.024	0.016	0.010	0.007	0.005	0.004	0.003	0.002	0.001	0.001			
26	0.772	0.598	0.361	0.220	0.135	0.084	0.053	0.033	0.026	0.021	0.014	0.009	0.006	0.004	0.003	0.002	0.002	0.001				
27	0.764	0.586	0.347	0.207	0.125	0.076	0.047	0.029	0.023	0.018	0.011	0.007	0.005	0.003	0.002	0.002	0.001	0.001				
28	0.757	0.574	0.333	0.196	0.116	0.069	0.042	0.026	0.020	0.016	0.010	0.006	0.004	0.002	0.002	0.002	0.001	0.001				
29	0.749	0.563	0.321	0.185	0.107	0.063	0.037	0.022	0.017	0.014	0.008	0.005	0.003	0.002	0.002	0.001	0.001	0.001				
30	0.742	0.552	0.308	0.174	0.099	0.057	0.033	0.020	0.015	0.012	0.007	0.004	0.003	0.002	0.001	0.001	0.001	0.001				
40	0.672	0.453	0.208	0.097	0.046	0.022	0.011	0.005	0.004	0.003	0.001	0.001										
50	0.608	0.372	0.141	0.054	0.021	0.009	0.003	0.001	0.001	0.001												

SOURCE: Reprinted with permission from R. N. Anthony, *Management Accounting: Text and Cases* (Homewood, Ill.: Richard D. Irwin, Inc., 1960), p. 658.

TABLE 3-4

Present value of $1 received annually at the end of each year for N years

Years (N)	1%	2%	4%	6%	8%	10%	12%	14%	15%	16%	18%	20%	22%	24%	25%	26%	28%	30%	35%	40%	45%	50%
1	0.990	0.980	0.962	0.943	0.926	0.909	0.893	0.877	0.870	0.862	0.847	0.833	0.820	0.806	0.800	0.794	0.781	0.769	0.741	0.714	0.690	0.667
2	1.970	1.942	1.886	1.833	1.783	1.736	1.690	1.647	1.626	1.605	1.566	1.528	1.492	1.457	1.440	1.424	1.392	1.361	1.289	1.224	1.165	1.111
3	2.941	2.884	2.775	2.673	2.577	2.487	2.402	2.322	2.283	2.246	2.174	2.106	2.042	1.981	1.952	1.923	1.868	1.816	1.696	1.589	1.493	1.407
4	3.902	3.808	3.630	3.465	3.312	3.170	3.037	2.914	2.855	2.798	2.690	2.589	2.494	2.404	2.362	2.320	2.241	2.166	1.997	1.849	1.720	1.605
5	4.853	4.713	4.452	4.212	3.993	3.791	3.605	3.433	3.352	3.274	3.127	2.991	2.864	2.745	2.689	2.635	2.532	2.436	2.220	2.035	1.876	1.737
6	5.795	5.601	5.242	4.917	4.623	4.355	4.111	3.889	3.784	3.685	3.498	3.326	3.167	3.020	2.951	2.885	2.759	2.643	2.385	2.168	1.983	1.824
7	6.728	6.472	6.002	5.582	5.206	4.868	4.564	4.288	4.160	4.039	3.812	3.605	3.416	3.242	3.161	3.083	2.937	2.802	2.508	2.263	2.057	1.883
8	7.652	7.325	6.733	6.210	5.747	5.335	4.968	4.639	4.487	4.344	4.078	3.837	3.619	3.421	3.329	3.241	3.076	2.925	2.598	2.331	2.108	1.922
9	8.566	8.162	7.435	6.802	6.247	5.759	5.328	4.946	4.772	4.607	4.303	4.031	3.786	3.566	3.463	3.366	3.184	3.019	2.665	2.379	2.144	1.948
10	9.471	8.983	8.111	7.360	6.710	6.145	5.650	5.216	5.019	4.833	4.494	4.192	3.923	3.682	3.571	3.465	3.269	3.092	2.715	2.414	2.168	1.965
11	10.368	9.787	8.760	7.887	7.139	6.495	5.988	5.453	5.234	5.029	4.656	4.327	4.035	3.776	3.656	3.544	3.335	3.147	2.752	2.438	2.185	1.977
12	11.255	10.575	9.385	8.384	7.536	6.814	6.194	5.660	5.421	5.197	4.793	4.439	4.127	3.851	3.725	3.606	3.387	3.190	2.779	2.456	2.196	1.985
13	12.134	11.343	9.986	8.853	7.904	7.103	6.424	5.842	5.583	5.342	4.910	4.533	4.203	3.912	3.780	3.656	3.427	3.223	2.799	2.468	2.204	1.990
14	13.004	12.106	10.563	9.295	8.244	7.367	6.628	6.002	5.724	5.468	5.008	4.611	4.265	3.962	3.824	3.695	3.459	3.249	2.814	2.477	2.210	1.993
15	13.865	12.849	11.118	9.712	8.559	7.606	6.811	6.142	5.847	5.575	5.092	4.675	4.315	4.001	3.859	3.726	3.483	3.268	2.825	2.484	2.214	1.995
16	14.718	13.578	11.652	10.106	8.851	7.824	6.974	6.265	5.954	5.669	5.162	4.730	4.357	4.033	3.887	3.751	3.503	3.283	2.834	2.489	2.216	1.997
17	15.562	14.292	12.166	10.477	9.122	8.022	7.120	6.373	6.047	5.749	5.222	4.775	4.391	4.059	3.910	3.771	3.518	3.295	2.840	2.492	2.218	1.998
18	16.398	14.992	12.659	10.828	9.372	8.201	7.250	6.467	6.128	5.818	5.273	4.812	4.419	4.080	3.928	3.786	3.529	3.304	2.844	2.494	2.219	1.999
19	17.226	15.678	13.134	11.158	9.604	8.365	7.366	6.550	6.198	5.877	5.316	4.844	4.442	4.097	3.942	3.799	3.539	3.311	2.848	2.496	2.220	1.999
20	18.046	16.351	13.590	11.470	9.818	8.514	7.469	6.623	6.259	5.929	5.353	4.870	4.460	4.110	3.954	3.808	3.546	3.316	2.850	2.497	2.221	1.999
21	18.857	17.011	14.029	11.764	10.017	8.649	7.562	6.687	6.312	5.973	5.384	4.891	4.476	4.121	3.963	3.816	3.551	3.320	2.852	2.498	2.221	2.000
22	19.660	17.658	14.451	12.042	10.201	8.772	7.645	6.743	6.359	6.011	5.410	4.909	4.488	4.130	3.970	3.822	3.556	3.323	2.853	2.498	2.222	2.000
23	20.456	18.292	14.857	12.303	10.371	8.883	7.718	6.792	6.399	6.044	5.432	4.925	4.499	4.137	3.976	3.827	3.559	3.325	2.854	2.499	2.222	2.000
24	21.243	18.914	15.247	12.550	10.529	8.985	7.784	6.835	6.434	6.073	5.451	4.937	4.507	4.143	3.981	3.831	3.562	3.327	2.855	2.499	2.222	2.000
25	22.023	19.523	15.622	12.783	10.675	9.077	7.843	6.873	6.464	6.097	5.467	4.948	4.514	4.147	3.985	3.834	3.564	3.329	2.856	2.499	2.222	2.000
26	22.795	20.121	15.983	13.003	10.810	9.161	7.896	6.906	6.491	6.118	5.480	4.956	4.520	4.151	3.988	3.837	3.566	3.330	2.856	2.500	2.222	2.000
27	23.560	20.707	16.330	13.211	10.935	9.237	7.943	6.935	6.514	6.136	5.492	4.964	4.524	4.154	3.990	3.839	3.567	3.331	2.856	2.500	2.222	2.000
28	24.316	21.281	16.663	13.406	11.051	9.307	7.984	6.961	6.534	6.152	5.502	4.970	4.528	4.157	3.992	3.840	3.568	3.331	2.857	2.500	2.222	2.000
29	25.066	21.844	16.984	13.591	11.158	9.370	8.022	6.983	6.551	6.166	5.510	4.975	4.531	4.159	3.994	3.841	3.569	3.332	2.857	2.500	2.222	2.000
30	25.808	22.396	17.292	13.765	11.258	9.427	8.055	7.003	6.566	6.177	5.517	4.979	4.534	4.160	3.995	3.842	3.569	3.332	2.857	2.500	2.222	2.000
40	32.835	27.355	19.793	15.046	11.925	9.779	8.244	7.105	6.642	6.234	5.548	4.997	4.544	4.166	3.999	3.846	3.571	3.333	2.857	2.500	2.222	2.000
50	39.196	31.424	21.482	15.762	12.234	9.915	8.304	7.183	6.661	6.246	5.554	4.999	4.545	4.167	4.000	3.846	3.571	3.333	2.857	2.500	2.222	2.000

SOURCE: Reprinted with permission from R. N. Anthony, *Management Accounting: Text and Cases* (Homewood, Ill.: Richard D. Irwin, Inc., 1960), p. 657.

The present value of the income stream at 5 percent would be $1,000.00. If we bought the bond at par with a 5 percent interest rate, we would enjoy a 5 percent yield to maturity. Since we paid less than par, and since the yield table does not calculate the 5 percent yield we find the present value by interpolating between the 4 and 6 percent rates. The present value of the income and principal at 6 percent is $894.85, which is less than the purchase price of $946.25. The present value at the 4 percent rate is $1,121.30. The present value interval is $226.45, which is the difference between the present value at 4 percent, $1,121.30, and the present value at 6 percent, $894.85. The difference between the purchase price and the present value at 4 percent is $175.05 ($1,121.30—$946.25). We convert this to percentage by multiplying 175.05/226.45 × 2 percent, which equals 1.555 percent (.7775 × 2). When this is added to 4 percent we arrive at a figure of 5.555 percent, the yield to maturity (YTM).

In spite of the fact that we did not use the actual time period of interest payment, usually every 6 months, we have a more accurate measure of yield than that which results from the use of the approximate method. By use of calculus, we could derive a continuous function that gives us the most accurate method of measurement. We should be familiar with these methods of measuring yield, since they help us understand better the yield alternatives from all investment media.

Government Securities and the Individual Investor

Individual investors do not own directly a large portion of marketable government securities. Government bonds are owned largely by institutional investors whose investment needs call for high-quality, fixed-income securities. Since most financial institutions deal in dollar claims, they are not much concerned about the possible decline in purchasing power of the dollar. They are interested in quality and certainty of income, marketability, and liquidity rather than in capital gains. These are the attributes of government securities. When we as individuals invest, we must accept the risk of inflation, and we would not solve this problem by investing in government bonds. The only way we can improve yield is to trade in government securities according to price movements. This is common practice among financial institutions.

We can use government securities as a conservative and defensive part of our investment funds. When security prices are high and the outlook for the stock market is pessimistic, we can shift our investments in stocks to an investment in government securities. We might use government securities as a permanent part of our investment program to give substance and security to our financial position and allow us to accept the risk associated with other types of investment securities. Long-term government securities provide us with a fixed yield only slightly lower than other fixed-income investments. The security and market-ability of government securities, particularly important for financial institutions, tend to outweigh the lower yields than might be earned by investment in other, higher-yield debt. A permanent investment in government securities can be considered desirable, therefore, even where common-stock investment is dominant, but where we wish to provide a hedge against the business risk and the market risk. This is important for all forms of private, corporate, and institutional investment. The very small investor would probaly not consider investment in marketable government bonds, since he could earn a higher rate of return on deposits in a savings and loan company and would not be able to purchase government securities in less than $1,000 amounts.

State and Municipal Bonds as Investment Securities

State and municipal securities offer investors a unique combination of investment qualities. They offer security of principal and stability of income. For the most part, their record of experience has been good. There have been some defaults on state and local debt historically, but they were small in relation to the total amount of debt outstanding. The second quality that makes these securities unique is their tax-exempt status. All state and municipal bonds are exempt from federal income taxes. Individuals and corporations in the high income brackets find this type of bond attractive for investment. Even though the rates of interest and yields on state and municipal bonds are relatively low, they offer a much higher yield when the tax effect is considered. If we were in the 56 percent bracket, for example, and bought a 4 percent municipal bond, we would have to buy a fully taxable bond for a yield of 9.09 percent to have the same after-tax yield. The fully taxable equivalent can be found by dividing one minus the marginal tax rate of the individual into the tax-exempt rate of interest times 100 to convert back to percentage. In this example, $1-.56$ is divided into $.04 \times 100$, which gives us 9.09 percent. This is the fully taxable equivalent an investor with the 56 percent tax bracket would need to yield 4 percent after taxes. If the investor were in the 77 percent tax bracket, the fully taxable equivalent rate would be:

$$\frac{.04 \times 100}{1-.77} = \frac{4}{.23} = 17.4 \text{ percent.}$$

If we can benefit from stability of income, safety of principal, and exemption from federal income taxes, then we will find state and municipal bonds an attractive outlet for our investment funds. The wealthy individual, corporate investor, or financial institution in the high tax brackets can obviously benefit from this type of investment.

The Growth of State and Municipal Debt

The total amount of state and municipal debt does not compare in amount to the total federal debt. The amount has been steadily increasing, however, and has been growing faster than our federal debt. In 1957, for example, the state and municipal debt outstanding totaled $52.0 billion. This figure represents the total debt of 102,352 government units that were in existence in January, 1957. By the end of 1967, the total debt had increased to $113.3 billion. The increase in state and municipal debt was far greater than the increase in federal debt for the same period.

Approximately 75 percent of the total debt outstanding has been issued by local government units, which include counties, municipalities, townships, and towns, as well as school districts and special districts. As state and local debts have increased, the number of government units has decreased. Special districts have increased, but the number of school districts has decreased dramatically. Between 1942 and 1957, 58,126 school districts were eliminated out of a total of 108,579. The trend toward consolidation of school districts continues at the same rate today, because of the mergers that have taken place to finance new school facilities. Often it is uneconomical or impossible for one school district to finance a new high school, for example. Through the merger of several districts into one large one, the financing of the new facilities becomes feasible.

The growth of state and municipal debt can be visualized clearly from the figures in Table 3–5. In each year from 1957 through 1966, except for 1960, the total amount of debt increased. We can see in the number of new issues sold that debt other than state debt dominated state and municipal financing. The increased amount of these securities coming into the market offers investors an opportunity to obtain quality investment with unique characteristics.

The Uses of State and Municipal Debt—Where the Money Is Spent

We need not search very long to find a reason for the growth of municipal debt. Since the end of World War II, the demand for public services of all types has skyrocketed. Our population has expanded, and for this population we have had to provide more schools, more roads, more colleges, and more utilities. Not all communities have been successful in solving their individual problems. Most likely the pressure for new services to meet the future growth of population will continue undiminished and compound the problems of these communities.

The pattern of the growth of state and municipal debt will be

TABLE 3-5

New issues of state and local government securities 1957–1966 (millions of dollars)

ALL ISSUES (NEW CAPITAL AND REFUNDING)

YEAR	TOTAL	Type of Issue				Issuing Authority			TOTAL AMOUNT DELIVERED[c]
		GENERAL OBLIGATIONS	REVENUES	PHA[a]	U.S. GOVT. LOANS	STATE	SPEC. DIST. & STATE AUTHORITY	OTHER[b]	
1966	11,395	6,804	3,955	325	312	2,590	4,110	4,695	11,538
1965	11,329	7,177	3,517	464	170	2,401	3,784	5,144	10,069
1964	10,847	6,417	3,585	637	208	1,628	3,812	5,407	10,496
1963	10,538	5,855	4,180	254	249	1,620	3,636	5,281	8,732
1962	8,845	5,582	2,681	437	145	1,419	2,600	4,826	8,298
1961	8,562	5,721	2,406	315	120	1,928	2,164	4,470	7,112
1960	7,302	4,677	2,097	403	125	1,110	1,985	4,207	7,423
1959	7,695	4,777	2,409	333	176	1,686	2,120	3,889	7,708
1958	7,526	5,447	1,777	187	115	1,993	1,371	4,162	6,568
1957	6,924	4,792	1,967	66	99	1,489	1,272	4,163	

USE OF PROCEEDS FROM NEW CAPITAL ISSUES

YEAR	TOTAL	EDUCATION	ROADS AND BRIDGES	UTILITIES[d]	HOUSING[e]	VETERANS' AID	OTHER PURPOSES
1966	11,294	3,738	1,476	1,880	533	—	3,667
1965	10,471	3,619	900	1,965	626	50	3,311
1964	10,201	3,392	688	2,437	727	120	2,838
1963	9,151	3,029	812	2,344	598	—	2,369
1962	8,568	2,963	1,114	1,668	521	125	2,177
1961	8,460	2,821	1,167	1,700	385	478	1,909
1960	7,257	2,411	1,007	1,318	425	201	1,895
1959	7,588	2,314	844	1,989	402	355	1,684
1958	7,441	2,617	1,164	1,412	251	339	1,658
1957	6,874	2,524	1,036	1,516	113	333	1,352

a Only bonds sold pursuant to 1949 Housing Act; secured by contract requiring Public Housing Administration to make annual contributions to the local authority.

b Municipalities, counties, townships, and school districts.

c Excludes U.S. Government loans.

d Water, sewer, and other utilities.

e Includes urban redevelopment loans.

SOURCE: *Federal Reserve Bulletin*, December, 1967, p. 2113.

similar to the pattern that has developed in recent years. The figures in Table 3–5 reveal the purposes for which debt was raised from 1957 through 1966. Educational facilities, which are predominantly a local expenditure, received the greatest amount of money. Most communities have had to expand their classroom facilities to meet the population bulge that was created by World War II. Over a third of the total amount of municipal debt sold in 1966 went for educational facilities. As we look at the future expected growth of the school-age population, we can be assured that even more facilities will be needed, requiring new and greater expenditures for classrooms and educational facilities.

New roads and bridges have also required states and municipalities to obtain money from the sale of debt securities. In 1966, 13.1 percent of the total new municipal debt was issued for this purpose. As our population expands, there will be a need for more new highways, and old avenues of travel will be improved to accommodate a record number of autos produced in recent years. This will require more money to be raised by local government units in addition to federal aid and state programs.

The need for all types of public utilities has expanded. Large sums of money have been spent annually for new water treatment stations, sewage plants, and trash removal facilities. In the future there will be a continued need for this type of facility, and expenditures should continue. As individuals and political leaders, independent of political affiliation, begin to recognize social and cultural needs, not only for the minimum public utilities but also for the amenities of life such as art and cultural centers and public recreation facilities, expenditures in this category will increase. In 1966, 13.1 percent of the total state and municipal debt was spent for utilities.

Housing and urban renewal projects have stimulated communities to borrow money to improve their cities and towns and to provide housing for low-income families. Many cities have embarked upon major redevelopment projects supported by public and private capital. New York, Philadelphia, Boston, and Cincinnati are a few of the cities that have undertaken such projects. In 1966, 4.7 percent of the total state and municipal debt was used for housing projects and urban renewal. In the future, we may look for greater expenditures for urban renewal and industrial development. Money will be needed to solve the housing problems of people living in the ghettos of our cities. The amount of money these programs will require is awesome.

Municipal and state funds raised from debt issues are used for a wide variety of other purposes. Veterans' aid including veterans' bonuses, received a modest but mentionable share of the funds raised in 1966. States have issued debt for mental institutions and state recreation facilities. These and similar projects accounted for 32.5 percent of the total debt in 1966.

State and Municipal Borrowers

States. States may issue debt to carry on their activities from time to time with the consent of the people. The laws vary among the states as to how debt shall be raised. Each state is sovereign and has absolute power to issue debt without interference from the federal government. The state of Ohio, for example, can issue debt as a direct obligation subject to approval by the people of the state. The source of the sovereign power given to the states in the issuance of debt comes from the Tenth Amendment to the Constitution.

The states have been, on the whole, excellent credit risks. There have been few times in history when states were forced to repudiate their debt. When repudiation occurs, the state simply tells the creditors that it will not pay. Since the state is the sovereign power and the individual cannot sue for payment, an investor could suffer a substantial loss. The creditor is in a weak position when he purchases bonds issued by a state. Since default is rare, however, and since states have excellent revenue sources, such as taxes on sales, gasoline, motor vehicles, income inheritance, and general property, they have enjoyed an excellent credit rating. In recent years, the states have been taking a more active supporting role in helping schools meet their financial commitments. This could place undue pressure on the states to raise funds and might eventually lower their credit position. Several states, such as Michigan and California, have experienced difficulties in meeting their current financial needs.

Municipalities. The creditor may be in a stronger position than the state in dealing with local political units depending upon the terms of the bond indenture but these units are limited in their source of revenues to pay for debt service and retirement. The cities, towns, and counties are heavily dependent upon property taxes to support their activities. In many cities, property taxes have not produced sufficient revenue, and the cities have resorted to income or sales taxes as a source of funds. The power to levy an income tax is given to most cities by the state, and the tax rate is usually limited by the state. The debt burden is great in many communities in the local political units, since they are constantly under pressure to increase community services and therefore constantly seeking new sources of revenue. The wealthier communities with a large tax base are obviously in a better position to meet the increased demands for services of all types.

Special Districts. School districts, road districts, and park districts represent another type of borrower. These districts are almost completely dependent upon the property tax. Usually when money is needed for special districts, the people in the district must approve an increase in property taxes to support the bond issue that will be used to finance the improvement. Without the approval of the voters, the project cannot be carried out. In wealthy communities with low debts and modest needs, few problems are involved in raising adequate funds for improvements. The districts that have the greatest difficulty are those with rapidly growing needs, a low tax base, and a large existing debt, where the people do not wish to or cannot extend themselves to meet the needs of the community. The dilemma for such communities is almost insolvable without aid from the state, other districts, or even the federal government.

Assessment Districts. Another classification of borrowers is the assessment district. These are usually formed to provide a single facility such as sewage, street lighting, or a street-paving project. Usually the obligation to pay the assessment bonds is assumed by the lot owner. He is given the choice of paying the lump-sum value of the improvement or paying the debt and interest over the life of the bond issue, which varies from 10 to 20 years, depending upon the amount of the expenditure. The position of the bond issue is strong if the dollar cost of the improvement is small in relation to the property.

Public Authorities. Public authorities also issue debt securities that are a part of the heterogeneous category called municipals. The public authority is usually established to operate one or several businesses. The New York Port Authority, for example, is perhaps the most widely known public authority in the United States. The Maine Turnpike Commission, the Ohio Turnpike Authority, the New Jersey Turnpike Authority, and the Pennsylvania Turnpike Authority are other examples of public authorities that have sold bonds to the public and have been attractive investment outlets. Where competitive economic conditions are favorable, the public-authority method of financing a project is an excellent way of meeting the needs of the people and allowing them to pay as they go. The credit ratings of most public authorities have been excellent, but a few have run into financial difficulties that could result in loss to the investor. The West Virginia Turnpike bonds, for example, sold at a substantial discount in 1968. The revenues from the Turnpike fell far below expectations. Possibly revenues will increase and the bonds will be paid at maturity, but there is a risk involved, and the bonds might not be paid.

Also in this category are the municipal development corporations that have been established to aid cities in their economic growth. The federal tax laws no longer provide exemption for the interest received from this type of bond. It is likely that the change in the tax law will result in diminished growth of this type of municipal activity.

State and municipal bonds are debenture contracts that do not have a pledge of either real or personal property. As we shall see, their credit rating rests upon their ability to pay principal and interest solely from tax revenues, solely from operating revenues of a special revenue facility, or from a combination of both. The debenture contract is simply a long-term written promise to pay. The bonds are issued both in straight maturities and in serial maturities. Serial maturities have advantages for both the investor and the issuer. A portion of the debt of serial bonds is paid off every six months from income or revenues. This insures the retirement of the debt and improves the credit rating of the bonds that remain in the hands of the public. The issuer of this type of bond meets his obligation, the investor has his contract completed, and the credit contract has been fulfilled. The varying maturities for these bonds make them attractive to many groups of investors rather than to just a limited segment of the investment market. Investors can choose the maturity in advance, so that if we wish to invest in six-month or six-year bonds, we can select the maturity that meets our requirements. If debt is not amortized through serial repayments, then a sinking fund is established to repay the debt. The sinking fund requires that monies be set aside for the retirement of the debt when it matures. The monies can be invested in other securities or in the securities of the bond issue itself. The sinking-fund payments have the same effect in the retirement of the bond issue as the period retirement of the serial bonds. The right to call the bonds for retirement or sinking-fund purposes is retained in the contract of the newer issues of municipal bonds to allow the municipality complete flexibility in its financial planning. If we exclude those bonds guaranteed by the federal government, there are two basic types of state and municipal bonds: (1) general-obligation bonds, and (2) revenue bonds. Even this classification is an oversimplification of state and municipal debt issues. Usually two other classifications are provided. Special-assessment bonds are considered as a separate, third class. However, these bonds are usually repaid from money received from the person assessed, and because of this we would put them in the revenue bond category. A fourth type is the combination bond, which is supported by revenues from a project but is also guaranteed by the pledge of revenues from tax sources. Bonds with this combined guarantee are also considered a type of revenue bond.

GENERAL OBLIGATIONS

General obligations are fully tax-supported bonds that are guaranteed by a political unit with the power to levy taxes. These bonds are sometimes referred to as "full-faith-and-credit bonds." There is no pledge of a specific property, but the bondholder receives the unconditional guarantee that both interest and principal will be paid at maturity. As we saw in Table 3–5, this type of bond represents the bulk of the debt issued by states, cities, counties, and special districts. The base for the tax that supports this debt is usually the assessed value of real estate. In cities, income-tax or sales-tax receipts might be pledged as the means of debt repayment, but property taxes are still the most important source of funds for the repayment of general obligations. The investment quality of general obligations depends upon (1) their legality and (2) the ability of the issuer to repay the debt.

The Legality of the Issue. The question of legality is quite important. At times, municipal bonds have been sold to investors when the issuing unit had absolutely no power to issue the debt. In some cases, because of legal technicalities, innocent investors have lost money. Today, legal consultants who are experts in matters pertaining to the issuance of municipal debt are employed to determine the legality of the bond issue before it is sold to the public. The municipal-bond lawyer employed by the bondholders investigates thoroughly the constitution, statutes, charters, and judicial procedure to determine if the bond issue has met all the necessary legal conditions for issuance. If the bonds are legal, he will make an unqualified statement of the fact. This "legal opinion" will not prevent loss if subsequent events prove the attorney to be wrong. However, his statement is good evidence that everything is in order about the bond issue. When the bonds are sold, the bondholder usually receives a copy of the legal opinion. It is wise for a potential purchaser of state and municipal bonds to know whether a legal opinion has been made for each bond issue in which he wishes to invest.

The Ability to Pay Debt Coverage and Income. Once it is known that the bond issue is legal, we must then look at the economic and financial position of the government unit issuing the debt. Essentially, we must learn whether the community has a broad, strong, and growing economic base, and we must know if debt and taxes are reasonable in relation to the present and future income and debt of the community. This is the critical point of analysis for state- and municipal-bond investing. We must obtain an affirmative answer to the question: Is it likely that the issuer will be able to pay the debt at maturity from its future tax receipts?

A guide to the ability of a state or municipality to pay its debt is the income level of its citizens, the existing debt per capita, the relationship of debt to the assessed valuation of the property, and the issuer's past record of meeting its debt obligation. The per capita income indicates the ability of the individual to pay his taxes once they have been levied. Debt per capita and its relationship to the assessed valuation of the property indicate the relative size of debt. A comparison with similar government units will give some idea of the size of debt. A state, county, city, town, or district with a low per capita debt and a low ratio of debt to assessed valuation will be in a much safer position than a similar unit with a high debt and high ratio.

A community that has had a record of default must be examined carefully to determine whether the conditions that created the previous default still exist. In modern times in the United States, the number of defaults has been at a minimum. Most of the defaults occurred prior to World War II. Table 3–6 indicates the type of information that would be helpful in determining the relative merits of a municipal bond issue. The cities selected are representative of the larger, better-known communities. New Orleans had the greatest overall debt to property valuation in 1963, and Cleveland had the lowest. Since overall debt represents an accurate picture of debt position of a community, this suggests that Cleveland is in a better debt position than New Orleans. New York had the largest per capita income but also the largest direct debt per capita. The large income was favorable for New York, but its large debt per capita would place it in a relatively lower credit category. Cleveland appears to be in the best position in regard to direct debt except for its temporary default, which did not mar its credit reputation. Cleveland, Houston, and Los Angeles rank best in regard to overall debt. This is the type of comparative analysis we would make in examining a specific community. Comparison with these large cities would permit us to make a quality judgment about the debt-paying capacity of a community.

Most municipal units have a limit imposed upon their taxing ability. The limit may be expressed as a percentage of the assessed value of the property or as a maximum tax rate. Under this limit the government unit can raise only a certain amount from general assessment—say 10 mills per $1,000 of valuation. Anything beyond this figure must be specially approved by the people. Where the debt is expressed as a percentage of the assessed property value, the rate has actually ranged from 1 to 20 percent of value, 7 percent being a common limit. These limits must be known to the investor when he makes an analysis of a particular debt to learn whether the community has exceeded its debt capacity. No standard debt limit or uniform guide exists to determine when debt is excessive, and the investor must make a decision based upon a relative rather than an absolute criterion.

Often, a certain type of debt will be excluded from the debt limits. Special-assessment bonds, although secured by revenues, are often secured also by a pledge from the municipality. These revenue bonds are not included as a part of the debt, and yet they should be added, since the municipality has pledged its security. Investors must be certain that the debt limits include all the obligations that have been issued or

TABLE 3-6

1963 state per capita income and city per capita debt and default record

City	State Income Per Capita	Net Tax-Supported Debt				Default Record
		Direct[a]		Overall[b]		
		Per Capita	Ratio to Property Valuation	Per Capita	Ratio to Property Valuation	
Boston	$2,853	$159	5.3 %	$299	10.0%	No
Chicago	2,948	75	2.6	157	5.3	No
Cleveland	2,474	124	1.9	172	2.6	Temporary delay in repayment
Detroit	2,541	305	4.9	464	7.4	Default and refunding
Houston	2,068	271	3.4	298	3.8	No
Los Angeles	2,974	94	1.12	324	3.9	No
New Orleans	1,776	153	9.7	242	15.6	No
New York	3,013	412	8.0	412	8.0	No
San Francisco	2,974	151	3.5	195	4.6	No
Median	2,449	167	3.9	266	5.7	—

[a] Debt supported by direct taxes upon real estate.

[b] Includes debt that is self-supporting, such as assessment bonds that are supported only partially or not at all by a specific tax.

source: *Moody's Municipal and Government Manual* (New York: Moody's Investors Service, 1965), pp. a37, a38, a42.

pledged by a municipality. Where the debt is secured by taxes other than property taxes, the investor must determine whether the revenue will be sufficient to service the debt. More and more cities are levying income taxes to meet the costs of government. This revenue may be pledged to support full-faith-and-credit obligations. Where income taxes are used as a source of revenue or where other sources are used, a careful analysis must be made to determine whether these sources are adequate. Again, the standard of comparison is relative. The best way is to compare debt-service costs to the amount of revenue expected from the tax. The greater the coverage of income over debt costs, the more secure the debt issue. Conservative opinion suggests, however, that debt service should not exceed 25 percent of the annual budget from all sources.

Ability to Pay and the Economic Growth of the Community. In addition to analysis of the debt burden, we wish to know about the community's growth potential and its attitude toward debt. We will ask if the community has a broad, strong economic base, well balanced between commercial and residential property, that will support debt in the future. Preferably we want a community where ownership is stable and is represented by a large percentage of homeowners, where the per capita income is increasing, and where the debt and public expenditures are reasonable in relation to their means. These might seem to be utopian criteria for the purchase of municipal bonds, but we do want adequate security before loaning our money. The majority of communities meet the prerequisites of financial stability and economic growth. We must guard against investing in the marginal community, where debt is excessive and likely to lead to loss.

REVENUE BONDS

Revenue bonds are bonds of a political subdivision, government unit, or public authority whose debt service is paid solely out of revenues from the project. They are not solely general-tax revenues, but some revenue bonds may have the additional support of a pledge of tax revenues. Revenue bonds fall into the categories listed below.

A UTILITY:
1. Bridge, Tunnel, or Toll Highway
2. Electric Light and Power
3. Gas
4. Public Transportation
5. Off-Street Parking Facilities
6. Water
7. Multiple Purpose, the more common combinations being electric and water and sewer

B   QUASI-UTILITY
1. Airport
2. Dock and Terminal
3. Hospital
4. Public Market
5. Public Garage

NONUTILITY:
1. Gasoline tax, Cigarette tax, Beer tax, Utility, Excise tax or similar tax.
2. Rentals of Public Buildings
    a. To another government agency
    b. To the public generally
       (1) Education Facilities
       (2) Recreation Facilities
    c. To private persons or corporations[1]

This list of categories indicates the broad use of this type of obligation in state and municipal finance. Revenue bonds possess certain advantages over other forms of municipal debt from the viewpoint of the municipality issuing them. First, they avoid an increase in the debt of the municipality that is payable out of general revenues. Second, revenue bonds can be issued where the legal limit of the debt has been reached by the municipality, as they do not ordinarily come under legal debt limits. Third, revenue bonds follow closely one principle of good taxation —the benefits-received theory—since the debt is repaid by those who use the service. Presumably, revenue bonds also represent ability to pay, which is another tenet of good taxation. Fourth, revenue-bond financing does not require approval from the citizens, and projects can be undertaken that ordinarily would not come under the responsibility of the local government. Fifth, some communities do not have the revenue to support debt from general tax revenues and must look to revenue bonds to finance the improvement. In principle, therefore, revenue bonds are an ideal way to finance needed projects.

The possibility exists that municipal projects will compete with private enterprise. This conflict must be settled by the individual communities involved. The principle that should be followed by municipalities and authorities is to undertake projects only where private enterprise cannot do the job efficiently.

The Value of Revenue Bonds. The basic criterion for the valuation of a successful revenue bond issue is the economic feasibility of the project. If a project is economically sound and will produce revenues adequate to service the debt, then it must be considered a successful

---

1 *Moody's Municipal and Government Manual* (New York: Moody's Investors Service, 1968), p. a26.

venture. We must be aware that equity securities as such do not exist when revenue projects are started. Thus debt repaid from revenues of community projects is subject to the business risk. Each project must be carefully examined to determine the likelihood of success and whether revenues will be adequate. There are many examples of issuance of revenue bonds by authorities. A partial list of these bonds appears in the *Wall Street Journal* with current price quotes. Many of the issues have suffered because of the general increase in money rates. A few have done poorly because the projects were unsuccessful. The West Virginia Turnpike bonds have been unprofitable for investors because the anticipated revenue from the project did not materialize. The Chesapeake Bridge and Tunnel and the Chicago Calumet Skyway issues are also in the class of unsuccessful bonds. The Mackinac River Bridge bonds, in contrast, were economically sound. The bridge replaced a ferry service whose revenues were adequate to provide debt service for the bond issue, and so the project was successful from the beginning. Even though care is taken in establishing the economic value of a project, errors may be made that lead to financial loss. Not all financing is as economically sound as were the Mackinac Bridge bonds. Complete bond quotations and information about state and municipal bonds may be obtained from a municipal bond dealer or from Standard and Poor's weekly "Bond Outlook" or Moody's weekly "Bond Survey." Quotes may be obtained from the "Pink Sheet" of over-the-counter-market bond prices in brokerage offices. The quotes are printed on pink paper; hence the name.

Bond Ratings

It is difficult for an individual to determine independently the legality and financial and economic position of a municipal bond issue. Bond-rating services are available, which can be consulted when an evaluation is made of a specific bond issue. *Moody's Municipal and Government Manual*, a factual, interpretative rating service, provides ratings for virtually all state and municipal bonds. Occasionally ratings are omitted or changed if information is available. The bonds are rated from Aaa to C. The Aaa (Triple A) bond issues are defined:[2]

> Bonds which are rated Aaa are judged to be of the best quality. They carry the smallest degree of investment risk and are generally referred to as "gilt edge." Interest payments are protected by a large or by an exceptionally stable margin, and principal is secure. While the various protection elements are likely to change, such changes as can be visualized are most unlikely to impair the fundamentally strong position of such issues.

2 *Moody's Municipal and Government Manual* (New York: Moody's Investors Service, 1968), p. vi.

The Baa bonds:

Bonds which are rated Baa are considered as lower medium grade obligations, i.e., they are neither highly protected nor poorly secured. Interest payments and principal security appear adequate for the present but certain protective elements may be lacking or may be characteristically unreliable over any great length of time. Such bonds lack outstanding investment characteristics as well.

These bonds represent the lowest quality that institutional investors may buy.

The C bonds:

Bonds which are rated C are the lowest rated class of bonds, and issues so rated can be regarded as having extremely poor prospects of ever attaining any real investment standing.

Reference to the bond rating will quickly provide a close approximation to quality. Before municipal bonds are purchased, the rating should be determined so that we may verify our independent analysis with the rating service and thus be able to balance the risks with the possible rewards. Standard and Poor's is a similar well-known investment information source that rates municipal and corporate bonds. An example of their bond ratings appears in Figure 3–1.

Yields on Municipal Bonds

The yields on state and municipal bonds are usually lower than the yields on comparable government bonds and other bonds that are subject to federal income taxes. We must not assume that because their yield is lower, they are a better risk. They sell on a lower yield basis because bond interest is exempt from federal income taxes. Interest and principal are usually exempt from the state taxes levied in the state in which they are issued. The pattern of yields follows very closely the movement of yields in the money market. The yield at any one time will depend upon two factors: (1) the supply of bonds, which is determined by the demand for funds from the municipalities and states, and (2) the demand for the securities, which is determined by the rates for other high-quality taxable bonds, the number of investors who will benefit from tax exemption, and the money-market conditions in general. The pattern of yields on the Aaa quality municipal bonds is presented in Chart 3–2 and compared there with yields on United States Government and corporate Aaa and Baa bonds. The money-market crisis, the Vietnam War, the outflow of gold, and the inflationary fiscal deficit brought about a sharp increase in long-term interest rates from 1966 through 1968. The main restraint during that period of time was the monetary policies of the Federal Reserve Banks, which were, of necessity, restrictive.

Following are Standard & Poor's ratings on some 7,000 municipal bonds, arranged alphabetically by states; and by state bonds, general obligations and revenue bonds within each state. See page 2 for explanation of ratings symbols. Ratings of direct state obligations are shown after each state name, if the state has such bonds.

ALABAMA

Ala. Corrections IFA	A
Ala. Trade School	A
Bldg. Auth. & Bldg. Corp.	A
Bldg. Finance Auth.	A
Education Authority	AA
Hwy. Auth. A–D; Fin.	AA
Hwy. Auth. E, H, I, N, O.	AA
Public Sch. & Coll.	AAA
Road & Bridge	AA
State Ind. Dev. A	AA

General Obligations:

Alexander City	BBB
Anniston	BBB
Athens	A
Baldwin Co. B.E. (5 Mil)	BBB
Bessemer	BBB
Birmingham	BBB
Colbert Co.	BBB
Cullman	BBB
Decatur (All G.O.)	BBB
Dothan (1963 Refunding)	BBB
Dothan (Other G. O.)	BBB
Etowah Co. Bd. of Ed.	BBB
Florence	A
Gadsden & Bd. Ed.	BBB
Homewood	BBB
Huntsville	A
Jefferson Co. & Bd. of E.	BBB
Mobile ('52 & '61-64 Ser.)	BBB
Mobile Co. & Hosp. Com.	BBB
Mobile Co. Sch. (3-mill)	BBB
Mobile Co. Sch. (5-mill)	A
Montgomery & County	BBB
Ozark	BBB
Prichard	BBB
St. Clair Co. BE (5-mill).	BBB
Scottsboro (10 mills)	BBB
Selma	BBB
Shelby Co. Bd. of Ed.	BBB
Talladega	BBB
Tuscaloosa & B.E., County	BBB
& Bd. Ed. (3-Mill)	BBB

* Funds available for call.

Tuscumbia	BBB

Revenue Bonds:

Anniston (Water)	BBB
Athens (W, G, S)	BBB
Atmore (W, G, S)	BBB
Auburn Univ (A-G)	A
Bessemer (Wtr. '58)	BBB
Birmingham (Ind. Wtr.).	BBB
Birmingham (Water)	BBB
Cullman-Jef'son Gas	BBB
Decatur (Sewer)	BBB
Decatur (Wtr. '62; '66)	BBB
Foley (Utility)	A
Florence (Rur. Elec.)	BBB
Florence (Wtr. & Swr.)	BBB
Gadsden (Water)	BBB
Gadsden Pub. B '65	BBB
Hartselle	BBB
Houston Co Hosp '65	AA
Huntsville (Electric)	BBB
Huntsville (Gas-1st)	BBB
Huntsville (Gas-2nd)	BBB
Huntsville (Water)	A
Marshall County (Gas)	BBB
Montgomery (Water)	BBB
Mobile Co. (Gas D.)	A
(W&F)	BBB
Mobile (IW & W&S)	A
Northwest Alab. Gas.	BBB
Opp (E. W. & S.)	A
Phenix City	A
Prichard (Wtr. & Swr.)	BBB
Southeast Alab. Gas	A
Sylacuga Util Bd.	BBB
Talladega (W&S)	BBB
Trussville (Gas)	A
Tuscaloosa (Util. '58)	A
Tuscumbia (Wtr. & Swr.)	BBB
Univ. of Alabama Dorm. Rev.—'62 (A-B)	A
Student Facil.	BBB

ALASKA

General Obligations:

Anchorage & I.S.D.	A
Gtr. Anchorage Area Boro	BBB
Fairbanks & I.S.D.	BBB
Juneau	A
Juneau-Douglas I.S.D.	BBB
Kenai	BBB
Ketchikan & I.S.D.	BBB
Kodiak Island Boro	BBB
Sitka I.S.D.	BBB

Revenue Bonds:

Alaska St. Dev. Cp.	BBB
Alaska St. Hsg. Auth.	BBB
Anchorage (Tel. & Wtr.).	BBB
Fairbanks (Utility)	BBB
Ketchikan (Utility)	BBB
Sitka (Util. Sr. Lien)	BBB

ARIZONA

General Obligations:

Apache Co. H.S.D.	A
Casa Grande U.H.S.D.	BBB
Cochise Co. Jr. Coll. D.	A
Coconino Co. S.D. #1	A
Coconino Co. U.H.S.D.	A
Flagstaff	BBB
Gila Co. HSD	A
Glendale, U.H.S.D.	BBB
Lake Havasu Irr. D.D.	BB
Maricopa Co. & Jr. Coll.	AA
Maricopa Co. Schl. Dists.:	
#3, 4, 5, 6, 31, 38, 40	A
#66, 69, 217	BBB
#48, 68, 80, 83	A
Mesa & H.S.D.	BBB
Mohave Co. S.D. #4	A
Phoenix & U.H.S.D.	BBB
Pima Co.; S.D.1 & HSD 1	A
Pima Co.; S.D. 8, 10, 12; H.S.D. 4, 8, 12	A
Prescot	BBB

Scottsdale & H.S.D.	A
Tempe & Union H.S.D.	A
Tucson	BBB
Yavapai Co. H.S.D.	BBB
Yuma & S.D. #1	BBB
Yuma Co.Jr. C.D. & U.H.S.D.	BBB

Revenue Bonds:

Arizona State U. '66	A
Arizona State U. '64	A
Chandler	A
Cochise Co. J.C.D.	AA
Flagstaff (Water)	A
Glendale (Wtr. & Swr.)	AA
Maricopa Co. J.C.D.	AA
Mesa (Misc.)	A
No. Arizona U. ('65)	A
No. Arizona U. ('66)	AA
Phoenix (Airport)	A
Phoenix (Fuel Tax)	A
Phoenix (Wtr.–Senior)	A
Prescott (Wtr-2d ln)	BBB
Salt River Project	AA
Scottsdale ('64 Swr)	A
Tempe (Wtr. & Swr.)	A
Tucson (Wtr. Tax)	A
Tucson (Wtr. Ref.)	A
Univ. Ariz (66)	AA
Yuma Co. J.C.D.	AA

ARKANSAS

General Obligations:

Blytheville S.D. #5	A
El Dorado S.D. #15	A
Fayetteville S.D. #7	A
Forest City S.D. #7	BBB
Fort Smith & S.D.	BBB
Garland Co.	A
Hulbert-W. Mem. S.D. #4	BBB
Jonesboro & S.D.	A
Little Rock & S.D.	A
Magnolia S.D. #14	BBB

Newport Spec. S.D.	A
North Little Rock & S.D.	A
Texarkana S.D. #7	A
Union Co.	A

Revenue Bonds:

Ark Rev. D. Bldg. C.	A
El Dorado (Wtr. & Swr.)	A
Fayetteville	A
Ft. Smith (Wtr., Swr.)	A
Hot Springs (Wtr. 1st)	BBB
Hot Springs (Wtr 2d ln)	BBB
Little Rock (Airport)	BBB
Little Rock (Sewer)	AA
Little Rock (Water, '64)	AA
No. Little Rock (Elec. '59)	AA
(Elec. & Sewer) (Wtr	AA
Pine Bluff (Sewer)	BBB
Springdale (Wtr.)	BBB
Texarkana (Wtr. & Swr.).	AA

CALIFORNIA

General Obligations:	AAA
ABC Unif. S.D.	BBB
Acalanes Union H.S.D.	BBB
Alameda & U.S.D.	AA
Alameda-Contra Costa Transit Spcl. Dist. #1	AA
Alameda Co. Fl. C. & Wtr.: Z2, Z3A, Z5, Z6, Z7, Z9	BBB
Alameda Co Wtr Impr #1	BBB
Alhambra City SD & HSD	AA
Alum Rock Union S.D.	AA
Alvord S.D.	BBB
Amador Vy U.H.S.D.	BBB
Anaheim & SD & UHSD	BBB
Analy Union H.S.D.	A
Antelope Valley Jt. U.H.S.	BBB
Antelope Vy. Jt. J.C.D.	BBB
Antioch U.S.D.	BBB
Apple Valley S.D.	A
Aptos San. Dist.	BBB
Arcadia Unif. S.D.	BBB
Arcata U.H.S.D.	BBB
Armijo Un. H.S.D.	BBB
Arroyo Grande U.H.S.D.	BBB

FIGURE 3–1

An example of municipal bond ratings

SOURCE Standard & Poor's Bond Guide, 1968

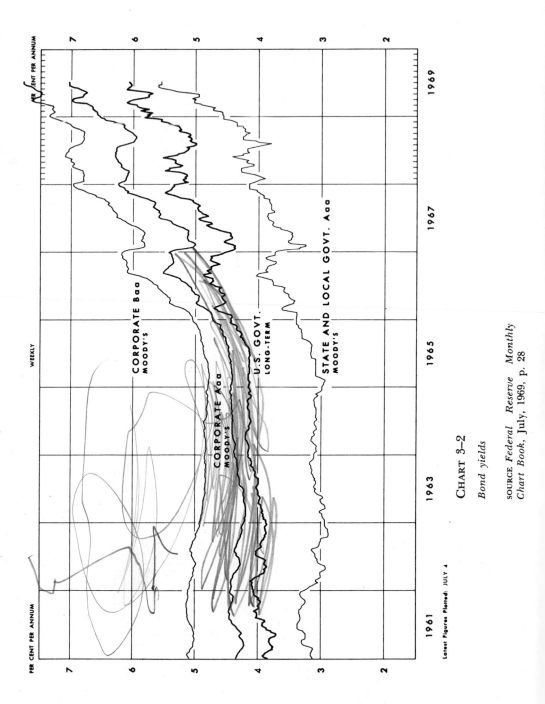

CHART 3–2

Bond yields

SOURCE *Federal Reserve Monthly Chart Book*, July, 1969, p. 28

Ownership of Municipal Debt

Commercial banks were the largest owners of state and municipal securities in 1967. Table 3–7 indicates the pattern of ownership for 1957, 1961, and 1967. The next two most important owners of municipals in 1967 were individuals and insurance companies. Institutional investors are attracted to state and municipal obligations because of the stability of income, the security of the investment, and the tax-exempt status of the bonds that affords them a high after-tax yield when they are in the top corporate-tax bracket.

Early in the 1960's corporate and personal federal income tax rates were reduced. The effect of the tax reduction was to make tax-exempt bonds less attractive than previously to wealthy individuals and corporations and make them more comparable to other fully taxable bonds. It had the effect of raising the cost of state and municipal financing. The rate of interest would have to be increased on these bonds in order to make them as attractive as they were before the rate reduction, compared to the fully taxable obligations. With the lower tax rate, municipal bonds would tend to sell more and more like fully taxable obligations. In 1968, however, with the increase in federal income taxes

TABLE 3–7

Distribution of ownership of state and municipal bonds, 1957, 1961, and 1967 (billions of dollars and percent)

HOLDER	1957		1961		1967	
Private:						
Individuals, partnerships, and personal trust accounts	$22.0	42.3%	$28.3	39.4%	$39.0	35.1%
Commercial banks	13.4	25.8	18.8	26.1	45.6	40.3
Mutual savings banks	0.7	1.3	0.7	1.0	0.3	0.3
Insurance companies	7.4	14.2	12.3	17.1	15.5	13.7
Other corporations	1.5	2.9	2.3	3.2	4.8	4.2
Miscellaneous investors*	1.0	2.0	1.6	2.2	2.1	1.8
Total Private	46.0	88.5	64.0	89.0	107.3	95.4
Public:						
United States Government agencies and trust funds	0.2	0.3	0.4	0.7	1.0	0.9
Sinking, trust, and investment funds of state and local governments	5.8	11.2	7.4	10.3	4.2	3.7
Total Public	6.0	11.5	7.8	11.0	5.2	4.6
Total Public and Private	$52.0	100.0%	$71.8	100.0%	$113.3	100.0%

* Includes savings and loan associations, corporate pension trust funds, dealers and brokers, and the like.
SOURCE: *Moody's Municipal and Government Manual* (New York: Moody's Investors Service, 1968), p. a16.

through a surcharge tax of 10 percent, the municipal bond became more attractive for investment.

The Place of Municipal Bonds in the Investor's Portfolio

In the introductory remarks we pointed out that state and municipal bonds are unique. The quality that makes them unique is their exemption from federal income taxes and from taxes imposed within the state of issue. Only five states impose an intangible tax on bonds issued within the state (Arkansas, Illinois, Missouri, Montana, Texas); Pennsylvania exempts state bonds but taxes local bonds. Where personal income taxes are levied against bond-interest income, most states exempt the income from state and municipal bonds. Colorado, Idaho, Indiana, Iowa, Kansas, Montana, Oklahoma, and Wisconsin, however, consider all bond-interest income subject to personal income taxes. Ohio and Utah include local but not state bonds as taxable for income tax purposes. Warrant interest is considered income in Arizona. However, the important exemption from federal income taxes makes municipal bonds attractive for investors in the upper income-tax brackets, particularly commercial banks and individuals.

These securities possess a great degree of quality, particularly those that enjoy the highest bond ratings. The bonds are readily marketable, and the short maturities have a high degree of liquidity. Wealthy individuals seeking stability of income and security of principal should look carefully at the advantages of state and municipal bonds to meet their needs. An individual, institutional, or corporate investor who is in the 52 percent bracket or above and who is interested in a high after-tax yield should consider municipal bonds. Even individuals in a lower income-tax bracket can benefit from tax exemption. If we were in the 20 percent tax bracket and bought a 4 percent tax-exempt bond, this would be the equivalent of a fully taxable yield of 5 percent. A 5 percent rate of return for a long period of time on a safe and secure investment is a modestly attractive return. As a further advantage, state and municipal bonds are not subject to the amount of market risk that accompanies the purchase of common stock.

The municipal bond does not offer an opportunity for future growth, however, and this must be considered when an investment is contemplated. The investor in a state or municipal bond will earn a satisfactory yield, his principal is secure and will be returned, but there is no possibility of capital growth. Municipal bonds do not provide against the possible loss of purchasing power if we suffer from inflation. Municipal bonds are subject to the money rate risk too, since the yields fluctuate with the pattern of yields in the money market. If we purchase revenue bonds, we must accept still another risk, the business risk. Since revenue bonds are supported by the revenues from quasi-competitive business ventures, the risk of failure always exists. Thus, in the purchase of municipal bonds, there is the possibility of a business loss but no possibility of a business gain. In spite of these disadvantages, state and municipal bonds offer attractive investment opportunities for individuals and corporate institutional investors in the higher income-tax brackets. These bonds should be considered investment outlets for the type of investor who wants a stable after-tax income.

Summary

The securities issued by the United States Government are excellent investment-grade securities. They provide the individual and institutional investor with marketability and liquidity and possess a high degree of safety of principal and stability of income with a modest yield. Marketable securities are sometimes used by individual investors to achieve liquidity and maintain a defensive position in their investment portfolios. The short-term securities are particularly adaptable to the temporary needs of the investor. Short-term bills are useful as a temporary haven for funds and are used substantially by corporations and financial and institutional investors. The long-term government securities may be used as the conservative portion of an investor's security holdings. Federal securities are fully taxable and do not offer the investor protection from the purchasing-power risk or the money rate risk. However, we avoid the risk of loss that is associated with the business risk and market risk when we purchase federal government securities.

Municipal bonds are unique. They possess the features of safety of principal and stability of income, and they are exempt from federal income taxes and the majority of state taxes. They are usually referred to as "tax-exempts." Some market risk is assumed when we purchase general-revenue bonds, particularly if they are associated with economically unfeasible projects. The business risk is present in revenue bonds, and they offer no protection from the purchasing-power risk or the money rate risk. The value of the securities depends upon the financial and economic position of the community or authority that is issuing the bonds. Their quality and tax-exempt position makes them attractive for individual and institutional investors in the high income-tax bracket who desire safety of principal and stable income with an adequate rate of return.

Review Questions

1. Who are the owners of marketable debt of the United States Government and what are the types of government issues owned?
2. What is the difference between a U.S. Treasury bill, a Treasury certificate of indebtedness, a Treasury note, and a Treasury bond?
3. How would we judge the basic value of a government security?

4. What are the basic risks inherent in the purchase of government securities?

5. What are the advantages and disadvantages of the ownership of long-term and short-term government securities?

6. What does the term *state and municipal bonds* mean?

7. What feature of state and municipal bonds makes them unique?

8. What are the purposes for which state and municipal securities are issued?

9. Comment upon the growth and ownership of state and municipal debt.

10. Indicate the basic types of state and municipal obligations. Be sure to contrast general obligations with revenue bonds.

11. What factors determine the investment quality of a state or municipal obligation? Explain in detail.

12. What part do legality and debt limit play in the valuation problem?

13. To what extent can we rely upon the bond ratings of the various investment services as an indicator of value? Be sure to differentiate between Aaa and Baa ratings.

14. What are the major risks inherent in the purchase of state and municipal bonds?

15. What type of investor would use municipal bonds?

16. Should municipal bonds be tax exempt?

Problems

1. Find the yield to maturity on the following marketable government securities from the *Wall Street Journal* or another source.
   U.S. Treasury bills
   U.S. Treasury notes
   U.S. Treasury certificates of indebtedness
   Treasury bonds
   Bank for Cooperatives
   Federal Home Loan Bank
   Federal Land Bank
   Federal Intermediate Credit Bank debentures
   Federal National Mortgage Association notes and debentures
   World Bank bonds

2. Compute the yield to maturity for the Maine Turnpike 4's due in 1989 and the New York State Power 3.20's maturing in 1995. Use the approximate method and the present value method. Explain the difference in the pattern and amount of interest compared to long-term governments.

3. From *Moody's Municipal and Government Manual* determine the following for a bond issue from your home town:
   (a) The type of bond and its rating.
   (b) The provisions of the bond indenture.
   (c) What are the unusual features, if any, of the bond issue?
   (d) Is the bond issue adequately secured? Is the community growing?
   (e) What is the per capita debt and income level of the taxing district, and are they respectively excessive or adequate?
   (f) Comment upon its overall attractiveness for investment.
   If *Moody's* is not available, get the information from the treasurer of the community.

4. If we bought a tax-exempt municipal bond to yield 4.2 percent to maturity, what would be the fully taxable equivalent yield if we were in the 20 percent tax bracket, the 38 percent bracket, or the 72 percent bracket? Use the formula 1 — the marginal tax rate divided into the yield.

Sources of Investment Information

Barron's
Commercial and Financial Chronicle
Standard & Poor's *Bond Guide*
Moody's Municipal and Government Manual
Federal Reserve Bulletin
Federal Reserve Chart Book
The Blue List of Current Municipal Offerings
Wall Street Journal

Selected Readings

Harries, Brenton W., "Standard & Poor's New Policy," *Financial Analysts Journal* (May-June, 1968), p. 68.

Homer, Sidney, "Spring Tide in the Money Market" (Keynote Review) *Financial Analysts Journal* (September-October, 1966), p. 101.

Matteson, Archibald C., "In Defense of Municipal Ratings," *Financial Analysts Journal* (July-August, 1968), p. 99.

Miller, Donald C., "Financial Markets Under Stress," *Financial Analysts Journal* (January-February, 1968), p. 81.

Packer, Stephen B., "Higher Interest Rates Forever?" *Financial Analysts Journal* (January-February, 1968), p. 84.

———, "Municipal Bond Ratings," *Financial Analysts Journal* (July-August, 1968), p. 93.

Reilly, James F., "The Outlook for Municipal Bonds," *Financial Analysts Journal* (September-October, 1967), p. 93.

Riehle, Robert C., "Moody's Municipal Ratings," *Financial Analysts Journal* (May-June, 1968), p. 71.

Sprinkel, Beryl W., "Measuring Impact of Monetary Policy," *Financial Analysts Journal* (September-October, 1967), p. 85.

Weidenbaum, Murray L., "Government Spending," *Financial Analysts Journal* (January-February, 1968), p. 77.

4

CORPORATE BONDS
Usual and Unusual

We turn now to a consideration of the investment characteristics of the securities of private corporations. A greater degree of risk is associated with corporate than with government securities, but greater profits are also anticipated. We will first continue our discussion of debt securities, in this chapter, by examining the investment qualities of regular corporate bonds and how they might meet the investment needs of either an individual or an institutional investor. Many corporate bonds possess no greater risk than fully taxable United States Government securities. Some corporate bonds are more attractive and offer the investor a high degree of stability of income and safety of principal. In addition, they provide a higher yield than government securities. Several special types of corporate bonds, such as convertible bonds and bonds with warrants, will be examined for investment opportunities. Individual investors might not show enthusiasm for the usual form of corporate bonds, but bonds with profit-sharing features, such as convertibles, are very attractive to individual and institutional investors alike. Individuals facing uncertainty will assuredly find bonds with unusual features attractive. In the two chapters following, we will examine the ownership securities of private corporations—preferred stock and common stock.

The Significance of Corporate
Debt Securities

When corporations go to the capital markets to obtain money for all corporate purposes, the single most important source of funds is the sale of debt securities. The figures in Table 4–1 represent the amount of money raised through the sale of bonds both to the public and to private investors, and the total amount raised by the sale of all types of securities between 1957 and 1967. The total sales of bonds in 1967 comparable to past years represented 88.5 percent of all new issues of securities sold. Two basic reasons exist for the heavy reliance upon debt financing to raise corporate funds. First, the sale of bonds is less expensive in terms of interest costs and issuance costs than any other form of security. In addition, under present tax laws, bond interest is deductible as an expense, reducing further the cost of financing to the corporation. If a corporation were in the 52 percent tax bracket, for example, the after-tax cost of issuing a 5 percent bond would be only 2.4 percent ($.05 \times .48$). This is because the company receives a tax credit of 52 percent of the interest expense, and so the net cost to the company is 48 percent of the interest cost.

The second major reason for the issuance of debt securities is the ready market that exists for them. Debt securities are an important investment outlet for all institutional investors and some individual

TABLE 4–1

Total corporate funds raised through the issuance
of all securities and bonds, 1957–67
(millions of dollars)

		Corporate Bonds			Stock	
YEAR	TOTAL CORPORATE SECURITIES NEW ISSUES	TOTAL	PUBLICLY OFFERED	PRIVATELY PLACED	PREFERRED	COMMON
1967	24,798	21,954	14,990	6,964	885	1,959
1966	18,074	15,561	8,018	7,542	574	1,939
1965	15,992	13,720	5,570	8,150	725	1,547
1964	13,957	10,865	3,623	7,243	412	2,679
1963	12,211	10,856	4,713	6,143	343	1,011
1962	10,705	8,969	4,440	4,529	422	1,314
1961	13,165	9,420	4,700	4,720	450	3,294
1960	10,154	8,081	4,806	3,275	409	1,664
1959	9,748	7,190	3,558	3,632	531	2,027
1958	11,558	9,653	6,333	3,320	571	1,334
1957	12,884	9,957	6,118	3,839	411	2,516

SOURCE: *Federal Reserve Bulletin,* December, 1957, p. 2114; and July, 1968, p. A44.

investors. Some of the financial institutions, as we pointed out previously, are permitted to own nothing but debt securities. They can buy only bonds rated Baa and higher. These requirements are imposed by law and by the nature of their own financial commitments. Whatever the reasons for the issuance of debt, corporate bonds represent an investment medium for many different types of investors. The advantage of debt as a source of funds is reflected in the total growth of debt as shown in Table 4–1, relative to the other sources of funds.

The Nature of Corporate Bonds

A corporate bond issue is a long-term debt of the corporation. It is a long-term written promise to pay under seal a certain sum of money at a certain time for a specified rate of interest. Since the amount of money borrowed is usually large, and since no one investor would be able to · lend the entire amount of money to the corporation, the entire loan is divided into a large number of parts or pieces and sold to many investors. These parts are bonds and in their entirety constitute the bond issue. The consolidated balance sheet and operating statement of Litton Industries and its subsidiary companies, with explanations and notes, appear in Figure 4–1. The place of debt and ownership of a corporation are clearly placed by the accountant to facilitate understanding. As we examine debt as an investment, we understand the relationship to the assets as well as to the ownership of the corporation. In the case of Litton, we note that long-term debt is substantially less than shareholders' investment and only slightly smaller than fixed assets. We also note that interest on debt is well secured by income after taxes. These are the relationships germane to the discussion of bond investment. At this point, it would be wise for the reader to review accounting and corporation finance to refresh his understanding of basic balance-sheet and operating-statement relationships.

A corporation issuing bonds is in effect selling its credit to the individual or financial institution that is willing to loan money by investing in its debt securities. The corporation agrees to pay interest on the money borrowed and to repay the loan at maturity. The interest paid represents compensation to the investor for the risk he assumes. The greater the risk, other things being equal, the higher the interest and the greater the cost to the corporation that is selling its credit. The lower the risk, the lower the interest and the lower the cost to the company.

When a corporation borrows money, it promises to do two things for the bondholder. It promises, first, to repay the money at a specified time, and second, to pay the interest on the money borrowed at a specified rate and at a specific time. The issuing company will make further

Consolidated Statement of Earnings

	Year Ended July 31, 1967	Year Ended July 31, 1966	
		After Adjustment for 1967 Poolings of Interests	Prior to Adjustment for 1967 Poolings of Interests
Sales and service revenues	$1,561,510,340	$1,340,964,413	$1,172,233,328
Costs and expenses (including depreciation of $33,778,000, $28,514,000 and $26,577,000):			
Cost of sales	1,147,719,716	975,117,860	851,546,658
Selling, general and administrative.	283,437,105	249,200,255	214,751,429
Interest	10,292,384	10,399,082	9,723,217
	1,441,449,205	1,234,717,197	1,076,021,304
Earnings before taxes on income	120,061,135	106,247,216	96,212,024
Federal and foreign taxes on income	49,991,008	45,318,778	40,597,821
Net earnings	$ 70,070,127	$ 60,928,438	$ 55,614,203

The 1966 data, "Prior to Adjustment for 1967 Poolings of Interests," represents the operations of Litton as shown on its 1966 report. The 1966 data, "After Adjustment for 1967 Poolings of Interests," gives effect to the restatement of the 1966 operations to include operations of businesses acquired in 1967 in poolings of interests.

See notes to financial statements.

Consolidated Balance Sheets

ASSETS

	July 31, 1967	July 31, 1966
CURRENT ASSETS:		
Cash, including certificates of deposit and treasury bills	$ 50,774,319	$ 45,200,145
Accounts receivable	297,904,664	274,964,863
Inventories, at lower of cost or market, less progress billings of $86,760,184 and in 1966 $88,201,223	275,933,009	259,272,085
Prepaid expenses	9,233,776	8,822,187
Total Current Assets	633,845,768	588,259,280
PROPERTY, PLANT, AND EQUIPMENT—See page 60	220,683,416	186,159,191
INVESTMENTS AND OTHER ASSETS—See page 60	90,495,288	64,459,943
	$945,024,472	$838,878,414

LIABILITIES AND SHAREHOLDERS' INVESTMENT

	July 31, 1967	July 31, 1966
CURRENT LIABILITIES:		
Notes payable to banks	$ 11,104,199	$ 8,304,971
Accounts payable	130,179,031	127,140,216
Payrolls and related expenses	47,580,722	41,887,830
Federal and foreign taxes on income	40,469,859	54,203,106
Current portion of long-term liabilities and debentures	3,087,110	3,930,275
Total Current Liabilities.	232,420,921	235,466,398
LONG-TERM LIABILITIES (Note C)	192,141,283	156,512,886
DEFERRED FEDERAL TAXES ON INCOME	22,840,993	18,051,019
DEFERRED SERVICE CONTRACT AND OTHER INCOME	21,650,737	20,766,861
CONVERTIBLE SUBORDINATED DEBENTURES (Note D)	48,984,000	57,897,000
SHAREHOLDERS' INVESTMENT—See page 60 (Note E)	426,986,538	350,184,250
	$945,024,472	$838,878,414

See statement of properties, investments and shareholders' investment and notes to financial statements.

FIGURE 4–1

Consolidated balance sheet and operating statement, Litton Industries, Inc., and subsidiary companies

Properties, Investments and Shareholders' Investment

	July 31, 1967	July 31, 1966
PROPERTY, PLANT AND EQUIPMENT—at cost:		
Land	$ 11,148,093	$ 9,877,207
Buildings	90,496,767	81,936,016
Machinery and equipment	263,040,380	223,957,742
	364,685,240	315,770,965
Accumulated depreciation	144,001,824	129,611,774
	$220,683,416	$186,159,191
INVESTMENTS AND OTHER ASSETS:		
Equity in unconsolidated finance subsidiaries (Note B)	$27,658,376	$ 20,687,195
Long-term investments—at cost	21,295,902	12,276,631
Excess of cost over related net assets of businesses purchased	37,913,264	28,171,415
Other assets, including patents	3,627,746	3,324,702
	$ 90,495,288	$ 64,459,943
SHAREHOLDERS' INVESTMENT (Note E):		
Capital stock:		
Voting preference, par value $2.50 a share, issuable in series:		
Authorized 8,000,000 shares		
Convertible participating series issued 5,162,040 shares, and 5,149,734 shares less 36,702 shares in treasury	$ 12,813,346	$ 12,782,581
Voting preferred, convertible, cumulative, par value $5 a share, issuable in series:		
Authorized 3,000,000 shares		
Series A issued 128,257 shares, and 169,292 shares	641,285	846,460
Common, par value $1 a share:		
Authorized 39,000,000 shares		
Issued 21,536,644 shares, and 20,687,116 shares	21,536,644	20,687,116
Additional paid-in capital	220,559,427	169,588,042
Earnings retained in the business (less $138,022,917 and $100,462,478 transferred to paid-in capital for stock dividends paid)	171,435,836	146,280,051
	$426,986,538	$350,184,250

See notes to financial statements.

Consolidated Statement of Earnings Retained in the Business

Year Ended July 31, 1967

Balance at beginning of year		$146,280,051
Net earnings for the year		70,070,127
		216,350,178
Deduct:		
Market value of 2½% stock dividend	$ 37,560,439	
Premium on redemption of convertible subordinated debentures	6,951,462	
Cash dividends on preferred stock—$3 a share	402,441	44,914,342
Balance at end of year		$171,435,836

Consolidated Statement of Additional Paid-In Capital

Year Ended July 31, 1967

Balance at beginning of year	$169,588,042
Excess of market value of stock dividend over par value of common stock issued	36,867,351
Excess of market value over par value of preference stock issued to purchase businesses	7,212,730
Excess of principal amount of debentures and par value of preferred and preference stocks converted over par value of common stock issued	6,891,304
Balance at end of year	$220,559,427

See notes to financial statements.

FIGURE 4-1 (continued)

Year Ended July 31, 1967

Notes to Financial Statements

NOTE A—Principles of Consolidation

The accounts of the Company and its wholly-owned subsidiaries (excluding its finance subsidiaries) are included in the accompanying financial statements.

During the year ended July 31, 1967, the Company acquired the net assets of businesses which have been accounted for as poolings of interests. The 1966 financial statements have been revised to include these businesses. The Company also purchased other businesses, the operations of which are included from dates of acquisition.

NOTE B—Equity in Unconsolidated Finance Subsidiaries

The Company's equity in its wholly-owned finance subsidiaries is stated at cost, represented by investments and advances, and undistributed earnings of $4,259,103 at July 31, 1967. These subsidiaries had total assets of $102,569,914 and liabilities to banks and others of $74,911,538 at July 31, 1967.

NOTE C—Long-term Liabilities

Long-term liabilities at July 31, 1967 consisted of the following:

Notes payable to insurance companies:	
Due to 1984 with interest from 3⅜% to 4⅞%	$ 89,435,120
Due to 1977 with interest from 5% to 6%	2,147,255
Notes payable to banks:	
Due 1970 with interest at 4¼%	35,250,000
Due 1972 with interest at 5¾%	39,750,000
Due to 1980 with interest from 3% to 5½%	3,776,457
Miscellaneous debt due to 1985 with average interest of 4½%	24,209,561
	194,568,393
Less current portion	2,427,110
	$192,141,283

The principal maturities due during each of the next five fiscal years is as follows:

Year ended July 31, 1968	$ 2,427,000
Year ended July 31, 1969	9,503,000
Year ended July 31, 1970	6,822,000
Year ended July 31, 1971	42,078,000
Year ended July 31, 1972	46,505,000

The Company has complied with its agreements to maintain specified ratios of assets to debt and shareholders' investment to debt.

NOTE D—Convertible Subordinated Debentures

Convertible subordinated debentures at July 31, 1967 were as follows:

3½% due April 1, 1987, issued 1962, 1963, 1964, and 1965	$ 43,669,000
5¼% due December 1, 1974, issued 1959	2,495,000
4¾% due June 1, 1974, issued 1959	3,480,000
	49,644,000
Less current portion	660,000
	$ 48,984,000

The debentures are convertible into common stock of the Company at conversion prices as follows: 3½% debentures—$40 a share until April 1, 1972, $42.50 a share until April 1, 1982, $45 a share thereafter; 5¼% debentures—$20 a share; 4¾% debentures—$16.25 a share. These conversion prices are subject to antidilution provisions.

The Company has agreed to retire annually principal amount of debentures as follows: 3½% debentures—$2,819,000 commencing April 1, 1972; 5¼% debentures—$600,000 commencing December 1, 1968; 4¾% debentures—$470,000. Required annual retirements of the 3½% debentures have been met through April 1, 1980.

The debentures are subordinated to all existing debt and future debt of the Company with limited exceptions. The Company has complied with the terms of the debentures.

NOTE E— Shareholders' Investment

Each share of preference stock is currently convertible into 1.0309 shares of common stock. This conversion rate increases by 3.09% in each of the years 1968 to 1989 and, additionally, is subject to antidilution provisions. If a cash dividend is paid on common stock, each share of preference stock is entitled to receive a cash dividend in an amount equal to the dividend per common share times the then applicable preference stock conversion rate. Each share of preference stock is redeemable at any time after January 31, 1976 at prices ranging from $67.75 in 1976 to $100.95 in 1989 and thereafter. The Company has the right, at its option, each calendar year to redeem shares of preference stock by offering to each preference stockholder the right to call upon the Company to redeem up to 3% of his shares at prices ranging from $51.65 in 1967 to $100.95 in 1989 and thereafter. In the event of liquidation each preference share is entitled to receive $25 a share plus accrued dividends.

Each share of preferred stock is currently convertible into two shares of common stock and is redeemable on or after April 1, 1972 at $100 a share plus accrued dividends. In the event of liquidation each preferred share is entitled to receive $50 a share plus accrued dividends.

At July 31, 1967, there were reserved 1,430,629 common shares for conversion of debentures, 256,514 common shares for conversion of preferred stock, and 5,283,711 common shares for conversion of preference stock.

Under certain acquisition agreements capital stock may be issued as additional consideration for businesses acquired. The number of shares to be issued is dependent, among other things, upon future earnings of acquired businesses and future market value of Litton stock. Based upon current estimates, the maximum number which could be issued as additional consideration is approximately 112,000 common shares, 41,700 preference shares and 2,300 preferred shares.

Under the terms of the Company's borrowing agreements, consolidated earnings retained in the business of approximately $124,359,000 were available for cash dividends on common stock at July 31, 1967.

A 2½% common stock dividend paid on November 8, 1966 is reflected in the July 31, 1967 financial statements but has not been retroactively reflected in the July 31, 1966 financial statements.

On May 19, 1967 the Board of Directors declared a common stock dividend of 2½% payable November 15, 1967, to holders of record of such common stock at the close of business September 29, 1967. This transaction has not been reflected in the financial statements.

NOTE F—Lease Obligations

Annual rentals under long-term leases expiring between 1970 and 1999 are approximately $8,236,000 plus property taxes and insurance in some instances.

FIGURE 4–1 *(continued)*

commitments, each of which is designed to improve the promise of re-payment, the security of principal, and the promise to pay the interest. The degree of uncertainty surrounding the repayment of the borrowed money and the payment of interest determines the risk involved and the rate of return that we will receive as investors. Some bonds offer a third promise to the investor—the promise of sharing in the growth of the company. The type of bond sold will obtain its identity from the nature of the promises made by the company.

The Bond Indenture

The specific promises that are made to the bondholder are set forth in the bond indenture. The bond indenture is an agreement between the corporation issuing the bonds and a corporate trustee, usually a com-mercial bank or trust company, who represents the bondholder. The trustee is necessary because it would be impractical and economically unfeasible for the corporation to enter into a direct agreement with each of the many bondholders. A single trustee who represents all bond-holders is also helpful for the purpose of working out any financial difficulties that should arise in the future.

The usual items found in the indenture are: the authorization of the issue; the exact wording of the bond; the interest or coupon rate; the trustee's certificate; the registration and endorsement; the property pledged as security, if any; and the agreements, restrictions, and remedies of the trustee and the bondholders in default. If there is a conversion right or a redemption right, this is usually stated. The information con-tained in the indenture usually relates to the promises made by the corporation to the bondholders. Correct legal language is used to avoid misunderstanding. Each of these promises will be discussed to indicate the usual features of a bond issue as well as to present the various types of bonds that may be issued.

The Repayment of Principal—The First Promise

The first promise the corporation agrees to make is to repay the borrowed money at a specified time and for a stated amount. The usual value of the bond is $1,000. This is referred to as the par value, face value, or maturity value. Corporate bonds can be and are issued in larger denomi-nations. There is nothing to prevent a large institutional investor who buys $1,000,000 worth of bonds from having one $1,000,000 security. But this might be undesirable, for in future years the investor might wish to dispose of the security or a portion of it, and the large denomi-nation might be difficult to sell. Smaller denominations would be much more marketable and convenient. For this reason, individual bonds are issued with lower face values than $1,000,000 or $100,000; most typical is the $1,000 bond, although some bonds are issued in units of $5,000 or $10,000 if they go to institutional investors.

MATURITY DATE

The time of repayment of the principal of the bond is another part of the pledge of repayment. When each bond issued is sold, a maturity date for the bond issue is established. The maturities vary from short term to long term, much like government bonds. The length of time to maturity for long-term bonds is from 20 to 100 years. It is this type of bond issue with which we are concerned. Short-term bonds will have a maturity of less than a year, and intermediate-term bonds mature in from 5 to 10 years. Ordinarily, we use the same time classification for government bonds that we do for private corporate bonds. Long-term corporate bonds will, therefore, mature in 20 years or longer. The actual time will be established in the bond indenture. A bond issue with a 20-year maturity is actually, in the market place, a bond with many different maturity dates. As it approaches maturity, it becomes first an intermediate-term bond and then a short-term bond. A long-term bond is in reality, then, a bond with varying maturity dates and yields.

CALL FEATURE

Most modern corporate bonds are callable at the discretion of the issuer. The call feature is designed to solve two problems facing the corporation. First, it allows bonds to be purchased by the corporation for retirement piecemeal, year by year, by reserving for the corporation the right to call the bond before maturity for sinking-fund purposes. This assures the corporation and the creditors of the eventual retirement of the debt. Second, the call feature is used to allow the bond issue to be retired in total before maturity. Calling a bond issue before maturity might be done by the issuing corporation to take advantage of lower interest rates in the money market or to make way for new financing. When a company calls the debt outstanding, the investment maturity is changed. The maturity value is also changed because the bonds are usually called at a higher price than the par value, to compensate the investor for the risk of reinvesting his money. A higher call price and a shorter time to maturity tend to increase the yield on bonds. The time at which the bonds can be called and the amount for which they can be called are stated in the bond indenture. When a bond is purchased, the investor should examine the bond indenture carefully to determine if and when it can be called for redemption. If a call feature were exercised, it could change the investment period and yield by a change in the maturity date and the maturity price. Both of these changes would affect the bond yield. If we were to purchase a bond, we would compute the yield to maturity and the yield to the first call date to determine what impact an early call would have upon the yield.

SERIAL BONDS

Some bond issues are retired serially, just like municipal bonds. A schedule of yields, interest rates, prices, and maturity dates is known before the bonds are purchased. The investor then selects the issue of bonds which best meets his needs. If he desires a long-term investment, he will buy bonds that will be mature in the later years. If the investor should desire a short investment period, he will buy the short-term securities. The basic purpose of the serial bond issue is to provide for the retirement of the debt in an orderly, easy, and direct fashion. It assures the eventual elimination of debt, and it tends to improve the credit rating of the remaining outstanding bonds. A serial bond issue meets the needs of many investors because of the range of maturities. The serial bond is a series of bond issues that have securities maturing every six months. A 20-year serial bond of $20,000,000, for example, is really 40 different bond issues of $500,000 each that have different yields to maturity ranging in time from six months to twenty years. Serial bond issues, like bond issues with a sinking fund, have an effect upon yields. The shorter maturities of serial bonds, under normal circumstances, have lower yields than the longer maturities. The investor must select the issue that meets his needs from the standpoints of both yield and maturity.

THE PLEDGE OF SECURITY

The third feature of the promise to repay the principal relates to the security of the pledge. To assure the investor that his principal is secure and that either he will be repaid at maturity or his bonds will be called before maturity, the corporation sometimes offers security in addition to a simple promise to pay. Several types of bonds are typed or classified by this additional pledge of real or personal assets. Actually the pledge to repay made by a corporation to the trustee who represents the bondholders is simply a formal promise, in writing and signed under seal. However, the promise to pay, without further comment in the bond contract, is simply a pledge.

DEBENTURE BONDS

The pledge to repay takes its highest form in the debenture bond, which is a full-faith-and-credit obligation. When a corporation issues a debenture bond, it says to the creditor: "I (the corporation) promise to repay the money you have loaned me at the maturity date. I give you my bond that I will repay, but I do not pledge a tangible, specific asset as security for the loan. I simply pledge my good faith and credit that I will repay the loan." The company, in making the pledge to repay, actually pledges its assets, its earnings, and its character to fulfill its obligation to the bondholder. If the company did not pay interest or principal at maturity, its assets could be sold to satisfy the claims. Debenture bonds are typically issued by corporations that have an unquestioned credit rating and by corporations that do not have a large amount of assets to pledge as additional security. The debenture bond bears the same relationship to the corporation as long-term government bonds bear to the federal government.

SUBORDINATED DEBENTURES

A subordinated bond is usually junior to all existing bond issues and actually reduces the investor's security of principal. It is sometimes junior to current liabilities or to bank loans. The exact relationship of the subordinated bond to other debt will be found in the bond indenture. Subordinated bonds usually have a claim upon assets that is superior to that upon preferred and common stock. They are often used with the conversion feature in which the final security will be an ownership claim that is junior to a debt issue. Subordinated debentures may offer greater income for the investor and other features, even though they offer a smaller amount of security of principal.

MORTGAGE BONDS

Some bond issues pledge additional security rather than reduce security, to support the pledge of principal repayment. A mortgage bond issue not only agrees to repay the principal at maturity but also pledges real property as additional security with the pledge. All the customary features of the bond issue are the same except for the pledge of general or specific assets. If the company defaults, the strict interpretation of the indenture states that the general or specific asset pledged can be sold to pay the creditors. If this is not sufficient, the creditor can sue the corporation on its bond. A mortgage on real property has substance only if the property is relatively marketable and if there are no claims on the property that take precedence over the claim that is being satisfied. Real property that has more than one use or a variety of uses would be a superior asset as security to an asset having only one use. The Marathon Oil Corporation, for example, has an excellent group of office buildings in Findlay, Ohio. If they were pledged as security for a bond issue, their value would be questionable. If Marathon Oil failed, it would be difficult to sell the buildings to pay the claims. No other industry in Findlay is large enough to afford or to use the office facilities, and it would be difficult to sell the buildings to another corporation outside of Findlay because of the costs involved in relocation and the adjustments in method such a move would involve. In practice, it is rare that assets are sold to satisfy creditors. Usually, the assets are kept in the business and the claims of the creditors are adjusted downward. As the claims are scaled down, it is possible that the junior bondholders or the stockholders might end up with nothing or only a modest share in the future earning power of the enterprise.

The type of mortgage is also an important consideration. A first mortgage on a property is usually more desirable than a second mortgage. The first mortgage is more secure since it has first claim on the specific asset pledged. If the company did not pay its interest or principal, the property could be sold to pay the claim. Not enough money might be left to pay the second mortgage or junior claim. Possibly the higher interest rate on the second mortgage would compensate for the added risk, but it is difficult to determine in advance if a 20 percent increase in yield is adequate compensation for the potential loss of the entire principal. Without balancing risk of loss with added compensation, we must conclude that a second or third corporate mortgage is less secure than a first mortgage. (There are times, however, when a second mortgage on a valuable property is relatively better and more secure than a first mortgage on a poor piece of property.) When we look for security of principal and expect repayment of principal in a mortgage bond issue, we must determine to what extent the property pledged adds materially to the fulfillment of the pledge of repayment of principal.

COLLATERAL TRUST BONDS

Some bond issues pledge stock or bonds as additional security for the money borrowed. This type is referred to as a collateral trust bond. The collateral is usually the personal property of the corporation that is issuing the bonds. This type of bond enables the investor to sell the property pledged to pay his claim should the corporation fail to pay interest or principal when it is due, thus adding to the security of the bond issue and providing something beyond a written promise to pay. A collateral bond issue usually arises out of the relationship between a parent company and its subsidiary. Let us assume, for example, that a parent company owns $10,000,000 of debt securities of a subsidiary company. The parent company needs money but does not wish to sell the bonds to the public. Instead, the parent company sells collateral bonds to the public and pledges its full faith and credit and the securities of its subsidiary. Thus, the parent company has a well-secured loan and still retains its ownership of the bonds of the subsidiary company. The quality of the collateral trust bond is determined by the credit position and asset-and-earnings positions both of the company issuing the debt and of the company whose securities are being pledged. Both common stocks and bonds can be used as collateral.

EQUIPMENT TRUST BONDS

Another way in which the principal of a bond issue is secured is through the pledge of equipment. The title to the property or machinery usually remains in the hands of the trustee until the debt is repaid. The best example of this type of debt issue is the equipment trust bonds commonly used in railroad finance. Railroads since the end of World War II have financed almost their entire purchase of new equipment through the sale of equipment trust certificates based upon the Philadelphia lease-plan method. Assume that the Penn Central wanted to purchase a new diesel locomotive, but did not have the full purchase price. The company would put up 20 percent of the equity and would borrow the remaining 80 percent through the issuance of equipment trust certificates that would be retired serially every six months over the next ten years. The title to the equipment would remain in the hands of the corporate trustee. Each six months after the purchase of the equipment, a principal and interest payment would be made to the trustee. The trustee in turn would retire some of the equipment trust certificates and pay the interest on the outstanding debt. If the Penn Central could not make the principal payment, the trustee could sell the property and pay off the creditors. The equipment can be easily sold: usually it is readily salable, and the trustee has the title and can sell it if necessary. The equity put up by the issuing corporation serves as a reserve to protect the lender, should the market value of the asset drop. These bonds have been prime investment securities and have served their purpose well. They have generally provided the institutional investor a safe and secure principal with an excellent yield to maturity. The ratings of several equipment trust obligations may be found in Standard and Poor's *Bond Guide*.

BONDS WITH SUPPLEMENTAL CREDIT

Some bond issues have an additional or supplemental pledge as added protection for the creditor. No specific asset or security is pledged, but the principal is secured by something more than the general credit of the company issuing the bonds. *Guaranteed bonds* are an example of this type. They are secured by the corporation issuing the bonds, and the principal, interest, or both are guaranteed by another corporation. This type of bond might be issued in a situation where the entire assets of a company are leased. The company leasing the assets guarantees that the interest and principal of the debt outstanding will be paid.

Joint Bonds. There is another type of supplemental credit bond that is jointly secured by two or more companies. Two companies that use a common facility and have raised money to finance it through the sale of debt would provide a good example of a situation where the bonds might be jointly secured. The investor has the additional security of another corporation's pledge. *Assumed bonds* are another type of bond with the pledge of additional security. The assumed bond results from a merger or a consolidation of two companies. Let us assume that

Company A is merged into Company B. Company A has a bond issue that has been issued prior to the merger. Once the merger has been completed, Company B assumes the obligations of Company A. The bondholder now has the pledge of two companies as security for a bond issue.

RECEIVERS CERTIFICATES

Receivers certificates are debt instruments that arise out of reorganization. When a corporation in reorganization needs capital, the receivers or the trustees have the power to raise additional funds. The securities issued are known as receivers certificates, and the principal value of these claims ordinarily takes precedence over any other debt outstanding. This priority places them in a superior position with respect to other debt. The risk of loss is still present, however, since the company may not be able to solve its basic problems that have resulted in loss. Any additional pledge of security in the form of real, personal, or intangible assets, or any additional pledge or guarantee by another corporation, will be covered in the indenture.

REGISTERED BONDS

One other safeguard might be indicated in the indenture which assures the basic security of the bond. A bond may be registered as to principal to protect the owner from loss. When the bond principal is registered, the name and address of the bondholder are recorded with the issuing company. The method of transferring a registered bond is much the same as transferring stock. The interest on a registered bond is usually paid by check. The registration of the principal does not guarantee that we will receive our principal repayment at maturity, but it does provide us with protection from loss should the bond certificate be lost or destroyed.

The Payment of Interest—The Second Promise

The second promise that is made to the purchaser of corporate debt securities by the issuing corporation is the promise to pay the interest on the debt. The promise to pay interest is of perhaps greater importance to the investor than the promise of repayment of principal. The rate of interest that is paid and the time of payment are stated in the indenture. Usually, the interest is paid semiannually in an amount based upon the stated rate of interest and is paid either by check directly to the bondholder or by coupon. The bond is usually registered as to principal when the interest is paid by check. The coupon bond is usually registered as to interest. The coupon is numbered, and each coupon represents one interest-payment period. As each coupon comes due, it is presented to a designated paying agent—usually a commercial bank or trust company.

Unfortunately, if the bond should be lost or stolen, it would be difficult to recover, since coupon bonds are usually *bearer* bonds, which are negotiable. The coupons are negotiable when due and payable, and proof of ownership is not needed to cash them in. Coupon bonds, then, require special care and safekeeping to prevent loss.

The rate of interest on coupon bonds—the *coupon rate*—is based upon the par value of the bond. The rate, of course, establishes the number of dollars of interest, the *nominal rate*, that will be paid to the bondholder. Whether the interest is paid by check or coupon, the amount is fixed for the life of the bond. The *interest rate* and *coupon rate* on the bond are terms that are often used interchangeably. Since the interest rate of the bond cannot be changed, the price is the only variable that can change, and this, as we noted earlier, changes the yields on the bond.

Today we assume quite naturally that the interest on bonds issued in the United States will be paid in dollars. At one time prior to 1933, however, bond principal and interest were sometimes payable in gold. These clauses were nullified by Congress in 1933 when we went off the gold standard, and now interest is payable in lawful money of the United States of America. Some foreign securities may be payable in the currency of the issuer or in American dollars.

We assume that the interest will be paid when it is due. If interest is not paid, the bond issue is in default. At this point all interest and principal is due and payable. It then becomes the job of the trustee to act for and protect all bondholders. This clause, which is a standard part of the bond agreement, is referred to as the *acceleration clause*. It does not insure repayment of principal, but it does protect the creditor and establishes his claim to assets. Where payments of interest and principal are made together, it accelerates all future payments and eliminates the need for selling on each defaulted payment.

INCOME BONDS

Bonds are sometimes issued which require that the interest be paid only if there are sufficient earnings to pay. These are referred to as *income bonds*. In some income bonds, the interest payment must be approved and declared by the board of directors, much the same way as dividends are paid on preferred stock. If the interest on the bond is not paid, it may be cumulative and payable at a later time. Income bonds are still debt instruments, but they are closely related to stock in the essential characteristic of interest payment. Income bonds in the past arose out of reorganization and are sometimes referred to as *adjustment bonds*. Today they are used for several purposes, one of which is to recapitalize a company by replacing preferred stock with tax-deductible income bonds. The effect is to lower the after-tax cost of financing the company by substituting for a nondeductible dividend a deductible interest payment that need not be paid if no earnings are present. In any debt instrument, the interest payment is secure only if the corporation issuing the debt has adequate income to cover all of its expenses including the interest cost on the debt. In determining the quality of the bond issue and the ability to pay interest, the best guide is the number of times the interest is covered by net operating profit or by net income after taxes. The lower the interest charges and the higher the net operating profit or net income after taxes, the more secure the interest payment. There are other assurances that are offered to increase the security of the interest payment. Often corporations will be required to maintain a minimum cash position or working-capital position. Occasionally, further guarantees of interest payment come from additional pledges to be found in a guaranteed, joint, or assumed bond.

PROTECTIVE COVENANTS

The dual promises of the corporation to repay principal and to pay current interest are also protected by other covenants in the bond indenture. The protective covenants, as they are called, do not pledge specific or additional assets, but they do bind the corporation to certain agreements that control their operations and protect the bondholders. One such agreement limits the dividends on common stock. The dividend is limited to protect the cash and working-capital position of the company, which in turn protects the bondholder. If cash or working capital drops below a certain limit, then no dividends can be paid. Other protective covenants are associated with specific types of bonds. Mortgage bonds usually include a protective provision that limits debt to a certain proportion of the new property. It might say that debt cannot be placed upon new properties in excess of 50 percent of value. These are only a few examples of the many possible protective covenants. Each covenant helps to improve the creditor's security position and increases the possibility that the two main promises of principal repayment and interest payment will be met.

Investment Quality of Corporate Bonds

The ultimate investment quality of a corporate bond issue depends upon the company's ability to repay the debt, pay the interest, and provide additional security or covenants to assure that the financial commitments will be met. This was discussed when we examined the promises that were made in the bond indenture by the company to the trustee acting for the bondholder. If we are to analyze a debt issue, therefore, we must test the ability to repay, the interest coverage, and the general, overall credit position of the company. In addition, we can use the rating services as a guide to investment quality.

The Ability to Repay the Debt

The first step in an analysis of a bond issue is to determine the ability of the company to repay the debt if the company fails or if the company continues to prosper and is to repay the debt at maturity or through periodic sinking-fund payments. Let us assume, first, that the company fails and is required to pay the creditors from the assets that remain. In the absence of prospects for earnings, our first consideration is whether the assets of the company are sufficient to pay the debt. We can examine the value of the assets and their relation to the specific debt issue and the total debt outstanding. A company with a small amount of debt in relation to the market value of its assets is in a much better position, other things being equal, to repay the debt than a corporation with a high debt relative to the market value of its assets. We must stress market value in our analysis and not book value, since an asset cannot always be sold for its book value or original cost. We have two tests to determine the ability to pay should the company fail. One is the ratio of debt to net worth; the other, of debt to fixed assets. In industrial finance, debt of all types should not exceed net worth. If railroads or public utility companies are being analyzed, the debt ratio can be higher. In regard to the second ratio, long-term debt should generally not exceed 50 percent of the value of the fixed assets of the company, based upon the market value of the assets. If debt does not exceed these limits, we may conclude that it is not excessive and would be properly secured. Practical debt limits for companies in a wide range of industries appear in Figure 4–2. It is obvious that few industrial, public utility, or railroad companies in practice have a ratio of debt to net worth or equity of one to one, even in the case of public utilities, which usually have a large amount of debt in the capital structure.

The Ability to Pay the Interest

The company must also be able to pay its interest, usually every six months, from its current earnings. Cash flow and earning power are both used as measures of the capacity of a company to pay its interest. These measures do double duty, since they tell us if the company can pay interest as well as principal. Without sufficient earnings or cash flow, or the prospect for earnings and cash flow, the bond interest is not secure nor is the bond issue. On the other hand, if interest is adequately covered, we can conclude that the bond issue is secure and interest will

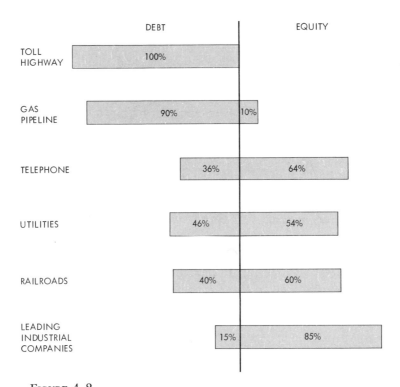

DEBT   EQUITY

TOLL
HIGHWAY   100%

GAS
PIPELINE   90%   10%

TELEPHONE   36%   64%

UTILITIES   46%   54%

RAILROADS   40%   60%

LEADING
INDUSTRIAL   15%   85%
COMPANIES

FIGURE 4–2

*Approximate division of capital
structures between equity and debt
financing—selected industries*

be paid according to the agreement. What is adequate coverage, of
course, depends upon the company and the industry. Usually we require
that net income after taxes in normal years cover interest payments at
least three times in the case of industrial companies, and two times in
the case of railroads or public utilities. If the interest rate is historically
low, however, the coverage limits should be raised. During World War
II, for example, long-term interest rates were below 3 percent. The interest-coverage ratios should be higher under this situation—perhaps five
times interest payments—than when interest rates are 5 percent. The
higher coverage will compensate for situations in the future when financing charges might be higher. There are two acceptable methods of computing the interest-coverage ratio, to determine the adequacy of the company to meet its future interest payments. One is the Combined Charge
Method and the other is the Cumulative Deduction Method. For purposes of illustration, assume the following situation: A company has
two bond issues outstanding, a $20 million first-mortgage 5 percent bond

issue and a $10 million 7 percent second-mortgage bond issue. Total interest charges are $1.7 million. The company earned, on the average, $8 million after taxes but before interest for the past five years. If we use the Combined Charge Method, we find that interest has been covered 4.7 times ($8.0 million/$1.7 million).

If we use the Cumulative Deduction Method, we calculate the fixed-charge coverage first on the first-mortgage issue, and then we add the interest amount for the second mortgage to that of the first-mortgage bond issue and compute the coverage on the combined amount. Using this method, the coverage on the first-mortgage bond is 8 times ($8.0 million/$1.0 million), and the coverage on the second mortgage, cumulatively, is 4.7 times ($8.0 million/$1.7 million). If there were a third bond issue outstanding with $.3 million of interest charges, then the coverage on the third mortgage would be 4 to 1 ($8.0 million/$2.0 million).

For all practical purposes, the Combined Method is most satisfactory and is that used by Standard & Poor's *Bond Guide* presented in Figure 4–5 on page 132. In fact, the interest-coverage ratio (times interest and miscellaneous charges earned) presented includes interest on loans as well as interest on long-term bonds.

If we applied our interest-coverage ratio to Litton Industries, presented in Figure 4–1, using the Combined Method, the ratio would be 121,863,026/1,801,891 = 67.6. In this case, we added interest charges to earnings *before* taxes on income. We would conclude that Litton's bond interest was adequately secured.

The Credit Position of the Company

The third step in determining the ability of a company to repay its debt, and hence the quality of the bond issue, is the overall credit position of the company. We must learn whether the company has demonstrated an ability to manage debt with prudence and conservatism in the past. What has been the debt paying experience of the company? Has the company ever defaulted? What is the character of the issuing corporation? Is the company in a strong financial position, and has it always been strong financially? These questions are subjective, but the answers will reflect either a good credit position for a company or a poor one. If the credit record has been good, then an issue might be considered satisfactory. Generally, strong companies—competitively and financially —with a strong equity position and a management that has a proven ability to manage debt have the best credit position. The Dun and Bradstreet reports can serve as an excellent guide to the credit position of the company and will tell if the company has been prompt in paying its bills. A good rating by Dun and Bradstreet would be an adequate indication of the overall credit position of the company.

Where debt is secured by the pledge of other corporate securities, as in the case of collateral trust bonds, or when another corporation guarantees an issue of bonds, we must anlayze carefully the security pledged and the credit position of the company that has issued the securities or the company that has given its additional pledge. This analysis is exactly the same as the credit analysis that would be performed on the company issuing the debt securities.

Bond Ratings and Investment Quality

Independent analysis by an investor to determine the quality of a bond is important. Some analysts are expert at making these valuation judgments; however, even under the best of circumstances a layman might find it difficult to judge private corporate bonds. It is therefore desirable to enlist the aid of professional services that provide investment ratings for bond issues. Moody's and Standard & Poor's are two well-known companies in this field. These services rate bonds just as public utility bonds are rated. The ratings range from high and unquestionable investment-quality bonds down to speculative bonds that might be unsuitable for investment. The ratings for corporate debt are similar to the ratings on municipal debt securities. The language of the ratings is almost identical with that used for municipal bonds in the previous chapter.

In *Moody's Industrial Manual*, the Aaa bond is defined as one that is "judged to be of the best quality." They carry the smallest degree of investment risk and are generally referred to as "gilt edge" securities. Interest payments are protected by a large or by an exceptionally stable margin of earnings, and the principal is secure.[1] The ratings service usually also states that "while the various protective elements are likely to change, such changes as can be visualized are most unlikely to impair the fundamentally strong positions of such issues."[2] The rating schedule applies to all types of private corporate obligations. The higher the investment rating, the more secure the bond issue. The investment quality of bonds diminishes in stages until ratings of C are reached. Standard & Poor's uses a similar rating system, which is described in Figure 4–3. Using such ratings and the analysis of interest coverage or debt, we can, within limits, judge the investment quality of a bond issue.

Bond Yields and Investment Quality

The yields on long-term private corporate bonds shown in Chart 3–2 (Chapter 3) and Figure 4–4 are higher than those for fully taxable government securities. The pattern of the yields, however, is much the same.

1 Moody's *Industrial Manual* (New York: Moody's Investors Service, 1968), p. vi.
2 Ibid., p. vi.

In the Standard & Poor's bond quality ratings system, interest-paying bonds are graded into eight classifications ranging from AAA for the highest quality designation through AA, A, BBB, BB, B, CCC to CC for the lowest. Bonds on which no interest is being paid, either because of default or because of "income" characteristics, are given C, DDD, DD and D ratings. Rating symbols are the same for corporate and municipal bonds, and every effort has been made to keep the two systems on a comparable basis. United States Government bonds are not rated, but are considered as a yardstick against which to measure all other issues.

BANK QUALITY BONDS

Under present commercial bank regulations bonds rated in the top four categories (AAA, AA, A, BBB or their equivalent) generally are regarded as eligible for bank investment.

AAA Bonds rated AAA are highest grade obligations. They possess the ultimate degree of protection as to principal and interest. Marketwise, they move with interest rates, and hence provide the maximum safety on all counts.

AA Bonds rated AA also qualify as high grade obligations, and in the majority of instances differ from AAA issues only in small degree. Here, too, prices move with the long term money market.

A Bonds rated A are regarded as upper medium grade. They have considerable investment strength but are not entirely free from adverse effects of changes in economic and trade conditions. Interest and principal are regarded as safe. They predominantly reflect money rates in their market behavior, but to some extent, also economic conditions.

BBB The BBB, or medium grade category is borderline between definitely sound obligations and those where the speculative element begins to predominate. These bonds have adequate asset coverage and normally are protected by satisfactory earnings. Their susceptibility to changing conditions, particularly to depressions, necessitates constant watching. Marketwise, the bonds are more responsive to business and trade conditions than to interest rates. This group is the lowest which qualifies for commercial bank investment.

SUB-STANDARD BONDS

As we move down the rating scale, beginning with BB, investment characteristics weaken and the speculative elements become progressively stronger. The fortunes of the obligors change rapidly with economic and trade conditions and in adverse periods interest requirements may not be earned. Investment in bonds in this group must be under constant surveillance. Prices fluctuate widely with changing business conditions and with little regard for the money market.

BB Bonds given a BB rating are regarded as lower medium grade. They have only minor investment characteristics. In the case of utilities, interest is earned consistently but by narrow margins. In the case of other types of obligors, charges are earned on average by a fair margin, but in poor periods deficit operations are possible.

B Bonds rated as low as B are speculative. Payment of interest cannot be assured under difficult economic conditions.

CCC-CC Bonds rated CCC and CC are outright speculations, with the lower rating denoting the more speculative. Interest is paid, but continuation is questionable in periods of poor trade conditions. In the case of CC ratings the bonds may be on an income basis and the payment may be small.

C The rating of C is reserved for income bonds on which no interest is being paid.

DDD-D All bonds rated DDD, DD and D are in default, with the rating indicating the relative salvage value.

CANADIAN BONDS

Canadian corporate bonds are rated on the same basis as American corporate issues. The ratings measure the intrinsic value of the bonds, but they do not take into account exchange and other uncertainties.

FIGURE 4-3

Standard & Poor's bond ratings

SOURCE Standard & Poor's *Bond Guide*, 1968

YIELD TO MATURITY, IN PERCENT

	PUBLIC UTILITY				INDUSTRIAL				RAILROAD				COMPOSITE				MUNICIPAL
	AAA	AA	A	BBB	AAA	AA	A	BBB	AAA	AA	A	BBB	AAA	AA	A	BBB	
Weekly Averages 1968																	
March 27	6.20	6.29	6.56	6.85	6.20	6.26	6.32	6.64	5.70	6.34	6.58	7.18	6.03	6.30	6.49	6.89	4.58
March 20	6.16	6.25	6.50	6.74	6.16	6.18	6.29	6.68	5.85	6.44	6.57	7.05	6.06	6.29	6.45	6.82	4.53
March 13	6.13	6.21	6.41	6.70	6.02	6.15	6.25	6.58	5.76	6.40	6.54	6.87	5.97	6.22	6.40	6.72	4.61
March 6	6.08	6.14	6.33	6.70	6.00	6.06	6.20	6.55	5.78	6.23	6.56	6.92	5.95	6.14	6.36	6.72	4.53
February 28	6.10	6.16	6.35	6.70	6.00	6.07	6.20	6.59	5.76	6.23	6.58	6.96	5.94	6.16	6.38	6.74	4.48
Monthly Averages 1967–68																	
March	6.14	6.22	6.45	6.74	6.09	6.15	6.27	6.61	5.77	6.35	6.56	7.01	6.00	6.24	6.43	6.79	4.56
February	6.10	6.16	6.36	6.70	5.98	6.06	6.21	6.53	6.01	6.35	6.65	7.41	5.94	6.15	6.36	6.73	4.39
January	6.15	6.21	6.41	6.74	6.01	6.10	6.25	6.59	5.77	6.19	6.47	7.20	5.98	6.17	6.38	6.84	4.36
December	6.26	6.35	6.55	6.82	6.13	6.24	6.34	6.73	5.94	6.32	6.56	7.14	6.11	6.30	6.48	6.90	4.49
November	6.13	6.20	6.42	6.59	6.01	6.11	6.22	6.54	5.88	6.19	6.38	6.98	6.01	6.17	6.34	6.70	4.36
October	5.88	5.95	6.15	6.34	5.76	5.85	6.00	6.30	5.87	6.01	6.17	6.74	5.84	5.93	6.11	6.46	4.31
September	5.81	5.87	6.00	6.24	5.65	5.68	5.88	6.22	5.61	5.88	6.12	6.55	5.69	5.81	6.00	6.34	4.15
August	5.74	5.83	5.97	6.17	5.60	5.64	5.84	6.13	5.63	5.80	6.06	6.48	5.65	5.75	5.96	6.26	4.03
July	5.66	5.73	5.87	6.13	5.55	5.57	5.74	6.04	5.51	5.64	5.93	6.45	5.52	5.67	5.74	6.21	4.05
June	5.62	5.64	5.78	6.04	5.43	5.51	5.60	5.99	5.51	5.68	5.84	6.40	5.52	5.45	5.57	6.15	3.99
May	5.48	5.51	5.61	5.86	5.26	5.33	5.44	5.97	5.32	5.52	5.67	6.30	5.35	5.35	5.43	6.05	3.91
April	5.29	5.32	5.41	5.72	5.11	5.18	5.29	5.88	5.15	5.56	5.57	6.08	5.18			5.89	3.66
Weekly Ranges																	
1968 High	6.20	6.29	6.56	6.85	6.20	6.26	6.32	6.77	5.85	6.44	6.58	7.38	6.06	6.30	6.49	6.99	4.58
1968 Low	6.08	6.14	6.33	6.33	5.96	6.01	6.19	6.47	5.70	6.02	6.36	6.87	5.93	6.10	6.32	6.72	4.23
1967 High	6.26	6.38	6.57	6.85	6.15	6.25	6.36	6.81	6.01	6.35	6.65	7.25	6.12	6.32	6.50	6.97	4.51
1967 Low	5.03	5.07	5.16	5.52	4.94	4.99	5.08	5.65	5.05	5.50	5.56	6.00	5.00	5.22	5.31	5.74	3.43
1966 High	5.57	5.64	5.79	6.28	5.44	5.56	5.63	6.02	5.44	5.74	5.79	6.61	5.46	5.58	5.66	6.25	4.26
1966 Low	4.73	4.77	4.85	4.95	4.67	4.75	4.83	4.94	4.76	4.94	4.99	5.24	4.72	4.83	4.89	5.06	3.51
1965 High	4.75	4.81	4.92	5.00	4.69	4.75	4.82	5.07	4.76	4.90	5.00	5.28	4.73	4.81	4.90	5.09	3.56
1965 Low	4.36	4.39	4.60	4.73	4.23	4.28	4.46	4.60	4.37	4.56	4.65	4.87	4.33	4.43	4.53	4.70	3.04
1964 High	4.45	4.49	4.51	4.55	4.32	4.40	4.53	4.65	4.50	4.73	4.78	5.44	4.41	4.51	4.61	5.09	3.35
1964 Low	4.35	4.37	4.42	4.38	4.19	4.22	4.34	4.56	4.38	4.59	4.68	4.95	4.32	4.43	4.50	4.87	3.13
1963 High	4.41	4.46	4.51	4.73	4.27	4.28	4.38	4.64	4.43	4.74	5.00	5.97	4.36	4.48	4.55	4.73	3.42
1963 Low	4.19	4.22	4.28	4.37	4.01	4.06	4.25	4.49	4.24	4.53	4.68	5.40	4.16	4.29	4.44	5.39	4.07
1962 High	4.41	4.47	4.58	4.88	4.32	4.33	4.51	4.77	4.52	4.84	5.18	6.81	4.41	4.54	4.74	5.02	
1962 Low	4.21	4.24	4.31	4.48	4.08	4.11	4.29	4.61	4.27	4.61	4.99	6.02	4.19	4.31	4.44	5.54	
1961 High	4.56	4.64	4.67	5.16	4.32	4.39	4.63	4.93	4.59	5.12	5.19	6.96	4.48	4.67	4.80	5.22	
1961 Low	4.33	4.38	4.52	4.56	4.06	4.13	4.38	4.77	4.23	4.62	4.90	6.30	4.22	4.39	4.61	5.49	
1960 High	4.72	4.73	4.86		4.47	4.50	4.68	5.27	4.70	4.92	5.09	6.61	4.62	4.71	4.87	5.16	
1960 Low	4.32	4.36	4.49		4.07	4.18	4.44	4.82	4.28	4.68	4.92	6.04	4.23	4.41	4.62		

FIGURE 4–4

Corporate and municipal bond yields

SOURCE Standard & Poor's Bond Guide, 1968

129

In fact, most bonds follow the same pattern if they are high-quality money rate bonds. The movement of long-term yields for all debt securities is variable, and the bonds do not remain as stable as the fixed interest rate suggested in the bond indenture. This variability in yields is reflected both in the price of bonds and in the yield. Bonds, therefore, have a certain instability of price just as common stocks do. In purchasing debt securities for long-term investment, the investor must carefully allow for this characteristic. Also, his timing of debt purchases is almost as important as it is in the purchase of the volatile common stocks.

Bond yields vary with changes in yields in the long-term money market. Differences in yields also occur because of quality differences in the rating of bonds; they differ also according to type of industry. Figure 4–4 indicates the yields of AAA to BBB bonds for each of the major groupings. Bonds with the lowest rating, which are still in the top investment categories for purchase by institutional investors, have a higher yield than the highest-rated bonds.

Over the entire period covered by Figure 4–4, the AAA bonds sold on a lower-yield basis than the BBB obligations—AAA industrials on a slightly lower-yield basis than either public utilities or railroads. Such relationships, however, vary over time, and we cannot assume that they will remain the same in the future.

The bond issues in Figure 4–5 (pp. 132–33) are examples of varying quality investment-grade debt securities that we might have considered attractive outlets for our investment funds. They ranged from AAA to BB, and all the bonds rated highest had adequate coverage of fixed charges. Only General Motors Acceptance Corporation had a fixed charge coverage that was below a ratio of 2 to 1; however, the 1.17 to 1 ratio under the annual earnings column provided adequate interest coverage at least in 1968. Most of the debt issued was either debenture bonds backed by the full faith and credit of the corporations or mortgage bonds secured by a first mortgage on real property. Some of these issues might continue to meet our investment needs today. Certainly, we should be impressed with the very high yields on all of these bonds.

The bonds in the highest-rating classes (AAA and AA) are often called money rate bonds because their yields fluctuate with changes in the money rates. The lower-grade bonds do not offer as high a degree of security, but they do offer a higher yield. These bonds possess, however, the credit risk or the business risk. In purchasing bonds below an AA rating, we are assuming a greater risk of loss of capital. It is possible that the company could not pay the debt at maturity or pay the interest, and hence the bond is generally in a lower category. These bonds might not fluctuate with changes in the market yield; they would change in price based upon shifts in their overall credit position. They would provide us with yields above 5 percent; some might, however, offer a degree of safety as well as yield and might prove attractive investments.

Advantages and Disadvantages of Corporate Debt Securities as Investments

Corporate debt securities of private businesses offer us certain definite advantages for the investment of our funds. They provide us with a high degree of safety of principal and stability of income comparable to that of government securities. The highest-quality bonds above a Baa rating are excellent investments for institutional investors too, particularly for those who can invest only in debt securities. Yields are higher than those offered by government securities, and for this reason we might be attracted to this type of security if it were needed in our investment program. Bonds rated BBB offer the individual investor a higher yield and represent an attractive investment for investors who need income.

The major disadvantages of corporate bonds are much the same as those for other debt securities. The investor has security of principal and does not assume the business or market risk with top-grade securities. On the other hand, these securities do not offer the promise of capital gains, nor are they a hedge against inflation. Corporate bonds are also susceptible to changes in money rates. Yields and prices fluctuate in sympathy with yields in the money market, and these fluctuations can be as severe as in the stock market. Poor timing in the purchase or sale of bonds could result in financial loss. Also, when buying debt securities, we must be on guard against the money rate risk. Some low-grade securities do not provide a great deal of security of principal, and we must accept the business or credit risk. We must also accept possible losses through the purchasing-power risk, since bonds do not increase in value as the purchasing power of the dollar declines; also, the unit of purchase is large, which might preclude individual purchases. These factors might force us to ignore debt as an outlet for our funds.

The nature of corporate debt securities makes them attractive investment securities for institutional investors. This is because of the security of principal and stability of income. Generally, the small investor is not a major purchaser of long-term bonds. Corporate bonds might be attractive, however, for the investor in the moderate income-tax bracket who needs stability of income and a higher yield than would be afforded on government bonds and who is willing to give up some security of principal to achieve the greater income.

KEEPING ABREAST OF CORPORATE BONDS

In addition to sources of information presented in this chapter, the *Wall Street Journal* provides a daily review of up-to-date bond information. Bonds listed on the New York Stock Exchange are quoted

INDEX	Exchange	BONDS Name and Description of Issue	Description, Interest Rate, Due	Interest Dates	S&P Quality Rating	Eligibility	LEGALITY Conn.	Me.	Mass.	N.H.	N.J.	N.J. tr	N.Y.	CALL PRICE For S.F.	Regular	Ref. Start	PRICE RANGE 1960-66 High	1960-66 Low	1967 High	1967 Low	1968 High	1968 Low	3-29-68 PRICE Sale (s) or Bid	Yield to Mty.
1	•	General Motors Acceptance....	Deb 3s '69	jJ15	A	X	–	–	–	–	–	–	√	....	100		98⅝	83	99¼	93¼	98⅛	94½	s96⅛	6.25
2	•	do	Deb 3½s '72	Ms15	A	X	–	–	–	–	–	–	√	....	100		96	84⅛	92¾	85½	90	87⅝	s89	6.60
3	•	do	Deb 3⅝s '75	mS	A	X	–	–	–	–	–	–	√	....	†100⅜		95¾	77¾	89¾	79	83¼	81	s82⅛	6.70
4	•	do	Deb 5s '77	fA15	A	X	–	–	–	–	–	–	√	....	†103		107¼	88⅝	100	86	90⅞	86¼	s88	6.74
5	•	do	Deb 4s '79	Ms	A	X	–	–	–	–	–	–	√	....	†100¾		98⅞	78	89½	76	81⅞	77½	s77½	6.96
6	•	do	Deb 5s '80	mS	A	X	–	–	–	–	–	–	√	....	†102¾		107	87	99¾	82¾	88⅝	82½	s84½	6.86
7	•	do	Deb 5s '81	Ms15	A	X	–	–	–	–	–	–	√	....	102½ '70	A	107½	88½	99¾	83⅛	88⅛	84¼	s84½	6.76
8	•	do	Deb 4⅝s '82	mS	A	X	–	–	–	–	–	–	√	....	102¼ '70	B	105	83	93	78¾	83½	78⅛	s78⅝	7.00
9	•	do	Deb 4⅝s '83	Ms	A	X	–	–	–	–	–	–	√	....	102.4 '71	C	105	84½	93½	78	83½	77¼	s77½	7.09
10	•	do	Deb 4½s '85	mN	A	X	–	–	–	–	–	–	√	....	102 '72	D	101⅝	77½	92⅞	76	81½	76½	s76½	6.78
11	•	do	Deb 4⅝s '86	Jd15	A	X	–	–	–	–	–	–	√	....	102½ '72	E	102¾	82⅞	93½	76⅝	82¼	77½	78	6.71
12	•	do	Deb 4⅞s '87	jD	A	X	–	–	–	–	–	–	√	....	102 '73	F	100¼	84	96½	78¼	84	80½	s80¾	6.63
13	•	do	Deb 6¼s '88	fA	A	X	–	–	–	–	–	–	√	....	102½ '77	G	....	....	103	97½	101¼	96	s96¾	6.54
14	•	General Motors Corp..........	Deb 3¼s '79	Jj	AAA	X	–	√	√	√	–	√	√	100.2	†101.2		95	81½	86¾	80¾	81¾	77	s78	6.00
15		Gen. Portl'd Cement......	Sub Deb 5s '77	aO	BBB	X	–	–	–	–	–	√	–	100 '68	†102½		142	83	90	73	81	78	81	7.75
16		General Tel. Co. Calif.........	1st I 3⅜s 85	Fa	A	X	√	√	√	–	√	√	√	....	†102.97		87½	73	79⅛	67⅛	69¾	67⅛	68⅞	6.40
17		do	1st J 4½s '86	mS	A	X	√	√	√	–	√	√	√	....	†103.72		102¾	85¼	91⅝	77⅞	80⅜	77⅞	79½	6.40
18		do	1st K 5s '87	Jd	A	X	√	√	√	–	√	√	√	....	†103.28		105	90⅞	97⅞	83	85⅜	83	84½	6.40
19		do	1st L 4½s '88	Ms	A	X	√	√	√	–	√	√	√	....	†103.56		97½	79⅞	86½	72⅞	75⅜	72⅞	74½	6.40
20		do	1st M 5s '89	jD	A	X	√	√	√	–	√	√	√	....	†103.62		105	89¾	97¾	81½	84¾	81½	83	6.45
21		do	1st N 4⅝s '91	jD	A	X	√	√	√	–	√	√	√	....	†103.97		104⅜	84⅝	92¼	76⅜	79¾	76⅜	77⅞	6.45
22		do	1st O 4⅝s '93	Mn	A	X	√	√	√	–	√	√	√	....	†104.14		100	80⅞	88⅜	72¾	76⅛	72¾	74⅜	6.45
23		do	1st P 4½s '94	Jd	A	X	√	√	√	–	√	√	√	....	†104.03	I	101	82½	89⅛	74	77⅜	74	75⅜	6.45
24		do	1st Q 4½s '95	Ms	A	X	√	√	√	–	√	√	√	....	†104.03	J	100¼	82	89	73¾	76¾	73¾	75¼	6.45
25		do	1st R 5s '95	jD	A	X	√	√	√	–	√	√	√	....	†104.94	K	103	86¼	95⅝	79⅞	82⅞	79⅞	80¾	6.50
26		do	1st S 6s '96	aO	A	X	√	√	√	–	√	√	–	....	†105.79	L	103¼	100	105½	92¼	95¾	92¼	93½	6.50
27		do	1st T 6¾s '97	jD	A	X	√	–	√	–	–	–	–	....	†106¾	M	....	....	99⅜	99⅜	103⅝	99¾	103¼	6.50
28		do	SF Deb 5¾s '92	Ms	BBB	X	√	√	–	–	–	√	–	100 '71	†105.51	N	....	....	100	86½	88¼	86½	86¾	6.89
29		General Tel. Co. Florida.....	1st G 5s '90	Ms	A	X	√	√	√	–	–	√	√	‡100	†103.62		104¾	89¾	97⅝	81⅜	84¾	81⅜	83	6.45
30		do	1st H 4⅝s '91	mN	A	X	√	√	√	–	–	√	√	‡100	†103.97		104⅜	84⅝	92¼	76⅜	79¾	76⅜	77⅞	6.45
31		do	1st J 4⅝s '95	Jd	A	X	√	√	√	–	√	√	√	‡100	†103.72	P	100	83⅝	90⅛	75¼	78¼	75¼	76⅜	6.48
32		do	1st L 6½s '97	mN	A	X	√	√	√	–	–	–	–	‡100	†106½	Q	....	....	100½	98½	102	98¾	100	6.50
33		General Tel. Co. Illinois ..	SF Deb A 6¾s '92	jD	BBB	X	–	√	–	–	–	–	–	....	†106	V	....	....	....	....	102	99¼	100¼	6.73
34		Gen. Tel. Co. Southwest........	1st s '98	Ms	A	X	√	√	√	–	√	√	√	....	....		....	....	....	....	SEC Rgstr'n		......	....
35	•	General Tel. Co. Wis............	1st 5s '96	Fa	A	X	√	√	√	–	–	–	√	100 '71	†104.66	R	99⅞	88¾	95⅝	81⅛	No Sale		80¾	6.50
36		Gen. Tel. & Electronics....	SF Deb 4⅞s '87	Ao	BBB	X	–	–	–	–	–	√	–	†100.22	†103.84	S	107	84⅞	90	80	82½	80	80	6.76
37		do	SF Deb 4½s '88	Ms	BBB	X	–	–	–	–	–	√	–	100.89	†104.35	T	101⅛	79⅞	86	76	78	76	76	6.70
38	•	do	SF Deb 6¼s '91	jD	BBB	X	–	–	–	–	–	√	–	101 '71	†107.07	U	105½	101⅛	107¼	95¾	100	95¾	93	6.84
39	•	Gen. Tire & Rubber......	Sub Deb 4¾s '81	Ao	BB	Y	–	–	–	–	–	√	–	105½	105¼		101¾	88	95	90	92	90	87	6.22
40		do	xw Sub Deb 6s '82	aO	BB	Y	–	–	–	–	–	√	–	100	†103½		105½	90	99¾	86	87	84	84	7.90
41		Georgia Power Co...............	1st 3½s '71	Ms	A	X	√	√	√	√	√	√	√	100	100		95	89	92¾	91	92½	91	91	6.75
42		do	1st 3⅜s '78	jD	A	X	√	√	√	√	√	√	√	†101¼	†102⅝		99¼	78½	85⅜	74¾	76¾	74¾	76	6.45
43		do	1st 2⅞s '80	Ao	A	X	√	√	√	√	√	√	√	†101¼	†102⅞		83⅜	72⅞	77½	68¼	70½	68¼	70¾	6.40

Uniform Footnote Explanations—See Page 4. Other: [1]Incl $7.2 M adv fr parent Co. A—■†101¾. B—■†101.65. C—■†102.15. D—■†101½. E—■101⅝. F—■101⅜. G—■102 '72. I—103.72 '69. J—103.72 '70. K—104.39 '70. L—104.97 '71. M—105.59 '73. N—104.55 '72. P—103.31 '70. Q—105.38 '72. R—104.14 '71. S—103 '72. T—103.89 '70. U—104.30 '76. V—104.75 '72.

FIGURE 4–5

Selected examples of investment-grade bonds, the facts and analysis

daily, and the price and volume relationships are summarized. The *Wall Street Journal* also carries "Bond Markets" and "Financing Business" columns that help keep the investor abreast of current events in the money and capital markets. Invaluable factual and advisory data are presented in Standard & Poor's *Bond Guide*. Provided too is a coded reference to underwriters who handle specific issues, if more information is needed by an investor.

Convertible Bonds

The majority of corporate bonds offer two promises to the investor; convertible bonds offer a third—the promise of sharing in capital growth. This is derived from the bondholder's right to exchange his bonds for common stock of the company. If the stock increases in price, the bond also will increase in price. If the stock price remains the same the bond will still provide a good yield. The right to convert the bond into common stock is stated in the bond indenture. This right may be expressed in terms of the price at which the shares of stock may be exchanged for the bond; it is then referred to as the *conversion price*. Or it can be expressed as the number of shares into which each bond may be converted—the *conversion rate*. It makes little difference how

INDEX	PRINCIPAL BUSINESS or General Information	UND'RWRIT'G Firm	Price	Year	OUTST'D'G Mil-$ This Issue	Long Term Debt	FINANCIAL POSITION —Mil-$— Cash & Equiv.	Curr. Assets	Curr. Liabs.	Balance Sheet Date	Ratio Debt to Net Prop.	Yrs. End.	ANNUAL EARNINGS Times Int. & Misc. Charges Earned 1963	1964	1965	1966	1967	INTERIM EARNINGS General Information Period	1966	1967	INDEX
1	This GM subsidiary is its financing	M25	100⅜	'54	75.0	3437	156	7837	3902	12-31-67	....	Dec	1.24	1.19	1.21	1.15	1.17				1
2	organization for installment sales.	M25	100	'55	200																2
3	It obtains about 35% of GM dealers'	M25	98¼	'55	200																3
4	installment sales business and some	M25	97½	'57	100																4
5	16% of all auto retail credit ext'd.	M25	98½	'58	150																5
6	Protective ratios are not quite as	M25	100	'59	125																6
7	good as those of other leading in-	M25	99½	'60	100																7
8	stallment finance concerns, but im-	M25	99¼	'60	150																8
9	plied strength from control by GM is	M25	99⅜	'61	150																9
10	an important offset. Loss experience	M25	99½	'63	150																10
11	has been unusually good	M25	99¾	'64	150													Dated June 15, 1964			11
12		M25	99	'65	150													Dated Dec 1, 1965			12
13		M25	100	'67	150													Dated Aug. 1, 1967			13
14	The strongest of corporate issues	M25	100½	'53	42.8	345	1783	6846	2840	12-31-67	7.2	Dec	89.79	120.0	106.8	65.05	45.51				14
15	Low cost southern cement producer	M19	100	'57	9.49	9.49	21.0	42.2	16.2	12-31-67	15.6	Dec	17.28	15.21	13.84	10.66	....				15
16	Largest independent tel company in	E17	102½	'55	12.0	542	9.86	60.1	69.7	12-31-67	52.4	Dec	3.68	3.49	3.05	2.87	2.44				16
17	US; serves southern & central Calif.	H6	101½	'56	20.0																17
18	All telephones are dial operated.	H6	100	'57	20.0																18
19	Debt conservative to net plant,	W15	100⅜	'58	20.0																19
20	which is relatively new. Area	F3	100	'59	30.0																20
21	growth prospects promising. 25%	F3	100	'61	25.0																21
22	of revenues applied to maint-depr.	P2	99¾	'63	25.0																22
23	Controlled by Gen. Tel & Electronics	P2	99	'64	35.0													Dated June 1, 1964			23
24		P2	100	'65	35.0																24
25		P2	100¼	'65	40.0													Dated Dec 1, 1965			25
26		F3	100	'66	45.0													Dated Oct 1, 1966			26
27		F3	99⅜	'67	55.0													Dated Dec. 1, 1967			27
28		F3	99⅜	'67	50.0													Dated Mar. 1, 1967			28
29	Serves St. Petersburg, Clearwater, Sar-	P2	99¼	'60	15.0	+1137	2.10	14.8	22.0	8-31-67	45.7	Dec	2.97	3.57	3.40	3.63	....	12 Mo Sep	3.21	3.06	29
30	asota, Lakeland, Venice. All dial op-	P2	100.4	'61	15.0																30
31	erated. Controlled by Gen. Tel. &	P2	99	'65	20.0													Dated June 1, 1965			31
32	Electronics	P2	100	'67	20.0													Dated Nov. 1, 1967			32
33	Telephone service in Illinois	P2	99¼	'68	20.0	+116	1.16	11.8	25.7	8-31-67	53.9	Dec	3.71	3.94	3.87	3.42	....	Dated Dec. 1, 1967			33
34	Serves parts of Tex, N.M. Oak. & La.	P2	....	'68	25.0	+156	1.27	15.1	46.9	12-31-67	45.8	Dec	3.27	3.18	3.29	3.06	2.82	Dated Mar 1, 1968			34
35	Serves various areas in Wisconsin	D27	99	'66	8.50	41.3	0.54	4.80	15.5	12-31-66	57.3	Dec	3.10	2.93	2.85	2.80	....	12 Mo Sep	2.73	2.42	35
36	Controls largest telephone group out-	P2	100¼	'62	45.5	2483	86.0	980	800	12-31-67	57.8	Dec	2.78	2.87	2.99	3.09	....	9 Mo Sep	....	2.45	36
37	side Bell System; important mfr.	P2	101	'63	47.9																37
38	Sylvania Elec lgst mfg subsidiary	P2	101⅛	'66	125													Bear interest from 12-1-66			38
39	Replacement and fleet tires; plastics; a	Pfd	Exch	'56	2.29	179	37.9	375	191	11-30-67	74.5	Nov	5.92	6.26	6.46	6.96	2.97	$61,300 called 5-1-67			39
40	leader in rockets and propellants	K7	100	'57	7.67																40
41	Subsid Southern Co; supplies elec	....	103¾	'41	79.9	+472	4.82	45.9	43.5	12-31-66	41.3	Dec	3.73	3.60	3.42	3.33	3.21	12 Mo Jan '68	3.35	3.19	41
42	to more than 3,700,000 in most of	F3	102⅜	'48	10.1																42
43	Ga. incl. (Continued on next page.)	H6	102⅛	'50	15.0																43

FIGURE 4–5 *(continued)*

SOURCE Standard & Poor's *Bond Guide,* 1968

conversion is established; whether it is stated as a price or in a number of shares per bond, the effect is the same. Let us assume, for example, that a bond can be converted into common stock at a conversion price of $50 per share. Since the par value of a bond is usually $1,000, each bond may be converted into 20 shares of stock. The conversion right could here be expressed as 20, which is technically referred to as the *conversion rate.* The conversion rate and the conversion price provide the same results, but each is expressed differently in the bond indenture.

Figure 4–6 provides a representative sample list of investment-grade and convertible bonds. These range from A to CCC bonds with yields comparable with nonconvertible bonds. Their conversion rate varies from bond issue to bond issue; this is noted in Figure 4–6.

The common stock price of a bond is found by multiplying the number of shares of stock into which the bond is convertible by the market price of the stock. Figure 4–6 shows Pan American World Airways 4 7/8s A of 1979, for example, as convertible into 133.33 shares of common stock through 1979. The current price of the bond is 261 5/8. The stock is 19 5/8, which gives the bond a stock price of $2,616.60 (133.33 × 19 5/8). In this case there is little difference between the price of the bond and the price of the bond in terms of stock into which it could be converted. Note however that bond prices are usually higher than the common stock price of the bond. The reason for this is the

CONVERTIBLE BONDS Issue, Rate, Interest Dates and Maturity	S&P Quality Rating	Outstdg. Mil. $	Conv. Expires	Shares per $1,000 Bond	Price per Share	Div. Income per Bond	1968 Range Hi	1968 Range Lo	Curr. Bid Sale(s) Ask(a)	Curr. Return	Stock Value of Bond	Invest. Worth	Conv. Parity	STOCK DATA Curr. Price	STOCK DATA P/E Ratio	Earnings Per Share Yr End	1966	1967	Last 12 Mos.	1967 Dil-u't'n
Nytronics Inc 6s Mn 1961	B	0.6	[3]81	73.48	13.61	....	403¼	260	286⅝	2.09	286⅝	....	39	♦39	26	Jl	q◻0.99	q1.52	[1]1.50	....
♦Nytronics, Inc 6s aO ;5 1982	B	10.0	[4]82	34.97	28.60	....	190	124	s137¾	4.36	136⅜	....	39⅜	♦39	26	Jl	q◻0.99	q1.52	[1]1.50	....
•Oak Electro-netics 4⅜s Ms 1987	B	10.0	1987	25.00	40.00	16.00	103½	81	s81⅞	5.34	62¾	....	32¾	•25⅛	15	Dc	2.56	1.73	1.73	1.64
Offshore Co 5s jD 1992	BB	35.0	1992	26.67	37.50	....	117	93½	98	5.10	80	70	35¼	30	19	Dc	1.02	P1.57	1.57	....
Ohio Water Service 6s mS 1977	....	2.0	1977	33.33	30.00	53.33	105	95½	102	5.88	101⅝	....	30⅝	30½	13	Dc	2.35	P2.29	2.29	....
OKC Corp 5¾s jD 1987	B	10.0	1997	41.67	24.00	22.92	100	89	90	6.39	62¾	....	22¼	♦19⅞	10	Sp	1.56	1.87	[12]2.05	....
♦Okonite Co 4¾s Jd 1992	B	30.0	1992	30.30	33.00	30.30	119⅝	90	s93	5.11	89¾	....	30⅝	♦29⅝	10	Dc	2.63	P3.03	3.03	....
•Outlet Co 5½s jJ 1986	B	7.5	1986	53.33	18.75	34.67	138	108¼	116	4.74	116	....	21¾	•21¼	13	Ja	1.85	....	[10]1.74	....
•Owens-Illinois 4½s mN 1992	BBB	50.0	1992	16.95	59.00	22.88	110⅞	99	s100¼	4.49	83	72¼	59⅛	•49	17	Dc	▴3.51	▵2.92	2.92	n/r
♦Ozark Air Lines 5¼s jJ 1986	CCC	9.16	1986	129.03	7.75	....	111	93	s96½	5.44	98⅜	....	7½	♦7⅝	32	Dc	▴0.20	▴0.24	0.24	n/r
♦Ozark Air Lines 6¾s jD 1988	CCC	15.0	1988	111.11	9.00	....	100¾	93	s95	7.11	84¾	....	8½	♦7⅝	32	Dc	▴0.39	....	[11]0.28	....
Ozite Corp 4½s mS15 1987	B	10.0	1987	19.67	50.83	11.80	127⅞	105	108⅛	4.16	108⅛	....	55	55	34	Dc	1.34	P1.62	1.62	....
[2]Pacific Airmotive 6s fA 1981	B	2.7	1981	66.40	15.06	47.81	245	195	214⅛	2.80	214⅛	....	32¼	•32¼	24	Jn	0.95	1.34	[12]1.37	....
Pacific Gas Transm'n 5½s Fa 1986	....	8.5	1971	70.00	14.28	56.00	101	92	98	5.61	98	....	14	14	13	Dc	1.01	P1.06	1.06	....
Pacific Power & Lt 4¾s mS 1974	BB	3.0	1974	60.00	[6]20.00	72.00	126¼	110	112½	4.22	112½	87	22	•22	14	Dc	1.53	1.53	1.53	n/r
•Pan Am World Airways 4⅞s fA 1979	BB	10.8	1979	133.33	7.50	53.33	307	261	261⅝	1.86	261⅝	77	19⅝	•19⅝	10	Dc	2.31	1.98	1.98	n/r
•Pan Am World Airways 4½s Jj15 1984	BB	40.9	1984	68.38	14.63	27.35	159	133½	s136¾	3.29	134¼	69½	20	•19⅝	10	Dc	2.31	1.98	1.98	n/r
•Pan Am World Airways 4½s fA 1986	BB	175.	1986	25.72	38.88	10.29	86¼	77¾	s80¼	5.61	50½	67½	31¼	•19⅝	10	Dc	2.31	1.98	1.98	n/r
Panoil Co 6s Jd15 1977	....	1.1	1977	200.00	5.00	....	167½	120	135	4.44	125	....	6¾	6¼	..	Au	◻0.03	0.02	0.02	n/r
Paradise Fruit Co 7s Jd 1978	....	1.5	1978	166.67	6.00	....	88	85	85	8.24	79⅛	....	5	4¾	30	Dc	0.16	....	0.16	....
•Parker-Hannifin 4s aO 1992	BB	20.0	1992	13.16	76.00	15.79	96	83¾	85	4.71	70⅜	58	64⅝	•53½	17	Je	3.06	q3.41	[12]3.22	n/r
Parkview Gem, Inc	....	See Gem International					....		....	....	....	....	....	....	..	...	....	....	....	....
Pauley Petroleum 5¾s Jd 1976	B	7.9	1970	47.62	21.00	....	119	85⅛	119	4.83	119	....	25	25	d	Au	▵d0.76	d1.90	d1.90	n/r
•Penn-Dixie Cement 5s aO 1982	B	30.0	1982	34.19	29.25	20.51	104¾	78½	s79¼	6.31	65	....	23⅛	•19	19	Dc	0.75	E1.00	[9]0.88	....
Penn Real Estate Tr 6¼s fA15 1979	....	1.4	[7]73	80.00	12.50	64.00	100	76	96	6.51	96	....	12	12	..	Au	■0.59	■0.76	0.76	n/r
Penton Publishing 5s mS 1982	....	2.0	1982	55.56	18.00	29.17	98	95	95	5.26	91⅝	....	17⅛	16½	18	Dc	1.16	0.90	0.90	n/r
Perfect Film & Chemical	....	See Perfect Photo					....		....	....	....	....	....	....	..	...	....	....	....	....
[1]Perfect Photo 5½s aO 1980	CCC	3.6	1980	21.55	46.40	....	156¾	90	100	5.50	98	....	46⅜	•45½	22	Dc	1.71	2.05	2.05	n/r
Pettibone Mulliken 4⅝s fA 1987	BB	15.0	1987	25.00	40.00	15.00	94	75	78	5.93	63⅛	64½	31¼	25¼	8	Mr	4.01	....	[12]3.05	....
Phoenix Steel 6s mS 1987	CCC	12.5	1987	37.85	26.42	....	111¾	97	98½	6.09	81⅜	....	26	♦21½	19	Dc	▵2.16	P1.15	1.15	....
Photon, Inc 5s jD 1971	....	1.4	1971	200.00	5.00	....	1780	1260	1550	0.32	1550	....	77½	77½	34	Dc	1.53	P2.25	2.25	....
Piedmont Aviation 5⅜s fA 1986	B	7.0	1986	51.28	19.50	10.26	86	81	83	6.48	60¼	....	16⅛	11¾	12	Dc	1.05	P▵1.02	1.02	....
Piedmont Aviation 7s Ms [15] 1988	B	15.0	1988	76.92	13.00	15.38	100½	100	100½	6.97	90⅜	....	13	11¾	12	Dc	1.05	P▵1.02	1.02	....
♦Pioneer Plastics 6½s Jd 1984	....	1.6	1984	90.91	11.00	....	138	101	s113	5.75	115⅞	....	12⅜	♦12¾	d	Ja	d0.15	....	[10]d0.17	....
Power Ind'l Prod 6⅛s fA31 1987	....	2.2	1987	100.00	10.00	....	110	82	82	7.47	67½	....	8⅜	6¾	13	Au	0.48	....	[6]0.52	....
Pueblo Supermkts N.Y. 5¼s Ms 1988	B	10.0	1988	27.78	36.00	12.22	101½	98	100½	5.22	91	....	36¼	•32¾	17	Ja	1.68	....	[10]1.78	....
Purex Corp	....	See Pacific Airmotive					....	....	....	....	....	....	....	....	..	...	....	....	....	....
♦Puritan Fashions 6s jD31 1979	....	3.7	1979	[9] Com & Deb		....	91½	81	80	7.50	....	....	....	....	..	Nv	◻1.46	P▵0.09	0.09	....
Racine Hydr (Mchy) 5⅛s Fa 1987	B	2.9	1987	43.48	23.00	30.44	134¾	100	102⅛	5.02	102⅛	....	23½	23½	16	Je	2.35	2.20	[12]1.46	n/r
•Radio Corp of Amer 4½s fA 1992	A	160.	1992	16.95	59.00	16.95	111	100½	s104¼	4.32	78⅝	74¾	61½	•46⅜	20	Dc	2.26	2.27	2.27	n/r
•Ralston Purina 4⅞s jD 1992	A	40.0	1992	37.74	26.50	22.64	106½	101¾	s103	4.73	86⅜	78⅝	27¼	•22⅞	25	Sp	1.49	0.99	[12]0.92	n/r

Uniform Footnote Explanations—See Page XV. Other: [1]Now Perfect Film & Chemical. [2]Now Purex Corp. [3]Thru 4-30-71; $15.42 '76; then $17.24. [4]Thru 10-14-72; $33.36 '77; then $38.12. [6]$1,000 in Deb. plus $200 cash for ea 60 shrs. [7]Thru 8-14-70; then $14.25 thru 8-14-73. [9]30 shrs com & $800 non Cv Deb due 12-31-79.

EXPLANATION OF COLUMN HEADINGS AND FOOTNOTES

MARKET: Unlisted except where symbols • or ♦ are used:
•—New York Stock Exchange ♦—Amer'n Stock Exchange.

ISSUE TITLE: Name of Bond at time of offering; otherwise issue footnoted with name change of obligor. Minor changes with old title indicated in brackets, i.e. Rohr (Aircraft).
#Prin & int payable in U.S. Funds. ‡Canadian funds.

CONVERSION EXPIRES: Footnote keyed to bottom of page when conversion price changes during life of the privilege.
§Indicates a change in next 12 months.

DIVIDEND INCOME PER BOND: If $1,000 Bond were converted, the annual amount of dividends expected to be paid by the company on the stock based on most recent indication of annual rate of payment.
‡Less tax at origin. g—In Canadian funds less 15% or 10% non-residence tax.

STOCK VALUE OF BOND: Price at which bond must sell to equal price of stock i. e., number of shares received on conversion times price of the stock.

INVESTMENT WORTH: The estimated value of a bond assuming it had no conversion privilege. An appraisal, determined by averaging the yields of similar quality issues which do not have a 'stock right' privilege.

CONVERSION PARITY: Price at which stock must sell to equal bond price. i.e., price of bond divided by number of shares received on conversion.

P-E RATIO: (Price-Earnings Ratio) Represents market valuation of any $1 of per share earnings i.e., the price of the stock divided by estimated or latest 12 months per share earnings.

EARNINGS, in general, are per share as reported by company. **FOR YEAR INDICATED:** Fiscal years ending prior to March 31 are shown under preceding year. Net operating earnings are shown for **banks**; earnings before appropriation to general reserve for **savings & loan associations**; net investment income for **insurance companies**; **railroads'** earnings are as reported to ICC. **Foreign** issues traded **ADR** are dollars per share, converted at prevailing exchange rate. Specific foot notes used:

▵Excl extra-ord income
▴Incl extra-ord income
◻Excl extra-ord charges
■Incl. extra-ord charges
‡Partial Year
‡Comparison 1967 vs 1968
b—Before depletion

d—Deficit
E—S&P Estimate
j—Currency at origin
P—Preliminary
p—Pro forma
q—On average shares
n/r—Not reported

LAST 12 MOS. indicates earnings through period indicated by superior number preceding fig. [1]for Jan. [2]for Feb., etc. Figure without superior number indicates fiscal yearend.

DILUTION: Earnings are pro-forma giving effect to conversion and exercise of other stock rights, as reported by Company.

FIGURE 4–6

Convertible bonds

SOURCE Standard & Poor's *Stock Guide*, 1968

expectation by the investor of a price rise in the stock at the time of the initial offering of the bond.

When a convertible bond is originally sold, the conversion rate is set below the value of the bond. This encourages investors to hold the bond for appreciation. As the price of the stock increases, the price of the bond moves above par, and expectation of a future price increase by the investor continues. So once again the bond sells higher than the equivalent value in stock. Under normal circumstances, the bond will continue to move up and sell above its conversion value in terms of common stock. Convertible bonds with quality ratings, therefore, offer a satisfactory investment, with income and a chance to share in company growth.

The major advantage of convertible bonds is their defensive–aggressive characteristic. They provide security of principal and interest income, and they offer the possibility of an increase in capital value. If the common stock of the company increases in price, the price of the convertible bond will increase also. If, on the other hand, the price of the stock drops, then the price of the bond will drop. However—and this is a further advantage of this type of security—as the stock price drops, the bond will decline in price until par is reached; then it will sell like a money rate bond rather than a stock, providing it is of money rate caliber. When it sells as a debt instrument, the price is supported, which puts a floor under the price and reduces the possibility of complete loss. In Figure 4–6 the bonds of the Off Shore Company sold close to par; yet the bond price in terms of the market price of stock was only $800. Why would we wish to buy a convertible bond at this price? An investor could purchase the bonds at par, receive a yield of 5 percent, and still hope for an increase in the stock price over a longer period of time; this would move the price up and result in a very satisfactory investment. A selected list of convertible bonds published by Standard & Poor's in *The Outlook* appears from time to time and may be used as a source of up-to-date convertible securities available for investment.

Another advantage of convertible bonds is their strength as collateral for loans. They provide much more stable security than common stocks. Most commercial banks will lend up to 85 percent of the market value of high-grade convertible bonds.

In 1968, the margin requirement for listed convertible bonds was 50 percent compared with 70 percent for listed common stock. When we borrow on margin, we take advantage of purchasing a large amount of bonds with a given amount of dollars. This leverage will help us if we are right in our decision.

A third advantage is the regularity and security of income from bonds. Many are convertible into stock which pays a small dividend or no dividend at all. The income from such common stock would be small or nonexistent, and the current yield extremely low. The interest income from the convertible bonds would be modest too, but substantially higher than that from the common stock. To attract capital, some convertible bonds that have low ratings will pay interest as high as 6 percent. The risk involved in this type of security is great, however, and should be thoroughly studied before a commitment is made.

A fourth advantage is that convertible bonds may protect individuals who wish to speculate by selling stock short. Assume we wished to sell a stock short at 100. We think it will decline to 80. We sell it at 100 and hope to buy it back at 80, making 20 points per share profit. At the same time we buy sufficient convertibles so that if the stock should rise in price, we can convert the bonds to stock and deliver it to the person from whom we borrowed the stock in the first place. If the price of the stock should decline, we still profit from the short sale and we still earn interest on the bonds. When the bond price moves back up, we can sell the bonds, and we have profited from both a falling and rising stock market.

A fifth advantage of convertibles is provided the institutional investor and financial institutions. Convertibles offer such investors an opportunity to share in the growth of common stock even though they cannot, by law, own a large amount of common stock. This feature makes them particularly attractive to this type of investor.

The Disadvantages of Convertible Bonds

The major disadvantage of convertible bonds is in the loss that might occur if they are purchased at too high a price. In order to be attractive for investment, they should provide a fair yield in terms of the bond or the stock price, and the risk of a sharp drop in price should be small. A convertible bond purchased at 160, for example, might have a negative yield to maturity. A person buying a convertible at this price loses the advantage of a price increase and at the same time accepts the possibility of a sharp decrease should the market price of the stock fall because of a decline in earnings or because of the market risk. If the bond offers a satisfactory yield in terms of the common stock value, then it may be purchased for investment. If there is little chance for the stock price to decline because earnings are strong, then the bond could be purchased at these levels.

A second disadvantage of convertibles is their relative lack of security. Most are rated lower than comparable nonconvertible bonds. Many convertible bonds are subordinated to other debts, giving them a junior claim to assets in case of failure. In essence, a convertible bond is a debt that serves as equity and it must be considered such when analyzed. Most convertible bonds are callable too; the corporation may call the bonds at its discretion. Should this happen, bondholders would be forced either to convert or to sell and take a profit if a capital gain exists. In a bond call, the decision to convert is taken away from the bondholder through the act of calling, which forces conversion. This might come at an inappropriate time for him and represents a third disadvantage of convertible bonds.

Bonds with Warrants

Warrant bonds are another type of security that offers the investor some of the same advantages as convertible bonds. A warrant attached to the bond gives the owner the right to buy a specified number of common shares at a stated price for a limited period of time. The time period might be as long as five years; therefore, it is not a short-term agreement. The warrants may be exercised separately from the bond, in which case they are called detachable warrants. If we owned a bond having detachable warrants, we could benefit in one of two ways if the warrant increased in value because of an increase in price of the common stock: (1) We could sell the warrant and realize our gains, or (2) we could exercise the warrant, buying the stock at the option price, then selling it at market price. If we bought the stock and retained ownership of the bond, our investment position would change. We would be a bondholder and a stockholder at the same time. The warrants, however, might be nondetachable, in which case we would be required to send the bond to the company's agent. He would detach the warrant and return the bond to us at the time we wanted to exercise our option.

Bonds with warrants allow investors to share in the growth of the company without undue risk, by participating in the potential increase in value of common stock. If the market price of the common stock remained below the subscription price at which it is usually set in the bond agreement, then we would not have to exercise our warrants and would continue to hold the bond. If the stock increased in price, we could exercise or sell our warrants and realize a profit. The simplest thing would be to sell the warrants and keep the bond. We would then have a profit on the warrants and also a safe debt-type security for investment.

The ability to share in price increases by means of warrants is not as great as it is for convertible bonds. But the bond with warrants offers protection against the purchasing-power and the business risk. It provides advantages that minimize risk. The quality of each bond issue must, however, be judged by the tests we used for other bonds, namely, the ability to repay the debt, the ability to pay interest, and the overall credit position of the company. The Consolidated Edison 4 3/8s issue maturing in 1992 is a good example of a bond with warrants listed on the New York Stock Exchange Bond Market. Bonds with warrants, however, are not as common in present-day markets as the more popular convertible bonds. The market price of the bond plus the market value of the stock from the warrants compared with the market price of the bond plus the cash cost of exercising the warrant will help decide the relative advantage of buying the bond or the stock. A bond with warrants selling on a high current-yield basis might be attractive because of the expected profit potential of the growth in common-stock price.

Summary

Debt securities are an important source of money for private corporations. Corporate bonds offer investors a stable rate of return higher than government bonds and provide security of principal. When we buy bonds for investment we receive two promises. The issuing corporation promises to repay the principal and pay interest on the debt. We can test the quality of a bond issue by examining the earning power and the cash-flow position of the company to determine whether it can carry out these promises. The debt-to-net-worth ratio and the debt-to-fixed-assets ratio allow us to determine whether debt is excessive. Generally a company's total debt should not exceed net worth, and long-term debt should not exceed 50 percent of fixed assets. Rating agencies provide us with standards that allow us to judge the quality of a bond issue. Interest, in normal times, should be covered three times by net income after taxes for industrial companies and twice for rails and public utilities.

Lower-grade bonds offer higher yields than AAA bonds. If the bonds are held to maturity, they offer security of principal and a stable income. Some of the lower-quality bonds are attractive for income. Top-quality bonds do not possess the market risk, but although business risk is only slight, these bonds do fluctuate in value because of the money rate risk. Lower-grade bonds below an AA rating suffer from the credit or business risk to a greater degree than top-quality money rate bonds. Lower-rated bonds also are susceptible to the money rate risk.

Convertible bonds and bonds with warrants offer the investor a third promise that is not possessed by ordinary bonds—the promise of an increase in capital because of an expected increase in the price of common stock. Convertible bonds close to par and offering a modest yield provide the investor with a unique combination of aggressive-defensive characteristics that provide an excellent hedge. Bonds with warrants offer the bondholder a way to share in the growth of the company by allowing him to subscribe to stock at a specified price. Convertible bonds are more numerous than bonds with warrants and offer attractive investment opportunities under varied market conditions. For all practical purposes, a convertible bond issue must be analyzed in the same way as common stock. Before purchase, all types of bonds must be carefully analyzed, and care must be exercised in timing the purchase to assure that risks are minimized.

Review Questions

1. When a corporation borrows money, what are the promises it makes to the investor who purchases the bond or bonds?
2. What do the terms *maturity, call,* and *serial* have in common, and how do they differ?
3. Discuss ways in which the security of the pledge to repay may be enhanced or weakened.
4. The company issuing bonds agrees to pay the interest, on a regular basis, to the bondholder. Distinguish between *interest rate, coupon rate,* and *current yield.*
5. What are protective covenants designed to do for the bondholder?
6. Discuss the ways in which we can assess the investment quality of a corporate bond.
7. Discuss the relationship between bond quality, bond ratings, and bond yields.
8. What risks are assumed when high-grade and/or speculative-grade bonds are purchased by the investor?
9. What advantages and disadvantages do corporate bonds hold for the investor?
10. What type of investor, typically, would be interested in corporate bonds?
11. How would you define the term *convertible bond?*
12. What are the advantages and disadvantages of an investment in convertible bonds? Where and when would they be most likely to be used by the investor?
13. What is meant by the term *bond with warrants,* and what advantages does such a bond hold for the investor?
14. Compare the yields on convertible bonds and nonconvertible bonds. What conclusion can you make from the comparison?
15. What is the difference in yield between an AAA and BBB bond?

Problems

1. What is the yield to maturity for the following types of bonds at the present time?
   AAA-rated
   BBB-rated
   Industrial
   Public utilities
   Railroads
   Convertible bonds
   Bonds with warrants
   (Where information on a large number of bonds is unavailable to

indicate market yields, select one or two specific issues and indicate yield to maturity.)

2. Select a high-grade bond, a medium-grade bond, a convertible bond, and a bond with warrants. For each specific bond issue, determine the bond rating, the nature of the pledge, the security of the issue, the adequacy of debt to assets and of bond interest to income, the specific protective covenants, and any other details that determine the character of the bond issue.

3. Find a current quote on the price of EG & G 3 1/2s convertible debentures due in 1987 and the price of the common stock.
   (a) What is the market price of the bond?
   (b) What is the value of the bond in terms of the price of the common stock?
   (c) Is the bond selling above, below, or at its conversion price? Explain.
   (d) If you owned the bond, would you convert or continue to hold it? Why or why not?
   (e) Is the bond attractive as a bond or in terms of common stock?

4. Examine the indenture provisions of the Consolidated Edison 4 3/8s due in 1992 with warrants.
   (a) Is the debt issue adequately secured?
   (b) Do the warrants have value?
   (c) Would it be desirable at this time to exercise the warrants?

Sources of Investment Information

Barron's
Commercial & Financial Chronicle
Dun and Bradstreet credit ratings
Federal Reserve Bulletin
Moody's Bond Record
Moody's Manuals
New York Stock Exchange listings statements
Prospectus of a bond issue
Standard & Poor's *Bond Guide*
Standard & Poor's *The Outlook*

Selected Readings

Harris, John T., "Discount & Current Coupon Bonds," *Financial Analysts Journal* (July-August, 1968), p. 81.

Jen, Frank C., and James E. Wert, "Sinking Funds and Bond Yields," *Financial Analysts Journal* (March-April, 1967), p. 125.

Johannesen, Richard I., Jr., "Coupon Bond Price Fluctuations," *Financial Analysts Journal* (September-October, 1968), p. 89.

Johnson, Robert L., "The Value of the Call Privilege," *Financial Analysts Journal* March-April, 1967), p. 134.

Kassouf, Sheen T., "Warrant Price Behavior, 1945–1964," *Financial Analysts Journal* (January-February, 1968), p. 123.

Klaman, Saul B., "The Plenitude of Scarcity," *Financial Analysts Journal* (July-August, 1967), p. 59.

Shelton, John P., "Warrant, Stock-Price Relations—Part I," *Financial Analysts Journal* (May-June, 1967), p. 143.

———, "Warrant, Stock-Price Relations—Part II," *Financial Analysts Journal* (July-August, 1967), p. 88.

5

PREFERRED STOCK
An Ownership Security

We now move away from the relative security and stability of corporate bonds to preferred stock. Preferred stock is an ownership security. As such, it shares in certain risks that an investor does not have with a fixed-income debt security; dividends are contingent upon earnings and are not mandatory as is the interest on bonds and preferred stock has a junior claim to corporate assets compared with bonds. In many respects, preferred stock is a unique investment security, which makes it attractive for investment. In this chapter we will look at these unique characteristics and attempt to understand the virtues and vices of preferred stock. We will examine how it guards against some of the investment risks and where it might fit into our investment program.

The General Nature of Preferred Stock

Historically, corporations have not relied heavily upon preferred stock as a major source of funds. Between 1957 and September, 1967, new preferred issues represented only a small portion of the money raised by corporations through the sale of new securities. Table 5–1 reveals that the amount of preferred stock sold comprised over 5 percent of the total new issues in only one of ten complete years. Usage of preferred in corporate finance has been limited because it does not possess the tax advantages of bonds; yet the payment of dividends is almost as binding as the interest payment on bonds. There are, however, two preferred-stock attributes which make them of interest to certain investors. The first and primary attribute is the preference of preferred dividends on

TABLE 5–1

Annual new corporate issues of preferred stock,
1957–1967

YEAR	PREFERRED STOCK ISSUED (MILLIONS OF DOLLARS)	PREFERRED STOCK ISSUES AS A PERCENT OF TOTAL NEW CORPORATE ISSUES OF SECURITIES
1967 (9 mos.)	531	2.8
1966	574	3.2
1965	725	4.5
1964	412	3.0
1963	343	2.8
1962	436	4.0
1961	449	3.4
1960	409	4.3
1959	531	5.4
1958	571	4.9
1957	411	3.2

SOURCE: *Federal Reserve Bulletin*, December, 1967, p. 2114.

the earnings of the company. The second is the preference to a claim on assets over common stock in the unusual case of liquidation and in the more usual case of reorganization, refinancing, or adjustment of a company's capital account. Let us look at these features more closely.

The First Attribute—First Preference to Dividends

Cash dividends on preferred stock have priority over those on common stock. This is of primary importance to preferred-stock owners. If a dividend is declared (even when earnings are adequate and cash is available, dividends must be declared by the board of directors) and the corporation does not have sufficient earnings to pay the dividend on both preferred and common stock, it is required to pay the dividend on preferred first. If any funds remain after payment of the preferred dividend, one may be paid on the common stock. This priority of dividends is in contrast to the interest payment on bonds, which is a fixed claim upon earnings and must be paid or the corporation will be in default. Dividends on preferred stock are paid from net income after taxes; bond interest is paid before taxes. And dividends on preferred are subordinate to federal income taxes and bond interest. This subordination tends to make preferred stock somewhat weaker than the dividend priority suggests.

The Second Attribute—Preference to Assets

Most preferred stocks have a par or stated value. The par value is stated in the charter of the corporation and may be changed by consent of the corporate stockholders. When preferred stock has no par value, the directors may, at their discretion, assign a value to it. This is referred to as the *stated value*. In the event of failure of the corporation, the preferred stockholder has the right to receive the par or stated value of his shares before any money is distributed to the common stockholders. The assets are usually not liquidated and distributed; rather the corporation is reorganized, and claims against the assets are scaled down. Preferred stock purchased in the market is obligated to receive in liquidation, reorganization, or recapitalization only the par or stated value, even though the purchase price was higher. Its relative security makes preferred stock attractive to those who desire greater security of principal and a higher current income than is supplied by common stock. Should the company fail, the investor would have greater assurance that his position with respect to common stock is superior. This guarantee is not absolute, however; the assets might not be sufficient to allow for any residual economic value for the preferred stockholders.

The Usual Features of Preferred Stock

Several other features are typically associated with preferred stock. The classes of stock a corporation has issued are described in the corporate charter; so is the description of preferred stock. If the charter were silent and common law were allowed to rule, the preferred stock of a company would not be significantly different from the common stock. Preferred stock would be an ownership security, it would be voting stock, it would have no maturity, and, in the event of liquidation, its owners would share in the assets of the company equally with the common shareholders. It would also be cumulative and nonparticipating. The charter and the preferred stock agreement are not silent, however, and detailed characteristics are clearly set forth. If we were to summarize them, we would find the following pattern emerging.

VOTING

Preferred stock is usually nonvoting. It does not vote to elect the directors. However, it does have contingent voting rights. In times of financial trouble, preferred stockholders would be given the right to elect some of the directors. The New York Stock Exchange will not list a preferred stock for trading unless it has the contingent right to vote. The Exchange rule states that if six quarterly dividends have not been paid, the preferred stockholders have the right to elect a minimum of two directors. Preferred stockholders usually have the right to vote approval on the issuance of additional preferred stock, mergers and consolidations with other companies, and charter amendments.

MATURITY DATE AND CALL DATE

Typically, preferred stock has no maturity date. In this respect it is similar to common stock. The usual preferred stock is callable, however, at the option of the company. The call or redemption feature allows the company to retire all or part of the issue at a price stated in the original agreement. This provides flexibility for corporate management, but it may be detrimental to the investor. Our discussion of bonds disclosed that a change in maturity date caused by activation of the call option will have an impact on yield. The change might be advantageous or harmful to the investor. The effect is the same for callable preferred stock. If we are to invest in such stock, we must be aware of the effect of the call date on our yield.

SINKING FUND

While we are on the subject of calling stocks and bonds for redemption, we might comment that a sinking fund is customarily provided in the modern preferred-stock agreement. Stock may be called for sinking-fund purposes to assure the retirement of the preferred stock. This is most often found in industrial preferred stock, where there might be some desire to eliminate the stock from the capital structure. Railroads and public utilities seldom provide a sinking fund in their preferred stocks.

DIVIDENDS

Dividends on preferred stock are stated as a percent of par value or as a dollar amount. The majority of preferred stocks have a par value. Usually, when it is low or when there is no par value, the dividend is stated in dollars. The $5 preferred stock of General Motors is a good example of this type of dividend. Where the par value is above $50, the dividend is stated as a percent of par. Reynolds Tobacco, for instance, has a 3.6 percent preferred-stock dividend.

The dividends of a company may be cumulative or noncumulative, but the usual preferred-stock dividend is cumulative. This means that if a payment is missed, the dividend accumulates and is added to future dividend payments. The accumulation of dividends, or dividend arrearage because of inability to earn enough to pay dividends, has caused financial difficulty for some companies. Dividend arrears often force the company to change its capital structure or to recapitalize to eliminate past unpaid dividends. When recapitalization is completed, the company once again will be in a position to pay dividends on the common stock. When dividends on preferred stock are in arrears, no dividends can be paid on common stock.

Preferred-stock dividends can be participating or nonparticipating; usually they are nonparticipating. A participating preferred stock will share beyond its stated dividend rate, in earnings with the common share owners. Participation might be equal with common stock, or there might be a limit. Most participation features allow preferred stock to share equally with common stock after a similar amount of dividend has been paid on the common stock. This is unlimited participation. Details of participation are not rigid, and, based upon the judgment of the corporation's directors, they can be set to meet the needs of investors.

Participating preferred would be an ideal security in which to invest, offering the same security of principal as regular preferred, together with an opportunity to share in future growth of the company. Few outstanding preferred issues, however, combine both quality and the participating feature.

CONVERTIBILITY

Preferred stock is typically nonconvertible. Only about one-third of the issues outstanding enjoy the conversion privilege—a feature that makes convertible preferred an attractive investment security. This conversion feature is almost identical with that of bonds. We have, in each case, an additional privilege of sharing in the potential increase in common-stock value plus some security of principal and stability of income. Convertible preferred, however, does not usually have security equal to that of convertible bonds. The corporation's subordinated convertible debentures have a claim senior to convertible preferred stocks. If a convertible preferred stock were the senior security with no debt outstanding, then it could be as strong as a senior convertible bond issue. With preferred stock, the conversion ratio is usually protected from dilution by stock splits and stock dividends in the same manner as with convertible bonds.

Table 5–2 provides a list of high-grade callable, noncallable, and convertible utility and industrial preferreds that possess most of the characteristics of preferred stock. The list of preferreds with the special convertible feature could offer advantageous investment opportunities. The convertible feature makes them more attractive than ordinary preferred for our individual investment requirements.

Yields on Preferred Stock

The yield on preferred stock is different from that on bonds because there is no maturity value for preferred. The yield is a current yield, which is found by dividing the current price or purchase price into the dollars of dividend income paid on the stock. The yield on the $7 Liggett & Myers preferred in Table 5–2, for example, is obtained by dividing the price of $114 into $7, which gives a current yield of 6.14 percent. We cannot do this with a bond because purchase price and maturity price might differ, resulting in either a gain or loss for the investor that would affect his profits or yield to maturity. Actually, in the case of preferred stock, we are saying that the purchase price is the average investment and that there will be no capital gain or loss because

P_p and P_m are the same. Dividend income then is the only income received, and it will be paid perpetually. This assumes, of course, that there is no call feature nor sinking fund. Based on these circumstances, the yield on preferreds and on bonds is comparable.

When a preferred stock has a call date and a call price and can be called for sinking fund purposes, then we would be required to compute its yield to maturity just as we compute the yield to maturity on bonds. This calculation will allow us to make a valid comparison about the expectations of a preferred stock investment for a period of time, compared with yield to maturity on bonds for the same period. This should enable us to make a better decision. Let us assume, for example, that the preferred stock of Consolidated Edison (in Table 5–2 under Callable Preferreds) will be called at 100 in five years. What then is the yield to maturity? The average investment is $(77 + 100)/2 = 88.50$. The average annual income is $5.00 + $4.60 = $9.60 (where $5.00 is the annual dividend and $4.60 the annual gain of principal over a five-year period). The yield to call date then is 10.85 percent ($9.60/$88.50), and this is a yield to maturity comparable with the yield to maturity on bonds. Yields on preferred stock quoted in the financial press are the current yield, which divides the current price into the dividend paid by the company, and they do not calculate yield to first call date or to maturity if there is a maturity date for the preferred stock.

Yields Compared with Bond Yields

Yields on preferred stock have usually been higher than on government or private corporate bonds; preferreds offer the investor a comparatively attractive yield with reasonable quality and security. This varies, of course, with the quality of the stock. It is possible that a high-quality preferred stock issue of one company would have a higher credit rating than a bond of a company with substantial debt. This is particularly true when the preferred is the senior stock issue of the company. Under these conditions, a preferred stock would offer a lower yield than a bond. Dividend income of preferred stock, however, may be offset by the dividend credit under present IRS regulations, which would make for lower rates than for bond interest that is fully taxable. The preferred yields in Table 5–3 reflect the relatively good rates of return that can be earned even on the top ten high-grade preferred stocks. Since 1957, one could have obtained more than a 5 percent yield on medium-grade preferred stocks. If we had been investing at the time and were willing to accept somewhat greater risk, we could have purchased ten specula-tive-grade preferreds to achieve a higher yield. Yields on preferreds since early 1956 and in the current market have exceeded the current yields on common stocks.

TABLE 5-2

Selected list of noncallable preferred stock, callable preferred stock, and convertible preferred stock

Noncallable Preferred Stock

Issue	Par Value $	1967-8 Price Range	Rating	Approximate Price	Times Charges Earned	Current Yield %
American Can 7%	25	32 3/4 – 29 1/2	AA	30	24.7	5.83
American Sugar Refining 5.44%	12.50	11 1/2 – 10 1/2	BB	11	11.7	6.18
Celanese 7%	100	120 3/4 – 115	BBB	114	14.8	5.88
Consolidated Edison of N.Y. 6%	100	102 5/8 – 95 7/8	BBB	98	4.6	6.12
Detroit Edison $5.50	100	106 3/4 – 97	AA	99	12.1	5.55
Ingersoll-Rand $6	100	137 – 118	AAA	131	341.9	4.57
Kaiser Aluminum 4 3/4%	100	108 – 89 1/2	BBB	99	21.0	4.80
Liggett & Myers $7	100	122 – 111 1/2	A	114	22.1	6.14
Montgomery Ward $7 CLA	No Par	114 – 108 1/2	BBB	112	16.9	6.24
Pacific Gas & Electric 6%	25	27 – 24 1/8	AA	24	9.1	6.25
Pacific Telephone & Telegraph 6%	100	108 1/2 – 100 1/4	AAA	102	30.8	5.88
Pittsburgh, Fort Wayne & Chicago Railway 7%	100	117 – 107 1/2	AA	108	1.1	6.48
Pittsburgh, Youngstown & Ashtabula Railway 7%	100	119 1/2 – 108	AA	112	*	6.25
Quaker Oats 6%	100	111 – 103	AA	105	31.0	5.71
United Shoe Machinery 6%	25	27 3/4 – 25	AA	25	48.8	6.00
United States Rubber (Uniroyal) 8%	100	140 1/2 – 124 5/8	BBB	127	8.9	6.30
Universal Leaf Tobacco 8%	100	137 – 128 1/4	A	131	19.7	6.11
Wisconsin Electric Power 6%	100	105 – 99 1/2	AA	102	30.0	5.88

* Dividends paid from rental guaranty under lease.

Callable Preferreds

Issue	Par Value $	1967-8 Price Range	Rating	Approximate Price	Times Charges Earned	Current Yield %
Armstrong Cork $3.75	100	70 3/4 – 64	AA	64	69.6	5.86
Atlantic Richfield $3.75	100	68 1/2 – 64	AA	65	107.9	5.77
Canada Dry $4.25	100	76 – 68	A	72	20.5	5.90
Consolidated Edison of N. Y. $5.00	100	84 7/8 – 77	A	77	4.6	6.50
Consumers Power $4.50	100	78 – 70 7/8	AAA	74	18.7	6.08
General Motors $5.00	100	93 – 84 3/4	AAA	85	131.8	5.88
International Paper $4.00	100	74 1/2 – 65	AA	68	219.1	5.88
Ohio Edison 4.56%	100	79 – 72 3/4	AAA	76	16.9	6.00
Philadelphia Electric 4.68%	100	83 – 76 1/2	AAA	77	16.4	6.08
Public Service Electric & Gas $6.80	100	108 1/4 – 103	AA	105	10.7	6.48

TABLE 5-2 (*Continued*)

Convertible Preferreds

Issue	Call Price ($)	No. Common Shares for Each Preferred	Recent Price Common	Value in Common	Recent Price Preferred	1967–1968 Price Range Preferred ($)	Yield-Preferred (%)	Rating	Times Charges Earned
Cities Service $2.25	52.50[a]	1.818	48	87 1/4	84	88 1/2– 81 3/4	2.68	BBB	47.1
Litton $3.00	100 [b]	2.00	66	132	140	217–126	2.16	A	34.8
Radio Corporation of America $4.00	105 [c]	2.00	53	106	119	120 1/2–104 1/4	2.52	BBB	204.4
Atlantic Richfield $3.00	85 [d]	.85	118	100 1/4	100	104 1/4– 81	3.00	BBB	107.9
Eaton Yale & Towne 4 3/4%	25.50[e]	.50	33	16 1/2	32	33 1/4– 26	3.72	A	79.0
Rexall Drug $2.00	55 [f]	1.00	32	32	40	43 5/8– 35	5.00	BB	10.8
Eltra Corporation $1.40	36 [g]	.915	35	32	62	71 1/8– 54 5/8	2.26	BB	56.6
Kaiser Aluminum 4 3/4%	105 [g]	1.200	46	55	99	108– 89 1/2	4.80	BBB	21.0

[a] Begin 1-1-70
[b] Begin 4-1-72
[c] Begin 5-11-72
[d] Begin 12-31-72
[e] Begin 7-1-69
[f] Begin 6-30-71
[g] Begin 1-1-72

SOURCES: *Barron's*, May 13, 1968, pp. 49–62; and Standard & Poor's *Stock Guide*, May, 1968.

TABLE 5–3

Preferred stock yields
Moody's averages (percent)

		Industrial Preferreds		Public Utility Preferreds	
YEAR	TEN HIGH GRADE	TEN MEDIUM GRADE	TEN SPECULA- TIVE GRADE	TEN HIGH GRADE	TEN MEDIUM GRADE
1967 (April)	4.90	5.09	5.48	5.23	5.52
1966	4.85	5.03	5.53	5.19	5.41
1965	4.30	4.60	4.93	4.53	4.72
1964	4.28	4.67	5.02	4.49	4.68
1963	4.29	4.69	5.10	4.38	4.58
1962	4.47	4.81	5.34	4.52	4.74
1961	4.60	4.82	5.41	4.71	4.90
1960	4.71	5.18	5.77	4.85	5.06
1959	4.62	4.99	5.58	4.79	5.01
1958	4.34	5.14	5.77	4.51	4.83
1957	4.48	5.28	5.91	4.72	5.01

SOURCE: *Moody's Industrial Manual* (New York: Moody's Investors Service, 1967), p. a25.

The Pattern of Preferred Yields

The pattern of yields on preferred stock is almost identical with that of yields on other fixed-income obligations. Higher-quality preferreds sell on a lower-yield basis than medium- and lower-grade preferreds. This is apparent from the average yield figures in Table 5–3. Yields on speculative-grade preferreds averaged almost 1 percent, absolute, above the yields on the highest-quality preferreds. Yields on industrial and public utility preferreds differ in an interesting way. High-grade industrial preferreds sold on a lower-yield basis than public utility preferreds. Medium-grade industrial preferreds, on the other hand, sold on a higher-yield basis than medium-grade public utility preferreds. This information is useful only to the investor who needs income and is willing to give up some security of principal and accept more risk to improve his income. Such an investor should buy medium-grade industrial preferreds rather than medium-grade public utility preferreds. The lower-quality preferreds do not follow the money rate pattern as closely as do the high-quality; they are influenced more by business risk than by the money rate risk.

Stability of Preferred Yields

Yields on high-grade preferred stocks are relatively stable, even though dividends are contingent upon earnings and must be declared by the directors. A careful, comparative analysis of yields on bonds and preferred stocks would reveal that preferred yields are as stable as bond yields. The bond yields in Chart 3–2 demonstrate no greater a degree of stability than the preferred yields, by quality, in Table 5–3. The stability of preferred yields is also reflected in Chart 5–1. From 1960 through 1968 yields on preferreds have ranged from 4 to 5 percent and have been much more stable than those on common stocks. Yields on both preferred stocks and long-term bonds moved up sharply in 1967 and early 1968, bond yields to a higher level than the stock yields. This was brought about by the severe tightness of money during that period.

The stability of yields suggests also a price stability somewhat greater than that of common stocks and possibly more stable than bonds, if the preferred stock is high quality. This stability of price and of income makes these securities attractive for individuals and institutions that require these features. The stability of price and yield on preferreds, however, particularly the lower-grade preferreds, still depends

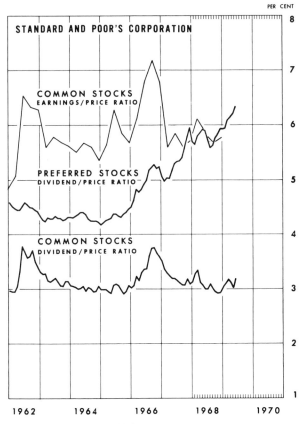

CHART 5–1

Corporate security yields, stocks—earnings ratio, end of quarter; dividend ratio, monthly

SOURCE *Federal Reserve Monthly Chart Book,* July, 1969, p. 29

on business conditions and conditions in the stock market. Convertible preferred stock would be affected more by conditions in the stock market than by those in the money market. When a good quality preferred possessing stability of yield can be purchased to yield 6 percent, it should be considered a satisfactory income investment. In times of stock market uncertainty, preferred stock with stable revenues and a relatively high rate of return comes into its own.

Analysis of Preferred Stock

When we analyze preferred stocks, what should we consider? The substance of the preferred-stock pledge is security of principal and security of income. We then must examine both these attributes—the earnings and the assets of the preferred stock—on a per share basis. Most preferred stocks have preference to assets in liquidation; hence, we must learn if the net assets per share are adequate to cover the par or stated value of the stock should the company fail. Since dividends are declared and paid before common dividends, we must know the amount of earnings per share available for the preferred stock and also the extent to which the earnings per share cover the preferred dividend requirements.

Assets Per Share

Assets per share of preferred stock are significant in determining liquidating value. One promise of preferred is the right to receive assets before the common stock of the company is liquidated. It is important to know whether the book value will be adequate to repay the par value of preferred stock. If so, then we can consider the stock adequately secured and protected. The book value or net assets per share is found by subtracting all debt from the total assets of the company and then dividing by the number of shares of preferred outstanding. Assume, for example, that a company has total assets of $110 million and short- and long-term liabilities of $50 million, leaving a net asset balance of $60 million. Assume further that there are 1,000,000 shares of $10 par preferred stock outstanding. The net asset value per share would be $60; this would cover par value six times. Such coverage would provide sufficient assets to repay preferred stockholders par value should the company be liquidated.

The company promises to repay the par or stated value of preferred stock only if the company is liquidated. If book value covers par value two or three times, this is adequate asset protection under normal circumstances. The marketability of the assets owned by the company, however, will determine whether the preferred stock is adequately secured. In case of liquidation, marketable assets are better security than assets that are difficult to sell. We must therefore determine not only the number of times net assets per share will cover book value but whether the book value figure is realistic in terms of the actual market value of the assets owned by the company. In our assumed case, the assets were valued at $110 million, however, in liquidation, they would bring only $80 million. The liquidating value of the company then is actually lower than the balance sheet value. The liquidating value of the preferred stock would also be less. It would drop to $30 million or $30 per share ($80–50 million, divided by 1,000,000 shares of $10 par value). Asset coverage remains more than adequate, but it is much less than the book value figures indicate.

If there is adequate asset coverage, preferred stock will be more secure. Adequate asset coverage exists when the dollar amount of preferred stock is small in relation to total assets; when net assets are liquid and marketable; and when there are few senior securities with prior claim on the assets of the company.

Dividend Coverage

The investor who buys preferred stock is interested in stability of income, and for this reason, might be more interested in the safety of his dividend than net assets per share. If the company is able to maintain adequate earnings on each share outstanding, the dividend will be secure. If a dividend is declared, it will be given first to the preferred stockholders. The dividend coverage ratio, a guide to the security of preferred stock dividends, is found by dividing the dollars of dividend into the net income per share after taxes. It may also be computed on a total basis, but before common dividends have been paid. It is expressed as the number of times contingent charges are earned. In the case mentioned above, 1,000,000 shares of preferred stock had been issued. Let us assume that the company had a net income of $2,500,000 after taxes. The preferred stock has a dividend rate of 5 percent, or $.50 per share, for a total dividend requirement of $500,000. Net income per preferred share was $2.50, and the dividend requirement of $.50 per share would result in a dividend coverage ratio of five times. Under normal circumstances, a two- or three-to-one dividend coverage ratio is entirely adequate for preferred stock. Thus, the times-contingent-charge earned ratio of five to one is adequate.

Where preferred stock represents only a small part of the capital structure, earnings per share will be extremely high and will provide adequate coverage for the investor's dividend, insuring stability of income. In 1968, for example, General Motors earned $610.80 per preferred share on the $5 and $3.75 preferred. We can see that the dividend on both preferreds is adequately secured. *Moody's Industrial Manual* computed the dividend coverage ratio on $5 GM preferreds for the investor as 133.95 times in 1968.[1] Most companies that issue preferred stock will not be in as good a financial position as General Motors. A

1 *Moody's Industrial Manual—American and Foreign,* July, 1969, p. 2284.

lesser coverage, however, will provide sufficient protection, and this has been achieved by many companies.

When two issues of preferred stocks are outstanding, the preferred dividends should be added together; and then the dividend coverage limit may be applied. If one preferred stock requires a dividend of $200,000 and another a dividend of $300,000, the dividends should be combined, and the net income after taxes should adequately secure both dividends equally. This method would be used even if one preferred stock had a prior claim over net income after taxes. The dividend coverage limit, when computed in this manner, provides a conservative measure of coverage.

When a bond issue is outstanding, the debt interest will take priority over preferred and common dividends. Where both bonds and preferred stocks are issued, interest charges and preferred dividends should be added together. Combined charges should be adequately covered by income. The total of interest charges and dividends is divided into net income after taxes to determine the number of times fixed charges and contingent charges have been earned. This is referred to as the times-fixed-and-contingent-charge earned ratio. It is easily computed by dividing total interest and dividend payments into net income after federal income taxes. Investment manuals such as Moody's and Standard & Poor's provide these figures for the investor, although they sometimes compute the ratio before taxes. The preferred stocks listed in Table 5–2 have a varying degree of earnings coverage of fixed and contingent charges. Most quality nonconvertible preferreds have adequate coverage; most of these companies earned the charges at least three times.

We should calculate interest and preferred dividend coverage and then preferred dividend coverage alone to determine how secure our preferred dividend stock will be. The computation should be made for several of the most recent years; one year is not sufficient to judge whether dividends are secure. This could be done for the companies listed in Table 5–2. An inadequate dividend coverage ratio or a ratio that fluctuates widely would not be satisfactory for our investment standards. The advantage of preferred stock ownership is its stability of income; if dividends are in jeopardy, then the investor will lose this advantage. The investor, in analyzing preferred stocks, should reject those that do not meet the dividend coverage requirements.

Preferred Stock Ratings

Standard & Poor's has developed quality ratings on preferred stocks similar to their bond ratings. The ratings represent a considered judgment of the relative security of dividends and the prospective yield stability of the stock. The ratings are: AAA, prime; AA, high grade;

A, sound; BBB, medium grade; BB, lower grade; B, speculative; and C, submarginal.

Preferred Stock as an Investment

When the subject of preferred stock is brought up in investment discussions, someone will always say that it is not a satisfactory investment. He will continue by saying that it is not attractive for the individual investor, that preferred stock should be purchased by institutions. When challenged, he will support his argument in the following way: "Preferred stocks are really a hybrid security. They do not possess the major advantage of common stock, which is the ability to share in the earnings of the company. Nor do they possess the major advantage of bond investment, which is security of principal and stability and security of income. Therefore, I cannot recommend them for the individual investor, and I'm not certain that institutions should invest a great deal of money in preferred stock either." If he were less charitable, he might state his case negatively by saying that preferred stocks possess all the disadvantages of common stocks and bonds and few of the advantages.

In many respects the critic is right. Preferred stock *is* a hybrid, it does not share in earnings of the company, nor does it have the security of a bond. However, this simply reflects its limitations for investment; its use is not completely precluded, and under some conditions is wholeheartedly encouraged. Some of the conditions in which different types of preferred stock might fit into an investor's portfolio will be discussed below.

Ordinary Preferred

Ordinary preferred stock is attractive to investors who want more income than they could receive from bonds. Usually the yield on high-grade preferred stocks is greater than that on investment-grade bonds above the Baa rating, and there is a comparable degree of price stability. These stocks would offer the investor somewhat more income with only a modest decrease in security. A high-quality preferred stock of a sound company with adequate asset and earnings coverage will be attractive for the investor having an immediate need for maximum current income and desiring stability as well. The high-grade preferred, as we have seen, does not fluctuate greatly in yield and follows closely the pattern of money rates. The major advantages of high-quality preferreds are (1) partial security from the business risk and (2) security from the market risk. Their major disadvantages lie in their inability to compensate adequately for the money rate risk and the purchasing-power risk.

Lower-grade preferred stocks offer larger income but also greater price instability. Their price range is much greater than that of preferred stock with the highest rating. Yields of almost 6 percent can be obtained on some speculative-grade preferreds, which are not as secure as high-quality preferreds. The investor must give up quality to obtain a high current yield. If the demand for current income is high, then lower-grade preferreds will satisfy the need. The investor must accept one additional degree of risk in getting additional income. Purchase of the lower-grade preferreds puts him in a position where he must accept the business risk. Additional income will compensate for, but not completely satisfy, the risk involved. Dividends on preferred stock do have a minor tax advantage over bond interest income. Preferred dividends can be offset by the dividend credit, whereas bond interest cannot be.

Thus, the investor who purchases speculative preferred stock accepts the market, business, and purchasing-power risk but eliminates the money rate risk, since this class of preferreds sells more like a common stock than a bond. The investor must balance his income needs against the additional risk he must assume.

Convertible Preferred Stock

Convertible preferred stock enjoys the advantage of being able to share in the profits of the corporation through capital growth of common stock. Such stocks offer the investor greater stability and security of income than do common stocks, and at the same time give an opportunity to hedge against loss of purchasing power caused by inflation if the common stock increases in price. High-grade convertible preferreds offer an opportunity to guard against purchasing-power risk. The investor retains the risk of loss, however, because of the business and market risks. Convertibles are not as susceptible to changes in the money rate as are top-rated preferred stocks. They provide good aggressive-defensive security for the investor and are an attractive investment when stock prices are high or when unusual uncertainty surrounds the market. Several times in the immediate past these conditions existed, and high-grade convertibles offered an ideal solution to this dilemma. In such cases, if the stock price rises, the price of the preferred will increase. The investor will share in the gain, since the preferred price moves with the price of common stock. Should the market decline, and along with it the price of common stock, preferred stock will then sell as regular preferred and will offer greater security of price than the common stock.

The investor must be careful about the price he pays for convertible preferred stock. If it is purchased at a substantial premium, it is vulnerable to the downward movement of prices. It is best to purchase a convertible preferred stock close to the original price or par value, or on an attractive yield basis, or if it is fairly priced in relation to common-stock expectations. Preferred stock will have more stability and security under these conditions, and will produce a good yield and an opportunity for capital gains, putting the investor in a favorable investment position.

A disadvantage of convertible preferred stock is that it might be called for redemption. Most preferred stock issued today, particularly convertible preferred, is callable at the option of the company. If it is called, the investor has the option of accepting the call or redemption price or converting his preferred stock into common stock. This will end his investment in preferred stock, and he will become either a common stockholder or the owner of an investable sum of cash. It will then be necessary to look for new investment opportunities. He may or may not have achieved the benefits he anticipated from preferred stock ownership. Of course, if he made money in the process of converting or in accepting the redemption price, he had a satisfactory investment.

Preferred Stock with Dividends in Arrears

Some investors consider preferred stock with large dividend arrearages an attractive outlet for their funds. They reason that the unpaid dividends might eventually be paid in cash, or the capitalization of the company might be changed and the dividend arrearages eliminated by issuing stock to replace the dividends. This type of reasoning may be true in certain unusual situations, but it does not generally hold. A company that has not paid current dividends from past earnings has not had sufficient earnings to meet its claims. The circumstances that created the arrearages in the first place often continue, so that these claims cannot be paid off in the future, and current dividends may not be paid. This is true of the majority of companies that have dividends in arrears. The investor who purchases the preferred with arrearages is speculating on the possibility of a windfall, which is unlikely to occur.

If the preferred dividend is eliminated by a recapitalization of the company, the investor continues to be in a relatively poor position. In the recapitalization process, preferred dividend arrearages are exchanged for either common or preferred stock. In some cases both the preferred stock and dividends are exchanged for a new preferred or a combination of preferred and common stock. These changes are made on the theory that the company will be able to afford to pay the new dividend rate on a regular basis. One typical arrangement is to exchange the old preferred with a new preferred having approximately the same dividend rate. The dividends in arrears are exchanged for common stock on which there is no dividend requirement. These changes help the company meet its immediate problem of being unable to pay dividends, but they usually impose more severe requirements on future dividends. The net effect is that the investor is in a junior position and does not receive any greater income than he would have if the recapitalization had not taken place. Preferreds with dividend arrearages are weak speculative securities that only on occasion offer the investor sufficient rewards to make them attractive for investment.

Summary

Preferred stock is an ownership security used infrequently by corporations to raise permanent capital. The preference concept arises from the nature of the agreement between the corporation and the preferred stock owners. Preferred stock has preference to the assets of the corporation over the common stock should the company be dissolved, liquidated, or merged. Preferred stock also has preference over common stock to the earnings of the company, and dividends on it must be paid before those on common stock. Preferred stock offers two promises: (1) a return of par or stated value in liquidation, and (2) a secure dividend superior in claim to the common dividend. In addition to its preference features, it is usually nonparticipating in the earnings of the company, but the earnings are cumulative. Preferred is nonvoting and has no maturity date, but a sinking fund and call feature are often provided for possible retirement of the stock.

Some investors consider preferred stock a hybrid security possessing all the disadvantages of debt and none of the advantages of common stock. However, we find in high-grade preferred stocks stability of income and security of principal. They do not share in the business or market risks to the extent of common stock. They do share the money rate and purchasing-power risks. High-grade preferreds offer higher yields than both common stock and bonds and would be satisfactory to meet needs of stability of income. Lower-grade preferreds offer higher income and are less affected by changes in the money rates, but are more susceptible to the business and market risks. This type of security offers greater current income relative to the size of the investment account.

Convertible preferred stocks offer not only income but the opportunity to share in the profits of the company. They are excellent securities for safety of income; they usually pay a higher dividend than common stocks; and they offer the possibility of appreciation. They possess the market and business risks but provide against the purchasing-power and money rate risks. They are a good aggressive-defensive security when the market is undecided. Preferred stocks with dividends in arrears offer a speculative opportunity for gain.

Review Questions

1. Discuss the nature of preferred stock and indicate the attributes that make it unique.
2. Describe the usual features of a preferred stock with respect to the typical rights given to it in the stock agreement.

3. Contrast the yield on preferred stock with that on government, municipal, and corporate bonds.

4. Comment upon the stability of the current yield on preferred stock.

5. Discuss the advantages and disadvantages of a convertible preferred stock for an investor.

6. Indicate how we can determine whether the preferred dividend is secure.

7. What would we emphasize in an analysis of preferred stock?

8. Under what circumstances would a preferred stock with dividends in arrears be an attractive investment?

9. Indicate the risks associated with the purchase for investment of preferred stock.

10. What special features does the Litton Industries stock presented in Fig. 4–1 possess?

Problems

1. What is the current level of yields for the following types of preferred stock?
   (a) High-grade industrial preferreds
   (b) High-grade utility preferreds
   (c) Convertible preferreds
   (d) Medium-grade industrial preferreds
   (e) Speculative-grade industrial preferreds
   (f) Medium-grade utility preferreds

2. Indicate the particular features of American Can 7% preferred stock (See Table 5–2). Is this a typical preferred? Comment.

3. (a) What is the current price of Cities Service $2.25 convertible preferred and its common stock?
   (b) What is the value of this preferred stock in terms of the common stock?
   (c) If we owned this preferred stock, would we be wise to convert? Explain.
   (d) What is the yield on this preferred stock?
   (e) How many times have fixed charges and preferred dividends been covered by current income?

4. Analyze the preferred stock of Litton Industries presented in Figure 4–1, Chapter 4, by answering the following questions:
   (a) What has been the net asset coverage per share for the period 1965 to the present?
   (b) How many times have preferred dividends been earned by net income after taxes from 1965 to the present?
   (c) If more than one preferred stock issue is outstanding, include the charges and compute dividend coverage from 1965 to the present.
   (d) Compute the number of times that net income covers the combined interest and dividend charges from 1965 to the present.
   (e) Is the preferred stock a good investment?

Sources of Investment Information

> Annual reports
> *Barron's*
> *Federal Reserve Bulletin*
> Moody's Manuals
> Standard & Poor's *Industry Surveys*
> Standard & Poor's *The Outlook*
> *Wall Street Journal*

Selected Readings

Schwartz, William, "Convertibles Get Realistic Image," *Financial Analysts Journal* (July-August, 1967), p. 55.

6

COMMON STOCK AS AN INVESTMENT

The security that offers the greatest rewards and the greatest risks is common stock; many individuals and institutions invest in it because of its advantages. Historically, the attitude toward common-stock ownership has varied from extreme optimism to extreme pessimism. In this chapter we will examine briefly the historical attitudes toward common-stock ownership. We will discuss the nature of such ownership, its advantages and disadvantages, the methods of valuation of common stock, and the part it might play in our own investment program. Emphasis will be on the analysis and selection of common stocks.

The Changing Attitude Toward Common-Stock Ownership

A major change in the attitude of individuals and institutions toward common-stock ownership has occurred in the past decade. The change has been favorable, and there are more common-stock owners today than at any time in the history of the New York Stock Exchange. Nowadays, when people discuss investment, they usually talk about common stock. There is also a predisposition toward common-stock ownership by those who do not own shares. The attitudes of investors, the environment in the United States, and the growing ability to invest, all favor common-stock ownership. What has brought this about? At times in the past, common stocks have been accepted and then rejected by the investing public. Before World War I the public actively invested in railroad shares. New issues of industrials and mercantile enterprises came into existence immediately after World War II, and the railroads declined in favor.

Interest at these times was modest compared with the bull market of the 1920's, when there was widespread public participation, ranking in impact with the speculative era of the Mississippi Bubble and the South Sea Bubble. The public became speculators, men mortgaged their homes and businesses to buy common stock. Everyone, including the Wall Street short-order cook, became an expert in the market. The relatively conservative investment rules of the past were swept aside, and common stocks were viewed as a method of getting rich quick. There was no limit to the height of the market because earnings and dividends and therefore prices would continue to move up ad infinitum. Then in October, 1929, the bubble burst and stocks tumbled down. A rally occurred shortly; then the market stopped its upward climb, shuddered, and dropped down until it reached a new low in 1932.

Those who had been so extremely confident about the ultimate success of common stock became completely disillusioned. Common stock lost its investment appeal, and investors began to look upon stock as a speculation, and not for the ordinary man. The market moved to higher ground between 1932 and 1936, but then it dropped again, even more sharply and suddenly than in 1929. Once again investors were disillusioned about common stock, those who did purchase it looked at the fundamentals rather than the promises.

Then World War II came, and common-stock prices were depressed. More interest was shown in winning a war and in government bonds than in the stocks and the market. World War II ended; everyone expected a postwar adjustment and its depression effects to lower stock prices. I remember vividly a conversation with my colleague, Dr. Henry Hawley, at the University of Maine in 1949. The Dow Jones Industrial Average was then close to 170. We discussed the market and concluded that it was too high. We had expected the postwar readjustment and lower prices. Of course, we were wrong. Gradually, from 1949 on, investor confidence increased. After 1955, the stock market surged forward, reaching an all-time high in 1961. In 1962, it dropped sharply, but by 1963, it had regained most of the lost ground, and once again there was interest in common stocks. This time, as before, investors talked about quality and fundamentals.

This brings us back to our original question, Why the interest in common stock? Basically several factors have brought it about. First, investors—individuals and institutions—have recognized the rewards of common-stock ownership. Many now believe the rewards overshadow the risks. Second, the government has taken a more active role in maintaining a high level of economic activity and employment, which has strengthened the economy and the securities market. Third, corporate earnings in the United States are more stable than in past periods, and the outlook for continued growth is much better than in the 1930's, 40's, and 50's. Fourth, the recognition by institutional investors of the value of common stock in their investment portfolios has helped to broaden common-stock ownership among individuals. Fifth, there has been greater emphasis by mutual fund managers upon performance and the measurement of performance.

The Nature of Common Stock

Fixed-income securities, such as debt, and contingent income securities, such as preferred stock, offer the investor stability of income but little capital appreciation potential, unless, of course, a special feature such as convertibility is added, allowing participation in future growth. Common stock is an ownership security. In reality, it guarantees nothing to the owner except the right to share in the earnings of the company. If earnings do not materialize or if losses are sustained, then the stockholder as a residual owner in the company must share the losses up to the asset value of the corporation. It is important that we realize the significance of this statement. Today we may be enthusiastic about the opportunities that exist through common-stock ownership, but we must be aware as well of the risks we assume—we might lose as well as gain. There is nothing certain about earnings on common stock, as we will learn.

Evidence of Ownership

Ownership of common stock is evidenced by a stock certificate, which is freely transferable by the owner. Established channels for transfer include the broker, who brings together buyer and seller, and the transfer agent, who transfers the stock of a company for a bona fide buyer or seller of securities and keeps an up-to-date list of stockholders on the books of the company. Figures 6–1 and 6–2 show the front and back of a common-stock certificate of the Armco Steel Company. On the front is such information as the name of the company, the number of shares represented by the certificate, the name of the owner, the type of stock, if it is fully paid and nonassessable, whether it has a par value or is no par, the registrar, the transfer agent, and the signature of the treasurer and the president of the company. The back of the certificate provides a form that must be completed by the seller when he transfers his stock.

If we purchase common stock, we can allow our broker to keep the certificate in "street" name for convenience and safety. This means that our certificates will be held by the brokerage firm for our account.

FIGURE 6-1

Specimen stock certificate—front

164

ARMCO STEEL CORPORATION

SHARES OF OTHER CLASSES ARE AUTHORIZED. A STATEMENT OF THE EXPRESS TERMS, PROVISIONS AND PREFERENCES OF THE SHARES OF SUCH OTHER CLASSES IS ON FILE WITH THE TRANSFER AGENT. THE COMPANY WILL FURNISH WITHOUT CHARGE, WITHIN FIVE DAYS AFTER RECEIPT OF WRITTEN REQUEST THEREFOR, TO EACH SHARE-HOLDER WHO SO REQUESTS A PRINTED COPY OF THE EXPRESS TERMS, PROVISIONS AND PREFERENCES OF EACH CLASS OF SHARES OR SERIES THEREOF WHICH THE COMPANY IS AUTHORIZED TO ISSUE.

The following abbreviations, when used in the inscription on the face of this certificate, shall be construed as though they were written out in full according to applicable laws or regulations:

TEN COM	—as tenants in common	UNIF GIFT MIN ACT — ....Custodian..............
TEN ENT	—as tenants by the entireties	(Cust) (Minor)
JT TEN	—as joint tenants with right of	under Uniform Gifts to Minors
	survivorship and not as tenants	Act.................................
	in common	(State)

Additional abbreviations may also be used though not in the above list.

For value received, _____ *hereby sell, assign and transfer unto*

PLEASE INSERT SOCIAL SECURITY OR OTHER
IDENTIFYING NUMBER OF ASSIGNEE

PLEASE PRINT OR TYPEWRITE NAME AND ADDRESS OF ASSIGNEE

_____ *Shares*
*of the capital stock represented by the within Certificate, and do hereby irrevocably constitute and appoint*_____

Attorney to transfer the said stock on the books of the within-named Corporation with full power of substitution in the premises.
*Dated,*_____

NOTICE: THE SIGNATURE TO THIS ASSIGNMENT MUST CORRESPOND WITH THE NAME AS WRITTEN UPON THE FACE OF THE CERTIFICATE, IN EVERY PARTICULAR, WITHOUT ALTERATION OR ENLARGEMENT OR ANY CHANGE WHATEVER.

THIS SPACE MUST NOT BE COVERED IN ANY WAY

FIGURE 6–2

Specimen stock certificate—back

When dividends are paid or annual reports and rights are received, the broker must credit our account or notify us. When we wish to sell the stock, we merely call the broker; he sells the stock and credits the proceeds to our account. If we elect to receive the stock certificate directly, when we sell the stock we must complete the form on the back of the certificate or sign a separate power of attorney. If we sell our stock through a broker, he will be appointed as attorney to transfer it. We do this by placing the broker's name on the line between *appoint* and *attorney*. (See Figure 6–2.) We date and sign the certificate and send it to our broker, usually by registered mail. If the broker wishes to transfer the stock to a buyer, he need only fill in the name of the person to whom it will be transferred and send it to the transfer agent. If we wish to sell stock to another individual directly, we must enter the name and address of the buyer who is to receive the stock. We then have his signature verified by a bank having a New York correspondent or by a brokerage firm and send the certificate to the transfer agent. Within a few weeks a new certificate will be sent to the new owner.

Many people lose securities each year or have them stolen. Since it is costly and time-consuming to replace them, certificates should be kept in a safe place. If they are lost, stolen, or otherwise destroyed, the transfer agent should be notified immediately. A new share may be obtained by filling out an evidence of loss form and by posting bond obtained from a casualty insurance company. The cost of the bond is based on the market value of the number of shares represented by the certificate. It is usually a perpetual bond and costs approximately 5 percent of the market value of the stock at the time of loss.

Maturity of Common Stock

Common stock has no maturity date; its life is limited by the length of time stated in the corporate charter. The corporate life might be for a stated or limited period, or it might be perpetual. Most corporations have a perpetual charter, which means there is no maturity date for the common stock. While some corporations do buy their own stock for various reasons, this is done in the market place, and not by a right retained by the corporation when the stock was originally sold.

Voting in the Modern Corporation

The owners of common stock have the right to elect the directors of the corporation and to vote on other important corporate matters. Granting stock options for management, approving mergers, issuing debt securities, waiving the right to subscribe to new shares, changing the par value of the stock, and increasing the authorized capital of the company are all matters upon which owners may—indeed, should—vote. In some cases the right to vote is taken away from a portion of common stock. Class A and Class B common, for example, are sometimes issued; one class usually has complete voting rights and the other limited rights or none at all. Historically, the nonvoting class of common stock was issued to allow the original voting stockholders to maintain control: nonvoting stock could be sold to raise additional money without losing control of the company.

Nonvoting shares are seldom used today for this purpose, as certain institutional changes have tended to work against their use. One of the conditions for listing on the New York Stock Exchange, for example, is that all common shares have voting rights. Since 1957 the Exchange may delist companies having nonvoting common stock that is being traded off the Exchange. In order not to jeopardize the privileges and advantages that go with listing, companies will not issue nonvoting stock for trading in the over-the-counter market.

Florida Telephone, traded over-the-counter, is an example of a company having two classes of stock outstanding. Its Class B common stock has limited voting rights, while Class A has full voting rights. The same is true of the Westgate-California Corporation, which has a Class B stock that does not have voting rights. Sometimes, however, Class B stock has the right to vote and Class A does not. Standard Milling has nonvoting Class A stock outstanding and a Class B voting stock.

What impact does the nonvoting feature have upon the market price of the stock? This question cannot be answered with certainty, but currently nonvoting shares seem to sell for a lower price than voting shares. This was true for Standard Milling. In 1969, its class B, the voting stock ranged from 3 to 6 1/2, and the Class A common (nonvoting) ranged from 3 to 6 1/4—a 1/4 point differential in price between voting and nonvoting stock.

ORDINARY AND CUMULATIVE VOTING

Typically, each share of common stock has one vote. This is referred to as ordinary voting. If we owned 100 shares of General Motors common stock, we would have 100 votes on corporate matters. In electing directors at the annual stockholders' meeting we would have the right to cast 100 votes for each of the number of directors to be elected; if fifteen were to be elected, we could cast 100 votes for each director. Some corporations allow cumulative voting, which would confer the right to vote our 100 shares for each director, or if we wish, to cast all our votes for one. If we were to elect fifteen GM directors, for example, we could cast 100 votes for each director or 1500 for one director. We could divide our total 1500 votes among the candidates in any way we saw fit. The advantage of this type of voting is that it allows a minority group of shareholders or an individual holding a large amount of stock to be represented on the board of directors. Under ordinary voting, a person with 49 percent of control fighting a group with 51 percent of control would be unable to elect a single director. With cumulative voting, the minority would be able to elect slightly less than half the number of directors. This is not a point of great concern for most small investors in large American corporations. It is important, however, to a large minority group of stockholders to whom control is important. The right to vote should not, however, be ignored nor should its importance be minimized by any stockholder. We must vote as we think best for our own needs and for the objectives of the company. And while this can be done only to the limit of our ownership in the company, giving up the right to vote is giving away a privilege of ownership.

Par Value

Like preferred stock, common stock can be par or no-par. If it is no-par, it can have a stated value at which it is carried on the company's books. Most corporations tend to place a low par value upon their shares. This gives them the advantage of paying low state excise and franchise fees when these are based on the par value of the stock. But many states tax no-par shares at $100 par, which makes it costly to issue no-par shares. Another advantage of low par value shares is the flexibility they provide in issuing new shares. Shares must be sold at or above par value. A low par value permits them to be sold at a price related to their market price. A high par value of, say, $100 might make it difficult or impossible to sell the stock if the market price was $80. A par value of $2 would allow the shares to be sold at $80 without any difficulty. The common stock of Litton Industries (see Figure 4–1) is a $1.00 par stock.

A low par value also dispenses with the idea that the common stock holder will receive a fixed amount of money if the company is liquidated. As residual owner, the common stockholder cannot expect to receive a fixed-dollar amount. A $100 par value common stock gives the impression that $100 should be available for distribution to the stockholder. This might not be the case. In any event a low par value focuses attention on earning power or earnings per share rather than on a par value that has little significance.

Book Value

A figure that has much more significance than par value is the book value per share. The book value of common stock is found by dividing the number of common shares outstanding into the total assets minus all debt and minus the value of preferred stock, when it exists. Some investors prefer to consider book value the net worth available for common stock. The figure obtained by using either method is divided by the number of shares of common stock outstanding. The book value figure provides us with some idea of the dollars per share that have been invested and that would be available should the company be liquidated. Of course, the book value is only an approximation, since the proceeds obtainable from assets sold in the marketplace might differ greatly from the book value of the assets.

Book value per share is often compared with market price by investors. This, however, is usually a poor guide to market value. The productivity of assets and a specific combination of assets and entrepreneurial ability often create greater earnings and greater values than the book value of the assets suggests. Where assets have greater value if sold in the marketplace than they have in their present and specific use for profit, we might consider book value to be significant. It would be better to liquidate such a company than to continue it as an operating unit.

Dividends on Common Stock

Owners of common stock have the right to receive dividends. The financial position of the company must justify the dividend, and the board of directors must also approve and declare the dividend. The amount and manner of payment will be decided by the company management and the board of directors, based upon the needs of the company. The dividend is not a contractual obligation between corporation and stockholder. Its amount is not fixed as a certain percentage of par value or as a stated number of dollars per share. The amount and type of dividend will depend upon the earnings of the company, its financial position, and the need for funds for investment in new plant and equipment. An established dividend policy suggests a fixed dividend rate; we can say, under these conditions, that a dividend is "certain." A company that pays a regular cash dividend can be said to have a fixed dividend policy of paying cash, even though the amount of the dividend will vary. One of the single most important characteristics of most common stock is the variability of the dividend and the variability of the factors that contribute to dividend policy over a long period of time. The dividend might increase as the company prospers, or it might decrease with financial adversity. It is the exceptional company that maintains the same dividend rate over a period of time.

The Cash Dividend

The cash dividend is the most familiar and expected type paid on common stock. Ordinarily, the word *dividend* is synonymous with *cash,* unless a company follows a different practice. It is not unusual to read, for example, that the dividend paid to stockholders is in the form of a 3 percent dividend based on the market value of the stock. The writer, in making such an announcement, does not bother to say a cash dividend, since it is assumed that a cash disbursement will be made. If another type of dividend is paid, then it is identified as either a stock dividend or a property dividend. In an ordinary year, more than 80 percent of the common stocks listed on the New York Stock Exchange will pay some cash dividend. More than a dozen companies have paid dividends for over a century, either in the form of stock or cash; the majority have been paid in cash. The First National City Bank, for example, has paid a dividend every year since 1813. Table 6–1 lists companies that have paid a dividend for over 100 years. These companies and others listed in Standard & Poor's *Stock Guide* have established an enviable dividend record.

The amount of the cash dividend is usually established in relation to the earnings and cash flow per share. The amount of the dividend that is a percentage of current earnings is referred to as the payout ratio. This ratio varies over time and from industry to industry. United States corporations pay out approximately 60 percent of their earnings in dividends—manufacturing corporations about 55 percent, railroads 12 percent, electric power companies about 75 percent, and telephone companies approximately 70 percent.

These figures are considered typical of the various industry groups over the past few years, even though payout ratios have varied over longer periods of time. The trend of railroads has been toward a higher payout ratio, and telephone companies have moved toward a lower one. Electric utilities have had relatively stable payout ratios; their historic rate is close to the levels mentioned above. This is true also for all corporations in the manufacturing category. Actual payout rates will vary from year to year depending upon economic conditions, the needs

TABLE 6–1

*Some companies that have paid dividends
each year for 100 years or more*

COMPANY	YEAR DIVIDENDS FIRST PAID
First National City Bank (N.Y.)	1813
First Penna. Banking & Trust	1828
Chase Manhattan Bank	1848
Providence Gas Company	1849
Manufacturers Hanover Trust	1852
Pepperell Manufacturing Co.	1852
Cincinnati Gas & Electric	1853
Springfield Gas Light	1853
Continental Insurance Co.	1854
United States Trust Co. of New York	1854
Scoville Manufacturing Company	1856
Agricultural Insurance Co.	1864
American News Co.	1864
Tranter Manufacturing Co.	1864

SOURCE: Standard & Poor's *Stock Guide*, August, 1969, p. 198.

of the company, and the expectations of the stockholders. During periods of economic recession, many companies maintain dividends payments even though they have no earnings. This results in a payout ratio of over 100 percent—a situation that occurred in the early 1930's.

The cash flow of a company can also be used as a guide to dividend policy. Cash flow per share is used as a broader measure of profitability than earnings per share. Cash flow is computed by adding depreciation, depletion allowances, and other noncash costs to the company's net income after taxes. This figure represents the return of profits from the company's investments, and it includes the return of capital as measured partially by investment in plant and equipment. The cash flow of companies in general has increased steadily and become more stable in recent years. This is somewhat different from the trend of corporate earnings after taxes.

Dividends tend to bear a more stable relationship to cash flow than to earnings after taxes. Therefore, when we purchase common stock for investment, we must consider cash flow as well as earnings per share to anticipate the future level of dividends.

Stock Dividends

The stock dividend is another type of dividend that may be paid on common stock. It is usually given as a percentage of the number of existing common shares outstanding. A 2 percent stock dividend would give the holder of 100 shares of common stock two additional shares. Stock dividends are given in the same type of share owned by the stockholder. If another type of security is given as a dividend it is technically considered a property dividend or an unlike stock dividend, and is therefore fully and immediately taxable as income, whereas the tax on like dividends is paid when the stock is sold, and then only as a capital gain.

Stock dividends are frequently used by smaller companies and growth companies. Stock of such companies is more likely to be traded on the over-the-counter market and on the smaller stock exchanges than on the New York Stock Exchange, where the majority of the companies listed pay cash dividends. Approximately 8 percent of the companies covered in Standard & Poor's *Stock Guide* pay some form of stock dividend, while only 3 percent of the companies listed on the New York Stock Exchange do so.

Stock dividends are issued by companies that wish to conserve cash in order to purchase equipment and plant facilities or to invest in inventory and receivables, to insure continued growth of the enterprise. A rapidly expanding growth company can use every dollar of cash it can generate to finance increasing sales. If a growth company did pay out dividends in cash obtained from cash sales and the collection of receivables, it would have to turn to the capital markets for funds, either borrowed or obtained by selling equity securities. The cost of obtaining funds, particularly through the sale of common stock, would be increased, since the expenses of registration and selling are substantial. So, rather than incurring additional expenses, the company simply retains its earnings. These earnings are acknowledged by issuing new shares of stock in an amount equal to the total dividend. The effect is to increase the amount of outstanding stock, which capitalizes the retained earnings. The stock dividend gives the share owner tangible evidence that his earnings have been permanently retained in the business, and the company has managed to maintain its cash position and its expansion program.

The Camden Trust Company of New Jersey provides us with an example of some of the mechanics involved in the declaration of a stock dividend. Its board of directors declared a 5 percent stock dividend on the capital stock of the company. The dividend was payable June 28, 1968, to stockholders of record at the close of business June 5, 1968, The board also stated that no fractional shares would be issued. Each shareholder entitled to a fractional share received an order card on which to indicate whether the fractional share should be sold or a fractional share purchased to allow him to receive one additional share. A trust company was named as agent to purchase and sell the fractional shares. If no order card was received from the stockholder, the trust company assumed that the stockholder wanted his fractional shares sold, and the dollar proceeds of the sale were sent to him.

STOCK DIVIDENDS AND STOCK SPLITS

The percentage rate for the usual stock dividend is below 10 percent, 2 to 5 percent being typical. A stock dividend above 25 percent is usually referred to as a stock split. There is, however, a technical difference between a stock dividend and a stock split. The usual stock dividend is reflected in the company's balance sheet by an increase in the amount of capital stock items and a decrease in the amount of retained earnings in the ownership or capital account and the book value per share is reduced. In the case of a stock split, the dollar amount of the capital stock account remains the same, the number of shares of stock increases, and the book value is reduced. A 25 percent stock dividend and a 5 for 4 stock split have the same effect upon book value. The 25 percent dividend increases the value of the capital account as well as the number of shares; the value of the capital account in a stock split remains the same, but the number of shares increases by 25 percent, with a lower capital value per share. Typical rates for stock splits are 3 for 2, 2 for 1, and 3 for 1. IBM, for example, has used a 2 for 1 and a 3 for 2 rate. The immediate effect of a stock split or a large stock dividend is to lower the price per share. The long-range effect is to provide a wider distribution of the shares at a more marketable price. Stock splits are helpful and profitable for the investor only if earnings and dividends continue to grow and result in higher stock prices.

STOCK DIVIDENDS AND FEDERAL INCOME TAXES

The Internal Revenue Code states that a stock dividend is exempt from federal income tax until the stock is sold. The dividend does not affect the tax base of the investor. A 10 percent stock dividend on 100 shares lowers the per-share cost and the tax base on the total 100 shares. If, for example, an investor paid $50 per share for 100 shares of stock, for tax purposes his cost basis per share would be $50. After the 10 percent stock dividend is declared, the investor spreads his cost over 110 rather than 100 shares, and his cost basis becomes $45.45 ($5,000 ÷ 110) per share. If the stock is sold subsequently, the adjusted cost becomes the tax basis from which the investor's taxable gains or losses are determined. There is no immediate tax effect when the stock dividend is paid.

If an investor sells his stock dividend shares or his fractional shares, there will also be a change in his tax base. The change will place the stock dividend in a position where it will be taxed as either a long-term gain or loss depending on the basis of computing the fractional interest and the holding period of the stock upon which a stock dividend was paid. Assume, in the example above, that the investor sold his 10 shares at $55. Would he pay federal income taxes on $550 or on only a fraction of that amount? The investor's cost basis was calculated to be $45.45 per share, and he would be required to pay a capital gains tax on the per-share difference between $55 and $45.45. He would pay tax on $9.55 per share times 10 shares or $95.50. If he had held the stock for more than six months, the gain would be taxable as a long-term capital gain. If it were held for less than six months, the gain would be a short-term capital gain and taxed as ordinary income. The method for computing such gain is set forth in the Internal Revenue Code.

SIGNIFICANCE OF STOCK DIVIDENDS

Some controversy exists over the importance and significance of stock dividends. If the company's stock maintains its market price, then payments of stock dividends offer several distinct advantages to the stockholder. They allow him to receive a dividend without the burden of paying income tax on it, as would be necessary with cash dividends. A wealthy investor would not have his current dividend income taxed at high rates. Or, if after six months, he sold the shares representing the dividend, he would pay a capital gains tax lower than his ordinary tax rate. Another advantage of greater share ownership is that it allows the investor's capital to grow at a compounded rate if the present dividend rate is maintained. Some people maintain that stock dividends merely give the stockholder something he has already received, that is, retained earnings that will be invested and allowed to grow to improve and build up his equity. Why then, they ask, is it necessary to pay any dividend at all? It is difficult to come to a definite conclusion about the value of a stock dividend; but a company that manages to continue its growth will, through a policy of stock dividends, allow the investor to improve his financial position and his tax position as well.

No amount of stock dividends, however, will turn a company with declining earnings into an investment success. Stock dividends are desirable when a company must conserve cash or is experiencing rapid growth; where per-share earnings and price will not be diluted; and where the investor is in a tax bracket where cash dividends are not wanted. Many companies paying only a stock dividend are in the savings and loan field. Table 6–2 lists some companies that pay only stock dividends.

Cash and Stock Dividends

Some companies pay a dividend of cash and stock that is attractive to all stockholders. The company recognizes that a policy of paying some dividends is desirable, and that some people desire stock dividends for tax advantages. The company itself might wish to conserve its cash for

TABLE 6–2

*Selected companies traded on the NYSE that
paid stock dividends in 1967*

PRICE RANGE JAN. 1–MAY 27, 1968		COMPANY	RECORD DATE	PAY-MENT DATE	DIVI-DEND RATE	EARN-INGS 1967 OR LATEST FISC. YR.
HIGH	LOW					
32 7/8	21 3/8	APCO Oil Corp.	12-9-67	1-31-68	4%	$2.37
62	42	Coastal States Gas	12-8-67	1-8-68	10	2.55
35 5/8	29 5/8	Cook Coffee	11-24-67	12-15-67	3	3.61
37 3/4	29	Crowell-Collier & Macmillan	9-26-67	11-14-67	4	2.21
63	22 1/2	DuPlan Corp.	12-26-67	1-15-68	2 3/4	.71
38 7/8	37	Eastern Gas & Fuel	12-1-67	12-29-67	3	3.52
35	21 3/4	First Charter Financial	10-25-67	12-14-67	5	1.42
63 1/4	40 1/8	General Instrument	4-24-67	5-24-67	2	2.18
34 1/4	19 1/2	Gibraltar Financial	4-3-67	5-1-67	5	1.70
19 1/2	11	Hotel America	12-26-67	1-26-68	5	.65
87	54	Kidde & Company	12-12-67	12-29-67	3	3.20
104 3/4	62	Litton Industries	9-29-67	11-15-67	2 1/2	2.54
16 3/8	11 3/8	Marquardt Corp.	1-12-68	2-2-68	2	.26
11 1/4	5 7/8	Publicker Industries	8-31-67	9-29-67	5	.17
37 1/4	23 1/8	Vornado, Inc.	11-20-67	12-20-67	2	1.83
51 3/4	33 1/2	Ward Foods	10-16-67	11-16-67	3	2.83

SOURCE: *Barron's*, May 27, 1968, pp. 49–56.

reinvestment in plant or working capital. Marathon Oil Company and IBM are good examples of companies that pay cash and stock as dividends. Marathon Oil has paid stock dividends from time to time since 1940, but not in every year. In 1962, Marathon paid a 2 percent stock dividend in addition to its cash dividend. In 1968, it paid a regular dividend of $1.60 per share. IBM has paid some dividends since 1916, and in 1968, it was paying a $2.20 annual cash dividend. In the past IBM has paid stock dividends as part of its regular dividend policy. Many corporations listed on the New York Stock Exchange pay some cash and some stock. Next to cash dividends alone this is the second most important form of dividend. Several of the more familiar companies that have paid both cash and stock dividends are listed in Table 6–3.

Dividend Policies

Typically, a dividend is either cash, stock, or a combination of both. Some companies, however, do not pay dividends at all because they wish

TABLE 6–3

Some representative companies that paid both
cash and stock dividends in 1968

PRICE RANGE JAN.–MAY 27, 1968		COMPANY	RECORD DATE	PAY-MENT DATE	DIVIDEND RATE		EARN-INGS 1967 OR LATEST FISC. YR.
HIGH	LOW						
33	22	Evans Products	1-29	2-15	4%	.60	2.29
32	21 3/8	Foster Wheeler	2-15	3-15	5%	.60	2.00
76 1/2	56 1/4	Georgia Pacific	2-9	3-26	1%	1.00	2.68
75 3/8	48 1/8	Metromedia, Inc.	2-23	3-15	2%	.80	3.15
48	43 1/4	National Starch & Chemical	2-9	3-11	5%	.80	2.13
44 1/2	29	Occidental Petroleum	3-15	4-16	2%	.40	1.01
63 7/8	43 1/2	Pittston Co.	1-10	2-9	3%	1.20	3.50
60	41 7/8	Disney Productions	3-15	4-1		.30	2.52
59 1/4	43 3/4	Columbia Broadcasting	3-1	3-15		1.40	2.14
33 7/8	24 7/8	Bulova Watch Co.	3-8	3-29	2%	.80	2.01
38 3/4	27 1/2	Purex Corp.	3-13	3-31		.72	1.34
37 5/8	26 1/8	Rexall Drug	2-9	3-6		.30	1.93
61 1/4	39 1/2	SCM Corp.	1-2	1-22		.60	3.13
53	24 1/4	Shulton, Inc.	3-4	4-1		.80	2.50
23	16 1/2	Southeastern Public Service	3-15	4-1		1.08	1.46
71 5/8	61	Standard Oil of Ohio	2-16	3-11		2.50	5.22
58 1/8	43 7/8	Transamerica Corp.	4-10	5-27	4%	1.00	2.78
72	53 3/4	U.S. Smelting, Refining & Mining	12-27	1-15	5%	1.00	4.79
53 7/8	45	White Motor Corp.	3-6	3-20		2.00	4.43

SOURCE: *Barron's*, May 27, 1968.

to retain the funds for expansion. They do not think it necessary to formalize the retention of earnings by declaring a stock dividend and would argue that there were no advantages in issuing more shares, thereby imposing a burden on management to maintain future earnings. If earnings could not be maintained, the dilution effect would take place. (The retained earnings, when invested, earn a smaller amount than previously invested funds, hence earnings are said to be diluted.) Or companies may not pay dividends because they cannot afford them with their present and future expectations of profit. Perhaps the company is in receivership or is being reorganized. Hydromatics, Inc., traded on the American Stock Exchange, is an example of a company that did not pay dividends in such a situation.

PROPERTY DIVIDENDS

Some companies, from time to time, declare property dividends. When Du Pont distributed its GM stock to its shareholders, the GM stock could have been classed a property dividend. Usually this type of dividend is the personal property of the company and takes the form of securities of other companies, or of one of the products of the company. A typical property dividend would be the stock of a subsidiary owned by the parent company. Rather than pay a dividend in its own stock, the parent company distributes stock of the subsidiary company to the parent company shareholders, to conserve cash and to effect a permanent change in the company structure.

Usually a property dividend is temporary and cannot be counted upon by stockholders as a permanent type of dividend. The tax upon property stock dividends is different from that on regular stock dividends. Property dividends are taxable as income to the investor. They are treated, for tax purposes, as a cash dividend. Very few companies today pay property dividends to their owners in the form of shares of stock of other companies.

Occasionally, a company will pay a property dividend in the form of the product of the company. During World War II one company in the liquor industry gave each shareholder some of the liquor it had produced. During the war alcoholic beverages were scarce, and this made the dividend attractive to many shareholders. However, this was not a regular dividend and could not be continued as a permanent practice. The property dividend in the form of company products is seldom used today.

LIQUIDATING DIVIDENDS

Liquidating dividends can also be paid to the owners of common stock. This is not a type of dividend that will continue over a period of time, nor will it be paid regularly. It is a return of capital to the owners of the business. If the company is going out of business, it may distribute its assets to the owners as a liquidating dividend. A mining company that uses up its minerals and an oil company that uses up the oil in the ground are both engaged in business requiring that an asset be "wasted" to render its service to the final consumer. Depletion allows a business such as an oil company to recover the expense of the wasted asset. If the funds retained because of depletion are no longer needed, then they can be paid out to the owners. Since they represent a return of principal, they may be free from ordinary income taxes and subject only to capital gains taxes. (The 27 1/2 percent depletion allowance was reduced to 20 percent in 1969.) Some public utility companies, financial institutions, and investment companies distribute capital and capital gains to their shareholders, and these capital gains are also subject to capital gains taxes. A real estate company, by the same token, might distribute a dividend based upon a depreciation allowance that retains within the business funds that are not needed for current operation. A dividend of this type would not be subject to ordinary income taxes but would be taxed as a long- or short-term gain based on the tax base of the property distributed. These examples represent a partial liquidation of company assets.

SCRIP DIVIDENDS AND BOND DIVIDENDS

These must be included as special types of dividends that the investor may receive as an owner of common stock. A scrip dividend is usually given when a company is short of cash. It is in the form of a transferable promissory note that may or may not be interest bearing. The scrip continues as a liability of the company until it is paid. Scrip is justified where earnings exist to pay a dividend but where the company does not have money to pay the dividends. It is not used frequently.

In some instances, bonds or notes are used to pay a dividend on common stock. The stockholder becomes a creditor of the company just as in the case of the scrip dividend. The weakness of this is that a stockholder in the process of receiving the dividend actually changes his relationship to the company. He becomes a creditor rather than an owner, and his fundamental position has changed. Both scrip and bonds may be used to pay a dividend when, as a matter of conservative financial policy, none should be paid. An investor could interpret both types of dividends as a sign of financial weakness rather than as a benefit.

We will learn when we examine our individual needs and investment policies that the type of dividend paid will have an important bearing upon which companies' stock we buy. A company that follows a policy of paying cash and stock dividends appeals to many investors. However, an investor who wants no current income and maximum capital gains would not care much for this type of compromise dividend. The income investor, on the other hand, would not be satisfied by a

14 All-Alt **STANDARD & POOR'S CORPORATION**

INDEX	Ticker Symbol	STOCKS NAME OF ISSUE (Call Price of Pfd Stocks)	Market	Earns & Div Ranking	Par Val.	★ Inst. Hold Cos	★ Inst. Hold Shs. (000)	STOCK CHARACTERISTICS Principal Business	PRICE RANGE 1936-66 High	1936-66 Low	1967 High	1967 Low	1968 High	1968 Low	Apr. Sales in 100s	April, 1968 O-C Recent Bid Ask High	Low	Last	% Div. Yield	P-E Ratio
1	ALA	Allegheny Airlines, Inc.	ASE	C	1	3	104	Serves Middle Atlantic area	26⅜	1¼	20⅞	12⅞	19⅛	13⅛	979	19⅛	13⅛	17⅛	....	d
2	WS	Warrants (Purch 1 Com at $13)	ASE	NR	....	5	238	local service air carrier	16	8¼	16	8¼	11⅜	7¼	365	11⅜	7½	10⅝	....	..
3	AG	Allegheny Ludlum Steel	[4]NYS	A−	1	36	969	Stainless & alloy steels	79¼	a6½	79¼	55⅛	72¾	61	1013	69¾	61	62⅞	‡3.8	14
4	Pr	$3 cm Cv Pfd ([5]65) vtg	NYS	....	1	....	....	hand tools; sporting goods	79	69¼	79	69¼	76⅜	69¾	24	71⅜	69¾	69¾	4.3	..
5		Allegheny Pepsi Cola Bottling	UNL	B	50¢	....	....	Pepsi-Cola; makes soft drinks	a9	a2¾	a10⅜	a4½	10¾	a7⅝	....	....	10½B	11A	2.5	13
6	AYP	Allegheny Power System	NYS, Bo, PB, PC	A−	2½	128	2784	Controls group elec companies	31	a3⅜	27¾	21	24¼	20⅞	1879	23½	21¾	23⅛	5.2	13
7	AY	Allegheny & Western Ry., Gtd	NYS•	•B	100	3	0.8	Leased line by B&O System	134¾	28	107	91	102	92	1.5	92	92	92	6.5	..
8		Allen Aircraft Radio, Inc	UNL	NR	1	1	8	Overhauls, mfg's. nav/com. eq	....	....	23¾	11¼	15⅜	9½	....	....	13¼B	13¾A	....	d
9		Allen (R. C.) Business Machines	UNL	C	1	....	....	Business machs; typewriters	16	4	13	6	12¾	9¼	....	....	12¼B	12¾A	....	27
10	ALN	Allen Electric & Equip	ASE, MW, PC	B	1	3	39	Motor tune-up eq; accessories	31⅛	⅛	68⅛	17½	69⅞	31	2009	44½	34	39	....	23
11	ANL	Allen Industries, Inc.	NYS	B+	1	....	....	Auto upholstery: rug cushions	a36⅝	a1	28½	21½	31⅞	24¾	195	30½	26	29⅞	4.7	10
12		Allen Organ, Cl B non-vtg	UNL	NR	1	1	1	Mfr electronic organs	a24½	a5⅛	17¼	9½	11½	8½	....	....	11½B	12½A	‡1.2	18
13	ATR	Alliance Tire & Rubber, Cl A	ASE	NR	j10	....	....	Israel producer tires & tubes	12⅞	3	9¼	3⅛	10⅝	4⅝	106	9¼	8⅜	9	3.3	7
14		Allied Aero Industries, Inc.	UNL	NR	25¢	....	....	Aircraft engines; mkt planes	2⅞	⅝	7	2¼	6	3½	....	....	4¾B	5½A	....	13
15	AAP	Allied Artists Pictures	ASE, PC	C	1	....	....	Motion picture producer	a9½	a¼	13⅜	1⅝	25	9¾	3205	13¾	10¾	12⅞	....	5
16	ACD	Allied Chemical Corp.	[3]NYS	A−	9	279	2647	Basic chemicals; plastics, fibers	66¼	a14¾	46⅞	33¼	43	34	9396	37½	34	36⅜	5.2	15
17	ACC	Allied Control Co.	ASE	B−	50¢	....	....	Makes relays and elec coils	a33	a3⅞	61¾	20¾	38½	27	1632	38½	28½	29⅝	†1.8	12
18		Allied Equities Corp.	UNL	NR	1	4	29	Precision castings; tankers	a70	a¼	22	10¼	16¼	9½	....	....	12¾B	13¼A	...	15
19		Allied Farm Equipment, Inc. Cl A	UNL	NR	1	....	....	Whlse farm eq, machy; mfg	7½	6	8	5	7	5	....	....	5½B	6A	‡...	11
20	AKD	Allied Kid Co.	NYS	B	5	....	....	Leather processor; 'Corfam'	21½	a3½	30¼	15¼	33¼	24½	217	29¼	25½	28	3.6	12
21		Allied Maintenance	UNL	NR	3	6	47	Cleaning serv; plane fueling	57½	12¾	38¼	13	47½	35¾	....	....	47½B	48½A	1.6	25
22	ADS	Allied Mills, Inc.	NYS	B+	No	6	0.8	Live stock & poultry feeds	58	8⅝	53¼	47½	49	44¼	29	45¾	44⅜	45¾	4.4	10
23	ADP	Allied Products Corp.	NYS, Bo	B	5	18	447	Fasteners, auto dies; invests	70½	a1¼	60⅜	26½	63¾	37¾	1383	50¼	40⅝	48	1.3	20
24	Pr	$3 cm Cv Ptc Pfd (100 fr '73)vtg	NYS	...	No	....	....	alum windows, bldg panels	....	....	....	....	114	77	26	98	84	94½	3.2	..
25	ALS	Allied Stores	NYS, Bo, Ci, PB	B+	No	61	938	Large company in depart-	a36	a1⅝	41½	22⅛	49½	35⅝	3432	49½	41¾	49	2.9	15
26	Pr	4% cm Pfd (100; SF100) vtg	NYS•	BBB	100	33	108	ment store field; nationwide	108	69½	77¾	64	68	64	5.5	68	64	66½	6.0	..
27	ASU	Allied Supermarkets	NYS, De, PC	B	1	15	332	Food mkts; Midwest	24¾	9¾	24	11	22	16⅛	2008	18⅛	16⅛	16⅝	3.6	16
28		Allied Thermal Corp.	UNL	NR	12½	1	4	Holding co., heating eqp mfrs	a36	a9½	43	26	41	34½	....	....	38½B	40A	‡3.8	10
29	AH	Allis-Chalmers Mfg. Co.	[1]NYS	B	10	34	412	Power, industrial, farm eq	a41¾	a10⅞	44	21⅝	38⅛	28⅜	7481	34⅜	29⅛	30¾	3.3	83
30	ASE	Allison Steel Mfg. Co.	ASE	NR	2	....	....	Fabricate & erect steel	a7	a2⅞	15⅝	7	15½	12⅛	279	13¼	12¼	12¾	3.1	8
31	AU	Alloys Unlimited, Inc.	ASE, PB	NR	10¢	8	256	Semicond'r parts; contacts	a30⅜	a1⅜	49¾	18	49¼	32⅛	4577	46½	39⅛	45⅛	0.2	33
32	ALR	Allright Auto Parks	ASE	NR	1	4	22	Park'g: S-SW, RkyMt, WCoast	15¾	a8¼	16¾	9¾	19	13⅝	423	18⅜	15⅛	17¾	2.9	16
33		Allyn & Bacon, Inc.	UNL	B+	50¢	5	68	Textbooks; audio-visual aids	44½	a2¼	30½	18¾	26½	21	....	....	25½B	26½A	1.5	28
34		Aloe Creme Laboratories, Inc.	UNL	C	1	2	3	Cosmetics, sun tan, ointment	7⅝	1⅞	10¾	4⅞	9	5½	....	....	6½B	7A	....	d
35		Aloha Airlines, Inc.	UNL, Ho	NR	25¢	....	....	Inter-island air service	2¾	⅛	5	2½	5¼	2⅞	....	....	3¼B	3½A	....	88
36	AHA	Alpha Industries	ASE	NR	50¢	....	....	Microwave comp., assemblies	a3⅝	a2⅜	16¾	a3½	16½	10⅝	537	14¾	10⅝	13¾	....	42
37	APC	Alpha Portland Cement Co	NYS	B	10	1	0.3	One of leading cement makers	47	a2¾	14⅞	7¾	16	12	1659	16	12	15¼	....	61
38		Alpine Geophysical Associates	UNL	NR	10¢	4	72	Oceanographic surveys & eqp	26	1⅝	44	15½	34½	19	....	....	32B	34A	....	..
39	ALO	Alsco, Inc., Cl A	ASE	NR	1	3	27	Rkt launch, alum siding, furn	8¾	3¼	15½	6⅛	17⅜	9	974	14	9	11¾	....	6
40	ASD	Alside, Inc.	NYS	NR	No	....	....	Alumin lap siding & paneling	49¾	5½	15¼	5¾	14¾	10⅝	1240	14	11	12	1.7	14
41	ALW	Altamil Corporation	ASE	NR	50¢	5	90	Alum airframe components	17⅝	2⅜	28¾	10⅜	28½	16	1496	21⅝	16¼	18⅞	1.1	17
42	ALF	Alterman Foods, Inc.	ASE	B+	2½	5	74	Super mkt chain, Atlanta area	a23½	a7¼	17½	12⅞	20¼	14½	618	20¼	17⅜	20	2.5	12

Uniform Footnote Explanations—See Page 1. Other: [1]Bo, Ci, De, MW, PB, PC. [3]Bo, De, MW, PB, PC. [4]Bo, Ci, MW, PB, PC, Pi. [5]From 7-1-72. [6]Approx. [7]Subsid pfd million $. f—▲$0.25, '65. m—□$0.57, '67. q—Partial year r—■$0.41, '63; ▲$0.45, '64; ■$0.21, '66; ■$0.19, '67. s—▲$0.45, '65; ▲$0.46, '67. t—Fiscal Jan '65 & prior. u—▲$0.92, '67. v—□$2.49, '64. w—▲$0.21, '66. x—□$1.17, '66, y—Aver shr. aa—Approx.

FIGURE 6–3

Common- and preferred-stock information

combination dividend policy either. His needs stress current income, and the stock dividend would be objectionable. A cash dividend policy might face the same type of objection.

Whatever type of dividend it distributes, a corporation should establish a stable dividend policy. The policy should reflect the needs of the company and of its shareholders. It should relate closely to the earnings or cash flow of the company. It should be changed infrequently, and then only to reflect a change in the economic position of the company and the needs of its shareholders. A haphazard policy of dividend payments will not allow a company or its stockholders to reach their financial objectives.

REGULAR AND EXTRA DIVIDEND POLICY

Dividends may be classed as regular or extra. Regular dividends are the usual amount of dividends paid on a regular (most often, quarterly) basis. Some companies like GM make it a practice to pay a regular dividend plus an extra, declared at the end of the year. The latter is based upon earnings and will be paid if the amount of earnings permits. If earnings are not much greater than expected, then it is likely that no extras will be paid. The company that pays a regular cash or stock dividend consistently tends to have greater appeal than one that has no stated policy about dividends or has an irregular policy.

COMMON AND PREFERRED STOCKS **All-Alt 15**

INDEX	Some Divs. Ea. Yr. Since	DIVIDENDS — Latest Payment — Per. $	Date	Ex. Div.	$ So Far 1968	Total Ind. Rate	$ Paid 1967	FINANCIAL POSITION — Mil-$ — Cash & Equiv.	Curr. Assets	Curr. Liabs.	Balance Sheet Date	CAPITALIZATION — Long Term Debt Mil-$	Shs. 000 — Pfd.	Com	Ended	EARNINGS — $ Per Shr — Years ▼ 1963	1964	1965	1966	1967	Last 12 Mos	INTERIM EARNINGS OR REMARKS — Period	$ Per Share $ 1967	1968	INDEX
1	......	0.06	10-14-66	9-27	....	Nil	....	8.22	19.4	11.8	9-30-67	76.5	....	1838	Dc	0.27	△0.19	0.81	0.57	Pd0.38	d0.38				1
2	......	Terms & trad. basis should be checked in detail										....	....	....	Dc	Price increase to $18 on 4-1-72						Expires April 1, 1987			2
3	1934	Q0.60	3-29-68	3-4	0.60	2.40	‡2.40	12.8	173	45.1	12-31-67	57.8	1307	4679	Dc	2.75	4.02	4.81	6.39	4.53	4.56	3 Mo Mar	1.36	1.39	3
4	1967	Q0.75	4-1-68	3-4	1.50	3.00	0.75	Conv into com sh for sh					1307		Dc	....	....	....	23.97	18.79	....	Issued for TrueTemper			4
5	1961	Sa0.13½	1-18-68	1-4	a0.13½	0.27	a0.23½	2.31	4.37	2.86	12-31-66	8.51	....	1112	Dc[25]	a□0.71	a□0.71	a□0.40	a□0.89	Pa△0.83	0.83				5
6	⊙'35	Q0.30	3-29-68	3-4	0.30	1.20	1.20	28.6	78.0	60.2	12-31-67	394	792	19292	Dc[14]	a1.34	1.41	1.52	1.54	1.72	1.73	12 Mo Feb	1.66	1.73	6
7	1899	S3.00	1-1-68	12-12	3.00	6.00	6.00	....	....	....	.....	1.97	....	32	Divs pd from rental g't'd under lease							Lsd Buff Rock & Pitts Ry			7
8	......	None paid			....	Nil	....	0.21	3.01	1.02	5-31-67	0.22	....	544	My	0.38	0.44	0.49	0.82	y0.62	d0.15	9 Mo Feb	0.71	d0.06	8
9	......	0.10	5-16-66	4-21	....	Nil	....	0.34	4.70	1.75	12-31-67	0.55	....	299	Dc	d1.10	d0.20	0.63	xd0.30	0.47	0.47				9
10	......	0.10	12-23-64	11-24	....	Nil	....	2.96	27.2	6.78	12-31-67	13.3	10	1461	Dc	0.63	0.93	0.87	□1.42	1.70	1.70				10
11	1939	Q0.35	6-15-68	5-24	0.70	1.40	1.40	2.69	26.7	11.6	12-31-67	4.29	....	1042	Dc[13]	a2.87	a2.80	a3.45	2.80	2.68	3.00	3 Mo Mar	0.63	0.95	11
12	1954	‡A0.15	3-15-68	[illegible]-1	‡0.15	0.15	a0.22½	0.22	3.43	0.46	12-31-67	0.97	....	+509	Dc[19]	+a0.83	+a1.25	+a1.16	+a1.35	+0.68	0.68				12
13	1966	0.30	12-29-67	11-21	....	0.30	0.30	3.89	29.4	17.0	j3-31-67	j3.22	....	+666	Mr	0.79	1.15	1.13	1.33	....	1.33				13
14	......	None paid			....	Nil	....	0.36	1.75	0.70	12-31-67	0.38	....	‡839	Dc	d0.004	0.08	0.01	△0.29	□0.41	0.44	3 Mo Mar	0.09	0.12	14
15	......	0.15	1-24-56	....	....	Nil	....	0.22	3.88	4.54	7-1-67	0.21	47	932	Je	d2.98	0.01	d1.63	0.52	u△0.79	2.40	6 Mo Dec△	d0.12	△1.49	15
16	1887	Q0.47½	6-10-68	5-6	0.95	1.90	‡1.90	38.6	474	217	12-31-67	‡548	....	27975	Dc[23]	a2.58	a2.91	a3.03	a3.25	△2.50	2.41	3 Mo Mar	0.66	0.57	16
17	1954	Q0.11	5-17-68	4-23	†0.32	0.54	0.44	1.04	5.94	1.17	12-31-67	....	....	489	Dc	c△1.03	c1.18	c1.45	c2.57	2.79	2.45	3 Mo Mar	0.68	0.34	17
18	......	None since 1942			....	Nil	....	1.47	2.83	0.89	12-31-66	8.76	....	1049	Dc[15]	ad1.12	ad0.02	d0.10	1.04	P0.86	0.86				18
19	1965	5% Stk	3-29-68	2-28	5% Stk	Stk	0.52½	0.98	15.5	9.61	10-31-67	3.97	....	+945	Oc	+q0.59	+0.70	+△0.64	+0.64	+0.56	0.56				19
20	1933	Q0.25	2-23-68	2-7	0.25	1.00	0.92½	1.35	17.4	7.00	12-31-67	2.10	....	478	Je	1.35	1.57	1.43	1.58	1.70	2.35	9 Mo Mar	1.22	1.87	20
21	1960	Q0.15	3-15-68	2-27	0.15	0.80	‡0.60	Vote May 9 on 2-for-1 split				....	....	925	Mr	1.24	1.53	1.77	1.85	....	1.94	9 Mo Dec△	1.36	1.54	21
22	1935	Q0.50	5-10-68	4-22	1.00	2.00	2.00	2.52	47.4	27.4	6-30-67	3.16	....	832	Je	3.69	3.16	3.82	6.02	4.77	4.43	6 Mo Dec△	2.80	2.46	22
23	1963	Q0.15	6-28-68	6-3	0.30	0.60	0.52½	4.44	49.1	27.0	12-31-67	9.31	212	1537	Dc	△0.41	0.99	1.32	△3.25	2.61	2.42	3 Mo Mar	0.64	0.45	23
24	1968	Q0.75	6-28-68	6-3	1.25	3.00	....	Conv into 2 shrs common				....	212	....	Dc	....	....	....	26.71	21.94	....	General Bronze merger			24
25	1942	Q0.35	7-20-68	6-14	1.03	1.40	1.32	29.9	371	163	7-31-67	‡315	176	7618	Ja[12]	a1.83	a2.34	a2.95	3.01	P3.26	3.26				25
26	1945	Q1.00	6-1-68	5-10	2.00	4.00	4.00						142		Ja	69.30	89.51	117.7	128.8	....	....				26
27	1957	Q0.15	3-27-68	2-29	0.30	0.60	0.60	6.87	60.9	34.1	6-24-67	‡28.7	....	3914	Je	1.25	q1.32	1.28	1.30	1.24	1.07	9 Mo Mar	0.92	0.75	27
28	1954	Q0.37½	4-1-68	3-12	‡0.37½	1.50	1.50	1.58	13.4	3.43	12-31-67	3.35	....	452	Dc[22]	r■2.29	r△3.21	a3.26	ar■3.74	r■4.08	4.00	3 Mo Mar	0.85	0.77	28
29	1936	Q0.25	3-29-68	2-26	0.25	1.00	1.00	25.3	423	169	3-31-68	119	....	10324	Dc	0.73	v□1.37	2.33	2.67	0.41	0.37	3 Mo Mar	0.30	0.26	29
30	1965	0.10	3-30-68	3-14	0.10	0.40	0.40	0.26	8.93	4.33	12-31-67	1.61	....	677	Dc[21]	a0.86	0.83	a0.95	1.42	1.51	1.51	3 Mo Mar	0.47	0.47	30
31	1964	0.07½	11-1-67	10-10	....	0.07½	0.07½	2.06	19.7	8.53	8-31-67	6.06	....	3645	Au[20]	a□0.02	a□0.21	a0.29	1.10	1.29	1.38	6 Mo Feb	0.67	0.76	31
32	1963	Q0.13	4-15-68	3-26	0.26	0.52	0.50½	3.73	4.28	4.28	6-30-67	4.44	....	1249	Je[16]	+△0.86	+△0.73	+△0.77	△0.93	△1.00	1.08	9 Mo Mar	△0.75	0.83	32
33	1959	S0.20	4-30-68	3-25	0.20	0.40	0.40	1.08	11.0	2.66	4-30-67	....	....	1434	Ap	1.09	0.74	1.01	1.08	0.96	0.96				33
34	......	None paid			....	Nil	....	0.06	0.92	0.19	7-31-67	....	....	884	Jl	d0.06	d0.27	t0.02	q0.12	d0.10	d0.10				34
35	......	None paid			....	Nil	....	0.40	2.61	3.24	12-31-67	3.81	1240	6531	Dc	0.08	0.09	0.09	0.02	0.04	0.04				35
36	......	None paid			....	Nil	....	0.14	1.15	0.36	9-30-67	‡1.00	....	977	Mr[24]	d0.002	a0.07	a0.16	ya0.28	....	0.33	9 Mo Dec△	a0.20	0.25	36
37	1935	0.06¼	6-9-67	5-10	....	Nil	0.12½	4.29	15.2	5.60	12-31-67	27.4	....	1808	Dc	1.20	□1.24	f△0.39	0.28	△0.03	d0.25	3 Mo Mar	d0.57	d0.85	37
38	......	None paid			....	Nil	....	1.35	4.21	1.34	10-31-67	0.42	....	919	Ap	0.12	0.20	0.10	y0.48	y0.52	0.33	6 Mo Oct△	0.38	0.19	38
39	......	a‡0.05	6-13-61	5-11	....	Nil	....	1.69	15.4	9.93	5-31-67	2.71	....	1886	My	△d2.43	0.46	d0.40	0.21	m□2.20	1.99	9 Mo Feb	□1.74	1.53	39
40	1960	Q0.05	2-29-68	2-16	0.05	0.20	0.20	6.73	20.8	5.83	9-30-67	2.19	....	2111	Sp	+0.85	□d0.30	s△0.88	0.74	s△0.71	0.86	3 Mo Dec△	d0.05	0.10	40
41	1962	S0.10	5-17-68	4-25	0.10	0.20	0.20	0.50	17.8	7.50	2-29-68	6.89	100	1636	Au	△0.59	△0.66	0.62	w△1.32	y1.24	1.09	6 Mo Feb	△0.55	0.40	41
42	1960	Q0.12½	5-1-68	4-8	0.25	0.50	0.50	5.72	16.8	9.51	4-29-67	3.07	....	1384	Ap[18]	a1.01	a1.17	a1.62	1.77	1.90	1.67	39 Wk Jan	1.37	1.14	42

▼Stock Splits & Divs: [12]2½-for-1, '66. [13]10%, '63, '66. [14]2-for-1, '64. [15]Reverse 1-for-20, '64. [16]10%, '64. [17]100%, '65. [18]2-for-1, '65. [19]10%, '66 & '67. [20]3-for-1, '66. [21]2½-for-1, '66. [22]2-for-1, '67. [23]Adj to 2%, '67. [24]2-for-1 twice in '67. [25]50%, '68.

FIGURE 6–3 *(continued)*

SOURCE Standard & Poor's *Stock Guide*

Current information about dividends may be found in the *Wall Street Journal* under "Dividend News." Information about the rate of regularity and type of dividends can be found in Standard & Poor's *Stock Guide.* An example of the type of information found there is presented in Figure 6–3 (a-b). An examination of the explanatory footnotes for price quotations in the *Wall Street Journal* will show the variety in dividends.

The Declaration of Dividends

Dividends are declared by the board of directors. The date of announcement usually precedes the date of record by several weeks. After the date of record, the stock sells ex dividends and a person buying it after this date does not receive the declared dividend. A person who buys stock in anticipation of receiving a dividend must make certain that he becomes a stockholder of record before the stock goes ex dividend. He must buy the stock with dividends "on." The actual date of payment will be sometime after the date of record as shown in Table 6–2.

The Pre-emptive Right

In addition to receiving dividends and voting on corporate matters, the stockholder has the right, called the *pre-emptive right,* to maintain his proportionate share in the assets, earnings, and voting power of the corporation. When additional common stock of the corporation is to be sold to raise capital, the pre-emptive right gives the present stockholder the opportunity, based upon the number of shares he owns, to subscribe to the new issue of stock. Selling stock to current stockholders is known as a privileged subscription or a pre-emptive rights offering of stock.

Common Law and Rights

The pre-emptive right is a matter of common-law doctrine rather than of statutory law; half the states in the United States permit this right to be limited or denied by statute. Raising money by first offering the stock for sale to the shareholders is common among United States corporations. If the shareholder does not elect to participate in the rights offering, he may sell his privilege in the marketplace to someone willing to buy the rights to purchase shares. Not all stock has the right to share in the pre-emptive right. If the stock issue is part of a continuing sale of stock, if it is Treasury stock, if it is issued to buy property or to settle a debt, it will not be subject to the pre-emptive right.

The Value of Rights

When rights are offered to the investor, they usually have value and should be exercised or sold in the market. Often we learn of share owners who actually throw away rights when they arrive in the mail. The value of the right depends upon the market value of the stock, the subscription price that the company establishes for the shares that are to be sold, and the number of rights necessary to buy one new share of stock. The right attached to each share of stock owned is called a New York right, and several New York rights are usually required to buy one new share of stock. The shares are offered at a price below the existing market price to make them attractive purchases. If a stock was selling in the market for $50 a share, for example, it might be offered to existing shareholders at $42.50 per share—a discount of 15 percent. If the discount were much smaller than 15 percent, it would be difficult to sell the stock. If the discount were larger, the total number of shares sold would not increase and the total amount of money raised by the company would be reduced. Now let us make an additional assumption in our above example. Assume ten rights are required to buy one new share of stock. The value of each right would be approximately $.75. Simply divide the number of rights needed to buy one new share into the difference between the market and subscription prices to arrive at the value of the right. If the market price changed after the conditions of the rights offering had been determined, the value of the right would also change.

The Time Period of the Rights Offering

The investor must keep in mind three dates that may have an effect upon the value of the right—the announcement date, the record date, and the expiration date. On the announcement date the board of directors gives details of the privileged subscription; these include the number of rights needed to buy one new share of stock, the price of the stock, and the record date, the day on which the list of stockholders is established. Owners of stock on the date of record receive the right to subscribe to new shares based upon their proportional share in the company. From the announcement date up to the date of record, the stock sells with rights attached or *cum rights*. After the date of record, it sells *ex rights* or without rights.

In some cases, an investment banker assists with the sale of any unsold shares of new stock through what is referred to as a standby underwriting syndicate. When a syndicate is used, the investor may sell his rights to a member of it. These rights may then be sold to other share owners who wish to acquire enough rights to buy a full share of stock. It is the underwriter's responsibility to make certain that all of the rights are exercised to insure the success of the offering. Between the date of record and the expiration date, the rights are traded; if the company is listed on the New York Stock Exchange, they will be traded there along with the stock of the company. The market price of the right will be quoted daily until the rights expire.

The last important date is the expiration date—on this date, rights no longer have value. The period between the date of record and the expiration date varies; two weeks to a month is typical. The time is sufficient for all shareholders to take the necessary steps to use their rights. Occasionally, stockholders do not exercise their rights. The author is aware of an individual who purchased rights to buy shares in a company, but before he acted, the rights had expired. The time period was adequate. The investor simply misunderstood the nature of the pre-emptive right and was careless in the details of his transactions. Therefore, there is real meaning in the admonishment to exercise or sell any rights received as part of common-stock ownership.

The Theoretical Value of the Right

The theoretical value of the right can be calculated by using a simple formula. If the stock is selling with rights, that is, between the announcement and date of record, the formula is $Vcr = (M - S)/(R + 1)$. Vcr is the value of the right when stock is selling cum rights. M is the market price of the stock, S the subscription price, and R the number of rights needed to buy one new share of stock. The 1 in the formula compensates for the value of the right in the market price of the stock after the announcement date. Theoretically, the market price of the stock goes up to include the value of the right on the day the privileged subscription is announced. Assume that a stockholder is given the right to subscribe to one new share of stock for each 5 shares he now owns, at a price of $25 per share. The announcement date is May 1, the record date May 30, and the expiration date June 15. The market price after the announcement is $31. What then is the value of the right? We find it by substituting in our formula.

$$Vcr = \frac{M - S}{R + 1} = \frac{\$31 - \$25}{5 + 1} = \frac{\$6}{6} = \$1$$

The theoretical value of the right, therefore, is $1. If the market price should drop before the rights are issued, the value of the right also drops. A sharp drop in prices in the market comparable to 1967 or 1969 might provide a set of circumstances where the market price of a stock dropped and resulted in a right having little value.

On the date of record, the stock sells ex rights or without rights. On that day, other things being equal, the price of the stock in the market should drop by the value of the right. In our example, the stock would drop from $31 to $30—assuming that there has been no price change. How do we calculate the theoretical value after the date of record? We use the same basic formula, but since a right is no longer attached to the shares in the market, we remove the 1 from the denominator and express the formula as $Vxr = (M - S)/R$, where Vxr is the value of the right ex rights. The results are:

$$Vxr = \frac{\$30 - \$25}{5} = \$1.$$

As before, the theoretical value of the right is $1.

THE MARKET VALUE AND THE THEORETICAL VALUE OF THE RIGHT

The actual value of the right in the market will vary from the theoretical value, depending on demand for the rights and interest in the new issue of stock. Under strong market conditions, a small issue of stock, and an ownership group that wishes to buy the new shares, the market for rights will be limited, and the only trading engaged in will be to take care of the purchase and sale of fractional shares. Occasionally a strong demand for rights forces their price higher than their theoretical value.

Rights Offering Favorable to Investors

When the investor can subscribe to new shares because of a pre-emptive rights offering, he is in a favorable position. He is afforded an opportunity to buy stock at an attractive price, with minimum effort and a minimum brokerage cost. This is true as long as the future prospects of the company seem to promise a satisfactory rate of return. Purchasing stock through a *rights offering* has the added advantage of lower margin rates. With a 70 percent margin requirement generally in effect, a much lower requirement of 15 percent for a right offering is attractive for investors who might not have cash immediately available or for those who wish to purchase a larger amount of stock with a given amount of cash. Not everyone is in a position to accept the risk. The actual margin requirements for a rights offering vary; the specific margin required must be determined at the time of purchase.

Yields, Investment Experience, and Investor Expectations

When we buy a bond or preferred stock, we know what we will earn on our investment. What will we earn if we invest in common stocks? One often hears how Joe Smith bought Moon Rocket common at 2 1/2 and it is now selling at 81. And IBM was selling at 196 in 1951; in 1969, after it had split several times, it was selling at well over 300. If an investor had purchased one share in 1951, he would have owned approximately 22.5 shares with a market value of over $7,000 in 1969. This represents an increase in value of over 35 times the original investment or a compound yield well above 35 percent. Is this usual? The answer is an emphatic *no!* Such growth is not usual, but some companies have achieved similar results. Let us examine what we might reasonably expect to earn on common stocks.

Current Yield

Current yields on the Dow Jones Industrial Averages offer a clue to what might be expected in terms of current income from a common-stock investment. Chart 5–1 in the previous chapter shows graphically the current yields on common stock. Table 6–4 presents them for the industrial, rail, and utility averages. Current stock yields have moved downward from 1950 to 1965, with a slight upturn in 1966. In recent years, because of inflation psychology, the current yields on common stocks have been lower than yields on bonds.

Low current yields, it would seem, should make common stock unattractive to individual investors; however, common stocks have been good investments. Current yields do not reveal directly the growth in capital value in common shares, but this growth can be established indirectly. Assume that an investor bought one share of an industrial common stock in 1950 on a current yield basis of 7.5 percent. Assume further that the company's earnings doubled during the period. In 1968, the stock sold on a current yield basis of 3.75 percent. The price of the

TABLE 6–4

Current dividend yields on common stock

YEAR	125 INDUSTRIAL COMMON STOCKS[a] %	25 RAILROAD COMMON STOCKS—MOODY'S AVERAGES[b] %	MOODY'S 24 UTILITY STOCKS[c] %
1966	3.44	4.80	3.99
1965	2.98	4.30	3.30
1964	2.98	4.05	3.15
1963	3.20	4.46	3.12
1962	3.39	5.30	3.25
1961	3.04	4.94	3.10
1960	3.48	5.65	3.84
1959	3.12	4.63	3.94
1958	3.88	5.74	4.33
1957	4.11	6.77	4.92
1956	3.89	5.51	4.68
1955	3.93	4.88	4.50
1954	4.70	6.20	4.81
1953	5.51	6.48	5.33
1952	5.55	5.88	5.89
1951	6.29	6.31	5.77
1950	6.51	6.50	5.66

SOURCE:

[a] *Moody's Industrial Manual* (New York: Moody's Investors Service, June 1967), p. A23.

[b] *Moody's Transportation Manual* (New York: Moody's Investors Service, September, 1967), p. A53.

[c] *Moody's Public Utility Manual* (New York: Moody's Investors Service, August, 1967), p. A9.

stock in 1968 is actually four times higher than in 1950. If earnings had remained constant and current yield had been reduced by one-half, the stock would have doubled in value. Because earnings doubled, there was a fourfold increase in price. It appears that the investor, on this current yield basis, is losing each year. Actually capital growth provided him with an exceptional rate of return. We should, therefore, look to the yield to maturity as a more important guide to common stock yields.

Yield to Maturity

Current yield does not take into consideration the price appreciation that many stocks traded on the New York Stock Exchange have experienced. The market has risen over the period 1950–1968 in spite of cyclical drops. The price that people have been willing to pay for a dollar of earnings and dividends has gone up, too. The trend of the market has brought about increased capital gains, which must be considered in measuring investment success. Studies have been undertaken to determine what a person would earn through common-stock investment, considering both dividend income and capital gains. Essentially, they use the present value method (see Chapters 3 and 7) to compute yields to maturity. The results of a major study sponsored by Merrill Lynch, Pierce, Fenner & Smith found that an average of all common stocks listed on the New York Stock Exchange earned 9.01 percent compounded annually between 1926 and 1960. The rate earned between 1950 and 1960 was 14.84 percent.[1] The author conducted a study on yields based upon random selection and random timing of purchases of stocks listed on the New York Stock Exchange during the period 1950–1962.[2] The results, based upon fifty investors who bought 5.6 different securities—mostly common stocks of industrial companies—and held them for 4 1/2 years, were significant. They had earned an average yield of 13.8 percent, with a range of from 33.04 to −12.67 percent. When stocks comparable to the Dow Jones Industrial Averages were purchased for the same time period, the average yield was 13.14 percent, with a range of from 32.01 to −2.80 percent. This study, of course, reflects only one time period in the history of the stock market.

Other studies indicate that a yield of 8 percent on common stock is possible over a long period of time. But more work must be done in this area. Whether the investor is interested in growth or income, yields that include current dividends and capital gains are far more important to investment success than current yields alone.

Measuring Performance of Common-Stock Investment

The focal point for common-stock investment is usually dividend income or capital gains but not yield. How often have we heard that a stock hasn't gained much in price but pays an excellent dividend. In 1968, when AT&T was selling at 48 after a long slide from 75, one investor used this "yield" defense for the stock. Actually, the stock had not performed well, the investor had suffered a loss, and the high dividend rate was being used to justify continued investment. Conversely, some investors ignore dividends completely and look only at capital gains. Think of the investor who states, "I bought the stock two months ago; it hasn't moved much, just up a few points." In reality, the stock was purchased at 10 and increased to 13—a 30 percent increase in two months, or an annual rate of 180 percent. Not bad for a stock that hasn't "done much." Another comment often heard is, "I bought U.S. Steel and it has doubled in price. Boy, that's been a good investment!" The truth of the matter is that the stock did in fact double in price, but it had been held for twenty years. Dividends were 4 percent on the average; the capital growth rate was approximately 3.5 percent, compounded. To-

---

1 Lawrence Fisher and James H. Lorie, *Rates of Return on Investments in Common Stocks*, Pamphlet, The Center For Research in Security Prices, Graduate School of Business, University of Chicago, 1963.

2 Frederick Amling, "Random Investment Decisions and Portfolio Yields," *Miami Business Review*, April, 1963.

gether, the dividends and capital gains provided a yield of 7.5 percent—
an excellent yield over a twenty-year period, but not as large or
glamorous as the investor suggested.

It is necessary to have a measure of performance that provides
comparability in yield for both common stock and bonds. The yield
formula presented in Chapter 3 provides a way for measuring yield and
also a standard of performance. Let's assume that we bought a stock
at $25, held it for seven years, and sold it at $60. During the seven years,
we received the following annual dividends:

YEAR	DIVIDENDS
1	$.50
2	.50
3	.60
4	.65
5	.65
6	.75
7	.80

What was our yield, and was the performance satisfactory? We
can calculate yield by the approximate method. The average investment
was $42.50, or ($25 + $60)/2, and the average annual income was $5.64,
where $5, or ($60 — $25)/7, was the average annual taxable capital gain
and $.64 the average dividend income. The yield from the investment
before federal income taxes was 13.3 percent ($5.64 ÷ $42.50). If we
assume that the investor was in the 60 percent tax bracket, then dividend
income, ignoring any dividend credits, would have been $.64 minus $.38
($.64 × 60 percent), or $.26 after taxes. The average annual capital
gain after taxes was $5 minus $1.25 ($5 × 25 percent), or $3.75. The final
investment value was $51.25 ($60 — $8.75), and therefore the average
investment after taxes was $38.13, or ($51.25 + $25)/2. (The $8.75 is the
tax on the capital gain of $35 over the seven-year period; tax rate was
25 percent.) The after-tax yield for the seven-year period was 10.5
percent, or ($.26 + $3.75)/$38.13. The use of present-value tables or cal-
culus would provide a more precise answer, but the approximate yield is
sufficiently accurate for our purposes.

The yield of 13.3 percent before taxes or 10.5 after taxes should
be considered satisfactory, since the investor had anticipated a yield
of 10 percent, and since according to the Lorie and Fisher study, 9 percent would have been acceptable as a yield over long periods of time.
Both criteria suggest that the investor's performance was favorable.
Without these criteria, he would not know how he had done in his
investment program. It is suggested that standards of performance be
established by the investor early to serve as a guide for decision making.

Bond and preferred-stock ratings emphasize the basic security of the issue, particularly with respect to interest and dividend coverage. The question of the security of principal is also important in the valuation and rating process employed by independent rating agencies, such as Standard & Poor's in its *Bond Guide* and *Stock Guide*. Symbols used in the *Stock Guide* for rating preferred stock are the same as those used for bonds. These ratings are presented in Figure 6–4.

Ratings for common stock cannot be so precise, so instead of rating them, Standard & Poor's uses a ranking system. The emphasis is upon earnings and dividend growth and stability as described in Figure 6–4. A company ranked A+ is one with the highest growth and stability of earnings and dividends. A ranking of C is given to a company with the lowest stability and growth of earnings and dividends. However, Standard & Poor's cautions that its ranking code is not a recommendation to buy or sell.

The Advantages and Disadvantages of Common-Stock Investment

The advantages and disadvantages of common-stock ownership should be apparent from the comments made previously. The major disadvantage of common stock is its lack of earnings and price stability. When we buy common stock, we have no guarantee, no contractual agreement, that the dividend will remain fixed, or even that a dividend will be paid. Since income is unstable and uncertain, the stock price will fluctuate widely, and we might lose both principal and current income. Another disadvantage of common-stock ownership is the difficulty in estimating future earnings and price, particularly by those who do not understand the nature of common stock. Since its price fluctuates and forecasting its earnings is difficult, it is an undesirable investment for certain investors, particularly institutional investors. The low current yield at present tends to make it unattractive to people who need substantial current income. When we buy common stocks, we must accept the market and business risks associated with such investment.

The advantages of common-stock ownership should also be apparent. First, the potential for profit is greater than with any other investment security. The current dividend yield is low, but potential for capital gain is great. The yield to maturity potential over a period of time is substantial; and expectation of yield considerably above that of government bonds would be reasonable. Common stock also offers tax advantages to the investor. The larger yield on most common stock

EARNINGS AND DIVIDEND RANKINGS FOR STOCKS

The relative "quality" of common stocks cannot be measured, as can that of bonds, which depends upon the degree of protection for interest and principal. However, there are differences in the nature of stocks and some of them are well worth measuring and comparing.

Standard & Poor's Rankings are designed to indicate by the use of symbols the relative stability and growth of earnings and the relative stability and growth of dividends. These measures of past records have a considerable bearing on relative quality, but do not pretend to reflect an examination of all other factors, tangible and intangible, that also bear on a stock's quality. *Under no circumstances should these rankings be regarded as a recommendation to buy or sell a security.*

The Common Stock Formula

Standard & Poor's point of departure is a scoring system based upon earnings and dividend records. The first step is to examine the earnings record of the past eight years. In measuring earnings stability, a basic score is given for each year in which net per share equals or exceeds that of the preceding year. For any year in which earnings declined, the score is reduced by the percentage of that decline. The average of these eight annual scores, weighted for frequency of earnings declines, becomes our first "basic earnings index."

This stability index is then multiplied by a growth index, based on the square root of the percentage by which earnings increased between the base years period and the most recent three years. To prevent growth in extreme cases from dominating the rating, the growth factor is "topped" at 150%.

Scoring for dividend stability and growth is similar, with the principal exception that a longer period is used and results are weighted for recency. A dividend reduction fifteen years ago is obviously a less serious current investment consideration than one that was voted recently. A further weighting is applied for frequency of dividend reductions, because an erratic dividend policy is a matter affecting investment standing. The result is multiplied by a growth factor similar to that for **earnings.**

When this is completed, the two factors—earnings and dividends—are combined into a single numerical ranking. All the common stocks so graded are then grouped into seven classes. To these we have assigned an easy-to-understand code, as follows:

A+ Highest	B+ Average	C Lowest
A High	B Below Average	
A— Above Average	B— Low	

These mathematically determined positions are modified in some instances by special considerations. Non-recurring costs, windfall profits, etc., "must sometimes be allowed for. There are certain other exceptions. In the oil industry, for example, so-called "cash flow" is used rather than final net profit in order to avoid the distortions that might be caused by differences in accounting practices.

Since earnings and dividends of regulated public utilities characteristically are more stable than those of most non-regulated industries, numerous other factors must be considered. Among these are capital structure, amount of depreciation reserves, condition of properties, growth potentialities for individual service areas, the regulatory environment, and the rate of return.

These scorings are not to be confused with bond quality ratings, which are arrived at by a necessarily altogether different approach. Additionally, they must not be used as a substitute for market recommendations; a high graded stock may at times be so over-priced as to justify its sale, while a low score stock may be attractively priced for purchase. Rankings based upon earnings and dividend record are no substitute for analysis. Nor are they quality ratings in the complete sense of the term. They cannot take into account potential effects of management changes, internal company policies not yet fully reflected in the earnings and dividend record, public relations standing, recent competitive shifts, and a host of other factors that may be relevant to investment status.

N.R. signifies No Ranking possible, because of insufficient data, non-recurring factors, or some other reason.

* Preceding ranking denotes railroad guaranteed stock quality rating based on S&P bond rating scale.

Preferred Stock Ratings

Quality ratings on preferred stock are expressed by symbols like these used in rating bonds. They are independent of Standard & Poor's bond ratings, however, in the sense that they are not necessarily graduated downward from the ranking accorded the issuing company's debt. They represent a considered judgment of the relative security of dividends, and—what is thereby implied—the prospective yield stability of the stock. These ratings are as follows:

AAA Prime	BBB Medium Grade	C Sub-Marginal
AA High Grade	BB Lower Grade	
A Sound	B Speculative	

FIGURE 6-4

Common-stock ranking and preferred-stock ratings

SOURCE Standard & Poor's *Stock Guide*

results from an increase in principal or capital gains, taxed at a lower rate than ordinary income. And common stock is a good hedge against inflation, even though it does not compensate perfectly for the diminished purchasing power of the dollar, for it is subject to the money rate risk if it is an income stock. When money rates and interest rates are high, income stocks tend to be less attractive, and prices tend to be depressed. The major advantage of investment in common stock is its ability to increase in value by sharing in the growth of company profits.

Sources of Information About Common Stock

One of the most frustrating aspects of investment analysis and management is the difficulty in obtaining up-to-date information about the earnings and dividends of a company. Certainly, earnings, dividends, and price are the focal point for the investment decision-making process. What we need is a relatively simple, reliable, available, and inexpensive information source. Standard & Poor's *Stock Guide*, a sample of which is presented in Figure 6–3, is an excellent source of up-to-date facts. The annual report of the company being considered should be a basic source of information. The annual report, coupled with interim reports in the *Wall Street Journal* under the subject "Digest of Earnings Reports," and reports mailed to shareholders by the company provide sources of sales and earnings information.

Other excellent sources of factual information include: Standard & Poor's *Listed Stock Reports* (see Figure 6–5), available from brokers and in most libraries; the *Value Line Investment Survey* (see Figure 6–6), in libraries; *The Outlook*, another publication of Standard & Poor's; and 3-Trend Security Charts. Brokerage firms will also supply up-to-date information to the investor.

This in no way exhausts the list of information sources available, but those mentioned are excellent examples of the more familiar sources.

Portfolio Needs and Common Stock

Common stock is looked upon as an aggressive type of investment. If the market is moving up and inflation threatens, then it is an excellent investment. It is versatile and can provide income, growth, or a combination of both to meet the needs of almost any investor. The risks of ownership are greater than with either bonds or preferred stock, but, over time, the rewards tend to outweigh the risks. Common stocks fit admirably into the investor's program when he does not need a great deal of current income or where a favorable tax status and capital growth are desired. In later chapters more will be said about its place in the investor's portfolio.

Avco Corp.

Stock —	Approx. Price	Dividend	Yield
COMMON	48¾	²$1.20	²2.5%
$3.20 CUM. CONV. PREFERRED	100	3.20	3.2

RECOMMENDATION: Although revenues from Government contracts remain important, more than 75% of this diversified company's profit is derived from commercial operations. Avco merged with Paul Revere Corp., a financial services holding company, in November, 1967. Paul Revere had previously owned 32% of Avco's common stock. The net effect of this transaction was to increase net income while reducing the number of common shares outstanding. The shares have interesting price appreciation possibilities.

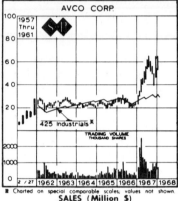

SALES (Million $)

Quarter:	1966-7	1965-6	1964-5	1963-4
Feb.........	150.4	118.6	94.0	109.4
May	176.7	147.3	107.7	107.7
Aug.........	182.2	150.4	109.8	106.5
Nov.........	273.7	227.5	131.7	107.5

Based on the preliminary report, sales of products and services for the fiscal year to November 30, 1967, rose to $783,017,000, from $643,815,000 a year earlier. Despite the sales gain, margins were under significant pressure, and net income from these operations declined to $22,041,000, from $27,964,000. While revenues from insurance operations, consisting of Paul Revere on a pooling of interests basis, increased, operating profits were lower. But this was more than offset by sharply higher net realized capital gains, and insurance earnings were $25,046,000, versus $19,105,000. And with equity in profits of Avco Delta at $7,084,000, against $5,531,000 in 1965-6, net income rose to $54,171,000, from $52,-600,000. Results for 1967 were before a special credit of $2.07 a share.

³COMMON SHARE EARNINGS ($)

Quarter:	1966-7	1965-6	1964-5	1963-4
Feb.........	0.56	0.54	0.43	0.50
May	0.54	0.60	0.40	0.56
Aug.........	0.49	0.50	0.43	0.47
Nov.........	⁴2.12	⁴1.66	0.52	0.52

PROSPECTS

Near Term— Further sales gains are expected in the fiscal year ending November 30, 1968. The large backlog of orders indicates that Government business will remain at a high level, while the expected improvement in the economy should aid commercial operations, including engines for civilian aircraft and broadcasting.

The higher volume and better product mix may result in wider margins in 1967-8. Earnings could also be substantially affected by capital gains from the sale of securities. Improvement in net income is likely from the $3.71 a share (preliminary) reported for 1966-7, before a special credit of $2.07. The dividend is $0.30 quarterly.

Long Term— The merger of Paul Revere has accelerated the trend toward more profitable commercial business. Further diversification in this direction is possible.

RECENT DEVELOPMENTS

On November 28, 1967, Avco merged with Paul Revere Corp. Under the plan, Avco exchanged 1.8 common shares and one share of a new $3.20 preferred stock (convertible into two Avco common shares) for each of Revere's 2.65 million shares. Revere had previously owned 32% of Avco's common stock. Holders of Avco common stock were then entitled to exchange half their common shares for the same preferred issue, receiving one share of preferred for each two common shares exchanged. The 4 million Avco shares owned by Revere (acquired through a tender offer at $33 a share) were retired.

On February 19, 1968, Avco announced it was negotiating to acquire Carte Blanche Corp., a national credit card operation controlled by the First National City Bank of New York. In 1966, Carte Blanche earned $1.9 million on volume of $123 million.

DIVIDEND DATA

Payments in the past 12 months were:

Amt. of Divd. $	Date Decl.	Ex-divd. Date	Stock of Record	Payment Date
0.30. .	Mar. 31	Apr. 25	Apr. 28	May 20'67
0.30...	Jun. 23	Jun. 25	Jul. 28	Aug. 19'67
0.30...	Sep. 29	Oct. 24	Oct. 27	Nov. 20'67
0.30...	Dec. 15	Jan. 23	Jan. 26	Feb. 20'68

¹Listed N.Y.S.E. & Midwest & Toronto S.Es.; also traded Boston, Cincinnati, Phila.-Balt.-Wash., Pittsburgh, Detroit & Pacific Coast S.Es.   ²Indicated rate.   ³Based on avge. shs. outstanding.   ⁴Incl. Paul Revere Corp. for 12 mos.

Vol. 35, No. 39   Tuesday, February 27, 1968   Sec. 2

FIGURE 6–5 (a)

Stock information fact sheet—front

SOURCE Standard & Poor's *Standard Listed Stock Reports*

260 AVCO CORPORATION

INCOME STATISTICS (Million $) AND PER SHARE ($) DATA

Year Ended Nov. 30	Net Sales	% Op. Inc. of Sales	Oper. Inc.	Depr. & Amort.	Net Bef. Taxes	[2]Net Inc.	-----Common Share ($) Data---- [2]Earns.	Divs. Paid	[1]Price Range	Price-Earns. Ratios HI LO
1968--	-----	---	---	---	----	----	---	0.30	---------	-----
1967--	[4]783.02	---	---	---	[4]89.05	[4]54.17	[4]3.71	1.20	65⅜-22½	18- 6
1966--	604.22	11.1	67.21	8.81	52.11	32.01	2.30	1.05	31½-20	14- 9
1965--	443.19	11.0	48.72	7.04	40.77	24.43	1.78	1.00	27¾-19	16-11
1964--	431.08	11.8	50.77	6.23	44.54	22.64	2.05	1.00	24½-19⅞	12-10
1963-	514.13	10.5	53.96	6.51	46.79	22.43	2.00	0.80	29¼-21⅞	15-11
1962--	414.28	11.3	49.96	6.93	39.34	18.79	1.72	0.67½	28⅞-16¾	17-10
1961--	323.14	10.3	33.43	7.15	25.51	12.98	1.24	0.57½	27⅞-13½	23-11
1960--	322.74	8.5	27.31	6.84	19.30	10.02	0.97	0.50	17¼-11¾	18-12
1959--	306.05	8.5	26.10	6.24	18.49	9.59	0.93	0.40	17⅝-10½	19-11
1958--	282.93	7.3	26.52	5.60	13.53	9.56	1.01	0.40	13⅞- 5⅝	14- 6
1957--	314.88	5.8	18.15	6.12	10.55	10.47	1.12	0.10	7¾- 4⅞	7- 4

PERTINENT BALANCE SHEET STATISTICS (Million $)

Nov. 30	Gross Prop.	[3]Capital Expend.	Cash Items	Inven-tories	Receiv-ables	——Current—— Assets	Liabs.	Net Workg. Cap.	Cur. Ratio Assets to Liabs.	Long Term Debt	($) Book Val. Com. Sh.
1966--	153.54	19.59	33.3	122.31	112.93	268.53	103.85	164.68	2.6-1	124.34	12.41
1965--	135.52	8.12	27.3	88.55	102.14	218.02	109.38	108.64	2.0-1	80.78	11.45
1964--	111.14	9.30	24.0	72.79	89.83	186.60	67.66	118.95	2.8-1	17.48	14.25
1963--	103.36	8.01	40.7	66.79	96.26	203.78	74.78	128.99	2.7-1	20.86	13.74
1962--	96.54	8.34	14.8	71.36	90.34	176.52	58.90	117.62	3.0-1	23.94	12.54
1961--	91.02	5.93	14.6	46.96	82.51	144.06	36.30	107.76	4.0-1	27.88	11.39
1960--	87.06	4.75	13.4	46.65	68.94	129.03	30.67	98.36	4.2-1	34.39	10.71
1959--	84.96	4.07	22.4	54.63	59.78	136.75	45.22	91.54	3.0-1	36.76	10.24
1958--	92.60	15.74	14.9	56.66	56.86	128.40	60.32	68.08	2.1-1	23.13	9.90
1957--	81.08	7.75	17.5	50.15	49.54	117.23	43.20	74.03	2.7-1	24.95	9.11

[1]Cal. yrs. [2]Earns. based on avge. shs. outstanding in 1961 & subsequently; excl. spec. credits of $0.26 a sh. in 1957, $0.22 in 1958 & $0.11 in 1962. [3]Net additions, excl. investments. [4]Preliminary; pro forma earns. reflecting $3.20 pfd. conv. were $2.63 a sh. d Deficit.

Fundamental Position

Although a large portion of revenues is derived from Government billings, commercial operations accounted for over 75% of net income in fiscal 1966-7, up from 64% a year earlier (excluding operations of Paul Revere). Following completion of the merger with The Paul Revere Corp. in November, 1967, the combined companies were restructured into four major groups.

The Government Products Group accounts for the major portion of revenues. Sales of the Lycoming Stratford division are primarily derived from manufacture of gas turbine engines for military helicopters, reconnaissance aircraft, and amphibious vehicles. The Missile, Space, and Electronics divisions produce combat communications systems, re-entry systems, heat shields, and numerous other aerospace items. Special ordnance items, munitions, and missile arming and fuzing devices are turned out by the Ordnance division. The Aerostructures division makes major structural components for C-130 and C-141 military cargo planes, and structures for space vehicles. It will be responsible for sizable portions of the C-5A and SST aircraft. Economic Systems Corp. operates job corps centers.

The Commercial and Industrial Products Group includes the Avco New Idea Farm Equipment division, which makes specialized farm equipment; Moffats, Ltd., a maker of home appliances and commercial cooking equipment in Canada; Avco Lycoming Williamsport, the nation's largest producer of aricraft engines for private and business aircraft; Avco Bay State Abrasives; and Thompson Wire. Avco Broadcasting owns and operates five VHF television stations and six radio stations. With Meredith Publishing, Avco is owner of a company engaged in CATV operations.

The Financial Services Group, composed of Avco Delta Corp. and its subsidiaries, is engaged in savings and loans, home finance, and personal finance. Avco Delta had receivables of $712 million at fiscal 1966-7 year-end, up from $580 million a year before.

The Insurance Group consists of The Paul Revere Life Insurance Co., which specializes in individual and group life and accident and health insurance and is among the top 50 U. S. insurance companies in terms of assets, and The Paul Revere Variable Annuity Insurance Co., which sells both individual and group variable annuity contracts.

Finances

At May 31, 1967, Avco had taken down $75 million of a $100 million revolving credit agreement to April 15, 1970.

CAPITALIZATION

LONG TERM DEBT: $200,231,000, including $1,573,000 of 5% subordinated debentures convertible into common at $11.50 a share.

$3.50 CUM. CONV. PREFERRED STOCK: 5,219,752 shs. ($6 stated value), each conv. into two common shs.

COMMON STOCK: 9,910,147 shs. ($3 par).

Note: Preferred and Common share figures assume full participation in exchange offer of Preferred for Common shares. Assuming full conversion of the Pfd. shares, fiscal 1966-7 earns. would have been $2.63 a sh.

Incorporated in Del. in 1959. **Office**—750 Third Ave., New York 17, N.Y. **Pres**—J. R. Kerr. **Treas**—F. S. Larson. **Secy**—G. M. Tuttle. **Dirs**—K. R. Wilson, Jr. (Chrmn), G. E. Allen, E. H. Blaik, J. Bruce, J. R. Gosnell, O. F. Grahame, F. A. Harrington, F. Harrington, Jr., F. L. Harrington, Sr., R. D. Harrington, E. R. Hodgkins, F. W. P. Jones, H. H. Kahn, A. R. Kantrowitz, J. R. Kerr, E. H. Litchfield, J. A. McDougald, M. A. McLaughlin, W. I. Myers, B. H. Namm, A. E. Rasmussen, R. W. Yantis. **Transfer Agents**—Schroder Trust Co., NYC; First National Bank, Chicago; Bank of America N.T. & S.A., San Francisco; Crown Trust Co., Toronto. **Registrars**—Bankers Trust Co., NYC; Harris Trust & Savings Bank, Chicago; Wells Fargo Bank, San Francisco; The Canada Trust Co., Toronto.

Information has been obtained from sources believed to be reliable, but its accuracy and completeness, and that of the opinions based thereon, are not guaranteed. Printed in U. S. A.

FIGURE 6–5 (b)

Stock information fact sheet—back

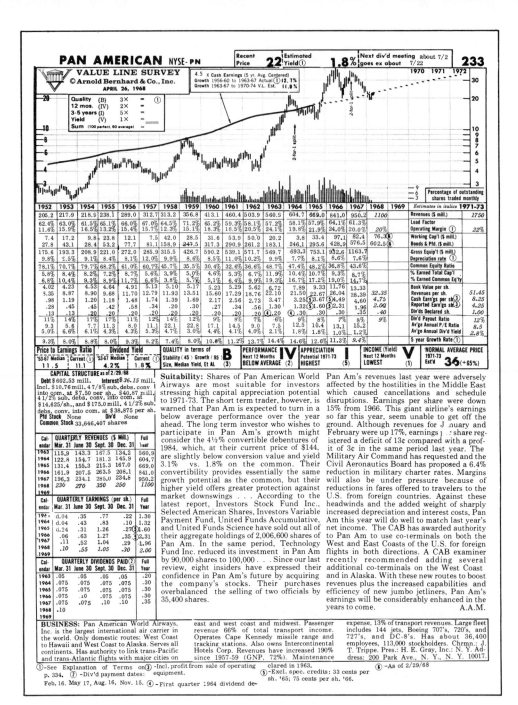

FIGURE 6–6

Common-stock information

SOURCE *The Value Line Investment Surveys*, Arnold Bernhard & Co., New York, April 26, 1968, p. 233

Summary

In the past decade, common-stock ownership with its inherent risks and potential rewards has been increasingly attractive to the public. In distinct contrast to bonds or preferred stock, the earnings and dividends on common stock are not fixed by contract or indentures but are determined by the success of the business. Since the common stockholder is the residual owner—the risk taker—he receives profits, but he also assumes the risk of loss. The stockholder has the right to receive a certificate as evidence of ownership, to receive dividends, to vote on corporate matters, and to maintain his proportional share in the earnings, assets, and voting control through the pre-emptive right granted in many states. Dividends received on common stock are in the form of either cash, stock and cash, or stock. The type of dividend will have an important effect on the investor's tax position. A stock dividend, for example, is not taxable until sold. A cash dividend is taxable in the year paid. Investors in the high tax brackets are interested in companies that pay a stock dividend.

The investor must make a valuation of common stock before he invests. The success of common-stock investment is determined by timing and by certainty of earnings. A company offering growth of earnings and a high degree of certainty of earnings will bear less risk than one that promises little growth and a great deal of uncertainty. Current yields on common stock have been low in the early sixties and have moved downward over the past decade; they are now less than bond yields. Current yield, however, has been only a small portion of investment return on many common stocks. The yield to maturity is more important, but little information exists about investment returns over time. Investors are wise to measure yield from a historical investment as a measure of performance. A yield of 9 percent over long periods is possible. This is comparable with and higher than the return on either bonds or preferred stock. Common-stock owners experience the business risk and market risk, but they do not assume completely the purchasing-power risk. Some common stocks are susceptible to changes in money rates. When money rates are high, income stocks tend to decline and do share the money rate risk. Common stock appears in portfolios that are aggressively seeking gains in an inflationary market. It also meets the needs of the growth and income investor. The major advantage of common stock is the capital gains that can be earned because the stock directly shares in the growth of the company. The major disadvantage is the greater risk of loss of capital and the lack of stability of income. Well-selected common stocks should, over time, overcome these risks.

Review Questions

1. Has there been a marked change toward ownership of common stock in recent years? Comment.

2. Common stock represents the residual ownership of the corporation. Explain.

3. How would you explain what we own when we own a share of common stock?

4. How do ordinary voting and cumulative voting differ?

5. What is the significance of the par value of common stock?

6. What is the significance of book value, and how does it differ from par value and market value?

7. What are the typical forms of dividend payments?

8. How is the dividend rate established?

9. What is the tax advantage in stock dividends? Is this true of dividends paid in securities of companies not held by the investor?

10. Some people think that stock dividends are unrealistic and unnecessary since they give the investor what he has already received. Comment.

11. What is meant by the following terms:
    (a) *Property dividend*
    (b) *Liquidating dividend*
    (c) *Scrip dividend*
    (d) *Bond dividend*

12. What are the advantages of the pre-emptive right that is associated with ownership of common stock?

13. Do rights have value? Discuss.

14. Might the market value and the theoretical value of a right differ? Discuss.

15. Explain the difference between current yield on common stock and yield to maturity.

16. What has been the trend of current yields from 1957 until the present?

17. What are the basic risks involved in the ownership of common stock?

18. What are the advantages and disadvantages of common-stock ownership?

19. What place does common stock have in the investor's portfolio?

20. How should we measure the performance and yield on a common stock?

Problems

1. In Moody's or Standard & Poor's manuals find the stated characteristics of the common stock of Dow Chemical, Springfield Gas
Light, and Atchison, Topeka, & Santa Fe.
   (a) Is the common stock of each of these companies typical?
   (b) Find the following for each of the companies:
       (1) Amount of the dividend
       (2) Date of record for dividends and date of payment
       (3) Current yield
       (4) Earnings per share since 1957
   (c) Comment upon the significance of the four items above.

2. As an owner of American Widget Company common, you are given
the right to subscribe to a new issue of stock that is being sold to
raise capital to expand plant facilities. The announcement of the
offering was made on January 1 for owners on record January 30.
The rights expire February 15. Subscription price for the new stock
was set at $45 per share. Each stockholder is allowed to buy one new
share at the subscription price for each eight shares of stock owned.
The market price January 7 was $54.
   (a) What was the theoretical value of the right on January 7?
   (b) If nothing disturbed the price, what would the value of the right
       be on February 1?
   (c) What value would the right have on February 16?

3. Would we expect the market price and theoretical price to be the
same in this case? Why or why not?

4. The Boatright Company expects its earnings and dividends to increase in the future. Several of the officers of the company have made
forecasts of earnings and dividends from 1969 through 1973 as follows:

Year	Estimated Earnings	Estimated Dividends
1969	$2.10	$1.05
1970	2.30	1.15
1971	2.50	1.25
1972	2.80	1.40
1973	3.10	1.55

The current market price is 63 and the current yield 1.66 percent.
The dividend yield and price-earnings ratio will remain constant and
close to present levels. Assume that these estimates are accurate.
Ignoring federal income taxes, what is the expected yield to maturity?

5. Plot the earnings of AT&T from 1962 to the present, and forecast
the earnings for the next five years. (A simple line fitted to the data
or the least-squares method will suffice.)

(a) Estimate future dividends for the five-year period based upon past relationships.
(b) Calculate yield to maturity.
(c) Would we conclude that the yield is satisfactory?
(d) Have the past earnings been stable? What effect would this have on the earnings forecast?

Sources of Investment Information

Annual reports of companies
Barron's
Commercial and Financial Chronicle
Clark Dodge Investment Reports
Forbes
Moody's manuals
New York Times and other daily papers
Standard & Poor's *The Outlook*
Standard & Poor's *Industry Surveys*
Standard & Poor's *Stock Guide*
3-Trend Security Charts
The Value Line Investment Survey
Wall Street Journal
Wall Street Journal Index

Selected Readings

Brigham, E. F., and J. L. Pappas "Growth Rate Changes and Common Stock Prices," *Financial Analysts Journal* (May-June, 1966), p. 157.

Keller, Philip R., "Utility Stock vs. Bonds," *Financial Analysts Journal* (May-June, 1968), p. 127.

Niederhoffer, Victor, "Some Properties of Stock Prices," *Financial Analysts Journal* (March-April, 1968), p. 105.

Smith, Keith V., "Option Writing," *Financial Analysts Journal* (May-June, 1968), p. 135.

Snyder, Gerard L., "A Look at Options," *Financial Analysts Journal* (January-February, 1967), p. 100.

Soldofsky, R.M., and C.R. Johnson, "Rights Timing," *Financial Analysts Journal* (July-August, 1967), p. 101.

Stevenson, Richard A., "The Variability of Common Stock Quality Ratings," *Financial Analysts Journal* (November-December, 1966), p. 97.

Young, Allan, "Common Stocks After Repurchase," *Financial Analysts Journal* (September-October, 1967), p. 117.

COMMON-STOCK VALUATION AND THE COMPUTER

7

THE VALUATION OF COMMON STOCK AND THE COMPUTER

The valuation of common stock is much more difficult than that of preferred stock and bonds. Much more uncertainty and instability surrounds common stock. Bonds have a superior claim on assets and income, and as long as the interest and principal on a bond is adequately secured and the yield satisfactory, the decision to invest is not difficult. The satisfying aspect of investing in bonds is the certainty of income and yield. We rely on this certainty, and, though the yields are relatively modest, we are willing to temper our expectations and be satisfied with these lower yields when we examine the advantages. Greater risk is associated with preferred stock investment. Dividends are less certain and do not represent a fixed commitment of the company. Yet even with this uncertainty, a proper valuation of preferred stock is relatively easy. Yields are easily determined, and we can readily establish if the dividend and principal value are secure. The tests involved are quite simple to apply. Within reasonable limits of accuracy, we know what to expect from a preferred stock investment. We can, therefore, make our decision whether or not to invest based upon expectations of the yield.

The Problem of Valuation of Common Stock

In the case of common-stock investment our position is more complicated. We must deal with three important variables that are not fixed by a bond indenture or a preferred-stock agreement. First, we do not know precisely the amount of future earnings or when they will be earned. Second, we do not know the amount and timing of dividend income. Third, we do not know for certain the value that will be given to future earnings and dividends of the company. What would an investor be willing to pay for a share of stock considering the risks involved? If we knew all these variables, our investment decisions in buying common stock would be quite simple. If we had complete knowledge and certainty about future earnings, dividends, price, and risk associated with common-stock investment, we would have a much more stable investment. It would be quite similar to making a decision about bond investment.

A great deal of uncertainty surrounds an investment in common stock, however. We must attempt to estimate future earnings and dividends. We must determine the risks involved, and we must then weigh the earnings consistent with the risks and arrive at a value for the stock. We discussed investment risks in the first chapter. The business and market risks are associated with investing in common stock. The business risk varies from company to company. A company involved with products that meet our basic needs would, if properly managed, involve a relatively small degree of business risk. A manufacturer of hula hoops, on the other hand, would face a great degree of uncertainty and a great deal of business risk.

In reaching a solution to the valuation problem, we attempt to establish a normal level of risk. We can then rank each company in relation to this level. This is accomplished within an acceptable margin of error by the majority of investors. Once the companies are ranked according to their risk characteristics, yields are estimated to determine whether they are commensurate with the risk. Those projects that are extremely risky would have a high rate of yield. Conversely, if the risk were very small, a low rate of return would be acceptable. The principle is to maximize yield and minimize risk, with the emphasis on maximum yield with a given level of risk.

The value of any common stock is determined by the future income that will be received by the investor in the form of dividends, either from earnings or capital distribution, and in the return of capital at some future time. The purpose of valuation is to determine whether the income or flow of funds will provide a satisfactory yield commensurate with risk. There are several methods of valuation; most are based on some form of the present-value method. The measurement of present value is identical with measuring the yield on bonds discussed in Chapter 3.

These calculations require an estimate of future earnings. Once these are estimated and a risk rate of return established, it is a relatively simple matter to determine the value of a share of a company's stock. This can be done in many ways. We could capitalize the income by the risk rate of return, by using the basic and simple capitalization formula $V = \frac{i}{r}$ where V is the present value of the future income, i is the expected future average annual income in dollars, and r is the capitalization or risk rate. The capitalization formula gives us the present value of all future earnings at the indicated rate of return. If we found that average annual future earnings per share were estimated at $2.50 and we considered the risk rate to be 10 percent, then a share of stock should sell for $25 ($2.50/.10 = $25). If the market price were above $25, the stock would be overpriced and not a satisfactory investment. If the price were below the estimated value, the stock would be considered satisfactory and underpriced or undervalued.

The above assumptions represent an oversimplification of the problem of valuation. No mention has been made, for example, about the variation in the tax bracket of the investor. Nor were the problems involved in estimating future earnings or the proper capitalization rate indicated. Some investors will be adversely affected by a large dividend payout, whereas others would welcome it. Some would enjoy stock dividends; other would need cash income. And even though each company had a known degree of risk and a known income pattern, each investor would appraise the results differently to meet his own needs. However, the amount of earnings a company will generate in the future is not certain in either amount or timing. Nor are the risks involved easily determinable or unchangeable. Earnings and risks vary over time, and this is one of the first assumptions we must make when considering investing in common stock or when attempting to value it. The fundamental problems facing the investor then are: (1) what will a company earn per share in the future, and (2) what value will these earnings have, based upon the risks inherent in the industry, the company, and the common stock itself? These are essentially problems of valuation.

Graham, Dodd, and Cottle[1] state that the basic variable components in the valuation of common stock are four:
1. The expected future earnings
2. The expected future dividends
3. The capitalization rates—or multipliers—of the dividends and earnings
4. The asset values

It is appropriate at this time to examine each of these variables to understand the part they play in the process of valuation.

Expected Future Earnings

All methods of common-stock valuation are based upon or related to an estimate of expected future earnings. Past earnings are a valuable

---

1 Benjamin Graham, David L. Dodd, and Sidney Cottle, *Security Analysis*, 4th ed. (New York: McGraw-Hill Book Company, 1962), p. 443.

guide to the future earnings of a company, but future changes and differences must be considered. Although it may be impossible to forecast future earnings with precision, and despite the uncertainties involved, an estimate must be attempted by anyone who seeks to be successful in investment.

Any realistic estimate of future earnings must give recognition to the stability of earnings, their rate of growth, and their timing. Expected earnings will be based on the "normal" operations of the company and will ignore unnecessary, extraordinary sources of income or expense that unduly influence "normal" earnings. The determination of future normal expected earnings is based upon an estimate of future sales and expenses, using realistic accounting practices and reliable sources of information. We will discuss in depth the various methods of estimating future expected earnings. This should be the central integrating force in all of our deliberations.

The future expected growth rate is important in forecasting earnings for growth stocks and stocks of quality comparable to the Dow Jones Industrial Average. Special valuation techniques are necessary to value growth shares, particularly where there is a strong possibility that growth rates might diminish in the future, as they tend to do.

Expected Future Dividends

The level of future expected dividends is related to future expected earnings, the payout ratio, and the dividend policy established by management to provide maximum benefits to the stockholders and the company. Many methods of valuation, particularly the present-value method, consider future expected dividends partially or wholly as the basis for the valuation of common stock. These will be explored under the Capitalization of Dividend Method in this chapter. Just as the timing of future earnings is important in the valuation process, so too is the timing of future dividends; these must be reflected in the valuation process.

The Capitalization Rate

What rate should be used to capitalize earnings, and for what time period in the future? Whether we are referring to the capitalization of earnings or dividends, or a combination of both, and whether for a definite period of years or in perpetuity, we must use the appropriate rate. The appropriate capitalization rate will take into consideration the risks involved, the stability of earnings and payment of dividends, the growth of earnings or dividends expected in the future, and the certainty of earnings and dividends. Other things being equal, a higher capitalization rate will be employed where the risk is greater and a lower one where risks are lower.

Nicholas Molodovsky found the average return on common stocks since 1871 to be slightly less than 8 percent.[2] This could be used as an average capitalization rate for all common stocks. In a subsequent article Molodovsky and others[3] suggest 7 percent as an attainable rate usable as an average capitalization rate.

Fisher and Lorie found stocks yielding 9 percent for the period 1926 to 1960,[4] which gives another clue to what might be considered an average risk capitalization rate for the valuation process. In the last analysis, the rate chosen will range around these suggested norms, but it will be determined by appraisal of the risks involved.

The price-earnings ratio reflects the amount of risk associated with a particular common stock. Up to a point, the higher the P/E ratio, the lower the risk, and vice versa. High P/E ratio stock is supposed to be less risky only because of the high growth rate of earnings. Obviously stocks that are selling at infinite P/E ratios because of no earnings are in a high-risk category. Under certain "normal" circumstances the reciprocal of the P/E ratio is the capitalization rate. This is demonstrated in Table 7–1. The P/E ratios are current and are based upon the current level of earnings and current price. Growth rates of earnings and future earnings are not considered, and so the reciprocal of the P/E ratio is not a true rate by which to capitalize future earnings.

TABLE 7–1

Selected capitalization rates translated into
equivalent price-earnings ratio and
degree of risk

CAPITALIZATION RATE (%)		EQUIVALENT PRICE-EARNINGS RATIO
1	High	100 to 1
2	degree of	50 to 1
4	certainty	25 to 1
5		20 to 1
6	Normal	16.7 to 1
8	degree of certainty	12.5 to 1
10	or uncertainty	10 to 1
15		6.7 to 1
20	High	5 to 1
25	degree of	4 to 1
33 1/3	uncertainty	3 to 1
50		2 to 1

2 Nicholas Molodovsky, "Stock Values and Stock Prices—Part I," *Financial Analysts Journal*, May-June, 1960.

3 Nicholas Molodovsky, CFA; Catherine May, and Sherman Chattiner, "Common Stock Valuation—Principles, Tables, and Application," *Financial Analysts Journal*, March-April, 1965.

4 Lawrence Fisher and James H. Lorie, "Rates of Return on Investments in Common Stocks," *Journal of Business*, January, 1964.

In order to make this adjustment, Graham, Dodd, and Cottle provide us with a conversion table that takes into consideration future earnings growth rates. They limit their estimates to seven years and use an average P/E multiplier in the fourth year. The relationships appear in Table 7–2. Table 7–3 presents the same type of information for both shorter and longer periods of time.

The relationships in Table 7–2 and 7–3 provide an explanation of why an investor would be willing to pay forty times current earnings for a stock that has an indicated capitalization rate of 2½ percent. Actually, the capitalization rate would be substantially higher, because future earnings are expected to increase at an annual rate of 20 percent, as shown in Table 7–2.

TABLE 7–2

Average P/E multipliers and growth rates

EXPECTED RATE OF GROWTH FOR PRESENT YEAR AND NEXT SEVEN YEARS	AVERAGE PRICE-EARNINGS MULTIPLIER IN FOURTH YEAR	CURRENT PRICE-EARNINGS MULTIPLIER
%	(TIMES)	(TIMES)
3.5	13	15
5.0	14	17
7.2	15	20
10.0	16	23 1/2
12.0	17	27
14.3	18	31
17.0	19	35 1/2
20.0	20	41 1/2

SOURCE: Benjamin Graham, David L. Dodd, and Sidney Cottle, *Security Analysis*, 4th ed. (New York: McGraw-Hill Book Company, 1962), p. 537.

TABLE 7–3

Price-earnings ratios and growth rates

ANNUAL RATE OF INCREASE OF PER SHARE EARNINGS	Justified P/E Ratios				
	5 YEARS	7 YEARS	10 YEARS	15 YEARS	20 YEARS
2	15	15	13	12	10
4	17	17	16	16	15
5	18	18	18	18	18
6	19	19	20	21	22
8	21	22	24	28	30
10	23	25	28	35	45
12	25	28	33	48	
14	27	32	40		

SOURCE: Benjamin Graham, David L. Dodd, and Sidney Cottle, *Security Analysis*, 4th ed. (New York: McGraw-Hill Book Company, 1962), p. 591.

The Asset Values

Modern techniques applied to common-stock valuation do not emphasize book value or assets per share. Virtually the entire emphasis is placed upon expected earnings or dividends. Even though a careful estimate of expected future earnings has been made, however, in the valuation process, attention should be given to asset values. An examination of assets per share might reveal the existence of assets not needed for production of present earnings, and which could be sold or reemployed to add to future earning power.

Assume that a company is expected to earn $1.70 a share, on the average, into perpetuity. If we capitalize these earnings at 8 percent, the value per share would be $21.25 ($1.70/.08). However, the company owns assets of $4.00 per share, which are not needed to produce the average earnings of $1.70. This residual value should be added to the capitalized earnings to provide a current value of $25.25.

This, of course, requires careful estimates and knowledge. Ordinarily all the assets will be needed to produce the estimated future revenues. The astute analyst will consider all factors in the valuation process and under proper circumstances pick up an added "kicker"— assets that will result in added value. Usually the reverse situation is true; asset values do not approach the capitalized earnings value.

The Methods of Valuation

Several basic methods can be employed to estimate common-stock value. Those used most frequently are: (1) capitalization of earnings, (2) capitalization of dividends, (3) capitalization of cash earnings, (4) the present-value technique, and (5) an appraisal of psychological forces affecting supply and demand.

Capitalization of Earnings Method

The capitalization of earnings valuation technique requires that an approximation of future annual earnings be established or estimated. This estimate is averaged and then capitalized to establish its present value. The capitalization rate is determined by the risks involved in the company and its industry. Presumably, the risk would be reflected in the marketplace by the ratio of price to earnings (P/E ratio). If a normal P/E ratio were 10/1, then the capitalization rate would be 10 percent. If future risks seem likely to be greater than past risks, then it would be necessary to raise the capitalization rate. If future risks are expected to be lower than past risks, then the capitalization rate would be lowered. Table 7–1 converts price-earnings ratios into capitalization rates and indicates the risk involved. A measure of risk, in part, then, is the level of the P/E ratio. The higher the P/E ratio, the lower the risk, other things being equal and assuming a compensating growth rate of earnings as in Tables 7–2 and 7–3.

Let us see how we would establish a value for a share of common stock with this method. Assume for a moment that a company is expected to earn $2.52 per annum, on the average, in the future. The average earnings result from the following income stream, where earnings are expected to grow at 5 percent per year.

Years in the Future	Earnings
1	2.00
2	2.10
3	2.21
4	2.32
5	2.44
•	2.56
•	2.69
•	2.82
•	2.96
n	3.11

The average for the period is $2.52. It was assumed that earnings would continue to grow in the future at a 5 percent rate. A normal risk rate for this company is 8 percent and an unchanging P/E ratio of 12.5 is assumed. Graham, Dodd, and Cottle[5] use a variation of the capitalization method by projecting earnings for the next seven years. Then they apply a multiplier to the average of the next seven years' earnings, which is the fourth year of earnings. The multiplier used depends on the rate of growth as shown in Table 7–2. Since the earnings growth rate is 5 percent in the example above, we can use this to convert future expected earnings into common-stock value. A 5 percent growth rate calls for a multiplier of 14. Fourteen times the fourth year's earnings of $2.32 provides a valuation of $32.48. This is Graham, Dodd, and Cottle's favored method of valuation for growth stock.

With a capitalization rate of 8 percent (or a P/E of 12.5 to 1), what should be the value of the stock, using the standard capitalization method? It is found by capitalizing the earnings using the formula $V_e = i_e/r_e$; V_e equals the value of the share of stock where earnings are capitalized, i_e equals the income, and r_e equals the risk rate of return, or the risk capitalization rate. When values are substituted in the equation, a capitalized value of $31.50 ($2.52/.08 = $31.50) is obtained; thus the indicated value of each share is $31.50. If the market price was $40, then we could conclude that the stock was overpriced. If the stock was selling at $20, it would be underpriced and an attractive pur-

5 Graham, Dodd, and Cottle, *Security Analysis*, Chapter 39.

chase. It would provide the investor with a yield, if the forecasted figures are accurate, of more than 8 percent.

We must emphasize that this is only an approximate indication of value. An investor would be wise to establish a range of earnings and then capitalize the high, low, and average earnings that are expected. Assume, for example, in the case above, that a 10 percent error was allowed in forecasting the earnings. Then the high earnings would be $2.77 and the low $2.27 ($2.52 ± 10 percent). The price range resulting when the earnings were capitalized at 8 percent would be between $34.62 and $28.37. Although this adjustment does not help in the decision-making process, it does provide more realism in the investment valuation and can still serve as a sound basis for judgment.

Capitalization of Dividends Method

Capitalization of dividends also can be used to estimate the value of common stock. Future dividends must be estimated and then capitalized at a rate that reflects the risk involved. Let us go back to the example we used when we capitalized earnings. Assume that the company had a payout ratio of 60 percent. Expected earnings in the future are $2.52 a share, which would provide an annual dividend of $1.51 ($2.52 × 60 percent). The dividend rate would then be capitalized at 7.5 percent. This rate is suggested by Graham, Dodd, and Cottle[6] and is similar to the rate used by Nicholas Molodovsky in his writings.[7] It is made up of a 2.5 percent growth rate and a historical dividend rate of 5 percent.

The capitalization formula is $V_d = i_d / r_d$, where V_d equals the value of the capitalized dividends, i_d equals the dividend income, and r_d the capitalization rate of dividend income. When the values are substituted in the formula, a value of $20.13 is obtained ($V_d = \$1.51/.075 = \$20.13$). If the stock was trading at this value, it would be considered reasonably priced. Above this price, it would be overpriced and below, it would be underpriced. The dividend capitalization method resulted in a lower value than the capitalization of earnings method.

John C. Clendenin takes a similar approach, using the rate of dividend growth, the duration of the growth trend, and the capitalization rate. He has devised tables that convert these variables into a multiplier. When this is multiplied by the dollars of dividends expected over a period of years, a reasonable value of common stock is obtained. Tables 7–4 and 7–5 provide these multipliers. Using Table 7–4, we can find the present value of the dividend at a 5 percent growth rate for 10

---

6 Graham, Dodd, and Cottle, *Security Analysis*, Chapter 39.

7 Nicholas Molodovsky, "Valuations of Common Stocks," *Financial Analysts Journal*, February, 1959; "Stock Values and Stock Prices—Part 1," *Financial Analysts Journal*, May-June, 1960; and "Dow-Jones Industrials—A Reappraisal," *Financial Analysts Journal*, March-April, 1961.

years. The dividend in the first year for the company illustrated above was $1.20 ($2.00 × 60 percent payout). Multiplying $1.20 × $24.85 from Table 7–4, we arrive at a value of $29.82. Our error limits of ± 10 percent would provide a range in values of from $26.84 to $32.80. Using the information in Table 7–5, we arrive at a value of $37.45 ($31.21 × $1.20) based upon the method used and stated in the table.

The various methods used produce a range of values from $20.13 to $37.45. We might have expected this, but it is disquieting to know that the results have such a wide range. A pragmatist faced with this dilemma would suggest that "if you could get it for 30 bucks a share, you've got a good investment."

The unfortunate aspect of the capitalization of dividend income is that some companies do not pay dividends and others pay stock dividends. Since neither policy represents dollar income, it is impossible to include these figures in the dividend capitalization calculation. In cases where a stock dividend is paid, the cash equivalent can be used to provide an estimate of cash income. However, this is not cash income to the investor. Since the purpose of the capitalization of dividends is to reflect the present value of cash income, then it is doubtful whether one should consider the cash equivalent of stock dividends. Where there are no declared dividends or only stock dividends, we should use the capitalization of earnings method of valuation.

Capitalization of Cash Earnings Method

More and more emphasis is being given to cash flow or cash earnings of the company as a broader measure of corporate profitability. *Cash earnings* does not mean that actual cash dollars will be available for the stockholder; management uses the term as a partial guide to capital expenditures or dividend policy. Since *cash flow* represents the return of

TABLE 7–4

Approximate present values of all future dividends on a stock now paying $1.00 per annum, if the dividend is expected to increase at the indicated compound rate for the indicated period of years and then remain stable until 100 years from today, and if the payments of the first decade are discounted at 4 percent, those of the second at 5 percent, those of the third at 6 percent, and those of the remaining 70 years at 7 percent.

GROWTH PERIOD	*Annual Growth Rates*				
	5%	4%	3%	1%	0%
None	$17.01	$17.01	$17.01	$17.01	$17.01
10 years	24.85	23.04	21.37	18.37	17.01
20 years	31.21	27.51	24.27	19.12	17.01
30 years	35.97	30.55	26.08	19.51	17.01
40 years	39.65	32.67	27.22	19.69	17.01
50 years	42.63	34.23	27.99	19.80	17.01

capital as well as income, it would be considered a broader index of profitability. Essentially, we raise the question, Rather than capitalize earnings at the risk rate, why not capitalize cash flow? Let us assume another case where the earnings per share are $2.52. Now add on $.50 per share, which represents depreciation, or the return of our invested capital over future years. This gives us a cash flow figure of $3.02. Now let us capitalize this figure at 10 percent, which is the risk rate appropriate for direct investments by businessmen where there is a return of capital by depreciation. Then substitute into our new equation, $V_{cf} = i_{cf}/r_{cf}$ where V_{cf} equals value of the cash flow; i_{cf} equals the cash flow income, which is net income plus depreciation or other noncash income per share; and r_{cf} is the risk rate of capitalization of the cash flow. We get a value of $30.20 $\pm$ 10 percent per share as the capitalized cash flow value per share. This provides a price range of $27.18 to $33.22.

The capitalization of cash flow method is useful, since it considers the impact of depreciation accounting on the estimate of profitability. Businesses are being urged more and more to increase their capital expenditures. To encourage more capital spending, the Internal Revenue Code allows companies to use accelerated depreciation in their

TABLE 7–5

Approximate present values of the future dividends on a stock now paying $1.00 per annum, if the dividends are expected to grow at the indicated rates for 20 years and then remain stable for the next 80 years, and if the dividends of the first decade are discounted at 4 percent, those of the second at 5 percent, those of the third at 6 percent, and those of the remaining 70 years at 7 percent.

GROWTH RATE PER YEAR	Present Values				
	FIRST DECADE	SECOND DECADE	THIRD DECADE	NEXT 70 YEARS	TOTAL
6 percent	$10.85	$11.36	$7.36	$5.96	$35.53
5 percent	10.35	9.84	6.09	4.93	31.21
4 percent	9.87	8.53	5.03	4.08	27.51
3 percent	9.40	7.37	4.14	3.36	24.27
2 percent	8.96	6.39	3.41	2.76	21.52
1 percent	8.53	5.52	2.80	2.27	19.12
0 percent	8.11	4.74	2.30	1.86	17.01

NOTE: Tables 7-4 and 7-5 are calculated on the assumption that each year's dividend is received at the year end, and that it contains the full year's growth element. The shortcut calculation methods that were used may underestimate some of the values by as much as 1 1/2 percent. Slide rule computations were used.

SOURCE: Paul F. Wendt, "Current Growth Stock Valuation Methods," *Financial Analysts Journal*, March-April, 1965, as it appeared in The Institute of Chartered Financial Analysts, *CFA Readings in Financial Analysis*, 1st ed. (Homewood, Ill.: Richard D. Irwin, Inc., 1966), p. 486. Based on an article by John C. Clendenin, "Theory and Technique of Growth Stock Valuation," Occasional Paper No. 1, Bureau of Business and Economic Research, UCLA, 1957.

accounting practices. As a result, earnings after taxes, depreciation, and noncash expenses are lower than they would be under more conventional accounting methods. By adding depreciation into net income after taxes, the analyst compensates for the larger amount of depreciation and has a clearer overall measure of profitability and the return of capital. In addition, he must adjust depreciation rates to obtain comparability. This method of valuation can be used even when the company does not pay a cash dividend. The capitalized value of cash earnings cannot be compared with the capitalization of dividends or earnings. It is best used as an index for comparison with other companies in the industry.

Present Value of Price and Dividends Method

The present-value method combines the capitalization of earnings and the capitalization of dividends techniques. It makes one or two assumptions about the pattern of income and the return of capital that are not made by the other methods. First, an estimate of future earnings and dividends is required. Second, this method assumes that the investor is interested in capital gains as well as income, therefore, he must estimate a future price. This price will be estimated for a finite number of years during which he will put his money to work. By way of contrast the capitalization process assumes an infinite number of years and future price is not estimated. But since an investment is usually made for a limited number of years, an assumption of a future price within a few years is more realistic. The Molodovsky, the Clendenin, and the Graham, Dodd, and Cottle methods all are approximations of the discount or present-value method.

The investor is interested not so much in the rate of capitalization as in knowing whether the income and capital gains he will receive will provide a satisfactory rate of return on his investment. He is also interested in yield after taxes, since tax rate will have an impact upon his decisions. In other words, the investor wants to know if an investment will provide him with an acceptable after-tax yield consistent with risk, based upon expected income and the future price of the stock. In short, what does he get out of it in cash?

Let us go back to our original example and use the assumptions about average future earnings and dividends to see how the present value of dividends and price works. Let us now assume the common stock is selling at $35 per share and earning $2 per share at present; within five years, earnings are expected to reach $2.44 per share. The company pays out 60 percent of its earnings as dividends; the present dividend is $1.20 per share. The stock is selling for a current yield of 3.43 percent, and it has a price-earnings ratio of 17.5 to 1. An investor examines the stock price and its future potential earnings. He knows that the earnings forecasts are only approximations and are subject to change. The company's earnings are increasing rapidly, but in five years they will probably not be growing at such an accelerated rate. In five years the P/E ratio will reflect this slower rate and will drop to 15 to 1 instead of the present 17.5 to 1. This is a realistic estimate, but of course it is not a certainty. The prospects of the company appear to be something like this:

		EARNINGS	DIVIDENDS	MARKET VALUE OF STOCK	P/E
Present year	1	$2.00	$1.20	$35.00	17.5/1
	2	2.10	1.26	————	————
	3	2.21	1.33	————	————
	4	2.32	1.39	————	————
Five years hence	5	2.44	1.46	$36.60	15/1

Now we may ask, What is the present value of the income from this investment, assuming the investor wishes a 10 percent yield after income taxes? Does the present market price allow him to earn 10 percent? He is in the 30 percent marginal tax bracket, and his after-tax income and capital gains on each share will be as follows:

YEARS	AFTER-TAX DIVIDEND INCOME (30% TAX RATE)		PRESENT VALUE OF $ AT A DISCOUNT RATE OF 10%		PRESENT VALUE
1	$ .84	×	.909	=	$ .764
2	.88	×	.826	=	.727
3	.93	×	.751	=	.698
4	.97	×	.683	=	.663
5	1.02	×	.621	=	.633
	36.36[a]	×	.621	=	22.579
			Total Present Value		$26.064

[a] After-tax value of stock sold at $36.60 in five years, which is the market price five years hence. The gain on the transaction would be $1.60. The tax would be $.24 because the investor would declare half the gain and pay ordinary income taxes on the remaining half. The dividend credit that is allowed by the IRS is ignored for these computations.

In these calculations a 10 percent discount rate applied to the income and return of capital after taxes provided a present worth of $26.06. Since this is lower than the $35.00 current price of the stock, the investor would earn less than 10 percent. The actual after-tax yield would be 3.3 percent. The investment therefore would be unsatisfactory, failing to meet the standards imposed by the investor.

At what price would the stock provide a 10 percent rate of return? A price of $26 would provide a yield of 10 percent after taxes. Therefore, the investor wishing to buy this stock would wait until it could be purchased for $26 or less. An investor wishing an 8 percent yield could buy between $28 and $30 and obtain such a yield.

Each year the investor would revise his estimates of future earnings, dividends, and price. As long as the stock continues to earn a yield that is satisfactory, he will hold the security. If the estimates provide a lower yield than he desires, he will sell the stock and look for a more attractive investment alternative.

The formula for the stock market value equation is as follows:

$$V = \frac{D_1}{1 + k} + \frac{D_2}{(1 + k)^2} + \cdots + \frac{D_5}{(1 + k)^5} + \frac{P_5}{(1 + k)^5}$$

where V = value,
D_1-D_5 = the future expected dividend by year,
k = the discount rate, and
P_5 = the future expected price, which is the product of earnings in the fifth year and a "normal" or current P/E ratio.

In actual practice, V represents the current market price. What we are trying to learn is whether the stock at its current price will provide a risk rate of return acceptable to the investor. Therefore k is the variable for which the equation is solved.

Dividends are based upon future expected earnings. In the illustration presented, a 60 percent payout rate was assumed. Actually this rate will vary in practice.

P is the product of earnings (E) five years hence and the P/E ratio or multiplier (M) that represents a realistic risk level for the company. A ten-year P/E ratio, pragmatically, has been found by the author to be a realistic multiplier; Arnold Bernhard of *Value Line*, however, uses a fifteen-year average. A stock selling at high P/E multiples has its P/E norms; over a ten-year period these are somewhat below its high P/E ratio. If one values a stock selling at a high P/E multiple, it is wise to assume that sometime in the future, the P/E ratio will be lower, since the rate of growth of earnings of a growth company will not continue to rise indefinitely. The growth rate tends to diminish, and the high P/E ratios caused by rapid growth of earnings usually come down. A stock with a 50 to 1 P/E ratio and a 25 percent growth rate is not likely to continue this relationship for a long period.

The five-year forecast period in the formula was used consciously. Five-years reflects the length of the corporate planning period and is long enough to overcome the effects of the stock market. It is also much closer to the investment period than we would ordinarily assume when we peer down the profit road to financial success. It is difficult to document the following statement, but as a working hypothesis it is correct: The investment period is much closer to 3–5 years than to any other period of time. Some mutual funds look for a substantial gain for one or two years and no farther, but "go-go" outfits are in the minority.

The formula used offers great flexibility just as do the Clendenin, Molodovsky, and Graham, Dodd, and Cottle formulas. The capitalization formula of dividends used by Molodovsky[8] is

8 Molodovsky, May, and Chattiner, "Common Stock Valuation."

$$V = D_0 + \frac{D_1}{1 + k} + \frac{D_2}{(1 + k)^2} + \cdots \frac{D_n}{(1 + k)^n}$$

where D_0 is the dividend initially

    D_n is the dividend in the year indicated, D_1 being the first and D_5 the fifth

    k is the discount rate, or the desired rate of return

The formula we have used simply asks investors to focus upon a realistic time period along with a dividend and future price expectation that are realistic.

The advantage of the present-value technique for the valuation of common stock is its versatility. It can be used with equal facility for companies that do not pay dividends and for those that pay cash or stock dividends. It also focuses attention on future price expectations as well as future earnings expectations. It considers the time period of investment, which is more realistic than assuming a perpetual investment period. The method considers the tax position of the investor, as well as his attitude toward investment risk. It can be used with a growth stock and with an income stock for a rich or an average investor.

The Psychological Aspects of Valuation

A number of people say that value is determined by the supply and demand for the stock and the psychological aspects related to the stock. Demand might or might not be an accurate reflection of value that considers only earnings. In past years investors have purchased stock for fear of inflation. This has tended to bid up the price beyond historic norms of P/E relationships. Institutional investors have played an important part in this process, since institutions account for more than 50 percent of market activity. They must invest their funds either in bonds or stocks. When they purchase equity securities, they insist upon high-quality stocks. Since a limited number of such stocks are available for investment, these are bid up higher than normal. Thus demand exceeds supply, and the price goes up. In short, the stock moves up in price because the psychology of the market toward the stock is favorable. Historically, institutional investors were more cautious on the down side of the market and most often invested in fixed-income obligations instead of stocks. They are "go-go" oriented and tend to follow each other. When the psychology of the market suggests "no buy," demand subsides and prices fall. In this situation, relative supply is greater than demand.

The psychological aspects of supply and demand help to explain short-range cyclical market effects. From time to time, too much or too little demand in relation to supply causes excessive price fluctuations. An example of this is Texas Instruments common, which was bid up to an inordinately high price, going to approximately 256 in the early 1960's, and then dropping back to the 60–70 price range. Short-term demand had moved the price too high in relation to earnings and investment position. Countless other examples could be given: General Dynamics, Alpine Geophysical, Leasco, and even IBM have been in this category. Unfortunately, the law of supply and demand is valid as it applies to common-stock prices. Demand should be based upon a realistic price for realistic earnings. Demand based upon extremely optimistic views of the future and a pie-in-the-sky philosophy is wrong. It is the author's thesis that demand should be determined by future earnings capitalized at a reasonable rate. There is a limit to what can realistically be paid for common stock. An excessive price created by an artificial demand-supply relationship can lead only to excessive loss by the investor. Supply and demand that is based on the fundamental earnings position of and the risks inherent in the company is a valuable way to approximate price and value.

Valuation and the Computer

The valuation formula of

$$V = \frac{D_1}{(1 + k)} + \frac{D_2}{(1 + k)^2} + \frac{D_3}{(1 + k)^3} + \frac{D_4}{(1 + k)^4} +$$

$$\frac{D_5}{(1 + k)^5} + \frac{P_5}{(1 + k)^5}$$

is well adapted to the computer if we are willing to accept the calculation of trends based on historical data. Certainly, projections that provide us with estimates of expected future earnings; expected future dividends; estimates of P/E multiples, stability of earnings, and yields to maturity and also provide clues to the earnings capitalization rate multiplier uphold all the variables recommended by Graham, Dodd, and Cottle[9]. Such projections are comparable with the ideas of valuation discussed by other financial and academic writers, like Clendenin,[10] Bauman,[11] Ferguson,[12] Hayes,[13] Malkiel,[14] Molodovsky,[15] and Walter.[16]

9 Graham, Dodd, and Cottle, *Security Analysis.*

10 John C. Clendenin, "Theory and Technique of Growth Stock Valuation," Occasional Paper No. 1, Bureau of Business and Economic Research, UCLA, 1957.

11 W. Scott Bauman, "Estimating the Present Value of Common Stock by the Variable Rate Method," Michigan Business Reports No. 42, Bureau of Business Research, University of Michigan, 1963.

12 Robert Ferguson, "A Monograph for Valuing Growth Stocks," *Financial Analysts Journal,* May-June, 1961, pp. 29–34.

13 Douglas A. Hayes, CFA, "Some Reflections on Techniques for Appraising Growth Rates," *Financial Analysts Journal,* July-August, 1964.

14 B. G. Malkiel, "Equity Yields and Structure Share Prices," *The American Economic Review,* December, 1963, pp. 1004–31.

15 Molodovsky, May, and Chattiner, "Common Stock Valuation."

16 James E. Walter, "Dividend Policy and Common Stock Prices," *Journal of Finance,* March, 1956, pp. 29–42.

If data can be provided quickly and accurately with a minimum of maintenance and updating, the investor, analyst, or portfolio manager has another valuable tool for analysis. The computer program presented here is applied to the valuation equation above. It produces results on the IBM 360–50 in about three seconds, with only one second devoted to computation. To do the same work by desk calculator would require approximately three hours; it is evident that the computer saves a tremendous amount of time.

The investment analysis profession in the United States has been moving toward new frontiers in the use of the computer in its daily activities. In the future, there will be greater emphasis on the large computer throughout the entire investment process—both analysis and management. There is an obvious need for use of the computer in assimilating the large quantity of data needed to assess the latest changes in price and earnings in relation to the short- and long-range investment positions of thousands of common stocks. With the computer, we can aid analysts in selecting from among seemingly attractive investment opportunities and in putting together the combination of securities offering maximization of reward. A program such as the following might be useful in the analyst's work.

The Computer Program

Figure 7–1 shows the output of a computer program developed by the author.[17] The company presented is Minnesota Mining and Manufacturing, in the office equipment industry. A description of the various items of output in the figure, following the alphabetic labels, will explain what is involved in the program and how it may be used. The input of the program is a set of cards, one for each year, giving the high price, the low price, the earnings per share, and dividends paid by the corporation. The input becomes part of the output and can be seen at Item A in Figure 7–1. In addition, the card for the last year includes the current price of the stock, the estimated earnings for the current year, and the current estimated dividend. This information must be provided by the analyst and will reflect his current interpretation of annual earnings data. The program is written to handle ten years of data, but shorter time periods may be used. The analyst would require ten years of data to make a meaningful analysis.

The actual output of the computer in terms of calculation is presented in Items B through P. In Item B we find a projected price

---

17 This program was developed by the author while Professor of Finance at Miami University. It was written originally by Dr. David Griffing, Professor of Physics, Miami University. Subsequent revisions in format were accomplished by graduate students at Miami. The present program and format were written by Jack Silver, Graduate Assistant in the College of Business Administration, University of Rhode Island.

MINNESOTA MINING AND MANUFACTURING				OFFICE EQUIPMENT	
YEAR	HIGH	LOW	EPS	DIVIDEND	
57	33.000	19.000	0.780	0.400	
58	38.000	24.000	0.860	0.400	
59	60.000	37.000	1.250	0.500	
60	88.000	53.000	1.380	0.580	
61	87.000	66.000	1.460	0.650	A
62	70.000	41.000	1.610	0.800	
63	73.000	52.000	1.730	0.900	
64	70.000	54.000	1.920	1.000	
65	71.000	54.000	2.180	1.100	
66	86.000	61.000	2.590	1.200	
67	83.880 (CURRENT)		2.750(EST)	1.450(EST)	

MINNESOTA MINING AND MANUFACTURING		OFFICE EQUIPMEN 10 YEARS OF DATA		
PROJECTED AND CURRENT PRICE		EARNINGS GROWTH RATES		
1-10	108.08	1-4	23.19	
6-1	90.10 B	4-7	8.07	C
8-10	88.82	7-10	14.31	
CURRENT	83.88			

PROJECTED 5 YEAR PRICE		EARNING GROWTH RATES		
1-10	176.52	1-10	13.05	
6-10	144.57 D	6-10	12.55	E
8-10	161.62	8-10	16.14	

AVERAGE AND CURRENT PRICE-EARNINGS RATIO		PROJECTED CURRENT EARNINGS AND ESTIMATED CURRENT EARNINGS		
10 YEAR	37.16	1-10	2.91	
5 YEAR	31.97	6-10	2.82	
3 YEAR	29.75 F	8-10	2.99 G	
CURRENT	30.50	ESTIMATED	2.75	

5 YEAR HIGH AND LOW PRICE-EARNINGS RATIO			
AVERAGE HIGH AND LOW PRICE-EARNINGS RATIO		PROJECTED LAST YEARS EARNINGS AND ACTUAL EARNINGS	
HIGH	59.59	10 YEARS	2.57
LOW	23.55	5 YEARS	2.50
HIGH AVERAGE	41.25 H	3 YEARS	2.57 I
LOW AVERAGE	29.53	ACTUAL	2.59

AVERAGE YIELD AND CURRENT YIELD				K
10 YEAR	1.34	GROWTH RATE STABILITY=	92.10	
5 YEAR	1.69	MAXIMUM EARNINGS DEVIATION=		1.15
3 YEAR	1.67 J			L
CURRENT	1.73	MINIMUM EARNINGS DEVIATION=		0.89

	EARNINGS GROWTH	10 YEAR PRICE EARNINGS RATIO	EARNINGS	PRICE	CURRENT YIELD	YIELD TO MATURITY	
10 YEAR RATE	13.05	37.16	4.75	176.52	1.28	21.00	M
3 YEAR RATE	16.14	37.16	5.43	201.88	1.28	25.07	N
	EARNINGS GROWTH	CURRENT PRICE EARNINGS RATIO					
3 YEAR RATE	16.14	30.50	5.43	165.70	1.56	19.15	O
10 YEAR RATE	13.05	30.50	4.75	144.89	1.56	15.29	P

FIGURE 7-1

*Input-output analysis of computer
valuation program*

for Minnesota Mining stock based on three different trends. The projected price for 1967 based on ten years of data is $108.08, for five years of data $90.10, and on the basis of the last three years, $88.82 per share. This was accomplished by fitting a curve to the price data and then extending it one year.

The earnings growth rate, so necessary in forecasting future earnings in modern financial analysis, is presented in Items C and E. In C we have the growth rate of earnings for 1957 to 1960, 1960 to 1963, and 1963 to 1966. The earnings growth rate under E covers the entire period from 1957 to 1966 as well as the last five years and three years. Item **K** shows that Minnesota Mining had a stability of earnings of 92.1 percent. Pragmatically speaking, anything above 80 percent is a highly stable growth rate. The maximum and minimum earnings deviations under Item L seem large compared with the amount of earnings realized by the company from 1957 to 1966. However, when we consider that the trend of earnings has been rising steadily, the earnings deviations are not as large as a first appraisal suggests, since the deviations were created by the growth of earnings.

What might we expect of future price if the relationships that existed for the past ten years were extended five years into the future? Item D represents such a projected five-year expected price based on ten years, five years, and three years of data. This, too, is a simple curve fitted to the price data and extended. It is not a sophisticated methodology, but nonetheless it gives us some idea of where we might be five years hence if the same conditions continue into the future, and it can make the *same* calculation in the *same* way for each company analyzed.

The price-earnings ratio is extremely vital to understanding the risks involved in any particular investment situation. Knowledge of the historical P/E ratio of a particular company, not available in the usual current financial periodicals for analysts and investors, would be an excellent tool for understanding the risk factor. Items F and H give some insight into the P/E relationship of 3M. The ten-year P/E ratio for 3M was 37, the five-year ratio was 32, and the three-year ratio 30, with a current P/E ratio of 30.5. This is a stable P/E ratio for a company. The range is presented in Item H, where we find the high, low, high average and low average P/E ratio. A stock like 3M would be selling at a high P/E ratio above 40 and a low P/E ratio around 20. This is helpful in understanding whether a stock is overpriced or underpriced.

Investors interested in current income would avoid Minnesota Mining. Its average and current yields are provided in Item J. The ten-year average yield was 1.34 percent, current yield is 1.73 percent. MMM is a growth stock and has made up in price what has been given up in current income. Nonetheless it wouldn't be recommended for income accounts. An item such as J is helpful when you're trying to determine where a stock should be used in a portfolio to meet the needs of the investor.

Item G presents a calculation of projected current earnings for 3M based upon ten, five, and three years of data along with the analyst's estimate. Based on the earnings trend for the past few years, the analyst's expectations are somewhat low.

In Item I we have a check on Item G. Earnings forecasted last year and what actually was earned are shown. It is interesting to note that actual earnings were close to the forecasts based on three and ten years of data.

If we put all these variables into the valuation equation, what do we get? In our Items M, N, O, and P, we find an example of what we might expect in the future, if past trends continue. Item M presents yield to maturity based on a ten-year earning growth rate and a ten-year average P/E ratio. (*Yield to maturity* used previously is a fictional phrase. There is no maturity for common stock, but it does assume a future selling price is the maturity price.) Earnings expected five years hence are computed, and the price expected five years hence based on this is calculated. Current yield based upon the expected future price is also calculated. The yield to maturity based on the current price of $83.88 and a future expected price of $176.52 is 21 percent. This is a substantial rate of return. The present value of the dividends on the basis of these earnings and the present value of the price of $176.52 discounted at 21 percent gives us the current price of $83.88. Again, the equating force is the discount rate for the yield to maturity rate expressed in the Yield to Maturity column for Items M, N, O, and P.

Item N is a repetition of item M except that it uses a three-year growth rate of 16.14 percent instead of the 13.05 percent ten-year growth rate. The 16.14 percent rate provides earnings five years hence of $5.43 and a price of $201.88. In this calculation the current yield remains the same and the yield to maturity increases to 25.07 percent. The ten-year P/E ratio of MMM is rather high—well above average. By using a more conservative P/E ratio in Items O and P, with the three- and ten-year growth rate, we get a more conservative, but nonetheless substantial, yield to maturity of 19.15 and 15.29 percent.

As we examine Minnesota Mining and Manufacturing based upon the computer output, we would have to agree that if the yield-to-maturity expectation for the next five years, between 15 and 25 percent, is correct, it represents a rather attractive investment opportunity. Certainly, we would not ignore it if we were interested in making profits in the stock market.

IS THERE PREDICTIVE VALUE IN THE COMPUTER PROGRAM?

As students of investment analysis and management, we might be interested in learning what success we would have had if we had used the results of the computer program in making investment decisions. We ask: If we focused only on the yield-to-maturity figures under Items M, N, O, and P, chose only the stock with the largest yield to maturity, and made investments only on the basis of this figure, how would we have done in our investment program? In order to find out, a study was conducted. We assumed that we bought stocks in the Dow Jones Industrial Average, which had the highest yield to maturity for the next five-year period as indicated by computer results. We assumed further that this process continued from 1916 through 1966. During that period, if we had bought all the Dow Jones Industrial Average stocks, we would have obtained an average yield of 14 percent—not a bad yield over a fifty-year period. If we had selected those companies in the top 25 percent of Dow Jones Industrial Average as ranked by yield, we would have achieved the following results:

If we used the current P/E ratio and the three-year earnings growth rate, we would have earned a yield to maturity of 16 percent.

If we used the current P/E ratio and the ten-year earnings growth rate, we would have earned 20 percent.

If we used a ten-year P/E ratio and a three-year earnings growth rate, we would have earned a yield to maturity of 18 percent.

If we used the ten-year P/E ratio and a ten-year growth rate, the yield would have been 23 percent.

On the basis of this study, we find that stocks in the DJIA selected by yield-to-maturity criteria provided by the computer would have resulted in yields above the DJIA yield to maturity. The yield based upon three sets of assumptions proved significantly higher, which indicates that other than chance factors were present in the selection process. It would seem then that the yield to maturity, as calculated by the computer, does have some predictive characteristics. It is not perfect and the variables must be examined with judgment, but it does give a valuable comparable guide to what we might expect in the future for a given set of variables if the past continues in the future. Actual experience with the program suggests that the greatest reliability is with the stable growth company. The program is not satisfactory for trading, new issues, or cyclical stocks. It is not particularly good for short-term market swings. It is helpful to investors who want fundamentals and a look at an uncertain future.

Summary

In summary, a valuation of common stock based upon an accurate estimate of future earnings, dividend, price, and appraisal of risk will tend to improve investment performance. Without these ingredients we cannot make a fair estimate of the worth of a share of common stock. The present-value method, in which we look at the expected behavior of earnings and dividends, focuses attention upon what the investor expects and will receive and his tax position, as well as the earnings capability of the company. When possible, we recommend that the present-value method be used in the decision-making process.

The computer program written is not a panacea for all investment decisions. It is a guide that can be used by the intelligent analyst and investor making investment decisions. If we are going to examine theoretical factors suggested in this chapter and writings about investment analysis, management, and the frontiers of investment, we should begin to adapt these practices to the computer and test the results. Without this exposure and study, the investment analysis profession will not progress. It is important to learn the work being done in using basic and theoretical valuation formulas and applying them via the computer to investment analysis and management by analysts. The discussion in this chapter suggests that future earnings, dividends, prices, and a proper capitalization rate plus residual asset values are the focal point for a valuation estimate of common stock. Our decision about the valuation of common stock is only as good as our estimates and judgment of the future.

Review Questions

1. What is the purpose of common-stock valuation?
2. Why is the valuation of common stock difficult?
3. What are the variables one must consider in the valuation of common stock?
4. Is there one best method of common-stock valuation?
5. The past market and yield action of a common stock does not necessarily tell us about the future. Comment.
6. If an investor who wanted an 8 percent return on an investment could buy at a current price that was exactly equal to the sum of all future dividends plus a price n years in the future, it would not be an attractive investment because it did not offer anything more than an 8 percent rate of return. Comment.
7. If we had perfect knowledge about the future earnings of a company and its dividend pattern, there wouldn't be any point in investing in the stock because the rate of return would be too low. Comment.
8. What other factors should we examine in making an estimate of the future?
9. What determines the amount of risk that is involved in making a forecast of earnings?
10. Explain how we might arrive at a valuation of a common stock by the use of the capitalization of earnings method, capitalization of dividends method, capitalization of cash earnings method, the present value method and the supply-and-demand psychological method. (Use specific details of each method described in the chapter as your source of information.)

Problems

1. National Business Incorporated had the following sales, earnings, and dividends for the last five years:

Earnings	Dividends	Sales (millions)	Stockholders' Equity
$1.67	$1.20	$7.67	$3.76
2.02	1.20	8.11	3.86
2.37	1.40	8.29	3.88
3.09	1.60	8.98	4.05
3.21	1.80	8.97	4.24

The stock is selling at $40.00 a share, and the ten-year price-earnings ratio for the company is 12.5. Based on this information, estimate future earnings and dividends. Be certain to establish an error limit for your estimates. The company is a chemical company involved in the production of agricultural chemicals, metals, and other products, nationally and internationally.

2. Make a valuation of the common stock of the company by assuming that there is no increase in shares outstanding and no new changes in the capitalization of the company. Use the capitalization of earnings method, the capitalization of dividends method, the capitalization of cash earnings method, and the present-value method and its variations in making the estimate.

3. Based on the valuation appraisal of the company, would you conclude that investment is worthwhile and profitable at $40 a share?

Sources of Investment Information

Annual reports
Barron's
Commercial and Financial Chronicle
Clark Dodge Investment Reports
Forbes
New York Times
Standard & Poor's *The Outlook*
Standard & Poor's *Industry Survey*
Standard & Poor's *Stock Guide*
3-Trend Security Charts
The Value Line Investment Survey
Wall Street Journal

Selected Readings

Bing, Ralph A., "Scientific Investment Analysis," *Financial Analysts Journal* (May-June, 1967), p. 97.

Callard, Charles G., "The Third Yield," *Financial Analysts Journal* (January-February, 1968), p. 114.

Eiteman, David K., "A Computer Program," *Financial Analysts Journal* (July-August, 1968), p. 107.

Margoshes, Sanford L., "Modified Present Value Profile," *Financial Analysts Journal* (March-April, 1968), p. 97.

Murphy, Joseph E., Jr., "Relative Growth of Earnings Per Share," *Financial Analysts Journal* (November-December, 1966), p. 73.

———, "Earnings Growth and Price Change," *Financial Analysts Journal* (January-February, 1968), p. 97.

Spriggs, Dillard, "Forecasting Oil Industry Profits," *Financial Analysts Journal* (September-October, 1966), p. 49.

Way, Peter F., "Forecasting by Probabilities," *Financial Analysts Journal* (March-April, 1968), p. 35.

IV

THE INVESTMENT ENVIRONMENT

The Securities Market and The Broker

8

THE SECURITIES MARKET

Once we have decided upon the type of securities that will meet our investment needs, we are faced with the practical problem of where to purchase them, from whom, and what it will cost. We must know a great many technical details about buying and selling securities before we can undertake an investment program. A knowledge of where securities are traded and purchased is essential to the investment function.

In Chapter 9, we will discuss the mechanics of buying and selling investment securities. The function of the broker will be examined, and the cost of buying and selling securities will be discussed. In Chapter 8 we will examine the places where securities are traded and the national exchanges where facilities are provided for brokers who conduct business for their customers. The "third," or "off-the-board," market and the broad over-the-counter market will be examined.

The Concept of the Securities Market

What is the securities market, and where is it located? Most knowledgeable individuals would agree that New York is the financial center of the United States and, perhaps, of the world. They would say that the securities market is the New York Stock Exchange, located on Wall Street. Others include the American Stock Exchange as part of the securities market, and still others would say that the Midwest Exchange in Chicago or the exchanges in Los Angeles or Philadelphia represent the securities market and its location. They relate their concept of the market to the specific place where securities are traded. Actually, *any place* where securities are bought and sold, where buyers and sellers come together to trade in securities, is a securities market. An individual who buys United States Treasury bonds from or through his commercial bank is part of the securities market. Residents of a village who buy bonds issued to build a new high school are part of the securities market. (A dealer in municipal bonds probably helps the community sell the bonds; they are not traded on an exchange. Negotiations are conducted in the village offices and in the offices of the municipal bond dealer.) A man purchasing the shares of a company traded on a local exchange is part of the securities market. And, of course, the woman who buys Procter & Gamble stock through a brokerage office doing business on a national exchange is part of the securities market. Even the casual sale of securities by one person to another without the aid of a broker is part of the securities market. These examples demonstrate the breadth of the market. It is not confined to Wall Street, even though this is its center. Its location is Main Street in any community in the United States.

The securities market is actually divided into two broad classes: the organized securities exchange market and the over-the-counter market. The organized securities market is further divided into national, and regional and local exchanges. The New York Stock Exchange and the American Stock Exchange, located in New York, represent the largest part of the organized national exchange market. The rest of it consists of the National Stock Exchange, a small national exchange also in New York. In 1967, transactions involving 4,504 million shares on all registered securities exchanges in the United States were recorded. The dollar value of all transactions amounted to $162 billion.[1] The New York Stock Exchange accounted for 64.1 percent of the number of total shares traded and 77.5 percent of the value of all shares traded in 1967— a decline from the 1961 dollar volume of 82.6 percent. The American Stock Exchange increased its percentage to 28.6 percent of the shares traded and 14.3 percent of the dollar volume in 1967. Regional exchanges accounted for 8.2 percent of the dollar volume.[2]

The over-the-counter market exists as the informal market that handles securities transactions in the offices of approximately 6,000 brokers and dealers registered with the SEC to engage in the securities business. Over 40,000 issues of stocks and bonds are traded in this market in a year. Almost all federal, state, and municipal securities are traded here, as are approximately two-thirds of all security resales in the United States. A substantial number of shares listed on exchanges are also traded in the over-the-counter market.

1 New York Stock Exchange, *Fact Book* (New York, 1968), p. 11.
2 *Ibid.*

Stock Exchange Functions

Early trading in securities in the United States was done informally, in the open or in public meeting places. Some securities transactions were conducted as early as 1725 in lower Manhattan at the foot of Wall Street. The first securities traded were bank stocks and government securities. Brokers met at a special time each day to buy and sell them. The amount of shares traded was small at first, but as the volume of trading increased, rules for commissions and trading were established. From these early agreements grew the New York Stock Exchange and the other national securities exchanges that provide facilities for buying and selling securities.

The functions of national exchanges have grown to include more than furnishing information about price and sales. National exchanges also assure the investor of basic financial information and protection. They require a company to provide its shareholders with a statement of earnings and a balance sheet that summarizes the asset and liability position of the company. National exchanges must register with the Securities and Exchange Commission (SEC) under the Securities Exchange Act of 1934. This affords added protection for stockholders along with the self-regulatory activities of the exchanges. The Special Study of the securities market, which will be referred to shortly, has improved the regulatory power of the SEC over the securities market through both regulation and the self-regulatory activities of the National Association of Securities Dealers (NASD). Several other functions (discussed below) performed by exchanges are even more important than price quotations, information, and protection.

Continuous Market

The exchange provides a continuous market for individual security issues. This is perhaps its most important function. A continuous market is predicated on a large volume of sales and a narrow price range between the bid price and the asked price and between the previous sale and the sale taking place at the moment. It also depends upon rapid execution of orders. These conditions are fostered by the trading rules of the exchange. There are also a sufficient number of buyers and sellers of the shares of stock of each company traded, and a sufficient number of brokers and other members of the exchange transacting orders, to assure a broad and active market. The effect of such a market is to improve the liquidity and marketability of securities that are traded. Few other capital assets possess such a high degree of marketability.

Fair Price and Collateral Value

The price of a share of stock is established in an auction market. It is not set by the traders on the floor of the exchange, nor by negotiation off the floor. It is established by a bidding process, and therefore, the price at any one time tends to reflect a fair market appraisal of the stock. Since the market for a security is continuous, and since the price is established by supply and demand, securities have good collateral value for loans. Obviously, the ability of an exchange to provide a fair market price is limited, because current news or events can have a tremendous effect upon stock prices. A specific price may or may not be fair when long-range investment values are considered. All that we can expect from a market is a price established freely by competitive forces. The price mechanism tends to improve marketability, which helps securities to be better collateral for loans.

Aid in Financing Industry

A continuous market for shares competitively priced provides a favorable climate to raise capital if it is necessary for a company to sell stock to the public. Even if the securities are sold to existing stockholders or to new stockholders by investment bankers off the exchange, the securities traded on the exchange establish a price pattern that serves as a standard of value. Such a comparison should aid in corporate financing. Since there is also a continuous market available after the securities have been sold, the new offering is more readily salable to investors. Most large corporations depend upon retained earnings or internally generated funds for financing. Their infrequent trips to the stock market, however, are aided by the formal organized stock exchange. Providing a continuous market, a fair market price with favorable collateral value, and aid in corporate financing are important functions performed by the exchange.

The New York Stock Exchange

Certainly the best-known, largest, and most important stock exchange in the United States is the New York Stock Exchange. Of the organized exchanges, it does the greatest volume of business, and its activities have a far-reaching impact upon financial centers in all parts of the world. The New York Stock Exchange is both national and international in character and operation. The Exchange itself neither buys, sells, owns, nor sets the prices of securities. All these are activities of members of the Exchange, initiated by investors who can express their investment needs quickly and economically through the physical facilities provided by the New York Stock Exchange.

History of the Exchange

Securities were traded in Wall Street long before the first official document was signed by twenty-four brokers on May 17, 1792.[3] The agreement, known as the Buttonwood Tree Agreement, clearly established a one-quarter of 1 percent commission and obligated the brokers to buy and sell only from each other. Before the agreement, trading took place under a buttonwood tree at 68 Wall Street. Afterwards, until 1817, the business of the Exchange was conducted in an office in the Tontine Coffee House. In 1817, the name was changed to the New York Stock and Exchange Board, and it moved to new quarters at 40 Wall Street. Later, in 1903, the Exchange moved to its headquarters at Broad and Wall Street.

The name, New York Stock Exchange, was adopted January 29, 1863. The first stock tickers were introduced in 1867. These were replaced by a new high-speed ticker service in 1930, and in 1963 new equipment was installed that could print out 900 characters per minute to handle 16,000,000 shares a day. (A volume greater than this had occurred only once before, on October 29, 1929, when 16,410,030 shares were traded.[4] Volume almost reached 16,000,000 when President Eisenhower had his heart attack; then 14.7 million shares were traded. April 10, 1968, was the first day on which the New York Stock Exchange recorded over 20 million shares.[5] To keep up with the volume, the Exchange closed for business on Wednesdays in 1968 to allow the back office to catch up with the paper work.) A continuous market was developed in 1871, and a stock clearing corporation was established in 1920 to facilitate sale of stock on the New York Stock Exchange. An investigation in 1933–34 by the Senate Committee on Banking and Currency—called the Pecora Investigation after Ferdinand Pecora, chief examiner for the committee—led to reorganization of the Exchange in 1937 and 1938, and suspension of Richard Whitney and Company for dishonest practices.[6] Shortly thereafter William McChesney Martin, Jr., who, as secretary, wrote the committee report, became the first salaried president of the reorganized New York Stock Exchange. The Pecora Committee had recommended that there be a full-time paid president of the Exchange, an entirely new Board of Governors with representation for nonmember brokers and out-of-town members, public representation on the board, and a drastic revision of the committee system of running the Exchange.

3 New York Stock Exchange, *Fact Book*, 1968, p. 62.

4 *Ibid.* p. 62.

5 *Ibid.* p. 62.

6 Based on George L. Leffler and Loring C. Farwell, *The Stock Market*, 3d ed. (New York: The Ronald Press Company, 1963).

The Exchange was investigated by the Fulbright Committee in 1955. Little criticism was expressed, and no new legislation was put into effect to regulate the stock market as a result of the study. A monumental report, referred to as the Special Study and prepared by the SEC, was published in 1963. The Special Study[7] in its four parts covers not only the activities of the New York Stock Exchange but the broad characteristics of the entire securities market and the activities of the SEC itself. The study was mild in tone but forceful. It criticized and upheld the many and varied activities of the securities market. To quote the authors,

> ... The report demonstrates that neither the fundamental structure of the securities markets nor the regulatory pattern of the securities acts requires dramatic reconstruction. The report should not impair public confidence in the securities markets, but should strengthen it as suggestions for raising standards are put into practice. Serious shortcomings are apparent and the report, of course, has concentrated on their examination and analysis.[8]

The report, received as a competent research job, upheld the concept of self-regulation in the securities business. The Special Study proposed 176 recommendations intended to raise the standards of the nation's exchanges, the National Association of Securities Dealers (the industry trade group that polices the over-the-counter market under SEC supervision), corporate issues, investment advisers, mutual funds, and others in the securities business. From all appearances, the SEC is intent on giving earnest consideration to each and every proposal.[9] The Special Study focused originally on improved protection for small investors and regulation of the activities of odd-lot dealers, specialists, short sellers, and floor traders. The study's dozen chapters range from the qualification of persons in the securities industry (not as high as one might think) to the responsibilities of investment advisers, to security credit and mutual funds, ending with the regulatory pattern and the market break of 1962. Many of the study's recommendations were adopted immediately. Others provided work for the SEC, which continues today under the able leadership and scrutiny of Milton H. Cohen. More will be said about this in subsequent chapters.

Organization and Management

The New York Stock Exchange is an unincorporated association of members. Its existence is not affected by the death of one of its members, but each member has unlimited liability. Membership is not freely

7 *Report of Special Study of the Securities Markets of the Securities and Exchange Commission*, House Document 95, 88th Cong., 1st sess. (Washington, D.C.: Government Printing Office, 1963).

8 *Ibid.*, p. 111.

9 Lee Silberman, "Critical Examination of SEC Proposals," *Harvard Business Review*, November, 1964, p. 123.

transferable. New members must be personally acceptable to the existing members. The Exchange is governed by a 33-man Board of Governors— 29 members and allied members elected by the membership and a president and three governors elected by the board.[10]

Three members of the board are public representatives; thirteen are from the New York metropolitan area. No fewer than seven of these must be general partners of member firms or holders of voting stock in member corporations having direct contact with the public. No fewer than ten must spend a substantial portion of their time on the floor of the Exchange.

Six members or allied members from within the metropolitan area of New York must be general partners of member firms or holders of voting stock in member corporations having direct contact with the public. Five of these must be allied members and one a member of the Exchange.

Nine must be members or allied members from outside the metropolitan area; they must be general partners of member firms or holders of voting stock in member corporations having direct contact with the public. No fewer than two of these must be members of the Exchange. The president of the Exchange and the chairman of the Board are automatically members.[11]

The balance of the membership gives representation to brokers on and off the floor of the Exchange, to brokers in and out of New York City, and to the general public. The Board of Governors is responsible for the overall policy of the Exchange, the discipline of members, and the approval of new members. It has authority over the listing of a new security and where it will trade. There are no standing committees, since the board works together as a whole. There are, however, several subcommittees including an advisory committee, an admission committee, and a subcommittee of governors on the floor that makes recommendations about the location of stocks and assignment of stocks to specialists. Committees may be established from time to time as they are needed.

The president and his executive staff manage the Exchange. Some idea of the size of the staff needed to carry out the functions of the Exchange can be obtained by examining Figure 8–1. The structure of the organization is much like any industrial company. The president and the other executives of the Exchange are full-time paid executives. Under the reorganized constitution the president has broad powers to carry out the internal and external functions of the Exchange. The Exchange and its subsidiaries employ about 2,300 people, who are paid from revenues obtained from services performed by the Exchange.[12]

10 New York Stock Exchange, *Fact Book*, 1968, p. i.

11 Leffler and Farwell, *Stock Market*, p. 107.

12 New York Stock Exchange, *Fact Book*, 1968, p. 49.

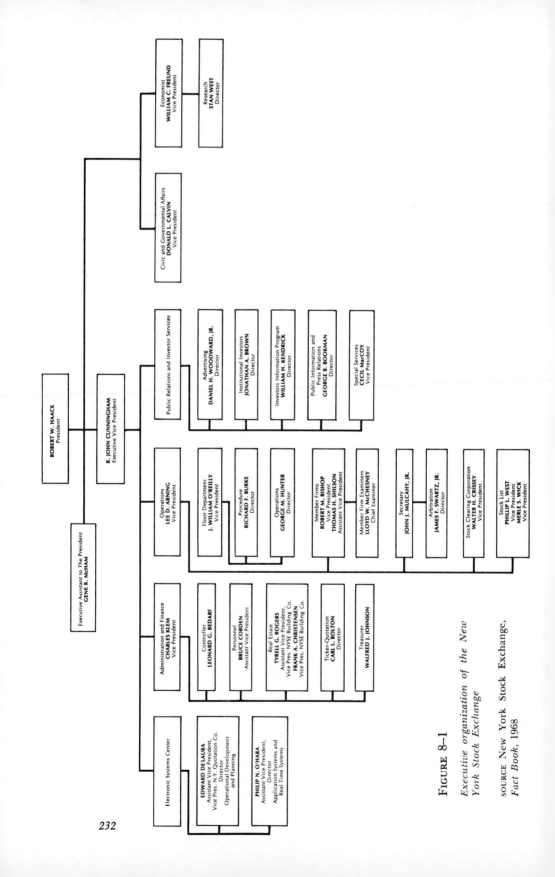

232

FIGURE 8-1

Executive organization of the New York Stock Exchange

SOURCE New York Stock Exchange, *Fact Book*, 1968

The Membership of the New York Stock Exchange

The Exchange has had 1,366 memberships since 1953. Memberships may be sold only with the approval of the Board of Governors. In 1967, 135 seats changed hands at prices ranging from $210,000 to $450,000. The highest price ever paid for Exchange membership was $625,000 in February, 1929.[13] The lowest price in the twentieth century was registered in 1942, when a seat sold for $17,000. In addition to the cost of the seat, a member organization doing business with the public must maintain a minimum net capital of $50,000; $60,000 if the member is a corporate organization. The member or member organization must also pay 1 percent of net commissions to the Exchange. In addition, there is an initiation fee of $7,500, annual dues of $1,500, and contributions to the membership retirement fund of $140 a year. A fund of approximately $20,000 is provided for each deceased member's family; each Exchange member contributes $15 to this upon the death of a member.[14]

The Legal Form of Membership

A member of the Exchange may conduct business as an individual, partnership, or corporation. If a member combines with other individuals to form a partnership or corporation, he must have prior approval of the Board of Governors. No one may become a partner or stockholder of a member company without permission and approval of the board. At the end of 1967, there were 462 partnerships and 185 corporations operating as member organizations. These accounted for almost 1,100 seats. The remainder were held by individuals; a dozen seats were held by deceased members. Corporate memberships were not originally allowed because of the limited liability aspect of the corporate firm. Since a change in rules in 1953, there has been a steady increase in the number of corporate members.

Types of Members

The members of the Exchange are divided into classes based upon the nature of their activity. The classes are: (1) commission broker, (2) odd-lot dealer or broker, (3) specialist, (4) floor broker, (5) floor trader, and (6) bond broker.

COMMISSION BROKER

From the investor's viewpoint, the commission broker is the most important member of the Exchange because he trades primarily for the public. Certainly he is the most numerous of the Exchange members.

13 *Ibid.*, p. 47.
14 Leffler and Farwell, *Stock Market*, p. 119.

It is his main function and responsibility to buy and sell stock for his firm's customers. He acts as agent for the customer and earns a commission for the service performed. Most of the business conducted on the floor of the Exchange by the commission broker is obtained through the registered representatives of the member firm. The registered representative is an employee of a member firm who is engaged in soliciting, handling, buying, selling, or trading in securities on behalf of his employer. At the end of 1967 there were 42,423 registered representatives in 4,130 brokerage offices.[15] When an investor buys stock through a brokerage firm, he most likely deals with a registered representative and not directly with the commission broker who transacts the business of the firm. (Each member firm must have one partner or stockholder who is an Exchange member.)

ODD-LOT BROKER

The odd-lot broker executes buy and sell orders for stocks in amounts of from 1 to 99 shares at post 30 on the Exchange. Only round lots of 100 shares are traded on the floor of the Exchange. The odd-lot broker buys and sells as a principal. The shares are not actually traded on the floor, but the price of the odd-lot sale is determined by the price of the round-lot sale at the time of the transaction. Odd-lot volume is a reflection of "public" participation in the stock market, since the "little man" typically does not buy in round lots. Two large member firms in New York City, De Coppett & Doremus and Carlisle and Jacquelin, carry out almost all the odd-lot transactions—a very important part of stock market activity. The only customers of these dominant odd-lot firms are other commission brokers that are member organizations and channel their odd-lot business to the odd-lot houses. Most firms rotated their business between the two firms before the merger. They were in the process of merging together in 1969.

Odd-lot trading varies as a percentage of round-lot trading. During the 1950's it amounted to an annual average of 10 percent of round-lot volume. Odd-lot transactions by New York Stock Exchange customers in 1967 totaled 302 million shares, an 18 percent increase over 1966. However, round-lot sales increased more rapidly, and odd lots as a percentage of round lots reached an all-time low.[16]

SPECIALIST

It is the basic responsibility of the specialist to make an orderly and continuous auction market in the stocks in which he specializes. He can buy and sell for his own account as a dealer, or for the accounts of other members or member organizations. He does not do business with

15 New York Stock Exchange, *Fact Book*, 1968, p. 51.
16 *Ibid.*, p. 5.

the public directly but handles transactions on a commission basis for other brokers who are acting for their clients. Approximately 25 percent of Exchange members are specialists, most of them members of specialist firms. Essentially the specialist must buy when stock is offered for sale, and he must sell when stock is requested for purchase, in order to maintain an orderly market.

In order to become a specialist, a member notifies the Exchange that he wishes to act as a specialist; he registers for that function subject to approval by the board. There are one or more specialists for each company listed on the Exchange. The average specialist handles three or four stocks and is a member of a specialist organization that handles a dozen or more stocks. Specialists account for about 15 percent of market volume for their own accounts as dealers and for more than that if we add transactions for other brokers. The commission on the transaction for other brokers ranges from $1\frac{1}{4}$ cents per share, for stock selling under $2, to 5 cents per share, for stock selling for $200 or more.

The Board of Governors selects specialists on their ability and also on the basis of sufficient capital. The specialist must have enough money to buy 400 shares of each 100-share-unit stock and 100 shares of each 10-share-unit stock for which he is registered. Although the usual unit of trading on the New York Stock Exchange is 100 shares, some high-priced stocks with slow turnover have a round lot of 10 shares. The 10-share units are traded as a round lot at post 30 of the Exchange.

The specialist can "take orders away from the market"; that is, he can receive orders to buy and sell at prices different from the existing market price. He keeps these orders in his book and executes them when he is able. Orders of other brokers take precedence over the specialist's orders as a dealer, and his activities are under scrutiny by Exchange officials. The specialist makes an orderly and continuous market; he opens the market, and operates in the capacity of both dealer and broker. His is a unique position, and he performs an important function in the market. Because he could take advantage of market knowledge or improve his own position to the detriment of his customers, he is closely regulated by the Exchange and the Securities and Exchange Commission.

FLOOR BROKER

The floor broker buys and sells shares for other brokers on the floor of the Exchange. He ordinarily does not belong to a member firm but owns his own seat and receives a commission on the orders he executes. He also helps other brokers when they are busy. Other firms depend upon him to conduct a portion of their regular business. Floor brokers once were called $2 brokers because this was their commission for executing an order. Today the commission averages closer to $4 per 100-share transaction. There are almost 200 floor brokers on the Exchange.

THE FLOOR TRADER

The floor trader buys and sells for his own account. He does not do business with either the public or other brokers. Some floor traders depend exclusively upon trading for income; others engage in trading as a part-time activity and devote the major portion of their time to commission work. Most full-time traders are members of a firm. When active, the floor trader helps to make a continuous market and stabilize prices. He has been criticized, however, as performing no important economic function, and it has been suggested that he acts to increase market instability. Since there are few full-time traders today, their direct impact on the market is not very important. In 1964, the management of the Exchange and the SEC were caught up in a bitter public argument over the Special Study recommendation to abolish floor trading. Differences were finally settled by an SEC ruling allowing it to continue under greatly circumscribed conditions.[17]

THE BOND BROKER

About a dozen members of the Exchange are bond brokers who handle the almost 1,400 bond issues traded on the Exchange. Bonds are divided into two classes, free bonds and cabinet bonds. Free bonds are actively traded issues, which include nine domestic rails and eighty-eight domestic industrial issues. All other listed bonds are called cabinet bonds, since trading involves using metal cabinets where records of bids and offers are kept. Orders are filled in the order of their receipt at the indicated prices. All trading in these issues takes place on the bond trading floor.

Listings on the New York Stock Exchange

To be traded on the New York Stock Exchange, a security must meet the Exchange's requirements for listing. At the end of 1967, 1,274 companies were listed[18] and a total of 1,700 different issues were traded, including preferred and common stock of United States and foreign companies. In addition, 1,388 separate issues of bonds were traded, including those issued by U.S. corporations, foreign companies, the U.S. government, the International Bank, and foreign governments. The bulk of those listed were U.S. Government and New York State and City bonds.

The assets of the companies listed on the Exchange equaled about 30 percent of the total capital invested by all corporations, and the companies employed approximately 20 percent of all civilian workers in the United States. As one would expect, these companies include many that are known to most people; American Telephone and Tele-

17 Silberman, "Critical Examination," p. 121.
18 New York Stock Exchange, *Fact Book*, 1968, p. 23.

graph, General Motors, and International Business Machines are among the more familiar companies that have met the listing requirements.

CONDITIONS OF LISTING

Each company applying for initial listing is selected on its own merits, but, in general, it must meet the conditions presented in Figure 8–2.

In addition to these specific requirements, the company must agree to provide an earnings statement to the public; dividend notices must be sent out; proxies must be solicited for all meetings of the stockholders; and the company must provide other information which may affect security values or influence investment decisions. All listed common stock must give its owner the privilege of voting. The requirements

FIGURE 8–2

Listing requirements of the New York Stock Exchange

SOURCE New York Stock Exchange, *Fact Book*, 1968, p. 22

To be listed on the New York Stock Exchange, a company is expected to meet certain qualifications and to be willing to keep the investing public informed on the progress of its affairs. The company must be a going concern, or be the successor to a going concern. In determining eligibility for listing, particular attention is given to such qualifications as: 1) the degree of national interest in the company; 2) its relative position and stability in the industry; and 3) whether it is engaged in an expanding industry, with prospects of at least maintaining its relative position.

Initial Listing

While each case is decided on its own merits, the Exchange generally requires the following as a minimum. (These requirements were approved in principle by NYSE Board of Governors on April 18, 1968.)

1. Demonstrated earning power under competitive conditions of $2.5 million before Federal income taxes for the most recent year and $2 million pre-tax for the preceding two years.
2. Net tangible assets of $14 million, but greater emphasis will be placed on the aggregate market value of the common stock.
3. A total of $14 million in market value of publicly held common stock.
4. A total of 800,000 common shares publicly held out of 1,000,000 shares outstanding.
5. Round-lot shareholders numbering 1,800 out of a total of 2,000 shareholders.

Continued Listing

The appropriateness of continued listing of a security on the Exchange cannot be measured mathematically, and the Exchange may at any time suspend or delist a security where the Board considers that continued dealings in the security are not advisable, even though a security meets or fails to meet any specified criteria. For example, the Exchange would normally give consideration to suspending or removing from the list a common stock of a company when there are:

1. 900 round-lot holders or less, with 1,000 shareholders of record or less.
2. 400,000 shares or less in public hands.
3. $4,000,000 or less aggregate market value of publicly-held shares.
4. $7,000,000 or less in aggregate market value of all outstanding common stock or net tangible assets applicable thereto, combined with an earnings record of less than an average of $600,000 after taxes for the past three years.

Listing Agreement

The listing agreement between the company and the Exchange is designed to provide timely disclosure to the public of earnings statements, dividend notices, and other information which may affect security values or influence investment decisions. The Exchange requires actively operating companies to agree to solicit proxies for all meetings of stockholders.

Voting Rights

As a matter of general policy, the Exchange has for many years refused to list non-voting common stocks, and all listed common stocks have the right to vote.

for continued Exchange listing are less stringent than these initial requirements; however, should a company no longer be worthy of listing, should it fail, or should there be too few investors interested in it, then for the good of the Exchange community—the members, the companies listed, the customers, and the public—its stock would be delisted.

LISTING FEE

A fee is imposed on corporations listing their shares for trading. This is divided into two parts, an initial fee and a continuing annual fee.[19] The initial fee provides for a charge of $100 per 10,000 shares, or fraction thereof, for the first 500,000 shares listed; $50 per 10,000 shares, or fraction thereof, for the next 1,500,000 shares; and $25 per 10,000 shares, or fraction thereof, for shares in excess of 2,000,000. The minimum initial fee is $2,000. The annual fee, which continues for fifteen years after the initial listing, is $100 per 100,000 shares, or fraction thereof, for the first 2,000,000 shares; and $50 per 100,000 shares, or fraction thereof, in excess of 2,000,000. The minimum fee is $500 per year. Should the company have two or more issues, the minimum fee would be $250 per issue.

Trading on the New York Stock Exchange

The purchase or sale of stock is initiated by a customer through a registered representative in a brokerage office, but the actual trading or negotiation is done by brokers on the floor of the Exchange.

WHO CAN TRADE

Only members of the Exchange or their officially invited guests may enter the trading floor. Only members can transact business at the posts where securities are traded. General Motors stock is traded at post 4 and Chrysler at post 2.[20] An investor wishing to buy 100 shares of GM would call his registered representative, who in turn would either wire or telephone the broker on the floor of the Exchange to buy the shares. About 1,800 telephones and teletypewriters are available around the perimeter of the Exchange for this purpose.

As the GM buy order was received, it would be given to the broker, who would go to post 4. The brokers and specialists would quickly convey price information about the GM stock. Then, verbally, a short auction would take place. The buyer would offer a price that is either accepted or rejected by the other brokers. This bargaining or auctioning takes place in a matter of seconds and continues until the buying broker and selling broker agree upon a price.

19 Leffler and Farwell, *Stock Market*, pp. 136–37.
20 *Ibid.*, p. 184.

A STOCK TRANSACTION

The broker is responsible for getting the best price for his customer at the time the order is placed. The price is established independently by brokers on an auction basis and not by officials of the Exchange. When a sale is completed, it is reported to the ticker operator, who transmits the transaction simultaneously to every ticker in the country. If we assume that 100 shares of GM were bought and sold at 70, the ticker tape would flash the following:

GM
70

This simply means that 100 shares of GM traded at 70. (Each stock has its own ticker symbol to identify it for trading; X, for example, is the symbol for U.S. Steel and C for Chrysler.) If another 100 shares traded at 70 1/8, the tape would look like this:

GM
70. 1/8

If 200 shares were traded at 70, the tape would look like this:

GM
2s 70

If a preferred stock is traded instead of common stock, the letters *Pr* will appear after the symbol. The following indicates that 100 shares of GM 3 3/4 percent preferred traded at $101 per share:

GM Pr
3 3/4 – 101

Upon completion of the transaction the broker wires a confirmation of the sale to the registered representative, who notifies the customer. The entire transaction is completed long before a rapid reader has finished this page.

A summary of some of the daily transactions of the New York Stock Exchange is reported in the *Wall Street Journal* as shown in Figure 8–3. A word of explanation is in order for those not familiar with the stock market page. The first two columns represent the high and low price per share for the period indicated. Next appears the name of the company in abbreviated form, then the dividend. Next is the number of sales in round lots of 100 shares, followed by the opening price for the day, the high, low, and closing price. The last column gives the net change over the previous day's closing price.

If you visit a brokerage office, you'll find at the desk of the registered representative one of the modern methods for obtaining price

New York Stock Exchange Transactions

Tuesday, June 25, 1968

—1968— High	Low	Stocks Div.	Sales in 100s	Open	High	Low	Close	Net Chg.
77½	41	EngelM .60b	443	76	80½	76	79½	+4
235	130	Eng M pf4.25	2	239	239	238	238	+6
36⅞	33½	EqutGas 2.10	10	36⅝	36⅝	36⅜	36⅝	....
32	24⅜	ESB Inc 1.20	16	27⅝	27⅝	27¼	27⅝	+ ⅛
36⅞	20½	Esquire .30	121	28¼	28½	28¼	28¼	.....
59	36⅞	Essex W 1.20	506	55	59	55	59	+4¼
37⅞	27¼	Ethyl Cp .60	117	32⅛	32½	32	32¼	− ⅛
54⅞	45¾	Ethyl pf2.40	15	50⅛	50½	50⅛	50½	+ ⅜
25¼	16	Eurofnd .30a	14	19¼	19⅜	19⅛	19⅛	+ ⅛
		Eurofd fn.30a	4	17½	17½	15½	15½	.....
37¾	22	EvansP .60b	80	36⅞	36⅞	34¾	34⅞	−1¾
20⅛	13¾	Eversharp	21	16	16¼	16	16	− ⅛
40⅛	28½	ExCellO 1.20	56	39⅜	39½	38¾	38¾	− ⅜
63½	46	FactorA .80b	68	60½	60⅞	60	60⅞	− ⅛
92⅜	52	FairCam .50g	499	67½	67¾	64	64¼	−3¼
23½	14⅜	FairHill .15e	338	17½	17⅞	17	17½	−1¼
20½	16	Fairmont 1	158	20¾	21½	20⅝	21¼	+1
22	18¾	Fairmnt pf 1	13	22¼	22¾	22¼	22½	+ ⅞
17⅛	10¼	Falstaff .40	58	14	14⅜	14	14¼	+ ⅜
23⅝	18	Fam Fin 1.30	489	23⅞	27	23⅞	26½	+2⅞
61⅞	29½	Fansteel Inc	74	41½	41½	04¼	40¼	−1¾
16	7⅞	Far West Fin	41	15⅞	16⅛	15⅝	15¾	+ ⅜
45⅝	28¼	FarahMfg .80	x15	41	41¼	41	41¼	+ ½
40⅞	29½	Fedders .60	342	[illegible]	[illegible]	33½	34⅞	−2¼

—1968— High	Low	Stocks Div.	Sales in 100s	Open	High	Low	Close	Net Chg.
40¾	30¾	Inland Stl 2	275	38½	38½	37¼	37½	− ¾
35¼	30½	Inspir Cop 2	3	33	33	33	33	+ ¼
38	30½	Interchm 1.20	5	34⅝	34⅞	34¼	34¼	− ½
50⅝	34¾	Interco .90	9	50½	50¾	50⅜	50½	+ ½
34¼	28⅛	InterlkSt 1.80	46	31⅜	31⅝	30¾	31⅝	+ ⅝
375	324	IBM	186	358	358	348	348¼	−10
64¾	48⅝	IntFlaFr .36b	24	57½	57¾	57¼	57¾	− ⅛
38	30⅜	Int Harv 1.80	160	32⅝	33	32½	32⅝	− ⅛
18¾	14⅛	IntHold 1.47e	23	18¼	18½	18	18½	+ ½
80⅜	37	Int Indust	121	66	69¼	65⅞	68¾	+4¼
30⅛	20¼	Int Miner 1	122	22	22½	21⅞	22⅛	.....
43¼	24½	Int Mng .10r	39	38⅛	38⅜	37⅛	37½	− ⅜
118	99⅝	Int Nickel 3	74	103¾	104¼	103¼	103¾	− ½
16⅝	9⅝	Int Packers	248	15⅛	15½	14⅞	15¼	.....
34¼	25⅞	Int Pap 1.35	1839	33⅜	34⅝	33⅜	34⅝	+1⅛
74½	65	Int Pap pf 4	z140	67¼	67¾	67¼	67¾	+2
26⅝	16⅝	Intl Rectif	45	21	21	20⅛	20⅛	− ⅞
56	41½	Int Salt 2.40	4	52⅜	52⅝	52⅜	52⅜	+ ¼
37⅜	26⅜	IntSilver .70	24	35⅛	35⅛	34¾	34¾	− ¼
38	27⅝	IntSilv pfA.75	1	35¼	35¼	35¼	35¼	+ ¼
59¾	44⅞	Int T&T .85	192	56¼	56⅝	56¼	56⅜	+ ⅛
167½	131	IntT&T pfF 4	1	160	160	160	160	−5
130	93	IntT&T pfH 4	3	113	113	113	113	− ½
109½	98¼	ITT pfI 4.50	13	109	109½	109	[illegible]	− ½

EXPLANATORY NOTES

(Footnotes apply to New York and American exchanges)

z—Sales in full.

Unless otherwise noted, rates of dividends in the foregoing table are annual disbursements based on the last quarterly or semi-annual declaration. Special or extra dividends or payments not designated as regular are identified in the following footnotes.

a—Also extra or extras. b—Annual rate plus stock dividend. c—Liquidating dividend. d—Declared or paid in 1967 plus stock dividend. e—Declared or paid so far this year. f—Payable in stock during 1967, estimated cash value on ex-dividend or ex-distribution date. g—Paid last year. h—Declared or paid after stock dividend or split up. k—Declared or paid this year, an accumulative issue with dividends in arrears. n—New issue. p—Paid this year, dividend omitted, deferred or no action taken at last dividend meeting. r—Declared or paid in 1968 plus stock dividend. t—Paid in stock during 1968, estimated cash value on ex-dividend or ex-distribution date.

cld—Called. x—Ex dividend. y—Ex dividend and sales in full. x-dis—Ex distribution. xr—Ex rights. xw—Without warrants. ww—With warrants. wd—When distributed. wi—When issued. nd—Next day delivery.

vj—In bankruptcy or receivership or being reorganized under the Bankruptcy Act, or securities assumed by such companies. fn—Foreign issue subject to interest equalization tax.

Year's high and low range does not include changes in latest day's trading.

Where a split or stock dividend amounting to 25 per cent or more has been paid the year's high-low range and dividend are shown for the new stock only.

FIGURE 8–3

Example of price reporting on the New York Stock Exchange

SOURCE *The Wall Street Journal*

information and a great deal of additional knowledge. The Stockmaster, introduced by Ultronic Systems Corporation, provides immediate access to price, volume, dividends, and earnings information. Teleregister Corporation has a telequote device that provides price data; Scantlin Electronics's Quotron provides similar information. Since 1965 the New York Stock Exchange has used a computer-based quotation processing system developed by IBM.[21]

21 Wilford J. Eiteman, Charles A. Dice, and David K. Eiteman, *The Stock Market*, 4th ed. (New York: McGraw-Hill Book Company, 1966), p. 115.

VOLUME OF STOCK TRADED

The reported total stock volume on the Exchange approached almost three billion shares in 1968. This represents round-lot and odd-lot transactions. The daily average number of shares traded was close to 11 million in 1967.[22] Table 8–1 provides a list of the 50 most active stocks traded in round lots on the New York Stock Exchange in 1967 and the 50 most active traded in odd lots.

The American Stock Exchange

The American Stock Exchange is the second largest stock exchange in the United States. The exact time of its beginning is not certain; it was sometime after the Gold Rush of 1849 but before the Civil War. Like the New York Stock Exchange, the American Stock Exchange began operations outdoors on Wall and Broad streets; it did not move indoors until 1921. The American Stock Exchange has had a colorful history; from 1929 until 1953, it was known as the New York Curb Exchange, from the curb on Wall Street where brokers met to trade shares. At the time, one would have found brokers decked out in colorful garb trading in the street. Their clothing identified them to their staffs in nearby offices. When an order was telephoned to a broker's office, it would be transmitted from the office window by hand signals or sign language to the broker below. This method is still used on the floor of the American Exchange. Clerks communicate with brokers on the floor by hand signals—an effective way of transmitting buy and sell orders.

Organization of the American Stock Exchange

The American Stock Exchange is organized in much the same way as the New York Stock Exchange. It is an association of individuals with a Board of Governors consisting of thirty-two members. This board represents regular Exchange members, associate members, the general public, and the administrative group. The executives of the Exchange are salaried. The chief executive officer is the president, who carries out policies established by the Board of Governors; he is supported in his actions by an advisory committee. The Exchange has five divisions: administrative, securities, transactions, floor supervision, and public relations.

Membership on the American Exchange

There are 499 seats or regular memberships on the American Stock Exchange that are accorded the full privileges of membership. A mem-

22 New York Stock Exchange, *Fact Book*, 1968, p. 6.

ber must be a U.S. citizen, 21 years or older, and have the approval of two-thirds of the Board of Governors. The cost of membership and the annual dues are lower than comparable costs on the New York Stock Exchange.[23] In 1968, for example, a seat on the American Stock Exchange sold for $260,000, a member's capital requirement was $10,000, both of which are substantially lower than those of the New York Stock Exchange.

In addition to regular members, there are approximately 400 associate members. These enjoy the privilege of conducting their business through a regular member at a substantial saving of commissions. The number of associate members on the Exchange is not limited, but each must be approved by the Board of Governors. An associate member pays approximately 10 percent of the market price of a seat for the privilege of using the facilities of the Exchange. This is considered an

TABLE 8–1

50 most active round-lot and 50 most active
odd-lot stocks on New York Stock Exchange, 1967

	Round Lots		
ISSUE	1967 REPORTED SHARE VOLUME*	ISSUE	1967 REPORTED SHARE VOLUME*
Sperry Rand (1)	25,550,500	American Cyanamid	9,766,800
American Tel. & Tel. (2)	23,467,200	American Airlines	9,705,100
American Motors (20)	20,001,600	International Paper (42)	9,694,200
Pan Amer. World Airways (5)	18,379,000	Ampex Corporation (26)	9,318,800
Brunswick Corp. (23)	17,951,400	Pacific Petroleums	9,274,200
Gulf & Western Industries (32)	16,593,100	Boeing Company (11)	9,051,400
McDonnell-Douglas (25)	16,211,900	Glen Alden	8,926,700
Occidental Petroleum (30)	16,107,600	Thiokol Chemical	8,869,800
Benguet Consolidated (15)	14,990,800	Ford Motor (16)	8,842,000
Standard Oil (N.J.) (36)	14,756,800	Ling-Temco-Vought	8,377,000
Control Data (14)	14,726,700	Martin Marietta (41)	8,271,200
Chrysler Corp. (4)	13,895,100	Monsanto Company	8,026,100
Avco Corp.	13,093,800	Union Carbide	7,961,400
Allis-Chalmers Manufacturing	12,704,900	Schenley Industries	7,865,000
Atlas Corp. (24)	11,961,500	Continental Air Lines (43)	7,846,500
Great Western Financial	11,771,700	Seaboard World Airlines	7,730,900
Studebaker-Worthington	11,368,400	Texas Gulf Sulphur (17)	7,577,700
Fairchild Camera & Instru. (7)	10,950,000	Trans World Airlines (22)	7,285,800
General Motors (6)	10,812,400	General Aniline & Film	7,141,500
American Photocopy Equip.	10,748,900	Commonwealth Oil Refining (31)	7,122,300
Radio Corp. of America (13)	10,535,300	Varian Associates (48)	7,080,600
Pan American Sulphur (40)	10,400,400	Amphenol Corp.	7,066,100
Magnavox Co. (21)	10,218,600	Flying Tiger Line†	6,939,900
SCM Corporation (3)	10,015,300	Polaroid Corp. (10)	6,900,500
Eastern Airlines (9)	9,773,700	Parke, Davis	6,834,900

NOTE: 1966 rank in parentheses, if among top 50.
* Old and new issues combined where applicable.
† Listed NYSE 8/7/67.

23 Leffler and Farwell, *Stock Market*, p. 307.

Odd Lots

(Customers' Purchases and Sales Combined)

ISSUE	1967 ODD-LOT VOLUME*	ISSUE	1967 ODD-LOT VOLUME*
American Tel. & Tel. (1)	8,986,522	Xerox Corporation (9)	1,298,599
General Motors (2)	3,579,038	Brunswick Corporation	1,255,912
Pan American World Airways (8)	3,100,783	Monsanto Co.	1,243,608
Standard Oil (N.J.) (13)	3,088,478	Continental Air Lines (45)	1,191,025
Sperry Rand (4)	3,026,230	Teledyne, Inc.	1,188,467
Radio Corp. of America (3)	2,434,120	General Electric (44)	1,163,351
Gulf & Western Industries (32)	2,398,588	Texas Gulf Sulphur (18)	1,099,062
Occidental Petroleum (19)	2,369,285	U.S. Steel (23)	1,084,627
McDonnell Douglas (15)	2,253,474	Tenneco Inc.	1,043,101
Chrysler Corp. (6)	1,892,279	American Cyanamid	1,019,198
Avco Corp. (48)	1,817,577	Martin-Marietta	1,011,714
Magnavox Co. (7)	1,740,337	Consolidated Edison (21)	1,010,860
Control Data (27)	1,593,679	General Aniline & Film (42)	954,213
Union Carbide (35)	1,543,358	Litton Industries (30)	945,151
Ford Motor (5)	1,501,072	Avnet, Inc.	937,923
Fairchild Camera & Instru. (12)	1,493,508	Eastman Kodak (40)	929,559
Ampex Corp. (39)	1,482,591	Bethlehem Steel (29)	920,827
Int'l Business Machines (14)	1,479,496	Communications Satellite (33)	917,627
American Motors (38)	1,472,247	Allied Chemical (28)	910,444
General Tel. & Electronics (17)	1,468,686	Westinghouse Electric	904,140
SCM Corporation (10)	1,353,702	Thiokol Chemical	903,581
Standard Oil of California (46)	1,353,065	United Nuclear	877,896
Ling-Temco-Vought	1,332,407	Pan American Sulphur	874,349
Allis-Chalmers	1,328,746	Itek Corp.	870,569
Boeing Co. (11)	1,321,065	du Pont de Nemours	853,906

* Old and new issues combined where applicable.
NOTE: 1966 rank in parentheses, if among top 50.

SOURCE: New York Stock Exchange, *Fact Book*, 1968, pp. 8 and 9.

initiation fee. The American Stock Exchange also has allied members, like the New York Stock Exchange.

CLASSES OF MEMBERS AND LISTING

The three classes of floor members on the American Exchange are: (1) specialists, who are most numerous; (2) commission brokers; and (3) floor traders. These members trade in both listed and unlisted securities.

Listed Companies. A listed company is one that has furnished the necessary information about its business and has paid its listing fee. The standards a company must meet for listing are: $1 million in net assets or net worth; 200,000 shares of stock outstanding in public hands; at least 750 share owners, of whom at least 500 own one or more round lots; a market value of its shares of at least $2 million, $1 million of which is owned by the public; and a net income of $150,000 in the year preceding listing with an average of at least $100,000 of net income for the three preceding years.[24] Listing must be approved by the Board of Governors. In general, the listing requirements follow the requirements of the New York Stock Exchange, but they are not as stringent. The average company listed on the American Exchange is likely to be less seasoned, smaller, and not as well established as companies on the NYSE.

Unlisted Trading. Over 800 issues are traded on the American Exchange; about 20 percent of them are unlisted. A company need not apply for unlisted trading of its securities. A specialist may be granted the right to make a market for unlisted stock. Unlisted trading is permitted by the SEC, but such trading has diminished.

Securities traded on the Exchange vary from old, established companies to new, highly speculative issues. Often companies list first on the American Stock Exchange and then move to the New York Stock Exchange, "The Big Board"; General Motors and Du Pont did this. Prentice-Hall and Technicolor Inc. are well-known companies that are actively traded on the American Exchange.

Foreign Securities. The American Exchange is the nation's leading market in foreign securities. It originated and uses American Depository Receipts for trading in these securities. ADR's, as they are known, are certificates issued by New York banks and trust companies against foreign shares that are deposited in the foreign branches of American banks.

The American Exchange engages in an important segment of the stock market and does an effective job in providing trading facilities for many important domestic and foreign companies.

The National Stock Exchange[25]

The National Stock Exchange is the third national exchange in the United States. In June, 1958, a committee of the Board of Governors of the New York Mercantile Exchange explored the possibility of forming another stock exchange; as a result, the National Stock Exchange, located in New York, began business on March 7, 1962. It is the first new exchange to be established under the Securities and Exchange Commission since that commision was created. Forty-five companies were listed for trading on the National Stock Exchange in July, 1968, with an equal number in the preliminary stages of application for listing. A list of stocks actively traded on the National Stock Exchange appears regularly in the financial press. Most have come from the over-the-counter market.

24 Leffler and Farwell, *Stock Market*, p. 309.
25 *Commercial and Financial Chronicle*, March 8, 1962, p. 6.

To be listed on the Exchange, a company must have a minimum of 500 stockholders, 100,000 shares of stock in the hands of the public, and total assets of $1,000,000. This is the size company that in the OTC market must report to the SEC in compliance with the Securities Acts Amendments of 1964. In addition, the company requesting listing must have demonstrated earning capacity, stability, and an acceptable record of management performance.

The National Stock Exchange gives investors an opportunity to trade on a regulated exchange with a national ticker service and national press coverage. It has over 260 members with a potential of 500 members. The price of a seat has ranged from $10,000 to $40,000, the latter figure reflecting the 1968 period. The Exchange uses stock specialists, whose financial requirement is set at $50,000 net liquid assets. There are two trading posts capable of handling 100 stocks each.

Regional and Local Exchanges

Regional and local stock exchanges provide a marketplace for a wide variety of securities with varying degrees of public participation and support. Such exchanges conducted approximately 7 percent of the market value of the total securities traded on exchanges in the United States in 1964. The Midwest Exchange in Chicago, the Pacific Coast Stock Exchange in Los Angeles and San Francisco, and The Philadelphia-Baltimore-Washington Stock Exchange generate almost 6 percent of the total business done by all of the regional and local exchanges. The remaining stock exchange business is done by the following local exchanges: Boston, Detroit, Cincinnati, Pittsburgh, Honolulu, Spokane, Salt Lake City, Richmond, Wheeling, and Colorado Springs.

These exchanges are registered with the SEC, except for the Honolulu, Richmond, Wheeling, and Colorado Springs exchanges, which are exempt primarily because their volume of business is so small. Regional and local exchanges are organized along the lines of the New York Stock Exchange. Each regional exchange deals with approximately 500 companies, while the smaller local exchanges list approximately 100. These companies are usually small, local or regional companies but may have their stock traded on a national exchange and also on one or more local stock exchanges. In recent years, member firms have listed on the regional exchanges as a way of combating the growth of the "third market," which is discussed later in the chapter. Fee splitting is permitted on the regional exchanges: rather than lose business to the "third market," the broker handles the purchase or sale of a stock listed on the NYSE on a regional exchange at a reduced commission. He then loses some of the commission, but not all. As a result of this activity, the volume of the regional exchanges has increased in 1968. The column "Markets in Other Cities" in the *Wall Street Journal* provides current price and volume information for companies in the regional market along with those on the Toronto Exchange.

The price of shares traded on local exchanges is usually low, the volume of trading is small, seats and membership fees are inexpensive, and there are few members of each exchange. Aside from the trading in securities also listed on the New York or American Exchange, trading is confined to local and regional issues or issues listed on more than one local or regional exchange. There is no duplication of listing among the New York, the American, or the National Exchange. A stock traded on the New York or National Exchange, for example, will not trade on the American Stock Exchange. Commission schedules for stocks traded on the regional and local exchanges and the New York Stock Exchange are identical. A variation in the total commission on stocks occurs primarily because the prices of shares on the regional exchanges are lower and therefore the commissions less. The type of security traded and the listing requirements vary among regional and local exchanges. Stocks that enjoy listed trading privileges on the American Stock Exchange or the New York Stock Exchange often enjoy *unlisted* trading privileges on local and regional exchanges.

Foreign Stock Exchanges

The Toronto Stock Exchange, the London Stock Exchange, and the Japanese stock exchanges have been important in world finance. The Toronto Stock Exchange has over 1,100 issues listed with nearly all of them trading every month. The London Stock Exchange lists and trades more than six times the number of issues listed on the New York Stock Exchange, and it has three times the number of members.

The stock exchanges in Japan are young compared with those in the United States. They have become important since World War II. There are nine stock exchanges in Japan; the Tokyo Exchange clearly dominates in stock volume, trading about two-thirds of the total transactions. This exchange has both listed and unlisted securities. Average prices of shares traded on both the London and the Tokyo exchanges are lower than those on the New York Stock Exchange. Average volume on the Tokyo Exchange is high in comparison with the New York Stock Exchange. Tokyo's annual share volume is well over 50 billion shares, with as many as 250 million trading in one day.

Trading on foreign exchanges is similar to trading on exchanges in the United States. Purchasing stocks on foreign exchanges, however, adds new risks for the investor. Information about securities traded on foreign exchanges is somewhat limited. Because of fluctuations in the foreign exchange rates among the various currencies, the risk is greater.

The market for foreign stock is narrow, and the instability of some foreign governments does not provide a favorable climate for buying and selling securities. Also, shares of foreign corporations that would appeal to conservative investors are available through exchange facilities in the United States. American Depository Receipts, mentioned above, can be purchased through the American Stock Exchange. In most cases, these allow investors to participate in the benefits of ownership of foreign securities without trading on foreign exchanges. But potential change in the political and economic climate is an additional risk that must be borne when foreign securities are purchased. The more actively traded foreign securities are reported in the *Wall Street Journal.*

Advantages of Buying Securities Listed on a National Securities Exchange

The functions of a stock exchange, the description of its membership, the issues traded, and the listing requirements imposed upon a company that desires to have its shares traded provide some indication of the advantages of buying and selling shares of companies listed on a national exchange. Such shares are usually more liquid and marketable than shares traded on smaller exchanges or in the over-the-counter market. The companies listed, except for those on the National Stock Exchange, are generally larger, more profitable, and more seasoned. Too, there is voluminous information about the financial and operating affairs of each company and about the price of the securities.

The national exchange, as exemplified by the New York Stock Exchange and the American Stock Exchange, provides high marketability for shares traded. The same degree of marketability is not generally found on smaller exchanges or in the equity security in the over-the-counter market. On the average, this makes the shares more acceptable as collateral for loans either from a broker or a commercial bank. Institutional investors usually favor purchases of stock on the New York Stock Exchange, which adds to the marketability of shares being traded there. The volume of business conducted on a national exchange is large, and a single transaction will have little effect upon the price of the stock. A large block of shares can be bought and sold with the same facility as a single 100-share transaction on a smaller exchange. This is important to the large institutional investors who might wish to buy large amounts of stock for their investment accounts.

There are also disadvantages of trading in the securities listed on a national exchange. A large national exchange is open to public scrutiny, and any adverse publicity might have a bad effect upon the market, which will affect the price of all shares traded. The rapidity with which information about listed companies and political and economic events is disseminated makes it difficult to keep good or bad news confidential.[26] The railroad in bankruptcy is given as much publicity as the photocopy company whose earnings are soaring. This may lead to excess price movements that might not have developed if the information had not become public.

The Over-the-Counter Market

The over-the-counter markets (OTC) are far more important in terms of the dollar volume of securities traded and number of issues traded than the national, regional, and local exchanges combined. Securities traded include bank stocks, insurance company stocks, United States Government securities, municipal bonds, mutual funds, equipment trust certificates issued by railroads, most corporate bonds except those listed on the New York Stock Exchange, and stocks of a large number of domestic and foreign industrial and public utility companies. The over-the-counter market includes all security markets except the organized exchanges. There is no organization structure of this market comparable with the New York Stock Exchange. Business is not conducted at any one place designated as the marketplace, although New York is the center of the over-the-counter market. Dealers and brokers do business directly with each other by telephone, telegraph, or teletype. The Wharton study[27] indicated that almost 90,000 different corporate and government securities could be traded in these markets; the number actually traded was 40,000. A typical trading day, according to the study, involved transactions of 3,000 different issues. Approximately three-fourths of these transactions were in corporate stock issues and one-fourth in corporate and government bond issues. The OTC markets did 100 percent of the United States Government, state, and municipal bond business in 1949. They did 82.4 percent of the corporate bond business and 33.5 percent of the corporate stock business, compared with 17.6 percent and 66.6 percent respectively for the organized exchanges.[28]

Many different types of securities are traded in the OTC markets. The largest banks and insurance companies are traded as well as smaller

26 The reaction of the stock market to President Eisenhower's heart attack and President Kennedy's assassination are examples of the speed with which bad news is conveyed to the marketplace. In both cases the market dropped sharply, then recovered. In the case of President Kennedy's death, it dropped 21 points before the New York Stock Exchange was closed early, Friday, November 22, 1963. On the next day of trading, Tuesday, November 26, 1963, the market gained 32 full points on the Dow Jones Industrial Averages by the close of trading.

27 Irwin Friend, G. Wright Hoffman, Willis J. Winn, Morris Hamburg, and Stanley Schore, *The Over-the-Counter Securities Markets* (New York: McGraw-Hill Book Company, 1958).

28 *Ibid.*, p. 116.

banks and some companies of poor quality. The market for securities of some companies might be limited because the company is small or unknown, the stock is closely held by one family, the security might be unseasoned or its price high, it might offer little or no investment or speculative interest, or the company simply might not wish its security to be listed on an exchange. The trading that takes place in such securities is done by negotiation, with the dealers or brokers bargaining directly to establish a price.

Of approximately 8,000 broker-dealers, 5,500 are registered with the SEC and engage in interstate commerce to effect security transactions. The bulk of the business is handled by broker-dealers who are members of the National Association of Security Dealers. These broker-dealers fall into six main classifications: (1) the OTC house that deals mainly in OTC issues and does not usually belong to an exchange; (2) the investment banking house that deals heavily in underwriting new issues of stocks and bonds; (3) the dealer bank, a commercial bank that makes a market for government securities; (4) the municipal bond house; (5) the government bond house; and (6) the stock exchange member house. Major functions of these broker-dealers are to make a market for securities outstanding, distribute new issues of securities, and help distribute large secondary offerings of stock in over-the-counter markets.[29]

Advantages of Trading in the Over-the-Counter Market

The OTC market is the only place where certain stocks can be purchased. Small local companies and good national companies that do not meet exchange listing requirements are traded OTC. Many of these securities are top-quality, investment-grade senior securities of federal, state, and local governments that fit into the investor's portfolio, particularly the institutional investor and the wealthy investor desiring fixed-income securities. The market for these securities is stable and continuous, providing marketability comparable with that of securities traded on a registered exchange. Securities that provide growth potential are also traded in this market, as are some local issues that are attractive for long-term investment. With the passage of the Securities Acts Amendments of 1964, with the improvement of self-regulation and of reporting requirements of corporations, stocks and companies in the over-the-counter market have been given a new dimension, making them more attractive for investment.

Risks associated with many stocks traded in the OTC have been reduced. With the reduction of risk, one aspect of the valuation process has been improved. Since we have always been interested in the balance in the equation of risk versus rewards, we are now in a position to make estimates of the future to reduce the penalty of risks or loss because of

29 Leffler and Farwell, *Stock Market*, p. 467.

improper practices or lower standards in the OTC market than in the New York Stock Exchange. A given dollar of earnings or rate of return of an OTC company would therefore have greater value than formerly. Increased regulation of the over-the-counter market has taken away some of the disadvantages of purchasing securities here.

The NASD revision of its retail quotation system was adopted in response to the congressional mandate based on recommendations of the Special Study.[30] In addition, automation in the over-the-counter market proposed by the National Association of Security Dealers will lead to better quotes. It is hoped that equipment will be provided from vendors for this activity.[31] Steps were taken to improve the surveillance of selling activities and to strengthen the self-regulatory agencies, so that clearer standards and stronger enforcement procedures would assure the effects of supervision of member firms in the over-the-counter market.[32]

Disadvantages of Trading in the Over-the-Counter Market

The disadvantages of OTC trading, by contrast, are imposing. Generally, the quality of securities, aside from municipal and federal government obligations, is not as high as of those traded on the New York Stock Exchange. It is more difficult to obtain information about price and the financial affairs of the companies. In general, the OTC market consists of smaller companies that have limited marketability and liquidity. The market is less well organized and the companies are smaller, leading to a lower degree of marketability for equity securities.

But in spite of these disadvantages, the OTC market is an important marketplace for securities transactions. Since the passage of the Securities Acts Amendments of 1964 that placed the market under regulation of the NASD, the over-the-counter market has taken on a new favor with the investor seeking adequate rates of return with a minimum of risk.

The "Third Market"

The "third" or "off-the-board" market is made up of nonmember firms that do not charge regular listed commissions on sales. To achieve these economies, shares traded are the same as those traded on the New York Stock Exchange. Clients of the third market are the large

30 Securities and Exchange Commission, *31st Annual Report* (Washington, D.C.: Government Printing Office, 1965), p. 18.

31 Securities and Exchange Commission, *32nd Annual Report* (Washington, D.C.: Government Printing Office, 1966), p. 4.

32 *Ibid.*, p. 5.

institutional investors who are price conscious in buying and selling securities and seek out the nonmember broker-dealer firms outside exchange facilities.

The institutional market is substantial. Institutional investors have a tremendous effect upon the stock market. Mr. Keith Funston, then president of the New York Stock Exchange, indicated their importance in an address to the American Management Association in New York City on November 6, 1966.[33] He indicated that institutional investors would increase their holdings of New York Stock Exchange listed stocks from 20 percent in 1966 to 27 percent in 1975 and 30 percent in 1980.

The brokerage community is "painfully aware that institutional investors, pension funds, insurance companies and the like—with large blocks of stock to buy and sell—are attracted to larger, nonmember, broker-dealer firms not only because those firms offer more advantageous net prices involving no commissions, but also because they usually are willing to quote a firm bid for the whole block. It is the rare portfolio manager who does not appreciate the convenience of being able to launch a sizable transaction with but one telephone!"[34]

The New York Stock Exchange's principal approach to competing against the third market has been to develop techniques for handling large block transactions quickly and with a minimum of price fluctuation. In addition, brokerage firms have taken out membership on regional exchanges that trade in stocks also listed on the Big Board. These exchanges permit commission cutting; the NYSE does not. This makes the brokerage firms competitive with third market firms.[35]

Regulation in the Securities Markets

The securities market, as it functions, is the outstanding example of the free enterprise, capitalistic economic system at work. But regulation has played an important part in its success. Regulations have been imposed upon stock market institutions to protect the investment public and society as a whole. They are carried out at the federal level through the Securities and Exchange Commission and at the state level through various departments that have been established to regulate the sale of securities within each state. These state agencies are often referred to as state securities commissions.

The SEC was established under the Securities Exchange Act of 1934. It consists of five members appointed by the President of the United States. The commission is assisted in its regulatory and inves-

---

33 Keith Funston, "Role of Institutions in the Stock Markets," *Commercial and Financial Chronicle*, December 29, 1966, p. 11.

34 Silberman, "Critical Examination," pp. 121–22.

35 *Ibid.*, p. 122.

tigation work by over 1,000 accountants, engineers, examiners, lawyers, security analysts, and administrative and clerical employees. SEC headquarters are in Washington, and there are ten regional offices. The activities of the SEC are designed to protect the investment public from losses owing to fraud, unfair competition, or unethical acts. It is the duty of the SEC to inform but not to advise the public about the investment worth of an individual company's securities.

The Securities Act of 1933, administered by the SEC, required corporations selling new issues of stock to the public to provide the purchaser with a complete statement of all pertinent financial and non-financial information relating to operations of the company. The 1933 act is sometimes referred to as the "truth in securities act," since companies selling stock to the public are required to tell the truth, the whole truth, and nothing but the truth about their past, present, and expected future activities. This act was the first important federal legislation regulating the stock market. Prior legislation at the state level was initiated in Kansas in 1911, with passage of the first "blue sky" law to protect investors from fraudulent or illegal promotion in intrastate security sales. Today state security commissions are very active in regulating the issuance of new securities.

The SEC administers the Public Utility Holding Company Act of 1935, which limits the scope and growth of public utilities by controlling the number of holding companies that can be pyramided upon an operating utility. It limits public utility holding company systems to well-defined geographic areas.

The Investment Company Act of 1940 and the Investment Advisers Act of 1940 are also administered by the SEC. These acts provide for the registration and regulation of activities of investment companies and investment advisers. Chapter X of the National Bankruptcy Act, providing for the reorganization of industrial companies, is also under the administration of the SEC. The Securities Exchange Act of 1934 not only established the SEC but also provided for the registration of national securities exchanges.

The seven major purposes and objectives of the SEC may be summarized as follows:

(1) SEC insures that the public will receive adequate information about securities traded in the various securities markets. All securities being sold to the public must be registered with the SEC except for certain exempt issues. Exempt securities include (a) the direct obligations of the federal government and the direct and indirect obligations of state and municipal governments, (b) other securities issued or guaranteed by corporations in which the United States has an interest, (c) securities issued by railroads, (d) security issues below $300,000 in amount, (e) security issues sold to one or a few institutional investors and

not to the public at large, and (f) any other securities that the SEC may deem necessary to exempt, such as unregistered securities and those of an intrastate character.[36]

(2) SEC provides for the registration of exchanges to regulate the activities of these markets. Any exchange that engages in interstate or foreign commerce or uses the mails in its activities must register with the SEC.

(3) Information is required by the SEC about inside trading and the activities of officers and directors in the securities of their company, with the aim of preventing manipulation in the securities market. SEC also attempts to prevent manipulation by brokers and dealers.

(4) SEC attempts to regulate the activities of investment companies and investment advisers by requiring their registration with the SEC. This is to insure that the market and its participants operate in an orderly fashion.

(5) SEC regulates the activities of the brokers and dealers that operate in the market.

(6) SEC provides for regulation to limit the amount of credit that is involved in the stock market. The control over margin requirements for stock market credit is exercised by the Federal Reserve Board of Governors. The margin requirement is changed by the Board of Governors from time to time to help maintain an orderly stock market.

(7) SEC is given the right of supervision over the NASD. The National Association of Security Dealers is the only self-regulatory association of brokers and dealers. The stated objectives of the NASD are: (a) To promote through cooperative effort the investment banking securities business, to standardize its principles and practices, to promote the high standards of commercial practice, and to encourage and promote among members observance of federal and state securities law. (b) To provide a medium through which its membership may be enabled to confer, consult, and cooperate with governmental and other agencies in the solution of problems affecting investors, the public, and the investment banking securities business. (c) To adopt, administer, and enforce rules of fair practice and rules to prevent fraudulent and manipulative acts and practices and in general to promote just and equitable principles of trade for the protection of investors. (d) To promote self-discipline among members and to investigate just grievances between the public and members and between members. The Special Study conducted by the SEC upheld the principle of self-regulation and broadened the scope of this practice of the NASD to include nonmember firms and firms involved in the over-the-counter market.

36 Securities Exchange Act of 1934, Section 3 (12).

All these specific areas of regulation are undertaken so that no unfair practices are engaged in that would result in losses to the investment public and so that capital markets may function properly. Enforcement of the Securities Exchange Act of 1934 may result in a criminal penalty with fines up to $10,000 for individuals and $500,000 for exchanges, and imprisonment up to two years for individuals. The SEC may also suspend a member, an exchange, or a company from trading activities or from the privilege of trading.[37]

The most recent amendment to the securities acts, the Securities Acts Amendments of 1964, was the result of the SEC's Special Study. It has had far-reaching implications for the securities business. The four-part Special Study was conducted by sixty-five lawyers, economists, and staffers under the direction of Milton H. Cohen, affectionately referred to by his colleagues and the President of the United States as "Manny." The first report of the study cited several abuses in the securities market: "(1) Some companies give only the scantiest information to stockholders. (2) Many securities salesmen are trained only poorly, if at all. (3) Many investment advisers are irresponsible. (4) Even the biggest and most reputable of brokerage houses were at times extremely careless. (5) Some publicity men and newspaper, magazine and broadcasting journalists were carefully cultivated by companies, usually by receiving allotments of hard-to-get 'hot' new issues that went up in price just after coming out. (6) 'A considerable number' of public relations men artificially pumped up their employer's or client's stock by issuing fantastic announcements of expected earnings, mergers, new products. (7) Some public relations men profited directly from trading in shares of client companies, a practice frowned on by the SEC because the public may not be aware that the 'information which it receives comes from an interested source.' "[38]

The second report indicated other abuses. "Investigators for the SEC reported that these men [insiders] often overcharge and insufficiently protect the small investor, and called many of the rules by which they work outmoded, ineffective, and in need of reform. . . . The SEC recommended that trading in stock issues that are 'unlisted' on any exchange be automated and perhaps made cheaper for the investor, and that the cost of trading in 'odd lots' of fewer than 100 shares be lowered. It asked for closer regulation of the stock exchange specialists and bearish 'short sellers' and suggested that the exchanges' anachronistic floor traders be abolished altogether."[39]

The third report of the Special Study dealt with the obligations

---

37 Leffler and Farwell, *Stock Market*, Chap. 28.

38 "Taking Stock," *Time*, April 12, 1963, pp. 91–92. Courtesy *Time*, Copyright Time, Inc., 1963.

39 "Modernizing the Market," *Time*, July 26, 1963, p. 71.

of the issuers of publicly held securities and brought important changes in the over-the-counter market. It recommended that unlisted securities come under regulation of the SEC and the original Securities Exchange Act and that companies with 500 or more security holders with two million dollars worth of securities should come under the jurisdiction of the Securities Act. The asset requirement later was changed to one million dollars. "The recommended legislation should not exempt any category of issuers merely because they file reports or are otherwise regulated under other laws, unless such reports or other regulations are clearly designed for the protection of investors."[40] It was indicated that insider trading activities of brokers should be enforced and no further exemptions should be provided for OTC companies.[41] The principle was followed that the widest disclosure of information is fundamental to federal securities regulation and that the disclosure of information and control of companies in the over-the-counter market would best be fulfilled by filing and providing the information required.[42]

The fourth part of the Special Study covered the subject of security credit, open-end investment companies, mutual funds, the regulatory pattern of the SEC, and the market break of May, 1962.

The Securities Acts Amendments of 1964, considered the most significant statutory advance in federal securities regulation relevant to investor protection since 1940, were a major boost to regulation in the over-the-counter market. The principal objective of the 1964 amendments was to provide investors in securities traded over the counter the same fundamental disclosure and protection as previously afforded by the Securities Exchange Act of 1934 to investors in listed securities.[43] The act was designed to strengthen the standards of the securities business and to make more effective the disciplinary controls of the SEC and the self-regulatory rules of the National Association of Security Dealers, having regulatory control over security brokers and dealers and persons associated with these groups. The 1964 Amendments extended regulation to a significant portion of the securities traded in the over-the-counter market, and covered registration, periodic reporting, proxy solicitation, and insider reporting and trading procedures of the Exchange Act that had previously been applicable only to listed securities on registered exchanges.[44] Companies with total assets of one million dollars or more and 750 stockholders became subject to regulation, as were listed corporations. Regulation of OTC security dealers

40 *Report of Special Study of the Securities Markets of the Securities and Exchange Commission*, Part III, p. 63.

41 *Ibid.*

42 *Ibid.*, p. 64.

43 Securities and Exchange Commission, *31st Annual Report*, p. 1.

44 *Ibid.*, p. 5.

was increased by requiring standards of training, rules for producing information and retail quotations, and broadening SEC's power to alter NASD rules and giving it the power to regulate both NASD members and nonmembers. The prospectus for a securities offering must be rendered ninety days after distribution begins and not forty days as previously. The non-NASD firm must meet the same qualification standards as the NASD firm.

Not all the recommendations of the Special Study have been carried out. But the SEC continues to protect the investor from fraudulent acts of unscrupulous operators in the securities market. In addition, the New York Stock Exchange continues to strengthen the normal regulatory procedures, both self-imposed and those existing under the securities acts administered by the SEC.

The Investment Company Amendments Act of 1967 is still pending. If enacted, it will result in a ceiling of 5 percent on sales charges or commissions instead of the current 9 percent on the purchase of mutual fund shares, fees paid by mutual funds being reasonable and subject to court review, and a ban on "front end loads." At the present time, 50 to 80 percent of the total sales commission paid on the first year mutual fund installment goes to the seller. Among lesser items of the act is the provision that the trading tactics of some mutual fund managers taking advantage of short-term market fluctuations be controlled to the extent that such actions are detrimental to shareholders.

In addition to this bill, other areas of investigation include disclosures required of tender offers and of persons who own 10 percent or more of the outstanding securities of the company. A tender offer is made by a group of purchasers wishing to buy a controlling interest in a company. They are willing to pay X dollars a share if the necessary shares are tendered by the present stockholders. Disclosure, required by the Securities and Exchange Commission, includes the identity, background, and plans of the purchaser, and the sources of information. The stockholder or person making a tender offer can withdraw the offer the first seven days after it has been made. If the offer was tied up by an undecided purchaser, it could be withdrawn up to sixty days after being made. Also any person or group obtaining more than 10 percent of the stock of a company would disclose its position and be subject to the tender rules.

The 1967 SEC report suggested that individuals who have willfully violated securities laws be barred from affiliation with investment companies.[45] A new section added to the act would empower the commission to adopt rules and regulations with respect to trading securities held or being acquired by investment companies by such a person. One amendment would prohibit the creation of mutual fund holding com-

---

45 Securities and Exchange Commission, *33rd Annual Report*, p. 4.

panies and acquisition of additional securities of registered investment companies by existing mutual fund holding companies. Another amendment suggests that directors of mutual funds be independent and disinterested in the management of the investment company; another would eliminate the possibility of transference of an investment advisory contract for the management of an investment company. In addition, suggestions were made for quantity discounts on the sale or purchase of large blocks of stock.

Summary

A marketplace for securities is any place where a buyer and a seller can be brought together in person or by an agent to engage in security transactions. The stock market is divided into two major segments, the organized securities exchange market and the over-the-counter market. The functions of a stock exchange are to provide a continuous market for individual security issues, to provide the mechanism whereby a fair price can be established with its accompanying improvements in collateral value, to aid in the financing of industry, and to provide information and protection for the investor.

The New York Stock Exchange is the largest and best-known exchange in the United States. It is an association of individuals governed by a 33-man Board of Governors. The membership of the Exchange is divided into commission brokers, odd-lot brokers, specialists, floor brokers, floor traders, and bond brokers. The most numerous group is the commission brokers. Commission brokerage firms employ over 42,000 registered representatives to transact business with the investing public. The larger, more profitable, more widely held corporations are listed on the New York Stock Exchange.

The American Stock Exchange operates much like the New York Stock Exchange except for certain institutional differences that are part of its historical development. The number of members and the corporations listed are smaller than for the New York Stock Exchange, but volume of shares traded is growing faster.

The National Stock Exchange is also growing rapidly but with a much smaller number of stocks. Local and regional exchanges deal mainly in local issues and in the unlisted shares on the American Stock Exchange. Stocks listed on a regional exchange may also be listed on a national exchange. The volume of business conducted on regional exchanges has increased substantially because of brokerage houses buying and selling on the "off-the-board" or "third market." The major advantages of trading in securities listed on a national exchange are the greater marketability, liquidity, availability of information, and stability of these shares. This is particularly true of securities on the New York Stock Exchange. There is simply a better market for stocks on the NYSE than on any other exchange. The advantages of trading in stocks on a national exchange have lessened with the passage of the Securities Acts Amendments of 1964 because of stronger regulation of OTC market stocks.

The over-the-counter market, the second major segment of the securities market, is much larger and possesses a greater variety of issues than the organized security markets. Typical securities traded are high-grade, high-quality government bonds and the securities of small companies not having a wide market for their shares. Government bonds can be purchased only in the over-the-counter market. The advantage of purchasing securities of smaller companies is their potential for growth. Many small companies originally traded over the counter and subsequently became excellent investment-grade companies.

The investor is protected in the stock market through the activities of the Securities and Exchange Commission. The main job of the SEC is to administer the Securities Act of 1933, the Securities Exchange Act of 1934, the Public Utility Holding Company Act of 1935, the Investment Company Act of 1940, the Investment Advisers Act of 1940, the Securities Acts Amendments of 1964, and the pending legislation of the Investment Company Amendments Act of 1967. The SEC regulates various individuals and institutions in the securities market in order to provide information for the investor to make an informed investment decision and to protect him from unfair and fraudulent activities. It does not judge the quality of the market or the investment security. The SEC supervises the activities of the NASD, the self-regulatory association of brokers and dealers in securities. The Special Study of the SEC and the actions of Congress have renewed, reemphasized, and strengthened the role of the SEC and NASD as watchdogs of the marketplace. It has also provided a blueprint for further protection of the investment public.

Review Questions

1. Where is the securities market, and what are its logical divisions?
2. What is the relative importance of the organized and the over-the-counter markets in terms of companies listed and number and value of shares traded?
3. Explain the functions of the organized stock exchange. Can you propose an alternative method of exchanging shares and raising capital for a corporation?
4. Discuss briefly the history of the New York Stock Exchange.
5. Describe how the New York Stock Exchange is organized and managed.
6. How many members belong to the New York Stock Exchange? What are their titles and functions?

7. What types of securities are listed and traded on the New York Stock Exchange?

8. What are the listing requirements of the New York Stock Exchange? Do they appear to be too stringent? Comment.

9. Who can buy and sell securities on the floor of the Exchange?

10. Compare the organization of the American Stock Exchange with that of the New York Stock Exchange. How are they similar?

11. Explain the nature of the membership and listing requirements of the American Stock Exchange as compared with those of the New York Stock Exchange.

12. What is the "off-the-board" or "third" market?

13. Why is the OTC market a safer place to buy stocks today than it was in 1963?

14. Explain unlisted trading and foreign securities as they apply to the American Stock Exchange.

15. Discuss the relative importance of regional and local exchanges. Should we do away with all regional exchanges? Comment.

16. What are block sales? How are they related to regional exchanges and the "third market"?

17. How important are foreign stock exchanges compared with American stock exchanges?

18. Discuss the advantages and disadvantages of buying securities on a registered exchange compared with buying securities in the over-the-counter market. Why must we be careful to compare specific securities and companies?

19. Explain how securities markets are regulated in the United States. Mention legislation enacted to protect the investor and the public. Is the legislation adequate? Comment.

20. What was the purpose of the Securities Acts Amendments of 1964?

21. Relate marketability and risk to the valuation and investment process.

Problems

1. Where is each of the following companies traded and what is its ticker symbol?
   (a) Alpine Geophysical Associates
   (b) American Telephone and Telegraph
   (c) Cessna
   (d) Continental Telephone
   (e) IBM
   (f) Richard D. Irwin
   (g) Litton
   (h) Prentice-Hall
   (i) Standard Dredging
   (j) Yoo Hoo

2. How many shares of common stock of each of these companies are outstanding and how many are actively traded?

3. As an individual investor, are the shares of each marketable? Would your answer be the same if you were an institutional investor?

Sources of Investment Information

American Stock Exchange
Annual Report of the SEC
Barron's
Commercial and Financial Chronicle
New York Stock Exchange *Fact Book*
Standard & Poor's *Stock Guide*
Wall Street Journal

Selected Readings

Kekish, Bohdan J., "Moody's Averages," *Financial Analysts Journal* (May-June, 1967), p. 65.

Molodovsky, Nicholas, "Building a Stock Market Measure," *Financial Analysts Journal* (May-June, 1967), p. 43.

Schoomer, B. Alva, Jr., "American Stock Exchange Index System," *Financial Analysts Journal* (May-June, 1967), p. 57.

West, Stan, and Norman Miller, "Why the NYSE Common Stock Indexes?" *Financial Analysts Journal* (May-June, 1967), p. 49.

9

THE INVESTOR
AND HIS BROKER

We usually purchase securities through brokers and dealers. The typical transaction is handled by a registered representative of the New York Stock Exchange who is an employee of a commission brokerage firm. Sometimes the transaction will be exercised in the over-the-counter market through a dealer. The commission brokerage firm, as was mentioned in the previous chapter, is a member of the New York Stock Exchange and other national, regional, and local exchanges and will transact business in the securities listed on these exchanges. Commission brokers also deal in securities that are traded only in the over-the-counter markets. In this chapter we will discuss the functions performed by commission brokers. We will examine the factors involved in selecting a broker, how to open an account with a broker, the commissions and fees involved in purchasing securities, and the types of orders we can give to the broker when we purchase them. Understanding the mechanical details involved in buying and selling securities should help us become better investors.

The Functions of a Broker

The fundamental function of a broker or a brokerage firm is to buy and sell securities for customers. When the broker trades in securities listed on a national, regional, or local stock exchange, he acts as an agent for his clients. He is asked either to buy or to sell a certain number of shares of stock and is compensated for this service by a commission. Most exchanges pattern their commissions on the commission schedule of the New York Stock Exchange. This was established by the Board of Governors of the NYSE and has been adjusted from time to time to reflect economic changes. Commission rates will be discussed later in the chapter.

The Broker's Obligation in Performing Basic Functions

As an agent representing a customer, the broker is first obligated to execute the customer's orders and, in the process, to exercise due care and demonstrate a reasonable amount of skill. The broker may be held liable for any losses resulting from his mistakes. The care with which he executes his orders is determined by what is reasonable practice in the brokerage business at the time the order is executed. The exercise of care and skill requires that the broker follow instructions and place the order in the market where the security is customarily traded. All securities listed on the New York Stock Exchange, for example, must be traded on the floor of the Exchange. Under this rule, the broker could not exercise the order off the floor unless he had permission from the Exchange. The broker is also obligated to refrain from making secret profits on the transaction, from crossing orders, and from acting as both broker and dealer in the same transaction. Secret profits might arise when a broker is asked to sell 100 shares of stock for $40 a share and instead sells them for $41 and pockets the $100 difference. Crossing orders comes about when a trade is made between buyer and seller without going through the exchange. This violates the principle of the auction market. The broker cannot act as broker and dealer in the same transaction since he would be both agent and principal. A conflict of interest could develop or a double commission would result, which would be unethical. The broker must at all times extend to the customer the right to cancel his order before it has been executed. Any case in which a dispute about the actions of a broker arises can be settled in a court of law and is governed by the law of agency.

The investor may trade in securities not listed on an exchange but traded in the over-the-counter market. In this situation, the broker or his firm might own the shares and would sell them to the customer. The broker would be acting as a principal or dealer in the transaction. Sometimes, when a brokerage firm owns stock that is traded in the over-the-counter market, it specializes in the stock and is said to be "making a market in the stock." When a firm does own the stock, it will sell it to the customer at the "asked" price and will not charge a commission for handling the transaction. The broker may also buy the stock from another broker at a slightly lower price and sell it to his customers, acting in this case as a principal. When stock is purchased in the market, the customer is charged the going price plus a commission and possibly other fees.

Information and Research and the Brokerage Function

Another function of the broker is to provide his customers with the best information that can be obtained about the securities in which he deals. Most brokerage firms provide their clients with information about individual companies and industries. The types of information can be divided into several categories.

THE MARKET LETTER

The first is the market letter, which is published twice a week by some of the larger brokerage firms in New York City. Lucien Hooper of W. E. Hutton and Co. writes such a market letter, commenting upon the activity of the stock market, the possible short-term direction of the market, stocks that are currently favored, and stocks that are recommended for purchase or sale. The emphasis is on the short-range outlook for the stock market. Walston & Company puts out a similar market letter.

COMPANY ANALYSIS

A second category is the special company report and industry analysis written by financial analysts employed by the larger brokerage firms. A Cincinnati brokerage and underwriting firm, for instance, had a special report on Drackett Company, a manufacturer of household cleaning products, including Windex, Drano, and O'Cedar cleaning equipment. The firm's analyst made a specific recommendation to buy Drackett Company stock at a price of 25 and provided the investor with supporting information that would lead him to purchase shares. This is typical of the reports published by the nation's leading brokerage houses. A list of such current reports and information available is found daily in the "Abreast of the Market" and "Heard on the Street" columns of the *Wall Street Journal*.

PORTFOLIO REVIEW

The research department of an investment firm provides some portfolio management for its customers. The service is usually provided without charge. If an investor wished to learn what a professional analyst would recommend regarding the securities he owned, he would simply write to the brokerage firm and ask for an appraisal of his investment portfolio. A firm like Merrill Lynch, Pierce, Fenner & Smith or Bache & Co. would send back a detailed analysis of each company and would make specific recommendations to the investor. The investor would not be obligated to act upon these recommendations. However, after receiving the information, the investor could expect a telephone call from the company's registered representative. A portfolio review is a very good way of obtaining expert advice on one's individual investment needs, but not all investment brokerage firms are equipped to provide this broad service. Most firms have one or more research analysts to help the investor with his investment problems, and often firms that do not employ their own analysts subscribe to the investment analysis services of New York firms. Robert W. Baird & Co. of Milwaukee, for example, uses the services of Clark, Dodge & Co. of New York.

FACT SHEETS

Almost all brokerage firms will provide information about any company for which data are requested. A service that is commonly used is Standard & Poor's *Stock Guide.* In addition to their investment manuals, Standard & Poor's publishes concise and informative reports about more than 4,000 companies traded on the stock exchanges and the over-the-counter market. An example of this material was presented in Chapter 6, Figure 6–5 (a) and (b). This type of service provides the investor with factual information upon which he can base his decisions. Seldom do brokerage firms give tips on the stock market, and they should not be expected to do so. They do, however, give factual information about investment-quality securities.

Chartered Financial Analysts

Analysts have grown in number and importance in the past decade. Most brokerage firms employ analysts who belong to analyst societies. Such societies are found in the major cities in the United States. New York City's is the most active, and it meets almost daily. At luncheon meetings, analysts gather to hear the presidents or top executives of prominent companies discuss their companies' economic and financial history and future. Not only do these meetings provide up-to-date information about the progress of the company, but they give analysts an opportunity to assess the abilities of management. In recent years the Financial Analysts Federation has established a formal training program with three stages of requirements for the analyst. The first level requires a thorough understanding of security analysis and the fundamentals of finance, investments, and the securities market; it is identified as Part I.

Part II has to do with applied security analysis. Topics included are practical applications of financial analysis, economic growth, business fluctuations, and industry analysis. In order to pass the examination, the candidate must develop competence in each of these areas, through study and experience.

Part III covers the subject of portfolio management for individuals and institutions. The examination in this area covers a wide range of subjects. The analyst must develop competence, judgment, and experience in answering questions presented in written form. Upon completing the training program and passing the required examinations, the analyst is designated a Chartered Financial Analyst (CFA).

The examinations for the title of CFA cover not only the substantive material in the field of investments, but also the judgment and experience of the analyst as well as attitudes toward the ethical standards of the industry. In order for the deliberations of the analyst about values, his forecasts for the future, and the economics of finance to make sense, an ethical business environment must prevail, where value judgments are not affected by artificial stimuli created by fraud, inside information, or other illicit activities unfavorably affecting the price of a security. The Chartered Financial Analysts have established a code of ethics and guidelines to the code. These form the basis of the ethical standards of 11,000 members of the Financial Analysts Federation in the United States and go a long way in helping to provide an ethical environment for decision making.[1]

The statements of the code of ethics of the CFA organization indicate both the aspirations and the integrity of the members, who are professionals highly oriented toward their discipline.[2] In the long run, adherence to the code of ethics and the spread of the CFA movement will add immeasurably to value decisions made by analysts.

The Securities and Exchange Commission has been vitally concerned with the ability of the customer's representative to act honestly and legally in his dealings with investors. One of the basic concerns of its Special Study was to establish standards for brokers and broker-dealer firms and to control their activities. The Securities Acts Amendments of 1964 provided emphasis in applying new rules and regulations. For the first time, the commission was authorized to proceed directly against individuals associated with broker-dealer firms and to impose sanctions on such individuals, including suspension or bar from being associated with broker-dealers. The sanctions, which included censure and suspension of registration for up to twelve months and statutory disqualification from being registered as a broker-dealer or from being associated with the broker-dealer, were expanded to cover certain additional types of injunctions, convictions, and violations.[3]

Nonmembers of the NASD who are brokers, and dealers who engage in over-the-counter business, also came under scrutiny of the Special Study and of subsequent legislation (the Securities Acts Amendments of 1964). The rules were amended to include the requirement that "persons associated with nonmember broker-dealers in certain capacities must successfully complete qualifications examinations; that nonmember broker-dealers file with the commission a personal form for each of their associated persons engaged in securities activities; and that they pay

1 The Institute of Chartered Financial Analysts, *Study Guide Examination to Applied Security Analysis* (Homewood, Ill.: Richard D. Irwin, Inc., 1968), p. 221.

2 *Ibid.*, p. 222.

3 Securities and Exchange Commission, *31st Annual Report*, 1965, p. 11.

fees to defray the additional costs of regulation."[4] Incidentally, the Special Study led to a change in the method of quoting security prices in the over-the-counter market. It recommended that the public receive improved quotations to reflect more accurately the prices received and given by dealers. This was made into law in the Securities Acts Amendments of 1964, and now the NASD system provides a national list published on the basis of the National Prevailing Interdealer Quotations as of a particular time; the statement is made that prices shown are subject to markups, markdowns, or commissions in retail transactions.

The Securities Acts Amendments of 1964 also regulate the areas of minimum net capital required by each broker, supervision of selling practices, research and investment advice, and financial responsibility.[5] After extensive discussion with the securities industry, the SEC adopted minimum capital requirements of $5,000 for firms engaged in the general securities business and $2,500 for firms engaged solely in transactions with share-registered investment companies. These are minimal figures, and brokers and dealers subject to this ruling must also comply with the requirement that their ratio of indebtedness to net capital not exceed 2,000 per cent.[6]

The NASD also established new rules to supervise its members. These "require an establishment and enforcement of written supervisory procedures and designation of a partner or officers responsible for their execution. Internal procedures must include periodic review of customer accounts and at least an annual inspection of each branch office. The rule governing discretionary accounts [such accounts are treated later in this chapter] is also being amended to require written customer authorization and supervisor review and approval of activity in such accounts." The NASD has prepared and distributed to its members a comprehensive supervision manual that contains detailed guidelines for effective procedures. New rules for research and investment advice have been adopted. These now generally provide that recommendations must have a basis that can be substantiated as reasonable; firms must accurately describe their research facilities and staff; and existing proprietary positions or other interests must be disclosed. In addition, many firms have adopted training programs for their registered representatives, which contain a great amount of information about the rules and regulations of the SEC and NASD and also provide grounding in the fundamentals of economics and finance.

The New York Stock Exchange and other major exchanges have amended their rules to provide special adjustments in the computation of members' net capital reflecting the commodities activities of their

4 *Ibid.*, p. 12.
5 *Ibid.*, pp. 14–16.
6 *Ibid.*, p. 14.

members. The NYSE has also established a special trust fund of 25 million dollars that can be utilized to satisfy the claims of customers in the event of the insolvency of any member organization.

The net effect of these activities is to ensure that the broker performs his basic functions honestly and fairly, that his activities are under supervision, and that there are rules of conduct that attempt to protect the investing public.

Investment Management

Some brokerage firms provide investment management services for their customers on a fee basis. These management services are performed either by the brokerage firm itself with the aid of its investment research department, or they are provided by another investment company. The brokerage firm performs this function to offer a wider service to its customers and to receive some of the business from the investment company in the way of purchase and sale of shares. One brokerage firm formerly permitted its customers to subscribe to the investment management service of Scudder, Stevens, and Clark by paying the regular investment counseling fees to the latter. Some firms offer their services on a fee basis as does Standard & Poor's. This type of service will be discussed in greater detail at a later time.

Types of Brokerage Firms

Many brokerage firms deal in securities that are not listed on a national exchange but are traded in the over-the-counter market; firms that buy and sell securities listed on an exchange may also deal in over-the-counter securities. Brokerage houses and dealers in securities can be separated into several distinct groups. First is the firm that performs the brokerage function but to some extent also helps new companies sell stock to the public. When it does the latter, the brokerage firm is acting as an underwriter and engaging in the activities of the investment banker by selling securities directly to the investing public without using the facilities of the exchange. Merrill Lynch, Pierce, Fenner & Smith and E. F. Hutton & Company are outstanding examples of this type of brokerage firm.

A second type of firm is predominantly engaged in underwriting new security issues, handling buying and selling orders for its customers only to a limited extent. These firms tend to underwrite the issues of the leading companies in the United States. Eastman Dillon, Union Securities & Co., and Paine, Webber, Jackson, and Curtis are examples of this type of company, although they are now beginning to emphasize their retail business.

A third classification of brokerage house is the smaller firm outside New York that trades in listed securities and underwrites the security issues of small, local companies. This type of firm provides an excellent service for the investor and for the small company that wishes to go public because it needs additional equity capital.

The fourth class of brokerage firm deals only in over-the-counter stocks. This type of firm helps the small company sell its stock, and it deals in other securities of the same type and size. Some of these firms become specialists in a particular company's stock, and they "make a market" for the stock. This simply means that the firm stands ready to buy and sell shares of the company's stock. This type of firm also might deal only in government securities.

Investment Banking

All of these types of firms, from time to time, act as managers of or participate in an underwriting syndicate. When a company wishes to raise capital by selling stock to the public or its own stockholders, it usually enlists the aid of an investment banking house. The investment banker or brokerage house advises the company on the type of security to offer and the price it should charge. The underwriter then brings together other firms to help sell the issue. Each member of the underwriting syndicate is given a portion of the total amount of shares to sell; each usually assumes the risk involved in selling the stock. The underwriter guarantees that the stock will be sold and a specific sum of money will be paid to the corporation. If any shares remain unsold after the initial sale, each participating underwriter will take a portion of the shares based upon his original participation in the total number of shares.

All new issues sold in interstate commerce, except those specifically exempt, must be approved by the SEC. To accomplish this, a preliminary prospectus—called a "red herring"—that contains all pertinent information about the sale of the stock and the company selling it is sent to the members of the syndicate. They, in turn, send it to persons who might be interested in purchasing the stock. Anyone wishing to buy the stock must be informed through the prospectus before he can complete the transaction. A final prospectus that includes the stock's selling price must also be seen by the investor. The prospectus is an excellent source of complete, recent, and objective facts.

Securities offered through investment syndicates consisting of brokers and dealers give the investor an opportunity to purchase securities without paying the usual stock exchange commission. The brokerage firm selling the shares does, however, charge the investor a higher price than it paid for the stock from the company—the underwriting commission, which may be 10 percent or higher. When a brokerage firm offers its customers an opportunity to participate in these new issues, it is offering them an additional service. We must hasten to add that this service is not provided without a *quid pro quo* in the form of a commission. And the risks involved in new and unseasoned stock issues of this type are somewhat greater than those of the average common stocks traded on the New York Stock Exchange.

Selecting a Broker

We must select our broker with a great deal of care. Many people ask, "Where can I find a good broker?" What they really ask is, "Where can I find a reliable person in a reliable brokerage firm who will provide me with adequate service?" This question might seem naive to the sophisticated investor, but represents a very real problem for many people who are investing their savings for the first time. If we raised this question, we might receive the following advice.

First, select a broker who can give prompt and efficient service. This means he must be able to confirm a purchase or sale within minutes and provide price quotes quickly. A broker who cannot give prompt service is not doing his basic job. Buying and selling securities is, after all, the basic function of the broker.

Second, select a broker who has unquestioned integrity. This requires that both the brokerage firm and the registered representative or dealer have an excellent reputation in the community. A lawyer, a banker, or an independent investment counselor can provide the investor with a list of brokers or dealers in the community who have a good reputation in the brokerage industry.

Third, select a brokerage firm that is in good financial condition. This is difficult for the average investor to assess. Discreet questioning in the financial community can determine the relative financial position of a brokerage firm. Generally, the newer, smaller broker-dealer firms have a tendency to be less well-financed than older firms.

Fourth, choose a broker who has experience in the brokerage business and who is working for a firm with an established record of good service over a period of time.

Fifth, select a broker who can provide information and research facilities. General economic information and data about companies and industries, along with economic forecasts, should be supplied to the investor. A research staff of financial analysts should be available to analyze the investor's portfolio and make unbiased recommendations to help him meet his investment objectives.

Sixth, the investment broker should be able to deal in securities listed on the major national and regional exchanges and, with equal facility, shares traded in the over-the-counter market. This requires membership in an exchange and in the National Association of Security Dealers. The brokerage firm should also participate in underwriting syndicates to give its clients the opportunity to purchase new stock issues.

Seventh, the broker should not bother the customer or attempt to change his mind after he has reached a well-thought-out decision. He should not suggest an active trading account or excessive switching from one stock to another. At all times the broker should have, and give evidence of having, the best interests of the investor uppermost in his mind. The broker must be able to render service, and to do this he must maintain a reasonable customer load. The broker-dealer who must service an excessive number of customers cannot perform his task efficiently.

In the final analysis, we must select a broker on his individual qualifications. We must investigate various brokers' experience and qualifications to find that person who will provide us with the best combination of qualities to meet our needs.

Institutional investors have a somewhat different set of criteria for selecting brokers depending upon their needs and the capability of their research staff. The first criterion is the broker's ability to transact business quickly and at a favorable price. Ability to handle a large order is also important. A brokerage firm that can handle block sales on the stock exchange and large "off-the-board" sales will have the competitive advantage in dealing with the large institutional investor. The second criterion for selecting a brokerage firm is the *quality* of the information it supplies, the ability of the brokerage firm to provide profitable information. Several large investment brokerage houses have institutional research departments. Eastman Dillon, Union Securities & Co., and Hayden Stone are among firms having such facilities. The ability to transact the business and to provide research are the two main criteria used by the institutional investor in selecting a brokerage firm. Whether the broker is a local firm and his proximity to the over-the-counter market are often considered in the selection process, but these are secondary.

To be competitive, the brokerage firm must provide profitable information; it will be compensated by brokerage commissions received. Usually a reciprocal arrangement is made between the broker and the institutional investor. The investor receives the research and the brokerage firm receives the commissions. The ethics of this tie-in arrangement are being tested, but at present it is the method of doing business.

An Account with the Broker

Opening an account with a brokerage firm is no more difficult than opening a checking account with a local commercial bank. To open an account, you fiill out a signature card. This card, which varies from firm to firm, provides space for your signature, home and business address, occupation and title, employer, bank, citizenship, and whether you are over twenty-one years of age. In addition, you fill out an information card, which will contain information about the type of account, the number of the account, and where notices and statement are to be sent. Credit references are always required; a bank and a friend or business associate are usually sufficient.

The simplest type of account is the cash account. In a cash account no credit will be extended nor will short sales be made. (See footnote on p. 554 for explanation of short sales.) All transactions must be settled within the time period given to the purchaser. The settlement date is stated on the confirmation of sale notice sent to the customer after his order has been executed. Another type is the general or margin account. This kind of account allows us to borrow when securities are purchased. We may sell short, and the broker will provide securities for the transaction. When this type of account is opened, you are required to sign a margin agreement or customer's agreement. This permits the broker to sell the securities if the margin requirement calls for such action. There are other types of brokerage accounts, but the cash or margin accounts are the most familiar.

You can close your account with the broker at any time, after a reasonable notice has been given and all obligations of the customer have been paid in full. A broker also has the right to terminate the relationship after proper notice. If you should die or become bankrupt, the broker will close your account, for the protection of your estate and your creditors.

You must be 21 or over to open an account with a brokerage firm because minors cannot enter into legally binding contracts. Parents may buy securities for a minor child, however, and hold them until the child reaches age 21. Many states have legislation that allows the stock to be carried in the name of the minor with the parent acting as custodian. The adult retains management rights over the investment until the minor comes of age.

Once an account has been opened, you are able to use the services of the broker. Orders are transacted through the registered representative, and a monthly statement of the results of transactions is sent to you. A copy of a confirmation of purchase appears in Figure 9–1. When securities are purchased you may have them registered in your name or you may at your option leave the securities with the broker. This is known as keeping the securities in "street name" for your benefit. Since the broker's name appears on the books of the corporation as the owner, he is sent all of the dividend notices, dividends, price statements, annual reports, notice of the annual meeting, and other notices. The broker must notify you of information or dividends received in the form of cash or stock. Keeping securities with the broker is convenient; the shares are safe from loss, and they are available for sale at a moment's notice. This arrangement is particularly desirable where there is more than one owner. An investment club, for example, would most likely

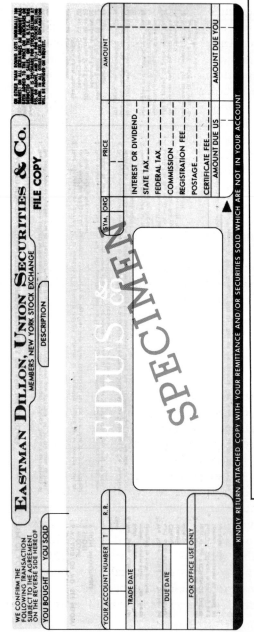

FIGURE 9-1

Sample of a brokerage purchase confirmation — front and back

leave its shares with the broker. It is the broker's responsibility and obligation to make certain that the owner enjoys all the rights of ownership when the stock is held in the name of the brokerage firm.

When the securities are sold, the proceeds of the sale may be kept by the broker for the account of the owner. The amount represents a credit balance with the brokerage firm, provided the owner has not engaged in other transactions that require payment from the account. The proceeds of the sale, after all expenses and commissions have been deducted, can be sent to the owner by check. It is to your advantage, however, as a customer of the brokerage house, to keep your funds on deposit if you are active in buying and selling securities.

Types of Broker's Orders

Once you open an account with a brokerage firm, you usually conduct most of your business by telephone. When placing an order to purchase or sell stock, you must be able to clearly communicate your intentions to the broker. He must know exactly what you wish to do, or he will not be able to carry out his job to the best of his ability. The task of communication is somewhat easier if you know and understand the types of orders you may give to a broker.

The Market Order

The market order is the simplest and most straightforward order to a broker to buy or sell a security. It is also the most common order carried out on the exchange. In giving this order, we expect the broker to obtain the best possible price for our shares at the time the order is given. When the order reaches the floor of the exchange, it is executed promptly by the brokers involved. The customer is certain that a market order will be completed. This is not the case with some other types of orders.

The Limit Order

A limit or limited order specifies the price at which stock is to be bought or sold. This is in contrast to the market order in which no price is specified. If a limit order is given to sell a round lot of General Motors common at 72, when the price is 70, the limit order becomes effective when the market reaches 72. A limit order given to buy 100 shares of GM at 60, when the market price is 70, will become effective at 60 and will be exercised by the broker.

The disadvantage of a limit order is that it might never be completed. For example, if we placed an order to buy GM at 60, and the price dropped to 61 and then went up again, the order would not be executed; we would not buy the stock. The price must drop to 60 before the order becomes effective and is exercised. And it is possible that when the market reached the limit price sufficient stock might not be available at the price. Under these circumstances it would be better to wait until the price of GM dropped. When it was close to the price we wished to pay, a market order could be placed which would assure the purchase of the stock. When the price of a limit order is established, it should be consistent and realistic with the present price range of the stock.

Stop Orders

An order that can be used to our benefit is the stop order or the stop-loss order. This is essentially a combination of a limit order and a market order. An order is placed to buy or sell stock at a specified price. When the limit price is reached, it puts into effect a market order. A stop order to sell becomes a market order at or below the stop price, and a stop order to buy becomes a market order at or above the stop price. The stop order may be used to protect profits and also to limit losses in an investment purchase or in a short sale.

An example of how the stop order may be used will be helpful. Assume that an investor has purchased a stock for investment purposes. He is said to be "long" in the stock. (This means that he is maintaining a long-term position and is not selling short.) He bought it at 50 and the price is now 65. The investor has a substantial profit and wishes to protect it. He places a stop order with his broker to sell at 60. If the stock should decline to 60, this order becomes a market order, and he will be sold out at 60 or below as the market allows. He still has a good profit and is protected from a greater drop in price.

The investor could have put in a stop-loss order when he purchased the stock. Assume, for example, that he bought the stock at 50 and was apprehensive about a possible drop in its price. He could put in a stop-loss order at 45 to protect his investment in case the market declined. The investor's position is "long" in this case; by putting in a stop-loss order, he will limit his loss to five points. The premise from which the investor is working is that if the market price drops five points, it will probably go lower, and he will be able to purchase his stock again at a lower price.

A speculator can use the stop-loss order to his advantage when he sells "short" or maintains a "short" position in the stock market. Assume that the speculator sells General Motors short at 70, hoping that it will drop. He will then be able to buy it back at a lower price, say 60, return the stock he borrowed and sold at 70, making a handsome profit. If the market should go up to 80, our speculator would lose an amount equal to what he had hoped to gain. In order to limit his loss, the speculator could place a stop-loss order with his broker at 75. When the market reached 75, the shares he needed would be bought, and his loss would be limited to five points per share instead of a large amount. If the stock dropped to 60, however, and the speculator thought it might go down further, he could place a stop-order at 65. If the stock did rise instead of dropping, his shares would be bought out at that level; he would still have almost a 10 percent profit on the transaction. Thus, if we were "long" or "short" in a particular stock, we could benefit by the use of a stop or stop-loss order.

Discretionary Accounts and Orders

A discretionary account is one that gives the broker a great deal of authority in making decisions for us. The assumption we make with a discretionary account is that, because of his knowledge and experience, the broker can do a better job in making decisions than we can. Under a completely discretionary account, we order the broker to decide what stock to buy or sell, when to buy or sell it, and the number of shares. Each order of this type must be approved by a partner of the brokerage firm, and the customer must give his written approval prior to execution of the order. This type of account and order is not widely used. Many people in the financial community do not favor it, nor do they want the responsibility. Its best use is for people who are ill, out of the continental United States, or away from home for an extended period of time.

Time Orders

In some cases we can use time orders when making purchases or sales. A time order is usually associated with a limit or limited order. Time orders are for a day, week, or month or are good until canceled (GTC). A day order is good until the end of the day, as is the market order. The week order is good for one week, the month order for a month. The GTC order simply remains in force until it is completed or canceled. The reason for time orders is that economic and market conditions may change and make it possible to buy or sell at a more attractive price. An investor who is interested in a long-range investment program would not be influenced by the daily price range of a stock and might be willing to wait quite long to obtain the desired price. Time orders are used infrequently by investors. If we wished to buy or sell a stock at a certain price, however, a GTC or open order would probably work most effectively.

The market order, the limit or limited order, and the stop and stop-loss orders are most frequently used by the investment community. These allow the investor a great deal of flexibility in meeting his needs. In our discussion we assumed that an order could be either a buy order or a sell order or a "long" or "short" order. It could also be a round-lot order, consisting of 100 shares of stock, or an odd-lot order of from

1 to 99 shares. The usual unit of trading, unless otherwise stated, is a round lot of 100 shares.

The Cost of Buying and Selling Securities

We must be aware of all the costs involved in buying and selling securities traded on a national exchange and in the over-the-counter market. We should know how to compute these costs and understand their impact upon our investment transactions, so that we can verify the commission and other fees charged by our broker. This does not suggest that brokerage firms are dishonest. But mistakes in billing can be made, and the investor must be able to verify and check his statement intelligently for his own protection. This is simply one of the facets of becoming an informed, intelligent investor.

Brokerage Commissions

The largest portion of the cost of buying and selling securities, excluding the market price, is the brokerage commission, which is charged all buyers and sellers. The schedule that determines the commission rate is established by the Board of Governors of the New York Stock Exchange. The schedule in effect in 1969 was:

Money Value	Round-Lot Commission	Odd-Lot Commission
Under $100	As mutually agreed	As mutually agreed
$ 100 to $ 399	2% plus $ 3.00	2% plus $ 1.00
$ 400 to $2,399	1% plus $ 7.00	1% plus $ 5.00
$2,400 to $4,999	1/2% plus $19.00	1/2% plus $17.00
$5,000 and above	1/10% plus $39.00	1/10% plus $37.00[7]

The commissions are given for transactions involving not more than 100 shares, but must be paid for each 100-share transaction or fraction thereof up to 1,000 shares. If less than a round lot of shares is traded, the commission will be reduced by $2.00, but an odd-lot fee is also charged. When the amount of the transaction is less than $100, the commission shall be as mutually agreed between broker and customer. When the amount in each transaction is $100 or more, the maximum commission shall not exceed $1.50 per share of $75 per single transaction, but in any event the commission shall not be less than $6 per single transaction.

A few examples will demonstrate how the commission is computed. Assume an investor buys 100 shares of Endicott-Johnson Corporation (EJN-NYSE) at 22 and 100 shares of Radio Corporation of America (RCA-NYSE) at 70. The initials in each set of parentheses are, first, the trading symbol of the stock and, second, those of the place where the

7 Standard & Poor's Corporation, *Stock Guide*, August, 1969, p. 252.

stock is traded. The total value of the Endicott-Johnson transaction is $2,200, which puts it in the 1 percent category of between $400 and $2,399. The commission is computed: $2,200 × .01 = $22; $22 + $7 = $29. The brokerage commission on the EJN is, therefore, $29.

The total value of the RCA purchase is $7,000, which puts it in the top rate of the commission schedule, 1/10 percent plus $39. The commission on RCA is: $7,000 × .001 = $7; $7 + $39 = $46.

If 100 shares of stock were purchased at $1 per share, the commission would be $6. If a stock sold above $360 per share, the commission would be $75 for a round lot, the maximum commission charged on a round-lot purchase or sale.

The New York Stock Exchange does not allow "give-ups" to other brokers. In a *give-up*, a major customer such as a mutual fund gives an order to a brokerage firm and directs the brokerage firm executive to yield part of the commission to another broker who has provided a service, such as selling mutual fund shares to the public, or is associated with the customer in some way.[8] The NYSE did not allow quantity discounts until early 1969, when such discounts were allowed on 100-share transactions over 1,000 shares. On the portion of an order that exceeds 1,000 shares, the following minimum rates apply:

Money Involved	Commission per 100 Shares
$100 to and including $2,800	1/2% of money involved plus $4.00
Above $2,800 to and including $3,000	Compute as $2,800
Above $3,000 to and including $9,000	1/2% of money involved plus $3.00
Above $9,000	1/10% of money involved plus $39.00[9]

The practice of not giving discounts led to the "third market" or the "off-the-board" market where listed stocks are traded in the OTC market at lower commission rates. Many brokerage firms have joined local exchanges that allow the practice of give-ups and lower rates. The New York Stock Exchange, before quantity discounts, countered the "third market" by encouraging block sales. The SEC continues to study the "third market" phenomenon, along with the entire level of compensation of brokerage firms and the rate structure.

Odd-Lot Commissions

If the investor bought only 10 shares each of Endicott-Johnson and RCA, computing the commission would be somewhat different. An odd-lot fee or differential is charged when less than a round-lot is purchased; this is in addition to the odd-lot brokerage commission. The odd-lot fee for 100-share unit stocks is 1/8 of a point per share for shares selling at

8 *Wall Street Journal*, Tuesday, July 9, 1968, p. 11.

9 Standard & Poor's Corporation, *Stock Guide*, August, 1969, p. 252.

54 7/8 or below per share and 1/4 of a point for shares selling at 55 and over per share. Stocks selling at 1/8 of a point or less pay half the price of the effective round-lot sale. For 10-share unit stocks, the odd-lot fee is:

Above 75	3/4 point
75	5/8 point
74 7/8	1/2 point
25 1/8 through 74 3/4	3/8 point
25 or below	1/4 point[10]

When stock is purchased, the odd-lot fee is added to the price, and it is subtracted when the stock is sold. The round-lot price determines the price that will be paid by the odd-lot buyer or seller. The odd-lot fee is added to or subtracted from this price. The odd-lot fee schedule for the American Stock Exchange is:

Stocks with a unit trading of 100 shares:	ODD-LOT CHARGE
When the Round Lot sells below $40 per share	1/8 point
When the Round Lot sells at $40 per share or over	1/4 point
Stocks with a unit of trading of 10 shares, regardless of selling price	1/2 point
Stocks with a unit of trading of either 25 shares or 50 shares, regardless of selling price	1/4 point
All American Depositary Receipts, American Shares or Block Shares, regardless of selling price	1/4 point
Stock selling *under* 1/2 of a dollar	1/16 point[11]

Assume that an investor wished to buy 10 shares of Endicott-Johnson and that the round-lot price determining the cost of the transaction was 22. The odd-lot price to the purchaser would be 22 1/8, since the odd-lot differential of 1/8 must be added. The total dollar amount of the purchase is $221.25. The commission would be 2 percent plus $1 and would total $5.43. Since this transaction involves more than $100, and the minimum commission is $6, the purchaser would be required to pay $6. His total cost of buying 10 shares at 22 is $227.25, which includes both the commission and the odd-lot fee.

The commission on a purchase of 10 shares of RCA is computed the same way as the example above. The price of RCA is 70 plus the odd-lot fee of 1/4 for a total of 70 1/4. The total amount of dollars involved is $702.50. The commission is 1 percent plus $5 for a total commission of $7.03 + $5 = $12.03. If the odd-lot fee is added to the commission, the total cost of buying 10 shares of RCA at 70 is $714.53 (market price + $12.03 commission + $2.50 odd-lot fee).

Commission on Stocks Selling Below $1 Per Share

The commission on stock selling below $1 per share is based upon the per-share value, as follows:

10 *Ibid.*
11 *Ibid.*

Price per Share	Rate per 100 Shares
1/256 of $1	$0.10
1/128 of $1	0.15
1/64 of $1 and above but under 2/32 of $1	0.50
2/32 of $1	0.50
Over 2/32 of $1 but under 8/32 of $1	1.00
8/32 of $1 and above but under 1/2 of $1	2.00
1/2 of $1 but under 5/8 of $1	3.00
5/8 of $1 but under 3/4 of $1	3.75
3/4 of $1 but under 7/8 of $1	4.50
7/8 of $1 but under $1	5.25[12]

The rate schedule for stock selling above $1 a share and that for stock selling below $1 a share are applied to stocks, rights, and commissions on the New York Stock Exchange and other major exchanges in the United States. The commissions apply to both the purchase and the sale of securities.

New York State Transfer Taxes

The state of New York imposes a transfer tax on all stock sales and transfers of stock not involving a sale. It is a small tax, and easy to compute, levied only on the seller. The rates are:

Shares Selling at	Tax	Shares Selling at	Tax
Less than $5	1 1/4¢ per sh.	$10 but less than $20	3 3/4¢ per sh.
$5 but less than $10	2 1/2¢ per sh.	$20 or more	5¢ per sh.[13]

The rate on transfers not involving a sale is $.02 1/2 per share. New York taxes stock transactions within the state but does not impose a tax on the sale of rights or warrants. The effect of the tax can be demonstrated by reference to the sales of stock that we used as examples. In each previous example the market price was above $20, which means the tax is $.05 per share. In each round-lot sale in these examples, the New York State tax is $5.00, and for each odd-lot sale consisting of 10 shares each, the tax is $.50. The tax is small when the value of the transaction is small, but it has been productive for the state of New York. A bill signed by Governor Rockefeller on June 22, 1968, provides for the gradual reduction of these rates. The schedule continued in effect until July 1, 1969; after that date a gradual reduction began, and by July 1, 1973, the rates will equal 50 percent of former rates.[14]

Other states impose transfer taxes. Florida, for example, charges $.15 per $100 of par value regardless of the selling price and $.15 per share on no par stock. South Carolina charges $.04 per $100 par value and $.04 on no par stock, regardless of selling price.

12 *Ibid.*
13 *Ibid.*
14 *New York Times*, Sunday, June 23, 1968.

The SEC Fee

The Securities and Exchange Commission imposes a transfer fee on all sales of securities on a registered exchange. It is paid by the seller and amounts to $.01 per $500 or fraction thereof of the value of the transaction. We can compute this tax on amounts from the previous examples, as follows:

COMPANY	TOTAL VALUE OF THE SHARES SOLD	SEC FEE
Round Lot—100 shares		
Endicott-Johnson	$2,200	$.05
RCA	7,000	.14
Odd Lot—10 shares		
Endicott-Johnson	220	.01
RCA	700	.02

The SEC fee is a small charge to the seller of the security for using the facilities of a registered exchange; yet it provides over three-quarters of a million dollars a year to the United States Treasury in years of active trading.

Summary of Costs of Buying and Selling Securities

Table 9–1 summarizes the total cost of buying and selling a round-lot and an odd-lot unit of the two companies used as examples in computing commissions and the various fees and taxes. In addition to the costs shown in the table, the brokerage firm usually makes a small charge to cover registration and postage.

The cost of buying and selling securities (a round-trip transaction) is high when a small dollar amount of stock is involved. The cost of the odd-lot transactions given as examples ranged from 4.3 to 6.8 percent. These costs are comparable to those in trading real estate or investment company shares. The round-lot transactions involving larger amounts of money, however, had much lower cost percentages. These appear to be reasonable for the size of the transactions.

One conclusion that can be drawn from these examples is that it is wise to purchase stock in round lots or in substantial dollar volume per single transaction to keep the cost of buying and selling within reasonable bounds. Otherwise the costs involved make it difficult for the investor to make a profit. In buying and selling 10 shares of Endicott-Johnson, for example, the stock would have to move up to 23 1/2 before the investor would break even on the transaction. The purchaser of small amounts of stock must allow 1 1/2 or 2 points per share to cover costs. Unfortunately, the practices of Wall Street do not lend themselves to economy. The New York Stock Exchange has established the MIP (Monthly Investment Plan) for the purchase of small amounts of

TABLE 9–1

Cost of buying and selling
Odd-lot and round-lot units of stock

	ENDICOTT-JOHNSON		RCA	
Price per share	$22		$70	
Number of shares in transaction	100	10	100	10
Total value of transaction	$2,200	220	$7,000	700
Buying cost:				
Brokerage commission	$29.00	$ 6.00*	$46.00	$12.03*
Odd-lot fee		1.25		2.50
Total buying cost	$29.00	$ 7.25	$46.00	$14.53
Selling cost:				
Brokerage commission	$29.00	$ 6.00*	$46.00	$11.98*
Odd-lot fee		1.25		2.50
New York State transfer tax	5.00	.50	5.00	.50
SEC fee	.05	.01	.14	.02
Total selling cost	$34.05	$ 7.76	$51.14	$15.00
Total cost of buy and sell transactions	$63.05	$15.01	$97.14	$29.53
Total cost as percentage of total value of securities purchased and sold	2.9%	6.8%	1.4%	4.3%

    * In computing the commission, the odd-lot fee was added to the purchase price and subtracted from the sale price.

stock each month. This is the most expensive method of buying stocks. Except for the element of thrift and forced savings, there is no advantage in buying stocks every month rather than every six or twelve months if investment continues over a long period of time.[15] No gain in appreciation occurs because of monthly purchases.

Commission on Bonds Traded on the New York Stock Exchange

When an investor purchases or sells bonds, a commission must be paid to the broker. The rates on United States Government bonds, bonds of Puerto Rico and the Philippines, bonds of the International Bank, bonds maturing within six months to five years, and bonds maturing or called for redemption within six months are determined by mutual agreement between the broker-dealer and his customer except where the exchange sets the rates. The commission on bonds traded on the New York Stock Exchange for nonmember and allied members is based upon the price of the bond. Members dealing with each other charge a lower commission. Rates for nonmembers are $.75 for bonds selling at less than $10; $1.25 for bonds selling above $10 but less than $100; $2.50 for

15 Frederick Amling, "Is There an Optimum Time Period for Dollar Averaging?" *Commercial and Financial Chronicle,* April 8, 1965, pp. 10–11.

bonds selling at $100 and above; and $1.25 as a special rate for bonds maturing in six months to five years. These rates are stated in Article XV of the New York Stock Exchange Constitution. These commissions are based upon the selling price of a bond with a principal of $1,000. If a person bought ten bonds quoted in the market at 102, he would pay $1,020 per bond, and the commission would be $25 (10 × $2.50). The cost of buying bonds is relatively small in comparison to the price of a bond.

Commissions on the Over-the-Counter Stocks

Commission charges on stocks traded over-the-counter are computed in the same way as those listed for securities. When a commission is charged, it is based upon the schedule established by the New York Stock Exchange. The customer buys on a net basis from the broker-dealer acting as a principal. The price quotation in the over-the-counter market is on a bid-and-asked basis. When buying on a net or dealer basis, the customer pays close to the asked price and would sell close to the bid price. The final price of the transaction depends upon the condition of the market when the transaction is completed.

Quotes for OTC securities are provided in major newspapers and by the National Quotation Bureau, which provides bid and asked prices daily for 7,000 stock issues and 2,000 bond issues. Brokers make these quotes available to their customers. The method of presenting bid-and-asked quotes on the OTC market has improved substantially because of changes made since the SEC's Special Study and the Securities Acts Amendments of 1964.

The volume of transactions in the OTC market and in registered exchanges has swamped many brokerage firms. The New York Stock Exchange closed on Wednesdays in 1968 to allow the back office to catch up with its paper work. The NASD is cracking down on its members[16] in the OTC market to ease the log jam.

Summary

The broker's basic function is to buy and sell securities for his customers. The modern brokerage house, however, offers more than this basic service. Most large brokerage firms provide investment information for customers through their investment research department. The research staff also gives customers advice about the management of their investment portfolios. From time to time, brokerage firms will make portfolio reviews and give specific recommendations to the customer. Some firms will provide investment management on a fee basis. Information and

16 "Testing the NASD," *Wall Street Journal*, Thursday, June 20, 1968.

research have become important brokerage functions. Brokerage firms help raise capital for corporations through the investment banking process, and they supply some investment-grade securities to investors. Some firms specialize in investment banking, others in brokerage.

In selecting a broker the investor should consider his reputation, size, credit standing, service, information and research facilities, the breadth of the type of securities he can provide the customer, and his general experience. A broker must not bother the customer or force him to make a decision based upon incomplete information. Institutional investors have two criteria for selecting a brokerage firm: first, the ability to buy and sell at favorable prices and volume; second, the facilities to provide information and research that prove profitable to the institutional investor. Some mutual funds tend to place their stockbrokerage business with those firms that do a good job of selling fund shares.

Opening an account with a broker is a simple matter. It requires the completion of a signature card and usually a credit reference. Once the account is opened, the investor can buy and sell easily. The brokerage firm will arrange to keep the securities for the investor in "street name" if he wishes and send a monthly statement of transactions. But if the investor prefers, he may have the securities he purchased sent to his business or resident address.

The customer must give the order to buy or sell. The most frequently used order is the market order, which allows the stock to be bought at the best price in the market at the time. A limit or limited order is frequently used by investors. This type of order directs the broker to buy or sell the stock at a specific price. Sometimes the customer might not get his price. Stop-loss orders and stop orders are used to protect profits or limit losses. Time orders are sometimes used and may be thought of as market orders suspended until the market reaches the price the customer desires. Some orders are in effect for a day, a week, or a month, or until canceled.

The customer must pay a brokerage commission on both the buy and the sell transaction. When the customer sells stock, he must pay the SEC fee and may be subject to a state transfer tax. If the transaction, whether a purchase or a sale, is for fewer than 100 shares, the customer must also pay an odd-lot fee. On purchases and sales of securities that are for a small dollar amount, the commissions, fees and taxes are substantial in comparison with the total amount of the transaction. On round-trip transactions below $1,000 the cost will vary from 4 to 6 percent, and the customer needs an appreciation of approximately two points per share to cover his costs. Round-lot transactions and the higher total dollar value odd-lot transactions have a relatively low round-trip cost as a percentage of total value, so the investor should, when possible, buy in round lots or larger dollar amounts to keep the costs of buying and selling to a minimum. The MIP is not the cheapest way of purchasing stock. There is economy in purchasing more than 1,000 shares of stock; such blocks are usually available to the institutional investor.

Review Questions

1. What are the functions performed by a broker? Should the broker perform all these functions? Comment.
2. To what extent do brokerage firms engage in investment management and investment banking? Should they engage in portfolio management?
3. How would you classify brokerage firms according to the types of securities they handle?
4. What are the factors we should consider when we select a broker?
5. What criteria does the institutional investor use to select a broker?
6. How might we go about opening an account with a broker, and would we be able to purchase stock on margin through the usual account? Explain.
7. What types of orders might we give to a broker when buying or selling stock?
8. What are the costs and commissions involved in the purchase of a security?
9. Is it expensive to buy and sell common stock?
10. Is it more expensive to buy and sell in odd lots or round lots? Explain.
11. What commission would we pay in buying and selling bonds on the New York Stock Exchange?
12. What would be the difference in commissions paid on shares traded on the New York Stock Exchange and in the over-the-counter market?
13. Are volume discounts provided by the New York Stock Exchange?
14. How do institutions decide where to place their brokerage business?

Problems

1. What would be the total costs and commissions in buying and selling the following common stocks?
   (a) Traded on the New York Stock Exchange:
       (1) Buy 100 Shares of Xerox
       (2) Sell 100 Shares of Xerox
       (3) Buy 10 Shares of Xerox
       (4) Sell 10 Shares of Xerox
   (b) Traded in the over-the-counter market:
       (1) Buy 100 Shares of Cross Company
       (2) Sell 100 Shares of Cross Company

     (3) Buy 15 Shares of Cross Company
     (4) Sell 15 Shares of Cross Company
  (c) Traded on the American Stock Exchange:
     (1) Buy 100 Shares of Prentice-Hall
     (2) Sell 100 Shares of Prentice-Hall
     (3) Buy 20 Shares of Prentice-Hall
     (4) Sell 20 Shares of Prentice-Hall

2. What would it cost to buy or sell the following securities?
  (a) Five United States Treasury bonds
  (b) Ten W. R. Grace convertible bonds
  (c) One Litton Industries convertible

Sources of Investment Information

American Stock Exchange *Fact Book*
Barron's
Brokerage firm market letters and research
Local commercial bank or brokerage office
New York Stock Exchange *Fact Book*
New York Times
Standard & Poor's *Stock Guide*
Wall Street Journal

Selected Readings

Cohen, The Honorable Manual F., "Disclosure: the SEC and the Press," *Financial Analysts Journal* (July-August, 1968), p. 21.

Securities and Exchange Commission release, *Financial Analysts Journal* (September-October, 1968), p. 67.

V

AN APPRAISAL OF THE NATIONAL ECONOMY AND INDUSTRY

Past, Present, and Future

10

AN ANALYSIS OF THE NATIONAL ECONOMY AND THE INDUSTRY

Up to this point in our studies of the investment process, we have examined the securities available for investment and pointed out the risks and yields we may expect from these securities. We have also discussed where securities are purchased and how the securities markets are being increasingly regulated—through the National Association of Security Dealers, the New York Stock Exchange, and the Securities and Exchange Commission—to make a more perfect market for investors. A lessening in inside manipulation and fraudulent practices that could result in substantial losses to unsuspecting investors will also lead to a more perfect market for analysis. We wish ultimately to focus on an analysis of the company, because it is here that we find the debt securities and common stocks to provide profitable investment outlets for our savings.

An Analysis of the National Economy

We do not analyze the company or the stock market in a vacuum. Investment in fixed-income and ownership securities is intimately associated with the economic activity of the nation. An investment in the common stock of any company is likely to be more successful and more profitable if the economy is strong and prosperous rather than declining. By the same token, strength in an industry that has evidenced rapid growth in the past suggests that companies within that industry and on the periphery of it will benefit from this growth and in the end provide the investor with substantial rewards. This has been true in the past of the telephone industry, the computer industry, the television industry, the automobile industry, the office equipment industry and, in today's society, the oceanography industry. Not all industries grow at the same rate, nor do all companies. The growth of a company or an industry depends basically on its ability to satisfy human wants through production of goods or performance of a service. How people earn their living and where they spend their money will, in the last analysis, determine which company and industry will grow and prosper and which will decline in importance.

In contrast, if expectations for the decline of the national economy are strong, the overtones and implications for investment in common stock or debt instruments are serious. If we could be certain that the next five years would bring a recession, then this fact would be reflected in our investment portfolio position. Certainly this would suggest greater attention to fixed-income obligations, because these would offer considerably more safety than common stock. It would not suggest a rush for equity securities. It is important, therefore, to analyze the national economy, attempt to determine its course over the next six to twelve months, and—to obtain some investment perspective—determine what the longer three- to five-year possibilities are. Once this has been accomplished, we can use the growth of the national economy to forecast the growth of an industry or company and thus determine those areas offering good investment opportunities. It will help to point out those that should be avoided since they appear to offer less attractive investment opportunities than suggested by the growth of the national economy and its components.

Measures of Economic Activity

In order to obtain investment perspective, we must first determine the stage of the nation's economy; second, its probable direction over the next six months to a year; and last, the long-range estimates of the growth of the economy. Certainly a forecast of where we are going in the next year or the next five or ten years is an extremely difficult process, requiring careful and intuitive studies, excellent judgment, and a tremendous amount of luck—particularly if we attempt to be precise in our estimates. Even the process of determining the state of economic development at the moment is not easy, simply because all the facts and figures are not available when we want them. Reporting methods provide us with an automatic lag in data and information. At best we have only estimates. With the improvement in reporting techniques from computerization of the data collected for the government by private enterprises that predict the future, we will be able to tell where we are with greater certainty. If we expect the economy to grow in the future at a substantial rate, compared with the past decade, then we will take one course of action. Obviously this will be to invest in common stocks. If we find one segment of the economy growing faster than the economy as a whole, we will attempt to concentrate in this rapidly growing area, assuming, of course that we accept this philosophy of investment.

If, on the other hand, we expect our economy to begin a period of cyclical or secular decline, such as we faced in the 1930's—for those who can't remember the 1930's, substitute 1957—then we must be more defensive in our investment policy. Under these conditions we would consider bonds to be much more appealing than all common stocks; we would select equity securities with extreme caution. Our reasons for examining the national economy are to forecast the direction of growth and to select those industries that are expected to share in or exceed the growth of the economy, and to identify those companies particularly that will allow us to earn a satisfactory yield on our investment commensurate with the risks involved.

THE GNP

There isn't a college student, financier, or broker today who doesn't know what the GNP is; the majority of housewives know. They certainly have heard that GNP stands for *Gross National Product*, and it is the broadest measure of economic activity we can use to measure where we are, where we've been, and where we might go. It represents the aggregate amount of goods and services that have been produced in the national economy for a period of time, usually one year. We have come to deal in terms of the GNP and the game of Growthmanship has developed using GNP as a measure of economic activity. For those who might not be familiar with the ingredients of GNP, reference is suggested to Figures 10–1 and 10–2. A review of a basic economics text will provide background information for understanding these accounts.

The dollar figures provide enough information to refresh our memories about the format of the items found in the National Income Accounts—where our total income is received and spent—and the method of arriving at these items. The data are presented both from the point of view of receipts to the various sectors of the economy, Figure 10–1, and of expenditures, Figure 10–2. The direction in which the various items in these accounts move can give us some insight into the direction not only of the economy but also of the industries that make up the economy. This is particularly true of the Gross National Product account in Figure 10–2. Here we find the amount of money spent in the form of final purchases, the types of goods purchased, where investment took place, what was spent for exports and imports, and what role the federal government played in the purchases of goods and services. In addition, we have some idea of the growth of GNP in current and constant 1958 dollars.

Item	1929	1933	1941	1950	1964	1965	1966	1967	1968	1968 I	1968 II	1968 III	1968 IV	1969 I
Gross national product	**103.1**	**55.6**	**124.5**	**284.8**	**632.4**	**684.9**	**747.6**	**789.7**	**860.6**	**831.2**	**852.9**	**871.0**	**887.4**	**903.3**
Less: Capital consumption allowances	7.9	7.0	8.2	18.3	56.1	59.8	64.1	69.2	74.3	72.3	73.7	74.9	76.2	77.5
Indirect business tax and nontax liability	7.0	7.1	11.3	23.3	58.4	62.5	65.3	69.6	75.8	72.8	74.8	76.7	79.0	81.2
Business transfer payments	.6	.7	.5	.8	2.5	2.7	3.0	3.1	3.3	3.2	3.3	3.3	3.3	3.3
Statistical discrepancy	.7	.6	.4	1.5	−1.3	−3.1	−3.3	−3.5	−4.8	−4.7	−3.6	−5.3	−5.5	−6.9
Plus: Subsidies less current surplus of government enterprises	−.1	......	.1	.2	1.3	1.3	2.3	1.6	.7	.5	.7	1.0	.6	.9
Equals: National income	**86.8**	**40.3**	**104.2**	**241.1**	**518.1**	**564.3**	**620.8**	**652.9**	**712.8**	**688.1**	**705.4**	**722.5**	**735.1**	**749.2**
Less: Corporate profits and inventory valuation adjustment	10.5	−1.2	15.2	37.7	66.3	76.1	83.9	80.4	89.1	83.8	89.2	91.6	91.8	90.6
Contributions for social insurance	.2	.3	2.8	6.9	27.9	29.6	38.0	41.9	46.9	45.8	46.5	47.4	47.8	51.8
Excess of wage accruals over disbursements	......	......	......	......	......	......	......	......	......	......	......	......	......	......
Plus: Government transfer payments	.9	1.5	2.6	14.3	34.2	37.2	41.0	48.6	55.3	52.5	55.0	56.3	57.5	59.0
Net interest paid by government and consumer	2.5	1.6	2.2	7.2	19.1	20.5	22.3	23.6	25.9	24.9	25.7	26.2	26.7	27.2
Dividends	5.8	2.0	4.4	8.8	17.8	19.8	21.7	22.9	24.6	23.6	24.4	25.2	25.4	25.4
Business transfer payments	.6	.7	.5	.8	2.5	2.7	3.0	3.1	3.3	3.2	3.3	3.3	3.3	3.3
Equals: Personal income	**85.9**	**47.0**	**96.0**	**227.6**	**497.5**	**538.9**	**586.8**	**628.8**	**685.8**	**662.7**	**678.1**	**694.3**	**708.2**	**721.7**
Less: Personal tax and nontax payments	2.6	1.5	3.3	20.7	59.4	65.7	75.3	82.5	96.9	88.3	91.9	101.6	105.8	112.5
Equals: Disposable personal income	**83.3**	**45.5**	**92.7**	**206.9**	**438.1**	**473.2**	**511.6**	**546.3**	**589.0**	**574.4**	**586.3**	**592.7**	**602.4**	**609.2**
Less: Personal outlays	79.1	46.5	81.7	193.9	411.9	444.8	478.6	506.2	548.2	533.5	542.3	555.6	561.6	572.3
Personal consumption expenditures	77.2	45.8	80.6	191.0	401.2	432.8	465.5	492.2	533.8	519.4	527.9	541.1	546.8	557.4
Consumer interest payments	1.5	.5	.9	2.4	10.1	11.3	12.5	13.1	13.7	13.4	13.6	13.8	14.0	14.2
Personal transfer payments to foreigners	.3	.2	.2	.5	.6	.7	.6	.8	.7	.7	.8	.7	.7	.7
Equals: Personal saving	**4.2**	**−.9**	**11.0**	**13.1**	**26.2**	**28.4**	**32.9**	**40.2**	**40.7**	**40.8**	**44.0**	**37.1**	**40.9**	**36.9**
Disposable personal income in constant (1958) dollars	**150.6**	**112.2**	**190.3**	**249.6**	**407.9**	**435.0**	**459.2**	**478.0**	**497.5**	**491.8**	**497.1**	**499.2**	**501.7**	**502.8**

NOTE.—Dept. of Commerce estimates. Quarterly data are seasonally adjusted quarterly totals at annual rates. See also Note to Figure 10-2.

FIGURE 10–1

Gross National Product information by receipts (in billions)

Item	1929	1933	1941	1950	1964	1965	1966	1967	1968	1968 I	1968 II	1968 III	1968 IV	1969 I
Gross national product	**103.1**	**55.6**	**124.5**	**284.8**	**632.4**	**684.9**	**747.6**	**789.7**	**860.6**	**831.2**	**852.9**	**871.0**	**887.4**	**903.3**
Final purchases	*101.4*	*57.2*	*120.1*	*278.0*	*626.6*	*675.3*	*732.8*	*783.6*	*852.9*	*829.1*	*842.1*	*863.5*	*876.8*	*896.4*
Personal consumption expenditures	**77.2**	**45.8**	**80.6**	**191.0**	**401.2**	**432.8**	**465.5**	**492.2**	**533.8**	**519.4**	**527.9**	**541.1**	**546.8**	**557.4**
Durable goods	9.2	3.5	9.6	30.5	59.2	66.3	70.5	72.6	82.5	79.0	81.0	85.1	85.1	86.8
Nondurable goods	37.7	22.3	42.9	98.1	178.7	191.1	206.7	215.8	230.3	226.5	228.2	232.7	233.7	238.1
Services	30.3	20.1	28.1	62.4	163.3	175.5	188.3	203.8	221.0	213.9	218.7	223.4	228.0	232.5
Gross private domestic investment	**16.2**	**1.4**	**17.9**	**54.1**	**94.0**	**108.1**	**120.8**	**114.3**	**127.7**	**119.7**	**127.3**	**127.1**	**136.6**	**139.0**
Fixed investment	*14.5*	*3.0*	*13.4*	*47.3*	*88.2*	*98.5*	*106.1*	*108.2*	*119.9*	*117.6*	*116.5*	*119.6*	*126.0*	*132.1*
Nonresidential	*10.6*	*2.4*	*9.5*	*27.9*	*61.1*	*71.3*	*81.3*	*83.6*	*90.0*	*88.6*	*87.0*	*90.1*	*94.3*	*99.6*
Structures	5.0	.9	2.9	9.2	21.2	25.5	28.5	27.9	29.2	29.6	28.5	28.8	29.9	32.2
Producers' durable equipment	5.6	1.5	6.6	18.7	39.9	45.8	52.8	55.7	60.8	59.0	58.5	61.3	64.5	67.4
Residential structures	4.0	.6	3.9	19.4	27.1	27.2	24.8	24.6	29.9	29.1	29.5	29.5	31.6	32.5
Nonfarm	*3.8*	*.5*	*3.7*	*18.6*	*26.6*	*26.7*	*24.3*	*24.3*	*29.3*	*28.5*	*28.9*	*28.9*	*31.0*	*31.8*
Change in business inventories	1.7	−1.6	4.5	6.8	5.8	9.6	14.7	6.1	7.7	2.1	10.8	7.5	10.6	6.9
Nonfarm	1.8	−1.4	4.0	6.0	6.4	8.6	14.9	5.6	7.3	1.6	10.4	7.3	9.7	6.2
Net exports of goods and services	**1.1**	**.4**	**1.3**	**1.8**	**8.5**	**6.9**	**5.1**	**4.8**	**2.0**	**1.5**	**2.0**	**3.3**	**1.0**	**.0**
Exports	7.0	2.4	5.9	13.8	37.1	39.2	43.1	45.8	50.0	47.5	49.9	52.6	50.1	46.6
Imports	5.9	2.0	4.6	12.0	28.6	32.3	38.1	41.0	48.1	46.0	47.9	49.4	49.1	46.6
Government purchases of goods and services	**8.5**	**8.0**	**24.8**	**37.9**	**128.7**	**137.0**	**156.2**	**178.4**	**197.2**	**190.5**	**195.7**	**199.6**	**203.0**	**206.9**
Federal	*1.3*	*2.0*	*16.9*	*18.4*	*65.2*	*66.9*	*77.4*	*90.6*	*100.0*	*97.1*	*100.0*	*101.2*	*101.7*	*102.4*
National defense	......	......	13.8	14.1	50.0	50.1	60.6	72.4	78.9	76.8	79.0	79.6	80.0	80.2
Other	......	......	3.1	4.3	15.2	16.8	16.8	18.2	21.1	20.3	21.0	21.5	21.7	22.2
State and local	7.2	6.0	7.9	19.5	63.5	70.1	78.8	87.8	97.2	93.4	95.6	98.4	101.2	104.5
Gross national product in constant (1958) dollars	**203.6**	**141.5**	**263.7**	**355.3**	**581.1**	**617.8**	**657.1**	**673.1**	**706.7**	**692.7**	**703.4**	**712.3**	**718.4**	**723.5**

NOTE.—Dept. of Commerce estimates. Quarterly data are seasonally adjusted totals at annual rates. For back data and explanation of series, see the *Survey of Current Business*, July 1968, and Supplement, Aug. 1966.

FIGURE 10–2

Gross National Product information by expenditures (in billions)

SOURCE *Federal Reserve Bulletin,* July, 1969, pp. A66 and A67

Table 10–1 dramatizes the growth of the Gross National Product for the past eleven years, along with the components of the National Income Accounts and personal consumption expenditures. From 1957 through the first quarter of 1968, we have enjoyed a 5.6 percent compound annual rate of growth in GNP and almost the same rate of growth for national income (NI), personal income (PI), and disposable personal income (DPI). In spite of the variation in the growth rate of GNP, the economy has sustained a substantial rate of growth. This reflects inflationary pressures brought about by an expanding economy engaged in the Vietnam war, the growth of the private sector and of the federal government, and the government's willingness to commit itself to a full employment economy. Table 10–1 reveals a slower rate of growth in 1967 and 1968 in spite of the fact that wholesale and retail prices increased during that period of time. A close look at the index figures in Table 10–1 indicates that durable goods, along with services, have kept pace with the growth of the national economy, but that nondurable goods have not. This suggests that investment opportunities exist in the national economy, particularly in the durable goods sector and in the service sector. Reference to Figure 10–2 also indicates a substantial growth in expenditures by state, local, and federal governments—in the case of the last, primarily for national defense. It also indicates a worsening in our balance of trade, which reflected conditions in the economy at that time.

An investor should be conversant with the National Income Accounts. Many of the forecasts published by brokerage houses, the federal government, and financial institutions—particularly commercial banks—are presented in the language of national income accounting. Many trade magazines publish this type of information and do make short-range forecasts of what to expect over the next year.

GNP and Other Indexes. Standard & Poor's, in the 1968 Annual Forecast issue of *The Outlook*, provided the 1966 data for the National Income Accounts, which they labeled Gross National Product, along with other indexes of economic activity such as the Federal Reserve Board (FRB) index of industrial production and corporate profits before and after taxes. Their own estimates of the expected 1967 and 1968 figures for GNP, personal consumption expenditures, gross private domestic investment, net exports of goods and services, and government purchases of goods and services were also provided. It is interesting to note that they indicated a GNP of 824.5 billion for the first quarter of 1968. In 1968, it actually was 826.7 billion—not a bad forecast at all. More will be said about this business of forecasting shortly. An investor examining Standard & Poor's data would have expected continued growth in the economy for all of 1968 at a rate comparable to the most recent activity of the GNP and substantially above that existing between 1957 and 1968.

Forecasts of Gross National Product for the coming year are

TABLE 10-1

Gross National Product, National Income, Personal Income, Disposable Personal Income and personal consumption expenditures in billions of dollars and index (1957–1959=100)

| | Gross National Product (GNP) | | | National Income (NI) | | Personal Income (PI) | | Disposable Personal Income (DPI) | | Personal Consumption Expenditures | | | | | |
| | | | | | | | | | | Durable Goods | | Nondurable Goods | | Services | |
	$	ANNUAL GROWTH RATE %	INDEX	$	INDEX	$	INDEX	$	INDEX	$	INDEX	$	INDEX	$	INDEX
1968[a]	826.7	5.3	181.0	686.2	181.4	659.0	180.4	571.5	177.9	83.3	206.2	230.6	162.3	222.8	194.2
1967	785.0	5.6	171.9	650.2	171.9	626.4	171.5	544.7	169.5	72.7	180.0	218.5	153.8	204.1	177.9
1966	743.3	8.8	162.8	616.7	163.0	584.0	159.9	508.8	152.4	70.3	174.0	207.5	146.1	188.1	164.0
1965	688.9	8.1	149.7	562.4	148.9	537.8	147.3	472.2	147.0	66.0	163.4	191.2	134.5	175.9	153.4
1964	632.4	7.1	138.5	518.1	137.0	497.5	136.2	438.1	136.4	59.2	146.5	178.7	126.7	163.0	142.6
1963	590.5	6.6	129.3	481.9	127.4	465.5	127.5	404.6	125.4	53.9	133.4	168.6	118.8	152.4	132.9
1962	553.9	6.8	121.3	458.0	121.1	440.5	120.6	382.9	119.2	47.5	117.6	162.0	114.0	147.1	128.2
1961	518.7	3.1	113.6	427.8	113.1	416.4	114.0	363.9	113.2	43.7	108.2	155.2	109.2	139.1	121.3
1960	503.4	4.3	110.2	415.5	109.8	400.8	109.9	349.4	108.7	44.8	110.9	151.8	106.8	131.9	115.0
1959	482.7	8.6	105.7	400.5	105.9	383.9	105.1	337.1	104.9	43.6	107.9	147.1	103.5	122.8	107.1
1958	444.5	—	97.3	367.4	97.1	360.3	98.7	317.9	98.9	37.3	92.3	141.6	99.7	114.3	99.7
1957	442.8	—	97.0	366.9	97.0	351.4	96.2	308.8	96.1	40.4	100.0	137.7	96.9	107.1	93.4
1957–59[b]	456.7	5.6[c]	100.0	378.3	100.0	365.2	100.0	321.3	100.0	40.4		142.1		114.7	

[a] 1st Quarter, except DPI for full year.
[b] Base year.
[c] Compound annual rate of growth 1957–1968.

SOURCE: *Federal Reserve Bulletin,* June 1963, p. 852; December, 1963, p. 1718; July, 1969, pp. A–66 and A–67; October, 1969, p. A–68.

readily abundant in the financial community, and in the president's annual State of the Union report. The Council of Economic Advisers usually provides its views of the economy for each coming year. First National City Bank prepares a forecast, which is available without charge, and also a monthly bulletin in which comments are made about the state of the economy. The Prudential Life Insurance Association provides an annual forecast in terms of Gross National Product figures for investors, giving a detailed forecast of the economic state of the union. Eastman Dillon, Union Securities & Co. usually provides semiannually an outlook that encompasses the state of the economy in terms of Gross National Product estimates.

Many other financial periodicals published by Mc-Graw-Hill, Forbes, and other investment services such as *The Value Line* provide economic forecasts that can be used in establishing investment policy and help in making decisions before individual companies are analyzed.

The Record of GNP Forecasting. Before we accept any forecast of the Gross National Product, however, we should understand the reliability of the estimate. Victor Zarnowitz[1] found that the average error in forecasting GNP during the period 1953–1964 was approximately $10 billion or about 2 percent of the Gross National Product during that period of time. Professor Maurice W. Lee[2] suggests that these seemingly accurate projections are not very good when you compare them to changes in GNP. When this is done, the error amounts to approximately 40 percent and the range of the error is between 28 and 56 percent of the change in GNP. Lee also points out that the declines are less often underestimated than are the increases. However, very few of the year-end forecasts missed the direction of change in the year ahead. A study done by Rozan Cole at the National Bureau of Economic Research indicated that it was difficult to be precise with measures of GNP.

The use of the forecast then becomes one of finding the direction of the national economy for the next year and planning investment actions accordingly. We should not be upset that our estimates are in error by as much as $10 billion, for the fact that we expect business to be good for the next six to twelve months gives us enough information to check our investment policy periodically and make any adjustments that seem to be needed, based on the projection of aggregate growth.

THE FEDERAL RESERVE BOARD INDEX OF INDUSTRIAL PRODUCTION

Another measure of economic activity is the Federal Reserve Board Index of Industrial Production.[3] The monthly index is published by the

---

1 Victor Zarnowitz, *Appraisal of Short-Term Economic Forecasts* (New York: National Bureau of Economic Research, 1967).

2 Maurice W. Lee, *Macroeconomics: Fluctuations, Growth and Stability*, 4th ed. (Homewood, Ill.: Richard D. Irwin, Inc., 1967), p. 638.

3 An index allows an easy comparison of the change in measurable data over

Federal Reserve Board in the *Federal Reserve Bulletin*. The index is perhaps the best-known and most widely used index of industrial activity. Its purpose is to indicate the current amount of industrial production relative to a base-year period. The base-year period used is 1957–1959. If the index was 163.7 in May, 1968, then we could say that the level of industrial production in real terms was 63.7 percent higher than in the 1957–59 period. The FRB Index is made up of many segments of the industrial economy that reflect the total economy. As seen in Figure 10–3, it is composed of consumer goods, equipment, and materials by major marketing groups and the major industry groupings of manufacturing, mining, and utilities. An examination of the components of the FRB Index indicates the relative growth over a period of time that reflects to some degree the direction of investment opportunities. For example, consumer goods have expanded somewhat less than total industrial production, and the mining industry has expanded least. In contrast, manufacturing has moved ahead substantially, with utilities showing the greatest growth over a long period of time. All of this growth is not translated into profits, but at least it is an indication of profitable areas for investment. A further breakdown by product and market groupings is given in each issue of the *Federal Reserve Bulletin*, again providing a basis for exploration and comparison for those looking for new opportunities for investment. Data are also available from the *Survey of Current Business*.

Each of the major categories of the FRB Index is divided into separate components. Indexes are computed, for example, in the consumer goods area for automotive products, home goods products, and consumer staples; and each of these categories is divided into separate product-oriented groups, based upon market groupings. Another grouping lists the major industry classes shown in Figure 10–3. These too are divided into major components. Manufacturing is divided into

a period of time. The data measured can be either dollars or units of production. A base year is usually selected for comparison. The year is selected both for its representativeness and its relationship to the immediate past. A base period that is extremely old has little merit, since few people are aware of the economic conditions that existed at the time. The typical index base used in 1969 was the 1957–1959 period. The base is given a weight of 100, and all other index numbers are related to it. Thus, an index of a 110 in 1960 would mean that the data being measured had increased 10 percent over the base period. The 1957–1959 base is found by adding the figures for 1957, 1958, and 1959 and dividing by 3. An example using Gross National Product information will demonstrate one way in which index numbers are computed. GNP for 1957 through 1959 was $442.8, $444.5, and $482.7 billions. The total for the three years was $1,370 billion. When divided by 3, the base-year index became $456.7 billion. The index for each year was found by dividing the base-year figure into the annual GNP figures. Thus, the index for 1957 was 97 (442.8/456.7) and for 1959 it was 105.7 (482.7/456.7) The main advantage of using an index number is that it allows one to compare large numbers easily.

(1957–59 = 100, unless otherwise noted)

Period	Industrial production									Capacity utilization in mfg. (per cent)	Construction contracts	Nonagricultural employment—Total [a]	Manufacturing [b]		Total retail sales [c]	Prices [d]	
	Total	Major market groupings				Major industry groupings							Employment	Payrolls		Consumer	Wholesale commodity
		Final products			Materials	Mfg.	Mining	Utilities									
		Total	Consumer goods	Equipment													
1951...........	81.3	78.6	77.8	78.4	83.8	81.9	91.3	56.4	94.0	63	91.1	106.1	80.2	76	90.5	96.7
1952...........	84.3	84.3	79.5	94.1	84.3	85.2	90.5	61.2	91.3	67	93.0	106.1	84.5	79	92.5	94.0
1953...........	91.3	89.9	85.0	100.5	92.6	92.7	92.9	66.8	94.2	70	95.6	111.6	93.6	83	93.2	92.7
1954...........	85.8	85.7	84.3	88.9	85.9	86.3	90.2	71.8	83.5	76	93.3	101.8	85.4	82	93.6	92.9
1955...........	96.6	93.9	93.3	95.0	99.0	97.3	99.2	80.2	90.0	91	96.5	105.5	94.8	89	93.3	93.2
1956...........	99.9	98.1	95.5	103.7	101.6	100.2	104.8	87.9	87.7	92	99.8	106.7	100.2	92	94.7	96.2
1957...........	100.7	99.4	97.0	104.6	101.9	100.8	104.6	93.9	83.6	93	100.7	104.7	101.4	97	98.0	99.0
1958...........	93.7	94.8	96.4	91.3	92.7	93.2	95.6	98.1	74.0	102	97.8	95.2	93.5	98	100.7	100.4
1959...........	105.6	105.7	106.6	104.1	105.4	106.0	99.7	108.0	81.5	105	101.5	100.1	105.1	105	101.5	100.6
1960...........	108.7	109.9	111.0	107.6	107.6	108.9	101.6	115.6	80.6	105	103.3	99.9	106.7	106	103.1	100.7
1961...........	109.7	111.2	112.6	108.3	108.4	109.6	102.6	122.3	78.5	108	102.9	95.9	105.4	107	104.2	100.3
1962...........	118.3	119.7	119.7	119.6	117.0	118.7	105.0	131.4	82.1	120	105.9	99.1	113.8	115	105.4	100.6
1963...........	124.3	124.9	125.2	124.2	123.7	124.9	107.9	140.0	83.3	132	108.0	99.7	117.9	120	106.7	100.3
1964...........	132.3	131.8	131.7	132.0	132.8	133.1	111.5	151.3	85.7	137	111.1	101.5	124.3	128	108.1	100.5
1965...........	143.4	142.5	140.3	147.0	144.2	145.0	114.8	160.9	88.5	143	115.8	106.7	136.6	138	109.9	102.5
1966...........	156.3	155.5	147.5	172.6	157.0	158.6	120.5	173.9	90.5	145	121.9	113.5	151.7	148	113.1	105.9
1967...........	158.1	158.3	148.5	179.4	157.8	159.7	123.8	184.9	85.3	153	125.7	113.5	155.0	153	116.3	106.1
1968........										173						
1968—May......	164.2	163.0	154.6	181.1	165.2	165.8	126.9	196.1	e ᵖ84.8	172	129.1	114.7	166.1	165	120.3	108.5
June......	165.8	165.2	156.8	183.2	166.7	167.3	129.2	197.9		160	129.5	115.3	167.7	167	120.9	108.7
July......	166.0	164.7	156.4	182.6	167.4	167.4	130.0	199.3	ᵖ84.0	187	129.8	115.2	167.2	168	121.5	109.1
Aug......	164.6	164.8	156.8	181.9	164.2	165.7	129.4	202.1		192	130.1	114.9	167.8	170	121.9	108.7
Sept......	165.1	165.7	157.3	183.6	165.1	166.3	127.0	204.8		183	130.2	114.9	171.2	169	122.2	109.1
Oct.......	166.0	167.0	159.6	183.0	165.7	167.8	120.7	208.9	ᵖ84.2	200	130.8	115.3	172.2	168	122.9	109.1
Nov......	167.5	167.9	159.2	186.5	167.6	169.1	126.4	206.9		183	131.3	115.7	173.8	168	123.4	109.6
Dec......	168.7	168.1	160.1	185.3	169.3	170.2	127.4	210.1		ʳ185	132.0	116.4	175.3	166	123.7	109.8
1969—Jan......	169.1	168.2	161.0	183.5	169.6	170.2	125.8	215.1	ᵖ84.5	191	132.6	116.6	175.8	170	124.1	110.7
Feb......	170.1	169.3	161.7	185.5	170.8	171.8	124.8	214.9		205	133.2	117.0	174.3	171	124.6	111.1
Mar......	171.4	170.8	162.8	187.8	172.1	173.1	126.7	215.1		177	133.6	117.3	178.2	169	125.6	111.7
Apr......	171.7	170.4	162.0	188.5	172.7	173.1	128.7	216.3	ᵖ84.6	183	132.9	117.0	177.8	172	126.4	111.9
May......	172.7	171.0	162.0	190.1	174.2	173.9	130.6	217.9		210	133.1	117.2	178.1	171	126.8	112.8
June ᵖ...	173.9	172.3	163.8	190.4	175.1	175.0	133.6	219.0			133.7	117.5	180.0	169		113.2

a Employees only; excludes personnel in the Armed Forces.
b Production workers only.
c F.R. index based on Census Bureau figures.
d Prices are not seasonally adjusted.
e Figure is for second quarter 1968.

NOTE.—*All series:* Data are seasonally adjusted unless otherwise noted.

Capacity utilization: Based on data from Federal Reserve, McGraw-Hill Economics Department, and Department of Commerce.
Construction contracts: F. W. Dodge Co. monthly index of dollar value of total construction contracts, including residential, nonresidential, and heavy engineering; does not include data for Alaska and Hawaii.
Employment and payrolls: Based on Bureau of Labor Statistics data; includes data for Alaska and Hawaii beginning with 1959.
Prices: Bureau of Labor Statistics data.

FIGURE 10–3

Selected business indexes

SOURCE *Federal Reserve Bulletin,* July, 1969, p. A60

durable and nondurable manufacturing and these are further broken down into individual industry categories. The relative growth of a specific industry group compared with the overall index of business or economic activity can easily be determined from this information.

OTHER INDEXES OF BUSINESS AND ECONOMIC ACTIVITY

Other indexes of business and economic activity are presented in the *Federal Reserve Bulletin*; some are included in Figure 10–3. In addition, other indexes are used to measure the output of our economy. A word of comment is appropriate about the selected indexes presented in Figure 10–3 and about some of the other indexes.

Construction Contracts. The index of construction contracts provides an indication of the relative level of building activity on an aggregate basis from one time period to another. Construction contracts include residential, nonresidential, and heavy engineering construction. The dollar volume of contracts has grown steadily each year since 1951. The rate of growth in housing was substantial during the 1950's. Then, in 1962, construction contracts increased sharply, up more than 10 percent over 1961 levels. The activity for 1963 was above the level for 1962, which was a bright spot in the national economy. Residential construction in the third quarter of 1963 was moving ahead at an all-time high. Housing construction conditions continued favorable until 1966 when, because of a combination of Vietnam and the lack of funds from the banking community, the rate of growth diminished. There was little or no change between 1965 and 1966, and 1967 was not a robust year. Housing picked up substantially late in 1967 and continued good through 1968, but slowed again in late 1969. There is substantial long-term future growth foreseen, as a commitment of the federal government to housing the poor offers an expectation for continued growth. The construction index is particularly beneficial as an indicator of activity in the building industry in its various phases. A sound building industry is one of the mainstays of the economic growth of our nation.

Nonagricultural Employment. A nation can prosper only to the extent that its citizens are employed in producing goods and services and are themselves demanding goods and services. Data on the growth of employment and the growth of payrolls, therefore, help to indicate the strength of the national economy. An index based upon information compiled by the Bureau of Labor Statistics is presented in Figure 10–3.

Total nonagricultural employment has increased modestly over the 1957–59 base period. Total employment has been cyclical and has not grown as fast as the GNP and the other aggregate measures of national income. Manufacturing employment declined somewhat from the 1957–1959 base period and did not regain that level until May of 1963. It increased substantially in 1964–1965 and through 1966, reaching a new plateau in 1967. Payrolls, on the other hand, jumped remarkably, an indication mainly of inflation.

Figures on employment supplied by the various industry divisions in nonagricultural establishments reveal some interesting trends. First, manufacturing employment has improved from the 1957–1959 base period through 1968.[4] Transportation, mining, and contract construction employment have reduced the number of people on their payrolls over the same period of time. The number of people employed in the trades and in the finance industry has increased somewhat during a comparable period of time.[5] The largest growth, however, has come

4 *Federal Reserve Bulletin,* July, 1968, p. A–62.
5 *Ibid.*

about in the service industry and in government employment. Employment in the service industry increased more than 25 percent between the base period 1957–1959 and May, 1968.[6] Government employment increased a substantial 23 percent for the equivalent time period. These figures correlate very closely with the dollar GNP components in each of the comparable areas.

Freight Car Loadings. Freight car loadings are another index of economic activity to help the investor determine whether business is favorable or unfavorable. A high level of freight car loadings indicates a high level of business and economic activity. An increase in freight car loadings would signify an upturn in business. This is based upon the simple premise that goods must be shipped from the manufacturer to the retail outlet and then to the consumer before they become sales. Freight car loadings reflect both sales and the anticipation of a change in sales. Because of the growth of other common carriers, mainly trucks, and the changes in the operating characteristics of the railroads, freight car loadings do not seem to be as good an economic indicator as they once were.

Total Retail Sales. Total retail sales represent another way of measuring the business health of the nation's economy. Just as employment incomes represent the ability of a customer to purchase goods and services, similarly, retail sales reflect the consumers' willingness to spend. Retail sales indicate consumer confidence, as well as profits for the sellers. If consumers are confident of the future, they tend to spend more freely. Thus, if consumers are spending now and retail sales have increased, it is a healthy sign for business now and in the near future. The level of retail sales should be of interest in those industries that are directly or indirectly related to retail store activity. The activities of department stores, discount houses, etc., vary widely from candy, drugs, and hosiery to furniture, boats, and swimming pools. Strength in retail sales would be a buoyant force in sustaining a high level of economic activity. As shown in Figure 10–3, total retail sales have increased each year since 1951 except for 1954. Unfortunately, the growth of sales has not been at an extremely high rate. Consumer goods have suffered from competition with services for the consumer's dollar.

The Price Level. The level of prices does not measure the aggregate economic activity of a nation. Price levels do measure the degree to which the nation's growth is the result of real increases in output or merely of inflation, in which more dollars are bidding up the prices of the same amount of goods. Economic and business growth is desirable only to the extent that this growth represents a real increase in the production of goods and services. No one benefits if the increase in

6 *Ibid.*

wages or GNP is brought about because of price increases. Stability of prices is a desirable goal of any national economy, and stability with growth is the ideal combination of economic goals.

An examination of the indexes in Figure 10–3 shows the trend of consumer and wholesale price indexes in recent years. From 1957 on there has been remarkable stability in the wholesale price index. In fact, wholesale commodity prices have remained virtually unchanged for that period of time, that is, until 1966, when there was a 3.4 point increase in the wholesale price index. Prices continued to rise quite rapidly in 1967 and 1968 because of the heavy financial commitments of the United States domestically and in Vietnam.

The consumer price index has moved up about 10 percent from 1957 through 1965. Then the index experienced a 3.2 point rise. The change has been much greater than the wholesale index and represents an inflationary increment of 1 percent per year from 1957 through 1965 and then a much more rapid rate of 3 percent per annum in 1966, 1967, and 1968. Although this is not a runaway inflation, it is creeping upward and will result in the loss of purchasing power for the individual. Within the past two decades our economy has suffered from both galloping and creeping inflation in consumer prices. Not all the growth reflected in the GNP and other indexes, therefore, has been a real gain for our economy. The GNP in constant 1958 prices reveals a relatively modest growth of the economy when inflationary elements are removed from the data.

The components of consumer prices varied in their degree of stability. Medical care, and reading and recreation, for example, increased 43.5 percent and 24.9 percent respectively from 1958 until April, 1968. Home ownership increased 24.0 percent for the same period. Food prices for the same period increased 18.3 percent; rent 14.4 percent; fuel oil and coal 14.0 percent; gas and electricity 9.5 percent; home furnishing 12.2 percent; and apparel and transportation 18.4 percent and 18.0 percent, respectively.[7] Housing costs and medical expenses have suffered the burden of inflation.

Business Week Indexes. FRB Indexes are not the only source of economic indicators. *Business Week,* a McGraw-Hill publication, provides each week an extensive list of production and trade figures plus an index of prices that helps one determine the health of the economy. It also gives information about finance and other statistics in a one-page "Figures of the Week" section. Over a period, trends can be ascertained from this information to help in making investment decisions and establishing investment policy. The unfortunate problem associated with individual statistics is the difficulty in forecasting. Unless we have access to industry forecasts, it is difficult to plan ahead with the same

7 *Ibid.* p. A–64.

degree of success we would have with the more familiar aggregate data such as the GNP and FRB indexes.

BUSINESS CYCLE DEVELOPMENTS

Gross National Product figures, Federal Reserve Board Index estimates of industrial activity, and other economic time series found in familiar sources provide the investor with a knowledge of where the economy is and the general direction in which it is going. However, the GNP is not a sensitive cyclical indicator, unless we focus on the rate of change of the annual rate of growth. The FRB Index is more cyclical, but forecasting with it has not been much more successful than short-range GNP forecasts. The National Bureau of Economic Research, through its studies of business cycles, has developed a substantial number of indicators to aid economists in forecasting the national economy. There are three basic groups of indicators: leading indicators, roughly coincidental indicators, and lagging indicators. The most significant indicators appear in the monthly publication *Business Cycle Developments* (BCD). A sample of the thirty-six leading indicators from BCD is reproduced in Figure 10–4. Information on how to read these charts is presented in Figure 10–5. Leading indicators include employment and unemployment; fixed capital investment; inventories and inventory investment; prices, costs, and profits; and money and credit. *Business Cycle Developments* also provides monthly information about twenty-five roughly coincidental indicators and eleven lagging indicators. The roughly coincidental indicators include job vacancies, comprehensive employment, comprehensive unemployment, comprehensive production (GNP and FRB), comprehensive income, comprehensive consumption and trade, backlog of investment commitments, comprehensive wholesale prices, bank reserves, and money market interest rates.

The lagging indicators include long duration unemployment, investment expenditures, inventories, unit labor costs, outstanding debt, and interest rates on business loans and mortgages.

Each of the time series must be interpreted by the economist or the investor. Skill here will pay off substantially. Fortunately comments are made from time to time in the *Wall Street Journal*, in "The Outlook" column that appears in Monday's issue. Results achieved by using the leading and lagging indicators suggest that one indicator cannot be used alone and that, in spite of the care in selecting indicators, results are not always consistent and reliable. Indicators are helpful but not infallible and forecasting is at best a hazardous activity.

The Future Growth of the National Economy

Where is the economy of the United States going? This is a question we must answer before we begin an investment evaluation of a company or establish an investment portfolio. We have learned that this is a difficult

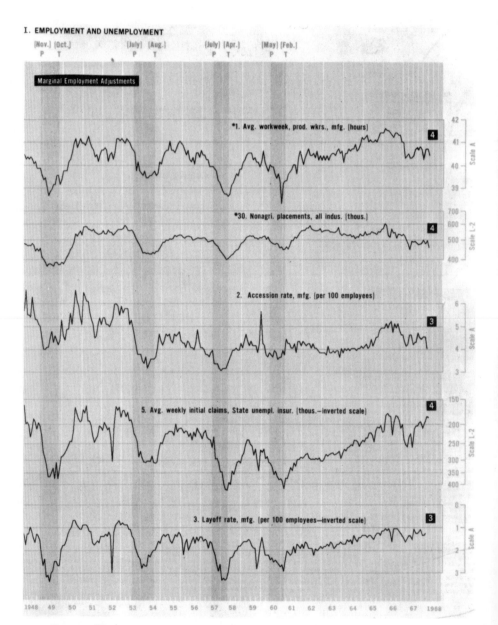

FIGURE 10-4

Business cycle series from 1948 to present—leading indicators

SOURCE *Business Cycle Developments*, May, 1968, p. 4, U.S. Department of Commerce, Bureau of the Census

HOW TO READ CHARTS

CHART 1 — Series

Peak (P) of cycle indicates end of expansion and beginning of Recession (shaded areas) as designated by NBER.

Series numbers are for identification only and do not reflect series relationships or order. Series are arranged in charts and tables according to their classification by timing and economic process.

Solid line indicates monthly data. (Data may be actual monthly figures or MCD moving averages.*)

Broken line indicates actual monthly data for series where an MCD moving average* is plotted.

Parallel lines indicate a break in continuity (data not available, changes in series definitions, extreme values, etc.).

Solid line with plotting points indicates quarterly data.

Trough (T) of cycle indicates end of recession and beginning of Expansion as designated by NBER.

Arabic number indicates latest month for which data are plotted. ("3" = March)

Roman number indicates latest quarter for which data are plotted. ("II" = second quarter)

Dotted line indicates anticipated data.

Various scales are used to highlight the patterns of the individual series. "Scale A" is an arithmetic scale, "scale L-1" is a logarithmic scale with 1 cycle in a given distance, "scale L-2" is a logarithmic scale with 2 cycles in that distance, etc. The scales should be carefully noted because they show whether or not the plotted lines for various series are directly comparable.

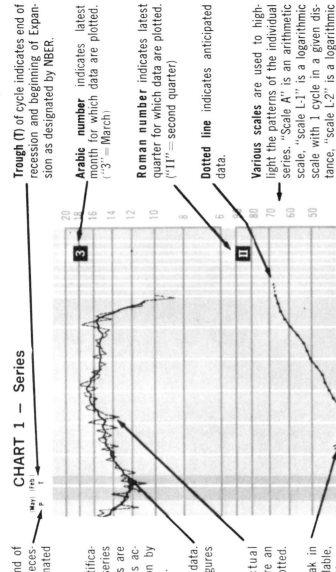

FIGURE 10–5

How to read business cycle development charts

SOURCE *Business Cycle Developments*, May, 1968, p. 9, U.S. Department of Commerce, Bureau of the Census

question to answer. Yet we have the evidence of the past to guide us. The 1968 Economic Report of the President, one source of economic information, has referred to the period 1957–1968. During 1967–68, for short periods, the rate of growth of the GNP was as high as 9 percent. A 9 percent rate cannot be sustained for any length of time. A range of growth between 3.5 percent in real terms and 5.6 percent in current dollars of the GNP is obtainable—and close to what happened between 1967 and 1968. Our expectations for the growth of our economy from the first quarter of 1968 compare favorably with the potential growth rate of 3.5 percent in real terms. The National Planning Association has agreed with this growth rate. (The Stanford Research Institute has used 3.7 and 4.0 percent as attainable growth rates for the national economy.) At these rates the following GNP figures in billions of dollars might result based on what is obtainable.

	5.6% GROWTH RATE (BILLIONS)	3.5% GROWTH RATE (BILLIONS)
1975	$1,212	$1,052
1974	1,148	1,016
1973	1,087	982
1972	1,029	946
1971	974	917
1970	922	866
1969	873	856
1968	827	827

The range in estimates for the year 1975 is from $1,052 billion for the 3.5 percent growth rate to $1,212 for the 5.6 percent rate. The relationships are presented graphically in Chart 10–1. In 1958 dollars, the GNP should reach $600 billion by 1975. In current year dollars it will reach almost 1 1/4 trillion dollars. There will be cyclical dips over the period. With business and government converted to a full employment economy these forecast figures are possible.

An Analysis of the Industry

The industries that contribute to the output of the major segments of the economy vary in their growth rate and in their overall contribution to economic activity. Some have grown more rapidly than the GNP and offer the expectation of continued growth. Others have maintained a growth comparable with the GNP. A few have been unable to expand and have declined in economic significance. If we are to succeed as investors, we must analyze the economic significance of the industries in which we wish to invest. We must make a value judgment about the future growth of each and invest in those that offer continued

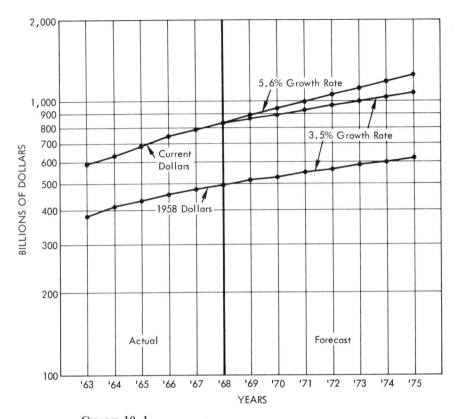

CHART 10–1

*Gross National Product 1963–1968
and forecasts for 1968–1975*

success, measured by the industry's ability to compete for its appropriate share of the GNP. One can find successful companies in industries that are not growing; these may make financially attractive investments. On the other hand, investment success is more likely to be found in growing and strongly competitive industries.

The Concept of an Industry

We have some general idea of what is meant by *industry*, but let us be sure that we understand its significance. Webster defines the word *industry* as "a department or branch of a craft, art, business, or manufacture; especially one that employs a large personnel and capital, esp. in manufacturing."[8] This definition could apply to almost any economic activity. In a broad sense, an industry might be considered a *com-*

8 *Webster's Seventh New Collegiate Dictionary* (Springfield, Mass.: G. & C. Merriam Co., 1967), p. 430.

munity of interests. The community of interests concept would reflect the idea of a group of people coming together because they did a certain type of work or produced a similar type of product. Such groups would include agriculture as well as manufacturing, mining, and merchandising.

In an economic sense these groups form into industries because of the nature of what is produced and the processes involved in its production. We tend to think of an industry as a product- or process-oriented unit. The automobile industry, for example, reflects both the concept of the end product—the automobile—and the method of manufacture—the manufacturing process. The banking industry also illustrates the industry concept. Basically it consists of commercial banks that make business loans. The product, of course, is money, and the process is the lending process.

The classes of industries we can have are unlimited. If we classify industries by the process of manufacture, then we can divide them according to the nature of their basic function, for example, the manufacturing industry, the transportation industry, and the public utility industry. These broad basic functional groups can then be further broken down into the end product. The manufacturing industry, for instance, would include such diverse products as autos, pianos, tin cans, strollers, and cribs. It would include all products that are manufactured. The transportation industry would include railroads, airlines, trucks, ships, and possibly pipelines. Automobiles would be excluded because, although they are a form of transportation, they are not available as a common carrier unless used as taxis. However, private transportation competes via the auto with other forms of transportation. In this case, the auto would fall into two classes of industry: the manufacturing class and the transportation class. For practical purposes, autos would be placed in the manufacturing industry.

The classification of an industry is important when we analyze its growth. Each industry takes its share of the GNP and competes with every other industry. Thus, the manufacturing industries compete with the agriculture, transportation, and public utility industries. This inter-industry competition is important. And within each major industry classification, the product- or service-oriented segments compete with each other for a share of the GNP; we are mainly interested in these service- and product-oriented industries. When we define an *industry*, then, as a limited set of productive functions or activities measured by the output of an end product or service, we can observe changes much more easily than if we used a broader industry classification. These changes and the expectation of change should cause the investor to react either favorably or unfavorably toward an industry for investment. As investors we are interested in competitive change. We are, however, more interested in the competitive position of the auto industry, for example, than in the competitive position of the manufacturing industry as a whole.

For careful analysis, each industry is broken down into its logical product class. The drug industry, for example, is usually divided into proprietary drugs and ethical drugs, the auto industry into passenger autos and trucks, and the rubber industry into tires and rubber products. The *Federal Reserve Bulletin* publishes production index figures for the various industries that make up the major industry groupings. A sample appears in Figure 10–6. These are useful in determining the level of economic activity of each industry group.

Howard B. Bonham, Jr., indicates the importance of input-output analysis on the demands for various products in the several industry groups. (An input-output system for the U.S. economy reflects in dollar terms the demands on our industries caused by certain amounts of final demand as represented by the national income accounts.) He considers such analysis "one of the most useful macroeconomic tools available for measuring the effects on equity investments of dynamic product flows within an economic structure."[9] Input-output analysis has evolved from the work of Professor Wassily Leontief of Harvard University and continues with research sponsored by the Office of Business Education. The OBE tables are the first to be integrated with the national income accounts.[10] The full implication of these studies can be learned by reading Mr. Bonham's article.

The Characteristics of Industry Growth

The growth of an industry usually begins with a major technological change. In the early years of the twentieth century in the United States, the automobile, the airplane, the radio, and the electric light were major technological developments that created new industries. In more recent years, rockets, computers, electronic equipment and communication devices, office equipment, automated control equipment, and ionic propulsion are developments that have created new industries and rapid technological change, resulting in rapid industrial growth. As an industry expands, the following growth pattern emerges, according to Dr. Simon S. Kuznets.[11] In the beginning, rapid growth takes place at extremely high rates. As the industry expands, over long periods of time, the percentage rate of growth diminishes. Industries never experience

9 Howard B. Bonham, Jr., "The Use of Input-Output Economics in Common Stock Analysis," *Financial Analysts Journal,* January-February, 1967, p. 19.

10 *Ibid.*

11 These comments are based upon class notes from Dr. Kuznets's course in Economic Development at the University of Pennsylvania. See also Simon S. Kuznets, *Capital in the American Economy* (Princeton, N.J.: Princeton University Press, 1961); *Modern Economic Growth* (New Haven, Conn.: Yale University Press, 1966); and *Economic Growth and Structure* (New York: W. W. Norton & Company, Inc., 1965).

(1957–59 = 100)

Grouping	1957–59 proportion	1967 average p	1967 Apr.	May	June	July	Aug.	Sept.	Oct.	Nov.	Dec.	1968 Jan.	Feb. r	Mar. r	Apr.
Total index..................	100.00	158.0	156.5	155.6	155.6	156.6	158.1	156.8	156.9	159.5	162.0	161.2	162.0	163.0	162.5
Manufacturing, total..............	86.45	159.6	158.2	157.2	157.0	157.6	159.4	158.1	158.3	161.1	164.0	162.7	163.6	164.4	163.7
Durable....................	48.07	163.8	162.5	162.2	161.5	162.5	163.6	161.1	160.7	164.1	168.1	167.2	167.6	168.2	167.3
Nondurable.................	38.38	154.4	152.8	151.1	151.4	151.5	154.0	154.2	155.2	157.2	158.9	157.1	158.6	159.7	159.1
Mining.....................	8.23	123.5	122.0	120.2	123.8	128.0	127.8	124.3	122.4	123.6	122.3	121.6	123.9	126.9	128.2
Utilities...................	5.32	184.4	182.7	182.7	183.2	184.1	184.8	184.8	187.6	190.5	191.8	195.9	197.5	196.8	198.0
Durable manufactures															
Primary and fabricated metals.....	12.32	145.4	143.0	142.8	142.9	142.8	142.3	141.8	143.3	145.8	150.3	148.3	150.8	151.8	152.2
Primary metals..................	6.95	132.5	129.1	128.9	129.0	129.6	129.3	129.2	131.7	135.0	140.9	136.3	139.3	140.2	144.5
Iron and steel..............	5.45	126.8	122.7	122.9	121.2	122.3	124.3	125.6	127.7	133.3	140.9	134.2	137.8	140.8	143.8
Nonferrous metals and products..	1.50	153.1	161.4	154.4	156.4	155.3	144.2	141.1	142.8	142.2	145.3	145.6	154.1	151.4	156.8
Fabricated metal products........	5.37	162.0	161.0	160.8	160.8	159.8	159.1	158.1	158.2	159.8	162.4	163.9	165.7	166.8	162.2
Structural metal parts..........	2.86	158.1	158.1	156.4	156.9	156.1	156.8	156.0	156.4	158.8	160.0	159.4	160.9	162.7	157.3
Machinery and related products.....	27.98	177.6	176.5	176.5	175.5	177.5	179.6	175.0	173.4	177.8	181.7	181.6	181.5	182.3	179.3
Machinery..................	14.80	183.4	182.1	180.5	177.5	180.0	182.8	182.2	179.6	183.2	182.2	183.4	183.2	183.3	179.6
Nonelectrical machinery.......	8.43	183.4	183.5	181.7	181.3	182.2	182.6	182.6	177.2	180.9	179.5	180.7	180.6	180.2	177.2
Electrical machinery..........	6.37	183.3	180.3	178.9	172.4	177.1	183.2	182.4	182.8	186.3	185.8	186.9	186.6	187.4	182.8
Transportation equipment.........	10.19	166.0	165.7	167.5	169.3	170.8	171.9	159.2	159.2	165.6	177.5	175.6	175.1	177.6	175.1
Motor vehicles and parts......	4.68	147.0	149.5	152.0	154.5	156.7	158.0	129.4	128.6	141.4	166.9	162.2	161.1	167.8	164.3
Aircraft and other equipment...	5.26	182.2	179.8	181.4	181.8	182.6	183.6	184.3	185.2	186.0	186.3	186.8	186.5	185.4	183.7
Instruments and related products...	1.71	184.8	185.2	185.3	184.1	182.9	183.2	183.1	183.2	185.4	186.3	186.7	184.7	183.8	181.4
Ordnance and accessories.........	1.28	......	......	......	......	......	......	......	......	......	......	......	......	......	......
Clay, glass, and lumber...........	4.72	130.6	129.8	127.8	126.7	127.3	126.7	129.6	131.4	132.4	137.0	132.5	130.7	129.1	137.5
Clay, glass, and stone products.....	2.99	138.7	136.0	134.8	133.5	134.1	136.9	138.4	139.7	139.2	143.6	140.8	137.3	131.0	144.9
Lumber and products..........	1.73	116.5	119.1	115.6	114.9	115.5	109.2	114.3	117.0	120.6	125.7	118.1	119.3	125.8	124.8
Furniture and miscellaneous........	3.05	162.6	162.9	162.3	161.5	159.1	159.9	161.4	160.9	161.5	163.3	165.2	166.9	166.9	166.8
Furniture and fixtures..........	1.54	167.8	166.5	166.5	166.3	162.7	164.8	166.3	166.6	167.8	170.7	171.3	173.0	173.7	174.1
Miscellaneous manufactures.......	1.51	157.4	159.2	158.1	156.7	155.4	154.9	156.4	155.0	155.1	155.7	158.9	160.7	159.9	159.3
Nondurable manufactures															
Textiles, apparel, and leather.......	7.60	139.6	135.5	135.3	134.8	135.3	137.6	139.1	140.4	143.0	145.9	141.0	141.9	143.7	143.6
Textile mill products..............	2.90	142.2	137.8	137.8	136.6	136.8	138.7	141.3	144.9	147.4	151.6	147.6	148.8	149.9	147.5
Apparel products.................	3.59	147.7	142.5	142.6	142.4	144.2	146.4	146.8	146.2	148.6	150.9	145.2	146.4	148.1	......
Leather and products.............	1.11	106.5	107.1	105.0	105.4	103.0	106.5	108.4	109.7	113.3	115.1	110.4	109.7	113.7	......
Paper and printing..............	8.17	149.6	149.9	149.1	149.4	148.6	150.3	148.5	148.6	149.9	149.5	148.6	150.6	151.3	151.3
Paper and products..............	3.43	153.6	152.1	151.4	151.6	149.0	152.8	152.9	154.5	156.1	157.0	155.9	157.1	......	......
Printing and publishing..........	4.74	146.8	148.3	147.4	147.8	148.3	148.6	145.4	144.3	144.5	144.1	143.3	144.9	146.8	146.2
Newspapers.................	1.53	134.2	133.8	133.1	134.3	136.1	137.0	135.7	134.0	134.4	129.9	129.9	131.4	133.7	130.8
Chemicals, petroleum, and rubber....	11.54	189.5	186.4	182.2	183.0	184.0	189.5	191.2	192.8	195.8	199.0	197.7	200.2	201.7	199.8
Chemicals and products..........	7.58	203.8	200.1	199.6	199.9	201.0	200.7	202.3	205.5	208.0	210.5	211.8	213.8	215.2	213.2
Industrial chemicals..............	3.84	234.8	228.3	228.8	227.5	227.6	231.4	234.2	238.8	242.3	246.9	250.9	251.8	252.7	......
Petroleum products..............	1.97	133.9	133.1	132.1	134.4	132.8	133.2	137.0	137.0	136.6	136.8	138.0	134.8	135.7	135.5	136.8
Rubber and plastics products......	1.99	190.3	186.9	165.7	166.9	170.1	170.1	203.1	202.4	199.1	207.5	215.4	206.7	212.3	215.7	......
Foods, beverages, and tobacco....	11.07	131.5	131.8	130.9	131.3	130.9	131.0	130.4	131.1	132.2	133.1	132.0	133.1	133.4	133.4
Foods and beverages............	10.25	132.4	133.1	132.0	131.9	131.5	131.7	131.2	132.2	133.5	134.1	133.5	133.2	134.2	134.2
Food manufactures............	8.64	130.1	130.6	130.3	129.9	129.4	129.0	128.9	129.3	130.2	130.5	130.7	130.7	131.5	131.7
Beverages.................	1.61	144.7	146.3	141.2	142.9	142.8	146.3	143.8	147.5	151.2	153.3	148.2	146.7	148.7	......
Tobacco products................	.82	120.0	116.0	117.4	123.9	123.6	121.4	120.2	118.0	115.5	120.5	114.4	132.1	122.9	......
Mining															
Coal, oil, and gas................	6.80	122.4	118.5	118.0	121.7	128.0	128.8	125.4	123.7	124.5	122.2	121.9	123.2	126.8	126.3
Coal.......................	1.16	118.1	125.5	120.1	122.5	122.6	117.2	115.5	112.3	115.3	116.1	113.4	116.8	126.0	124.4
Crude oil and natural gas.........	5.64	123.2	117.1	117.5	121.6	129.1	131.2	127.5	126.1	126.4	123.5	123.6	124.5	126.9	126.7
Oil and gas extraction..........	4.91	131.4	125.3	125.3	129.5	138.0	141.9	137.7	135.4	133.9	131.7	132.5	134.8	137.3	136.8
Crude oil..................	4.25	126.4	119.6	119.6	123.6	133.9	138.0	133.1	130.3	128.7	126.4	127.4	129.7	132.8	131.3
Gas and gas liquids..........	.66	163.3	161.5	161.3	167.3	......	......	......	......	......	......	......	......	......	......
Oil and gas drilling...........	.73	67.9	61.8	65.5	67.7	69.0	58.9	58.5	63.4	76.1	68.0	63.5	55.0	56.7	......
Metal, stone, and earth minerals....	1.43	128.8	138.7	130.8	133.6	127.7	123.4	119.1	116.2	119.5	122.7	120.3	127.0	127.4	137.3
Metal mining...................	.61	119.9	149.5	132.9	133.9	119.7	105.7	95.6	93.8	93.2	95.7	100.0	102.8	108.7	138.2
Stone and earth minerals..........	.82	135.4	130.6	129.2	133.3	133.7	136.6	136.5	132.9	139.0	142.7	135.3	145.0	141.2	136.7
Utilities															
Electric......................	4.04	191.7	189.9	189.7	190.3	191.4	192.1	192.1	195.8	199.4	200.8	205.2	207.3	206.4	......
Gas........................	1.28	161.2	......	......	......	......	......	......	......	......	......	......	......	......	......

NOTE.—Published groupings include some series and subtotals not shown separately. A description and historical data are available in *Industrial Production—1957–59 Base*. Figures for individual series and subtotals (N.S.A.) are published in the monthly Business Indexes release.

FIGURE 10–6

Industrial production by industry groupings

SOURCE *Federal Reserve Bulletin,* June, 1968, p. A57

unretarded or accelerated growth for long periods of time. To analyze the growth pattern, we will define the industry in terms of its end product and confine our discussion to a simple product in order to see the long-range effects of the changes in growth and the growth rate.

Professor Kuznets gives several reasons for the decreasing rate of growth of an industry. First, the major technological changes that created the industry are concentrated in the early stages of the life of the industry. If we have a limited number of production functions to use in the industry and their use is changed rapidly, strong economic pressures occur that bring about rapid upward growth. These major changes are reinforced by minor changes and improvements, which come about early in the development of the product as the bugs are being worked out. This definite bias toward early development tends to make the impact of change greatest in the early years. A good illustration of this is found in the auto industry, whose rate of growth was extremely high in the early years of its development, between 1900 and 1920. Production rates increased rapidly, and the percentage rate of change was extremely high as production techniques and products improved. After the early period of development, the growth rate subsided. In 1963, although the number of autos and trucks produced was far greater than in the formative years of the industry, the rate of increase was much less. In other words, the auto industry is increasing at a decreasing rate, even though annual production is impressive.

A second reason for a diminution in the industry growth rate is in the nature of the technological change itself. The basic types of major technological changes help to produce an old product more cheaply or a completely new product on a mass basis. A high-priced commodity or service is changed into a low-priced one, making it available to a larger market. A luxury good might be changed into a necessity good. Using the auto industry as an example, both changes increase the immediate demand for the product. In the early years of technological development these changes have a remarkable impact upon growth. Beyond the early years and the immediate reduction in costs and price, the changes have little effect upon the growth of the market and the output of the industry.

The relative growth of other industries tends to reduce the impact of cost reductions, which, in turn, tends to limit the continued growth of a market. If other industries do not grow as fast as that in which the rapid expansion takes place, prices will not drop in the other industries. This will limit the decline in price in the rapidly expanding industry. Assume, for example, that a technological innovation occurs, such as the development of automated equipment, that permits a reduction in the price of transistors from $2.00 to $.90 per unit. The demand for transistors expands, and the number produced increases dramatically. However, germanium, a raw material for the transistor, does not have a corresponding expansion in demand, since there are no new economies or developments that will allow germanium to be produced at a lower price and the amount used in producing transistors is not sufficient to bring about mass production economies. Since the raw material cannot be lowered in price, there is also a lower limit to the price of the transistor. Any price changes that would help increase output in the future will be negligible, and the accompanying rate of expansion will be diminished. The general effect of this example can be transferred to the economy as a whole: an industry growing at a rapid rate, faster than the national economy, will eventually have its growth dampened because of the slower growth of the economy.

A third factor that tends to limit the growth of an industry is the competitive pressure from other industries. A new industry might develop, having a restraining influence upon the old industry that first experienced the technological change. The new industry might compete directly for raw materials, tending to raise the costs of the original industry and limit its expansion potential. Sometimes new industries are directly competitive with the old product or original product. For example, one material becomes a substitute for another, as aluminum was substituted for steel, stainless steel for chromium, and plastics for aluminum or metal. For that matter, all metals can be substituted for each other, depending upon their use. One type of power can be substituted for other types of power, depending upon the cost–price relationship involved. Someday, when the cost becomes low enough, atomic or solar power will be substituted for oil-generated steam to produce electricity. Other examples can be cited. The woolen industry lost part of its market to cotton. Then cotton lost part of its market to silk and rayon. Then rayon and silk began losing their market to nylon, and so forth. The net effect of these changes is that the competitive position of one product or service is often lost to a competitive product that indirectly or directly does a better job than the old product. This competition tends to diminish the growth of the industry.

Another manifestation of this competition is international competition that develops for a national product. The transistor can be used as an illustration. Transistor production in the United States was growing rapidly with stable prices. Suddenly the Japanese developed production techniques allowing transistors to be mass-produced. Virtually overnight the market price was cut in half, to the detriment of the United States producers, and the competitive position of the transistor industry in the United States rapidly diminished.

A fourth and final factor which might reduce the rate of increase of a new technological development is a decrease in population growth. In order for a product to expand its output at an increasing rate, per capita output would have to grow at an increasing rate. For this to occur, the consumer would have to spend more of his income. The consumer's income does not increase as fast as the growth of the product because the economy grows more slowly than an industry experiencing rapid growth, and so it is unlikely that the industry's growth rate can be sustained. If we have declining population growth, the industry's growth will slow down even more quickly.

The diminishing percentage rate of growth of the output of an industry is depicted in Chart 10-2. The solid curved line on the semi-log graph represents a constantly decreasing rate of growth. If the same data were plotted on regular graph paper, the line would be straight. If the line in Chart 10-2 were straight, the growth rate would be constant. A constant growth rate is possible over short periods of the growth life of an industry but not for long periods of time. The time period in the chart does not depict one-year intervals. The intervals represent time but not a specific number of years. No uniform time period exists that represents the life-cycle growth of an industry.

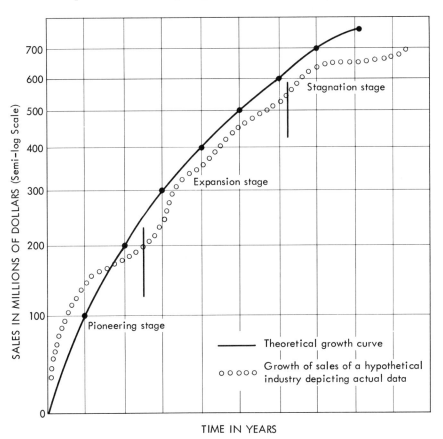

CHART 10-2

The industrial growth curve

THE INDUSTRY GROWTH CYCLE

The growth of an industry is sometimes divided into stages. Professor Grodinsky in his book on investments[12] and Professors Mead and Grodinsky in a previous book[13] divided the growth cycle into the pioneering stage, the expansion stage, and the stagnation stage. Actually, this division of industry growth is quite similar to Professor Kuznets's concept. Chart 10–2 demonstrates graphically the growth of an industry by the dotted line, which is divided into the three stages. Professor Grodinsky, however, relates the stages of growth more to the characteristics of the company than to the industry as a whole. His concepts should be of interest to the investor.

The Pioneering Stage. The pioneering stage, as presented by Professor Grodinsky, is comparable with the discovery stage or the stage, according to Professor Kuznets, when the technological development takes place. Its primary characterisics are a rapid increase in production and a rapidly expanding demand for the product. Many companies enter the market to produce the product, and the market is extremely competitive. Profits are large for those firms that first introduce the product, but as competition increases, prices decline rapidly and profits fall. This tends to force out the less efficient firms. There is little price stability in the pioneering stage, and risk capital is supplied more by speculators and promoters than by investors.

As competition forces out some of the firms, they are acquired by the competitively strong companies. As a result, when the end of the pioneering stage comes about, only a few leading companies remain in the industry. In Chart 10–2, the dip in sales represents the circumstances that force many firms out of the industry. Numerous examples of this competitive struggle can be found in American industry. The auto, radio, television, and electronic industries offer excellent illustrations of the pioneering stage as part of the growth cycle.

The Expansion Stage. The expansion stage in the growth cycle is characterized by an expanding demand for the product, but the rate of growth is less than in the pioneering stage. There is greater stability of prices, products, and production during this phase. Competition is keen, and a small number of larger firms dominate the industry. These large firms have been put together through merger and acquisition and by their competitive superiority. The companies that remain have successfully weathered the financial adversity of the later phases of the pioneering stage and remain in business turning out the products of the

---

12 Julius Grodinsky, *Investments* (New York: The Ronald Press Company, 1953).

13 Edward S. Mead and Julius Grodinsky, *Ebb and Flow of Investment Values* (New York: Appleton-Century-Crofts, 1939).

industry. These larger companies are well financed, have strong financial structures, and their current financial position is excellent. They also have an established dividend policy and, in addition, are able to expand from internally generated funds and are independent of the long-term capital markets except for major capital expenditure programs.

The investor can invest his funds during the industry's expansion stage in the knowledge that substantial growth potential remains in the industry, yet there is safety and security, since the larger companies have been able to retain a sizable share of the market. The competitive position of the firm is not automatically insured by its initial success, but it is in a strong position to maintain its status in the industry. The investor has some assurance that he will profit from his investment without the threat of a complete loss of principal. This period of industry growth is sometimes referred to as the period of investment maturity because of the stability and status of the firms within the industry.

The Stagnation Stage. In the later phase of the growth cycle of an industry, the rate of growth subsides. For some industries there is no growth at all in this phase and output actually declines. An example of this phenomenon can be found in the passenger and transportation segment of the railroad industry. The number of railroad passengers has declined, and the revenues generated have not been sufficient to allow some railroads to earn a profit. Even some freight railroads are not profitable. Unless costs can be reduced through eliminating unnecessary labor and operating costs, even the more successful railroads will become profitless. Many other industries could be given as further illustrations of the stagnation stage; the above will suffice. In this phase, the industry simply loses its power to expand. When the national economy shows economic strength, the growth of an industry in the stagnation stage does not keep pace; and its output falls faster than the economy when the economy declines. The transition from the expansion to the stagnation stage comes about gradually, and unless the investor is aware of the changes taking place in an industry, he will be taken by surprise.

REASONS FOR DECLINE IN THE COMPETITIVE POSITION OF AN INDUSTRY

In the stagnation stage, demand for the product is reduced by competition from other products or by factors that influence the profits of the industry by increasing costs. Professor Grodinsky[14] refers to these as factors of latent obsolescence that tend to destroy the competitive position of an industry. Included in this category are increasingly high labor costs, changes in social habits, changes in government regulation, and improved technology or automation.

High Labor Costs. High labor costs might force an industry out of a profitable existence. With a lessening of demand for a product, prices

14 Grodinsky, *Investments*, p. 71.

must be reduced to keep the product competitive. However, prices cannot be reduced because of relatively high production costs, and labor costs in particular. Unless changes can be made that reduce labor costs and total costs, the industry will decline in economic significance. The coal mining industry is an example of obsolescence brought about by a combination of factors. Increased wages forced automation, but competition from oil and gas reduced demand for the product, making price increases mandatory and further lessening the demand for coal.

Changes in Social Habits. The tobacco industry suffers from latent obsolescence because of a change in social habits. Cancer and cigarette smoking have been closely linked, as demonstrated by several studies in the United States and England. When results of the early studies became known to the public, a change occurred in demand—from regular cigarettes to filter-tip cigarettes. In 1969, the U.S. Government released the results of a study on the positive link between cigarette smoking and cancer. While this has not yet had a significant effect upon cigarette sales, the relationship between lung cancer and other fatal diseases and smoking has become more positive, and a strong advertising campaign has been launched by the American Cancer Society. The long-range result should be a diminishment in smoking.

Changes in Government Regulation. A change in governmental regulation or new regulations might operate against an industry and cause it to lose its competitive position. The outstanding example of this was Prohibition, which made an industry obsolete almost overnight. Price support programs undertaken by the government will also influence the competitive position of an industry. The enactment of minimum wage legislation will affect an industry's wage costs and reduce its competitive effectiveness. A tax on foreign investment was proposed by the federal government as a partial solution to the outflow of gold and the worsening of our balance of payments. This had a detrimental effect on the competitive position of foreign companies such as Royal Dutch-Shell and Aluminium, Ltd. A change in the method of depreciating or depleting an asset, as in the oil industry, or a change in costing an asset, as in the cement industry, will also adversely or favorably affect the economic position of an industry.

Automation. Automation can bring about changes that will influence the competitive position of an industry. Because of this automation is a problem; it is a social problem as well, and demands an answer to the question, "What can we do with workers who are displaced by the automatic machine?" Automation leads to tremendous benefits for the nation and for specific industries because it allows us to be competitive in world markets. At present the United States is undergoing a technological explosion in the field of automated equipment. One automated machine, for example, can take material from a press and transfer it to another machine for fabrication. The one automatic machine replaces twenty men, and this is only one phase of the assembly operation. The results, when magnified throughout an assembly plant, achieve considerable savings. At the same time, the new machine replaces older types of machines and causes a decline in demand in other industries. Technological change is not an unmixed blessing. John J. Snyder, Jr., former chairman of the board of U.S. Industries, put the problem this way:[15]

> Optimists like to compare this [technological change] to the Industrial Revolution—but this analogy is wrong. People got hurt then because we were breaking out of an agrarian society to build an industrial society, but with these new tools we are obsoleting not only our conventional machines but modern men as well. The Industrial Revolution created jobs. Now we're using sophisticated machines to destroy jobs.
>
> Well then, why are we doing it? Because we must. It can't be stopped. They tried it in the Industrial Revolution. They even legislated against the powered spindle—but it didn't work because England had to export. It won't work today for the same reason. We're living in a competitive world.

Other Factors. Other signs point to a worsening of the competitive position of an industry. Excessive productive capacity and rising prices are symptomatic of a decline. An industry that is no longer expanding will not need new plant and equipment. If the industry needs only 60 percent of its capacity to meet the demand for its product, it may be operating close to its breakeven point. The only course remaining will be for the industry to raise prices or even to seek government help or protection. The overcapacity suggests, too, that the growth of the industry is not keeping pace with the national economy. With unused capacity and rising costs, an industry has difficulty maintaining its competitive position.

Selecting the Expanding Industry

An understanding of the growth pattern of an industry and of the stages of growth—pioneering, expansion, and stagnation—as well as of the signs of obsolescence should provide a solution to the problem of where to invest. We should select industries that are in the expansion stage of the growth cycle and should concentrate our investigation in these areas. Except for special circumstances brought about by individual portfolio needs, we should not invest in industries in the pioneer-

15 Keith Wheeler, "Impact of Automation," a quote from an interview with John Snyder, Jr., *Life*, July 19, 1963, p. 77.

ing stage unless we are prepared to accept a great deal of speculative risk comparable with that assumed by the innovator or businessman. By the same token, we should ignore industries that are in the stagnation stage or are actually declining in economic importance. We should invest in those industries that have developed a strong competitive position with little threat of obsolescence influencing their future. Obviously this is simpler to suggest than to accomplish. A careful analysis of industries is important to determine which ones are competitively strong. This recommendation does not assume that we will buy growth industries and ignore industries that are not growing more rapidly than the national economy. The selection of an industry that is maintaining its competitive position equal with the GNP is entirely consistent with the recommendation. The growth concept assumes a rate of growth much greater than that of the national economy. The suggestion that we invest during the expansion stage of the growth cycle suggests growth-type industries as well as those that are growing at a rate equal to the rate of growth of the national economy.

COMPARISON OF INDUSTRY SALES WITH THE GNP

The competitive position of an industry can be measured in one of two ways: (1) by comparing the industry growth over time with the growth of the national economy, or (2) by measuring the growth rate of the industry itself. The first step would be to obtain reliable estimates of the physical output and dollar sales of the industry. This is relatively easy where the product involved is homogeneous and the data are available. The electric utility industry is one for which it is relatively easy to obtain production and sales figures. Based upon the sales figures obtained, an index can be constructed to reflect the relative growth of sales for the industry. The industry index of sales can then be compared with the index of growth of GNP, national income (NI), or disposable personal income (DPI), whichever is most appropriate and comparable to the industry in question. If an industry is growing at the same rate or more rapidly than the national economy, this will be apparent from a comparison of the indexes.

Table 10–2 provides an example of this type of comparison. The GNP in dollars and in index form is compared with the sales of the six leading companies in the tire industry. Care must be exercised in selecting the companies to make certain that they are truly representative of the industry under study. These six tire companies are large and adequately represent the industry. Often we cannot obtain data about total sales for an industry, and we must construct an index to represent the industry's growth. The relationship between tire industry sales and the GNP can be clearly seen in Chart 10–3. This type of relationship is helpful in predicting future sales of an industry, assuming there is an adequate and accurate forecast of the GNP.

TABLE 10–2

Comparison of industry sales growth
with Gross National Product and FRB index
of manufacturing production

	Gross National Product[a]			Manufacturing Sales of Six Tire Companies[b]		
YEAR	BILLIONS OF DOLLARS	INDEX 1957–59 BASE	FRB INDEX	BILLIONS OF DOLLARS	INDEX 1957–59 BASE	SALES AS PERCENT OF GNP[c]
1968	826.7	181.0	168.7	8.8	183.3	1.06
1967	785.0	171.9	158.1	8.0	166.7	1.02
1966	743.3	163.2	156.3	7.7	161.8	1.03
1965	683.9	150.0	143.4	7.0	146.9	1.02
1964	632.4	139.1	132.3	6.5	136.2	1.03
1963	590.5	129.5	124.3	6.0	125.8	1.02
1962	553.9	121.3	118.3	5.7	118.0	1.03
1961	518.7	113.6	109.7	5.2	108.0	1.00
1960	503.4	110.2	108.7	5.3	110.0	1.05
1959	482.7	105.7	105.6	5.2	109.0	1.09
1958	444.5	97.3	93.7	4.5	94.0	1.02
1957	442.8	97.0	100.7	4.7	97.0	1.05
1957–59 av.	456.7	100.0	100.0	4.8	100.0	1.05

[a] Seasonally adjusted.
[b] The six companies are Firestone, General, Goodrich, Goodyear, Lee, and U.S. Rubber.
[c] Data have been rounded and percentage figures are only approximate.
SOURCE: *Federal Reserve Bulletin*, June, 1963, p. 852; November, 1962, p. 1506; January, 1968, pp. A52 and A53; July, 1969, p. A60; and Standard & Poor's *Industry Survey—Rubber Fabricating*, April 10, 1969, p. R126.

The growth of sales in the tire industry has been somewhat less than the growth of the GNP. This is seen by comparing the index of the GNP with the index of sales. The growth of sales of the tire industry is more cyclical and less stable than the growth of the national economy. We notice in Table 10–2 that sales in the tire industry declined in 1958 and in 1961, whereas the GNP index increased steadily over the same period. Tire industry sales followed more closely the manufacturing section of the FRB Index. But the FRB Index was somewhat more stable than the tire industry index.

The conclusions to be drawn from this comparison are: First, the tire industry might be classed as a growing industry comparable with the national economy growth; second, it possesses stronger cyclical characteristics than the national economy; third, this growth pattern will probably continue and will aid us in estimating future performance of the industry; and fourth, we certainly might find a satisfactory outlet for investment among the companies making up the tire industry.

The relationship between industry sales and the GNP is more clearly shown in the last column of Table 10–2, in which industry sales

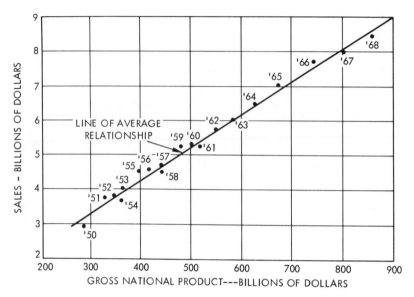

CHART 10–3

Relationship of tire industry sales (six companies) to Gross National Product

SOURCE Standard & Poor's *Industry Survey—Rubber Fabricating,* April 10, 1969, p. R126

are calculated as a percentage of GNP. Sales as a percent of GNP have varied over time, pointing up the cyclical character of the industry. In 1959, tire sales represented 1.09 percent of the GNP; in 1961, only 1.00 percent; and in 1962, 1.03 percent. The percentages were almost constant through 1967 and improved substantially in 1968. If the tire industry had grown at the same percentage rate as the GNP, the ratios in the last column would be a constant. If, on the other hand, sales were increasing faster than the GNP, the ratio would be increasing; if sales were decreasing, the ratio itself would be declining. The percentage relationship between the sales of an industry and the GNP is not as important as the trend: Is the percentage increasing, decreasing, or constant? The stability of the relationship is most important: Is it cyclical, counter-cyclical, or does it follow the trend of growth with a high degree of stability?

It is sometimes difficult to obtain industry sales figures that allow adequate comparison with the growth of the national economy. We must then use the combined sales data of the companies in the industry as we did in the case of the tire industry. We might also use the FRB Index of Industrial Production as a guide to the relative growth of an industry. The danger in this type of comparison is that the specific FRB Index might not describe the industry adequately. As a way of indicating major areas of industry growth in the economy, however, the FRB Index is a desirable tool. Figure 10–6 provides data on the output of many industries. Each index can be compared with the total output of the manufacturing industries. Structural metal parts, aircraft and other equipment, lumber and lumber products, textile goods, leather products, printing and publishing, petroleum products, food manufactures, beverages, tobacco products, coal, oil, metal mining, and stone and earth minerals have tended to grow less than the national economy. The other industries have grown at a rate equal to or greater than that of the national economy. This analysis quickly points out the product-oriented industries that are growing rapidly. We should find among these industries satisfactory securities for investment.

Investment Classification of Industries

The discussion up until this point has been about the economic classifications of industries. Economic data have been used that were obtained from readily available sources. In actual practice, investment services provide basic industry information more closely related to our needs. The investment services concentrate more on companies within the industry. Most of the services discuss the economic significance of the industry and its future outlook. If an industry appears to offer attractive future benefits, we can easily translate this into a company's common stock that will allow us to share in the industry's prosperity. We must be aware of the industry classifications used by the investment services. A great deal of valuable factual information is presented that will help us make intelligent decisions about investment securities. We must learn in detail the characteristics, problems, and practices of each industry. It is extremely important that we be informed about the present and future development and operating features of a given industry. This is vitally necessary for establishing the proper perspective in attempting to determine the future success of the industry and of a specific company within that industry. But we cannot discuss completely every industry; an outline of the industries and a brief discussion of the broader aspects of some industries must suffice.

The banking and finance industry, industrials, public utilities, and transportation represent the way in which Moody's manuals classify industries.[16] Standard & Poor's *Industry Surveys* use the index to industry classification presented in Figure 10–7. These classifications help us narrow our field of inquiry. We can analyze the effects of change in a given product without losing significance of the change in a mass of combined data.

16 *Moody's Industrial Manuals* (New York: Moody's Investors Service, 1969).

INDEX TO SURVEYS

Dates of Latest Surveys

Only Surveys with dates the same or later than those listed below
have reference value. Discard old Surveys as new ones arrive.

*Tentatively scheduled for publication during September. †The Food Processing I Survey combines the Food Products and Meats & Diary Products surveys. ★ The Retailing I Survey combines the Retail Dep't. Survey with elements of the Retail Chains.

Guide to Industries, General Subjects and Commodities

VOLUME 1 CONTAINS PAGES A 1 THROUGH L 40.   VOLUME 2 CONTAINS PAGES M 1 THROUGH U 50.

Discard Previous Index to Survey (Buff)

FIGURE 10–7 (a)

Industry classification
SOURCE Standard & Poor's *Industry
Surveys*

FIGURE 10–7 (b)

Industry classification (cont.)

321

An example of division into major groups and subgroups is found in the drug and cosmetic industry—one of the industries classified as an industrial by Moody's. Drugs, medical care, and cosmetics, as classified by Standard & Poor's,[17] consist of four basic parts. Drugs are divided into two parts, ethical pharmaceuticals and proprietary drugs; cosmetics and razors and blades are listed separately and represent the third and fourth parts. They are grouped in this way because of the basic method of distribution of these products. The insurance industry serves as another example of how an industry is identified. It is divided into two basic groups, life insurance companies and fire and casualty companies. These are all part of the banking and finance industry. It is important that these subgroups be used in making a comparative analysis, even though a knowledge of the broad classifications is also necessary. Let us look briefly at the major industry classifications.

BANKS AND FINANCE

This major segment of American industry supplies money to other segments of the economy, both private and public, to meet their long- and short-term capital needs. It also provides protection for individuals in our society and investment management for investors. Each of the components of banks and finance is discussed below.

Banking. Banking includes commercial banks and savings and loan associations. Commercial banks make loans primarily to business and depend on prosperous business conditions to support their growth. In recent years commercial banks have become "department store" banks. They now make mortgage and home-improvement loans and loans to consumers for the purchase of durable consumer goods. Banking has become more competitive, and banks now offer a wider range of services to individuals than in the past. Included in these subsidiary activities are short-term trusts, investment trusts, investment management, complete data processing and record keeping services, and management consulting and financial planning both for individuals and corporations. Banks also have increased the number and amount of term loans they extend to business. The success of a commercial bank depends, first, on its ability to attract demand and savings deposits and, second, on its ability to invest or loan the money profitably. The profitability of banking depends upon the level of interest rates and the relative success of business.

Savings and Loan Associations. Savings and loan associations, particularly through savings and loan holding companies, have expanded rapidly in the post–World War II era. Originally they made mortgage

17 Standard & Poor's *Industry Survey—Drugs, Medical Care, and Cosmetics,* May 8, 1969 (Section 2).

loans, but their lending and investing activities have broadened. Many savings and loan associations have expanded into leasing, consumer loans, and other types of loans in the housing area, including home-improvement loans. They have become much more competitive with the commercial banks, and their growth of deposits has been at a greater rate than those of commercial banks. Savings and loans are tied to the building industry and require large amounts of savings to meet the demand for loans. An adequate differential must be maintained between interest paid on savings accounts and the interest earned on loans.

Consumer Credit. Consumer credit is the mainstay of the small-loan finance industry, and it has grown twice as fast as disposable personal income. The industry expanded rapidly after World War II because of the growth of installment contracts to finance autos, home appliances, and other durable consumer goods. Continued growth is likely because of (1) projected increases in personal income, which reflect our ability to borrow; (2) population growth, with a higher proportion of younger families; (3) more emphasis on home and auto ownership; and (4) new applications of consumer credit.

Personal Loans. Personal loans have grown as fast as the general use of credit. These loans represent nonautomobile and nondurable-goods types of loans. Growth of the industry has been increasing steadily and faster than the national economy.

Insurance Companies. The insurance industry includes both life insurance and fire and casualty companies. Insurance in force has experienced a dramatic growth since World War II. Part of this growth in the life insurance industry is attributable to National Service Life Insurance, which was underwritten for members of the armed services in World War II by the United States Government. Rising personal incomes have also contributed to the growth of the life insurance industry.

Fire and casualty companies have also grown by offering a wider range of policies and attractive rates. Disability income policies and medical and accident insurance are becoming commonplace. Major medical insurance is even provided by many employers. The tendency on the part of insurance companies is to offer complete coverage to an individual in one policy, which would include auto, home, life, and accident and sickness insurance. Companies supplying one type of insurance are also tending to broaden their activities into other areas. Growth appears to be greatest for companies that sell both life and casualty insurance.

Investment Companies. There are two kinds of investment companies—closed-end or investment trusts and open-end or mutual funds. They offer the investor the opportunity to obtain diversification and management plus ease of reinvestment of dividends. Investment companies have grown substantially since the late 1940's. This growth was restrained by the dip in the stock market in 1962, but it moved back sharply with market improvement in 1963. Since then it has been phenomenal. Some mutual funds, although not all, have done exceptionally well, moving ahead of the stock market and the national economy. Many insurance companies are starting mutual funds to utilize their marketing organization and counter the competition from mutual funds and other investment companies. Investment companies will be discussed more fully under the subject of portfolio management.

INDUSTRIALS

The industrials represent a broad collection of industries in manufacturing, mining, and merchandising. The growth pattern of these industries covers all phases of the industrial growth cycle. Some of them established outstanding growth records during the late 1950's and early 1960's. Some areas of the following industries had experienced growth equal to or greater than the national economy: aerospace, amusements, drugs and cosmetics, electronics, miscellaneous (which includes the vending industry and such companies as Procter & Gamble and Minnesota Mining and Manufacturing), office equipment, publishing, and the retail trade.

Some industries have actually declined in economic importance. Coal, for example, has lost its competitive position to oil and gas. Leather and shoe production has not expanded its sales significantly. Agricultural machinery, rail equipment, and textiles and apparel have not grown as rapidly as the national economy.[18] The growth of other industries has been more or less equal to the rate of growth of the national economy.

PUBLIC UTILITIES

The telephone and electric and gas utilities industries have shown remarkable growth during the 1960's. Few industry groups have achieved the growth rates or stability of growth that these industries have experienced in the past. At the same time, their service rates have been controlled by regulatory bodies including the ICC, the FCC, and various state public utility commissions. Rate legislation and the determination of a fair return rate on a fair investment are very important to the public utility industry as a whole. In spite of a low maximum rate of return on invested capital (about 6 percent), these industries have provided very profitable investment opportunities. And the outlook appears to be favorable.

18 In spite of the declining competitive position of these industries, some companies in the various classes have been exceptionally good investments.

TRANSPORTATION INDUSTRY

The transportation industry has been undergoing a tremendous change in its competitive position. The passenger railroad industry as a whole has been unprofitable in the past decade, and some railroads are in receivership. Only a few major long-haul freight railroads offer the investor secure and stable opportunities for investment. In examining this industry, the investor must make a clear distinction between freight and passenger transportation. Some of the transportation companies, however, have maintained their competitive position.

Shipping and shipbuilding have been heavily subsidized and offer relatively unstable opportunities for investment dollars.

The air transport industry, both passenger and freight, has shown substantial growth of sales, but expenses and capital costs have increased much more rapidly than revenues. Growth potential exists for this industry, but many problems must be solved first. Air freight offers substantial profit opportunities if the industry can solve some basic problems. Some passenger airlines appear to offer attractive investment opportunities.

The trucking industry has continued to grow at a rate faster than the national economy, and this growth is likely to continue in the future. The trucking industry consists of companies that transport freight for short hauls. The growth of containerized shipping and piggyback operations should provide a further stimulus for growth in this industry and should help the railroads as well.

The hydrofoil transportation industry might now be in the pioneering stage of its life cycle. Hydrofoil commuter service was offered in New York in mid-1963 on a limited basis. This might be a partial solution to mass transportation in cities that have a network of waterways surrounding their borders.

CONGLOMERATES

A substantial increase in mergers in the United States has led to a renewed emphasis on the conglomerate form of business organization. A conglomerate company is one that has grown by adding diverse or unrelated types of companies producing unrelated products. The economic basis for conglomerates is the economy of management and the financial leverage for the parent company. Textron, based in Rhode Island, and Litton Industries, in California, are examples of successful conglomerates. Textron has brought together a wide array of companies such as Bostitch, Gorham, Bell Helicopter, Homelite, Sheaffer Pen, Speidel, Fafnir, Spencer Kellogg, and Pittsburgh Steel Foundry and Machine. These are successful component companies. Under one management, they represent a powerful source of earning power. When this earning power is connected into the higher P/E ratio (usually) of the parent company, substantial profits are obtainable. The reason for a separate classification is the difficulty of classifying a conglomerate as one industry. In spite of this difficulty of classification conglomerates should not be ignored as a way to financial success.

SIGNIFICANCE OF INDUSTRY COMMENTS

The comments made above are designed to indicate, in broad terms, the nature of an industry and its relative growth position. We must become familiar with these industries in order to wisely select companies that might become satisfactory investments. Standard & Poor's *Industry Survey* and *The Value Line Investment Survey* provide excellent factual data that will provide us with ample and accurate information about each industry. Each service uses different industry categories, but once we become familiar with these sources of information, this will not be a handicap. We should consult a basic source such as these to understand clearly the investment capabilities of an industry. *The Development of American Industries* by Professors Glover and Lagai[19] provides excellent background information that should be helpful to us in our analysis.

Future Industry Growth

The basic reason for determining the growth rate of an industry and analyzing its relationship to the GNP or the appropriate National Income Account is to aid in predicting the future growth of that industry. Economic forecasts are made in terms of GNP and NI estimates. If the sales of an industry vary directly with national income, then, barring major changes, these relationships should continue in the future. In the case of the tire industry referred to in Table 10–2, sales ranged between 1.00 and 1.09 percent of the GNP. This is expressed clearly in the line of average relationship in Chart 10–3. If we estimated that the GNP would be $1,250 billion in 1975, then sales of the six tire companies would be approximately $12.9 billion. The relationship of 1.03 percent was used to arrive at this figure. But since the growth of an industry is not constant, we might expect sales to be slightly lower than $12.9 billion. This, like all forecasts, is not a certainty, but it does provide a way of obtaining an estimate of future industry sales.

We could use per capita industry sales to estimate future sales of an industry. This would require two ingredients: (1) the trend of per capita sales, and (2) population trend analysis. Thus if per capita industry sales are about $50 and we believe that the population will be almost 240 million by 1975, then the 1975 sales estimate for the industry should be close to $12 billion.

19 John C. Glover and Rudolph L. Lagai, *The Development of American Industries*, 4th ed. (New York: Simmons-Boardman Books, 1959).

Since the investor's success is based upon future sales and profits of an industry and a specific company, he must make a reasonable estimate of future sales. Based upon this, he should select those industries that offer the greatest possibility of future sales and future earnings. This type of estimate will help the investor compare his chosen company with the industry as a whole. It will help him forecast the earnings of the company—a fundamental step in the valuation process. In the next section, we will analyze companies in an attempt to determine future earnings and to establish a realistic price to pay for these earnings. We will establish an investment decision process through company and market analysis that should lead to successful investment.

Summary

We should make an analysis of a company to estimate its future earning potential and its possibilities for investment. The correct relationship between current price and future earnings of a company is the key to investment success. It is important, however, to know something about the direction of growth of the economy. This can be measured by GNP figures, the FRB Index of Industrial Production or the lead-lag series published by the Department of Commerce as *Business Cycle Developments*. The GNP growth rate has been substantial in past years. Over the long term we can expect a growth of 3.5 percent in real terms and 5.6 percent in current dollars, which is comparable to past growth rates of GNP. The industries within the growing economy vary in their growth rates and growth characteristics. The usual growth pattern of the product-oriented industry is one of rapid growth in the early stages of the industry, with a diminution of the growth rate as the industry becomes more established. Over long periods of time the rate decreases. The growth cycle of an industry may be divided into three stages: the pioneering stage; the expansion stage or stage of investment maturity; and the stagnation stage or stage of decline, in which factors of latent obsolescence begin to destroy the competitive position of the industry. In the stagnation stage, the competitive position of the industry has deteriorated because of inter-industry and intra-industry competition and also factors that increase costs. We would be wise to invest in industries that are in a strong competitive position and in the expansion stage of their growth cycle. Within this group we will find companies that offer both growth and income. The relative growth position of the industry can be determined by comparison with the GNP, NI, or DPI. This is done using an index of industry sales or an index of sales of companies in the industry or by computing industry sales as a percentage of the GNP or another appropriate national income measure. In depicting relative growth rates of an industry, a line of average relationship is helpful.

We should be aware of the characteristics and growth rate of each industry. Several investment services provide excellent information about industries. Industries may be divided into four major groups: banks and finance, industrials, transportation, and public utilities. Each of these is broken down into industries and subindustries. Several industries have experienced outstanding growth and are likely to continue this growth in the future; a few have declined in economic importance.

It is essential that we attempt to forecast industry sales so that we may estimate future company sales and earnings. Sales can be estimated by: (1) a trend line fitted to past sales, (2) a line of average relationship between industry sales and the GNP, (3) sales as a percentage of the GNP, and (4) per capita industry sales related to population growth.

Review Questions

1. Distinguish between the Gross National Product and the Federal Reserve Board Index of Industrial Production as a measure of economic activity.
2. Explain how the FRB Index of Industrial Production is used as a measure of economic activity.
3. What has been the trend of the growth of the national economy as measured by the GNP and the FRB Index?
4. Is this growth trend likely to continue? Explain why or why not.
5. Are all sectors of the national economy growing at the same rate? Discuss.
6. How can the *Business Cycle Development* reports help us in selecting industries for investment?
7. Discuss what is meant by the term *industry*. Why is a knowledge of the industry concept so important in our analysis?
8. Explain the growth pattern established by the typical industry.
9. Why do industries tend to grow at a decreasing rate? Discuss.
10. (a) Explain the industry growth cycle thesis presented by Professor Grodinsky.
    (b) In what phase of industry growth should investment take place?
    (c) Discuss possible limits to the Grodinsky thesis.
11. (a) What are the reasons for the decline in the competitive position of an industry as it enters the stagnation stage?
    (b) What is meant by the term *latent obsolescence?*
12. Explain how we might determine the current phase of growth of an industry. Specifically, how do we determine if an industry is expanding?
13. What is the logic behind the investment classification of industry?

14. Explain what type of company would be found in the following industries:
    (a) Banks and finance   (c) Public utilities
    (b) Industrials   (d) Transportation

15. Explain how we might forecast the future growth of sales and the competitive position of a conglomerate.

16. How does an analysis of the national economy and of an industry help in the valuation process of a company?

Problems

1. Select an industry for study from among banks and finance, industrials, public utilities, and transportation. Define the industry carefully.
    (a) What has been the sales growth of the industry from 1957 to the present?
    (b) What has been the sales growth for each subindustry classification within the industry?
    (c) From the sales figures, compute an index of sales for the industry and each of its subcategories. Use 1957–59=100.
    (d) Compute an index of physical growth as well as dollar growth.
    (e) Compare these indexes to the index of the GNP, NI, or DPI where appropriate and to the FRB Index of Industrial Production.
    (f) Does the industry appear to be growing as rapidly as the national economy? What about the subindustries? Is the industry cyclical in character?

2. Compute industry sales and subindustry sales as a percentage of national income. What do the results reveal?

3. Forecast the growth of the industry and each subindustry. This can be done by several methods, including the fitting of a trend line to the data by visual inspection, the least squares method, using the line of average relationship between the GNP and industry sales, computing industry sales as a percentage of GNP, and by using per capita sales. Evidence submitted by industry experts may also be used as an indication of the expectation of future growth. Indicate methods and sources used.

4. What percentage of industry and subindustry sales are due to price changes, foreign sales, and military sales?

5. Are the industry and its subindustries in the pioneering, expansion, or stagnation phase of growth?

6. What factors account for the growth pattern of the industry and its subindustries?

7. What factors of latent obsolescence are present within the industry?

8. Based upon this analysis, which of the subindustries offers the greatest prospects for continued growth and for investment?

Sources of Investment Information

BUSINESS PERIODICAL SOURCES:

Business magazines classified by subject
Business Periodicals Index
Public Affairs Information Service

GOVERNMENT PUBLICATIONS:

Basic information sources
Catalog of United States Census Publications
Construction Review
Mineral Industry Surveys
Statistical Abstract of the United States
Survey of Current Business

INDUSTRY STATISTICS AND TRADE ASSOCIATION PERIODICALS:[20]

American Gas Association Monthly
American Machinist
American Petroleum Institute Statistical Bulletin
Automotive Industries
Baking Industry
Best's Insurance Reports
Broadcasting—Telecasting
Business Executives of America
Coal Age
Directory of National Trade Associations
Dodge Reports
Electrical Merchandising
Electrical World
Engineering and Mining Journal
Engineering News—Record
Fibre Container and Paperboard Mills
Implement and Tractor and Farm Implement News
Industrial and Engineering Chemistry
Iron Age
Leather and Shoes

NATIONAL ASSOCIATIONS OF THE UNITED STATES:

Oil and Gas Journal
Paper Trade Journal
Polk's National New Car Service
Printers' Ink
Railway Age

---

20 Many of these sources were found in Lester V. Plum, Joseph H. Humphrey, and John W. Bowyer, Jr., *Investment Analysis and Management* (Homewood, Illinois: Richard D. Irwin, Inc., 1961), Chap. 6.

Rock Products
Television Digest
Textile Organization

INVESTMENT SOURCES:

Clark-Dodge Reports
Standard & Poor's *Investment Surveys*
The Value Line Investment Survey

MAGAZINES AND OTHER PERIODICALS:

Barron's
Business Cycle Developments
Business Week
Commercial and Financial Chronicle
Federal Reserve Bulletin
Forbes Magazine
Fortune
Magazine of Wall Street
Monthly Economic Letter—The First National City Bank of N.Y.
Wall Street Journal
Wall Street Journal Index

Selected Readings

Ahern, David P., "Auto Industry," *Financial Analysts Journal* (May-June, 1968), p. 96.

Barges, A., and B. R. Hickey, "Drug Industry Profits," *Financial Analysts Journal* (May-June, 1968), p. 75.

Biggs, Barton M., "New Print-Out Horizons," *Financial Analysts Journal* (January-February, 1967), p. 75.

Brandon, Dick H., "Computer Leasing Industry," *Financial Analysts Journal* (May-June, 1968), p. 85.

Bretey, Pierre R., "Coal Industry's Expansion," *Financial Analysts Journal* (March-April, 1968), p. 61.

Burkhead, J. Gary, "Investing in the Shoe Industry," *Financial Analysts Journal* (March-April, 1968), p. 41.

Butler, Hartman L., Jr., "Aerospace Industry Revisited," *Financial Analysts Journal* (September-October, 1967), p. 57.

Conklin, G. Howard, "Evaluation of Savings and Loans," *Financial Analysts Journal* (July-August, 1967), p. 39.

Cunniff, Richard T., "The Magnetic Tape Industry," *Financial Analysts Journal* (January-February, 1967), p. 65.

Goldstein, Lawrence J., "Investment in Business Services," *Financial Analysts Journal* (July-August, 1968), p. 71.

Goodfriend, Herbert E., "Life Insurance Company Earnings," *Financial Analysts Journal* (November-December, 1966), p. 57.

Greer, Carl C., "Commercial Broadcasting Industry," *Financial Analysts Journal* (November-December, 1967), p. 51.

Gumperz, Julian, "The Therapeutic Factory" (Keynote Review), *Financial Analysts Journal* (September-October, 1966), p. 109.

Gunness, Robert C., "The Economics of Energy," *Financial Analysts Journal* (January-February, 1968), p. 47.

Hart, Orson H., "National Economic Policy," *Financial Analysts Journal* (November-December, 1967), p. 101.

Johnson, Leonard W., "The Offshore Service Industry," *Financial Analysts Journal* (March-April, 1968), p. 58.

Karo, Margherita, "The Jewelry Business," *Financial Analysts Journal* (March-April, 1968), p. 49.

———, "Cosmetics/Toiletries Industry," *Financial Analysts Journal* (September-October, 1968), p. 34.

Koeneman, John K., "Outlook for the Aerospace Industry," *Financial Analysts Journal* (September-October, 1968), p. 25.

Kopp, Bennett S., "Conglomerates in Portfolio," *Financial Analysts Journal* (March-April, 1968), p. 145.

Lempert, Leonard H., "Do the Leading Indicators Lead?" *Financial Analysts Journal* (November-December, 1967), p. 19.

Londoner, David J., "Steel Industry Profit Outlook," *Financial Analysts Journal* (July-August, 1968), p. 63.

Mackin, John J., "Machine Tool Industry," *Financial Analysts Journal* (September-October, 1968), p. 53.

Manus, Peter C., "The Inventory Syndrome," *Financial Analysts Journal* (July-August, 1967), p. 27.

Meiselman, David, "New Economics and Monetary Policy," *Financial Analysts Journal* (November-December, 1967), p. 95.

Mennis, Edmund A., "Economics and Investment Management," *Financial Analysts Journal* (November-December, 1966), p. 17.

Neidig, C. P., "World Chemical Companies," *Financial Analysts Journal* (January-February, 1968), p. 51.

O'Leary, James J., "The Economic and Investment Outlook," *Financial Analysts Journal* (January-February, 1966), p. 22.

———, "Economic Outlook for 1968," *Financial Analysts Journal* (May-June, 1968), p. 17.

Olsen, John A., and Terry A. Blaney, "The Copper Industry," *Financial Analysts Journal* (March-April, 1968), p. 36.

Salz, Frank, "Gross National Product and the Investor's Focus," *Financial Analysts Journal* (July-August, 1966), p. 28.

Sarlo, G. S., and F. A. Longley, "Current Trends in Integrated Circuits," *Financial Analysts Journal* (September-October, 1967), p. 65.

Scanlan, F. V., and C. S. Goodwin, "The Advertising Industry," *Financial Analysts Journal* (January-February, 1968), p. 71.

Schwartz, William D., "The Domestic Toy Industry," *Financial Analysts Journal* (September-October, 1968), p. 45.

Spigelman, Joseph H., "Technological Transformation of the Drug Industry," *Financial Analysts Journal* (September-October, 1966), p. 113.

Steiner, J. E., "Aircraft Evolution and Airline Growth," *Financial Analysts Journal* (March-April, 1967), p. 85.

Sullivan, Timothy J., "Significance of Population Changes on Investment Trends," *Financial Analysts Journal* (November-December, 1966), p. 25.

Ward, Frank F., "The Color Television Industry," *Financial Analysts Journal* (November-December, 1966), p. 39.

Weidenbaum, Murray L., "The Inflationary Impact of the Federal Budget," *Financial Analysts Journal* (July-August, 1966), p. 35.

Williams, William D., "Industrial Gases," *Financial Analysts Journal* (January-February, 1968), p. 66.

Yakowicz, Joseph V., "Glass & Metal Containers," *Financial Analysts Journal* (May-June, 1968), p. 92.

VI

COMPANY ANALYSIS,
YIELD, AND THE
INVESTMENT DECISION

11

COMPANY ANALYSIS AND THE COMPETITIVE POSITION OF THE COMPANY

Securities of companies in competitively strong industries should provide investment qualities capable of fulfilling the needs of most investors. Some of these securities offer growth of principal, others provide income, and still others offer a combination of both. All should offer quality to minimize the risks of investment. The purpose of this chapter is to discuss the important variables that determine whether the common stock of a company will be a satisfactory investment. We will discuss the emphasis and purpose of company analysis and attempt to establish a methodology of comparative analysis that will help us make better investment decisions. We will also began an analysis of a company by discussing its competitive position within the industry. We will then appraise a few leading companies within a strongly competitive industry as part of the analysis process.

The Valuation Process

When we are ready to invest in the common stock of a company, we must decide if the price we must pay for the expected earnings of the company's stock will provide a satisfactory rate of return. In order to determine if a price for a particular stock is reasonable, we will follow the present-value method presented in Chapter 7. The basic formula that will be used is $V = d_1/(1 + k) + d_2/(1 + k)^2 \ldots + d_5/(1 + k)_5 + P_5/(1 + k)^5$. This requires an estimate of earnings and price at some future date. We will use a five-year forecast of earnings, and future earnings will determine future dividends. Price will be determined by ex-

337

pected future earnings multiplied by a price-earnings ratio reflecting the basic risks inherent in the common stock. Risk is determined to a great extent by the amount, stability, and certainty of earnings. The greater the certainty of earnings, the lower the possible loss owing to the business risk. The greater the uncertainty and instability and the smaller the amount of earnings, the greater the business risk. This is the heart of the valuation process. Our major activity as analysts or investors is to make decisions based upon the product of these variables. The process will be demonstrated in this section and in the chapters following.

When we have estimated the amount and stability of future earnings and have established an expected market price based upon these estimates, we will be able to compute the yield from the investment. The present value of the dividend and the price, both based upon earnings, will provide a yield rate, which we will judge to be satisfactory or unsatisfactory, depending on the risks involved. If we find a company, for example, that has stable and certain earnings, is in a strong competitive position, possesses an excellent profit margin, has experienced an excellent operating rate, is in a strong current financial position, is adequately financed, has a capable and imaginative management, and provides us with a 10 percent yield, we would consider it a satisfactory investment.

Figure 11–1 depicts the valuation process. The balancing factor, the risk rate of return, will vary among individuals. Some investors would consider a return of 5 percent satisfactory, others 8 percent, and still others might require a 15 percent yield before they would invest. As the risk associated with the venture increases, the yield required

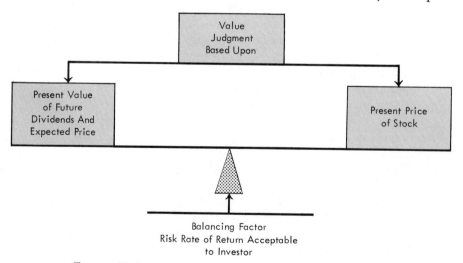

FIGURE 11–1

The valuation of common stock

would, of course, increase too. A company that provides quality but an unacceptable yield would be rejected. In any event, we must analyze each company to determine its quality of management and products, and we must attempt to predict the amount, quality, and variability of future earnings.

When we make a company analysis and attempt to determine its future earnings, their amount and certainty, there are tools and tests we can use. Much as the doctor examines his patient, we study and analyze the company and its earnings to determine its strengths and weaknesses and its investment quality. As a result of these tests, we draw conclusions about the company. By balancing price and earnings with risk yield, we either accept or reject it as an investment candidate. This is a continuing process because we must give the company frequent checkups to make certain its earnings health remains satisfactory.

Factors to Consider in Company Analysis

In order to translate the valuation process into a concrete reality and determine the present and future amount and quality of earnings, we must examine several important variables. Figure 11–2 pictures the

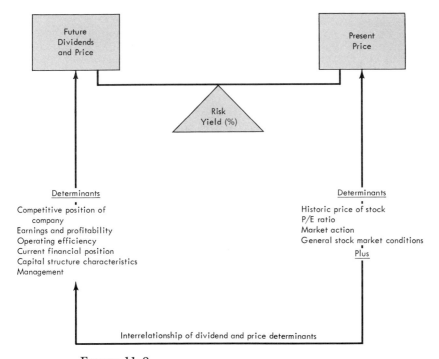

FIGURE 11–2

The major influences upon yield

transition from valuation of common stock in Figure 11–1 to the subject of company analysis. The important variables that influence future earnings of the company and hence future earnings on the common stock are presented in Figure 11–2. They are: (1) the competitive position of the company based on the record and prospects of growth; (2) company profitability; (3) the operating efficiency of the company; (4) its current financial position; (5) the capital structure characteristics; and (6) company management—perhaps the most important variable of all. Without capable management to carry out the programs of the company, future forecasts or numbers given are meaningless. (Chapter 15 will be devoted to this subject.) Each of these six factors has an influence, directly or indirectly, on future earnings. These variables must be considered whether the company is in the railroad industry, is a public utility or an industrial company, or is in the finance industry. Products and services produced in each industry are different. Operating characteristics vary, and each industry has its peculiarities and idiosyncrasies. All of these can be translated into their impact upon future earnings; therefore, we should be aware of them and understand them.

The other aspect of the analysis process has to do with an examination of influences upon the present price of the stock. Obviously, future earnings are the dominant force in price, yet expectations about earnings and the value of earnings vary among companies. Each stock has its own price history, its own price-earnings ratio, and its own market action. Each stock is also influenced by the general condition of the market. These influences are also depicted in Figure 11–2. The indicated balance between future earnings and price is an obvious oversimplification. All of these factors operate simultaneously upon each other; management, for example, works upon all the variables that influence earnings. This, of course, makes the analytical process difficult and complex. Let us now consider the variables that influence future earnings and price more closely.

The Competitive Position of the Company

The first variable that influences future earnings both in terms of quantity and quality is the competitive position of the company, or simply the company's past growth of sales, its future expected growth, and its position within the industry. We wish to know the type of product or service produced by the company and expected future demand for the product. Then we wish to translate this demand into its effect on the company. Is the company a leader in its industry, and does it have prospects for continued growth and leadership? How does the company compare in size and growth rate to its leading competitors? A company in a strong competitive position will provide greater earnings with more certainty than a company in a poor competitive position.

Company Earnings and Profitability

Generating a dollar of sales costs money before earnings result to the common stock. The expenses of operating the plant and raw materials used in the manufacturing process must be paid for before profits are achieved. Uncle Sam must also be paid, so taxes must be deducted. We use these expenses and profitability relationships to determine the future earnings of the company. We are also interested in the variability of future earnings. The higher and more stable the earnings of the company, the greater and more stable its value. Profit margins have a strong impact on future earnings. Since dividends are directly influenced by earnings, the higher the earnings and the more stable they are, the greater the dividends and also the greater the future value. A company that enjoys a high profitability rate has a management that has demonstrated its ability to control expenses and ensure earnings to the common stockholder.

Operating Efficiency

Operating efficiency is another factor in determining a company's quality and ability to earn money in the future. Operating efficiency attempts to relate real input to real output. To determine efficiency, in the majority of cases we must work through financial data. The operating efficiency of a company is measured by its operating ratio and its breakeven point. The lower the operating ratio, the higher the earnings, other things being equal. The lower the breakeven point and the higher the level of operations in relation to plant capacity, the higher the profitability of the company. Knowledge about a company's operating efficiency and ability to expand its plant provides further information about future earnings.

Current Financial Position

A company should be in good financial position to maintain its profitability and earnings for the common stockholder. The basic financial problem of the corporate business management is to maintain a balance between liquidity and profitability. Inability to meet current bills as they come due and to take advantage of discounts offered by suppliers immediately raises the possibility of failure. Too much cash or liquidity, on the other hand, does not help profits: idle funds are not productive funds. The ideal current financial position is one of balance. Current funds should be sufficient to meet the regular needs of the business, but cash should not be excessive. Several tests are available to help us decide what is an adequate cash and current financial position.

How a corporation raises funds to finance its needs and growth will have an impact upon the amount of future earnings because of its effect upon the stability of earnings. Debt financing is a low-cost source of funds for the company, providing financial leverage for the common stock. As long as the earnings of the corporation are above the cost of the borrowed funds, the earnings per share of common stock are increased. Unfortunately, the use of large amounts of debt in the capital structure tends to make earnings unstable. A large amount of debt might result in financial failure if the earnings do not materialize. Thus, a judicious amount of debt in the capital structure is desirable for the greatest amount and stability of corporate earnings.

Management

Quality and depth of management are essential to the future profitability of a business. Many analysts consider the quality of corporate management the single most important factor influencing future earnings and overall success. Without good management a company cannot maintain its competitive position or introduce new products. It cannot control costs of operation nor maintain its earnings or financial position. We must, therefore, carefully assess management's ability to direct the affairs of the company to a profitable future. We may buy a dollar of future earnings, but capable management is what will make our expectations a certainty.

Current Price of the Stock

We must analyze carefully the price we pay to make certain that it will provide us with a satisfactory investment. Whether the price is attractive depends upon the risks involved and the yield that will be received. Yield, of course, is dependent upon future expected dividends and future anticipated price. Future earnings will affect the future price of the stock; therefore, a study of price cannot be made without a study and analysis of future earnings, as we mentioned before.

Besides earnings, we must examine several other influences that might affect the price of a stock at any given moment of time. There are any number of variables; here we will consider:

1. The historic level of prices, including the price range.
2. The price-earnings ratio, and what might be a fair future ratio, as an acceptable measure of risk. We are interested in knowing what investors are paying for a dollar of earnings of a company, what they have paid in the past, and what they might be willing to pay in the future based upon these past relationships.

3. The market action of the stock. We ask, Is the price stable or unstable? Does it move with the stock market or does it move against the market?

4. The general level of the market and its future expected course.

Once we have made an analysis of the quality of the company, the quality of earnings, and the price, have calculated the yield expected, and have balanced these subjectively with the risks involved, we can determine whether the investment is satisfactory. It is wise to make a comparative analysis of several companies within the industry. Such an analysis better enables us to select a company offering a satisfactory outlet for our funds. We are always dealing in relatives—not absolutes—in analyzing a company's common stock. No one company at any given moment of time will necessarily be the best investment. Several securities might satisfy our requirements. One security in a specific industry might appear to be more attractive than another, even though it is not the only satisfactory investment for *all* industries. When we analyze a company and its common stock, we will select several of the strongly competitive, dominant companies from an industry and then attempt to select the one offering the best opportunity for investment success. We shall begin our discussion by examining the competitive position of the company within the industry and then its past and future growth characteristics. In subsequent chapters we will complete the analysis and reach a decision about which company to select.

The Competitive Position of the Company in the Industry

Major industries in the United States are composed of hundreds of individual companies. There are, for example, over 42,000 businesses in the petroleum industry, excluding service stations. The chemical industry has over 7,000 companies. In the pharmaceutical industry, over 1,100 companies manufacture medical preparations. Most are small, privately owned, and share a very small percentage of the market. The majority do not have securities outstanding, and investors are unable to share in their future. Their size alone, even if they were stock companies, would preclude them from consideration. Nor do they possess the amount, quality and stability of sales we want in a company for investment.

Within each industrial group a few firms control the major portion of the output. In the chemical industry, 175 firms account for over 90 percent of the entire output. Seven firms are dominant—du Pont, Union Carbide, Allied Chemical, Monsanto, Dow, Olin Mathieson, and American Cyanamid. In the auto industry, three companies, Chrysler, Ford, and General Motors, control over 90 percent of the passenger market in the United States. Together with American Motors, these companies virtually control the domestic automobile market. Fewer than ten companies, led by United States Steel, dominate the domestic market for steel. In the paper industry, approximately eight companies have captured the bulk of the market for paper and allied products. With the exception of banking and finance, dominance by a few firms persists in virtually all industries in the United States.

We should be interested in those companies that have reached positions of dominance. They are the largest companies in the industry and have been successful in meeting competition. They have demonstrated over time their ability to lead and have established their position by obtaining a significant share of the market for their products. They have demonstrated profit potential too, having grown because they have been profitable. Once such companies obtain a position of leadership within an industry, they seldom lose it.

Selecting the Competitively Strong Company in the Industry

The competitive position of a company within an industry can be determined by the use of several criteria: (1) the amount of annual sales, (2) the growth of annual sales, and (3) the stability of annual sales.

AMOUNT OF ANNUAL SALES

The dollar amount of annual sales helps to determine a company's relative competitive position within an industry. The greater the annual sales, the more successful the company has been in meeting competition. The relative position of the companies in an industry can be easily determined by obtaining sales figures for each, and then ranking them according to their sales.

If we had done this for the steel industry in 1962, we would have found that the four largest companies were United States Steel, Bethlehem Steel, Republic Steel, and Jones and Laughlin. In the paper industry, International Paper Company was dominant in sales, followed in order by St. Regis, Mead, Crown-Zellerbach, Scott, West Virginia Pulp and Paper, Union-Bag, and Kimberly Clark Corporation. Many more examples could be given; these few illustrate what is meant by the dominant firm.

One problem we face when we rank companies by size is to make certain that the companies are comparable. The paper industry affords an example of this. It is divided into several subindustry groups oriented around different products. When comparing the companies in an industry, we should compare them by like-product groups. We would rank the leading producers of sanitary papers together and the leading producers of corrugated board together, rather than the leading producers of paper and allied products. If we do not, our conclusions may be erroneous and may lead to poor selection of a company for investment.

Size is an excellent guide to competitive position. The leading companies of today will most likely be leaders in the future; smaller companies might not survive the competition. U.S. Steel was the leader in 1957 as it is now.

GROWTH OF SALES

In an attempt to determine the competitive position of a company, size is not the only criterion; the annual rate of growth of sales is equally, if not more, important. A company with rapidly expanding annual sales and adequate financing would be in a better position to earn money for the stockholder than one large in size but with no prospects for growth. Ideally we want both size and rapidly expanding sales in the companies in which we invest. The size of the company protects it from the vicissitudes of economic fluctuations. Growing sales give it growing profits. We want a company that is expanding. Growth is a relative concept, and the standard of growth is how one company in an industry compares with the others. Whether a company expands from within by building new plants, or from without by acquisition of existing plant capacity, is not extremely important at this point. What is important is that the company demonstrates an ability to obtain a large share of the market, leading eventually to greater profits.

How do we decide when a company is growing more rapidly than other companies in the industry? We usually compare its sales growth with that of the industry, in terms of both dollars and physical units. Not only do we desire our company to grow in dollar terms, we also want a significant growth in real terms—in goods and services produced. We can compare the growth of a single company with the growth of the national economy: GNP, NI, and DPI can be compared with the dollar sales of the leading company in the industry. We would make certain that the national income indicator is appropriate. A comparison with disposable personal income, for example, would be a good measure of growth in the retailing industry. The Gross National Product would be excellent for comparison with the industrial construction industry. The FRB indexes would be appropriate for comparing growth in real terms.

For our comparisons we should establish a base period for sales. If we convert data to an index number using 1957–1959 equivalent to 100, we will readily see how the company has grown in real and dollar terms compared with the industry and the national economy. We are also interested in annual growth rate. We would like a company that is growing at a rate faster than the industry in which it competes. In doing so, it will increase its share of the market over time and will be competitively stronger than the other companies. We can compute a company's sales as a percentage of industry sales. If a company is getting a larger share of the market—General Motors was a good example of this in early 1968—we know it is doing better competitively. However, if we have a very rapidly expanding industry, we might find a company growing less rapidly than the industry but becoming larger and larger in importance within the industry. It is still profitable and still expanding, but not as fast as the industry.

The reason for comparing growth in dollar and in physical terms is to determine the degree of inflation. We want a company that is expanding in units produced and in dollars of income received, and we would like this growth in constant prices without inflation. A rapid price change can materialize if there is a sharp increase or decrease in demand. The electronics industry illustrates what can happen when competitive forces reduce prices. We therefore want to know the relative growth rate of our company in real and in dollar terms, to determine if there is growth and stability of prices.

An example of the process of determining rate of growth of companies in a hypothetical industry is presented in Table 11–1. Here the two leading companies in the industry are compared with the growth of the hypothetical industry and the national economy. In actual practice the number of companies dominating an industry will vary from a few to as many as twenty. There are eight leading companies in the steel industry and approximately twenty in the drug industry. We should determine the growth rates for all leading companies in the industry to be aware of those in a dominant position that possess more of the attributes of growth.

An examination of the data in Table 11–1 reveals that the industry is increasing its share of NI and that sales per capita, another measure of market penetration and competitive position, are increasing. We also find that Company #1 is growing faster than Company #2 and the industry in dollar and physical sales. It also had a bigger share of the market, which increased over time.

COMPANIES WITH DIVERSIFIED SALES

Our hypothetical companies produce only a single product. Production records indicate how many units of the product are produced each year. In reality most companies produce many different items within a product classification, and some produce many unrelated goods. Procter & Gamble is a soap company but also produces packaged cake mixes and toothpaste. General Motors is the leading producer of passenger automobiles and trucks, and also a leading producer of refrigerators and diesel locomotives. Coca-Cola leads in production of carbonated beverages, yet it has a big stake in the frozen foods industry through its Minute Maid division. Companies that produce in more than one industry must be examined in such a way that we know the percentage of sales contributed by each division.

TABLE 11-1

Sales of two companies in a hypothetical industry compared with industry sales and national income (1957–1959 = 100)

Year	Index of National Income	Index of Industry Sales	FRB Index of Industry Production	FRB Index of Total Industrial Production	Industry Sales as a % of National Income	Industry Sales Per Capita ($)	Index of Dollar Sales of Company		Index of Physical Sales of Company		Company Sales as a Percent of Industry Sales	
							Company No. 1	Company No. 2	Company No. 1	Company No. 2	Company No. 1	Company No. 2
1963	127.2	147.2	138.0	125.1	.042	110	158.2	140.3	158.0	133.0	13.0	5.0
1962	121.0	137.3	133.0	118.3	.040	109	145.6	131.6	144.0	130.0	12.5	4.8
1961	113.1	129.4	128.6	109.8	.039	108	132.4	123.1	132.0	127.0	12.3	4.8
1960	109.8	118.9	115.0	108.7	.038	107	121.2	117.4	117.0	114.0	12.1	4.9
1959	105.8	109.4	106.0	105.6	.038	107	109.7	108.2	107.0	105.0	11.2	5.1
1958	97.2	105.2	101.0	93.7	.036	104	106.1	104.1	103.0	101.0	10.3	5.0
1957	97.0	98.1	98.7	100.7	.035	102	99.3	99.1	100.0	99.0	10.2	4.9

Let us assume that Company #1 diversifies its productive activities by acquiring a drug company and a chemical company. In the first year after acquisition, we find that 38 percent of its sales are in drugs, 22 percent in chemicals, and 40 percent in food. The company is still predominantly a producer of food, but now 60 percent of its sales are contributed by other products in other industries. It is necessary then to examine the growth characteristics of the company in all its classes. We must no longer consider it a food company, but a food-drug-chemical company. This will prevent the false assumption that the company is in only one industry. We must examine competitive position in all phases of the company's activities, if possible.

An example will suggest the problems involved. Once W. R. Grace & Co. was considered solely a steamship company. Today 86 percent of its sales are in chemicals—basically, agricultural chemicals—and the remaining portion is generated from other activities such as its bank ownership and its oil ventures in Libya, to mention only two. If we did not examine W. R. Grace in all of its activities, we might not realize the changes that have taken place in its competitive position. We might not consider the company in its proper industry class and might misunderstand its investment significance. Today W. R. Grace should be considered a chemical company rather than a steamship line.

One additional problem of comparison should be mentioned. Often a company is producing so many different products that it is difficult to classify it according to a major product group.[1] This is particularly true of conglomerates such as Bangor Punta, Litton, and Textron. Thus it is difficult to compare each segment to obtain a relative growth comparison. We cannot in some cases, for competitive reasons, obtain a breakdown of sales for the company. Then the only recourse we have is to examine the overall sales figures for the company without the benefit of an industry comparison or to make an assumption as to what the primary activity of the company is and compare it with the comparable industry. If no industry is discernible, the growth of sales can be compared to national income or Gross National Product. This will provide a standard of comparison to determine the relative growth position of the company in the national economy.

STABILITY OF SALES

The stability of sales is important in addition to the amount and rate of growth of sales. A firm with stable sales revenues, other things being equal, will have more stable earnings. A wide variation in sales will not allow for the advantages of financial planning, expansion,

---

1 Accountants recognize the problem of accounting for firms with diversified operations. Schachner suggests that assets and earnings be broken down by product line for easier analysis and understanding. Leopold Schachner, "Corporate Diversification and Financial Reporting," *The Journal of Accountancy*, April, 1967.

plant utilization, or dividends to stockholders. The degree of stability of aggregate sales of various industries may be noted in Figure 11–3. Company sales should follow the pattern of the industry. The revenues of all industries in Figure 11–3 have been stable upward and have ranged from modest to rapid growth except for railroads. Revenues of industries that provide a basic service of necessity goods tend to be more stable than those of other industries. Industries offering capital goods or high-cost durable consumer goods tend to have less stable revenues. Ideally we would desire growth and stability of sales in companies in which we might invest our funds. Large companies usually offer safety along with the possibility for future growth.

A Forecast of Sales

The above analysis assumes that a company that has been in a strong competitive position in the past and has demonstrated a superior rate of growth in sales both in dollars and physical units should continue this pattern in the future. There is no certainty in this assumption. We must, therefore, make the best forecast we can about future sales. Five methods can be used to forecast company sales. First, we can fit a trend line to past sales, either visually or mathematically, by using the least squares method.[2] Second, we might relate company sales to industry sales by percent or by a line of average relationship. Third, we might relate company sales to population growth. This would require an estimate of sales per capita. Fourth, we might analyze demand for the products of the company by analyzing the types of customers. In this case, we would consider military and nonmilitary demand, commercial, industrial, and consumer demand, and foreign and domestic sales; and we would need to identify the product as either a luxury or a necessity, durable or non-durable, high- or low-priced, and then assess the impact these factors would have on demand for the product. Fifth, we can use estimates of sales provided by company economists, investment analysts, and management.

Since these estimates vary in their reliability, we must use them only as an approximation of the future. Where no estimates for the company exist, we might assume that its growth will parallel the growth of the industry. Hence, if it is anticipated that the industry will double its sales within the next decade, then we can assume that the company under consideration also will. We might compare our growth of sales with the growth of the national economy, using past national economy–industry relationships to estimate the future. This is the real reason for developing these relationships. If we assume that the national economy is going to expand by $100 billion in the next decade, then an industry

---

2 The reader might review Frederick E. Coxton, Dudley J. Cowden, and Sidney Klein, *Applied General Statistics*, 3rd ed. (Englewood Cliffs, N.J.: Prentice-Hall, Inc., 1967), Chap. 15, "Analysis of Time Series," particularly pp. 399–411, or a later edition of this text or other texts on statistics.

Industry	1964	1965	1966	1967	1968	1967 I	1967 II	1967 III	1967 IV	1968[1] I	1968[1] II	1968[1] III	1968[1] IV
Manufacturing													
Total (177 corps.):													
Sales........................	158,253	177,237	177,738	201,399	225,027	48,585	51,679	48,317	52,818	53,781	57,767	53,760	59,719
Profits before taxes...........	18,734	22,046	23,487	20,898	25,492	5,153	5,608	4,232	5,867	6,045	6,938	5,526	6,982
Profits after taxes............	10,462	12,461	13,307	12,664	13,754	2,918	3,190	2,268	3,268	3,312	3,624	2,975	3,842
Dividends....................	5,933	6,527	6,920	6,989	7,196	1,670	1,701	1,721	1,897	1,712	1,719	1,731	2,034
Nondurable goods industries (78 corps.):[2]													
Sales........................	59,770	64,897	73,643	77,969	84,598	18,743	19,535	19,695	19,996	20,304	21,060	21,325	21,910
Profits before taxes...........	6,881	7,846	9,181	9,039	9,982	2,153	2,250	2,209	2,427	2,447	2,553	2,490	2,492
Profits after taxes............	4,121	4,786	5,473	5,379	5,765	1,319	1,323	1,313	1,431	1,442	1,426	1,416	1,481
Dividends....................	2,408	2,527	2,729	3,027	3,050	720	756	770	781	743	742	752	812
Durable goods industries (99 corps.):[3]													
Sales........................	98,482	112,341	122,094	123,429	140,429	29,842	32,144	28,622	32,821	33,477	36,707	32,435	37,809
Profits before taxes...........	11,853	14,200	14,307	11,822	15,510	3,000	3,358	2,024	3,440	3,598	4,386	3,036	4,490
Profits after taxes............	6,341	7,675	7,834	6,352	7,989	1,599	1,847	1,068	1,838	1,871	2,198	1,559	2,361
Dividends....................	3,525	4,000	4,191	3,964	4,146	950	945	952	1,117	968	977	979	1,222
Selected industries:													
Foods and kindred products (25 corps.):													
Sales........................	15,284	16,427	19,038	20,134	22,109	4,963	5,060	5,131	4,980	5,184	5,389	5,737	5,799
Profits before taxes...........	1,579	1,710	1,916	1,967	2,227	447	482	526	512	498	563	590	576
Profits after taxes............	802	896	1,008	1,041	1,093	236	253	284	268	255	260	285	293
Dividends....................	481	509	564	583	590	148	144	146	145	150	146	146	147
Chemical and allied products (20 corps.):													
Sales........................	16,469	18,158	20,007	20,561	22,808	4,998	5,163	5,117	5,284	5,436	5,697	5,782	5,893
Profits before taxes...........	2,597	2,891	3,073	2,731	3,117	694	700	636	701	760	807	806	744
Profits after taxes............	1,400	1,630	1,737	1,579	1,618	396	404	363	416	390	419	412	398
Dividends....................	924	926	948	960	1,002	238	235	235	252	236	236	243	287
Petroleum refining (16 corps.):													
Sales........................	16,589	17,828	20,887	23,258	23,955	5,390	5,808	5,985	6,075	6,038	6,048	5,874	5,995
Profits before taxes...........	1,560	1,962	2,681	3,004	2,983	684	741	744	835	827	753	685	717
Profits after taxes............	1,309	1,541	1,898	2,038	2,173	505	504	504	540	606	534	506	527
Dividends....................	672	737	817	1,079	1,036	232	280	286	281	253	255	258	271
Primary metals and products (34 corps.):													
Sales........................	24,195	26,548	28,558	26,532	29,721	6,801	7,040	6,525	6,166	7,150	8,427	7,461	6,683
Profits before taxes...........	2,556	2,931	3,277	2,487	2,921	693	670	477	647	669	915	601	735
Profits after taxes............	1,475	1,689	1,903	1,506	1,750	395	411	290	410	376	550	343	482
Dividends....................	763	818	924	892	924	222	214	228	228	224	230	233	237
Machinery (24 corps.):													
Sales........................	22,558	25,364	29,512	32,721	35,660	7,704	7,933	8,994	8,994	8,371	8,864	8,907	9,517
Profits before taxes...........	2,704	3,107	3,612	3,482	4,134	868	807	837	970	936	1,008	1,112	1,079
Profits after taxes............	1,372	1,626	1,875	1,789	2,014	421	417	438	513	448	499	537	531
Dividends....................	673	774	912	921	976	232	233	227	229	243	244	244	245
Automobiles and equipment (14 corps.):													
Sales........................	35,338	42,712	43,641	42,306	50,526	10,413	11,785	8,354	11,664	12,343	13,545	9,872	14,767
Profits before taxes...........	4,989	6,253	5,274	3,906	5,916	1,050	1,436	216	1,204	1,507	1,851	640	1,918
Profits after taxes............	2,626	3,294	2,877	1,999	2,903	583	782	62	572	783	847	330	943
Dividends....................	1,629	1,890	1,775	1,567	1,642	363	365	362	477	364	364	364	550
Public utility													
Railroad:													
Operating revenue...........	9,778	10,208	10,654	10,366	10,854	2,536	2,628	2,529	2,673	2,610	2,757	2,707	2,781
Profits before taxes...........	829	980	1,088	391	632	145	163	83	1	125	205	115	186
Profits after taxes............	694	816	902	325	566	121	143	78	−17	110	174	108	174
Dividends....................	438	468	496	539	517	124	156	103	155	116	136	98	166
Electric power:													
Operating revenue...........	15,156	15,816	16,959	17,954	19,421	4,709	4,291	4,417	4,537	5,106	4,553	4,869	4,892
Profits before taxes...........	3,926	4,213	4,414	4,547	4,789	1,278	1,026	1,155	1,088	1,351	1,040	1,271	1,125
Profits after taxes............	2,375	2,586	2,749	2,908	3,002	798	665	717	728	863	641	764	733
Dividends....................	1,682	1,838	1,938	2,066	2,201	516	508	513	529	539	555	543	565
Telephone:													
Operating revenue...........	10,550	11,320	12,420	13,311	14,430	3,229	3,312	3,341	3,429	3,486	3,544	3,629	3,771
Profits before taxes...........	3,069	3,185	3,537	3,694	3,951	869	923	953	949	971	989	990	1,001
Profits after taxes............	1,590	1,718	1,903	1,997	1,961	472	498	515	513	525	441	493	502
Dividends....................	1,065	1,153	1,248	1,363	1,428	334	337	341	351	351	318	396	363

[1] Manufacturing profits after taxes are partly estimated to reflect a 10 per cent surcharge each quarter.
[2] Includes 17 corporations in groups not shown separately.
[3] Includes 27 corporations in groups not shown separately.

NOTE.—*Manufacturing corporations:* Data are obtained primarily from published reports of companies.
Railroads: Interstate Commerce Commission data for Class I line-haul railroads.
Electric power: Federal Power Commission data for Class A and B electric utilities, except that quarterly figures on operating revenue and

profits before taxes are partly estimated by the Federal Reserve to include affiliated nonelectric operations.
Telephone: Data obtained from Federal Communications Commission on revenues and profits for telephone operations of the Bell System Consolidated (including the 20 operating subsidiaries and the Long Lines and General Depts. of American Telephone and Telegraph Co.) and for 2 affiliated telephone companies. Dividends are for the 20 operating subsidiaries and the 2 affiliates.
All series: Profits before taxes are income after all charges and before Federal income taxes and dividends.
Back data available from the Division of Research and Statistics.

FIGURE 11–3

Sales, profits, and dividends of large corporations (in millions of dollars)

SOURCE *Federal Reserve Bulletin,* July, 1969, p. A46

that obtains 0.6 percent of the GNP will increase its sales by $600 million in the next decade. A company that generates 10 percent of industry sales will, assuming its competitive position remains unchanged, share 10 percent of the growth of industry sales; thus, its sales in the example will increase by $60 million. Continuing our hypothetical case, if the industry's sales were at the $500 million level, then the company would be likely to have a 12 percent increase in sales in the next decade. We could arrive at a similar estimate by fitting a trend line to past sales and projecting them into the future. Here we would have to recognize that companies do not grow at a constant rate but that their growth rates tend to diminish.

We need not use all of these methods; each will serve to provide the necessary forecast. But all estimates of future growth of a company must be constantly revised. Its competitive position can deteriorate. We must periodically reappraise and be informed about the sales position of the company in which we have invested. We must learn to anticipate changes in demand for its products and services. These are not simple tasks and judgment must be carefully exercised.

Selecting the Competitive Firm—A Summary

In summary, there are several rules we may use as a guide to selecting the best company for investment. First, we want a company that is dominant in the industry—one that is a leader, that has obtained a position of dominance, that is not likely to lose its position. We want a company that offers size, stability, and growth of sales. Second, we want a company that is growing as fast or faster than its competitors, a company that has demonstrated its growth over time. Other things being equal, we will select the company that offers the greatest growth potential. Third, we desire a company that has been competitive in all areas of its productive activity. A company that has a diversified specialty is perhaps better than one producing a large group of unrelated products. Fourth, we want a company that has good prospects for continued growth. Past growth suggests growth in the future, but we must constantly appraise the company to make certain it is succeeding. At this point we make certain tentative decisions based on the competitive position of the company. This type of analysis allows us to narrow our field of inquiry to only the leading companies in an industry.

Selecting the Leading Competitive Companies in the Industry—An Actual Case in the Drug Industry

We will begin the company analysis by examining the leading competitive companies in the drug industry. The drug industry case will be continued in each of the chapters following until it is completed and we have arrived at an investment decision. We will eventually decide to buy or not to buy one or all of three leading companies in the industry. If we do not buy, we still might select the "best" company, and then try to buy it eventually at the right price.

The Drug Industry[3]

The drug or pharmaceutical industry has shown dramatic growth over the past two decades. It is highly competitive and depends upon research and a high degree of technical and scientific knowledge for its existence. There were over 1,100 companies in the industry in 1954; today there are probably close to 1,300, mostly manufacturers. The leading companies in the industry account for approximately 60 percent of the business.

Outside of cosmetics and razors the industry is divided into two main groups, ethical drugs and proprietary drugs. Ethical drugs are sold only by prescription, and advertising is directed toward the medical profession. Probably the most familiar ethical drugs are penicillin and other antibiotics such as Aureomycin, Terramycin, bicillin, tetracycline, and polycy. In addition, we would include hormones, prescription vitamins, hematinics, biologicals, cancer drugs, cardiovascular drugs, and polio vaccines.

Proprietary drugs are sold without prescription, mainly in drug stores. Advertising is directed to the consumer. The familiar proprietary drugs are vitamins, cold remedies, analgesics, laxatives, and cathartics. We know proprietary drugs by their popular names, such as Anacin, Bufferin, Pepto-Bismol, Rem, and Hadacol.

Cosmetic companies are usually considered part of the drug industry. They do not fall into the category of ethical and proprietary drugs and are analyzed separately. Some cosmetic companies do produce proprietary medicines. Chesebrough-Pond's is a good example; it produces Vaseline and Pertussin, as well as Pond's Cold Cream and Prince Matchabelli and Simonetta perfumes.

Two other branches of the drug industry are razors and razor blades and a miscellaneous category that includes distributors and drug chains, such as Johnson & Johnson, McKesson and Robbins, and Rexall Drugs. Leaders in the blade and razor field are Eversharp and Gillette. These two classifications round out what we refer to in the broad sense as the drug and cosmetic industry. If we wish to make a study of the relative growth of a cosmetic or razor blade company, we would do best to compare it directly with companies in the same category rather than with the broad category of drugs and cosmetics. Here we will examine only the ethical and proprietary drug groups.

3 Much of the data presented were obtained from Standard & Poor's *Industry Surveys—Drugs and Cosmetics*, May 2, 1968, and John G. Glover and Rudolph L. Lagai, *The Development of American Industries*, 4th ed. (New York: Simmons-Boardman Books, 1959).

The growth of sales in the ethical and proprietary drug industry has been excellent since 1957. Total sales were $3.4 billion in 1957 and $8.1 billion in 1967. By 1970, they may increase to approximately $10.9 billion, and if the trend continues, to $17.7 billion in 1975. See Chart 11–1 for the projected growth of the drug industry.

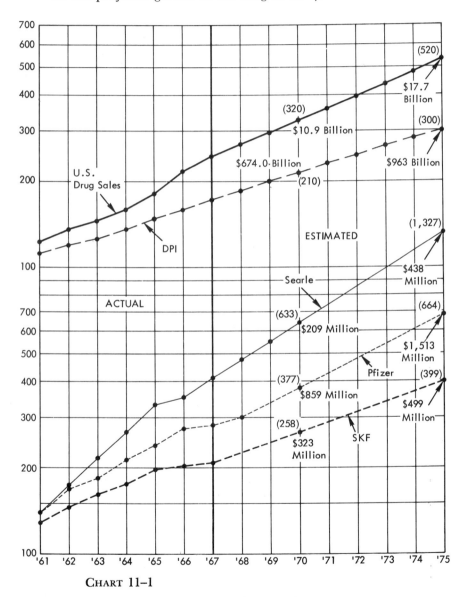

CHART 11–1

Projection of drug industry sales, DPI, and sales of Pfizer, Smith Kline & French, and G. D. Searle, based on index of sales (1957–1959 = 100)

The industry has grown faster than disposable personal income. Total industry sales continually increased between 1957 and 1967, and the industry increased its share of DPI from 1.03 percent in 1957 to 1.51 percent in 1967. Industry growth in real terms was greater than that of all manufacturing companies.

TABLE 11–2

Index and annual growth role of sales in drug industry[a] compared with disposable personal income (DPI) (1957–1959 = 100)

YEAR	DPI		U.S. Drug Industry Sales		ANNUAL % INCOME	DOLLAR SALES OF DRUG INDUSTRY AS A PERCENT OF DPI
	$ BILLION	INDEX	$ BILLION	INDEX		
1967	548	170	8.1	240	12.2	1.51
1966	509	158	7.3	214	16.9	1.43
1965	472	147	6.2	183	15.1	1.31
1964	438	136	5.4	159	10.4	1.23
1963	405	125	4.9	144	6.7	1.21
1962	383	119	4.5	135	8.9	1.17
1961	364	113	4.2	124	7.8	1.15
1960	349	109	3.9	115	5.5	1.12
1959	337	105	3.7	109	9.0	1.10
1958	318	99	3.4	100	6.3	1.07
1957	309	96	3.2	94		1.03
1957–59 average	321		3.4		10.6[b]	

[a] Federal Trade Commission–Securities and Exchange Commission data includes all domestic drug sales, all consolidated sales of foreign subsidiaries, all exports, and all sales of new drug stores. In 1967, ethical products represented 63% of total, and proprietary 27%.
[b] Ten-year average of annual growth rates.
SOURCE: Standard & Poor's *Industry Survey—Drugs, Cosmetics*, May 2, 1968, p. 22.

The Leading Companies in the Drug Industry

The leading companies in the ethical and proprietary drug industry are presented in Table 11–3, ranked according to their 1967 sales. American Home actually is in both industries. Many ethical companies have branched out into proprietary medicines, and the proprietary companies have moved into the ethical drug field. Little change occurred in the relative position of the companies in the ethical drug industry between 1957 and 1967. Eli Lilly, however, moved from third place in 1957 to second in 1967. More changes took place in the proprietary drug industry. Sterling Drug moved from first to fourth. Warner-Lambert moved from second to third place. Mead Johnson moved down to number seven position in 1967, Miles Laboratories moved up a notch into fifth place, and American Home Products was first.

TABLE 11-3

The leading ethical and proprietary drug companies ranked by 1967 sales in order of size (sales in millions of dollars and index 1957–59 = 100)

ETHICAL DRUG COMPANIES	1967 SALES	INDEX	RANK BY SIZE	RANK BY GROWTH RATE
Chas. Pfizer & Co.	637.8	280	1	4
Eli Lilly & Co.	408.4	216	2	8
Merck & Co.	337.5	260	3	5
Smith Kline, & French	259.9	208	4	9
Abbott Labs	220.6	260	5	5
Upjohn Co.	202.1	190	6	11
U.S. Vitamin	194.3	254	7	7
Parke-Davis Co.	176.4	136	8	12
G.D. Searle & Co.	132.7	402	9	2
Schering Corp.	112.8	191	10	10
Baxter Labs	75.5	403	11	3
Cutter Labs	36.8	256	12	6
Syntex	17.0	917	13	1
PROPRIETARY DRUG COMPANIES				
American Home Products	1055.0	259	1	5
Bristol-Myers Co.	730.1	792	2	1
Warner-Lambert	482.7	374	3	2
Sterling Drugs	33.2	228	4	8
Miles Laboratories	146.4	310	5	4
Richardson-Menill	142.5	254	6	6
Mead Johnson & Co.	131.1	231	7	7
Plough, Inc.	61.5	337	8	3
Norwich Pharmacal	56.1	310	9	4

SOURCE: Standard & Poor's *Industry Survey—Drugs, Cosmetics*, May 2, 1968, pp. D 6 and D 22.

Three Leading Companies in the Ethical Drug Industry

Three of the companies presented in Table 11-3 will be analyzed, with competitive position of the company, size, and growth rate serving as criteria. If we selected the top five companies based upon size alone, we would pick Pfizer, Lilly, Merck, Smith Kline & French, and Abbott. If we based our selection upon growth rate, we would select Syntex, Searle, Baxter, Pfizer, and Merck. A combination analysis would suggest that we focus on Pfizer and Merck only because they have the best combination of size and growth. If you are a conservative investor, you will stick to this combination of qualitative factors. If you are aggressive, you would select Syntex and Searle because of their aggressive growth rate. In actual practice I would examine Syntex and Searle and then Pfizer and Merck. In the first edition of this book, Pfizer, Searle, and Smith Kline & French were used for analysis. We will use them again to draw some comparison of past analysis and to reexamine how we have done. They are among the top companies in the ethical drug industry. *The Value Line Investment Survey* provides concise and comprehensive data for these companies. An example is shown in Figure 11–4. Their growth of sales is seen in Table 11–4 and in Chart 11–I.

CHAS. PFIZER & CO.

Chas. Pfizer manufactures and markets a full line of packaged pharmaceuticals. It is the largest company in the ethical drug industry and has a strong position in antibiotics. It produces penicillin, synthetic penicillin, streptomycin, oleandomycin, tranquilizers, biologicals, antihistamines, veterinary drugs, and Terramycin. The company has a strong marketing organization. Its foreign sales are expanding and account for almost half its total sales. It has been licensed to produce Sabin oral polio vaccine and has introduced a dietary food called Limmits.

G. D. SEARLE

G. D. Searle & Co. manufactures drug specialty items primarily for use in degenerative ailments. Enovid, Searle's major product, was the first oral contraceptive approved by the Food and Drug Administration. Searle also has Banthine for peptic ulcers, Dramamine for motion sickness, Momidine for morning sickness, Nilevar for body tissue, Aldactone, a diuretic, and Lomotil for diarrhea. These products, with Enovid, account for the major share of sales.

SMITH KLINE & FRENCH

Smith Kline & French Laboratories manufactures ethical drugs for the treatment of mental illnesses. Thorazine, Compazine, and Stelazine are its best-known tranquilizers. Tranquilizers and nervous system stimulants provide approximately 50 percent of sales. It has moved into the veterinary drug and steroid fields, antihistamines, analgesics, and synthetic hormones to avoid overspecialization and to expand sales.

Searle and Pfizer have the best indicated growth rate. Searle has demonstrated an excellent annual average growth of 16 percent. Pfizer follows with an annual growth rate of 12 percent and, as indicated before, Smith Kline & French (SKF) ends up in third place with a growth rate of 8.5 percent, which is better than the national economy. If past rates of growth are an indication of the future, and they are, then Searle and Pfizer have excellent future prospects. SKF was among the top three contenders for investment in 1963, based upon 1957 to 1963 data. It remains one of the top ten companies but has slipped in its growth rating. Of course, this change must be carefully watched.

A Tentative Decision

The data that have been presented now allow us to make a tentative decision about our investment choice. We have learned that the drug industry is growing faster than the national economy. The dominant

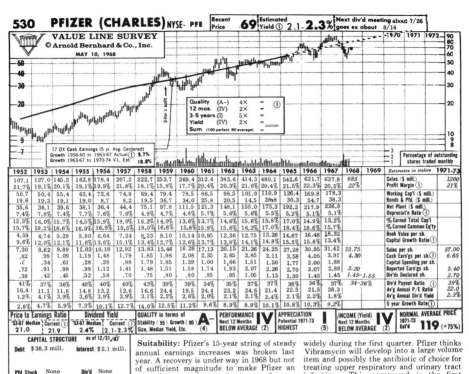

530 PFIZER (CHARLES) NYSE- PFE | Recent Price **69** | Estimated Yield ① 2.1-**2.3%** | Next div'd meeting about 7/26 goes ex about 8/14

VALUE LINE SURVEY
© Arnold Bernhard & Co., Inc.
MAY 10, 1968

Quality (A-) 4× =
12 mos. (IV) 2× = ①
3-5 years (I) 5× =
Yield (IV) 2× =
Sum (100 perfect, 60 average)

17.0X Cash Earnings (5 yr. Avg. Centered)
Growth 1956-60 to 1963-67 Actual ① 9.7%
Growth 1963-67 to 1970-74 V.L. Est. 10.0%

Percentage of outstanding shares traded monthly

	1952	1953	1954	1955	1956	1957	1958	1959	1960	1961	1962	1963	1964	1965	1966	1967	1968	1969		1971-73
	107.1	127.0	145.2	163.8	178.4	207.2	222.7	253.7	269.4	312.4	383.6	414.3	480.1	542.6	621.7	637.8	685		Sales ($ mill.)	1200
	21.7%	19.1%	20.1%	19.1%	19.9%	21.8%	18.1%	15.8%	17.7%	20.4%	20.3%	21.6%	20.4%	21.5%	22.3%	20.5%	22%		Profit Margin ①	21%
	50.7	50.4	55.4	63.4	72.6	74.9	69.4	79.4	78.5	86.5	98.5	101.0	110.9	126.4	169.8	178.3			Working Cap'l ($ mill.)	
	19.6	19.3	19.1	19.0	8.7	8.2	19.5	36.7	34.0	25.8	20.5	14.5	28×8	30.3	54.7	38.3			Bonds & Pfd. ($ mill.)	
	35.6	36.1	39.6	38.1	36.4	44.4	75.1	97.8	111.5	121.3	148.1	155.0	175.3	192.2	217.9	226.8			Net Plant ($ mill.)	
	7.4%	7.8%	7.4%	7.7%	7.6%	7.6%	4.9%	4.7%	4.8%	5.7%	5.6%	5.5%	5.5%	5.2%	5.1%	5.1%			Depreciat'n Rate ①	
	12.3%	16.0%	15.7%	14.5%	15.9%	18.0%	16.2%	14.0%	13.6%	13.7%	14.6%	15.6%	15.8%	17.0%	14.9%	13.2%			% Earned Total Cap'l	
	15.7%	19.2%	18.6%	16.9%	16.9%	19.5%	18.0%	16.6%	15.6%	15.6%	15.6%	16.2%	17.0%	18.4%	18.6%	15.7%			% Earned Common Eq'ty	
	4.59	4.74	5.28	5.80	6.64	7.24	8.23	9.10	10.14	10.95	12.36	12.75	13.26	14.67	16.48	18.32			Book Value per sh.	
	9.6%	12.0%	12.1%	11.6%	13.6%	13.5%	14.0%	12.7%	12.0%	13.7%	13.8%	14.1%	14.8%	15.5%	15.8%	13.4%			Capital Growth Ratio ①	
	7.30	8.62	9.89	11.03	10.18	12.92	13.83	15.46	16.28	17.13	20.15	21.26	24.25	27.28	30.95	31.42	33.75		Sales per sh.	57.00
	.82	.99	1.09	1.19	1.48	1.79	1.85	1.96	2.08	2.35	2.65	2.85	3.11	3.58	4.05	3.91	4.30		Cash Earn'gs per sh.①	6.85
	.C	.34	.61	.28	.28	.88	1.79	1.85	1.39	1.00	1.66	1.51	1.50	1.77	2.00	1.88			Capital Spending per sh.	
	.72	.91	.98	.98	1.12	1.41	1.48	1.51	1.58	1.74	1.93	2.07	2.26	2.70	3.07	2.88	3.20		Reported Earn'gs sh.	5.40
	.38	.42	.45	.52	.58	.70	.75	.80	.80	.85	.95	1.05	1.15	1.30	1.45	1.45	1.45-1.55		Div'ds Declared sh.	2.70
	41%	37%	36%	40%	40%	40%	43%	39%	39%	34%	35%	37%	37%	36%	36%	37%	34-36%		Div'd Payout Ratio ①	39%
	16.4	11.1	11.8	14.8	13.2	12.6	16.6	24.4	19.5	24.4	23.2	24.6	21.4	22.5	21.5	28.3			Av'g Annual P/E Ratio	22.0
	3.2%	4.1%	3.9%	3.6%	3.9%	3.9%	3.1%	2.2%	2.4%	2.0%	2.1%	2.1%	2.4%	2.1%	2.2%	1.8%			Av'g Annual Div'd Yield	2.3%
	2.8%	4.7%	5.9%	7.3%	10.1%	12.7%	14.0%	12.5%	11.2%	9.6%	8.9%	8.9%	10.1%	10.8%	10.3%	9.2%			5 year Growth Rate①	

Price to Earnings Ratio		Dividend Yield		QUALITY in terms of	PERFORMANCE	APPRECIATION	INCOME (Yield)	NORMAL AVERAGE PRICE
'53-67 Median	Current ①	'53-67 Median	Current ①	Stability (55) Growth (80) **A-**	Next 12 Months **IV**	Potential 1971-73 **I**	Next 12 Months **IV**	1971-73 Est'd **119** (+75%)
21.0	21.9	2.4%	2.1-2.3%	Size, Median Yield, Etc. (4)	BELOW AVERAGE (2)	HIGHEST (5)	BELOW AVERAGE (2)	

CAPITAL STRUCTURE as of 12/31/67

Debt $38.3 mill.   Interest $2.1 mill.

Pfd Stock None   Div'd None

Common Stock 20,298,123 shares

Cal-endar	QUARTERLY SALES ($ Millions)				Full Year
	Mar. 31	June 30	Sept. 30	Dec. 31	
1963	105.2	102.5	97.3	109.3	414.3
1964	114.3	117.5	112.0	136.3	480.1
1965	132.3	131.0	127.0	152.3	542.6
1966	148.8	153.6	150.1	169.2	621.7
1967	149.7	154.4	148.4	185.3	637.8
1968	158.4	167.6	162.0	197.0	685
1969					

Cal-endar	QUARTERLY EARNINGS (per sh.)				Full Year
	Mar. 31	June 30	Sept. 30	Dec. 31	
1963	.56	.47	.48	.56	2.07
1964	.59	.52	.50	.65	2.26
1965	.70	.65	.60	.75	2.70
1966	.72	.73	.72	.90	3.07
1967	.65	.61	.69	.93	2.88
1968	.73	.72	.75	1.00	3.20
1969					

Cal-endar	QUARTERLY DIVIDENDS PAID②				Full Year
	Mar. 31	June 30	Sept. 30	Dec. 31	
1963	.20	.20	.20	.45	1.05
1964	.20	.20	.25	.50	1.15
1965	.25	.25	.25	.55	1.30
1966	.30	.30	.30	.55	1.45
1967	.30	.30	.30	.55	1.45
1968					
1969					

Suitability: Pfizer's 15-year string of steady annual earnings increases was broken last year. A recovery is under way in 1968 but not of sufficient magnitude to make Pfizer an attractive commitment in terms of year-ahead market performance. Pfizer will appeal chiefly to the patient investor willing to wait 3 to 5 years for significant capital appreciation. Pfizer now rivals American Home Products as the largest company in this industry group. Much of the company's sales growth in the past decade has come from a large number of acquisitions. However, many of these new additions have not yet begun to realize their full potential. We think they will by 1971-73 . . . Funds reported a net selling balance of 7,900 shares in the fourth quarter . . . Insiders have reported no transactions in recent months.

Pfizer made a gratifying comeback in the first quarter when earnings hit a new high. Antibiotics made a significant contribution. Such products benefited significantly from a higher than normal incidence of upper respiratory infections throughout the country. Pfizer's newest antibiotic, Vibramycin, which was introduced in the United States and 23 other countries in 1967, was prescribed widely during the first quarter. Pfizer thinks Vibramycin will develop into a large volume item and possibly the antibiotic of choice for treating upper respiratory and urinary tract infections. This compound is the first antibiotic that can usually be administered at a very low dosage on a one-time-a-day basis after the initial day of therapy.

Pfizer's stock, however, is likely to remain under a cloud for some time because of uncertainty regarding the company's potential liability under a number of price damage suits filed against it. Last December Pfizer, along with Bristol-Myers and American Cyanamid were found guilty of restraint of trade, conspiracy to monopolize and actual monopoly of the manufacture of tetracycline. The companies are appealing the verdict and hope that the Court of Appeals in New York will reverse it. It is difficult to estimate what Pfizer's potential liability might be if the verdict is upheld; however, it is not likely that the company's financial stability will be seriously impaired. We estimate the potential damages might approximate $1.00 a share which would probably be accounted for by a charge against earned surplus.   R.P.G.

BUSINESS: Charles Pfizer & Co., Inc. is a leading manufacturer of antibiotics (Tetracyn, Terramycin, Signemycin). Also produces steroids, antidiabetics, synthetic penicillins, vitamins, antihistamines, citric acid, fine organic chemicals, agricultural chemicals. Product mix in 1967; Pharmaceuticals, 45% Chemicals, 17%; Agric. prodcts., 13%; Consumer products, 18%; minerals, pigments and metals, 7%. Foreign sales 48% of total volume, largest of any U.S. drug producer. Began marketing under own labels in 1950. Since 1957-59, sales have increased 180% (GNP, 72%). In 1967 research outlays totaled $23.9 million, or 3.7% of sales. Directors own 3.2% of stock. Employs 34,000; has 63,000 stockholders, Chrmn.: J.E. McKeen; President: John J. Powers. Inc.: Del. Add.: 235 E. 42nd St., New York, N.Y. 10017.

①–See Explanation of Terms on p. 577.   ② –Div'd payment dates: Mar. 24, June 23, Sept. 22, Dec. 14.

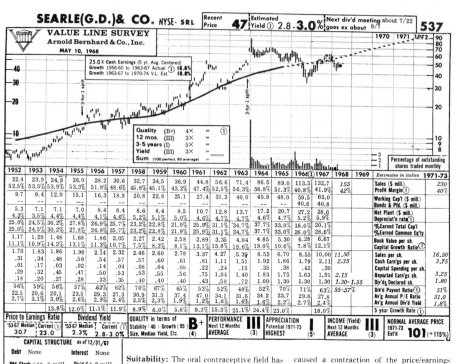

SEARLE(G.D.)& CO. NYSE- SRL

VALUE LINE SURVEY
Arnold Bernhard & Co., Inc.
MAY 10, 1968

| Recent Price | **47** | Estimated Yield ① **2.8-3.0**% | Next div'd meeting about 7/22 goes ex about 8/7 | **537** |

25.0 X Cash Earnings (5 yr. Avg. Centered)
Growth 1956-60 to 1963-67 Actual ① **16.0%**
Growth 1963-67 to 1970-74 V.L. Est. **10.0%**

Quality	(B+)	4×	=	①
12 mos.	(III)	3×	=	
3-5 years	(I)	5×	=	
Yield	(III)	3×	=	
Sum	(100 perfect, 60 average)		=	

Percentage of outstanding shares traded monthly

	1952	1953	1954	1955	1956	1957	1958	1959	1960	1961	1962	1963	1964	1965	1966①	1967	1968	1969		1971-73
	22.4	23.9	24.3	26.0	28.2	30.6	32.7	34.5	36.9	44.8	56.6	71.4	86.5	89.0	113.5	132.7	155		Sales ($ mill.)	230
	52.5%	53.5%	53.9%	53.3%	51.8%	48.6%	45.8%	45.1%	43.2%	47.4%	52.5%	56.3%	56.8%	51.3%	40.8%	41.9%	42%		Profit Margin①	40%
	9.7	9.4	12.0	15.1	16.3	18.9	20.8	22.8	25.1	27.4	31.3	40.0	45.9	48.0	59.5	65.0			Working Cap'l ($ mill.)	
	--	--	--	--	--	--	--	--	--	--	--	--	--	--	40.6	40.8			Bonds & Pfd. ($ mill.)	
	5.3	7.1	7.1	7.0	8.4	8.4	8.6	8.4	8.5	10.7	12.8	13.7	17.2	20.7	27.2	28.6			Net Plant ($ mill.)	
	4.3%	3.5%	4.4%	4.4%	4.1%	4.6%	5.2%	5.1%	5.0%	4.6%	4.7%	4.7%	4.6%	4.7%	5.2%	5.9%			Depreciat'n rate①	
	25.0%	24.5%	30.2%	27.8%	26.9%	25.7%	23.2%	22.8%	21.9%	25.9%	31.1%	34.7%	37.7%	33.0%	18.0%	20.1%			%Earned Total Cap'l	
	25.0%	24.5%	30.2%	27.8%	26.9%	25.7%	23.2%	22.8%	21.9%	25.9%	31.1%	34.7%	37.7%	33.0%	26.0%	28.6%			%Earned Common Eq'ty	
	1.17	1.29	1.48	1.68	1.86	2.05	2.27	2.42	2.58	2.89	3.35	4.04	4.85	5.30	6.28	6.67			Book Value per sh.	
	11.1%	10.9%	14.2%	13.1%	11.3%	10.7%	7.5%	8.3%	8.1%	13.1%	15.8%	19.6%	19.0%	10.6%	7.8%	12.1%			Capital Growth Ratio①	
	1.70	1.83	1.86	1.98	2.14	2.32	2.46	2.60	2.78	3.37	4.27	5.39	6.52	6.70	8.55	10.00	11.50		Sales per sh.	16.50
	.31	.34	.48	.59	.54	.57	.57	.60	.61	.81	1.11	1.51	1.92	1.86	1.79	2.11	2.35		Cash Earn's per sh.	3.75
	.01	.17	.03	.02	.14	.04	.08	.04	.08	.22	.24	.15	.35	.38	.42	.30			Capital Spending per sh.	
	.29	.32	.45	.47	.50	.53	.53	.55	.56	.75	1.04	1.40	1.83	1.75	1.63	1.91	2.15		Reported Earn's per sh.	3.25
	.18	.20	.27	.28	.33	.35	.40	.40	.40	.43	.58	.72	1.00	1.30	1.30	1.30	1.30-1.35		Div'ds Declared sh.	1.80
	56%	59%	56%	57%	62%	62%	70%	67%	65%	53%	52%	48%	52%	70%	71%	63%	55-57%		Div'd Payout Ratio①	51%
	22.5	20.6	20.1	23.5	29.3	27.3	30.9	31.5	37.4	47.0	34.1	31.6	34.2	33.7	29.6	27.8			Av'g Annual P/E Ratio	31.0
	2.7%	3.1%	3.0%	2.6%	2.3%	2.4%	2.5%	2.3%	1.9%	1.2%	1.6%	1.6%	1.6%	2.2%	2.7%	2.4%			Av'g Annual Div'd Yield	1.8%
				13.8%	12.0%	11.1%	11.9%	8.9%	6.0%	9.3%	15.3%	21.1%	24.4%	23.0%	18.0%				5 year Growth Rate ①	

Price to Earnings Ratio		Dividend Yield		QUALITY in terms of		PERFORMANCE	APPRECIATION	INCOME (Yield)	NORMAL AVERAGE PRICE
'53-67 Median ① 30.7	Current ① 23.0	'53-67 Median 2.3%	Current ① 2.8-3.0%	Stability (40) Growth (95) Size, Median Yield, Etc.	**B+** (4)	Next 12 Months III AVERAGE (3)	Potential 1971-73 I HIGHEST (5)	Next 12 Months III AVERAGE (3)	1971-73 Est'd **101** (+115%)

CAPITAL STRUCTURE as of 12/31/67

Debt None   **Interest** None

Pfd Stock $40. 8 mill.   **Div'd** $1.2 mill.
1,532,149 shs., $1 cum. conv. into 1/3 share common. Redeemable at $26.50 a sh. after 7/29/71.

Common Stock 13,275,660 shares

Cal- endar	QUARTERLY SALES ($ Millions)				Full Year
	Mar. 31	June 30	Sept. 31	Dec. 31	
1963	15.1	17.2	19.7	19.4	71.4
1964	21.3	21.7	22.0	21.5	86.5
1965	23.2	21.7	22.1	22.0	89.0
1966	29.0	28.2	27.4	28.9	113.5
1967	30.3	34.1	34.2	34.1	132.7
1968	33.8	39.2	39.0	43.0	155
1969					

Cal- endar	QUARTERLY EARNINGS (per sh.)				Full Year
	Mar. 31	June 30	Sept. 30	Dec. 31	
1963	.31	.34	.39	.36	1.40
1964	.45	.46	.46	.46	1.83
1965	.46	.46	.42	.41	1.75
1966	.48	.41	.39	.35	1.63
1967	.48	.49	.49	.45	1.91
1968	.49	.55	.55	.56	2.15
1969					

Cal- endar	QUARTERLY DIVIDENDS PAID (per sh.)				Full Year
	Mar. 31	June 30	Sept. 30	Dec. 31	
1963	.167	.167	.167	.217	.72
1964	.225	.225	.275	.275	1.00
1965	.325	.325	.325	.325	1.30
1966	.325	.325	.325	.325	1.30
1967	.325	.325	.325	.325	1.30
1968	.325	.325			
1969					

Suitability: The oral contraceptive field has become increasingly crowded in the past two years. No less than eight companies are now marketing birth control pills and prices have been cut more than 80% since Searle marketed the first oral contraceptive in 1960. However, Searle's newest introduction in this market, Ovulen, has bolstered the company's position and reversed a decline in earnings that set in during 1965. These shares will appeal to the investor seeking a leading ethical drug equity offering superior capital growth over the 3- to 5-year pull. Searle is also likely to perform as well as the average equity in the 12 months immediately ahead . . . The Funds bought stock on balance recently to the tune of 55,700 shares.

Searle currently sells at but 23 times current earnings; over most of the past 15 years this stock has commanded a capitalization rate of more than 30 times. The unlikelihood of any significant new product introductions in the next two years plus fear of a large new competitor in the oral contraceptive market (American Home Products) has undoubtedly

caused a contraction of the price/earnings multiple. However, steady growth of the present product line will enable Searle to post a 13% profit increase this year, it is estimated; and we think entrance of American Home will serve to broaden the entire market for birth control pills rather than cause large scale switching from Searle's compounds. Long range, the company has a lot of developments working to its benefit. Searle has embarked on an ambitious diversification program that should begin to pay off over the next 3- to 5-years. Through acquisitions this company has entered the fields of nuclear instrumentation and medical electronics (Nuclear-Chicago Corp.), enzyme production and research (Fermco Laboratories) and medical testing equipment for use in doctors offices (Berkeley Medical Instruments). All of these areas offer exciting potential. In addition, Searle does possess a strong research organization. Research has been going through a transitional state away from heavy concentration on oral contraceptives and toward the development of a broad range of new products. R.P.G.

BUSINESS: G. D. Searle and Company manufactures pharmaceutical specialties (about 30), principally for use in degenerative ailments. Enovid, the first oral contraceptive approved by the FDA, has become company's largest selling product. Other major products include Banthine (peptic ulcers) and Dramamine (motion sickness); also Mornidine (morning sickness), Nilevar (for building body tissue), Aldactone (an important diuretic) and Lomotil (for control of diarrhea). Foreign sales, 23% of total. Main plant at Skokie, Illinois. Since 1957-59, sales have increased 307%. Gross National Product, 72%. Has 4,500 employees, 27,000 stockholders. Searle family controls 46% of stock. Chairman; J. G. Searle. President; D. C. Searle. Incorporated; Delaware. Address: P. O. Box 5110, Chicago, Illinois 60680.

①-See Explanation of Terms on①-Includes Nuclear Chicago Corp.
p. 577. ② -Div'd payment dates:
Feb. 25, May 25, Aug. 25, Nov. 25.

FIGURE 11–4 (b)

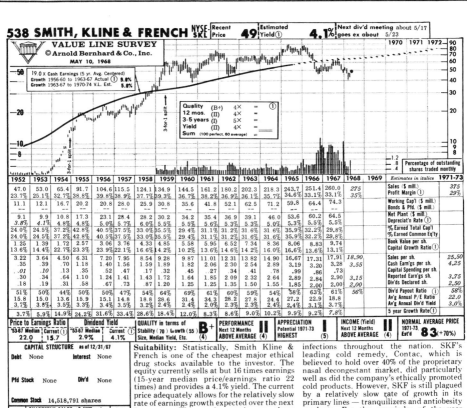

538 SMITH, KLINE & FRENCH

NYSE–SKF | Recent Price **49** | Estimated Yield① **4.1%** | Next div'd meeting about 5/17, goes ex about 5/23

VALUE LINE SURVEY
© Arnold Bernhard & Co., Inc.
MAY 10, 1968

19.0 X Cash Earnings (5 yr. Avg. Centered)
Growth 1956-60 to 1963-67 Actual ① **9.0%**
Growth 1963-67 to 1970-74 V.L. Est. **5.0%**

Quality			
12 mos.	(B+)	4×	= ①
3-5 years	(II)	4×	
Yield	(I)	5×	
Sum (100 perfect, 60 average)	(II)	4×	=

	1952	1953	1954	1955	1956	1957	1958	1959	1960	1961	1962	1963	1964	1965	1966	1967	1968	1969	Estimates in italics 1971-73
Sales ($ mill.)	47.0	53.0	65.4	91.7	104.6	115.5	124.1	134.9	144.5	161.2	180.2	202.3	218.3	243.7	251.4	260.0	275		375
Profit Margin ①	23.7%	25.1%	32.7%	38.8%	39.8%	38.9%	37.7%	39.3%	36.7%	38.2%	36.9%	36.1%	35.7%	34.6%	33.1%	33.1%	35%		29%
Working Cap'l ($ mill.)	11.1	12.1	16.7	20.2	20.8	28.0	25.9	30.8	35.6	41.8	52.1	62.5	71.2	59.8	64.4	74.3			
Bonds & Pfd. ($ mill.)	--	--	--	--	--	--	--	--	--	--	--	--	--	--	--	--			
Net Plant ($ mill.)	9.1	9.9	10.8	17.3	23.1	28.4	28.2	30.2	34.2	35.4	36.9	39.1	46.0	53.6	60.2	64.5			
Depreciat'n Rate ①	3.8%	4.1%	4.8%	4.8%	5.0%	5.7%	6.0%	5.5%	5.5%	5.6%	5.3%	5.3%	5.0%	5.3%	5.5%	5.5%			
% Earned Total Cap'l	24.0%	24.5%	37.2%	42.8%	40.5%	37.5%	33.0%	35.5%	29.4%	31.1%	31.2%	31.6%	31.6%	35.9%	32.2%	29.8%			
% Earned Common Eq'ty	24.0%	24.5%	37.2%	42.8%	40.5%	37.5%	33.0%	35.5%	29.4%	31.1%	31.2%	31.6%	31.6%	35.9%	32.2%	29.8%			
Book Value per sh.	1.25	1.39	1.72	2.57	3.06	3.76	4.33	4.85	5.58	5.95	6.52	7.34	8.36	8.06	8.83	9.74			
Capital Growth Ratio①	13.6%	14.4%	22.7%	23.3%	23.9%	22.1%	16.6%	14.2%	10.2%	13.6%	14.6%	14.2%	14.8%	13.6%	13.1%	13.1%			
Sales per sh.	3.22	3.64	4.50	6.31	7.20	7.95	8.54	9.28	9.87	11.01	12.31	13.82	14.90	16.67	17.31	17.91	18.90		25.50
Cash Earn's per sh.	.35	.39	.70	1.18	1.40	1.56	1.59	1.89	1.82	2.06	2.30	2.54	2.89	3.19	3.28	3.55			4.25
Capital Spending per sh.	.01	.10	.13	.35	.52	.47	.17	.32	.45	.27	.34	.41	.78	.99	.86	.73			
Reported Earn's per sh.	.30	.34	.64	1.10	1.24	1.41	1.43	1.72	1.64	1.85	2.09	2.32	2.64	2.89	2.84	2.90	3.15		3.75
Div'ds Declared per sh.	.18	.19	.31	.58	.67	.73	.87	1.20	1.25	1.25	1.35	1.50	1.55	1.85	2.00	2.00			2.50
Div'd Payout Ratio ①	51%	50%	44%	50%	50%	47%	54%	64%	69%	61%	60%	54%	54%	58%	63%	61%	56%		58%
Av'g Annual P/E Ratio	15.8	15.0	13.1	15.9	15.1	14.8	18.8	28.6	31.4	34.3	28.2	27.8	24.4	27.2	22.9	18.8			22%
Av'g Annual Div'd Yield	3.7%	3.8%	3.5%	3.3%	3.4%	3.5%	3.2%	2.4%	2.4%	2.0%	2.3%	2.3%	2.4%	2.4%	3.1%	3.7%			3.0%
5 year Growth Rate①	3.7%	5.9%	14.9%	24.2%	31.6%	33.4%	28.6%	18.4%	12.0%	8.3%	8.6%	9.0%	10.2%	9.9%	9.2%	7.8%			

Price to Earnings Ratio		Dividend Yield		QUALITY in terms of	PERFORMANCE	APPRECIATION	INCOME (Yield)	NORMAL AVERAGE PRICE
'53-'67 Median	Current ①	'53-'67 Median	Current ①	Stability (70) Growth (55) **B+**	Next 12 Months **II**	Potential 1971-73 **I**	Next 12 Months **II**	1971-73 Est'd **83** (+70%)
22.0	15.7	2.9%	4.1%	Size, Median Yield, Etc. (4)	ABOVE AVERAGE (4)	HIGHEST (5)	ABOVE AVERAGE (4)	

CAPITAL STRUCTURE as of 12/31/67

Debt None   Interest None

Pfd Stock None   Div'd None

Common Stock 14,518,791 shares

Calendar	QUARTERLY SALES ($ Millions)				Full Year
	Mar. 31	June 30	Sept. 30	Dec. 31	
1963	51.0	46.5	52.6	52.2	202.3
1964	51.7	49.4	59.7	57.4	218.2
1965	61.0	54.3	67.5	60.9	243.7
1966	63.5	58.7	67.0	62.2	251.4
1967	65.8	61.0	67.5	65.6	259.9
1968	70.1	65.0	71.9	68.0	275
1969					

Calendar	QUARTERLY EARNINGS (per sh.)				Full Year
	Mar. 31	June 30	Sept. 30	Dec. 31	
1963	.56	.57	.61	.58	2.32
1964	.59	.62	.75	.68	2.64
1965	.76	.62	.77	.74	2.89
1966	.74	.64	.77	.69	2.84
1967	.70	.68	.79	.73	2.90
1968	.80	.80	.80	.75	3.15
1969					

Calendar	QUARTERLY DIVIDENDS PAID②				Full Year
	Mar. 31	June 30	Sept. 30	Dec. 31	
1963	.30	.30	.30	.60	1.50
1964	.30	.30	.30	.65	1.55
1965	.40	.40	.40	.65	1.85
1966	.45	.45	.45	.65	2.00
1967	.45	.45	.45	.65	2.00
1968	.45				
1969					

Suitability: Statistically, Smith Kline & French is one of the cheapest major ethical drug stocks available to the investor. The equity currently sells at but 16 times earnings (15-year median price/earnings ratio 22 times) and provides a 4.1% yield. The current price adequately allows for the relatively slow rate of earnings growth expected over the next few years. This equity carries an above average rank for probable market performance in the next 12 months and it offers superior appreciation potential to 1971-73 ... It must be cautioned that earnings estimates for this company must be highly tentative. The patent on SKF's largest selling product, the tranquilizer Thorazine, expires in 1970. The company's results over the next few years will depend in large measure on how far Smith Kline decides to cut prices on Thorazine in anticipation of, or subsequent to, the arrival of competition ... Two of the 70 leading Investment Companies purchased 97,900 shares while two others sold 77,000 according to our latest report ... Insiders reported no significant transactions in this stock in recent months.

Smith Kline reported a strong first quarter. Share earnings rose 14% on a 7% increase in sales. The gain can be attributed primarily to the increased incidence of upper respiratory infections throughout the nation. SKF's leading cold remedy, Contac, which is believed to hold over 40% of the proprietary nasal decongestant market, did particularly well as did the company's ethically promoted cold products. However, SKF is still plagued by a relatively slow rate of growth in its primary lines — tranquilizers and antiobesity products. For the remainder of the year SKF's earnings may increase only 5% we estimate vs. the 14% increase reported for the first quarter.

Smith Kline's chief problem will be to increase earnings sufficiently in its non-tranquilizer lines to offset an expected sharp decline in Thorazine profits. Concern over the future course of earnings from its major product group, tranquilizers, is undoubtedly the principal reason for the relatively low price/earnings ratio which SKF now commands. Prices on Thorazine were cut 7.5% last year. It is conceivable that additional price reductions will be imposed before the patent finally expires. As yet, SKF's research department shows no signs that it is likely to come up with any important new products before 1970 despite rather large research expenditures ($28 million last year). R.P.G.

BUSINESS: Smith, Kline & French Laboratories manufactures ethical drug specialties for the treatment of mental illnesses. Best known are the tranquilizers Thorazine, Compazine and Stelazine. Other products include analgesics, synthetic hormones and antihistamines. Norden Laboratories Div. manufactures veterinary medicines. Tranquilizers and central nervous system stimulants provide 50% of sales. Since 1957-59, sales have increased 108% (GNP, 72%). In 1967, research outlays totaled $26.0 million, or 10% of sales. Main plant at Phila., Pa. Branch plants in Mexico City, London, Cal., and Montreal. Stockholders: 27,000, employees: 7,600. Directors control 24% of stock. Chrmn.: W.A. Munns. Pres.: T. M. Rauch. Incorporated: Pennsylvania. Address: 1500 Spring Garden St., Philadelphia, Pennsylvania 19101.

①—See Explanation of Terms on p. 577. ② -Div'd payment dates: Mar. 17, June 11, Sept. 10, Dec. 13.

FIGURE 11–4 (c)

TABLE 11–4

*Sales in millions of $ and index of sales
of three leading ethical drug companies*

Year	Chas. Pfizer & Co.			G. D. Searle & Co.			Smith Kline & French		
	SALES $	INDEX	% ANNUAL RATE	SALES $	INDEX	% ANNUAL RATE	SALES $	INDEX	% ANNUAL RATE
1975	1513E[b]	664		438E	1327		499E	399	
1974	1351E	592		378E	1145		460E	368	
1973	1206E	529		326E	988		424E	339	
1972	1077E	472		281E	851		391E	313	
1971	962E	422		242E	733		360E	288	
1970	859E	377		209E	633		323E	258	
1969	767E	336		180E	545		298E	238	
1968	685E	300		155E	470		275E	220	
1967	638	280	2.6	133	402	17.0	260	208	3.5
1966	622	273	14.2	114	348	4.8	251	201	2.6
1965	545	239	13.3	89	270	2.3	244	196	12.0
1964	480	211	15.3	87	265	21.0	218	175	7.4
1963	418	183	8.9	71	219	25.9	204	163	13.2
1962	384	168	22.6	57	174	26.1	180	144	11.6
1961	312	137	7.9	45	138	21.1	161	129	8.4
1960	290	127	14.4	37	114	7.5	148	119	10.2
1959	254	111	13.3	35	106	6.0	135	108	9.1
1958	223	98	7.7	33	100	6.4	124	99	6.5
1957	207	91		31	94		115	93	
Average Annual Growth Rate 1957–1967		12.0			13.8			8.5	

[a] Rounded
[b] E is estimate of future sales based upon projection of trend of index
of sales using ten-year average annual growth rate.
SOURCE: Standard & Poor's *Industry Surveys—Drugs, Cosmetics,* May 2,
1968, pp. D 22, D 27, and D 28.

TABLE 11–5

*A comparison of Searle, Pfizer, and SKF,
ranked by growth and competitive position*

COMPETITIVE POSITION OF COMPANY AND GROWTH CHARACTERISTICS	Company and its Relative Position		
	PFIZER	G. D. SEARLE	SMITH KLINE & FRENCH
Size of company	1	3	2
Growth of sales of company	2	1	3
Stability of sales of company	1	3	2
Future growth of sales	3	1	2
Product diversification	1	3	2

firms in the industry in sales have been found. From among these Pfizer,
Smith Kline & French, and G. D. Searle were selected for several reasons.
All have size, and Searle and Pfizer have excellent growth rates as shown

in the projected growth figures in Chart 11–1. If this growth continues, the companies will increase their share of the market and maintain their competitive position. We would choose Searle and then Pfizer, based on the criteria established. This is a tentative, preliminary decision. A final decision will be made only after all other factors of an analysis have been examined. This is the same conclusion reached five years ago in the first edition of this book. The relative position of the companies is summarized in Table 11–5.

Summary

Company analysis establishes a forecast of future expected earnings, dividends, and price. We must determine expected yield and then decide if the stock is a satisfactory investment based upon the risks involved. The analysis of future earnings requires that we examine: (1) the competitive position of the company based upon past and future growth; (2) earnings and profitability; (3) the operating characteristics and efficiency of the company; (4) current financial position; (5) capital structure characteristics; and (6) company management. Each has an effect upon earnings and price, but management is the most important variable. Independent of the interrelationship between earnings and price, we must examine the price characteristics. Here we must consider: (1) past price range; (2) the price-earnings ratio; (3) the market action of the stock; and (4) the general level of the stock market.

We began the analysis process by examining the competitive position of the company. We demonstrated the analysis by a hypothetical example, then we began an actual case to show how we might tentatively select a company in an industry for investment. We concluded that we want a dominant firm within the industry. Second, we want one that is growing faster than its industry and that is growing domestically as well as in foreign markets. Third, we must examine a company in all its activities to determine its true competitive position. Fourth, we must examine it to determine if it will continue to grow in the future. And we assume that this growth will be both in terms of dollars and in terms of real output. We suggested several methods of forecasting including: (1) trend, (2) average relationship between industry sales and company, (3) sales per capita, (4) an analysis of customers, and (5) expert forecasts. The examination of the competitive position of a company is only the first step in analysis. We began a case study of the drug industry and selected three leading companies. We chose two, tentatively, for investment. The final decision must await a complete analysis.

Review Questions

1. What are the factors we must examine in estimating the future earnings capability of a company?
2. Explain briefly what is meant by:
   (a) Competitive position
   (b) Company profitability
   (c) Operating efficiency
   (d) Current financial position
   (e) Capital structure characteristics
   (f) Management
3. Why should we be concerned with the price of a common stock and how does this relate to earnings?
4. How do we go about determining the competitive position of a company within an industry?
5. Explain the significance of size, stability, and rate of growth for an investor.
6. In defining the competitive position of a company, why is it so important to understand the nature of and type of products produced?
7. (a) How would you analyze a company that produced more than one major product?
   (b) How would you analyze a company that did not have one major product?
8. What does the character of the product, that is, luxury or necessity, high-priced or low-priced, have to do with the competitive position of a company?
9. Explain how we might forecast the sales of a company if we did not have an expert to tell us how the company's sales were expected to grow?
10. (a) What conclusions do you draw from the competitive position of the companies in the drug industry?
    (b) Why were Pfizer, Searle, and Smith Kline & French chosen for analysis?
    (c) Could the same type of analysis be applied to a company that is not a leading company? Explain.

Problems

1. Identify the leading companies in one of the subindustries discussed in Chapter 10.
2. Rank each company on the basis of dollar sales and sales in units of goods produced for 1957 and the most current year.
3. Based upon an index of dollar or physical sales using 1957–59=100, compare the overall growth between 1957 and the present year for

each of the leading companies. Select the companies that have shown the greatest competitive strength as evidenced by their growth of sales. Based upon size and growth rate, select the three leading companies in the industry.

4. Compute an index for the years 1957 to the present for each of the companies. Compare with the growth of the industry.
   (a) Which company appears to have the highest rate of growth?
   (b) Which company has the greatest stability of sales?
   (c) Rank each of the companies according to these qualitative characteristics.

5. (a) What products are produced by each of the three companies? Include in the answer the percentage composition of product sales of each company.
   (b) Does the company produce a luxury or necessity product?
   (c) What percent of sales are military and nonmilitary; foreign and domestic?

6. To what extent has inflation affected the sales of each of the companies?

7. Which company has the best diversification of sales?

8. Forecast the sales for each company for the next five years. Use one of the methods presented in this chapter.

9. On the basis of this analysis, which company would you select? Use criteria comparable to those presented in the chapter in answering this question.

Sources of Investment Information

Annual reports of company
Barron's
Forbes
Moody's manuals
Standard & Poor's *Industry Surveys*
Standard & Poor's *Listed Stock Reports*
The Value Line Investment Survey
Wall Street Journal
Wall Street Journal Index

Selected Readings

Bauman, W. Scott, "Investment Analysis: Science or Fiction?" *Financial Analysts Journal* (January-February, 1967), p. 93.

Bonham, Howard B., Jr., "Input-Output in Common Stock Analysis," *Financial Analysts Journal* (January-February, 1967), p. 19.

Clay, Landon T., "Investment Analysis," *Financial Analysts Journal* (January-February, 1966), p. 70.

Doan, Herbert D., "Challenges in Petrochemicals," *Financial Analysts Journal* (July-August, 1967), p. 35.

Kennedy, James R., "Challenges in Chemical Fibers," *Financial Analysts Journal* (July-August, 1967), p. 31.

Leslie, Neale, "A New Approach to Life Insurance Evaluation," *Financial Analysts Journal* (September-October, 1966), p. 75.

Savoie, Leonard M., "Financial Reports," *Financial Analysts Journal* (March-April, 1968), p. 67.

12

CORPORATE EARNINGS AND PROFITABILITY

We assumed in the last chapter that the company in a strong competitive position would prove desirable for common-stock investment. Strong competitive position helps ensure growth of earnings. However, before sales can be converted into earnings, certain costs and expenses must be met. A corporation must be able to produce goods or services cheaply and efficiently in order to convert sales into profits. There is a physical limit on the amount of goods and services that can be produced. Beyond this, new plants must be added to allow production and sales to expand. To determine how much a company can earn in the future we must analyze the expenses and costs that are required to generate sales. Earnings are the result of the interaction of income and cost and expenses. Future earnings can be estimated only if we are aware of this relationship. We continue, in this chapter, our analysis of the company by examining directly the relationship between earnings and sales and how expenses might vary independently of sales. We will also examine methods of forecasting future earnings per share, using current statistical techniques.

The Relationship Between Sales and Earnings Per Share

When we buy a common stock, we are buying the right to future earnings. We are interested in the amount, stability, and growth of sales only to the extent that they will provide a stable and growing amount of earnings per share. We assume that the dominant companies in an industry will provide these. We are particularly concerned with the amount of future earnings and when they will be received. If we could know for certain the future earnings per share, we could quickly compare price and earnings and decide whether the stock is a satisfactory investment.

We usually assume that earnings will follow the growth of sales. Therefore, if we choose for investment those companies that have stable and growing sales, they should provide stable and growing earnings per share. This assumption rests on the premise that expenses will not vary; that is, that profitability, the relationship between sales and expenses, will remain constant. This also assumes a constant utilization of plant and equipment above the breakeven point so that the effects of operating leverage will be the same. The relationship also assumes no changes in debt in the capital structure, and finally that the combination of products produced will remain the same. Obviously if any of these variables changes in the future, independent of sales changes, earnings per share will change. That is why we must carefully analyze costs and expenses in estimating future earnings.

Unfortunately earnings do not always follow the path of sales. Sometimes earnings actually move in a direction opposite to sales. The financial press frequently reports that a company's sales have increased but its earnings per share have declined. Allied Paper is a good example of this phenomenon. A few years ago Allied announced that its net earnings per share would decline to about $1.00 compared with $1.09 in the previous year. It further stated that sales for the corresponding period of time would increase to about $50 million, up from approximately $46 million. This is a case of approximately a 10 percent increase in sales with a 10 percent decrease in earnings per share. Obviously this is not a desirable position to be in.

Another problem of analysis is the relationship between earnings and sales relates to differences in their relative rates of growth. The rate of change of earnings can be different from the change of sales, depending on operating and financial leverage and changes in costs and expenses. Sales might, for example, increase 10 percent but earnings per share increase only 4 percent. We still have a correlation between earnings and sales, but it is not perfect.

An even more frustrating situation occurs when earnings increase with a decreased volume of sales. Hallicrafters, a manufacturer of radios and electronic components, had this experience in 1962. During one period sales decreased, but earnings per share remained the same. In some cases earnings per share have even gone up with a decrease in sales.

The illustrations dramatize the perplexing problems we face in estimating earnings. We would be in error to place complete reliance upon size and growth of sales without inquiring into the ability of the company to earn. We cannot assume that fixed relationships will always exist between sales and profits. Earnings must be carefully examined and their derivation must be understood if we are to be reasonably certain of the future earnings capability of a company in which we propose to invest. The company's earnings should be compared with those of the industry and to the national economy. Our basic problem is to determine whether companies selected for future sales growth will also be profitable and provide future earnings of sufficient amount, quality, and certainty.

Aggregate Corporate Profits and the National Economy

We have some idea of how the national economy has grown in the past decade. We also realize the course that sales of large corporations have taken between 1963 and 1968. Corporate sales, profits, and dividend figures were presented in Figure 11–3. The relationship between corporate profits and sales and the national economy on an aggregate basis is helpful in providing background for discussion about the relationship between company sales and earnings per share. We know that the GNP and NI have expanded between 1957 and 1968. Intermittent periods of recession, however, have occurred when the rate of growth slackened. At other times industrial activity declined, resulting in a decrease in corporate earnings. Corporate profits before taxes, shown in Figure 12–1, reflect these changes in business activity. Corporate profits have not been stable but cyclical in character. There has been a tendency for them to expand. Corporate profits before and after taxes increased substantially between 1961 and 1966. Profits declined sharply in 1967 and then increased in 1968 to the 1966 level. First quarter profits in 1969 were almost 10 percent higher than in 1968.[1]

During the same time period, cash dividends steadily increased,

Year	Profits before taxes	Income taxes	Profits after taxes	Cash dividends	Undistributed profits	Corporate capital consumption allowances[1]	Quarter	Profits before taxes	Income taxes	Profits after taxes	Cash dividends	Undistributed profits	Corporate capital consumption allowances[1]
1961	50.3	23.1	27.2	13.8	13.5	26.2	1967—III...	80.8	33.2	47.6	23.5	24.1	44.1
1962	55.4	24.2	31.2	15.2	16.0	30.1	IV...	85.4	35.1	50.3	22.5	27.9	44.9
1963	59.4	26.3	33.1	16.5	16.6	31.8	1968—I....	88.9	39.8	49.1	23.6	25.5	45.7
1964	66.8	28.3	38.4	17.8	20.6	33.9	II....	91.8	41.1	50.7	24.4	26.3	46.7
1965	77.8	31.3	46.5	19.8	26.7	36.4	III...	92.7	41.5	51.2	25.2	26.0	47.6
1966	85.6	34.6	51.0	21.7	29.3	39.7	IV...	95.7	42.8	52.8	25.4	27.5	48.5
1967	81.6	33.5	48.1	22.9	25.2	43.4	1969—I....	96.5	43.2	53.3	25.4	27.9	49.3
1968	92.3	41.3	51.0	24.6	26.3	47.1							

[1] Includes depreciation, capital outlays charged to current accounts, and accidental damages.

Note.—Dept. of Commerce estimates. Quarterly data are at seasonally adjusted annual rates.

Figure 12–1

Corporate profits, taxes, and dividends (in billions of dollars)

1 *Federal Reserve Bulletin,* July, 1969, p. A47.

as did depreciation and amortization allowances. Cash flow, the broader measure of corporate earnings, has steadily improved, and the trend has been upward between 1961 and 1968 except for a slight pause in 1967. There was a substantial increase in 1968.[2] Figure 11–3 provides insight into the profit pattern of various industry groups. Foods, petroleum, electric power, and telephone profits increased in 1967, whereas the other industry groups followed the pattern of the national economy just described. In 1968, only foods, machinery, and electric power continued with increased profits. What is true of the companies in Figure 11–3 is true of the earnings pattern of the individual companies traded on the New York Stock Exchange. We might conclude that, while we do have an expanding economy, the earnings of individual companies do not follow a consistent growth pattern. A more realistic approach is that earnings will vary, and it is the exceptional company that will have a continual increase in its profits. Keeping this in mind will be helpful when we attempt to forecast future earnings per share.

Determination of Corporate Earnings

Aggregate corporate profits of United States corporations are presented only to provide a point of orientation. We have the basic problem of analyzing earnings to learn if they closely follow the pattern of sales. We wish to establish the ability of a company to earn money. This will be helpful in estimating the future earnings per share of the company's common stock. A careful examination of the profit and loss statement or the operating statement of a company will help our analysis of earnings.

Operating Income

Simplified operating statements of two hypothetical companies—an industrial and an electric utility—are given in Table 12–1 to review how net income and earnings per share are computed. The operating statement of Industrial, Incorporated is presented in two ways, both used by industrial companies. All three operating statements are typical of companies in their industry.

Individual items in the operating statement vary from industry to industry. Electrical, Incorporated has only a service to sell. No tangible product is involved. Therefore, the income is considered operating revenues rather than sales. Water and gas companies, railroads, toll highway companies, and the like use the term *operating revenues* to denote their major source of income. Commercial banks, which derive their income from interest on loans to business and interest on invest-

2 *Ibid.*

ments, usually refer to interest income as operating revenue. Insurance companies have two main sources of income—premiums from policy owners and interest, dividends, and rents from investments. This income could also be referred to as operating revenue. Manufacturing companies in a class similar to Industrial, Incorporated sell a tangible product. Their revenues are referred to as sales, since the production of income requires that an actual good be sold.

Nonoperating Income

Most industrial companies receive, in addition to sales revenue, other income that is considered nonoperating income—usually interest income from bonds, lease rental income, or dividend income from securities of subsidiaries. This can be an extremely important source of revenue to some companies. The presentation of operating revenues or sales and operating and nonoperating income and expenses differs from company to company. Alternate #1 for Industrial, Incorporated, and the operating statement of Electrical, Incorporated, follow the same approach. First, they present operating income and operating expenses, then nonoperating income and expenses, and finally net income after federal income taxes.

Another way of presenting an operating statement is shown in Alternate #2 of Industrial, Incorporated. All sources of income are given; then all costs and expenses are deducted; then net income before and after taxes is established. Both methods lead to the same earnings per share.

An understanding of these methods will be useful later in the chapter when ways of measuring profitability are discussed. In addition, an individual making an analysis of a company must be thoroughly familiar with the terminology used by the company being considered. A standard accounting pattern is followed in reporting income. The significance of each item in the statement and variations in accounting must be determined if successful results are to be obtained. An illustration might help clarify the point under discussion. The insurance industry uses terms that may not be familiar to the investor, for example, *premiums for policy owners* and *policy proceeds left with the company.* Actually premium income is quite easily understood, for it represents payment for the life insurance benefits, puts the insurance policy into effect, and continues it in effect. Thus when we pay life insurance premiums, they are income to the insurance company. Proceeds left with the company represent one option included in some life insurance policies. The beneficiary may have several alternatives when receiving the proceeds of the policy. He can leave the funds with the company to earn interest at a guaranteed rate, or he can receive a life income, with several years certain. If he draws interest only, the policy proceeds are left with the company. One cannot make a proper analysis of the earning potential of the company unless he understands the terminology used.

Earnings Per Share

Since the unit of measurement in investment is a share of stock, it is important that net income after taxes be converted into per share figures. Earnings per share are found by dividing the total outstanding shares into corporate net income after taxes. If preferred stock exists, preferred dividends must first be deducted. Earnings per share should not be confused with dividends per share. Dividends represent the amount actually paid to the share owner. In the case of Industrial, Incorporated, total earnings after taxes were $6 million. Since 2,000,000 shares were outstanding, earnings per share amounted to $3.

Cash Flow or Cash Earnings Per Share

Today, in the field of finance and investment, increasing attention is being given to the cash flow of the business enterprise. The term *cash flow* is used to describe the funds, generated from operations, that remain after all other cash expenses have been subtracted. The usual way of estimating cash flow per share is to add all noncash expenditures to net income after taxes, then divide by the number of shares outstanding. The most important noncash expense for most companies is depreciation, which, in many cases, is the only noncash expenditure; all other items of expense are assumed to be cash items. Reference to Table 12–1 will show how cash flow or cash earnings are determined for Industrial, Incorporated. Net income after taxes was $6 million and depreciation expense $3 million, which provided a cash flow of $9 million or $4.50 per share for the 2,000,000 shares outstanding. The same computation was made for Electrical, Incorporated, which has a cash flow of $129 million, or $12.90 per share on the 10,000,000 shares outstanding.

Cash earnings are significant because they give an estimate of the amount of discretionary funds over which management has control. Many corporate managements, when planning for the future, look upon depreciation—a noncash expense—as a source of funds. In reality, sales are the original source of funds, but depreciation expenses keep funds within the company. These depreciation funds, when consciously used to govern management's capital expenditure policy, may buy or build new plant and equipment or even increase working capital. Cash earnings then are a good guide to the availability of internally generated funds that can be used for plant expansion. By considering cash earnings or cash flow rather than net income, we can appraise more realistically the earning power of a company, as well as its future ability to earn. It is conceivable that a company with a small net income per share might have a sizable cash flow that would turn a seemingly unprofitable venture into a profitable one, using the term *profitable* broadly.

TABLE 12–1

Methods of presenting income statement
for industrial and public utility companies

Industrial, Incorporated
Operating Statement, May 31
(Millions of Dollars)

ALTERNATE #1			ALTERNATE #2			
Net sales		197	Net sales		197	
Cost of goods sold		160	Other income		1	
Gross profit on sales		37	Total income			198
Operating expenses:			Cost of goods sold		160	
General administrative	10		Operating expenses		21	
Selling	7					
Depreciation	3		General administrative	10		
Retirement funds	1		Selling	7		
Total		21	Depreciation	3		
Profit from operations		16	Retirement funds	1		
Other income		1	Interest and other			
		17	nonoperating expenses		5	
Interest expense		5	Total cost and			
Net income before taxes		12	expenses			186
Federal and state income			Net income before taxes			12
taxes (50%)		6				
Net income after taxes		6	Federal and state			
			income taxes (50%)			6
Earnings per share		$3.00				
(2,000,000 shares outstanding)			Net income after taxes			6
Cash earnings per share		$4.50*				
			Earnings per share			
			(2,000,000 shares			
			outstanding)		$3.00	
			Cash earnings per share			
			(cash flow)		$4.50*	

Electrical, Incorporated
Operating Statement, December 31
(Millions of Dollars)

Operating revenues		655
Operating expenses:		
Operations	268	
Maintenance	62	
Depreciation	58	
Property taxes	118	
Total		506
Operating income		149
Nonoperating income		1
Gross income		150
Interest on debt		39
Net income before taxes		111
Federal income taxes		40
Net income after taxes		71
Earnings per share	$ 7.10	
(10,000,000 shares outstanding)		
Cash earnings per share	$12.90*	

* Net income after taxes plus depreciation and other noncash expenses.
Here we add depreciation only because it is difficult to establish the
amount of the other items.

Another point in favor of studying cash earnings relates to the company's productivity of capital. Cash earnings consider not only the net income from the investment but the timing of the return of principal. The greater the amount of cash earnings, the more quickly are capital and income returned and the more profitable the investment; in this case, the more profitable the company. Companies requiring large amounts of capital, such as public utilities, oil pipeline companies, chemical companies, and heavy machinery companies, are particularly affected by their cash earnings position and would be expected to have larger depreciation allowances than most companies. To the extent that cash flow represents return of capital, it tends to measure profitability.

Figure 12–1 indicates how important depreciation and amortization allowances are to corporations and the economy on an aggregate basis. Over the years presented in Figure 12–1, depreciation allowances were almost equal to net profits after taxes in most years. Cash earnings per share should be examined as closely and carefully as earnings per share; in many respects, they are just as important to the financial well-being of the company.

The Quality of Corporate Earnings

Much of the work that we do in analysis is based upon information published by the company we are studying or by an investment service. In the discussion on corporate earnings we assumed that the earnings reported by the company were accurate and a true reflection of corporate profitability. Just what constitutes a "true" measure of earnings is difficult to determine. We want to know if the reported earnings are realistic or whether they have been influenced unduly by temporary changes in income or costs and expenses. We should be willing to pay full value for a dollar of quality and recurring earnings. A dollar of temporary, transitory earnings would not be worth very much, since the earnings will not occur in the future and will be of little benefit to us. In our analysis of earnings, therefore, we must examine income and costs and expenses to make certain that they are accurate measures of the company's ability to earn. We must also understand depreciation policies and accounting practices, since they might affect the current earnings report of the company. To the extent that it is possible, reported earnings should be adjusted either up or down to reflect permanent changes in earnings. Temporary influences upon earnings resulting from changes in income or changes in expense should be disregarded in estimating future earnings.

Opinions of the Accounting Principles Board

The American Institute of Certified Public Accountants, through its boards and committees, reviews corporate financial statements to improve their usefulness. Opinions are given from time to time by the Accounting Principles Board, which has taken a stand on controversial items in an attempt to clarify some problems confronting the accounting profession and the analyst. Several of its opinions are of significance to investors and financial analysts.

The board has found that net income should reflect all items of profit and loss recognized during the period, with extraordinary items segregated and shown separately in the income statement. It suggests the following presentation:

Income before extraordinary items

Extraordinary items

(Less applicable income tax)

Net income[3]

The board strongly recommends that earnings per share be disclosed in the statement of income and approves of historical reporting of net income and earnings per share. It recommends that earnings per share be based upon the average number of shares outstanding for the period. It also suggests that earnings per share reflect the potential dilution created by a convertible preferred stock or convertible bond issue outstanding, and potential dilution from warrants, stock options, and agreements for issuing new shares for little or no value.[4]

Variation in Income

Many times a company's earnings have changed sharply because of a nonrecurring change in sales. Assume, for example, that a company suffered a strike in a particular year, the first in its history. It caused a reduction in output and lower sales for the year, reducing earnings by $.50 per share. Now the strike has been settled; peaceful coexistence prevails. The influence upon earnings was temporary. We would conclude that earnings ability had not been fundamentally impaired and would adjust the stated earnings to reflect the fundamental earnings of the company. On the other hand, if the strike that brought about the decline in earnings was an annual event for the company and brought to the surface a basic antagonistic difference in labor-management relationships, then the decrease in earnings could be expected again in the years ahead. Since the strike is recurring, the decline in earnings is recurring, and accordingly we would not adjust the earnings deficit. We would not add back the temporary decline in earnings. We would be unwilling to pay much for stock because of the high variability of earnings and because future earnings would be lower with recurring

3 The American Institute of Certified Public Accountants, *Opinions of the Accounting Principles Board*, December, 1966.

4 See also Leopold A. Bernstein, Ph.D., CPA, "An Analysis of APB Opinion No. 9, Reporting the Results of Operations," *The New York Certified Public Accountant*, March, 1967; and Frank T. Weston, CPA, "Reporting Earnings Per Share," *Financial Analysts Journal*, July-August, 1967.

strikes. In any appraisal of earnings, therefore, we must take cognizance of the reliability and dependability of the major source of the company's revenues.

Often the income of a company rises sharply because of a temporary increase in sales. Just as we discount a temporary decline in sales revenues, so should we discount a temporary increase in net income. The auto industry in 1962 reached new highs in sales levels that exceeded 1955; 1963 was also an extremely good year, along with 1967 and 1968, in spite of the fact that profits were not always as good as sales. Forecasts in mid-1968 suggested 9.6 million units would be sold in 1969. However, these should not be construed as ordinary years. More realistically they should be considered exceptional—much better than normal.[5] We may adjust earnings downward in those years, and be more likely to approximate long-range earnings than if we accepted these earnings at their face value. The auto industry has cyclical-type earnings even though the trend of earnings is up.

Variation in Expenses and Costs

The other cause of a change in earnings is changes in costs and expenses. Each item of the expense account should be examined to determine if the increase or decrease will have a transitory or permanent impact on earnings. This will help analysts determine future earnings. An example of this type of adjustment is taken from the 1961 annual report of Mead Johnson & Company, which stated: "The principal factor contributing to lower profits in 1961, when compared with 1960, was the investment of expense dollars required to create, staff, and organize the new division—Edward Dalton Company—formed to concentrate on the marketing of Metrecal and other special purpose nutritional products." This gives the distinct impression that the long-range earnings potential of the company has been improved although short-term expenses have been increased temporarily. The investor would classify this as a temporary nonrecurring expense and adjust the earnings per share accordingly. (Most companies report the occurrence of a temporary change in earnings in their annual report.) The stated earnings of Mead Johnson were $7.27 in 1960 and $5.13 in 1961. The adjustment in effect would tell the investor that a better earnings figure would be closer to $7.27 than to the reported $5.13 per share. Looking to a forecast of future earnings, we would conclude that earnings per share would be increased because of the present level of expenditures.

Other expenses not usually labeled in the operating statement have an impact upon corporate earnings. Many corporations make engineering changes that have a disastrous impact on earnings. In past years the

5 Contrary to the view that automobile production is no longer cyclical and that an eight-million-car year is normal.

crashes of the Lockheed Electra not only were of grave concern to the manufacturer but also created a great expense. Lockheed made exhaustive tests to determine the cause of the crashes. Then, based on the results, they modified the existing Electras still in service. This cost the company millions of dollars and reduced earnings sharply. It would be logical to assume that such inordinately high expenses would be non-recurring. And earnings would have to be increased if they were to reflect future earning power.

Depreciation

A more familiar business expense that can either raise or lower corporate earnings is depreciation. We must ask whether the method of computing depreciation expense or changes in depreciation expense will have a temporary effect upon the company's net earnings. Each company has a wide variety of assets that are depreciated over varying time periods under different rates established by the Internal Revenue Service. This makes it difficult to accurately determine an overall depreciation rate for a company. However, through observation and evaluation you can learn to determine the impact of depreciation accounting on the company's earnings.

A few examples will demonstrate how depreciation may affect expenses and cause variations in company earnings. Some oil companies, for example, capitalize their drilling expenses and write them off as an expense over the life of the asset. Other companies write off all their drilling expenses as current expenses. The method used will have an effect upon reported earnings. Assume that a company had drilling expenses of $1,000,000. Instead of writing off the expense this year, the company wrote it off over a period of five or ten years. This would have the effect of reducing the drilling expenses in the first year as a charge to income. However, if drilling continued for a five- or ten-year period at the same rate, eventually the annual amount written off would equal the actual annual expenditure. The effect in the first years of this practice would be to overstate earnings. If a company changed from one method to the other, say from the capitalization of earnings method to writing off the capital expenditure as current expense, it would reduce earnings because current expenses would be increased. This would be a permanent change in depreciation policy that would have a momentary effect of reducing earnings.

Another change in depreciation that would affect the earnings of a company occurs when a company changes from the straight-line method of depreciation to a form of accelerated depreciation, such as the sum-of-the-digits method, double-declining balance method, or uses the investment credit now provided under the IRS Code. Any form of accelerated depreciation tends to understate net income in early years and overstate it in later years. If cash earnings are considered, they will be greater in the early years compared with the straight-line depreciation method because of the reduced taxes that will be paid and because of the increased amount of depreciation. Where changes from one form of depreciation to another occur, we must adjust the earnings of the company accordingly. This would be particularly important where a corporation added large amounts of plant and equipment because of an expansion in services. Making these adjustments is important to be certain that when two companies are compared they are actually comparable even though their methods of depreciation are different.

Depletion

Some companies, notably those in the oil, mining, and forest products industries, are permitted to write off a portion or all of the assets used in production. The logic of depletion is that a company loses its ability to produce in the future when it uses irreplaceable oil, gas, or minerals. The company using depletion is allowed to write off a fixed asset as a current expense. Some controversy exists over the exact rate that should be used for determining the depletion allowance and how it should be computed in the oil and cement industries. Historically, the Internal Revenue Code allowed a depletion rate in the oil industry of 27 1/2 percent of gross income from oil sales. This was to be reduced to 20 or 23 percent in 1970. We must understand the method used in computing depletion allowances and assess the impact of depletion in earnings or the effect of any impending change upon the earnings of the company. The reduction of the depletion allowance from 27 1/2 percent would have the same effect upon earnings as an increase in taxes.

Inventory

An awareness of the method used in accounting for the cost of goods sold is important for the investor. A change in inventory policy could have a marked effect upon earnings. The method used in computing inventory is usually explained in a footnote to the financial accounting section of a company's annual report. Few problems would exist in inventory accounting practices if prices remained stable, but prices of inventory do vary. In the last decade there has been an upward trend in the price level. Business, from time to time, has changed its method of costing inventory to adjust for changes in price level, and these changes have had an effect upon earnings. Two methods of determining the cost of inventory are first-in-first-out (FIFO) and last-in-first-out (LIFO). The traditional practice is to use the FIFO method. This assumes that goods are sold in the order in which they are acquired. Any inventory on hand is assumed to be that most recently purchased. Thus if a company purchased 200 units of inventory during the year and sold 100 units, the remaining 100 units would have a cost based upon the most recent price. If the company bought 100 units at $10 in the first part of the year and another 100 at $11 later in the year, then when 100 units were sold, they would have a cost of $10 and the remaining 100 units would have a cost of $11.

The LIFO method assumes that the inventory going out bears a cost comparable to the last items of inventory purchased. Thus, in the above illustration, the inventory cost would be based upon the price when the inventory was sold. If 100 units of inventory were purchased at $10 and another 100 units at $11 per unit and then 100 units of inventory were sold, they would have a unit cost of $11. The next 100 units have a cost of $10. The effect of LIFO inventory accounting is to raise costs when prices are rising and lower corporate income. The FIFO method, under the same circumstances, would tend to lower prices and raise net income. FIFO lowers net income when prices are declining. Another method of costing inventory is to use an average cost method. All of these methods are acceptable in determining inventory cost for federal income tax purposes, but the method adopted must be used consistently.

The valuation of inventory can be based upon one of the cost methods or upon cost or market price, whichever is lower. *Cost* is the price paid for the goods, and *market price* is the price at which the goods can be replaced. Cost is a realistic value for inventory since it represents the cost of an actual transaction. Some accountants follow a more conservative approach and use market price if it is lower than cost. The lower-of-cost-or-market-price method uses the lower price for inventory, which tends to increase earnings. Thus, if prices are rising, FIFO as a cost method tends to increase net earnings. The combination of FIFO and lower-of-cost-or-market-price further increases net income. A change from one method to another, even though the new method will be used consistently, might result in a nonrecurring change in earnings that must be adjusted. We should understand these differences in inventory accounting methods and adjust for them to make an accurate comparative analysis of two companies.

Wages

For many companies, labor costs are a significant portion of total operating costs. In making an analysis of the impact of labor costs upon corporate earnings, we must consider the trend and the immediate impact of a change in wage costs. The impact of these changes will be more strongly felt by a company that has a larger proportion of wage costs to total costs than one that uses a small amount of labor. Generally speaking, the average hourly earnings of wage earners have increased over the last decade, as indicated by the Bureau of Labor Statistics. Bureau figures indicate an upward trend of labor costs in the

United States. Each company has its own peculiar wage cost requirements and must be examined separately from the trend in the economy
as a whole. We usually ask what effect a wage increase of $.40 per hour
in the automobile industry, for example, will have upon operating costs
and profits of companies in the industry. Or we ask the broader question,
What effect will an increase in the minimum wage have upon profits
of the industry? Changes of this type have a permanent and recurring
effect on earnings, as well as the immediate effect of lowering earnings.
This assumes, of course, that the wage increase cannot be offset by a
price increase.

Once direct labor costs and fringe benefits have been added to
employee wages, they are seldom reduced. As long as a company grants
wage increases to correspond to the productivity of the employee, a
balance is maintained between profitability earnings and costs. Should
a company continue to grant wage increases beyond the scope of productivity, then the profits of the company will be in jeopardy and
decline. In recent years, many companies have experienced this difficulty.
Champion Paper and Diamond National in the paper industry have
had to adjust to the competitive position in their industry—as have all
companies. By cutting total wages and by reducing the number of
employees, they have reduced wage costs as a percent of total costs and
have improved productivity.

Federal Income Taxes

Several areas in federal income tax accounting allow special adjustments
that will either understate or overstate a company's earning. Depreciation, already discussed, has an impact upon earnings. Another is the
provision of the IRS Code that allows a company to carry back a loss
incurred in one year to adjust the past three years' income and then if
necessary write off any remaining loss over the next five years. The loss
carry-forward or carry-back provision tends to overstate the amount of
earnings in previous and future years because of the tax credit for losses.
It is possible that in a year when a company has earnings to carry forward, the provision will balance out the taxable earnings. No federal
income taxes will be paid, and in that year earnings will be overstated
by the amount of the tax credit. Obviously, this will not be continued
in the future, and an appropriate adjustment must be made.

Examples of special tax treatment are found in some industries.
Taxes in the oil industry are different from other industrials because
of the depletion allowance. Mutual funds and investment companies
have a certain percentage of their income taxed as capital gains. Some
of the securities they have purchased allow them to earn a capital gain.
Public utility companies often have a portion of their income taxed as

a capital gain. Some also have switched from a practice of *normalizing* earnings to allowing the earnings to *flow through* to net income. Under the normalizing concept, public utilities are allowed a fast tax write-off for capital expenditure purposes, but for rate-making purposes they actually average the amount of depreciation. The Ohio Commission since 1960 has been allowing the flow-through method, which permits the fast tax write-off to flow through and is used to determine the rate base. This tends to reduce taxes and reduce net income, but it increases cash flow and has the impact of improving the profitability of the utility.

The items of income and expense and their variations have an impact upon corporate earnings. These are not all the possible factors an investor must consider. They are merely representative of a species of change that might affect corporate earnings. Before the investor accepts too readily the stated earnings of a company, he must make a judgment of the quality of the earnings and determine if they are recurring and permanent. If not, they should be adjusted so that they reflect the true earnings potential of the company.

An example of the type of change we are discussing is demonstrated in Table 12–1. The items of expense for Industrial, Incorporated, appear to be normal. However, its annual report stated that operating expenses were $2,000,000 above normal because of a temporary increase in costs associated with a plant expansion program. Thus earnings after taxes are temporarily reduced by $1,000,000 or $.50 per share (Industrial is in the 50 percent tax bracket). The earnings for that year then would have been closer to $3.50 per share than $3.00. The other expenses did not change and were considered normal. Adjustments of this type are not always as simple as this illustration, but they should be undertaken to improve the accuracy of reported earnings.

Measuring Profitability

In addition to determining the trend of earnings and cash earnings of a company in the past, present, and future, we must also examine profitability. The measures of profitability permit comparison among the companies of an industry to determine which appear to be most profitable. All profitability measures relate profit either to company sales or assets. These ratios become a measure of the financial efficiency or earning efficiency of a company. They tell much more than the direction of earnings: they help show what will happen to earnings if sales or investment in operating assets is increased. The measures usually given a great deal of attention in financial circles are profit margin, earning power, and the ratio of net income to sales.

The profit margin is found by dividing operating income into operating profit. It is usually expressed as a percent of operating income and directs attention to the profitability of the sales or the revenue dollar. The operating profit represents the amount of money remaining from operating income after all operating expenses and the cost of goods are subtracted. Income taxes, interest, and other nonoperating expenses and income are not deducted. The operating statement of Industrial, Incorporated, in Table 12–1 will serve as an example of how the profit margin is computed. The company's operating profit was $16 million, and it had operating revenues of $197 million. The profit margin is 8.1 percent ($197 million divided into $16 million).

Several investment services emphasize cash flow. They do not deduct depreciation as an operating expense, considering it part of the profit margin, since it represents a return of capital available for general corporate purposes. The cash flow for Industrial, Incorporated, was $9 million, and on this basis it has a profit margin of 4.6 percent ($197 million divided into $9 million). The profit margin figure computed in this way is readily available from most investment services.[6] It is also a satisfactory and comprehensive measure of profitability. We will, however, use the broader measure of the profit margin in analysis because of its breadth and availability.

Earning Power

Another way of measuring profitability is to divide operating assets into operating profits. This measure is known as earning power, and it provides a way of determining how profitable the uses of operating assets of a company have been, based upon the net book value of the assets. Some proponents of this method think it is a much better way of measuring profitability than through profit on sales. There is a good deal of logic in this measure. A direct relationship exists between investment in operating assets on the one hand, and sales and profits on the other. The higher the earning power and the higher the profit margin, the more profitable the company.

Table 12–2 presents the balance sheet for Industrial, Incorporated. Total assets are $110 million. Since we are not interested in nonoperating assets, they must be deducted to arrive at the dollar amount of operating assets. Any assets not directly needed to produce operating income should be excluded as operating assets. Operating assets are not always labeled precisely. A knowledge of their nonoperating character, however, will help you eliminate most of these items quickly. Since the

6 Standard & Poor's *Industry Surveys* and *The Value Line Investment Survey*
  indicate profit margins in this way.

TABLE 12–2

Typical balance sheet of an industrial company

INDUSTRIAL INCORPORATED, DECEMBER 31
(MILLIONS OF DOLLARS)

Current Assets:			Current Liabilities:	
Cash	$ 2		Trade Accounts	$ 8
Governments	2		Bank Loan	2
Receivables	8		Total	$ 10
Inventory	8			
Total		$ 20		
Fixed Assets:			Debt:	
Plant (Net)	60		Bond Issues	40
Equipment (Net)	20			
		80	Capital Stock	40
Nonoperating Assets		10	Retained Earnings	20
		$110		$110

operating profit of Industrial, Incorporated is $16 million (Table 12–1) and operating assets are $100 million ($10 million of nonoperating assets have been deducted), the earning power is 16 percent.

The Ratio of Net Income to Sales

The profit margin and the earning power measures of profitability consider only the relationship between income from operations and the costs and expenses of obtaining the income. Nonoperating income is excluded. Most corporations, however, earn additional income from ownership of nonoperating assets or from temporary investment in short-term securities. These assets and investments are not the primary source of revenue, but for some companies they add a significant amount to corporate earnings. Armco Steel in 1968 had operating revenues of $1,375 million. Revenues from dividends, royalties, interest, and other sources amounted to $20.6 million. Since Armco is in the 52 percent tax bracket, only about one-half of this $20.6 million was carried through to net income; it represented 12 percent of net income after taxes for Armco.[7]

Nonoperating expenses are not considered in the profit margin. Many companies have nonoperating expenses, such as interest on debt that must be paid each year. Such expenses can have a significant impact on earnings. The first impact of interest, for example, on operating expenses is that it reduces net income available for the share owner. However, since the payment of interest represents low-cost capital and financial leverage results, the earnings to the owner are actually increased. Without a detailed explanation of this leverage process at this

7 Armco Steel, *Annual Report*, 1968.

point, let's say we simply hire capital at 6 percent with an after-tax cost of approximately 3 percent. The money is then invested to earn 10 percent after taxes. This process is advantageous to the stockholder if it is not carried to extremes. If excessive debt is employed, it will have an unsettling impact upon per share earnings. More will be said about this subject when the capital structure of a company is analyzed.

Net income after taxes as a percent of sales is a measure that is designed to consider all income and all expenses rather than only operating income. Depreciation is deducted in arriving at net income. The higher net income is as a percent of sales, the more profitable the company. Industrial, Incorporated, has a net income to sales ratio of 3.05 percent. This figure, which would be considered low by business management, is found by dividing sales of $197 million into $6 million, the net income after taxes. This ratio examined over time gives one more clue to the profitability of a company for investment.

Significance of Profitability Measures

The significance of the profitability measures can be determined only by an analysis of their behavior and direction. The profit margin focuses attention on the ability of a company to produce goods and services at a profit. The problem of analysis could be solved if we could say that a company should have as high a profit margin as possible, but a high profit margin is only one part of the equation, particularly when the future is being examined. We must know what to expect from sales. A company that has a profit margin of 10 percent and prospects of its sales doubling in five years will be a better investment than a company having a 15 percent profit margin with no prospect for increased sales. It is desirable to invest in a company that has a growing profit margin and expanding sales, but this is not always possible. We might then select a company that has expanding sales with a stable profit margin.

The significance of earning power and the significance of the ratio of net income to sales are similar in our analysis of the profit margin. Earning power recognizes a company's ability to earn profits on its operating assets. The ratio of net income to sales provides a measure for determining the overall profitability of corporate sales. It is desirable to have an expansion of operating assets that will ensure future profitability. It is desirable to have an increasing earning power and net income as a percent of sales. However, these ratios themselves need not increase as long as sales are increasing. Large plant expenditures and greater sales with profit stability will assure future profits for the shareholder even if the profitability measures are not improving.

Perhaps the best way to determine the quality of the ratios is to compare one company with other leading companies within the industry. We can then make a value judgment; the company that has done best can easily be determined, and changes that have occurred will allow comparative standards to be adjusted. The criteria for excellence should be the stability and improvement of the profitability measures.

Future Earnings

We have been discussing the amount, stability, and quality of earnings, but what about future earnings? Are not expectations about future earnings more important than past earnings? The purchase of a capital asset gives us the right to future benefits. Future earnings then are clearly the most important part of the valuation equation, and the most important influence management has is on future earnings. No matter what has happened to a company in the past, future earnings and expectations about future earnings really determine the current value of its common stock. This does not mean that the investor will necessarily act rationally about future earnings, but he will nonetheless focus his attention on the earnings capability of a company he is investigating.

The impact of future earnings upon price and the impact of change in expectation of future earnings on price are very difficult to comprehend. Sometimes long-run and short-run changes that occur do not seem to be rational. For example, how does a person explain why a stock drops three points on the announcement of a sharp increase in earnings? Is this rational? asks the investor. Should not the price of the stock increase? Actually, the action of the stock is logical because the investment community had foreseen a good earnings report. Investors and probably some speculators had purchased the stock, anticipating a rise in price. The stock did rise in price, and on the announcement date the stock was sold by many owners to establish a short-term gain. Selling pressure forced the price down.

Texas Instruments, an electronics company, had such an experience in the price of its common stock. The company's earnings had increased, and based on expectation of continued growth, the price of the stock rose from 27 to approximately 240. Subsequently, increased foreign competition resulted in a decline in prices, which changed the level of future earnings. At the time of the decline in price, current earnings were adequate. Why then should the stock drop in price? One important factor was the change in expectation about future earnings. The neophyte investor might conclude that this is irrational behavior; in reality it is quite rational. Investors are simply reacting to a change in expectations about a company's earnings.

Thus, a careful analysis of a company will include an estimate of future earnings as well as an examination of past earnings. We assume that the past behavior of earnings will provide a clue to a company's future. There are many methods of estimating future earnings. We will consider three: (1) a forecast of future earnings per share based on past earnings, (2) a forecast based on the past relation between sales and earnings or the line of average relationship, and (3) an estimate based upon profit margins and forecasted sales.

A Projection of Earnings Per Share

To estimate future earnings, we may project their growth based on the past record by fitting a trend line to the earnings per share and extending the earnings into the future. An example of this can be seen in Chart 12–1. The trend line results in estimated earnings per share between 1969 and 1975. The danger of this approach is that the trend line might not actually describe the pattern of earnings per share. Earnings might decline or increase as a firm experiences internal or external changes, which have not been a factor in past earnings. In this category might be a merger, the development of a revolutionary new product, or a major modernization and mechanization program that will reduce costs and increase earnings. Each time changes occur that affect earnings, we must make adjustments in the trend line. We must be constantly aware of new developments that might change future earnings.

Line of Average Relationship Between Sales and Earnings

A second approach is to forecast earnings based upon the expectation of growth in sales and the relationship between past sales and earnings. In the previous chapter, we made a forecast of sales from which we could determine future earnings per share. Past earnings and sales are plotted as in Chart 12–2. A trend line is fitted to the data and projected

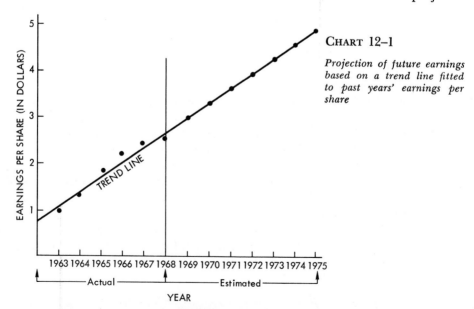

CHART 12–1

Projection of future earnings based on a trend line fitted to past years' earnings per share

until it intersects with the estimated sales line. Earnings per share are read from the bottom of the chart by dropping vertically to the horizontal axis. This method, as well as the one discussed above, is valid only for short-range forecasts in which the variables influencing sales and expenses are relatively constant. In investment analysis, the professional usually discusses earnings for the next year but refers only vaguely to the earnings potential over a longer period of time, say, five to seven years. A five-year or longer forecast is quite difficult to make with any accuracy.

Sales and Profit Margin Forecast

In this method we use sales forecasts to estimate future earnings per share. Assume that sales five years hence will be $400 million and the average profit margin is 18 percent and has been quite stable. The

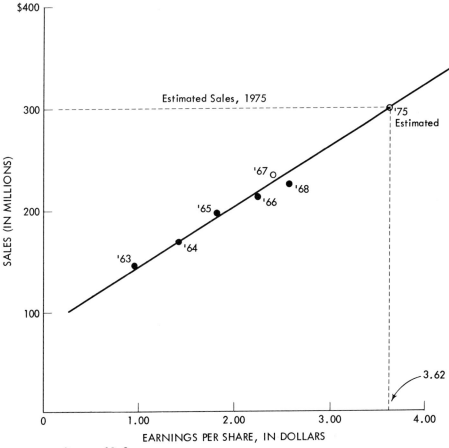

CHART 12–2

Line of average relationship between sales and earnings per share as a method of estimating future earnings per share

profit margin from sales will be $72 million. Since this figure includes depreciation, interest, and taxes, these items must be deducted before we obtain net income after taxes. Assume that depreciation requires a deduction of $17 million and interest $5 million. This will provide us with income before taxes of $50 million. The tax rate is 52 percent; thus, taxes will be $26 million, and net income after taxes, $24 million. If there are 12 million shares outstanding, then the estimate of earnings per share will be $2.00. If a greater number of shares are outstanding we must adjust earnings per share.

Measuring the Growth of Earnings and Profitability—A Hypothetical Case

The investor's problem is that of deciding which company among the competitive leaders of an industry is most profitable. Such a decision can be demonstrated by using the data in Tables 12–3 and 12–4. The two companies presented are leading companies in a hypothetical indus-

TABLE 12–3

Earnings, adjusted earnings, and cash earnings, per share for two hypothetical companies (in dollars, 1962–1968)

	EARNINGS	ADJUST-MENTS TO EARNINGS	ADJUSTED EARNINGS	ANNUAL PERCENT CHANGE IN EARNINGS	DEPRECIA-TION AND NONCASH EXPENDI-TURES	CASH EARNINGS ADJUSTED	ANNUAL PERCENT CHANGE IN ADJUSTED CASH EARNINGS
Company D							
1968*	$2.92	—	$2.92	10.0%	$.40	$3.32	10.7%
1967	2.65	—	2.65	10.4	.35	3.00	9.1
1966	2.40	—	2.40	6.7	.35	2.75	7.8
1965	2.20	+.05	2.25	4.7	.30	2.55	6.2
1964	2.15	—	2.15	7.5	.25	2.40	4.3
1963	1.75	+.25	2.00	33.0	.30	2.30	31.4
1962	1.50	—	1.50	—	.25	1.75	—
1962–1968 average	$2.22		$2.27	11.7%	$.31	$2.58	11.6%
Company E							
1968*	$2.46	—	$2.46	7.0%	$.30	$2.76	6.1%
1967	2.30	—	2.30	9.5	.30	2.60	8.3
1966	2.10	—	2.10	6.7	.30	2.40	—6.0
1965	2.25	—	2.25	7.1	.30	2.55	6.3
1964	2.10	—	2.10	2.4	.30	2.40	2.1
1963	2.05	—	2.05	7.9	.30	2.35	6.8
1962	1.90	—	1.90	—	.30	2.20	—
1962–1968 average	$2.17		$2.17	6.8%	$.30	$2.47	3.9%

* Estimated

try. Both have demonstrated growth potential of sales, and in this respect they are comparable.

The first step is to analyze the trend of earnings and then the cash flow. The earnings of both companies are almost identical. Company D has average earnings of $2.22 per share and Company E of $2.17, from 1962 through estimated 1968. However, the earnings of Company D have been adjusted upward somewhat because of inordinate development expenses in 1963 and 1965. In these years the company was developing new products that required above-normal expenditures but that would improve long-range earnings. The adjustments in earnings raised the average earnings to $2.27 per share, putting Company D in a somewhat better position than Company E.

The significant difference in the companies is not in their average earnings but in their different rate of growth. The sales growth rate of both has been about the same. Company D, however, has demonstrated better growth in earnings and shows the greater gain in the estimated earnings of 1968. We assume that the new products developed by Company D in 1963 and 1965 improved sales and profits substantially in 1968 and will continue to do so in the future. Cash flow per share is also better for Company D. Based upon past earnings, rate of growth of earnings, and rate of growth of cash flow, Company D is better than Company E.

An examination of the profitability ratios in Table 12–4 also indicates clearly that Company D is superior to Company E. Its average

TABLE 12–4

Profit margin, earning power, and net income to sales ratio for two companies in a hypothetical industry (in percent, 1962–1968)

YEAR	Profit Margin[a]		Earning Power[b]		Net Income as a Percent of Sales[c]	
	Co. D	Co. E	Co. D	Co. E	Co. D	Co. E
1968	13.0	11.0	18.0	16.0	14.0	12.0
1967	13.0	11.0	18.0	16.0	14.0	12.0
1966	13.0	11.0	18.0	16.0	14.0	12.0
1965	12.0	10.0	17.0	15.0	13.0	11.0
1964	12.0	10.0	17.0	15.0	13.0	11.0
1963	11.0	9.0	16.0	14.0	12.0	10.0
1962	12.0	10.0	17.0	15.0	13.0	11.0
1962–1968 average	12.3	10.3	17.3	15.3	13.3	11.3

[a] Profit margin is operating profit as a percent of operating revenues. Some investment sources such as Standard & Poor's include depreciation as part of operating profit.
[b] Earning power is operating profit as a percent of operating assets.
[c] Net income is income after taxes and all costs and expenses have been deducted.

profitability, as well as its improvement of profitability, is greater than for Company E. The assumption about 1968 and the future is that each company will be able to maintain its position with respect to profit margins, earning power, and net income to sales. If we projected earnings and assumed that there would be little change in the sales and earnings of each company, we would conclude that Company D's future earnings growth would be superior to Company E's.

Some Leading Companies in the Drug Industry—An Earnings Analysis

We will continue our actual company analysis by examining the earnings, profitability, and future earnings of Pfizer, G. D. Searle, and Smith Kline & French. We will assume that the analysis is being made in the third quarter of 1968.

Earnings

The earnings and cash flow per share for each of these companies are presented in Table 12–5 along with the annual rate of growth of earnings and cash flow, expressed in terms of an index with a 1957–1959 base = 100 and in terms of percentage of change. The growth of earnings for each company was excellent. G. D. Searle demonstrated an outstanding growth of earnings between 1961 and 1964, experienced a deficit in earnings in 1965 and 1966, and then improved remarkably in 1967 and early 1968. Pfizer reached a peak in its growth rate of earnings in 1966, experienced a decline in 1967, and was recovering in 1968. Smith Kline & French did not have a good earnings growth rate from 1966 through early 1968, but has had an excellent growth rate history. Based on the average annual rate of growth for the 1957 through 1968 period, we would conclude that Searle had the best growth of earnings, followed by Pfizer and Smith Kline & French. Pfizer had the most stable earnings and Searle the second most stable.

Cash Flow

When we consider the ability of these companies to generate cash flow per share, we find almost the same relationship as in our analysis of profits. Searle had the highest rate of cash flow generation, followed by Pfizer and Smith Kline & French. Pfizer had the greatest stability of rate of growth of cash flow followed by Smith Kline & French and Searle in that order.

Profit Margins

An analysis of the profit margin, earning power, and net income as a percent of sales indicates some interesting relationships. Searle had the highest profit margin of the three companies, the highest net income

TABLE 12-5

Adjusted earnings and cash flow per share for
Pfizer, Searle, and Smith Kline & French
(in dollars, % change, and index 1957–59 = 100)

ADJUSTED EARNINGS PER SHARE

YEAR	Pfizer $	Pfizer IND.	Pfizer %	Searle $	Searle IND.	Searle %	SKF $	SKF IND.	SKF %
1968[a]	3.20	218	11	2.15	400	13	3.15	207	8
1967	2.88	197	(7)[b]	1.91	354	17	2.90	191	2
1966	3.07	211	14	1.63	302	(6)	2.84	187	(2)
1965	2.70	184	8	1.75	318	(6)	2.89	190	10
1964	2.26	156	10	1.83	340	31	2.64	174	13
1963	2.07	139	6	1.40	216	11	2.32	153	12
1962	1.93	132	10	1.04	191	24	2.09	137	12
1961	1.74	119	10	.75	138	33	1.85	122	11
1960	1.58	108	5	.56	104	2	1.64	110	(5)
1959	1.51	103	2	.55	101	4	1.72	113	20
1958	1.48	101	5	.53	97	0	1.43	94	1
1957	1.41	97		.53	97		1.41	93	
1957–59 Average	1.47			.54			1.52		
Actual Average (1957–67)			8			12			8

CASH FLOW PER SHARE

YEAR	Pfizer $	Pfizer IND.	Pfizer %	Searle $	Searle IND.	Searle %	SKF $	SKF IND.	SKF %
1968[a]	4.30	230	10	2.35	405	11	3.55	211	8
1967	3.91	209	(4)	2.11	364	18	3.28	195	3
1966	4.05	217	14	1.79	309	(4)	3.20	190	0
1965	3.58	191	15	1.86	321	(3)	3.19	190	10
1964	3.11	166	9	1.92	331	27	2.89	172	14
1963	2.85	152	7	1.51	260	36	2.54	151	10
1962	2.65	142	13	1.11	191	36	2.30	137	11
1961	2.35	126	15	.81	140	33	2.06	123	14
1960	2.08	110	5	.61	105	1	1.82	108	(4)
1959	1.96	105	6	.60	104	5	1.89	113	16
1958	1.85	99	3	.57	99	0	1.59	95	2
1957	1.79	96		.57	99		1.56	93	
1957–59 Average	1.87			.58			1.68		
Actual Average (1957–67)			9			17			8

a Estimated.
b Parentheses represent negative numbers.
SOURCE: *The Value Line Investment Survey*, Arnold Bernhard and Company, Edition 4, May 10, 1968, pp. 530, 537, and 538.

as a percent of sales, and is second to Smith Kline & French in earning power. All of the companies had the same relative degree of stability in their profit margins, with a tendency for margins to decrease. This appears to be a continuing problem in the ethical drug industry. If we had to rank these companies on their ability to earn a profit based on the data in Table 12–6, we would rank G. D. Searle first, Smith Kline & French second, and Pfizer third.

TABLE 12–6

Profit margins, earning power, net income
as a percent of sales for Pfizer, Searle,
and Smith Kline & French

	Profit Margins %[a]			Earning Power %[b]			Net Income as a % of Sales[c]		
YEAR	PFIZER	SEARLE	SKF	PFIZER	SEARLE	SKF	PFIZER	SEARLE	SKF
1968[d]	22.0	42.0	35.0	17.0	46.0	40.0	9.1	20.1	16.3
1967	20.5	41.9	33.1	17.2	45.7	40.4	9.1	20.1	16.2
1966	22.3	40.8	33.1	24.5	72.8	80.7	9.9	20.1	16.4
1965	21.5	51.3	34.6	38.4	54.6	70.1	9.8	22.2	17.2
1964	20.4	56.8	35.7	35.2	41.7	64.5	9.3	28.0	17.7
1963	21.6	56.3	36.1	37.8	38.6	59.6	9.7	25.9	18.7

[a] Operating earnings before deduction of depreciation, interest, and income tax, as a percentage of sales.
[b] Operating profits before taxes, interest, and depreciation as a percentage of operating assets.
[c] Net income after taxes.
[d] Estimated.
SOURCES: *The Value Line Investment Survey*, Arnold Bernhard and Company, Edition 4, May 10, 1968, pp. 530, 537, and 538; *Moody's Industrial Manual*, June, 1967, pp. 653, 1701, and 1584, and July, 1968, pp. 1732, 66, and 1460; Standard & Poor's *Industry Survey—Drugs, Cosmetics*, May 2, 1968, pp. D23 and D24.

Future Earnings

Future earnings for each company are projected in Charts 12–3 and 12–4 and in Table 12–7. The 1968 forecast is based upon data presented in *The Value Line Investment Survey* fact sheets. The forecasts in Chart 12–3 simply extend the past growth of earnings per share. Chart 12–4 develops the average relationship between sales and earnings per share. The forecast of sales for the drug industry developed in the previous chapter (Chart 11–1) was used to estimate per share earnings in the years through 1975. The earnings forecasts by two methods appear in Table 12–7, on page 394.

The earnings forecasts based on past growth illustrate the methods used to estimate earnings for the drug companies. The companies anticipated an increase in sales and earnings in 1968 and in future years. New product development would be responsible for this growth. G. D.

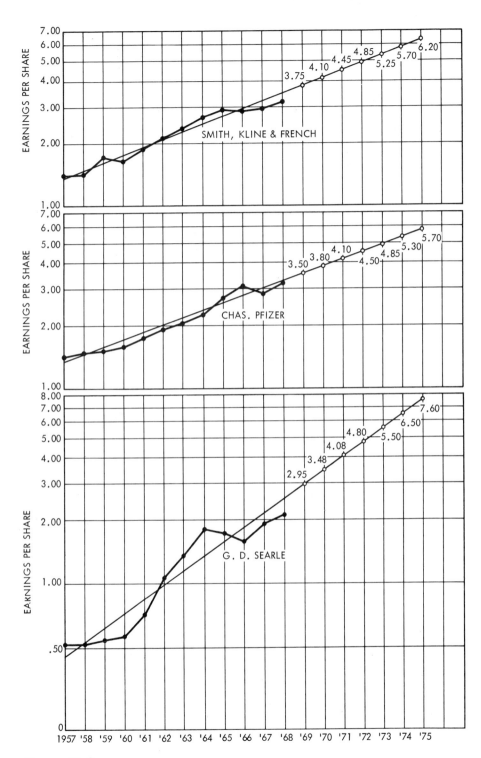

CHART 12-3

*Estimated future earnings of Pfizer,
Searle, and Smith Kline & French*

Searle expected improved earnings because of increased sales of Enovid, an effective oral contraceptive. Despite competition from American Home Products and other manufacturers, Searle felt that the market had been relatively untapped, since only about 2 1/2 percent of the married women in the U.S. had used any type of oral contraceptive. This position was held in spite of Pope Paul's encyclical affirming the ban on artificial birth control in 1968, which hampered the future growth outlook for Searle. Smith Kline & French expected the sale of Thorazine to remain strong. However, the patent on this tranquilizer runs out in 1970, making earnings forecasts only tentative. New products will have to be developed to take up the slack in sales and earnings of Thorazine. SKF also expected that sales of Contac, a cold remedy, would add materially to its sales and profit margins. Pfizer has developed several new products, including Limmits, that help ensure future growth. Pfizer's newest antibiotic, Vibramycin, promises to develop into a big earner. Anticipations such as these are subject to error and must be revised frequently, and new developments must be assessed for their effect on forecasts of earnings.

In making forecasts based on reported earnings for the three companies, we need not adjust for temporary and inordinate changes in income or expenses. Each company was active in developing new products and markets during the period upon which the forecasts were based. Pfizer acquired several new firms to diversify its output, Searle developed another oral contraceptive and also achieved greater diversification through the acquisition of several firms, and Smith Kline & French brought out a series of new drugs in the tranquilizer field. All these activities have their impact upon expenses and income and have reflected themselves in earnings per share. But since the competitive position of the companies is similar, no adjustments in past earnings were necessary.

How do estimated future earnings of these companies compare? G. D. Searle appears to be in the best position in terms of earnings growth over the period 1969–1975 (Table 12–7). Pfizer appears to have better prospects for earnings growth than Smith Kline & French.

Summary of Analysis

The results of the analysis of earnings and profitability are summarized in Table 12–8. The stability of earnings, cash flow, and profitability refer to the variation of earnings around the trend line. If there is a great variation in earnings or profitability then we can say that they are unstable. Stability is judged on the basis of past relationships.

The tabular presentation only helps to show the relative positions of the companies. When later we relate price to the quantity of future earnings, we will be able to make a decision about the desirability of investing in one of the companies. The beginning investor and analyst must recognize that these estimates are made at a given moment of time,

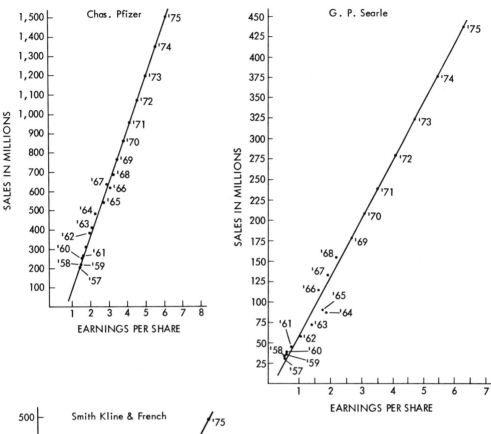

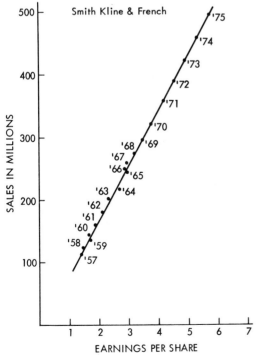

CHART 12-4

*Estimated future earnings of Pfizer,
Searle, and Smith Kline & French,
using the line of average relationship technique*

TABLE 12–7

Forecast of earnings per share for 1969–1975
for Pfizer, Searle, and Smith Kline & French*

	Pfizer		Searle		SKF	
YEAR	PROJECTION OF EARNINGS METHOD	LINE OF AVG. RELATIONSHIP METHOD	PROJECTION OF EARNINGS METHOD	LINE OF AVG. RELATIONSHIP METHOD	PROJECTION OF EARNINGS METHOD	LINE OF AVG. RELATIONSHIP METHOD
1975	$5.70	$6.12	$7.60	$6.25	$6.20	$5.70
1974	5.30	5.50	6.50	5.42	5.70	5.22
1973	4.85	5.00	5.50	4.72	5.25	4.83
1972	4.50	4.50	4.80	4.08	4.85	4.50
1971	4.10	4.10	4.08	3.50	4.45	4.15
1970	3.80	3.75	3.48	3.05	4.10	3.75
1969	3.50	3.40	2.95	2.65	3.75	3.43

* The earnings of these companies are not completely stable. A range of earnings based upon a 10 percent (±) variation would be minimal but realistic.

TABLE 12–8

Companies ranked by past and future earnings

	Company by Rank		
PAST AND FUTURE EARNINGS AND CASH FLOW	PFIZER	SEARLE	SMITH KLINE & FRENCH
Past Earnings			
Amount per share	2	3	1
Rate of growth	3	1	2
Stability	1	3	2
Profitability			
Profit margin	3	1	2
Earning power	3	2	1
Net income to sales ratio	3	1	2
Stability	1	1	1
Cash Flow			
Amount per share	2	1	3
Rate of growth	2	1	3
Stability	1	3	2
Future Earnings			
Growth	2	1	3
Stability	1	3	2

are subject to errors of judgment, and must be continually revised to keep the future in perspective. Our analysis will continue in the next chapters.

Summary

The investment potential of a company is influenced significantly by its past earnings and the future expected growth of earnings. A company that has experienced a growth in earnings and cash flow per share is highly desirable for investment. By the same token, a company must demonstrate a stability and quality of earnings if it is to be a desirable investment. The past growth of earnings and stability of earnings are measured by comparing the trend of earnings with the other leading companies in the industry.

Future earnings and the expectation about them are the central theme of investment value. The usual assumption made by investors is that the past trend of earnings will continue in the future, so we attempt to assess the future earnings capability of a company by fitting a trend line to the earnings, fitting a regression line to the past relationship between sales and earnings, or estimating earnings per share based upon expected sales and profit margins. These methods should lead to satisfactory results in forecasting, but they are only estimates and must be changed when current changes occur within the company.

Companies that have adequate profit margins, earning power, and ratio of net income to sales will most likely maintain their earnings per share. The company that has the best profitability ratios should provide the greatest profit to the investor as sales increase.

The reported earnings of a company should be adjusted to reflect the recurring and permanent earnings and to eliminate the nonrecurring and temporary earnings. Each item of income and expense should be examined to determine as well as possible if it is temporary or permanent. When a company has temporary additions and deductions from earnings, we must make adjustments accordingly.

The basic problem is to compare several companies and to select the one that appears to offer the best earnings. This process was demonstrated with hypothetical and actual cases. To guide the investor, we suggested that each company have:

1. Stability or growth of cash flow and earnings compared with its competitors.
2. Stability or growth of future cash flow and earnings when compared with competitors.
3. A high degree of permanency and quality of earnings.
4. Stable or improving profit margins, earning power, and net income as a percent of sales.

These attributes will then be related to future earnings per share, price per share, and risk. The quantity and quality of future earnings and the price we pay for a security will determine if the investment is satisfactory when balanced with risk. Investors and analysts are cautioned about forecasting future sales and earnings per share. The margin of error is great, and the forecast requires constant evaluation and revision to be successful.

Review Questions

1. Corporate earnings always follow the direction of sales. As sales increase, corporate profits increase; as sales decline, corporate profits decline. Should we agree with these statements? Why or why not?

2. What has been the pattern of aggregate corporate earnings in the United States? Has cash flow followed the same pattern? Explain.

3. Is there any truth in the observation that dividends follow cash flow more closely than they do earnings? Comment.

4. Discuss the various ways we can compute earnings per share from sales and other income minus costs and expenses.

5. Why should we be concerned about the level of cash flow per share? Comment.

6. What is meant by the term *quality of corporate earnings?*

7. To what extent may we rely on earnings reported by the company in estimating the true earning power of the company?

8. What types of variations in income might be considered of low quality and hence nonrecurring?

9. List the major items of costs and expenses a corporation might report. To what extent might each of these vary and be either recurring or nonrecurring and hence reflect themselves in recurring or nonrecurring profits? Include in your discussion the following:
   (a) Depreciation
   (b) Depletion
   (c) Inventory
   (d) Wages
   (e) Federal income taxes

10. Explain the difference between profit margin, earning power, and net income to sales ratio as measures of corporate profitability.

11. (a) Discuss the methods by which we may forecast corporate earnings and arrive at a five-year estimate of future earnings.
    (b) To what extent may we rely on these estimates?
    (c) Can you suggest an improved technique for estimating earnings?
    (d) How do we forecast earnings of companies that have a cyclical character?

12. Review the earnings, cash flow, profitability, quality of earnings and adjusted earnings, and the forecasted earnings of the three drug companies presented for analysis. Comment upon the analysis.

13. Based upon the information presented about each company's profit position, do you agree with the relative ranking in the summary of analysis?

14. What position has the Accounting Principles Board taken with respect to corporate reporting of earnings?

Problems

1. Obtain the earnings per share from 1957 until the present year for the three companies selected in the Problems in Chapter 11.
2. Adjust the earnings per share of each company for any nonrecurring items of income or expense.
3. Add to earnings per share any noncash expenditures per share to arrive at an estimate of cash flow per share.
4. Plot the adjusted earnings per share of each company on semi-log paper (3 cycle).
5. (a) Which company appears to have the greatest rate of growth of earnings?
   (b) Which has the greatest amount of earnings per share?
   (c) Which appears to have the greatest stability of earnings per share?
   (d) Rank each company in order of rate of growth of earnings, amount of earnings per share, and stability of earnings per share.
   (e) Which company appears to be best?
6. Determine the profit margin, earning power, and net income to sales ratio for each of the three companies from 1957 to the present.
   (a) Which company has the highest profit margin?
   (b) Which company has the highest earning power?
   (c) Which company has the highest net income to sales ratio?
   (d) Which company has the greatest overall profit stability as measured by the three ratios of profitability?
7. Estimate future earnings per share based upon forecasted sales and profit margins, the line of average relationship between sales and earnings, and a trend-like projection of earnings. Plot the results.
   (a) Which company appears to have the expectation of the greatest amount and growth of future earnings?
   (b) Which company has the greatest stability of earnings?
   (c) Rank each company on the basis of stability and amount of future earnings.
8. Examine the product of each company. Are any developments under way that might change these forecasts? Include in your answer developments in the domestic and foreign economy and in the military and nonmilitary sector.
9. Based upon this analysis and relative ranking process, which company appears to be best for investment?

Sources of Investment Information

Annual reports of companies
Barron's
Clark Dodge Investment Surveys

Commercial and Financial Chronicle
Moody's manuals
Standard & Poor's *Industry Surveys*
Standard & Poor's *Listed Stock Reports*
Standard & Poor's *Outlook*
Standard & Poor's *Stock Guide*
The Value Line Investment Survey
Wall Street Journal

Selected Readings

Amos, William W., "New Accounting Rules for Fire and Casualty Companies," *Financial Analysts Journal* (September-October, 1966), p. 41.

Axelson, Kenneth S., "Accounting for Deferred Taxes," *Financial Analysts Journal* (September-October, 1966), p. 23.

Briloff, Abraham J., "Pooling of Interests Accounting," *Financial Analysts Journal* (March-April, 1968), p. 71.

Clark, John N., Jr., "The Adjustment of Life Insurance Company Earnings," *Financial Analysts Journal* (September-October, 1966), p. 71.

Corcoran, Eileen T., "Reporting of Leases," *Financial Analysts Journal* (January-February, 1968), p. 29.

Hall, William D., "Accounting for Installment Sales," *Financial Analysts Journal* (September-October, 1966), p. 27.

Harmon, David Perry, Jr., "Pooling of Interests: Case Study," *Financial Analysts Journal* (March-April, 1968), p. 82.

Leveson, Sidney M., "Have We Solved the Dilution Problem?" *Financial Analysts Journal* (September-October, 1968), p. 69.

May, Marvin M., "The Earnings Per Share Trap," *Financial Analysts Journal* (May-June, 1968), p. 113.

Morrison, Paul and James Morrison, "Accounting and Business Acquisitions," *Financial Analysts Journal* (January-February, 1967), p. 51.

Myers, John H., "Depreciation for Fun and Profits," *Financial Analysts Journal* (November-December, 1967), p. 117.

O'Glove, Thornton L., "Finance Company Accounting," *Financial Analysts Journal* (January-February, 1968), p. 37.

Weston, Frank T., "Reporting Earnings Per Share," *Financial Analysts Journal* (July-August, 1967), p. 45.

Weston, Frank T. and Sidney Davidson, "Accounting Changes and Earnings," *Financial Analysts Journal* (September-October, 1968), p. 59.

Williams, William D., "A Look Behind Reported Earnings," *Financial Analysts Journal* (January-February, 1966), p. 38.

13

OPERATING EFFICIENCY

The profitability of a company and its earnings are directly affected by the efficiency with which it conducts its business. We can measure operating efficiency in terms of profit margins, earning power, and earnings per share as we did in the previous chapter. Or we can measure it by comparing revenues with expenses or by comparing input (expenses) with output (the sales generated as a result of the expenditures). We have developed the operating ratio to help us understand the relative degree of efficiency with which a company operates. Other measures, such as output per employee, output per dollar of plant, operating rate, and the breakeven point, help us to understand how efficient a company is in performing its tasks. Obviously, each of these factors has an influence upon earnings per share.

The Operating Characteristics of a Company

The operating efficiency and the earnings of a company are influenced directly by the company's operating characteristics. A company, for example, that is constantly expanding its physical facilities and continues to operate at full capacity is more likely to produce profits and earnings in the future than one that is not utilizing all of its operating capacity. A company that is expanding and is maintaining a high operating rate with a low breakeven point will be a profitable company. A company that operates at a low level of capacity with a high breakeven point will be less profitable or might even suffer a loss. A company with a stable operating rate will have more stable revenues than a company with an unstable operating rate. There is no magic about the source of revenues for any company. Income from sales is the result of the efficient use of capital assets combined with raw materials, labor, and management. If a company is to expand sales or revenues, it must also expand its capital asset base. The assets will be purchased from funds generated internally through company operations or from the sale of debt, preferred stock, or common stock. The addition of new assets will affect the breakeven point of a company and its range of profitable operations. Expanding plant investment, for example, raises the breakeven point, and until sales expand, temporarily reduces profits. These are the effects of operating leverage. If the money to buy the assets came from the sale of additional common stock, then earnings per share might be reduced even further. This is the effect of financial leverage. We shall begin our discussion by examining what is meant by the operating capacity of a company, its operating rate, and its breakeven point, and we will relate these concepts to earnings per share.

Productive Capacity of a Company

What is the capacity of a company to produce a product or service? This is easy to ask, but the answer is not quite so simple. If we asked the president of the American Can Company what was his company's capacity to produce, he might counter with another question, "What is our capacity to produce which product?" Many companies produce more than one product. Therefore, when we raise the question of productive capacity, we must specify a product or a group of products produced together that utilize the existing plant and equipment. Some companies produce so many products that we cannot come up with any answer except in broad dollar terms. The answer we would receive under these conditions would be something like this: "With our present plant and combination of products, we have the capacity to produce $325 million worth of sales." Thus the capacity is measured in terms of dollars of output. In spite of the difficulty involved in determining plant capacity, we are interested in knowing the capacity of a firm to produce and how much it can earn if it operates at full capacity. Let us examine further the concept of plant capacity.

When a company produces one product or a few that are homogeneous, plant capacity should be readily determined. Consider an electric utility, for example. The output is measured in kilowatt hours. Each company can produce a certain number of kilowatt hours of electricity, determined by the rated capacity of the generators used to produce the electricity. But even under these circumstances, it is difficult to determine the actual capacity to produce. Most generators have a rated capacity but can be operated safely above this rate. Let us assume, for instance, that Cleveland Electric Illuminating has a generator with rated capacity of 100,000 kilowatts. It would be possible for CEI to generate 110,000 to 115,000 kilowatts of capacity for short periods of time without harm to the generator. Thus it would be possible for the company to operate 10 to 15 percent above rated capacity. The same is true in the steel and paper industries. During national emergencies, the steel industry in particular has operated at 104 or 105 percent of capacity. This is possible only because of the method used in determining the capacity of blast furnaces. A change in technology can change the capacity of a blast furnace. In modern steel mills, oxygen is used in one phase of the production cycle. This increases the speed with which impurities are removed from the molten ore and speeds up the production cycle, which increases the output of the blast furnace far beyond its rated capacity. When making an estimate of capacity, these ancillary factors must therefore be considered.

The production capacity of companies in many other industries is more difficult to determine, particularly when a company produces more than one product. What is the plant capacity of a drug company or department store, for example? The capacity of such a company to produce would depend upon the product being produced and in what portion of the total plant. Let us look at a simple case. A drug company produces Products *A* and *B*. Its total capacity to produce will be different if 50 percent of the space is devoted to each product than if 40 percent of productive space is devoted to Product *A* and 60 to Product *B*. When we attempt to measure plant capacity for this type of company, we must make certain assumptions about the balance of its productive facilities between products.

A department store, with its many individual departments and products, would be forced to consider floor space as the capacity of the store. The square feet available suggests the capacity of such a company to produce. Hence, the store having a greater amount of floor space would have a greater capacity to produce. The most efficient company, of course, would generate most dollars of sales per square foot.

Some companies have no capacity limit other than the imagination or energy of their management and staff. What, for example, is the capacity of a life or casualty insurance company to produce? We could determine average sales per employee for the industry, multiply this figure by the number of people employed in the company, and allow this to serve as the capacity figure. But it would not be a satisfactory measure for a specific company.

The commercial bank, contrary to what we might expect, does have a limit (imposed by the capital–deposit ratio) to its capacity to lend. In banking, the typical capital–deposit ratio is close to 1:10. This is imposed by principles of conservative bank management and is not a state or federal reserve requirement. In order to expand plant, a bank must have more capital. If a bank operates below a 1 to 10 ratio, it is operating below capacity. If it operates above this ratio, more capital is probably needed.

If the unit of measurement is known, the capacity of a firm can be estimated through careful study. Where a physical capacity is nonexistent or difficult to determine, we can often substitute dollar figures of capacity. In this case we might say that the capacity of a firm to produce is $500 million. Before the company could expand its output beyond this amount, it would have to add to plant capacity or to sales personnel. Table 13–1 gives the units of measure for some industries. These can be used as an aid in determining plant capacity.

The Operating Rate[1]

Manufacturing equipment is usually designed to be most profitable when operated at or close to full capacity. A high operating rate is so important for some companies that they do not earn a profit if they go below 95 percent of capacity. Other companies become less efficient as they

TABLE 13–1

Units of measure for selected industries to aid in establishing plant capacity

Containers	Tons
Utilities—Gas	Thousand Cubic Feet (MCF)
Utilities—Electric	Kilowatt Hours (KWH)
Shoes	Number of Pairs
Drugs & Drug Products	Lbs., Gram Units
Meats	Lbs.
Passenger Airlines	Passenger Seats Available on Scheduled Flights
Coal	Tons
Baking & Milling	Lbs.
Retail Trade	$
Liquor	Gallons
Textiles	Yards
Sugar	Tons
Metals:	
Aluminum	Lbs.
Steel	Tons
Paper	Tons
Rubber	Lbs.
Electronics	$ and Number of Machines
Tobacco	Billions of Cigarettes
Soft Drinks	Cases
Candy	Lbs.
Aerospace	$ and Number of Engines
Office Equipment	$ and Numbers of Machines
Oil	Barrels $\times$ Operating Rate
Railroads	Ton Miles
Insurance	$
Banks	$

1 *Operating rate* is defined as output or production expressed as a percent of plant capacity.

approach full capacity because they must use inefficient equipment. One public utility, for example, uses its old equipment only when the demand for electricity exceeds normal demands. When this company increases its production from 95 percent to 100 percent of capacity, its increase in profit is less than if the more efficient, low-cost equipment were used. With many corporations, profits increase with increased production only to a point. As they approach 100 percent of capacity, expenses increase faster than income, and revenues decline. In short, most companies are most profitable as they expand production and operate at a high level of capacity, but not necessarily when they operate at or above 100 percent of rated capacity. Operating characteristics differ from company to company. The profitability level might be 60 percent of capacity for one and 90 percent for another.

We are concerned about operating rate because of its impact upon earnings per share. This effect manifests itself in two ways. First, the higher and more stable the operating rate, the higher the per share earnings. Second, the effect of a change in the operating rate of a company from one level to another will have differing effects upon earnings per share. As a company moves toward full capacity, a given increase in output, other things being equal, will have a smaller and smaller effect upon earnings. This will be discussed more fully when we examine the breakeven point of a company.

Our first concern is to learn what the historical operating rate of the company has been. We ask, "Has the company been able to operate at a high level of capacity during both depression and prosperity?" A knowledge of the operating characteristics of the industry is helpful in evaluating the operating rate of a company. Excellent operating data for the steel industry are reported regularly in the financial press, since steel is a basic industry important to the national economy. During and after World War II this industry operated at full productive capacity, sometimes above full capacity. In 1961, operations dropped, and the industry as a whole operated at about 70 percent of capacity. It did not increase its operating rate until the first half of 1963. From 1963 to 1968 the level was around 85 percent of plant capacity. Actually there was an increase in plant capacity, a substantial increase in steel-making facilities, during this period. What can we do with this knowledge?

The first and more obvious point is that the steel industry has had a severe decrease in its rate of production and the production rate has varied in the past. The industry has a cyclical tendency coupled with growth, and the modern mill operates at 100 percent of capacity only in times of national emergency. Firms in the industry, on the average, are not as profitable as when they operated at almost 100 percent capacity. When a decline in output takes place, however, the behavior of the individual company is of more importance. Some firms in the steel industry operated at far less than full capacity, while others operated above the level of the industry. Some companies, therefore, remained profitable, others lost money. We want to know which were able to maintain a strong operating rate. Armco is a good case in point. During this period, Armco had a tendency to maintain a higher operating rate than the industry as a whole. At times, when the industry operating rate was low, Armco managed to run at a higher percent of capacity. Granite City Steel, a smaller company in St. Louis, also had a favorable operating rate compared with that of the industry during the same period. Strong firms usually will tend to maintain their operating rates during periods of recession better than the industry as a whole. We consider a good operating rate over time a sign of corporate strength that will help the company maintain its earnings and profitability.

To be considered a growing company, a company must have a favorable operating rate. It will constantly expand its facilities to meet the growing demand for its product. It will probably operate close to full capacity. Growth is not limitless, but while the company is expanding, its level of operations will not be a problem. The biggest problem will be to keep up with the demand. Producers of color television in the 1960's were good examples of expanding production in an expanding industry. Companies not in growth industries may experience a decline in demand for their product, will be plagued with unused capacity, and will operate well below productive capacity. Earnings, too, will decline. The alternative is to develop new products that will allow the plant to be used in a more profitable way; otherwise the unused facilities will provide a low profit for the owners. Several Small Business Investment Companies (SBIC's)[2] were in this position early in 1964. Only one-quarter to one-half of their funds were invested profitably; the other funds remained idle. The profitability of these companies was low. They were only partially productive and not operating at full capacity. Although not manufacturing plants with a fixed capacity, SBIC's still have a total capacity to invest. Since 1964, the operating rate of the SBIC's has improved, and many have become fully invested.

The problem of unemployed capital assets is not confined to an industry or to a company but is a national problem. In the late 1950's, the national economy operated around the 90 percent level with a peak of 97 percent in 1955. In the 1960's, after billions of dollars had been spent on new plant and equipment, the operating level of industrial operations was between 85 and 90 percent.

We should invest in those companies that maintain a high rate of production and employ their resources to their fullest advantage. The most productive firms should be the most profitable firms for investment. An example of the type of analysis that should be made and

---

2 SBIC's are essentially mutual funds that specialize in raising capital for the small, growing company with the aid of government financing.

conclusions that may be drawn are presented in Table 13–2. Operating capacity, output, and operating rate are presented for Company *A*. Compared with the industry and Company *B*, Company *A* has enjoyed a higher and more stable operating rate. Based on this factor alone, we would conclude that Company *A* was a better quality company. Unfortunately, data of this type are not available for all companies or all industries. Paper, oil, steel, metals, water, electric, gas, autos, transportation, hotels, and similar industries have readily available data on an industry level. Many companies, however, are reluctant to indicate their operating rates, and company information is difficult to obtain.

The Breakeven Point, Operating Capacity, and Leverage

The breakeven point is that place in the level of operations where revenues just equal the total costs. Total costs include both fixed and variable costs. The usual theoretical way of presenting the breakeven point is shown in Chart 13–1. The vertical axis represents both dollars of revenue and dollars of expense. Usually only the percent of capacity or the number of units produced are shown on the horizontal axis. Some companies, however, do not produce a tangible product and do not have a well-defined capacity in units or percent of output; the only figures available are dollars of sales. We must assume that at some dollar volume of sales the company will break even. To accommodate companies of this type, dollars of revenue were put on the horizontal axis.

The revenue line in Chart 13–1 represents the amount of revenue received at each level of production or percent of capacity of the firm. If dollars of sales are used, obviously dollars will be on the horizontal axis as well as the vertical. The variable costs line is the total of the variable costs as they change with total output. Ordinarily, we assume that these expenses increase directly with output; in reality they tend to increase

TABLE 13–2

Operating capacity, output, and operating
rate compared with operating rate of a
competitive company and the industry*

	Company A			Operating Rate (%)	
YEAR	OPERATING CAPACITY (UNITS)	OUTPUT (UNITS)	OPERATING RATE (%)	COMPANY B	INDUSTRY
1963	450	425	94	87	92
1962	400	380	95	90	93
1961	350	325	93	89	89
1960	315	300	95	91	91
1959	280	260	93	90	90
1958	250	240	96	92	92
1957	200	180	90	89	87

* Companies are hypothetical.

at a slower rate than output because of the economies of large-scale production. The economies achievable with volume vary from company to company and depend a great deal on the size of the firm and its ability to benefit from such economies. Fixed costs are added to variable costs to establish the total costs of the firm. Fixed costs are constant and do not vary within the productive range of the firm. As output increases, however, they do decrease per unit. If new plant were added, then fixed costs would increase, and the breakeven point would be changed. For example, an increase in fixed cost would, without any offsetting changes in volume of output or variable costs, tend to raise the breakeven point.

At the breakeven point the costs of doing business have been met, but there are no rewards for the owners. Only after the company moves beyond the breakeven point does it become profitable. Therefore, a company that has a low breakeven point and a consistently high operating rate will be a very profitable company for investment. If we add to this equation a degree of certainty of the operating rate, we have an attractive investment possibility. The importance of the operating rate is once again brought into focus.

The knowledge that a company is operating at a specific percent of capacity is, however, only an indication of relative profitableness. We

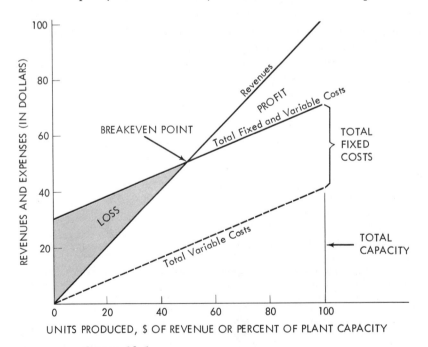

CHART 13–1

Typical breakeven chart for a company

can say that a company would be more profitable if it operated at 95 rather than 85 percent of capacity. We cannot say that one company operating at 85 percent of capacity is more profitable than another operating at 78 percent. The relative degree of profitability of the two companies depends not only upon the operating level but upon the breakeven point. A firm operating at 78 percent of capacity, with a 50 percent breakeven point, will be more profitable than a firm operating at 85 percent of capacity with an 80 percent breakeven point. We must relate the operating rate to the breakeven point to determine profitability. It is important, therefore, to try to estimate the breakeven point of the company in which we are to invest and assess its impact upon earnings per share.

The determination of a breakeven point is not a simple task. We must attempt to determine the relative degree of profitability based upon the existing level of plant, price, and cost structure that remain fixed. We then vary the output of the company. By doing this we can estimate at what volume of sales or at what percent of capacity the company will cover all of its costs and break even. Unfortunately prices vary, costs vary, and the mixture of the products produced varies over short periods of time, making the task of calculating the breakeven point difficult. And we are beset by another problem. The classification of fixed cost and variable cost is arbitrary, since some costs fall into both categories. Telephone expenses are a good example of this. The charge for basic service is fixed, but long distance calls and calls beyond the basic number are additional and variable charges. As the volume of business increases so do telephone expenses. Hence, telephone and similar charges are both fixed and variable, yet we must try to put them into either one or the other category. Again, in spite of these difficulties, breakeven analysis is important in estimating earnings.

We must understand the influence of a variation of the operating rate upon the variation of earnings of a company. The change in earnings brought about by a change in operating rate is referred to as *operating leverage*. It can be related to the breakeven point and helps to explain why a 10 percent increase in sales might lead to a 20 percent increase in earnings per share or possibly to a 5 percent decrease in earnings. The concept of operating leverage can be demonstrated by an example. Assume that a company is operating at its breakeven point and experiences a 10 percent increase in sales. The effect on earnings is phenomenal. They increase from $0 per share to, say, $.25 per share. An infinite percentage of increase in earnings results—($.25 − 0/$.0) × 100. Now let us assume that sales increase another 10 percent and earnings increase to $.50 per share. Sales increase 10 percent but earnings per share increase 100 percent—($.50 − .25/$.25) × 100. If sales increase another 10 percent, earnings will increase another $.25 per share to $.75, but the percentage increase is only 50 percent—($.75 — .50/$.50) × 100. Thus, as production increases and moves toward full capacity away from the breakeven point, earnings increase but at a decreasing rate of increase. Earnings might actually decrease if inefficiencies enter into production.

Operating leverage in each company must be studied to assess its impact upon earnings. A company could have a sharp increase in earnings, which might not be permanent. This is true for cyclical companies in which a decline in revenues automatically sets the stage for a sharp increase in earnings (after a sharp decrease) that might give the appearance of a growth situation or basic improvement. Assume, for example, that Company *A*'s revenues declined by 10 percent because of a cyclical decline, that earnings dropped sharply, and that there was a greater percentage drop in earnings than in revenues. An analysis of the operating characteristics of Company *A* will help us anticipate what will happen to earnings based upon changes in sales and operating revenues. The following year, however, business improves and so do the revenues of Company *A*. The improvement in business brings about a sharp increase in profits for Company *A* because of operating leverage. If one noticed only the increase in profits and ignored the operating leverage, one might draw a wrong conclusion about the profit characteristics of the company.

Breakeven analysis has significance for the investor. The breakeven point related to the operating rate of the company gives us a measure of profitability. The company that has a low breakeven point will be more profitable both at lower and higher levels of operation. Earnings will persist in spite of a decline in business, and the company will be better able to succeed even in periods of depressed business. The company with a high breakeven point is extremely susceptible to a profit decline in periods of recession; a slight decline in revenues could eliminate profits completely.

We are wise, therefore, to select for investment a company having a low breakeven point, a high operating rate, and high stability of revenues. This ensures future profitability. We must look for this type of company in our analysis.

The steel industry operates around a breakeven point of 50 percent. The auto and electronics industries have an estimated breakeven point of 60 percent. The drug industry has an estimated breakeven point of 65 percent and the paper industry about 75 percent. These examples are only estimates and are subject to current review.

LIMITS TO THE USE OF BREAKEVEN POINT

Breakeven analysis can be effectively used by the investor in establishing the profit range of a company. Given the breakeven point and the operating rate, we can easily establish the range of profitability to use in forecasting profits. If we know what operating rate to expect in the future, then we should be able to predict future earnings. However, we can also estimate profits based upon detailed forecasts of expense and revenues by projecting past relationships between profits and sales and by projecting earnings.

Breakeven analysis is essentially static. We assume that prices, wages, capital, and interest are constant over the range of production. Yet we know that these variables do change. Once we have calculated the breakeven point, we might find that it has changed; and this, of course, destroys the validity of the analysis. We also assume that the relationships between revenues and expenses or costs are linear, yet they might not be so simply described. Previously we said that variable costs might not change at the same rate because of economies of large-scale production. If this is true, our profit forecasts will be inaccurate if we use a straight-line projection.

In spite of these limitations, breakeven analysis focuses attention upon operating rates, profitability, and operating leverage. To the extent that it approximates levels of profits, it has accomplished a good deal to help support the analysis and forecast of earnings per share.

Measures of Operating Efficiency

Several other measures in addition to the operating rate and the breakeven point are available to establish the relative operating efficiency of a company. Three familiar measures are: (1) operating ratio, (2) sales or profits per employee, and (3) sales or profits per dollar of plant investment. In addition to these ratios, each industry has its own measures that can be used to advantage.

The Operating Ratio

The operating ratio is found by dividing operating revenues into operating expenses plus cost of goods sold. It is directly related to the profit margin: if we subtracted the profit margin from 100 percent, we would have the operating ratio.

The operating ratio is a good measure of operating efficiency, for it relates costs and expenses directly to revenues. It is easily understood. The lower the operating ratio, the more efficient is the company and, of course, the more profitable. However, overall profitability and efficiency must also be related to operating assets. The fact that the operating ratio of a company is low and a sign of operating strength is valid only for comparable corporations within the same industry. The operating ratio does change over time; it is important in any analysis to consider the direction of the change. An increasing operating ratio should be interpreted as a sign of weakness. A constant or decreasing operating ratio would be a sign of strength. Both these statements assume that other conditions remain constant. An increasing operating ratio brought about by a decrease in revenues that expands volume and improves revenues as a percent of assets would be desirable, even though the operating ratio increased.

Sales and Earnings Per Employee

Sales per employee, measured in terms of dollar sales or units of output, provide another indication of corporate efficiency. The greater the sales per employee, the greater the relative efficiency of a company. Profit or earnings per employee might also be used as a measure of efficiency. The greater and the more stable the earnings per employee, the greater is the overall efficiency of the company. Earnings per employee is actually a financial ratio, but it can be used as an efficiency ratio. We may use both sales per employee and earnings per employee as measures of the quality of a company. The higher the output and earnings per employee over time, the better the company.

Sales and Earnings Per Dollar of Plant Investment

The same comments that were made about sales and earnings per employee can be made about these measures of efficiency and profitability. The greater the sales or earnings per dollar of plant investment, the better the company. These ratios are considered by some analysts as more important than net income to sales. They reflect the return derived from expenditures on new plant equipment. In some industries you can measure sales by expenditures for plant. In the chemical industry, for example, a dollar of plant should produce a dollar of sales. A higher or lower ratio would reflect relative degrees of operating efficiency. A decrease in sales and profits per dollar of plant would indicate a weakness in the efficiency and profitability of the company.

Using the Measures of Operating Efficiency

Table 13–3 presents the operating ratio and the sales and earnings per dollar of plant and per employee for two companies. Based upon the criteria we have established, which company appears to be better? A careful examination of the data in Table 13–3 reveals that Company *B* appears to be better. It enjoyed the lower and more stable operating ratio. Sales and profits per employee increased between 1957 and 1968 as did sales and earnings per dollar of plant. All of these changes were better relative to those experienced by Company *A*. This was easy to decide, since the evidence was so clear-cut in favor of Company *B*. Often the data will be mixed, and the right decision will not be as apparent. Our criteria here, however, are simply which company had the best sales and earnings per employee and per dollar invested and had the lowest operating rate.

TABLE 13–3

*Operating ratio and sales and profit per
employee and per dollar of plant investment
for two hypothetical companies*

	Company A		Company B	
	1957	1968	1957	1968
Operating ratio	74%	76%	65%	65%
Sales per employee	$1,025	$1,200	$1,000	$1,250
Earnings per employee	65	58	66	67
Sales per dollar of plant	1.25	1.15	1.30	1.32
Earnings per dollar of plant	.08	.10	.10	.11

Capital Expenditures

Future earnings depend upon the ability of management to invest new corporate funds wisely and to manage the old efficiently. The investment of corporate funds is referred to as *capital expenditure.* All expenditures for plant and equipment will not be equally profitable, but we can assume that the greater the expenditure for new plant and equipment and the improvement of old facilities, the better able the company will be to deliver future earnings. Therefore, we can use capital expenditure as one guide to determine the profitableness of a company in the future. A positive and definite relationship exists between capital equipment and sales and future earnings. There is a physical limit to a firm's ability to produce and sell. Once that limit is reached, the firm cannot expand without more expenditures for new plant and equipment or for improving old plant and equipment. The relationship between sales and plant is not the same for each industry. In the steel industry, for example, a dollar spent for plant has the potential of generating a dollar of sales. A dollar spent for new plant for an electric utility might produce only $.20 of sales.

The magnitude of capital expenditures is important. Perhaps more important is the relationship between capital expenditure and the existing plant. One company might spend $1,000,000 on new plant and a second company $10,000,000. The second company made the bigger expenditure and our attention would be called to it. If the expenditure made by the first company increased its fixed assets by 50 percent and the second company increased its assets by only 10 percent, then we would conclude that the first company had made the larger relative expenditure. The first company actually had $2,000,000 of plant and equipment to begin with, whereas the second company had $100,000,000. The relative impact on earnings would be greater in the first company than in the second.

Table 13–4 provides us with capital expenditures as a percent of gross plant for several leading industries. This data will give some idea of what capital expenditure we can expect from individual companies in these industries. Xerox Corporation in the office equipment industry spent as much as 50 percent of its gross plant for new capital expenditure. Underwood Corporation, in a somewhat allied field, spent less than 10 percent of gross plant for new capital expenditure in the same year. Xerox has been expanding rapidly, doubling in size almost every two years, placing it in a superior position to Underwood, which has since merged with Olivetti and changed its name.

TABLE 13-4

Capital expenditures as percent of gross plant
for selected industries, 1966

	1966 AVERAGE
Aerospace	
Major prime weapons	19.8
Subsystems	15.5
Propulsion	9.5
Aircraft engines	14.0
Private planes	19.0
Auto Parts	16.5
Baking and Milling	
Flour milling[a]	24.8
Bread baking	9.9
Specialty baking	14.8
Breakfast cereals	6.5
Containers	
Paper containers	9.8
Metal containers	11.1
Glass containers	26.0
Drugs	
Ethical	15.7
Proprietary	16.0
Cosmetics	14.1
Razors & blades	19.6
Miscellaneous	20.7
Electrical and Electronic	
Industry leaders	18.8
Electrical products	18.5
Electric control & utility equipment	8.7
Household appliances	12.6
Radio & television	28.2
Food Products	
Canning	10.5
Packaged foods	10.3
Corn products	7.0
Meats and Dairy Products	
Meat packers	7.1
Dairy products	9.6
Metals	
Aluminum	13.3
Copper	10.8
Copper-mining cost	6.7

TABLE 13–4 *(continued)*

Wire fabricators	17.9
Other fabricators	14.2
Office Equipment	
Accounting & tabulating	16.6
Miscellaneous	12.6
Office supplies	30.5
Rubber fabricating	13.8
Telephone & Telegraph	11.9
Textile and Apparel	
Textile weavers	14.1
Rayon & acetate	12.9
Apparel	16.4
Utilities-Gas	
Pipelines	8.3
Distributors	6.9

[a] 1965 average

SOURCES: Standard and Poor's *Industry Surveys* in order presented; *Aerospace*, August 31, 1967, p. A 28; *Auto Parts*, September 7, 1967, p. A 101; *Baking & Milling*, September 7, 1967, p N 12; *Containers*, December 21, 1967, p. C 100; *Drugs, Cosmetics*, May 2, 1968, p. D 22; *Electronics, Electrical*, December 14, 1967, p. E 29; *Food Products*, November 30, 1967, F 37; *Meats & Dairy Products*, May 25, 1967, p. M 71; *Metals*, September 14, 1967, p. M 109; *Office Equipment*, May 25, 1967, p. O 18; *Rubber Fabricating*, April 25, 1968, p. R 134; *Telephone*, May 9, 1968, p. T 15; *Textiles and Apparel*, December 7, 1967, p. T 48; *Utilities-Gas*, June 1, 1967, p. U 45.

The conclusions we can draw from the data in Table 13–4 are not norms or standards. The impression we have is that capital expenditures as a percent of plant typically range from 7 to 30 percent, with a norm of 15 percent. An expenditure above 20 percent would be high and below 10 percent would be low. Office supplies, radio and television, glass containers, and flour milling appear to have made the largest capital expenditures. Industries such as gas distributors, copper-mining cost, meat packing, and breakfast cereals made relatively small capital expenditures. In the last analysis, what constitutes a large or a small capital expenditure depends on how the individual company compares with the industry in which it functions.

Capital expenditures undertaken by a company should reflect an increased demand for a product or an attempt to improve plant so that costs can be reduced, making the firm more competitive. Fully expensed annual capital expenditures also add to the stock of capital to make the firm more competitive. The needs of each corporation will vary, depending upon its competitive position. Capital expenditures made in anticipation of increased demand for a product must be analyzed carefully. Anticipated demand can decline. This results in excess capacity, a poor operating ratio, and impaired earnings and profitability. The initial capital expenditures were evidence of strength, yet they became a sign of weakness because of incorrect anticipation of demand. This type of situation existed in the past in the aluminum, paper, and plywood industries. It was temporary, but when demand did not materialize to maintain the capacity of the firms, the impact was severe. These industries suffered from excess capacity and temporary overexpansion. When we examine capital expenditures, we must realize that a latent and potential threat of overexpansion exists.

An Analysis of Operating Efficiency Applied to the Ethical Drug Companies

Thousands of products are produced in the ethical and proprietary drug industry. One source estimates that between 1956 and 1967, 2,976 totally new drug products were introduced nationally in the United States in the pharmaceutical industry.[3] The amount of money spent for research has increased substantially in the last decade, but the number of new drugs introduced annually has declined. These products differ to such an extent that a definition of a single production or consumption unit is prohibited. Any attempt to determine the operating capacity of the industry or of a particular company in physical units is impractical. We must use dollar figures of capital expenditures, sales, and operating ratio as a guide to overall productivity.

The Operating Rate and Operating Capacity

Pfizer, Searle, and Smith Kline & French all operated at full capacity during the period 1957 through 1968. This is reflected in both their growth of sales and growth of plant. The net plant (Table 13–5) of each company has expanded substantially between 1957 and 1967. Pfizer has demonstrated the greatest growth. G. D. Searle and Smith Kline & French experienced quite similar rates of growth, but Smith Kline & French had a somewhat larger net plant over the period. If these companies had not demonstrated such dramatic growth, we would have examined their operating capacity more closely. The implication here is that the greater the growth in net plant the better the company for investment. This assumes, of course, that a company can operate an expanded net plant profitably. It also assumes comparability in accounting practices and reporting of expenditures.

The Breakeven Point

The breakeven point is difficult to calculate for the three companies because of the heterogeneous nature of their products. Approximate estimates of the breakeven point for the companies are presented in

3 Paul de Haen, Standard & Poor's *Industry Surveys—Drugs, Cosmetics,* May 2, 1968, Table 7, p. D11.

TABLE 13–5

Net plant and capital expenditures as a percent of gross plant for Pfizer, Searle, and Smith Kline & French (millions of dollars and percent)

Net Plant in Millions $

	1957	1958	1959	1960	1961	1962	1963	1964	1965	1966	1967
Chas. Pfizer	44.4	75.05	97.72	116.39	121.35	148.1	154.8	175.2	192.0	217.7	239.7
G. D. Searle	8.4	8.60	8.40	8.50	10.70	12.8	13.7	17.2	20.8	27.2	32.3
Smith Kline & French	28.4	28.20	30.20	34.20	35.40	36.9	39.1	46.0	53.6	60.2	65.2

Capital Expenditures as a Percent of Gross Plant

	1957	1958	1959	1960	1961	1962	1963	1964	1965	1966	1967
Chas. Pfizer	15.6	22.5	19.3	11.0	9.1	10.78	7.4	9.6	10.3	10.4	9.3
G. D. Searle	4.4	8.3	3.7	7.9	17.8	11.04	9.5	17.7	16.2	13.6	9.0
Smith Kline & French	21.2	6.0	13.0	13.3	7.4	8.69	9.6	15.8	17.5	13.4	10.4

SOURCE: Standard & Poor's *Industry Surveys—Drugs, Cosmetics,* January 4, 1964, pp. D22 and D23; and May 2, 1968, p. D22.

Table 13–6. The data were based upon the 1968 income and expense items of the three firms. The breakeven point was calculated on the present size of the company. It did not take into consideration any proposed additions to plant. Searle had the lowest breakeven point, Pfizer the highest. If we look upon the lowest breakeven point as being most desirable, we would rate G. D. Searle first, Smith Kline & French second, and Pfizer third.

Operating Ratio

G. D. Searle enjoyed the lowest operating ratio of these three leaders in the ethical drug industry. Smith Kline & French also had an excellent operating ratio. We notice (Table 13–6) that Searle's operating ratio has been relatively stable except that there was a tendency in 1965, 1966, and 1967 for it to increase. Pfizer had the highest operating ratio of the three companies.

Operating Efficiency and Capital Expenditures

When we examine the operating efficiency of these companies in Table 13–7, we find that G. D. Searle appears to hold the position of leadership. It demonstrated the highest net income per employee, the highest earnings per dollar of plant, and highest sales per employee. Its sales per dollar of plant were close behind Smith Kline & French. Based upon these criteria, we would place Smith Kline & French after Searle, followed by Chas. Pfizer. Once again we have an indication of overall efficiency and investment quality.

The percent of capital expenditures per dollar of gross plant is not stable, nor does it show a definite trend for these companies. This is revealed in Table 13–5. In 1961, 1962, 1964 and 1966, G. D. Searle had a higher capital expenditure as a percent of gross plant than Pfizer or Smith Kline & French. Each company over the period spent substantial amounts on capital expenditures, which would help to ensure future profitability.

Summary of Operating Characteristics

A summary of the observations about the relative position of each of the three companies appears in Table 13–8. The physical data about operations and operating efficiency augment our quantitative knowledge about these companies. The analysis suggests that G. D. Searle is a well-run company and first in operating characteristics compared with Smith Kline & French and Chas. Pfizer. The analysis reinforces our value judgement about Searle and about the ability of each company to meet its future earnings estimate. The valuation appraisal will continue in the next chapter, where we will examine current and long-term financial position of each drug company.

TABLE 13-6

Operating ratios and breakeven points for Pfizer, Searle, and Smith Kline & French (percent)

	ESTIMATED BREAKEVEN POINTS 1968	Operating Ratios										
		1957	1958	1959	1960	1961	1962	1963	1964	1965	1966	1967
Chas. Pfizer	80	77.2	81.8	84.1	85.1	79.6	79.6	82.1	79.5	78.7	77.7	79.5
G. D. Searle	50	51.4	54.2	55.0	56.8	53.0	49.2	43.7	43.2	56.0	59.2	58.1
Smith Kline & French	60	61.2	62.3	61.8	64.1	61.8	55.4	64.1	64.3	65.4	66.9	67.1

SOURCE: Standard & Poor's *Industry Surveys—Drugs, Cosmetics*, January 9, 1964, pp. D24 and D25; and May 2, 1968, p. D23.

TABLE 13–7

Net income or earnings and sales per dollar of plant and per employee for Pfizer, Searle, and Smith Kline & French

	Net Income or Earnings Per Employee in Thousands of Dollars			Sales Per Employee in Thousands of Dollars			Net Income or Earnings Per Dollar of Plant			Sales Per Dollar of Plant		
	1957	1962	1966	1957	1962	1966	1957	1962	1966	1957	1962	1966
Chas. Pfizer	1.2	1.8	1.9	10.4	19.2	18.9	.52	.25	.30	4.7	2.6	3.1
G. D. Searle	4.3	8.6	9.5	19.1	35.4	47.4	.82	1.07	.84	3.6	4.4	4.2
Smith Kline & French	4.3	6.3	5.6	23.1	37.1	33.9	.72	.83	.69	4.1	4.9	4.2

SOURCE: *Moody's Industrial Manuals, Moody's Investors Service*, New York, 1963, pp. 772, 2309, and 2323; and 1958, p. 809; and June, 1967, pp. 1583, 1584, 1700, 1701, 651 and 652.

TABLE 13–8

Companies ranked by operating characteristics,
operating efficiency, and capital expenditures

	CHAS. PFIZER	G. D. SEARLE	SMITH KLINE & FRENCH
Operating Characteristics			
Productive capacity	1	1	1
Operating rate	1	1	1
Growth of plant	1	2	3
Breakeven point (lowest)	3	1	2
Operating ratio (lowest)	3	1	2
Operating Efficiency			
Sales per dollar of plant	3	2	1
Sales per employee	3	1	2
Earnings per employee	3	1	2
Earnings per dollar of plant	3	1	2
Capital Expenditures			
Total spent for net plant, 1963–67	1	3	2
Total spent as a percent of gross plant, 1963–67	3	2	1

Summary

A thorough analysis of a company requires an examination of operating characteristics and efficiency. One of the first steps in this analysis is to learn the capacity of the firm to produce its product or services. A second step is to understand its operating characteristics and its historical operating rate. The third point of analysis is the breakeven point. Knowledge of the breakeven point based upon existing capacity and historic operating rate tells us a good deal about the profit expectation of the company. Fourth, capital expenditures tell us something about the firm's ability to expand and be more profitable in the future. Expanding plant capacity should reflect an increased demand for the products of the company. The fifth step is to analyze the operating efficiency of the company. This is expressed in dollar terms and is used with the financial ratios and profitability ratios. The ratios used are the operating ratio, sales and net income per employee, and sales and income per dollar of plant. As investors we want a company that has an expanding plant capacity, high operating rate, and low breakeven point. These are indicative of the profitability of the company and help improve future earnings. The measures of operating efficiency are also indicative of profitability. The company with the lowest operating ratio, the highest sales and net income per employee, and the highest sales and net income per dollar of plant investment should be the best company. It is helpful when examining these ratios to compare them with those of other companies and, if available, comparable data for the industry. The analysis adds a qualitative dimension to our value analysis based upon estimates of future profitability.

Review Questions

1. What is the usual relationship between the operating efficiency of a company and its earnings; for example, as operating efficiency improves, do earnings improve? Comment.

2. How do we determine the productive capacity of a company? What are the problems in establishing productive capacity, in the companies in the following industries?
   (a) Banking and finance
   (b) Industrial
   (c) Public utility
   (d) Transportation

3. How would you measure the capacity of a company to produce if it made several different types of products? Explain.

4. Define what is meant by the term *operating rate*.
   (a) Why is the historic operating rate of a company important?
   (b) Why is a change in operating rate important?

5. Is it desirable for a company to operate consistently above its rated capacity? Explain.

6. Explain what is meant by the term *operating leverage*.

7. To what extent is breakeven analysis helpful in determining the earnings of a company? What are its limits?

8. Explain how the operating ratio, sales or profits per employee, and sales or profits per dollar of plant investment are used as measures of operating efficiency.

9. Explain the extent to which capital expenditures are indicative of a growing company. Can the level of capital expenditures be used as the sole criterion for estimating future growth of sales? Comment.

10. Review the analysis of the operating characteristics of the drug companies. Do you agree with the results?

Problems

1. What is the physical capacity to produce for the three companies you selected for analysis in the previous chapters? If units of capacity are not available, use dollar sales as a measure of capacity.

2. Has operating capacity in physical units or dollars increased for each company between 1957 and the present?

3. (a) How much did each of the companies spend annually on capital expenditures for the period 1957 to the present?
   (b) What percent of plant was spent annually for capital expenditure?
   (c) Rank each of the companies. Which one was best?

4. (a) What was the operating rate for each of the three companies from 1957 to the present?

(b) Rank each company on the basis of its operating rate. Which was best?

5. How does the operating rate and growth of capacity of the three companies compare with growth in the industry?

6. How do the breakeven points of the companies compare with each other and with the industry?

7. (a) What has been the profit and sales per dollar of plant and per employee for each of the three companies?
   (b) Which company appears to be best?

8. Based upon this analysis, which company would you consider to be best?

9. Does the information obtained in this chapter change your valuation appraisal of the company?

Sources of Investment Information

Annual reports of company
Barron's
Clark Dodge Investment Survey
Commercial and Financial Chronicle
Forbes
Moody's manuals
Standard & Poor's *Investment Surveys*
The Value Line Investment Survey

Selected Readings

Bennett, William M., "Capital Turnover versus Profit Margins," *Financial Analysts Journal* (March-April, 1966), p. 88.

Murphy, Joseph E., Jr., "Some Effects of Leverage," *Financial Analysts Journal* (July-August, 1968), p. 121.

Walsh, Philip F., "Engineering and Operation Problems," *Financial Analysts Journal* (March-April, 1967), p. 49.

14

CURRENT AND LONG-TERM FINANCIAL ANALYSIS

The function of financial analysis is to determine a company's ability to pay its current bills and long-term debt as they come due. This requires a company to have adequate liquidity, which comes about through a regular conversion of inventories into sales, sales into accounts receivable, and receivables into cash. It is achieved through adequate balances kept at the bank and monies invested in short-term government securities. The liquidity of a firm has obvious effects upon its earnings. If current assets are not converted regularly into cash, or if cash or equivalent balances are not maintained, the company will not be able to pay its bills. Default on contracts and debts will result in the failure of the company. On the other hand, if the company has too much cash or too many government securities—in short, is too liquid—earnings will be lower than if assets were invested more profitably.

The second focus of financial analysis is upon the ability of the company to support or repay long-term debt. Borrowing money for working capital and plant expansion has very obvious advantages for common-stock earnings. On the other hand, excessive debt can have a disastrous impact upon the company's future and, in fact, can result in complete corporate failure. The problem of financial analysis is to determine the short- and long-run financial solvency of the company. In this chapter we will discuss how we can test, through ratio analysis, the current financial position of the company. We will attempt to relate this to the quality of the company and to its future earnings. We will also examine ways in which we can test long-range solvency by an examination of long-term debt in the capital structure and its impact upon the amount and stability of a company's earnings.

Financial Objectives of the Company

The basic financial objectives of the company are long-range profitability and short-run liquidity. Long-range profitability is achieved by intelligently investing money in productive and profitable business ventures. The source of this money is from the sale of securities to investors, or from funds generated internally through sales but kept as depreciation expenses and retained earnings. The liquidity function is performed by management, which makes certain that money is on hand to pay for raw materials, to finance credit sales, to pay salaries as they are required, and to repay current debt.

The problem of financial management is one of balance. If all monies were kept on deposit at the savings bank or in a checking account, the company would be completely liquid. However, this would not constitute a very profitable investment of funds. At best, the funds would earn 5 percent—not a very attractive rate of return for a business corporation. The other alternative is to invest all the funds in buildings, land, machinery, and equipment, without any investment in working capital or cash to pay bills as they come due before receivables have been collected. The return on such investment could be 20 percent or higher, but the company could not function long without liquid funds to meet operating expenses. Somewhere between the condition of all cash and no fixed assets and that of all fixed assets and no cash is the solution to the dilemma; money is usually employed most profitably in both short-term investment and long-range projects to assure both liquidity and profitability.

To accomplish the objectives of profitability and liquidity, management engages in financial planning. This involves planning for the short-term needs of business by use of the cash budget as well as planning capital expenditures and acquisitions that require long-range budgeting. Often the company must obtain money—short-term or long-term, debt or equity—to meet its needs. It might borrow temporary cash from a commercial bank or possibly open-book credit from a supplier. This will increase its short-term indebtedness. Occasionally, a company will raise funds for plant and equipment expenditures or for working capital. This money will come either from reinvested earnings or from the sale of debt or equity securities. We are concerned whether the company can pay off its indebtedness, both short-term and long-term. We want to know if this can be done safely and in a method beneficial to our position as owners. And, of course, we want to know if, while the company borrows, it is able to earn a satisfactory rate on its common stock.

Judging the Short-Term Financial
Position of the Company

When the current financial position of a company is being analyzed, a series of questions are raised about its overall liquidity and its ability to pay its short-term obligations. Does the company have adequate current assets to pay its debts? Does it have sufficient cash to maintain a smoothly functioning organization that takes advantage of discounts and similar savings? Does the company have adequate working capital? Is inventory excessive? Are credit sales too high? Are accounts receivable exorbitant? Answers to these questions are obtained from a detailed examination of the balance sheet and income statement by using financial ratio analysis.

No company should be considered for investment unless it has a good current financial position, which contributes to earning power and stability of earnings. Let us now examine the ratios we use to determine the adequacy of the current financial position of a company. Data used in these ratios are supplied by the company, through its annual report. Explanations of variables and exceptions are also provided in this publication. Usually annual reports are issued at a time selected by the company, and discretionary variables are explained at the option of the company. These conditions and circumstances must be thoroughly understood when we make any attempt to determine the financial condition of a company based only upon ratio analysis.

The Current Ratio

The current ratio helps us determine the ability of a company to pay its short-term debts. Current ratio is found by dividing current liabilities into current assets and is expressed in the form 2.5 to 1 or 3.5 to 1, meaning that the company has 2.5 or 3.5 dollars of current assets for every dollar of current liabilities. The American Widget Company's balance sheet and operating statement presented in Table 14–1 allows us to see how the ratios are computed. American Widget has $220,000 of current assets and $100,000 of current liabilities. Its current ratio, therefore, is 2.2 to 1 ($220,000/$100,000). What does this mean? The purpose in comparing current assets with current liabilities is to determine whether sufficient current assets are available to pay current liabilities should they be presented for payment. The higher its current ratio, the better a corporation is able to pay its current debt; and the lower the ratio, the less able. Often a 2 to 1 ratio is considered adequate, however, no single standard can be applied that will be the same for all companies. A public utility, for example, would have a much different current ratio from that of a manufacturing company.

American Widget's current ratio of 2.2 to 1 is better than the 2 to 1 standard, but rather than accept an arbitrary ratio, let's consider the extent to which current assets when converted into cash will pay

TABLE 14–1

American Widget Company balance sheet and
operating statement, December 31
(thousands of dollars)

BALANCE SHEET

CURRENT ASSETS			DEBT		
Cash	$ 10		*Short Term*		
Government Securities	20		Accounts Payable	$40	
Accounts Receivable	70		One-Year Loan	60	
Inventory: Finished 60					
In Process 30			Total Current		
Raw Materials 30	120		Liabilities		$100
Total Current Assets		$220			
			Long Term		
FIXED ASSETS			6% Mortgage Loan	200	
Buildings and Land	$200		Total Debt		$300
Reserve for Depreciation	50				
Net Buildings & Land		$150	OWNERSHIP		
Machinery & Equipment	$150		Common Stock	150	
Reserve for Depreciation	20				
Net Machinery &			Retained Earnings	50	200
Equipment		130			
Total Fixed Assets		280			
Total Assets		$500	Total Debt &		
			Ownership		$500

OPERATING STATEMENT

Sales			$1,000
Cost of Goods Sold			600
Gross Profit on Sales			400
Selling Expenses		$150	
General Expenses		50	
Depreciation		10	210
Net Profit			190
Other Income (Interest Income)		1	
Other Expense (Interest Expense)		16	15
Net Income before Federal Income Taxes			175
Federal Income Tax (Estimated)			85
Net Income			$ 90

current liabilities. In reality this is a better and more basic test of corporate financial well-being. American Widget's inventory does not appear to be excessive. If the receivables are collectible, we would conclude that the current ratio reflected a good current position. But if we found, on closer inspection, that a high percentage of the current assets were not salable, then we would realize that the 2.2 to 1 ratio was not really adequate. This is the type of value judgment we must make.

The acid test ratio is designed to focus attention on the liquid assets of the company. It ignores those current assets that might not be easily converted into cash. The acid test ratio is found by dividing current liabilities into cash plus short-term securities plus accounts receivable; in short, current liabilities are divided into current assets minus inventory. Inventory is excluded, since its cash equivalent might not be available to pay short-term debts. If a company is having difficulty because it cannot sell its product, then a large inventory that cannot be sold will not help the company pay off its current debt. A high current ratio might result because of the large inventory, but the company still will not possess liquidity. The acid test ratio, therefore, is a better indication of ability to pay current debts than the current ratio.

If liquid current assets, current assets minus inventory, are equivalent to or exceed current liabilities, then theoretically at least, the company has an excellent current financial position. Practically speaking, the acid test ratio of above 1 to 1 is adequate only if receivables can be easily converted into cash. If accounts receivable include a large percentage of bad debts or uncollectible accounts, then even the acid test ratio would not adequately describe current liquidity. To be certain that current assets can pay off current debts immediately, the amount of the accounts receivable must be adjusted to eliminate bad accounts. As investors, we usually do not have such detailed information about the accounts. We must assume that the cash and equivalent in government securities and a reduced amount of receivables will be able to meet current liabilities. If we add the dollars that might be obtained from a distress sale of the inventory, then we will be able to judge whether a company will be able to meet its current debts.

The American Widget Company has a favorable acid test ratio based upon the criterion that suggests that current assets minus inventory should equal or exceed current liabilities. Cash, government securities, and accounts receivable total $100,000 compared to current liabilities of $100,000. The acid test ratio is 1 to 1 ($100,000/$100,000). The ratio is favorable because the most liquid of current assets equals the total of current liabilities. Even if the accounts receivable could not be collected, the company would be able to sell some inventory, which would probably be sufficient to meet current liabilities when combined with cash and government securities.

Composition of Current Assets

The composition of current assets is also important in determining the overall liquidity of a company. A very large proportion of inventory in current assets would suggest that the current assets were not as liquid as they should be. It might also indicate that management is following a poor inventory policy. Of course, some companies must maintain large inventories because of the nature of their operations. Tobacco companies, for instance, have an extremely high ratio of inventory to total current assets and to total assets. Actually, to the tobacco company, tobacco should be looked upon as a fixed investment.

On the other hand, a company might have a high percentage of its current assets in cash and government securities. This might be a good policy, since it allows the company to take advantage of cash discounts and provides emergency funds for periods of distress. Adequate cash balances work to improve the company's credit rating and general good standing with commercial banks. A large cash balance and investment in government securities might mean that a company is building up funds to acquire new plant and equipment. Large balances are justified under these circumstances. Large cash balances and temporary investments, however, do not improve the long-run profitability of the company; and excessive cash balances, unless they are to be invested in the near future, should be avoided. If in our analysis we find a company with an excessive cash balance, we might look upon it unfavorably.

The American Widget Company appears to be in a favorable position with respect to the composition of its current assets. Cash represents about 4.5 percent of the current assets, which is low based upon a rule of thumb used in the past. The rule suggests that the amount of cash should equal at least 10 percent of the current assets. It originated at a time when financial managers did not invest the company's funds directly. Today, many financial managers would not let this large an amount of cash remain idle and unproductive. Funds not needed even for a short period are invested in short-term securities to improve the company's earnings position. Therefore, in using the 10 percent cash rule today, we should include short-term investments. When we do this for American Widget we find that its cash and government security account equals 13.6 percent of total current assets, which is clearly above the 10 percent limit:

	Thousands of Dollars		% of Total	
Cash	$ 10	⎫	4.5	⎫
		⎬ $30		⎬ 13.6
Government securities	20	⎭	9.1	⎭
Accounts receivable	70		31.9	
Inventory	120		54.5	
	$220		100.0	

The accounts receivable position does not seem extraordinary at about 32 percent of current assets; 50 percent or above would be high. If American Widget had 70 percent of its current assets in accounts receivable, on the basis of reason alone, it would be too high. Inventories of American Widget are not excessive either. A level of 50 to 60 percent can be expected. American Widget's ratio is 54.5 percent, which might be considered normal. However, inventory ratios vary from industry to industry, and a final conclusion would be made after comparing this ratio with other companies in the industry. Comparison is always helpful in arriving at a decision.

Credit Sales Carried as Receivables

The observations about the reasonableness of the amount of cash, government securities and other short-term securities equivalent to cash, receivables, and inventory as a percent of total current assets are based on practices accepted in the field of accounting and finance that were thought to be reasonable. Receivables and inventory, respectively, vary with the credit sales and the total sales of the company. Therefore, to establish the limits of receivables and inventory in a more logical way, they must be compared with sales figures.

We can best determine whether receivables are excessive from the number of days that credit sales are carried on the corporate books as accounts receivable. This is computed by dividing the average amount of daily credit sales into the average amount of accounts receivable on the books, as reflected in the balance sheet and operating statement of the company. In making an analysis of a company we use data from the annual reports, which do not usually provide credit sales figures, nor the average amount of receivables carried. As a practical matter, the net sales figure can be used in place of the credit sales figure. Most corporate sales are done on open-book account; therefore, credit sales usually differ little from total sales. The receivables figures provided in the annual report are also used instead of the average accounts receivable carried, simply because the average figure is usually unavailable.

The American Widget Company had sales of $1,000,000 and receivables of $70,000 for the accounting period ending December 31. During the year, the company averaged about $2,780 of daily sales ($1,000,000/360). It had 25.2 days' sales on the books in the form of receivables ($70,000/$2,780) at the end of the year. This calculation can be expressed simply as: $DSO = (R \times 360)/S$ where DSO equals days' sales outstanding, R equals the amount of accounts receivable on the books, and S equals the credit sales or simply the sales of the company. In the case of American Widget this would be: $DSO = R \times 360/S = (\$70,000 \times 360)/\$1,000,000 = 25.2$. The significance of this figure is established only when it is compared with the credit period extended by the company. If the credit terms of American Widget are 30 days, then we can conclude that the DSO are small in relation to what is expected. Assume, for the moment, that another company has 60 days' sales outstanding. Compared with American Widget, this is an extremely high ratio. We would say that the other company was in a poor credit position. Upon closer examination, however, we learn that the credit period of American Widget is 30 days and that of the other company is 60 days. Relatively, American Widget is in the better position, but only because it has fewer days' sales outstanding compared with the credit period and not because it has less than half as many days' sales outstanding compared with the other company. The other company might be criticized for being too generous in its extension of credit, but probably the amount of receivables on its books is not excessive when compared with the credit period.

Net Sales to Inventory Ratio

The net sales to inventory ratio provides a way to determine whether a company's inventory is too high or too low. It is computed by dividing the inventory on the books into the annual net sales. The ratio for American Widget Company would be 8.33 to 1 ($1,000,000/ $120,000). This ratio simply shows that, for each dollar invested in inventory, the company generates $8.33 of sales. The true significance of the ratio, however, can be ascertained only by noting its direction of change and how it compares with other companies. If the sales to inventory ratio were decreasing for American Widget, yet increasing for other companies in the industry, this would be a sign that American Widget suffered excessive inventory in relation to sales or that sales were too low for the inventory carried. To be most efficient, a company should keep its sales to inventory ratio as high as possible consistent with the demands imposed by its competition.

Inventory Turnover Ratio

Closely related to the net sales to inventory ratio is the inventory turnover ratio, computed by dividing finished goods inventory into net sales at cost. This is somewhat difficult to compute, since, in published data, the inventory is not always broken down by major components—finished goods, goods in process, and raw materials. Where figures are available, however, the ratio does provide a measure of efficiency upon which to judge a company. We usually use the total inventory given in the annual report for the calculation. When a corporation sells $8 of a product for every $1 invested in finished goods inventory, it is doing a better job than if it sells only $6 of a product for every dollar of inventory. However, before any significance can be attached to the ratio, a comparison must be made with other companies in the industry.

The figures for the American Widget Company can be used as an example of how we use the inventory turnover ratio. The finished goods inventory of the company is $60,000 and the cost of goods sold is

$600,000, which gives an inventory turnover ratio of 10 to 1 ($600,000/$60,000). If this breakdown were not available, we would use total inventory—in this case, $120,000. Then the inventory turnover ratio would be 5 to 1 ($600,000/$120,000). Whether this turnover ratio is high or low will depend upon a comparison with other companies in the industry and the previous experience of American Widget.

Net Sales to Net Working Capital

A ratio significant in determining the ability of the company to finance sales growth is the ratio of net sales to net working capital. The net working capital of a company is found by subtracting current liabilities from current assets. In the case of American Widget, working capital is $120,000 ($220,000 — $100,000), and the net sales to net working capital ratio is 8.33 ($1,000,000/$120,000). Again, whether this is good or poor depends upon American Widget's position compared with that of other companies in the industry. It is desirable to maintain the level of working capital at a point where new sales can be financed easily. Many firms have a great deal of difficulty maintaining this working capital position. As sales expand, a company may be unable to finance, from bank loans and open-book accounts, all the growth of inventory and receivables needed to support the sales, so it must supply working capital to finance receivables and inventory. Working capital is supplied only by long-term capital in the form of retained earnings, the sale of common or preferred stock, and the sale of bonds. The prime consideration in the use of the net sales to working capital ratio is whether it maintains a degree of stability and grows with sales. It tells us if a company has the ability to obtain adequate working capital to finance its sales and the future growth of sales. A declining ratio would indicate the need for a more efficient use of previously invested capital. A ratio that was too high would reflect that more working capital was needed.

Cash Budget

The cash budget has become a valuable tool of modern corporate and business financial analysis. Long- and short-range budgets now are used to help plan and control the future of well-managed companies. These budgets are invaluable guides to financial solvency. When and where available, they make ratio analysis somewhat superfluous. If such data are available, they can shed light into corporate financial affairs. Unfortunately, such data are not readily available to investors and analysts.

The Significance of Ratio Analysis

Usually the neophyte investor or analyst cannot immediately assess the value of the current ratio, the acid test ratio, the number of days' credit sales outstanding, or the inventory turnover ratio, nor can he readily assess their impact upon earnings. A question often asked is, "What do I do with these ratios after I have computed them?" Or more simply, "What do they mean?"

Relative Comparison

The significance of the ratios rests in their performance over time and how they compare with other companies in the industry on a collective basis. The measures are all relative. The test of reasonableness must be added to these measures. As analysts we must ask, "Is the ratio reasonable based on the objectives of the firm?" For example, would it be reasonable to have 90 percent of the current assets in inventory, or 90 percent in accounts receivable, or, for that matter, 90 percent in cash and government securities? By the same token we would not have a reasonable situation if cash represented only 2 percent of current assets or if inventory or receivables each represented 10 percent of current assets —unless, of course, the company sold only for cash or produced not a tangible product but a service that required little inventory. Thus, in making an analysis of the current position of a company, a sense of proportion and reasonableness must be maintained. This comes from experience and judgment by using and applying the ratios we have discussed.

Year-to-Year Change

A second criterion for judgment is what happens to the ratio from year to year. Actually, stability in the financial position once the proper relationships have been established is more important than growth or change. Once a corporation has obtained an adequate working balance in its current assets position and between current assets and liabilities, then this ratio should be maintained as sales and plant investment increase. An increase in the current ratio or acid test ratio would indicate an increase in liquidity and an increase in working capital. An improvement in the working capital position of the company might be temporary and a result of long-term financing in anticipation of growth in sales. It might mean an increase in liquidity, in which case funds would be available for investment or even paid to the stockholders in the form of dividends. A decrease in the current ratio or acid test ratio would indicate the need for long-term working capital funds. Stability in the current ratio and acid test ratio is expected and important.

CHANGES IN THE RATIOS

Sharp changes in these relationships might be temporary, but they might also be indicative of long-range changes that forecast decreased earnings.

Inventory. An increase in inventory usually indicates that a company is not selling as much of its product as formerly. A company cannot profit from a buildup in inventory over time unless it is a temporary buildup in anticipation of increased sales volume. Most companies are trying to keep inventory in balance with sales so that available funds can be used effectively. A decline in inventory, on the other hand, might indicate an improvement in sales, a need for more productive capacity, or a basic internal change in inventory policy. A company can have too little inventory as well as too much. If it has too little, sales might be lost. If it has too much, earnings will be lost on unprofitable funds invested in inventory.

Receivables. An increase in receivables would indicate an increase in credit sales or possibly a slowing down in the collection of receivables. The days' sales outstanding (DSO) in receivables is a good test for determining whether or not receivables are excessive. If credit sales increase and receivables on the books increase in the same proportion, this is a highly desirable situation. If, on the contrary, sales do not increase but an increase in receivables occurs, then the company will be forced to increase its investment in receivables without an increase in profit. This, of course, is undesirable.

Cash Position. The cash position of a company can improve; that is, a company has more cash and government securities as a percentage of current assets. However, the improvement can come only within a well-defined range. Any company that has permanent excess balances in the commercial bank really has only two alternatives: (1) The money can be invested in more productive assets, or (2) the money can be paid out to stockholders in the form of dividends. Here the problem is one of a balance between liquidity and profitability and not of the actual amount of the cash balance.

Summary. The comparisons involved in the analysis of the current position over time suggest that stability of relationships is more important than growth. The keynote of these comparisons is in balance of the various items. Therefore, it is not desirable to have a buildup of inventory or receivables or cash per se, but only if there is a corresponding increase in sales. The best we can expect from the current and long-term assets of the company is that they correspond directly with an increase or decrease in sales and that the company be in a position to finance any changes.

Current Analysis in a Hypothetical Case

The current analysis process can be demonstrated using data on two companies in a hypothetical industry. Table 14–2 presents the various ratios for the industry and for two companies in the industry. The figures are given for two different time periods so that changes over time may be examined.

TABLE 14–2

Current analysis of two companies in a hypothetical industry

RATIO	Five Years Ago			Current Year		
	INDUSTRY AVERAGE	COM-PANY R	COM-PANY W	INDUSTRY AVERAGE	COM-PANY R	COM-PANY W
Current ratio	2.4	2.3	2.1	2.2	2.3	1.8
Composition of current assets (%):						
Cash	8.0	9.0	9.0	7.0	10.0	5.0
Short-term investments	12.0	14.0	15.0	8.0	12.0	4.0
Receivables	25.0	24.0	28.0	35.0	28.0	43.0
Inventory	55.0	53.0	48.0	50.0	50.0	48.0
Acid test ratio	1.1	1.0	.9	1.0	1.0	.7
DSO (Number of days' sales outstanding)	41.0	43.0	44.0	45.0	44.0	55.0
Inventory turnover	5.0	5.0	4.0	4.0	5.0	4.0
Finished goods inventory turnover, at cost	6.0	6.0	5.0	5.0	6.0	5.0
Net sales to working capital	8.0	9.0	6.0	8.5	9.0	4.0

A study of the ratios of five years ago reveals little basic difference between Company R and Company W. Each appears to have a satisfactory current ratio, acid test ratio, and composition of current assets. The inventory turnover ratio, the finished goods turnover ratio, and the number of days' sales outstanding are also in line with the industry. Company W, however, has a lower net sales to working capital ratio than either Company R or the average for the industry. This is the only ratio that is out of line for Company W.

In the current year, however, the comparative analysis shows that Company W has suffered a deterioration in its financial position as seen in the current ratio, acid test ratio, and composition of current assets. The deterioration is relative to Company R, the averages for the industry, and its own position five years ago. Company W has a large amount of receivables outstanding as well as a large DSO. Its net sales to working capital has decreased even though the inventory turnover ratios have been constant. Company R has changed very little in the six-year period and maintains a good current position in relation to the industry and its own position over time.

The general concluding comments made about the current financial position of Company R and W is simply that R, based on changes over time and the industry, has a good current position, is not burdened by excessive debt, appears to have adequate cash, does not have excessive inventory or receivables, and has maintained its working capital in relation to sales. Company W, on the other hand, has suffered some deterioration in its financial position. It has suffered a decrease in liquidity and an increase in receivables outstanding. More than that, its net sales to working capital ratio has declined. Certainly it is not a bankrupt company. It is still able to pay all its obligations. However, it has not maintained its previous good position, and its current position has worsened compared with the industry and Company *R*. If a choice had to be made between the two companies, Company *R* would be the right choice, based on its current financial position. It should be suggested to Company *W* that it improve its sales volume as well as collections of receivables and its cash position. At this point, the current position of Company *W* will not seriously impair future earnings. If the trend continues, however, both the earnings and solvency of the company will be in jeopardy. We would, therefore, give little consideration to Company *W* unless there were good reason for the decline in its liquidity. If the company needs working capital, then the management is not doing its job.

Current Analysis of the Drug Companies— Continuation of an Actual Case

A continuation of the study of the ethical drug industry will prove somewhat more rewarding as an illustration of current financial analysis than a hypothetical situation. The criteria established to test the current financial position are basically those of solvency and financial strength. The specific task we face is to determine if Chas. Pfizer, G. D. Searle, and Smith Kline & French have an adequate current financial position and if this enhances or reduces their earnings.

A current analysis was made for the ten leading companies in the ethical drug industry and for the three companies we have been analyzing. The results are presented in Table 14–3. We see that the data for the ten leading companies in the industry are remarkably similar and extraordinarily stable between 1957 and 1961. The current ratio, for example, has not changed at all. Except for the net sales to working capital ratio, there was little variation in the other ratios. The leading companies were in an excellent liquid position with a rather large average current ratio and acid test ratio and a high percent of the current assets in liquid assets. Inventory, for example, was less than one-third of the current assets. The average days' sales outstanding suggests that credit terms varied from 30 to 60 days among the leading companies. Between 1957 and 1961, the net sales to inventory ratio improved, which indicates more sales per dollar of inventory—a desirable trait for an industry. At the same time, net sales to working capital has declined, which indicates the leading companies have more than adequate working capital in relation to sales. Overall, the leading companies in the ethical drug industry were in an excellent current or short-term financial position in 1957 and 1961.

Chas. Pfizer and G. D. Searle are at opposite ends of the spectrum in their current financial position. Pfizer's current position declined somewhat between 1957 and 1968. Its current ratio went down from

TABLE 14–3

Comparison of the financial analyses of
Pfizer, Searle, and Smith Kline & French with
the average of ten leading ethical drug companies

Current Financial Analysis Ratios	Ten Leading Ethical Drug Companies		Chas. Pfizer			G. D. Searle			Smith Kline & French		
	1957	1961	1957	1961	1968	1957	1961	1968	1957	1961	1968
Current ratio	3.6	3.6	2.5	2.1	2.1	9.3	9.6	4.7	2.1	2.3	2.5
Composition of current assets (%):											
Cash & equivalent	41.4	41.0	20.5	15.8	18.0	67.2	62.4	47.7	56.0	60.6	44.9
Receivables	21.8	24.0	26.9	34.5	41.0	14.3	20.2	29.3	15.6	19.0	30.5
Inventory	33.3	31.3	49.3	49.7	41.0	18.5	17.4	23.0	24.8	18.6	24.6
Acid test ratio	2.5	2.7	1.3	1.1	1.2	7.6	8.0	3.7	2.0	1.9	1.8
DSO*	45.2	48.4	65.0	65.5	85.0	35.4	47.1	72.0	27.6	31.2	50.0
Net sales to inventory	5.6	6.4	3.4	3.8	4.2	7.9	8.9	6.7	8.7	11.8	8.9
Net sales to working capital	3.8	2.8	2.8	3.6	3.4	1.6	1.6	1.9	4.1	3.9	3.6

* Number of days' sales outstanding.

SOURCE: *Moody's Industrial Manual*, Moody's Investors Service, New York, 1963, pp. 792, 2309, 2310, 2323, and 2324; *Ibid*, 1958, p. 809; *Ibid*, July, 1969, pp. 1547, 1548, 1552, 1993, and 1994; and Standard & Poor's *Industry Survey—Drugs, Cosmetics*, February 8, 1968, pp. D 27, 28, 29, and 30.

2.5 to 2.1, cash as a percent of current assets went down, and receivables increased. The acid test ratio has declined. All of this suggests a decline in liquidity and a decline in the collection of receivables. Pfizer's net sales to working capital ratio increased for the period, and it was above the industry level at the end of the period. All of the ratios put Pfizer in a good current position, but it was not as liquid as other leading companies in the industry.

G. D. Searle is the most liquid of the companies presented. Its current ratio was high but declined sharply between 1957 and 1968. The 1.6 and 1.9 net sales to working capital ratios suggest an extremely low working capital ratio compared to the other companies, although it could have been lower without putting the company in jeopardy. Searle's receivables position changed substantially from 1957 to 1968, and at the same time an increase occurred in days' sales outstanding over 1957. This suggests the possibility of an increase in credit terms or a slowdown in the payment for credit sales. Whatever the reason, Searle's position worsened, but it would be able to finance increases in receivables if needed.

Smith Kline & French is also in an excellent current financial position. Its cash position was high and accounted for almost 50 percent of the current assets. Inventories and receivables were almost insignificant, although receivables increased substantially from 1957 to 1968. The current ratio was good at better than 2 to 1 and had improved. The acid test ratio was good. The DSO was low, and both the net sales to inventory and to working capital ratios remained about the same, but adequate, between 1957 and 1968.

This appears to be a rather detailed discussion of financial trivia. However, this could not be further from the truth. In the data presented in Table 14–3 we see the extremes of current financial position among companies that are in excellent financial condition. Searle was almost too liquid until 1968 and might invest the liquid assets more productively. If more productive investments were unavailable, a larger dividend could be paid to the stockholders. Chas. Pfizer, on the other hand, needs no working capital to improve its current financial position, but it should not go lower. Pfizer had a larger inventory than the rest of the companies and also extends more liberal credit. This accounts for the completely adequate yet comparatively less liquid position of Pfizer. In the final judgment of these companies Searle would be judged somewhat fat, Pfizer too lean but in all respects adequate, and Smith Kline & French would be just right. Searle, therefore, is penalized somewhat for being too liquid but its position has improved in 1968. Pfizer's position is somewhat more tenuous than that of the other companies, but completely adequate.

In conclusion, the analysis simply tells us that each of the companies has an adequate current financial position, one that will not harm the future earnings potential of the company. The liquidity of Smith Kline & French and Searle put these companies in an excellent position to expand their sales. The position of the companies is summarized in Table 14–4.

TABLE 14–4

Companies ranked by current financial position

COMPARATIVE CURRENT FINANCIAL ANALYSIS	CHAS. PFIZER	G. D. SEARLE	SMITH KLINE & FRENCH
Current ratio[a]	3	1	2
Acid test ratio[a]	3	1	2
Composition of current assets[b]	3	1	2
DSO[c]	3	2	1
Net sales to inventory[d]	3	2	1
Net sales to working capital[d]	2	3	1
Overall liquidity	3	1	2

     [a] Based on highest.
     [b] Based on greatest percent of cash and equivalent.
     [c] Lowest ranked first.
     [d] Highest ranked first.

Capital Structure Analysis

The method of financing corporate growth and expansion is extremely important for the common stockholder. How the corporation obtains funds has a direct effect upon the earnings per share of common stock. Debt financing at the present time is the cheapest way for a company to obtain capital. A heavy reliance upon debt financing then tends to raise the rate of return to the common stockholder. Of course, the funds must be invested profitably and at a higher rate than the interest that is paid for using these funds. Borrowing money at a low rate and investing it at a higher rate is referred to as *trading on the equity.* A large debt creates a high degree of financial leverage. If the revenues of the company are unstable, the presence of a large amount of debt tends to further increase the instability of earnings per share. Companies with a high degree of operating leverage and a high degree of financial leverage might have a high degree of earning instability if revenues are unstable. If a company experiences a wide fluctuation of earnings because of its revenue pattern, it will experience an even wider and more unstable fluctuation of earnings if there is a large amount of debt in the capital structure.

The impact of debt in the capital structure upon valuation and earnings is subject to a wide difference of opinion. Two views indicate the breadth of current thought. One group thinks that capital structure can affect the aggregate market value of a company's securities apart from the tax impact. The second group thinks that, except for tax factor, the capital structure has no effect on the total market valuation of a company's securities.

It is the author's view that an *optimum* amount of debt leads to both a tax advantage and an increase in total company value; that debt in the capital structure increases the risk of failure of the common-stock owners; that with increased debt the P/E ratio of common stock is lowered because of the additional risk; and that at the *optimum* debt level the P/E ratio is lowered, but the percentage drop is less than the tax advantages and increase in value. It is, therefore, important for the investor to ascertain if debt is excessive by an analysis of debt in the capital structure.

If a company depends solely upon the sale of common stock to raise capital, the impact on common-stock earnings per share is somewhat different. The sale of common stock might have the effect of reducing earnings per share. It might also have the effect of reducing total value because the advantages to the common-stock owners of having some debt in the capital structure are lost. Some debt is desirable, the optimum amount lying between the maximum leverage in earnings and the maximum amount of increase in risk. If, for example, the present rate of return earned on the common stock is 10 percent and the new funds from the sale of additional common stock earn only 8 percent, then the earnings of the existing shares have been diluted. Raising capital by the sale of common stock under these conditions reduces overall earnings on the common stock. This has the effect of reducing per share market prices. It is not desirable from the point of view of management and of the investor to have a set of conditions that reduces earnings per share. If a company proposes to raise capital by selling common stock, we must examine and estimate the effect upon per share earnings.

Of course, capital raised through the sale of common stock, although expensive, can be invested in such a way as to improve the earnings per share for all outstanding shares. Money can be raised by sale to the public or to the existing stockholders. If there is a danger of dilution in earnings and assets and it is necessary to obtain funds, this might be accomplished by selling stock to the existing stockholders. In this way funds are obtained without the fear that dilution will harm the shareholders' previous position since the old shareholders, if they subscribe to the stock, will maintain their relative position in the company.

Often corporations will finance by the sale of common stock even though it might be advantageous to finance through the use of borrowed funds. This is done by the more conservative management that does not wish to jeopardize its company's corporate existence through the default of a bond issue. Therefore, such a company engages only in equity financing. Companies that have widely fluctuating earnings or companies that are new and somewhat speculative tend to finance through the sale of common stock. This does not mean that they are unaware of the advantages and disadvantages of debt financing, but as a matter of policy they decide against it. Their position is such that the advantages of debt financing are outweighed by its disadvantages and by the advantages of equity financing.

The Capital Structure

The problem we must face is whether the corporation in which we invest has an adequate source of capital to finance its long-range growth. The source of capital should enhance and improve the per share earnings of the common stock. Steps must be taken to make certain that debt or preferred stock charges, both interest and dividends, are not excessive in relation to earnings and that debt alone is not excessive in relation to the total assets and capital of the company.

When we analyze how a corporation has raised its long-term capital, we look at the capital structure of the company. We define *capital structure* simply by saying that it is the sum of the net worth plus any outstanding long-term debt. The capital structure of Bristol-Myers in 1961 and 1966 is presented in Table 14–5 as an example of how one company has raised its long-term funds. Actually, 85.3 percent of Bristol-Myers' long-term funds in 1961 came from common stock, capital surplus, and retained earnings; 96.8 percent came from these in 1966. Debt was reduced in the 5-year period and preferred stock was eliminated from the capital structure. Less than 6 percent of the capital structure had come from debt issues. The amount of debt was certainly modest, and the company was able to double its capital structure in a short period of time. However, what is an excessive amount of debt for one company would be normal for another.

TABLE 14–5

Composition of the capital structure of
Bristol-Myers, 1961ᵃ and 1966ᵇ

	Million of Dollars		*Percent of Total*	
	1961	1966	1961	1966
Long-term debt (corporate bonds)	7.9	5.4	9.4	3.2
Preferred stock	4.6	0	5.3	0
Common stock	5.2	25.2	6.2	14.9
Capital surplus	16.1	6.6	19.1	3.9
Retained earnings	50.2	132.3	60.0	78.0
Total long-term capital	84.0	169.5	100.0	100.0

ᵃ *Annual Report*, Bristol Myers, 1961.
ᵇ *Moody's Industrial Manual*, June, 1967, p. 1267.

Preferred Stock in the Capital Structure

Preferred stock has never been a significant source of capital for the majority of corporations. It accounts for approximately 10 percent of the source of capital of the railroads and the public utilities and about 5 to 6 percent for the industrial companies. Although usage of preferred stock has been somewhat limited, it still can have a significant impact upon common-stock earnings. Its presence in the capital structure must be analyzed from the points of view of both the common- and the preferred-stock investor. Since bondholders have a prior claim on earnings and assets, their position is more secure than that of preferred stockholders. Let us look briefly at each point of view.

THE VIEWPOINT OF OWNERS OF PREFERENCE SHARES

The owners of preferred stock are interested in knowing if the dividend is secure and if the preferred claims will be satisfied if the company should fail. The preferred-stock owner ascertains whether the earnings of the company, after taxes and after prior interest claims have been paid, are sufficient to pay a dividend on the preferred, assuming normal as well as adverse or abnormal fluctuations in corporate earnings. The preferred-stock owner also examines the nature of the company's assets and the claims on assets to learn if the preferred claims will be paid if the company should fail. Any other contractual obligations must also be satisfied, and the preferred stockholder must verify the certainty of these other conditions. Investors who buy ordinary preferred stock want stable revenues and security of principal.

PREFERRED STOCK AND THE COMMON STOCKHOLDER

The presence of preferred stock in the capital structure of a corporation leads to some degree of leverage of earnings just as does the use of debt. The leverage impact upon common stock is not as great as debt because the preferred dividends are not tax deductible. They are paid out of net income or earnings after taxes have been deducted. Nevertheless, if 15 percent can be earned on funds raised by the sale of a 6 percent preferred stock, then the common owners will receive the difference, and the per share earnings will increase even after allowance for income taxes. A low-cost preferred, then, has a positive effect upon the common-stock earnings through the leverage effect if the trend of earnings is stable, higher than the dividend rate, and increasing.

An excessive amount of preferred stock in the capital structure tends, however, to create a situation of instability. A high degree of preferred leverage leads to a high degree of earnings variation in the common stock if the earnings of the company fluctuate. Another limit imposed on the common stockholder by the preferred-stock agreement is in the matter of dividend payments. Where earnings and working capital limits are not met or where dividends are in arrears, no dividends will be paid to the common stockholder. Preferred stock in this case would be detrimental to the common stockholder.

One other effect occurs on the per share common-stock earnings in the special case of convertible preferred stock. The possibility of a conversion of preferred stock into common stock might dilute the earnings of common stock. When common stock is purchased from a company with a large amount of convertible preferred stock outstanding, the possible effect of conversion must be determined. The amount of stock converted might result in a sharp increase in the number of shares of stock outstanding and a sharp decrease in earnings per share that could result in lower common-stock prices.

LIMITS TO THE USE OF PREFERRED STOCK

No hard-and-fast rules exist for the use of preferred stock as a source of capital for the corporation. However, several comments can be made as a guide for a company analysis. First, preferred stock should not be a large part of ownership securities or of the capital structure. When preferred stock is used, it should add to the financial strength of the company. Excessive use of preferred would impose a dividend burden on the company that would be difficult to meet. Second, preferred-stock dividends and bond interest should be adequately covered by the earnings of the corporation after taxes. Third, the use of preferred stock should enhance and maximize the earnings of the common stock, leading to stability rather than instability of earnings per share. Where earnings are already unstable, preferred stock should not be used in an amount that would add to this instability because of financial leverage. Fourth, the use of special types of preferred stock, such as convertible preferred shares, should not lead to the dilution of common stock in the corporation. Fifth and last, preferred stock and debt should not exceed the net tangible assets of the company. These general rules will serve as a guide in making an analysis. If a company should have an excessive amount of preferred stock, reducing the amount of common-stock earnings or adding to their instability, then we might not consider the common stock for investment.

Debt in the Capital Structure

Debt plays an important part in the long-term financing of most corporations. As we have noted, debt has certain advantages in terms of cost and market acceptability that makes it attractive as a source of funds. The use of debt results in a form of earnings leverage that can be highly beneficial to common-stock owners. On the other hand, leverage can be detrimental to the common stockholders by causing a great deal of instability of earnings per share and can actually force a company into bankruptcy.

The leverage impact can be demonstrated by the following example. Assume that two companies each have the same amount of sales and expenses, resulting in an identical profit margin of $20 million. Sales are $100 million and neither company has any other income, so the profit margin is 20 percent of operating revenues. One difference exists between the two companies: one company has a capital structure consisting entirely of common stock and retained earnings; the other has a capital structure consisting of 50 percent common stock and 50 percent debt with an interest rate of 5 percent. The capital structure of each company appears graphically in Figure 14–1.

Each company earned 20 percent before taxes on its capital structure ($20/$100). However, we must consider federal income taxes, which are assumed to be 50 percent, and we must consider interest expense. When we do this, Company *A* is found to earn $10 million after taxes, providing the common stockholder a return of 10 percent after taxes. Company *B* is in a somewhat different situation. Before taxes are paid, interest of $2.5 million (5 percent of $50 million) must be deducted. Taxable income, therefore, is $17.5 million, income taxes are $8.75 million, and Company *B* has an income after taxes of $8.75 million. The rate of return on common equity is 17.5 percent ($8.75 million/ $50 million). Therefore, two companies that have the same profit margin have two different rates of return on common equity, simply because one has used low-cost tax-deductible debt and the other has used either common stock or retained earnings.

The leverage aspect is more dramatically demonstrated when a change in profit margin occurs. Assume that both Companies *A* and *B* experience an increase in profit margin to 30 percent and in dollars from $20 to $30 million. This represents a 50 percent increase in the profit margin. What happens under these assumptions to the rate of return of common stocks? Company *A* pays a $15 million federal income tax on its profits, which leaves $15 million net income after taxes. This is a 15 percent rate of return on owners' equity. Company *A*, therefore, realizes a 50 percent increase in the return on owners' equity with a 50 percent increase in its profit margin. Company *B* has the same increase in the profit margin. The net income available for the common stockholder, however, increases dramatically. Taxable income is $27.5 million ($30 — $2.5 million), and net income after taxes amounts to $13.75 million ($27.5 — $13.75 million taxes). This amount is available to the owners and provides them with a 27.5 percent rate of return on their equity in the business. A 50 percent increase in the profit margin of company *B*, therefore, leads to a 57.1 percent increase in the return

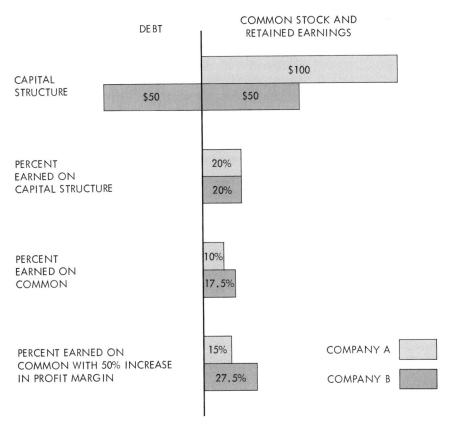

FIGURE 14–1

Percent earnings on common stock of two companies with the same operating profits but different capital structures ($ in millions)

to the common stockholders. The rate of return increases from 17.5 percent to 27.5 percent. This is the leverage principle at work. The results of leverage are pictured in Figure 14–1.

The unfortunate part about leverage is that it works when the profit margin declines. In a highly leveraged capital structure (one that employs a great deal of debt or fixed-payment preferred stock), the effect on earnings for the common stock will be great. With a given change of earnings up or down, the rate of return to the common stockholders will change more than the change in earnings. Just how damaging or beneficial a highly leveraged capital structure is depends not only on the amount of debt or preferred stock in the capital structure but upon the stability of earnings. Technically, a gas pipeline has a highly leveraged capital structure. Yet since its earnings are stable, the leverage has little effect on the earnings per share of the company. An industrial company, however, that has 30 percent debt in its capital structure does not have excessive debt, although the company's earnings vary widely and the leverage effect brings about an accentuation of the variation of earnings per share. The leverage factor in the capital structure must be assessed in terms of the stability or instability of revenues. Where revenues are stable and certain, as in the telephone or public utility industry, a large amount of debt can be carried and is beneficial to the stockholder. Where earnings fluctuate considerably, debt should be modest in relation to the capital structure, so that earnings fluctuation will not be reinforced to the detriment of the common stockholder. We must decide whether debt in the capital structure is reasonable or excessive, and try to avoid situations where debt is excessive in relation to the capital structure when earnings are unstable, or at least we should not be willing to pay as much for a dollar of unstable earnings.

DEBT LIMITS

The limits to the amount of debt a company can support varies, not only because of the characteristics of the industry but because of the characteristics of the company. Not all public utilities should have a large amount of debt, nor should all industrial companies be debtless. The limits of debt that are imposed usually relate to the ability of the company to pay interest and the ability of the assets to repay the debt should the company default.

Fixed Asset Limit. The fixed asset limit imposed upon debt states that debt should bear some reasonable relationship to the assets of the company. It is usually suggested that long-term debt in the balance sheet of a railroad or public utility not exceed 50 percent of the fixed assets. Some analysts would limit debt to 40 percent for the railroads and 60 percent for public utilities as a group. The industrial company also follows the debt-to-fixed-asset limit. We suggest that debt should not exceed 50 percent of fixed assets. In addition, we impose on industrial companies a working capital limit that states that long-term debt should not exceed the working capital of the company.

Earnings Limit. The amount of earnings provides another way of determining whether debt is excessive. Here we are interested in how many times bond interest is covered by net income after taxes. The basic premise is that if a company has adequate income to pay the interest on the debt, it will be in a good financial position, interest will be secure, and failure unlikely. The greater the number of times bond interest is covered by net income after taxes, the more secure is the debt position of the company. The wider the margin of protection between income and interest, the safer is the position of the bond issue. The common stockholder is in a better position too, since inability to pay the debt will not result in the failure of the company. The number of times fixed charges are covered will vary from time to time because of the level of the interest rate. The suggested limit for interest coverage in industrial companies is three times, and for public utilities and railroads two times. Thus, if the net income after taxes for industrials covers fixed charges (interest on debt) three times, this is adequate margin to protect the interest payment.

Where a junior and a senior debt are outstanding or where debt and preferred stock are outstanding, the interest and preferred dividend charges should be combined. The combined interest figure should be adequately covered by net income after taxes. The number of times these combined charges should be covered by net income can be reduced somewhat for the industrial company to approximately 2 1/2 times and probably to 1 1/2 times for public utilities and railroads. These limits refer only to the limits of total fixed and contingent charges, not to the combination of junior and senior interest charges. The interest limits must be applied to the total interest payment. The limits are reduced when preferred dividends are combined with interest charges because they are not a fixed charge on earnings but only a contingent charge.

Debt to Net Worth Ratio. Debt to net worth is also used as a guide to whether a company's debt is excessive. The word *debt* refers not only to long-term debt, which we have discussed, but to short-term debt too. This limit, usually imposed in the field of industrial financing, suggests that total debt (short-term and long-term) should not exceed the net worth of the company. This is a realistic limit. It prevents lenders from supplying more long-term capital than the owners. In a risk venture the owners should provide the residual risk taken, not the creditors. It would be unwise for the creditors to provide more capital— in the usual business situation—than the owners. Of course, situations exist where debt does exceed the net worth of the company. In cases like this, the debt must be justified by the peculiar circumstances surrounding the future growth and financial position of the company. If no realistic justification can be found for an inordinately large debt, it would be wise to avoid the company as an outlet for investment funds.

Convertible Debt and Debt Limits. When convertible debt is used to raise capital for a company, we should be interested in two questions: Is debt excessive? What impact will the conversion of the debt have upon the earnings of the common stockholders? The immediate impact of selling convertible bonds might be to increase earnings because of leverage and the profitability of the investment. After the bonds are issued, earnings might be diluted when the bonds are converted into common stock. Whether the debt is excessive under these circumstances can be judged by the ratios we have discussed. The result of conversion must be calculated, giving full effect to the change in the level of corporate taxes as it might affect future earnings and the increase in common shares that will result. Should conversion of the debt reduce future earnings, we have a dilution effect. We must adjust future earnings downward and compensate for this adjustment in the price we would be willing to pay for a share of stock. The purchaser of convertible securities should make the same calculation, for it is not to his advantage to have earnings diluted, resulting in lower market prices for his bonds or shares.

Rule of Reason and Debt. We must use reason in applying the debt limits that have been discussed. Under certain conditions a company, on the surface, might have excessive debt in its capital structure. Yet when the financial position and growth prospects of the company are analyzed and understood, the debt appears to be reasonable and an aid to growth. In fact, it might be a necessity for growth. Many public utilities are in this position. They are growing and need debt funds to finance their growth. However, even a small amount of debt, well below the debt limits we have suggested, might in some cases result in permanent damage to the long-range financial position of the company. A utility that is in a transitional area, with declining revenues, for example, could not support even a modest amount of debt, much less the amount suggested by the rules we apply. In all matters of debt we must use our business and financial sense to aid us in deciding what is or is not excessive debt.

An Example of a Capital Structure Analysis

An analysis of the capital structure and debt position of two companies is presented in Table 14–6. An examination of the table reveals that neither Company I nor Company II now has or had five years ago a large amount of debt in its capital structure. However, Company I has reduced its debt over the period, whereas Company II has increased debt in its capital structure. Company I has apparently expanded through the use of internally generated funds, whereas Company II has expanded through the sale of debt. We cannot, however, make a value decision and say that Company I is better than Company II. All we can say is that, in the current year, both companies have about the same amount of debt in the capital structure and that this debt is not too high in relation to other capital. Preferred stock represents a small portion of the capital structure of Company I, and there is no preferred stock in the capital structure of Company II. Both companies, therefore, have a rather modest amount of leverage in their financial structure, which should have only a small effect upon the earnings leverage of the company.

TABLE 14–6

Long-term debt analysis of two industrial companies (dollars in thousands)

	Company I				Company II			
	FIVE YEARS AGO		THIS YEAR		FIVE YEARS AGO		THIS YEAR	
	$	%	$	%	$	%	$	%
Capital Structure								
Long-term debt	10.0	25.0	5.0	11.1	0.0		10.0	25.0
Preferred stock	5.0	12.5	5.0	11.1	0.0		0.0	
Common stock	5.0 ⎫		5.0 ⎫		2.0 ⎫		2.0 ⎫	
Capital surplus	5.0 ⎬ 62.5		5.0 ⎬ 77.7		10.0 ⎬ 100.0		10.0 ⎬ 75.0	
Retained earnings	15.0 ⎭		25.0 ⎭		18.0 ⎭		18.0 ⎭	
Total	40.0		45.0		30.0		40.0	
Fixed assets	30.0		35.0		10.0		20.0	
Working capital	10.0		10.0		5.0		5.0	
Net worth	30.0		10.0		30.0		30.0	
Total debt	20.0		15.0		5.0		15.0	
Interest charges	0.5		0.5		0.0		0.6	
Preferred dividend requirements	0.3		0.3		0.0		0.0	
Net income after taxes	4.0		4.5		2.4		3.2	
Debt Limits								
Number of times fixed charges earned	8.0		9.0		infinite		5.3	
Number of times fixed and contingent charges earned	5.0		5.6		infinite		5.3	
Total debt to net worth (%)	66.6		37.5		16.6		50.0	
Long-term debt to fixed assets (%)	33.3		14.2		0.0		50.0	
Long-term debt to working capital (%)	100.0		50.0		0.0		200.0	

The number of times fixed charges and fixed charges plus contingent charges were earned for both companies is more than enough to meet the standards we have imposed—three times for interest coverage and two and one-half times for interest and preferred dividend coverage. The debt to net worth ratio and long-term debt to fixed assets and working capital ratio are adequate for Company I but not for Company II. The debt to working capital is presently excessive for Company II if we impose the 100 percent of working capital limit; that is, debt should not exceed 100 percent of working capital. Thus we would suggest that Company II had too much debt. All the other tests are adequate, suggesting that each company was well financed and that we might ignore this one test. However, this weakness suggests that Company II might improve its working capital position by the addition of retained earnings or more equity capital.

The overall conclusion about Companies I and II is that they are both in a good long-term financial position. There are no convertible preferred or bonds that might dilute future earnings. Leverage is not at the point where a great deal of instability is created in the earnings of the companies. The trend of Company II appears to be toward more debt. This should be watched carefully. Otherwise, both companies have an adequate capital structure.

An Analysis of the Capital Structure of Three Ethical Drug Companies

The capital structure of three leading ethical drug companies is composed almost entirely of common stock and retained earnings. Except for Pfizer, long-term debt of these companies represented less than 5 percent of the capital structure in 1966. The bulk of the funds raised came from retained earnings. The industry has been conservatively financed, and little or no leverage existed; the earnings of the companies were not aided or disturbed, therefore, by large amounts of low-cost debt financing. G. D. Searle issued a $1 cumulative convertible preferred late in 1967, not reflected in the balance sheet. The stock is redeemable at $26.50 a share after July 29, 1971, and is convertible into 1/3 share of common stock. This has added leverage to Searle's capital structure and will eventually lead to some dilution in per share earnings. The earnings of the industry should be relatively stable and vary only with variations in sales. The earnings fluctuations should not be increased because of substantial financial leverage.

An analysis of Pfizer, Searle, and Smith Kline & French for 1968 is presented in Table 14–7. Smith Kline & French had no long-term debt and no preferred stock in its capital structure. The capital of each of the three companies increased greatly in the period between 1957 and 1968 and continued to increase through 1969. Virtually all the increase was financed from retained earnings. Pfizer had some debt in its capital structure but not a significant enough amount to affect earnings fluctuation or the long-range profitability of the company. Pfizer, from an income-tax point of view, lowered its cost of capital by redeeming preferred stock that existed in 1957 and financing with bonds. This shift reduced the cost of funds and helped to improve earnings on the common shares. Searle's shift to convertible preferreds has increased its cost of capital and operating leverage.

Fixed charges were adequately covered for all companies, and the debt to net worth ratio was completely satisfactory. Debt to fixed assets and debt to working capital is not excessive in any of the companies. This suggests that their method of financing has been satisfactory. Some leverage exists in Pfizer and Searle but not enough to cause

TABLE 14–7

Long-term debt and capital structure analysis of Pfizer, Searle, and Smith Kline & French, 1968 (in millions of dollars and percent of total capital structure)

	CHAS. PFIZER		G. D. SEARLE		SMITH KLINE & FRENCH	
Capital structure:	($)	(%)	($)	(%)	($)	(%)
Long-term debt	$ 36	7	$ 20	17	—	—
Preferred stock	—	—	2	1	—	—
Common stock	7	2	13	11	7.1	4.0
Capital surplus	111	22	3	2	—	—
Retained earnings	348	69	86	69	171.6	96.0
Total	$502	100.0	$124	100.0	$178.7	100.0
Fixed assets	319		44		89	
Working capital	213		77		99	
Net worth	465		98		170	
Long-term debt	36		36		—	
Short-term debt	203		21		53	
Total debt	239		57		53	
Long-term debt interest charges	2		1		—	
Preferred dividends	—		2		—	
Net income after taxes	65		27		42	
Debt Limits:						
Number of times fixed charges earned	35		27		—	
Number times fixed and contingent charges earned	35		9		—	
Long-term debt to net worth (%)	8		37		—	
Long-term debt to fixed assets (%)	11		72		—	
Long-term debt to working capital (%)	17		47		—	

SOURCE: *Moody's Industrial Manual*, Moody's Investors Service, New York, 1969, pp. 1547, 1548, 1552, 1993, and 1994.

TABLE 14–8

Rate of return earned on total capital and common equity by Pfizer, Searle, and Smith Kline & French

	Rate Earned on Common Equity (%)			Rate Earned on Total Capital (%)		
YEAR	PFIZER	SEARLE	SKF	PFIZER	SEARLE	SKF
1968	13.9	25.5	25.7	14.0	27.5	24.7
1967	15.7	28.6	29.8	13.2	20.1	29.8
1966	18.6	26.0	32.2	14.9	18.0	32.2
1965	18.4	33.0	35.9	17.0	33.0	35.9
1964	17.0	37.7	31.6	15.8	37.7	31.6
1963	16.2	34.7	31.6	15.6	34.7	31.6

alarm. The capital structure analysis of the three companies demonstrates a sound, conservative method of financing an industrial company. Of the three, Smith Kline & French has relied most heavily on short-term debt to raise money. Based on the analysis, we could place each company in its relative position as in Table 14–9. The rate earned on common equity and on total capital (presented in Table 14–8) suggests that Searle is the best company with respect to these ratios. For all the companies, it is apparent that return on capital is diminishing.

TABLE 14–9

Companies ranked by debt limits

DEBT LIMITS	PFIZER	SEARLE	SMITH KLINE & FRENCH
Times fixed charges earned	2	1	1
Times fixed and contingent charges earned	2	1	1
Total debt to net worth (smallest amt.)	2	3	1
Long-term debt to fixed assets	3	2	1
Long-term debt to working capital	3	2	1
Rate earned on common equity	3	1	2
Rate earned on total capital	3	1	2

Using Table 14–9, we would conclude that all companies were adequately financed with the relative ranking of Smith Kline & French, G. D. Searle, and Chas. Pfizer, in that order.

Summary

As investors we must judge the current financial position of the company. Tests that are available for this purpose are the current ratio, the acid test ratio, the composition of current assets, the number of days' sales outstanding (DSO), net sales to inventory, and net sales to working capital. The current ratio and acid test ratio indicate the ability of the company to pay its current debts. The composition of current assets helps to determine if the company possesses sufficient immediate liquidity to meet its debts. The number of days' sales outstanding indicates the effectiveness with which accounts receivable are collected. If the days' sales outstanding (DSO) compared with the credit period is high, the company is jeopardizing its liquidity. The net sales to inventory ratio, as well as net sales to working capital, indicates liquidity and the ability of a company to adequately finance its sales growth with its funds. The basic concern in current analysis is to make certain the company can pay its bills and finance its sales growth easily and quickly. No absolute standard will ensure success. Each company must be compared with the other companies in the industry and with its own position over time. Stability in these relationships is desirable, for a marked change in any ratio might indicate a weakness in the company that is a latent threat to future profits. Balance in the current financial position assures that earnings will not be reduced either because of too little cash, which might result in failure, or too much cash, which will not contribute to maximum earnings.

The ability of a company to raise long-term funds often determines its future success. Expenditures for improvement in plant and equipment and for working capital also require adequate financing. How a corporation raises long-term capital has an impact upon earnings. A large amount of debt or preferred stock in the capital structure tends to increase the per share earnings of the common stockholder. However, these also tend to increase the instability of corporate earnings. This is particularly true in the case of industrial companies that have unstable operating conditions. As profits increase or decrease, the earnings per share on common stock fluctuate much more than the original change in profits. This phenomenon is referred to as *operating* or *financial leverage*. A company that has a large debt in the capital structure is said to have a high degree of financial leverage in its capital structure. Leverage has a greater impact on earnings per share if revenues of a company are unstable than if they are stable.

Debt in modest amounts is desirable. Excessive debt is to be avoided as the long-range profitability of the company might be jeopardized. The tests of whether debt is excessive are: (1) debt to fixed assets, (2) debt to net worth, (3) debt to working capital, and (4) an adequate coverage of interest charges and an adequate coverage of preferred dividends and interest charges by net income after taxes. Rate of return on total capital and equity capital is also an indication of profitability and financial leverage. Companies that have excessive debt in the capital structure in comparison to the practice in the industry and the assets and earnings of the company should be avoided, since earnings might be highly unstable. These companies in addition have a tendency to sell at lower P/E ratios.

Review Questions

1. What are the basic financial objectives of a company?
2. What is the significance of each of the following, and what does each indicate?
   (a) Current ratio
   (b) Acid test ratio
   (c) Percentage composition of current assets
   (d) Days' sales outstanding (DSO)
   (e) Net sales to inventory
   (f) Inventory turnover ratio
   (g) Net sales to net working capital

3. What would a comparison of these ratios for each company reveal?

4. What would a sharp change, either higher or lower, in each of the ratios reveal to the investor?

5. Can a company have too much cash, or liquidity? Explain and indicate the significance of excess liquidity upon company earnings per share.

6. Review the analysis of the current position of the drug companies. Do you agree with the conclusions reached? Explain.

7. What impact might the source of funds for capital growth have upon the common-stock earnings per share?

8. Explain what is meant by the term *capital structure.*

9. Does the use of preferred stock lead to leverage in the earnings on common stock?

10. What are the limits to the use of preferred stock in the capital structure?

11. (a) Explain how the use of debt brings about financial leverage in the earnings on common stock.
    (b) What are the advantages of leverage from the point of view of the common stockholder?
    (c) What are the disadvantages of leverage?

12. Define and explain the significance of the following debt limits:
    (a) Fixed asset
    (b) Earnings
    (c) Debt to net worth

13. What effect would the conversion of convertible bonds have upon leverage and future earnings on common stock?

14. What is meant by the *rule of reason* in debt analysis?

15. Review the analysis of the capital structure of the three drug companies. Do you agree with the results?

16. The percentage of debt in its capital structure has no impact on the valuation and earnings of a company. Comment.

Problems

1. Compute the following for each of the three companies you are analyzing for the year 1957 and the present year:
    (a) Current ratio
    (b) Acid test ratio
    (c) Percentage composition of current assets
        (1) Cash
        (2) Receivables
        (3) Inventory
        (4) Other
    (d) Days' credit sales outstanding (DSO)
    (e) Net sales to inventory
    (f) Net sales to working capital

2. Are the companies in a good current financial position?

3. Which of the three companies appears to be in the best current financial position in each category of analysis?

4. If possible, compare the current financial position of each company with the industry's position as found in *Dun's Review and Modern Industry.*

5. Compute the percentage composition and dollar amount of the following items as a percent of the total capital structure for the three companies chosen for analysis, for 1957 and for the current year:
   (a) Long-term debt
   (b) Preferred stock
   (c) Common stock
   (d) Capital surplus
   (e) Retained earnings

6. Obtain the following figures in dollars for the three companies under analysis for 1957 and the present year:
   (a) Fixed assets
   (b) Working capital
   (c) Long-term debt
   (d) Short-term debt
   (e) Net worth

7. Compute the following debt limits of the companies:
   (a) Total debt to net worth
   (b) Long-term debt to fixed assets
   (c) Long-term debt to working capital
   (d) Times interest earned by income after taxes
   (e) Times preferred dividends and interest earned by income after taxes
   (f) Rate earned on total capital
   (g) Rate earned on equity

8. Is the debt of any one company excessive? Explain.

9. Which company has the greatest leverage? Which has the most conservative capital structure? Explain.

10. If a company has convertible preferred stock or convertible bonds outstanding, indicate the effect upon earnings of the common stock if the securities were converted.

11. (a) Rank the companies in order of preference as in Table 14–9.
    (b) Based on the above information, which company would you select for investment?

Sources of Investment Information

Annual reports of companies
Clark Dodge Investment Survey
Dun's Review and Modern Industry
Moody's manuals
Standard & Poor's *Investment Surveys*
The Value Line Investment Survey

Selected Readings

Barges, Alexander, "Growth Rates and Debt Capacity," *Financial Analysts Journal* (January-February, 1968), p. 100.

Briloff, Abraham J., "The CPA and Fair Corporate Accountability," *Financial Analysts Journal* (May-June, 1966), p. 51.

Brown, H.A. and R.W. Estes, "Comparability vs. Flexibility: A Practical Solution," *Financial Analysts Journal* (May-June, 1966), p. 65.

Feuerstein, A.E. and P.G. Maggi, "Computer Investment Research," *Financial Analysts Journal* (January-February, 1968), p. 154.

Gal, Joseph J., "Man-Machine Interactive Systems and Financial Analysis," *Financial Analysts Journal* (May-June, 1966), p. 126.

Rua, Ernest J., Jr., "Analyzing a Motor Carrier's Balance Sheet," *Financial Analysts Journal* (May-June, 1966), p. 57.

Stone, Donald E., "Computer-Aided Financial Analysis," *Financial Analysts Journal* (January-February, 1968), p. 149.

15

MANAGEMENT AND COMPANY ANALYSIS

The future earnings of a company, which will determine the success or failure of an investment, do not come about automatically. They are primarily the results of the thinking and productivity of hundreds or thousands of employees who are directed by capable management. We as stockholders hire professional management to handle our corporate affairs. We expect from them excellence in their respective jobs in order to allow us to obtain maximum returns on the shares we own. It is not an easy task to determine the competence of management, yet excellent management is paramount to investment success. A corporation, though it may hold a substantial share of the market for its products, must meet the competition of other companies. Our basic problem is to determine the quality of company management, and whether it is capable of maintaining the competitive position of the company and successfully running the affairs of the company to produce a profit.

Company Objectives and Management Functions

As one book on the subject of management states, "management is the accomplishing of a predetermined objective through the efforts of other people."[1] While a primary objective of most companies is the maximization of its profits, we cannot assume that this is the only objective that

---

1 George R. Terry, *Principles of Management* (Homewood, Ill.: Richard D. Irwin, Inc., 1956), p. 19.

a company considers. Other objectives concern other groups of individuals within the corporate family. The employees and the public must be recognized as well as the owners of the company.

The public wants, for example, a continuous supply of goods and services at fair prices, with improvement in these goods and services to obtain greater utility and a better way of life. The employees want a safe place to work, fair wages, steady employment, satisfaction from their jobs, security in their old age, and information about what is going on. As owners we want an efficiently operated and adequately financed enterprise, a fair return on our investment, full utilization of existing facilities, information about current developments, and a long-range program for the company. The goals of the three major groups, public, employees, and owners, must be unified by the management so that in reaching the major objectives of the company all groups will be satisfied.[2]

The managers achieve their objectives through the careful performance of the fundamental management functions of planning, organizing, actuating, and controlling. If the overall objectives of the company are achieved, then we investors will have a profit. It might not be in the amount that we wish, but we must understand that profit is only one of the goals of management and receives varying degrees of attention from company management. Some companies are more profit-oriented than others. A management that ignores profits, however, might do more harm to the future of the company than one overemphasizing it. If profits are not obtained, new capital will not flow to the enterprise, or, what is worse, capital will leave and the success of the company will end. It is imperative, in the long run, that the public, employees, and owners share in the fruits of their efforts.

The successful management will state as an objective the participation of each group in the success of the venture. Northern Illinois Gas is a good example of what a company can do to make its policies and objectives known to the investor through its annual report.[3] Northern Illinois Gas Company's basic purpose "is to perpetuate [its] effort as an investor-owned, free enterprise company rendering a needed, satisfactory service and earning optimum, long-range profits."[4] The investors, customers, employees, and the public are considered individually, and a set of principles, purposes, and objectives are provided for each group, as follows:

---

2 *Ibid.*, p. 45.

3 Dr. Corliss D. Anderson, *Corporate Reporting for the Professional Investor* (Auburndale, Mass.: Corporate Information Committee of the Financial Analysts Federation, 1962).

4 *Ibid.*, p. 18.

INVESTORS

The Company will:

A. Strive to provide to its owners, the holders of its common stock, a growing per share value, measured in terms of both income and appreciation and to be the maximum, in the long run, consistent with the Company's responsibilities to its customers, employees and the public.

B. Seek to continue to hold the interest of its broad, diversified, well-balanced and stable family of shareholders, and to attract others who will maintain this balance.

C. Provide for its stock a ready, convenient and technically sound market to ensure optimum flexibility for its owners.

D. Keep present and potential investors in the Company and their representatives well informed about the Company and its prospects, in order that they may make their investment decisions with full knowledge and that the Company's securities will be appraised fairly.

E. Keep its books in accordance with accepted, conservative accounting principles and practices.

F. Soundly employ, control and safeguard Company funds and property.

G. Maintain a sound, conservative capital structure to support the quality of all its securities, assure its ability to attract new capital when needed, and provide good protection to the investors in its senior securities. Maintenance of a sound capital structure, coupled with strong earnings, should assure optimum preservation of the investments of both the shareholders and senior security holders.

H. To develop strong earnings:

 1. Promote aggressively the sale of its product and of appliances and equipment utilizing its product.

 2. Maintain a close control over expenses, and constantly seek means to reduce them.

 3. Recover, as an operating expense, a realistic allowance for depreciation.

 4. Engage in and support research to improve the utilization of gas, develop new uses, provide a substitute when needed and find better ways to transport, store, deliver, measure, bill and collect for it.

 5. Provide capable, well-trained and enthusiastic managers, with adequate replacements ready when needed.

 6. Enter other phases of the energy business which have economic risks compatible with existing operations, which conform with the Company's Basic Purpose and supplement or complement its principal business.

I. Pay to the holders of its common stock in dividends a reasonable proportion of the earnings. The dividend rate will be reviewed thoroughly at least once a year. Establishment of a rate that can be continued despite possible adverse economic, regulatory or other developments will be the goal.

J. Promote private enterprise and endeavor to minimize municipal or other governmental ownership of business.

CUSTOMERS

The Company will:

A. Deliver to its gas customers, safely and dependably, a gas of uniform heating value that will burn cleanly and efficiently.

B. Provide this gas at a fair and reasonable price, as low as possible consistent with prompt, courteous and dependable service, and consistent with its responsibilities to its investors, employees and the public.

C. Provide an adequate and dependable supply of gas over both the short- and the long-range.

D. Either provide prompt, courteous, dependable service on customer appliances and equipment itself, or assure itself that satisfactory service is otherwise available to customers and they have been so informed.

E. Endeavor to maintain the right of the customer to use the form of energy he prefers.

F. See to it that better, even more modern appliances and equipment utilizing its energy are being developed and are brought to the customers' attention.

G. Keep abreast of technological change.

H. Constantly seek out and utilize innovations and improvements to hold down and reduce costs.

I. Maintain its facilities and equipment well from the viewpoints of both operation and appearance.

J. Be staffed with personnel who are friendly, neat, well-informed, helpful and promptly attentive to the customers' individual problems.

EMPLOYEES

A. The Company will hire employees with good education, appearance and attitude.

B. The Company will hire and treat all employees without discrimination as to race, creed, nationality background, or physical handicaps not detrimental to performance or general health.

C. The Company, in return for the fulfillment by the employees of their responsibilities, as outlined later, will pay:

  1. Fair and just wages, comparable to what others are paying for like work.

  2. Increased wages from time to time as. merited by improved productivity or performance.

D. The Company will provide:

  1. Job security to the greatest extent possible, consistent with continued satisfactory performance and adherence to Company work rules.

2. A comprehensive, modern benefit program.

3. Safe and, so far as possible, pleasant working conditions and practices. Tools and equipment provided by the Company will be safe and efficient.

4. Job training and educational opportunities to help employees perform better in their jobs and prepare for advancement.

5. Promotions on the basis of ability and experience, not solely on seniority.

6. An opportunity for employees to become shareholders in the business.

E.   The Company will bargain fairly and realistically with recognized representatives of non-management employees.

F.   The Company will administer discipline fairly, equitably and firmly.

G.   The Company will:

1. Seek to promote a working climate in which the Company's objectives and management's decisions are understood and accepted, and the supervisors are motivated to implement them.

2. Keep employees informed of matters of interest to them pertaining to their jobs, the Company, its product and service.

3. Endeavor to merit the pride of all employees in the Company and its management.

4. Provide good, well-trained supervisors at all levels, with respect both for the individual and the need to get the job done.

5. Provide its managers with a sound organization structure and clearly defined duties.

6. Delegate responsibility and authority as nearly as possible to the point of action.

7. Encourage self-reliance, initiative and decision-making.

8. Urge supervisors to discuss matters freely with their subordinates and encourage employees to feel free to discuss problems with their supervisors.

9. Encourage the search for new, more efficient ways of doing its business, to the end of reducing costs, increasing productivity and freeing manpower from the tasks of greatest drudgery to those more challenging and better paying.

10. Strive to utilize every employee to his maximum capability in the long run.

H.   The Company will let each employee know what is expected of him and how well he is doing it. The Company will expect the employees:

1. To provide a fair day's work for a fair day's pay, but the Company will only pay for the performance of work required to be performed.

2. To be quick to suggest improvements and to be adaptable to change.

3. To uphold the highest standards of integrity.

4. To be loyal, supporting Company objectives and policies.

5. To be goodwill ambassadors of the Company at all times.

6. To be enthusiastic about the Company's business and to promote it diligently.

7. To be good citizens, and to participate in community activities of their choice, consistent with Company policies.

PUBLIC

The Company will be imbued with a sense of public interest. In discharging its responsibility to the public, it will endeavor to be a good citizen in every way, constantly seeking means to be of service and to deserve and enjoy the highest measure of public confidence and esteem. It will:

A. Keep its properties and equipment in good condition and appearance.

B. Plan ahead so that its operations will be performed with a minimum of public inconvenience.

C. Inform the public of construction to be performed and the reasons for it.

D. Restore property if disturbed.

E. Maintain a safe system.

F. Provide adequate capacity for the present utility needs of the communities it serves and be ready to meet their growth.

G. Promote the development of the area it serves.

H. Pay its fair share of taxes.

I. Encourage its employees to be leaders in community and civic activities to the extent consistent with Company policies.

J. Contribute to worthwhile community activities, to a reasonable extent considering its public utility status.

K. Keep the public informed of its problems and achievements which affect the public.

L. Be nonpartisan but speak out on issues where interests of the business, its investors, employees or customers are seriously affected.[5]

The Qualities of Good Management

What is meant by the term *good management*? What qualities must a manager or the management of a company possess in order to be considered good, adequate, or excellent? There is no golden rule for determining management success, just as there is no trait or list of traits in an individual that will lead to success. Professor Davis uses a list that has been helpful in determining executive success. It includes such traits as "intelligence, experience, originality, receptiveness, personality, teaching ability, initiative, tenacity, courage, human understanding, and a sense of justice and fair play."[6]

5 Anderson, *Corporate Reporting for the Professional Investor,* pp. 19–21.

6 Ralph Currier Davis, *Industrial Organization and Management,* 3rd ed. (New York: Harper & Row, Publishers, 1957), p. 35.

Terry[7] suggests that a successful manager possesses the following traits:

1. An ability to direct and motivate people.
2. A good background of the general and special field of management.
3. A broad point of view.
4. The ability to make decisions.
5. A desire for responsibility.
6. Completely dependable and thoroughly trustworthy.

Wald and Doty,[8] in a study of top executives, summarize the traits that lead to executive success as follows:

1. The successful or likely to be successful executive has experienced a happy home life in his earlier years, conducive to the development of security and self-confidence.
2. He is extremely interested in and feels very much attached to his present family unit.
3. The educational level completed by the typical executive is far above the average of the general population.
4. He takes full advantage of varied educational opportunities.
5. He is an active participant in and leader of social organizations during childhood and throughout his career as a worker.
6. He is interested in religion as a force toward developing high moral and ethical standards.
7. He has experienced and continues to experience good health.
8. He is interested in people—particularly in selling them on the idea of fundamental cooperation. He is interested in the written and spoken word as a means of communicating his ideas. He is not preoccupied with the technical phases of his work, but rather with promoting harmonious human relationships.
9. He possesses very superior mental and analytical ability.
10. He is serious and conscientious in his approach to work. He is willing to take risks only after full consideration of the available facts.
11. He is forceful and intense, actively seeking new work to be done and new methods of doing it.
12. He is objective in facing his personal problems, frank and straightforward in his dealings with people and spontaneous in his interpersonal relationships.
13. He is ambitious and able to identify his ambitions with those of his company to an outstanding degree.

Stating the good qualities and traits of management is a difficult job. No two experts will agree on just what will lead to executive and company success. An even more imposing task is to learn if the executives of the company in which we are to invest our funds actually possess

7 Terry, *Principles of Management*, p. 14.
8 Robert M. Wald and Roy Doty, "The Top Executive—A First-Hand Profile," *Harvard Business Review*, July-August, 1954, p. 53.

the desired traits. Many investors do not know who the president of their company is. Few investors know that James C. Donnell II is the President of Marathon Oil Company, that John Dykstra is President of Ford Motor Company, or that Eugene J. McNeely is President of American Telephone and Telegraph. These men are known to security analysts and businessmen, but not to most nonprofessional investors. Obtaining information about the officers and directors of a company, except for information published in the annual report or available in public statements, is difficult. Most small investors depend upon the advice of professionals in making investment decisions and feel they do not need to know the management of the company, assuming in most cases that management is good. But because we desire greater proof of excellence of management in our analysis, we investigate more thoroughly the qualities of management than would the average investor.

Determining Management's Ability

We need two types of information to understand the ability of management. First we want to know something about the men who manage. Who are they, and what is their background of experience and development? Second, we want some tests to judge the management's ability and to determine how well it has done.

THE BACKGROUND OF MANAGEMENT

Let us see what we wish to know about the man who manages. It is difficult to learn much about a manager from a sheet of vital statistics. We can find out his age, his educational background, his advancement within the corporation, the levels of responsibility he has achieved, and his activities in social, cultural, civic, educational, philanthropic, and charitable organizations. This will provide some insight into his abilities. An example of the personal data that are helpful in learning about management is found in the background of the president of Rio Algom Mines, Ltd. The Hon. Robert H. Winters, president of the company, held in 1962 a B.A. degree from Mt. Allison and an M.S. from Massachusetts Institute of Technology. In addition he had been awarded several honorary degrees. He was born in Luxemburg, Nova Scotia in 1910. He had held many positions of responsibility, including: president, Rio Tinto-Dow, Preston Mines; vice-president and director, Canada Permanent Toronto General Trust Company; director, Bathurst Power and Paper Co., Canadian Imperial Bank of Commerce, Crown Life Insurance Company, Ford of Canada, Globe Indemnity Co. of Canada, The Liverpool-Manitoba Assurance Co., Rothmans of Pall Mall Canada, and British New Foundland Corporation; member, Corporation of MIT; chairman, Board of Governors, York University, Toronto; federal cabinet minister,

1948–1957.[9] All these activities suggest Mr. Winters is an exceptionally able and intelligent corporate executive.

THE RECORD OF MANAGEMENT

The facts we read about management and its abilities and qualities are in reality impressions, most of them based upon the individual and collective achievement of management. When we read *Who's Who in Business*, we use the comments to help us determine what the man has accomplished. A familiar statement, "We measure a man by his deeds and not by his years," seems to apply here. We want management to be intelligent, hard-working, socially oriented to groups, interested in work, home, society, and religion. But we also want it to achieve the objectives of the company by performing efficiently and effectively the functions of management—planning, organizing, actuating, and controlling. We hope that these objectives will be consistent with the objective of profits and result in income and capital gain for securities we own.

We are quick to ask what the top management has done during its tenure in office. Has it accomplished the goals of growth, diversification, profits, and benefits to society and employees alike? If management's record has been good, then we can say the management is good. If the record has been poor, our conclusion must reflect this. There is no personal assessment here of its moral aptitude; we are simply assessing management's ability to achieve its objectives. Our test then is the record of the accomplishments.

The appraisal of the record of management covers many of the same topics we have already discussed. The ability to maintain the competitive position of the company, capital expenditures, profits, and financing are used as criteria to determine if management is capable. This might seem like circular reasoning and to some extent it is. However, in modern-day business management, the officers of the company acting as managers make the decisions about what will be done as well as when, where, how, and why. They *are* in reality the company; to assess their activities is to assess the activities of the company. We must use the record of accomplishment because it is difficult to find other information that will tell us whether management is capable. Testing management might be possible for the personnel officer or the plant psychologist, but it is not suitable for the analyst or the investor.

Management and the Competitive Position of the Company. One of the first questions to raise as a test of the effectiveness of management is whether management has been able to maintain the competitive position of the company. If we follow the growth concept, we want our company not only to maintain its competitive position, but to grow faster

9 Anderson, *Corporate Reporting for the Professional Investor,* p. 72.

than its competitors. If management can achieve a growth of sales superior to that of other companies in the industry, we can conclude that it has done a good job.

We must impose a different criterion upon the company that is not purchased for growth but for its stability and regularity of sales and profits. In this case we must determine if it is maintaining its competitive position. This type of company need not obtain a greater share of the market as long as it maintains its relative position in the market. A railroad, for example, might be purchased because of its income and yield. The railroad may not be increasing its sales every year, yet it may provide enough revenue to maintain adequate dividends and earnings. The management is meeting the objectives imposed and is considered to be successful.

Ability to Expand. Merger and consolidation often provide a clue to a management's ability to succeed. A firm may expand from within through expenditures for new plant and equipment. Another and sometimes more efficient way of expanding is through the acquisition of other companies. Many firms have grown larger and have developed a stronger competitive base through merger—Litton Industries, for example. Whether profitable benefits are always achieved through mergers is a moot point. Merger or consolidation is one way in which an aggressive and capable management can direct the growth of a company. A more competitive management would use merger as an immediate step for improving its competitive position. Thus we look upon merger as a sign of strength for some companies and an indication that management is doing a good job.

Ability to Maintain Profit Margins. One important function of the financial and corporate management is to maintain costs and profit margins. In performing the selling function, management cannot and must not ignore costs. If a company can increase sales only by increasing costs and reducing profits, then we would say that the management was not very efficient. On the other hand, a management that increases sales and maintains costs without decreasing profit margin is doing a good job of controlling the company and maintaining profits.

The concept of earnings and profitability is relative to the company and the industry, including changes over time. If the profit margin for an entire industry is declining, we cannot condemn one management because it is not able to maintain its profit margins. However, if a company could reduce its operating expenses and costs and maintain or improve the profit margin at a time when profit margins were declining, this would demonstrate a real show of strength on the part of management.

There is another side to this story. The ability to reduce costs cannot always be considered an advantage. Suppose, for example, costs and expenses were reduced but the long-range profitability was impaired because it was done at the expense of new product development. This type of reduction in costs and expenses might reduce long-range profits far more than a temporary reduction in expenses would add to profits and earnings.

Ability to Maintain Efficient Production. Output per man or operating efficiency as measured by the operating ratio can provide a basis to determine how well management has done in maintaining the company's productive efficiency. A management that is able to improve its output or sales per employee and maintain its operating efficiency is a good management. This is particularly important when the company is doing a better and more efficient job than its competitors. Another aspect of the question of efficiency is the ability of the company to operate at or close to full capacity and to maintain its level of operations above the breakeven point. In the steel industry Armco is a good illustration of a company that, typically, has operated at a rather high percent of capacity and has done a somewhat better job in maintaining its level of operations than the industry as a whole.

Ability to Finance the Company Adequately. Management must be able to sell and produce its product or service and to finance the production and sale of its product. How it accomplishes the financing is a direct reflection on its own ability to manage. A company that maintains an adequate profit margin, retains a sufficient amount of profits within the enterprise, maintains adequate commercial and investment banker relations, and provides funds when needed can be considered a well-managed company.

Companies differ as to their ability to provide adequate funds. The characteristics of each industry vary so that a variation in the method of financing is to be expected. Companies with large profit margins are in a much better position to finance their operations; internally generated funds might satisfy the needs of such a company. A business that is not growing at a rapid rate has an easier job of financing than a company that is growing rapidly. The important consideration is that the company's management provides funds when needed, regardless of the amount or timing of those funds.

The corporate management must maintain realistic dividend and capital expenditure policies in relation to earnings. A dividend policy that requires an excessive payment of earnings can be harmful to the future of a company, as can a policy of overexpansion. Conversely, a company that pays out little in dividends, spends little for plant expenditures, and builds up excessive liquid balances is not managing corporate funds adequately. Such a company is not as profitable as it could be, and management is not doing a good job.

Management must be able to finance the company's needs without resorting to excessive debt financing. One cause of corporate failure is the inability to repay debt. Debt has the unhappy faculty of coming due at the wrong time; many companies have gone into receivership because they were not able to pay their debt obligation. One commercial airline recently merged with another company. The airline company had borrowed heavily to finance the purchase of medium-range jets to improve service and stay ahead of the competition. The jets were not suitable for the company's operation, and revenues were not satisfactory. The debt burden was too great, and the company failed. The only way out was merger. A good management will have demonstrated over time an ability to manage debt successfully.

Ability to Work with Employees and Unions. The growth of unions and collective bargaining has placed management in a position where the employees must be recognized—sometimes to the exclusion of other groups. Management must present the company's position strongly so that the public, the owners, and the management do not suffer as a result of benefits to labor. Therefore, good labor relations—a mark of good management—mean that labor receives a wage and fringe benefits in some relation to productivity and that a fair share of productivity goes to the owners, the management, and the public. A management that consistently acquiesces to labor demands that are not based upon increases in productivity is a weak management. A management that does not consider labor at all or has poor working conditions and frequent strikes is also inconsiderate of the overall objectives of the company and is doing a poor job. An inconsiderate management jeopardizes the long-range profitability of the company. A company that has good management will have good labor relations. Good labor relations can be defined as that relationship that is fair to the public, to the stockholder, and to the employee in direct relation to each group's contribution to productivity.

Scientific Management. Management is much more complex than it was fifty years ago. Then, decisions were based upon the intuition of management, and little scientific methodology was used. Today the corporate manager has been trained through experience, through development programs, and through education in colleges and universities to perform his task effectively and profitably. Today computers aid in performing routine repetitive tasks, and office equipment is now being used to provide almost instant data to help management reach the best decision from among the alternatives. Cost controls have been and are being imposed by management, and time and motion studies are being undertaken to improve productivity while improving the compensation of the worker and his working conditions. Quality control is a common word in industry, and more frequently we hear such words as the planning division, linear programming, and psychological testing. The truth of the matter is that a good management is using all the tools of scientific management that are available. These will, in the long run, provide generous benefits to all the groups within the corporate family.

The corporation management that constantly applies new techniques, that searches for new and better ways to produce goods and services, that attempts to develop its own abilities through development programs and training, and that attempts to apply scientific techniques is a good management. Again, determining the extent to which a management is developing scientific principles is difficult. It requires diligence and perseverance on our part to learn of management's activities. Some will be learned from the annual report, others only from the current articles that appear in the financial press. Such information is highly subjective and depends upon a knowledge of management itself.

Management and the Government. Modern corporate management must be able to work with government officials in two important areas. One is in the complicated process of entering into contracts with the federal government to produce goods needed by civilian and military personnel. The second is in the area of anti-trust suits brought by the Justice Department against illegal competitive practices.

Not all managements possess the ability to negotiate and compete for government contracts. Many companies think that government business is unprofitable and do not care to engage in this activity. Others consider contracts with the government uncertain. Several aerospace companies, for example, have been affected recently because of cutbacks in military appropriations for their products. The pitfalls of government contracts are many, and it takes an experienced management to understand this phase of business activity and operate within the environment created by the government. We as investors must determine if the company is engaged in government business and what skills management has in this area.

The federal government has always been concerned with unfair competitive practices. The Justice Department attempts to carry out the letter if not the intent of the anti-monopoly laws. We wish the companies in which we invest to be large and stable with growth possibilities. The large corporations usually have a dominant position in the market. Actually, the leading companies might collectively "control" the market for particular goods and services. This position can be desirable for the investors in these companies, for they will profit because of this leadership. This monopolistic, or even oligopolistic, competition that develops, however, must be carried on without collusion, conspiracy, or fraud. Where there is restraint of trade and conspiracy, comparable to the situation in the electrical equipment industry in the early 1960's, then the Justice Department has every right to bring the guilty party to terms. Otherwise the public will suffer, possibly to the benefit of the shareholders and the employees. It is the duty then of management to maintain competitive conditions without collusion or conspiracy. It is the job of shareholders to make certain that the corporate management carries out these competitive conditions. A management that does not possess honor, integrity, and character is not worth the trust placed in it by the shareholders, and certainly it is no place for an investor's funds.

When management is accused wrongly by the federal government of unfair competitive practices, it should have the ability to pursue the charge until it has been cleared. Several important suits in recent years have been brought by the Justice Department against large corporations, where the Justice Department has found what it considers to be restraint of trade or where there will be a material lessening of competition because of a merger. In these cases, management must use every fair, legal means available to repudiate the charge and defend its competitive practices. Thus, management is charged with the responsibility of not engaging in collusive activities and unfair competition, and with the duty to protect the public, the employees, and the owners from unfair charges brought against them by the government. To the extent that it fulfills these obligations, it will be considered a good management.

Additional Tests of Management's Abilities

We can judge the quality of management by several additional yardsticks in the area of management activities. Does management, for example, engage in research and product development that will improve and insure future profits? Is there a training program at all levels of management to keep and attract managerial talent? Does management take an active part in community projects, and does it foster and encourage questioning by the owners? These are yardsticks that are subject to a wide variation in interpretation. They are intangibles, and yet an affirmative answer to each of these questions would suggest that management is capable and doing a good job.

RESEARCH AND PRODUCT DEVELOPMENT

Many corporations are producing products today for mass consumption that did not exist ten years ago. We live in a day of invention and innovation. In order for a company to survive, it must constantly produce improved products to maintain its competitive position. A management that recognizes its responsibility to the share owners will be in constant search of new and better products that will benefit and protect mankind and prove profitable for the company. The good management accepts the challenge of product development and translates this challenge into action by the expenditure of funds for product development and research. Without expenditures for new products many firms will not exist in the future. A management that does spend efficiently for product development can be considered a good management.

We must look to the research activities of our company. The company that spends for research has alert management that recognizes its responsibility to all groups in the corporate unit.

EXECUTIVE DEVELOPMENT AND MANAGEMENT

The management of a company not only has the obligation to manage well in the present but must also provide for the future. This means active recruitment of potential business executives from colleges and universities and the school of experience. Most large corporations, with the cooperation of college placement bureaus, interview hundreds of likely management trainee prospects each year to find men and women who will fill future positions of responsibility. Many companies have well-defined training programs designed to provide a wide range of experience for the newly hired person. Through exposure in several areas, the company hopes to develop the recruit so that he will eventually make the greatest contribution to the company. The personnel department's task is to see that the training program is fruitful for the trainee and the company. Merrill Lynch, Pierce, Fenner & Smith, for example, has an excellent training program for aspiring sales executives and financial analysts. Each year only a few out of the total number who apply for selection are taken. Those who succeed quickly learn many facets of the securities business. Industrial and utility companies such as Marathon, AT&T, Procter and Gamble, and Cleveland Electric Illuminating Company have excellent training programs.

Not only must management be concerned with younger executive trainees, they must also be concerned with the development of middle and upper management. Many companies have their managers take part in executive development programs. Harvard, Columbia, Stanford, and many other schools of business in the United States have provided industry with executive development programs designed to improve the abilities and capabilities of management to assume more important responsibilities in the corporation. Many corporations encourage their executives to take advantage of the educational opportunities within the community, both to broaden their vision and to enable them to do a specific task more easily. Some send their management to three-month or one-year programs to freshen their perspective and exchange views with their contemporaries within and without their own discipline in business.

All the programs mentioned lead to better trained, better informed, and more perceptive management. Some even provide the executive with a more liberal, socially oriented education. Bell Telephone, early in the 1950's, began a seminar program at the University of Pennsylvania.

It was not a program to train the manager to do a specific job but to help him understand the broad areas of his activities. The extent to which these programs prepare management to do a better job today, tomorrow, and in the future is beneficial for all groups within the corporation.

MANAGEMENT AND THE COMMUNITY

A good management accepts the responsibility of helping the community in which it lives. This help comes from the members of management as individuals as well as from the corporation. It would be impossible to list all the activities of the many corporations in the United States. A few examples will convey the meaning of community responsibility. The president of the Marathon Oil Company, James C. Donnell, is active in the Boy Scouts of America and holds an executive position with that organization. Charles A. Jackson, former treasurer and director of the company, had been president of the Board of Education in Findlay, Ohio. In fact, all of the management of the company are active in community affairs. In addition to this, the company helps Findlay College, provides scholarship assistance for the children of employees, has a summer Fellowship Program for University Faculty, and through its donation committee supports other charitable and educational work.

Contrast this to a company that offers little in the way of assistance to community activities or growth. Some time ago a report was published about a company that took no part in community activities. The stated policy of the company was completely *laissez faire*—let the community take care of its problems, we will take care of ours. The report discussed ways in which the company was cutting costs and improving its profit margin. We cannot help but think that the company might be profitable, but the management was not giving its full measure of time and effort to the broad social responsibilities it must share. This management could not be considered adequate in fulfilling its reasonable, long-range responsibility to society and the corporate owners.

Learning About Management's Ability

Information about the qualities and abilities of management can be obtained from many sources. Here are several of the usual places where we can learn about management.

The Annual Report

The annual report usually presents information about the top executives —both the board of directors and the officers—of the corporation. The plans of management for the years to come are presented, and the events of the past year are examined. When significant management changes occur, they too are reported. The 1969 annual report of the American Greetings Corporation mentioned that a restructuring of top management had taken place in January. Several officers were given new or added areas of responsibility. The reorganization was for the purpose of allowing the designated officers more time for planning future growth.[10]

The 1968 annual report of W. R. Grace & Co. stated:

> At the annual stockholders' meeting in May, 1968, E. Ainsworth Eyre and Francis G. Kingsley, having reached the retirement age for Directors, did not stand for re-election. They had been Directors for 35 and 8 years respectively. We are fortunate that both will continue to serve as Directors Emeritus. During the year, O. C. Carmichael, Jr., Chairman of Associates Investment Company; George J. Leness, formerly Chairman of Merrill Lynch, Pierce, Fenner & Smith, Inc.; George P. Gardner, Jr., General Partner of Paine, Webber, Jackson & Curtis; and John A. Puelicher, President of Marshall & Ilsley Bank, were elected to the board.[11]

This does not seem to be a great deal of information about the officers, but it does suggest that the men advanced to positions of responsibility have had experience and demonstrated their abilities in other positions of responsibility. In most of the annual reports the officers are pictured and some indication of their service to the company, their education, and their background are given.

The Financial Press

Often the excellence of management can be obtained from articles in the financial press and periodicals, such as *The Wall Street Journal, Barron's, Fortune, Commercial and Financial Chronicle, Business Week, US News and World Report, and Forbes. Fortune* magazine is a good source even though it does glamorize the information. Each month it provides in its column "Businessmen in the News" a commentary on what the country's active businessmen are doing. The August 1, 1969, issue commented:

> Despite industry-wide strikes that have halted operations for nearly nine months during the past two years, Phelps Dodge Corp. has stayed profitable, earning $64 million on sales of $550 million last year. With the company's mining operations reasonably secure from interruption because of labor contracts that run through 1971, George B. Munroe, 47, takes over as chief executive from sixty-eight-year-old Robert G. Page, who moves to chairman of the executive committee. Munroe said he intends to maintain and strengthen

10 American Greetings Corporation, *Annual Report,* 1969, p. 3.
11 W. R. Grace & Co., *Annual Report,* 1968, p. 5.

Phelps Dodge's position as a copper producer despite the company's diversification into aluminum and uranium in recent years.[12]

In the same issue, *Fortune* reported the activities of another businessman, Jacques de Fouchier:

> When Jacques de Fouchier, 58, takes control of Compagnie Financière de Paris et des Pays-Bas ("Paribas") he will relieve the man whose name has become synonymous with the dramatic postwar growth of this French banking complex. Jean Reyre, who spent twenty-one of his forty-five years as president of Paribas, saw the bank's assets grow from $115 million in 1947 to $2 billion at the end of last year. During the same period profits increased twenty-fivefold to $20 million.
>
> Jacques de Fouchier takes over what Reyre aptly calls "an exceptional instrument ready for further developments." Often called the "banking matchmaker," de Fouchier is the kind of financial mover who will not allow the "exceptional instrument" to become rusty. His special talent, displayed as president of the lending arm of Paribas, has been his ability to put together French credit resources for ambitious programs, including postwar industrial reconstruction, housing, and foreign investment.[13]

Articles of this type provide some insight into the qualities of the men managing a company. Men of this caliber should prove adequate in leading the companies in which we have invested our funds.

Analyst Meetings and Public Comments

Often an impression of the caliber of management can be determined by public meetings with the corporate executives. There is, of course, the possibility of bias either against or for management. A dynamic corporate president might radiate optimism and well-being and leave the investor confident of success. Another executive, equally qualified, may not convey the same qualities of leadership. Although his job has been filled with excellence and dispatch, a somewhat less flattering conclusion is drawn by the investor. Unless the analyst is somewhat knowledgeable about assessing the qualities of management, it might be better not to judge from a possible personal bias but from the performance of management.

Analysts' society meetings in recent years have served as an excellent way for professional analysts to become acquainted with the qualities and abilities of management. Almost every day in New York City, and at least once a month in the major cities in the United States, the members of the analysts' societies meet to learn more about the companies they are recommending to their clients. Usually a report is given by

---

12 "Businessmen in the News," *Fortune*, August 1, 1969, p. 36.
13 *Ibid.*

members of the top management of the company followed by a question-and-answer period. Keen interest is shown in new products and services being developed and the anticipated level of earnings in the coming year. From meetings such as these and from personal contacts, the analyst over the years becomes thoroughly informed about the activities of the companies and the quality of management. Only members and guests are permitted admission to these meetings, but investors can read the comments made by the officers who speak for the company. The talk is usually published and sent to other analysts and investors. The *Commercial and Financial Chronicle* customarily publishes the complete text of the speeches.

Personal Interviews with Management

Personal interviews with management are of great help in assessing their abilities. Direct and pertinent questions asked in good faith will usually be answered in the same way. Information that might be confidential and might weaken the competitive position of the company will not, of course, be given.

Many companies follow a policy of providing information to analysts and investors. RCA, for example, involves itself in these activities with two fundamental objectives in mind:

> The first is to provide full, accurate and timely information to the investing public and their representatives in order to provide them with sound information and to minimize the chance of judgments formed on rumor or speculation.
>
> The second is to encourage the investment community to disseminate this information as broadly as possible among investors.[14]

The success of the personal interview depends upon the knowledge and skill of the person interviewing the officer of the company. If the interviewer has a good deal of background about the company before the meeting, a common ground is reached immediately. A wise course when planning an interview is to outline the questions that are to be asked; we should not waste the time of the manager by asking questions that could be answered by reading the annual report. Emphasis should be placed on new developments.

Before you visit the company, you might follow the advice of one of the financial analyst societies in its recommendations to fellow analysts:

> Do your homework. (This has become an overworked admonition in view of the improvement in the last decade. Many quality analysts

14 John A. Hearharg, "Corporate Management and the Analysts," *Financial Analysts Journal*, September-October, 1967.

do such a good job now that many of their remaining questions are the ones for which we all wish we knew the answers.)

Clearly identify yourself and your objectives to the company.

Keep the length of any interview within reasonable limits. (In an ideal situation, the amount of time management spends over a period of time with analysts would vary with the quality of the analysts' questions.)

Don't push for information the company is not prepared to make available to its share owners.

Have experience and maturity appropriate to the level of the management contact.[15]

When you get to talk with management, you might wish to focus on the organization of the management team and its planning role, which is vital to the success of the company.[16] If you don't wish to follow the focus in this chapter, you might examine the following questions:

Can management make money when the economy has leveled off?
What does the analysis of trends reveal with respect to the quality of management?
Does the company use its own resources effectively?
Has the business a future?
Are the objectives clearly defined?
Is there sound planning to meet the objectives?
Is the organization structure sound?
Does the company have vital leadership?
Is the chief executive timid or aggressive?
What are the kinds and qualities of the persons in top management positions and how old is management?
Is there a sound executive development program?
Does the company plan effectively for merger and growth?
Is management research-minded?
Does the company have modern systems of quality control?
Is management close to its market, to the public, and to its customers?
Does management have sound analytical controls?
Are facilities up to date?
Does management do a good job with labor?
Finally, what do other managements think of the management?[17]

THE TREASURER SPEAKS

Many corporations have a planned program for visiting shareholders and investors, allowing each person to ask questions about the

---

15 *Ibid.*

16 William P. Hall, "Management Appraisal," *Financial Analysts Journal,* September-October, 1967.

17 Harlow J. Heneman, "The Financial Analyst and Management," *Financial Analysts Journal,* September-October, 1967.

company and obtain valuable information in a short period of time. There are programs and supplementary data designed specifically for stockholders as well. General Mills holds mock regional shareholders' meetings to inform the shareholders of the progress of the company. Other companies have had rather elaborate annual meetings where the shareholder was invited to attend and ask questions of management. Programs such as these allow the shareholder to meet management as well as to obtain up-to-date information about the company. Most of us will not be able to scientifically test management's ability at these gatherings, but impressions of excellence and ability can be obtained. All corporations hold annual meetings, but many do not encourage stockholders to attend.

The chief financial officer of many corporations considers it one of his activities to keep the financial community informed about company developments, and holds meetings with analysts at the company's executive offices. Often he and his staff will visit the major financial centers and present the most recent developments of his company to the financial analysts and managers. Meetings of both types provide current information about a company and an opportunity for the financial community to judge the qualities of the top financial management of the company. Special reports, in addition to annual reports, are also sent to financial analysts.

Management and Change

Secular Change

Recently, several of the author's associates were discussing the subject of company management. One man said that many companies fail because they do not have a product to sell or the demand for the product has declined to a point where it can no longer be produced profitably. He thought that the management in such cases was capable, but that factors external to the company and beyond management control brought about the failure. The example he used was a company in Ohio that had made wooden and metal propellers for small and large aircraft. He suggested that a secular change in the demand for the product beyond management's control had forced the company to close its doors. With the advent of the jet plane, presumably without warning the demand for propellers dropped sharply. The author's colleague could have been even more nostalgic in his example if he had referred to the village smithy, carriagemakers, and buggy-whip manufacturers and their battle with the horseless carriage.

The commentator had missed the whole point of the function of good management, however. Management must plan ahead and must anticipate the change in demand for the product to assure the future earning power of the company. Any reasonable manager of a buggy-whip company or propeller company should have been able to see new and competitive products being developed and to forecast a declining use for existing products. What should the manager do under these circumstances? He should attempt to find new products that can be manufactured with the facilities then owned by the company. Nothing would prevent these companies in question from making new products for automobiles or for jet aircraft. Management has the responsibility— for the benefit of shareholders—of changing its product line to adjust to the economies and changes in demand of a given industry. If one product does not sell, then new products must be developed that will maintain the sales of the company. The tobacco industry is in a position today where they must make product changes to insure future profits. If management is good and can make these secular changes, the company will not fail. Good management and failure appear, therefore, to be inconsistent.

Many companies have failed because they did not change or were slow or unable to change. A watch company in the East is an example of a company that did not change quickly enough. They did not wish to continue the development and improvement of their product; they were resting on their laurels of past product development. This conscious decision of management not to develop caused the company serious financial difficulty and eventual failure.

Montgomery Ward is another example of a management slow to change. It has been a profitable company. When its major competitor, Sears, Roebuck and Co., expanded the number of its stores in the 1950's, Montgomery Ward stood still. The management under the late Sewell Avery would not change. Eventually Avery stepped out of control, and new management improved the company. Montgomery Ward, with earlier more aggressive management activities, could have done a much better job of expansion than it did.

Many companies are changing constantly to maintain their competitive position. General Mills is actively searching for new products. When one product loses its profitability, another more profitable product is substituted. This helps the company realize its profit objective. W. R. Grace, mentioned earlier in the text, is an excellent example of what an aggressive management can do to change the destiny of a company.

Cyclical Changes

We cannot ignore the business cycle and its impact upon corporate earnings. Cyclical changes are another change with which management must cope. Cyclical changes are not regular, but they may be periodic. The nature of most postwar recessions has been that of inventory adjustments. When inventory becomes excessive, production must slow down or stop until the inventory is brought in line with sales. The impact of this type of cyclical decline is not measured by change in Gross National Product or National Income Account figures, but by the Federal Reserve Board Index of Industrial Production. Usually National Income is maintained during the period of inventory liquidation, but industrial activity declines.

Management, in planning and controlling corporate activities, must be able to adjust easily to changes in business activity. Many industries are affected very little by the business cycle. Food, electricity, gas, and utilities are not cyclical, whereas autos, machinery, and building industries are. A good management operates satisfactorily during recessions and cyclical dips and manages its inventory in line with sales. If inventory is larger or smaller than needed and not managed adequately, then management is not doing a satisfactory job.

Management of the Three Drug Companies

Any study of the management of a company will be limited to the availability of information, and inferences must be made from the data. The drug industry is no exception. The comments below about the management of the three companies under analysis are not complete, but we can try to judge management from the things they do and say and what the company has done in the past. Our comments are divided into two parts. The first part mentions the experience of the individual officers in each company; the second discusses the overall activities of the companies, which reflect the job management has done.

Management Background and Experience

The management of Chas. Pfizer, G. D. Searle, and Smith Kline & French vary in background and temperament, but they have certain things in common. They have had a wide range of executive experience in and outside the company, they seem well educated, and they take part in fraternal, professional, cultural, benevolent, and social activities, in which they have held positions of leadership. The top officers of each company in 1968 were:

> *Chas. Pfizer & Co., Inc.*
>   J. E. McKeen, Chairman of the Board
>   J. J. Power, Admin. President
> *Searle (G. D.) and Company*
>   J. G. Searle, Chairman of the Board
>   D. C. Searle, President
> *Smith Kline & French*
>   W. A. Munns, Chairman of the Board
>   T. M. Ranch, President

Although we cannot present a complete biographical sketch of each officer of these companies, a brief sketch of the top officer of each will provide some valuable information to help us assess the management quality of the company:

Chas. Pfizer & Co., Inc. John E. McKeen was born June 4, 1903. He received his Chemical Engineering degree from the Polytechnic Institute of Brooklyn in 1926 and an LL.D. degree from St. John's University in 1950. He was a department head at Pfizer from 1935–38, assistant superintendent 1938–42, superintendent 1942–45, Vice President 1945–48, Executive Vice President 1948–49. Mr. McKeen was President 1949 to 1965 and Board Chairman since 1950.

Mr. McKeen is a director of the Polytech Corporation and Health Information Foundation. He is a member of the Spies Committee for Clinical Research, Polytechnic Alumni Association, and member of the Board of Brooklyn College of Chemists. He is director of the Manufacturing Chemists Association, American Chemical Society, American Institute of Chemists, and American Institute of Chemical Engineers.

Mr. McKeen assisted in the design and construction of a fermentation plant in London, 1936–37. He presented a paper on the production of penicillin at the meeting of American Institute of Chemical Engineers in 1944.

He has been active in many social and fraternal organizations as well as his above accomplishments.[18]

Searle (G. D.) and Company. J. G. Searle was born March 18, 1901. He received a Bachelor of Science Degree in 1923 and began his career as a buyer for G. D. Searle in 1923. He subsequently moved up to Office Manager, Treasurer, and President, General Manager, and Chairman of the Board of the company in 1966.

Mr. Searle is a director of Harris Trust and a trustee of Sprague Memorial, Chicago Natural History Museum, and Northwestern University.

Mr. Searle was in the U. S. Navy in World War I. He received an award from the Citizen Fellowship Institute of Medicine of Chicago. He was a member of the Code Authority—Pharmaceutical and Biological Industry under the NRA. He was a member of the drugs advisory commission to Army-Navy Munitions Board.

Mr. Searle is a member of the drugs and medical supply committee of National Research Council, Advisory Board of Michigan Memorial, Phoenix Digest, and University of Michigan. He was past chairman of the Board of Health Information Foundation and a member of the Board of Directors of Evanston Hospital and a member of American Pharmaceutical Manufacturers Association. Mr. Searle has been active in many social and fraternal activities.[19]

18 World's *Who's Who in Commerce & Industry,* Fifteenth Edition (Chicago: Marquis—Who's Who, 1968), p. 927.

19 *Ibid.,* p. 1239.

Smith Kline & French. W. A. Munns was born June 23, 1902. He attended the Wharton School of the University of Pennsylvania and the Advanced Management Program at Harvard. He was with N. W. Ayer and Son 1922–25, B. F. Goodrich 1925–26, and National Metal Edge Box 1926–28. He went with Smith Kline & French in 1929. From 1945 to 1956 he was Vice President in charge of medical promotion. He was made a Director in 1950, became Executive Vice President in 1956, was President 1958 to 1966 and became Chairman of the Board in 1966.

Mr. Munns is a director of SKF, Inc., SKF Inter-American Corporation, SKF International Company, SKF Overseas Co., Avoset Co. and Fidelity, Philadelphia Trust Company. Mr. Munns was director of U. S. World Medical Association in 1957 and is a member of the board of Franklin Institute. He has been active in civic and social affairs.[20]

The background of the top leaders of the three companies shows experience, leadership, and growth as well as an interest in the broad scene of society. These men have demonstrated good management capabilities.

Company Activities

CHAS. PFIZER & CO., INC.

Chas. Pfizer, one of the dominant firms in the drug industry, had an anti-trust suit filed against it in 1958 for alleged price control. In 1962 the Federal Trade Commission dismissed the complaint and stated, in effect, that Pfizer had not engaged in the violation of the act as alleged in the complaint. This was good news to Pfizer and its shareholders. It has had an excellent growth of sales and profit margins, and management has kept costs in line. There is little debt in its capital structure, and it has maintained a good financial position over the past years. Recently the company has broadened its agricultural drug base and expanded its plant facilities. Management spends about 5 percent of sales on research. It is working in the area of cancer research and an anti-tubercular drug, is the largest producer of both types of Sabin polio vaccine, and has a measles vaccine, an oral diuretic, Renese, and a dietary supplement called Limmits. The company has paid a good cash dividend. Employees are enthusiastic about the company. Management has done an aggressive job in foreign selling, and improved its foreign tax problem by bringing the earnings home. Since the settlement of the anti-trust case, management looks strong and is moving forward in many new areas.

20 *Ibid.*, p. 993.

G. D. SEARLE AND COMPANY

G. D. Searle is a 51 percent family-owned company that makes about thirty drugs. It has no long-term debt, its profit margin is the highest in the industry, and its sales have grown rapidly in the past few years. The company has achieved success with Enovid, an oral contraceptive, and management is aggressively moving for wider market penetration of this product. The management has exercised good control over costs and is interested in product development. About one-third of the plant capacity is devoted to research activities. Management is apparently aware of the problems associated with one successful product and is searching for new products. In the past the company has had a good record of product introduction and is working in the area of degenerative diseases. Financial position is extremely good and highly liquid. The company has enjoyed good labor relations and is able to work with government. Planning programs include plant expansion. The company has acquired Nuclear-Chicago Corp., Fermco Laboratories, and Berkeley Medical Instruments. This would broaden its competitive position.

SMITH KLINE & FRENCH

The Smith Kline & French management is aggressive in the area of product development and research. Management has spent about 10 percent of sales for research. The company has enjoyed an outstanding growth of sales, particularly in tranquilizers, but it is trying to avoid overspecialization and is moving into veterinary drugs, steroids, and proprietary drugs. New products include Contac; mental illness drugs; Ornade, a nasal decongestant; and Eskatrol, a weight control drug. Smith Kline & French has acquired Julian Laboratories, a producer of steroid intermediates, Norden Laboratories, which produces veterinary drugs, and formed Menley & James Laboratory to handle the sale of

TABLE 15–1

Comparative rank of company management

MANAGEMENT ATTRIBUTE	CHAS. PFIZER	G. D. SEARLE	SMITH KLINE & FRENCH
Ability to maintain competitive position	2	1	3
Ability to expand	3	1	2
Ability to maintain profit margin	3	1	2
Ability to maintain efficient production	1	1	1
Ability to finance growth	3	1	2
Stockholder, employee, and community relations	2	1	1
Ability to meet secular and cyclical change	2	2	2
Expenditures on R & D	3	1	2
Adequate government relationship	3	1	2
Overall capabilities	3	1	2

proprietary items. The company plans continued promotion of sales and expansion into foreign markets. Management has been able to widen profit margins and keep expenses down. There is no debt in the capital structure, the company's working capital position is good, and it pays out about 66 percent of its earnings in dividends.

The quality of the management of these companies is excellent based on the individual achievements of the officers and the collective activities of the companies. Smith Kline & French and Pfizer appear to be the most aggressive and market-oriented managements. However, with the merger with Abbott, Searle has demonstrated equal management ability to compete. A summary of the attributes of management of each company is given in Table 15–1. These relationships are arbitrary; the differences in rank are slight.

Summary

The basic function of management is to plan, organize, actuate, and control the activities of the corporation to meet the needs of the stockholders, the public, and the employees. We as shareowners are interested in the profits that will come to us through good and capable management. To assess its qualities, we learn about management through information obtained in published sources, through the comments of others, and through interviews.

Management is judged by the past record, since few objective tests exist to tell us if it is good. A management that has brought about increased sales at a profit, maintained a good financial position, and been able to raise long-term capital is a good one. In addition, a trained management that can change with secular and cyclical changes, that can maintain good community, employee, stockholder, and union relationships, and that can be flexible in its work with government can be considered a good management.

In the final analysis, a management that is good is one that can grow profitably, perpetuate excellence of management, and introduce new products to insure continued and growing profitability. Management has the greatest impact upon future earnings, which is at the center of the valuation and appraisal process.

Review Questions

1. What are the basic objectives of a company's management? Is profit maximization the only objective of management? Discuss.
2. Explain why we should understand the stated objectives of a company with respect to employees, customers, the public, and investors.
3. What are the qualities of good management?
4. How do we go about determining the ability of management?

5. Explain what significance each of the following has in regard to a determination of management's ability:
   (a) Competitive position of company
   (b) Ability of company to expand
   (c) Maintenance of profit margins
   (d) Maintenance of efficient production
   (e) Adequate financing
   (f) Harmonious and productive employee relations
   (g) Use of scientific management
   (h) Maintenance of harmonious government relations

6. To what extent does research and product development indicate good management?

7. What do executive development programs and community responsibility reflect about corporate management?

8. What can we learn about management's ability from annual reports and the financial press?

9. Explain the importance of analyst meetings and public comments in assessing management's ability.

10. Explain how information might be obtained through personal interviews with the company treasurer and top management.

11. Management must demonstrate its ability to meet the secular and cyclical change in the demand for the company products. Explain.

12. (a) Review the analysis of management of the three drug companies in this chapter.
    (b) Do you agree with the results?
    (c) What information is missing? Explain.

Problems

1. What are the backgrounds of the chief executive officers of the three companies analyzed in past assignments?

2. How well has each company's management performed in the following activities?
   (a) Ability to maintain profits and earnings
   (b) Sales expansion
   (c) Ability to finance the company adequately
   (d) Labor relations
   (e) Government relations
   (f) Ability to apply scientific management techniques
   (g) Ability to develop new products

3. What percent of sales was spent on research and development in 1957 and in the present year?

4. What has been the ability of the company to build and maintain good community, employee, and owner relations?

5. Has management been able to meet the cyclical and secular trends of the industry? Explain.

6. After a thorough study of the companies, interview management about future prospects. What conclusions do you draw?

7. Which company has the best management? Explain.

8. Rank the companies on the basis of their overall management ability.

Sources of Investment Information

American Institute of Management—Corporate Director
American Management Association
Analysts' reports
Barron's
Business Week
Clark Dodge Investment Survey
Commercial and Financial Chronicle
Dun's Review and Modern Industry
Executive Investor Digest
Forbes
Fortune
Magazine of Wall Street
Managements' speeches to analyst societies, New York and other areas
Newsweek
Personal interviews with management
Standard & Poor's *Investment Surveys*
Time
U.S. News and World Report
Wall Street Journal
Wall Street Journal Index

Selected Readings

Collier, James R., "Management Business Planning," *Financial Analysts Journal* (September-October, 1967), p. 33.

Fisch, Gerald G., "Management in Financial Analysis," *Financial Analysts Journal* (July-August, 1968), p. 43.

Gearhart, John A., "Corporate Management and Analysts," *Financial Analysts Journal* (September-October, 1967), p. 31.

Hall, William P., "Management Appraisal," *Financial Analysts Journal* (September-October, 1966), p. 85.

Hayes, Douglas A., "The Evaluation of Management," *Financial Analysts Journal* (July-August, 1968), p. 39.

Heneman, Harlow J., "Financial Analysts and Management," *Financial Analysts Journal* (September-October, 1967), p. 27.

Priest, William W., Jr., "Evaluating Research and Development Expenditures," *Financial Analysts Journal* (July-August, 1966), p. 43.

Strong, George H., "Management's Fourth Dimension," *Financial Analysts Journal* (March-April, 1967), p. 97.

16

STOCK PRICE, THE PRICE-EARNINGS RATIO, AND THE INVESTMENT DECISION

So far, we have considered companies for investment on the basis of earnings and those qualities that would ensure future earnings. We suggested that a company of investment caliber would be a dominant firm within its industry, would possess stability and growth of earnings, would have an adequate profit margin and net income to sales ratio, would be efficiently operated at a level above the breakeven point, and would be expanding its plant capacity. The company would also have an adequate current financial position that would aid the improvement of earning power, have demonstrated an ability to finance its growth without excessive debt, and possess a good management that would help to assure its future competitive position and earning power. In short, the company in which we wish to invest is a quality company in the industry.

Now we must examine the price we have to pay for the stock of the company. We are willing to pay for quality, but we must be certain that the price we pay will provide a satisfactory yield. This requires comparison of present price with the dividends and price we hope to receive in the future.

The Importance of Price

One can pay too much for even a quality company. The purchase of a stock at the historic peak of the market would not usually be a satisfactory investment. Many of the stocks that were bought and sold before the crash of 1929 did not regain their pre-crash prices until the last half of the 1950's, some never regained their former price level. In the first half of 1962 the stock market declined sharply; many stocks declined 50 percent. IBM, for example, the leading producer of office equipment, dropped from a high of 578 1/2 down to 300. At 300 to 320 it was an attractive investment. In 1969, IBM sold at 336 after a two-for-one split. AT&T sold as high as 150 at about the same time, subsequently splitting two for one. In 1968, it sold for 50, and begin to pick up strength only in late 1969. General Motors, Litton, Textron, and Xerox suffered substantial losses in the bear market of 1969. Many more examples could be presented to demonstrate the impact of price changes on the quality stocks.

Quality alone does not prevent the loss of principal in the stock market. The price of a common stock changes frequently. We must be as careful about the price we pay as we are about seeking companies that are ably managed and enjoy a strong financial position. We must be familiar with the current price range as well as the range of prices over a period of time. Each company's stock has developed its own price pattern; familiarity with the price history helps in determining the reasonableness of the present price, which, in the final analysis, will depend upon what we expect in terms of the amount, stability, and quality of future earnings and the expectation of the future price.

The Price Range of Common Stock

Since the price of a stock varies, we would be wise to consider not a single price for a stock but price as a range. Two separate round-lot transactions could be executed at the same price, but if 200 round-lot transactions took place over a period of time, it would be most unlikely that they would trade at the same price. The price of a stock may be considered reasonable if it is low relative to its most recent price range and its historic price range. Let us take an example of how this might be used to help in establishing the reasonableness of a given price. In a stock market break we find that the Dow Jones Industrial Averages had declined to a point where market prices correspond to the peak of the previous market high. At the bottom of the market, we find prices to be reasonable in terms of the current range of market prices and reasonable compared with prices that were considered favorable four and five years before. Individual stocks such as IBM followed the market down. When the bottom was reached, the price of IBM was attractive in its then current price range and its historical range. The point we must make here is that the comparative market price, without considering future earnings and future prices, is an indication of whether a stock price is high or low. Thus, if GM had traded between 40 and 60 per share over a recent period and then increased to 80, we would conclude that the price was high. If we could purchase GM at 40 or 50, it would be reasonably priced compared to its most recent market. If nothing fundamental had changed about GM, and we knew that the stock had traded between 40 and 50 five years before and was now back to that level, we would conclude that we had a rare opportunity to buy a quality company at a low price.

The General Level of Market Prices

The trend of the stock market as reflected by the Dow Jones Averages is shown in Figure 16–1. Table 16–1 provides a list of the yearly highs and lows of the averages discussed in Chapter 1. We can see that there has been an upward movement in stock prices, with recurring cyclical dips, since the 1947–49 period, with the greatest growth since the end of 1949. The prices of public utilities appear to be much more stable than either industrials or railroads, but each group has the cyclical characteristics that we commented on before—in the case of the railroads, without the substantial growth achieved by the industrials. We are concerned here not so much with the general level of prices as with the behavior of the various market groups compared to the market as a whole. Let's examine the market performance of these groups.

Market Performance

We are interested in market performance because it helps us understand the nature of the company in which we invest. We want to know if the stock moves with the market; that is, when the market rises, does the stock of the company rise too? Or is the stock defensive in character?

TABLE 16–1

Yearly highs and lows of Dow Jones Averages
and Dow Jones Composite Averages

| | Yearly Highs and Lows of Dow Jones Averages | | | | | |
| | Industrials | | Railroads | | Utilities | |
	HIGH	LOW	HIGH	LOW	HIGH	LOW
1968	924.98	825.13	269.61	214.58	135.93	119.79
1967	897.05	756.91	235.17	205.16	140.43	134.49
1966	995.15	744.32	271.72	184.34	152.39	118.86
1965	996.36	848.59	249.55	187.29	163.32	149.84
1964	891.71	766.08	224.91	178.81	155.71	137.30
1963	767.21	646.79	179.46	142.03	144.37	129.19
1962	726.01	563.00	149.83	118.98	130.85	104.35
1961	734.91	610.25	152.92	131.06	135.90	99.75
1960	685.47	566.05	160.43	123.37	100.07	85.02
1959	679.36	574.46	173.56	146.65	94.70	85.05
1958	538.65	436.89	157.91	99.89	91.00	68.94
1957	520.77	419.79	157.67	95.67	74.61	62.10
1956	521.05	462.35	181.23	150.44	71.17	63.03
1955	488.40	388.20	167.83	137.84	66.68	61.39
1954	404.39	279.87	146.23	94.84	62.47	52.22
1953	293.79	255.49	112.21	90.56	53.88	47.87

TABLE 16-1 *(continued)*

	Dow Jones Composite Average—65 Stocks	
	HIGH	LOW
1968	334.42	290.09
1967	316.23	282.69
1966	352.40	261.27
1965	339.98	290.37
1964	314.15	269.09
1963	264.51	228.67
1962	245.80	195.48
1961	251.43	204.77
1960	222.62	189.84
1959	224.35	200.09
1958	202.43	147.41
1957	179.87	142.49
1956	184.11	164.29
1955	174.21	144.39
1954	150.22	106.03
1953	113.96	98.24
1952	113.56	96.05
1951	100.04	86.92
1950	87.23	70.34
1949	71.92	57.75
1948	71.85	59.89
1947	67.10	57.33
1946	79.44	58.53
1945	73.48	55.86
1944	56.55	47.01
1943	50.89	39.84
1942	39.62	31.46

SOURCE: *Barron's,* September 2, 1963, pp. 43 and 45; December 30, 1963, p. 45; November 4, 1963, p. 53; May 1, 1968, p. 48; December 26, 1966, p. 46; December 27, 1965, p. 45; December 28, 1964, p. 41; and September 23, 1968, pp. 40 and 63.

Does it move up when the market as a whole declines, and vice versa? Or perhaps the stock or stock group moves ahead of the market both on the up side and the down side of the market. We also want to know what groups are leading the market and are considered market favorites. At any given time the stock market tends to have its likes and dislikes, its fads and fancies. Past likes were airlines and motion pictures in 1946, titanium in 1951, uranium in 1955–1957, aluminum in 1956, oil producers in 1957, steel and chemicals in 1959, and in 1961 electronics, savings and loan, leisure time, publishing, and vending companies. In 1963 motors and oils led the advance and in early 1964 steels, airlines, and railroads were strong issues in the market. In 1968 and early 1969 new issues and the computer leasing stocks captured the fancy of the speculative investment public. In each case a particular group of stocks moved sharply ahead of the market.

The favorable market action of one group of stocks might result in some extreme price fluctuations, which might in turn result in losses to the investor. Assume, for example, that the auto company shares favored in the market were bid up out of all proportion to the long-range earning power of the companies, and that prices subsequently declined because the earnings of the autos declined. This time, however, the pendulum swings back, and prices drop as sharply as they have risen. But they have swung back too far, and although they are now relatively low, there is not a great deal of demand for the stocks, so the

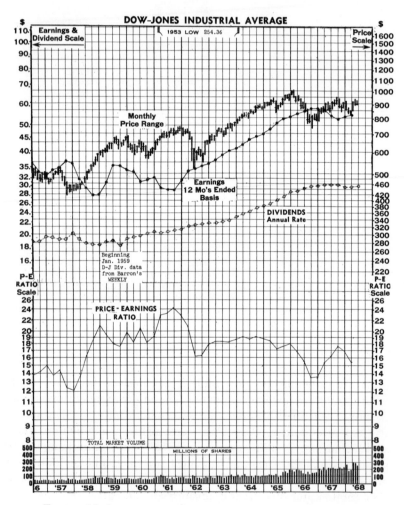

FIGURE 16–1

Dow Jones Industrial, Rail, and Utility Averages

SOURCE *3-Trend Cycli-Graphs,* Quarterly Edition, July, 1968, Securities Research Co.

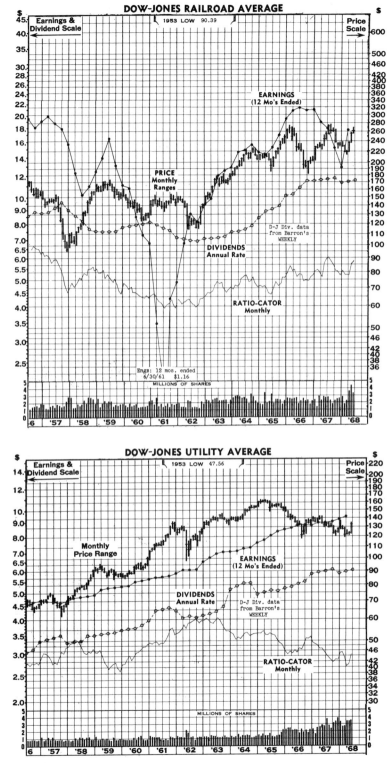

FIGURE 16–1 (continued)

prices remain low. An investor in this price fluctuation might lose by buying too high and selling too low. If a trained or sophisticated investor were accurate in the timing of purchase and sale, a good profit could be made by buying and selling the market favorites at the appropriate time. This, of course, takes a great deal of skill. It might be better simply to buy on strength in a rising market rather than attempt to anticipate a cycle and trade in it.

The market action of some of the major stock groups appears in Figure 16–2 for the period 1967 through the first quarter of 1968. The market as a whole is reflected in the major index of 500 industrial companies in the upper left-hand corner of the figure. It is an easy matter to find the industry groups with the strongest market action. Standard & Poor's, in *The Outlook,* provides one source of information about the most favored groups in the stock market at one moment of time.

If timing could be perfect, it would be better to invest in those companies that demonstrate market strength over a period of time than to select weak market performers. We must observe the market carefully, as an investment management function, to make certain the securities we have selected remain strong relative to the market.

The Price-Earnings Ratio

The market action and relative price position of a stock can help to determine if the price is high or low, but not in relation to the future earnings of the company. The price range or market strength does not help decide if the investment will provide a satisfactory yield to the investor. What we really must learn is the relation of the price to the future earnings. But before we can do this, we must ask what price an investor is willing to pay for a dollar of earnings per share of a particular company's stock. The answer to this question is found in the past relation between price and earnings, comparing the price an investor was willing to pay for a dollar of earnings in the past and then compare this historic rate with the current price for a dollar of earnings. This relationship is referred to as the price-earnings (P/E) ratio. The theoretical relationship of the P/E ratio and growth rates of a company were discussed in Chapter 7. What follows is a practical application of the P/E ratio analysis. (A review first of Chapter 7 is suggested.)

The price-earnings ratio is computed by dividing the current price of the common stock into the current annual per share earnings of the company. A stock that is selling for $34 per share, for example, with earnings of $2 per share, would have a current price-earnings ratio of 17 to 1 ($34/$2). Because the price of the stock is strongly influenced by the earnings expected in the year ahead, it is wise to compare the present

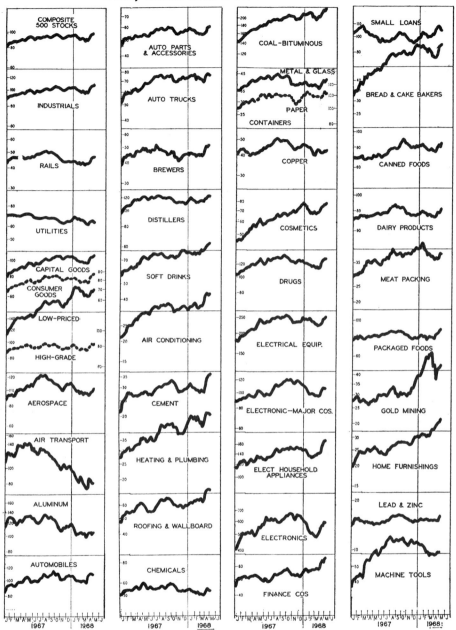

FIGURE 16–2

Price movements of leading stock groups and relative position in the market

SOURCE Standard & Poor's *The Outlook, Relative Appeal of Stock Groups,* Section 2, May 6, 1968, p. 810

price to the estimated annual earnings as well as the past year's earnings. Assume that in mid-year the expected earnings for the entire year were $2.50, and the earnings of the previous year were $2. We would compute the price-earnings ratio on the basis of the $2.50; the price-earnings ratio then would be 13.6 based on a current price of $34. The reason for using next year's earnings to compute the price-earnings ratio is that investors who purchase and sell the stock are doing so on the basis of next year's estimated earnings as well as the years beyond. Investors do look ahead, and they do anticipate earnings and prices, usually for six months to a year. Beyond this period vision is blurred. Some might be accused of being myopic and even sightless, but estimating future earnings is no easy task and should be considered only an approximation of the future. Since expectations play such an important part in investments, we must look ahead to future years and consider the price-earnings ratio for a longer period of time.

The Significance of the P/E Ratio

Once we have computed the price-earnings ratio, what do we do with it? If the P/E ratio is 5 to 1, do we automatically sell? Just what is the significance of the price-earnings ratio? The concept is similar to the capitalization rate that we discussed in the valuation process for common stock. The capitalization rate converts future earnings into a present capital value at a rate consistent with the risks involved. Assume, for example, that we are told that the earnings per share of stock will be $1 per year for every year in the future. If we were to buy the stock, the price we would be willing to pay would depend upon the rate of return we would be willing to accept after we had considered the risks involved. If a great deal of risk were involved in the amount and certainty of earnings, we would want a high rate of return. If little or no risk were involved in our expectations about future earnings, then we would be willing to accept a lower rate of return. Therefore, if the risk involved justified a 10 percent rate of return, the per share value of earnings would be $10 ($1/$.10). If the risk rate of return was 4 percent, then the value per share of $1 of earnings would be $25. Therefore, the share of stock would have a value of between $10 and $25, depending upon the risk involved.

Based on the above assumptions, the price-earnings ratio is really the reciprocal of the capitalization rate, as we pointed out in Chapter 7, if the growth rate of earnings is considered. If the capitalization rate is 5 percent, the price-earnings equivalent is 20 to 1; if the capitalization rate is 2 percent, the price-earnings ratio is 50 to 1. The price we are willing to pay for earnings is based on uncertainty. The greater the uncertainty, the lower the P/E rate to compensate for risk. The higher the P/E ratio, the greater the degree of certainty about the future earning power. A P/E ratio of 10/1, therefore, is much less certain than a ratio of 40/1, assuming the same amount of earnings per share in the future. If earnings grow at the rate of 20 percent a year, a stock could sell for a 30-to-1 current P/E ratio, but at a 15-to-1 P/E ratio based on the growth rate of earnings. Reference to Chapter 7 is again recommended for understanding of growth stock and the P/E ratio.

A stock selling at a high P/E ratio, theoretically at least, is one that investors will buy because of the faith they have in the ability of the company to maintain and improve earnings. Suppose a company's stock is selling at 60 times earnings when the securities in the market as a whole are selling at 20 times earnings. Such a P/E ratio indicates the expectation that the future earnings per share for the company will be much higher than they are at present. In the example investors. are saying that future earnings will be four times greater than the typical stock in the market. The only logical way to view the P/E ratio is to think in terms of certainty and uncertainty. A company that possesses a high P/E ratio, other things being equal, has more certain earnings and a higher growth rate than a company with a low P/E ratio. In essence, the P/E ratio is a measure of the confidence investors have in the future earnings ability of the company.

The Trend of Market P/E Ratios

The trend of the P/E ratio for the Dow Jones Industrials has been down since a peak in 1961, in spite of the increase in earnings and dividends. The Dow Jones Rails performance has been somewhat better, as indicated by the Ratio-cator line in Figure 16–1. The Dow Jones Utilities have performed more poorly than the industrials. The downward trend of the price-earnings ratio came about because of decreased confidence in the securities market as a whole.

From 1955 until 1961 the P/E ratios continued to increase. Corporate earnings did not move ahead as fast as stock prices. Confidence in the stock market was high, fed by the threat of inflation. During the latter half of the 1950's it was basically assumed that we would have continued inflation and that the securities market was a hedge against inflation. This was fine until the prospects of the economy changed during 1961. Economic growth was slow, steel and auto output was low, and increased foreign competition led to a less optimistic outlook for our national economy. Stock prices dropped with the result that P/E ratios declined too.

In 1962 the P/E ratios came tumbling down. Some companies, before the stock market decline of 1962, had sold as high as 60 to 100 times earnings. In March, 1962, only a few leading companies sold at 40 or more times earnings. Among these companies were Avon Products, Corning Glass, Hewlett Packard, IBM, 3M, Polaroid, Sanders Associates, Tampax, Technical Material, Transitron, Varian, and Xerox. In June,

1962, these ratios were much lower, but still indicated the investing public's confidence in these companies. Transitron is an exception. It had a higher P/E ratio because of a deficit in its earnings and not because of greater expectations for earnings in the future.

After 1962, company earnings continued to move up substantially. Investor confidence did not come back in spite of an upward movement of prices. In 1966 the market suffered another setback and P/E ratios declined once again. The market circumstances in 1962 and again in 1966 and 1968 clearly forewarn that one can pay too much for earnings. If too much is paid for future earnings and these earnings do not materialize, confidence will be broken and the price will come down.

What Is A Normal P/E Ratio?

We should at this point question what a normal P/E ratio is. This is a difficult question to answer. Are we talking about a normal P/E ratio for a company, an industry, or the market as a whole? After all, the investor will show varying degrees of confidence in the ability of different companies to provide future earnings. Therefore, we must ask, "What is a normal price-earnings ratio for a company or the market?" But even when we ask the question about one company, we find it difficult to answer. The normal P/E ratio varies from time to time, and we must inquire about what is normal at a specific time. What constitutes a high, low, or normal ratio depends upon a comparison of the P/E ratio of a company with the market at various times and also upon a comparison of the past P/E ratios of the company to the present level of the ratio.

THE PRICE-EARNINGS RATIO COMPARED TO THE MARKET

The market P/E ratio is measured by the Dow Jones Industrial Average or some other stock group that reflects the overall market. One investment counseling service attempts to judge the relative position of the price of a company's stock by comparing the P/E ratio of the company to the P/E ratio of the Dow Jones Industrial Average. It also compares the earnings per share of the company to that of the DJIA. The ratios that result are then plotted on a chart comparable to Chart 16–1. The P/E ratio is indicated on the vertical axis, and the earnings ratio is recorded on the horizontal axis. Let us see how we arrived at the 1962 relationship in Chart 16–1. The ratio of the P/E ratio of the company was 1 to 1, or 1. Thus the company had the same P/E ratio as the market in 1962. Earnings per share were 1/1 also. When we plot our point we move up the vertical scale until we reach 1/1 and we move out the horizontal scale until we reach 1/1. Then we mark the point where these two lines intersect and label the point with the date of the year it occurred. If the earnings of the company increase relative to the market and the P/E ratio also increases, we can conclude that the company is doing better than the market as a whole. As we move up and to the right on Chart 16–1, the company improves relative to the market. If it moves down and to the left, the company is not doing as well as the market. Thus in 1968, earnings were 2.6 times those of the market and the P/E ratio was 2.3 times.

The relationship between the P/E and earnings of the company and the DJIA can be looked upon as a confidence index. The higher the ratio of earnings and P/E to the market, the greater the confidence

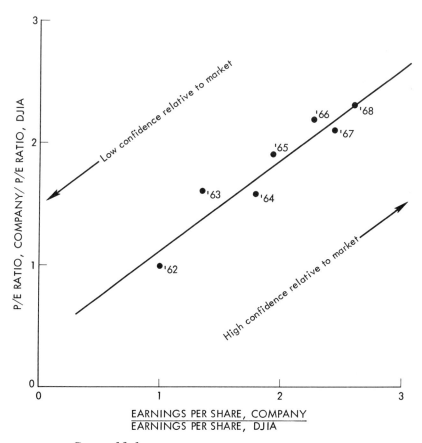

CHART 16–1

Regression line between ratio of company earnings per share to DJIA earnings per share and ratio of P/E ratio of company to P/E ratio of DJIA, as a guide to investor confidence

the investment public has in the company. As long as this confidence is maintained, we can say that the company is better than the market. Actually we are saying that either the earnings or the P/E ratio is higher than the market as a whole, and this would help us to learn if the P/E ratio were high, low, or normal. In this case we would define normal as the P/E ratio existing in the market at a given moment of time.

From these brief comments we realize that the market P/E ratio changes. The data we examined in Figure 16–1 indicated this. A P/E ratio of 10 to 1 might be low in one market and high in another. During the stock market of 1948–1949 a 10 to 1 P/E ratio was high; at that time the P/E ratio for the industrials was close to 7 to 1. In 1961–62, however, a 10 to 1 P/E ratio was low, since the market average P/E ratio was closer to 19 to 1. In 1968, a P/E ratio of 8 or 10 to 1 was considered low, but 30 to 1 was high with a market P/E ratio average of 16 to 1.

PRICE-EARNINGS RATIO AND THE INDUSTRY

Whether a ratio is high or low is also a matter of comparison with the industry in which the company functions. In 1951, for example, a 5 to 1 P/E ratio for a railroad would have been equivalent to the P/E ratio of the railroad industry, but it would have been low compared to the industrials. A 10 to 1 P/E ratio for a railroad company in the same year would have been high to the railroad industry but normal for an industrial company, as represented by the Dow Jones Industrial Averages. The P/E ratios of the companies in the various industrial classifications vary over time, just like the market as a whole. Therefore, whether a P/E ratio of a company is high or low depends upon the relative performance of the ratio compared to the industry as well as to the market.

P/E RATIO AND THE COMPANY

Just as we can compare the P/E ratio of a company to the market and the industry, we can also examine the trend of the P/E ratio to the company itself. Litton Industries is an example of a company that has sold consistently at a high P/E ratio compared to the industry and the market as a whole. There is no guarantee that this high P/E ratio will continue. But, until now, the high P/E ratio has been an expression of confidence of the investor in Litton stock. Its P/E ratio ranged from 14 to 166. Its average P/E ratio for the ten-year period 1958 to 1967 was 32 to 1. If we could have bought the stock at 30 times earnings we would have purchased it at a relatively low P/E ratio. During the same period of time the Dow Jones Industrial Averages sold at an average P/E ratio of 18 to 1. The reason for the higher P/E ratio for Litton was its superior growth rate and high stability of earnings. These ratios changed substantially in 1969.

IS THERE AN ABSOLUTE HIGH AND LOW PRICE-EARNINGS RATIO?

We cannot say with any degree of certainty whether a ratio is high or low in the absolute sense. In the stock market of 1962, a low price-earnings ratio for investment quality companies was below 10 to 1 and a high ratio was above 40 to 1. Average or "normal" was approximately 19 to 1. In 1948 a low P/E ratio would have been 3 to 1 and a high ratio 15 to 1, with the average around 7.5 to 1. This would suggest that there can be no absolute low or high P/E ratio just as it is difficult to say that there is a normal ratio. In 1947 there was not the investor confidence that existed in 1962. Investors remembered too clearly the depression of the 1930's and the two World Wars. In the 1950's and early 1960's the threat of inflation governed the attitudes of investors, which helped to raise P/E ratios. In 1968, 16 was a reasonable P/E for the Dow Jones Industrial Averages. Then, too, the growth of the economy and prosperity and the search for security caused securities to sell higher in relation to earnings than they did in the past.

The P/E ratio can be judged high or low only relative to the market, the industry, and the company's experience over time. A ten-year average P/E ratio is thought by the author to be a realistic average P/E ratio for a company; *The Value Line* uses a fifteen-year P/E ratio as "normal."

The experience of the stock market does, however, suggest certain upper limits to the P/E ratio. The investor in 1962 appeared reluctant to pay more than 22 times earnings for the DJIA. In 1962 resistance in the market developed when stocks in the DJIA approached a point where they were selling at close to 20 times earnings. Thus in that market, a P/E around 10 to 1 would be low and 25 or 35 to 1 would be high, with a 20 to 1 P/E ratio in the upper reaches of normal. Certainly then, a P/E ratio of 50 to 1 would be extreme not only in relative terms but in absolute terms as well. A P/E ratio of 5 to 1 would be absolutely and relatively low in almost any market; in the stock market of 1966 through 1969, an average or normal P/E ratio would have been 15 or 16 to 1.

AVERAGE P/E AS A GUIDE TO NORMAL

P/E ratios can be averaged over long periods of time to establish what we may refer to as "normal" P/E ratios. Table 16–2 lists the ten-year average P/E ratios for the individual DJIA stocks for 1953 through 1962 and from 1957 to 1966. Several of the stocks changed substantially from one period to the other. These ratios might be considered norms but they cannot be blindly accepted. Each company must be examined to ascertain whether the average P/E ratio reflects the risk involved in the company. It would be dangerous to draw conclusions based on the general trend and movement of an industry group or the market as a whole.

TABLE 16–2

P/E ratios for the individual Dow Jones
Industrial companies 1953–1962* and 1957–1966

COMPANY	AVERAGE P/E RATIO 1953–1962	AVERAGE P/E RATIO 1957–1966
Allied Chemical	18.5	19.7
Alcoa	26.9	29.2
American Can	16.0	16.1
AT&T	15.5	18.1
American Tobacco	11.6	12.3
Anaconda	11.6	11.6
Bethlehem Steel	12.9	15.2
Chrysler	15.7	13.1
du Pont	23.2	18.9
Eastman Kodak	22.6	28.6
General Electric	23.3	26.4
General Foods	16.8	21.3
General Motors	13.1	14.7
Goodyear	13.3	16.6
International Harvester	12.0	12.2
International Nickel	16.2	20.2
International Paper	16.3	23.1
Johns-Manville	14.4	16.0
Owens-Illinois	16.5	19.2
Procter & Gamble	19.5	23.9
Sears, Roebuck	16.6	22.6
Standard Oil (Calif.)	11.0	12.8
Standard Oil (N. J.)	13.5	15.7
Swift	15.9	16.1
Texaco	11.7	14.3
Union Carbide	23.3	21.9
United Aircraft	13.9	16.6
United States Steel	13.9	16.4
Westinghouse Electric	20.0	21.6
Woolworth	14.2	13.4

* Excludes 1958 and 1959.

SOURCE: *The Value Line Investment Survey*, October 25, 1963, pp. 118, 119, 140, and 145; November 8, 1963, pp. 321, 322, and 324; November 15, 1963, pp. 406, 410, and 422; November 29, 1963, pp. 618 and 637; December 6, 1963, pp. 713, 732, and 734; December 13, 1963, pp. 807, 823, 826, 828, and 837; December 27, 1963, pp. 1009, 1017, and 1020; October 4, 1963, pp. 1113 and 1120; and October 11, 1963, pp. 1208, 1216, 1223, and 1229, Arnold Bernhard & Co., Inc. New York. Standard and Poor's *Industry Survey—Aerospace*, April 25, 1963, p. A31 for United Aircraft, *Moody's Handbook of Common Stocks*, 1968 (First Quarter), pp. 25, 32, 40, 66, 67, 73, 122, 206, 314, 327, 400, 401, 405, 429, 511, 513, 515, 533, 721, 765, 830, 868, 870, 896, 908, 938, 945, 962, 996 and 1007.

The Price-Earnings Ratio and the Quality of the Company

SPECULATIVE COMPANIES AND P/E RATIO

We have been discussing firms that are considered investment-quality or investment-grade companies. These companies are well-managed, well-financed, quality companies. But what about the P/E ratio of the more speculative companies? What is the behavior of their P/E ratios? Generally, the speculative companies tend to sell at either extremely low or extremely high P/E ratios. This might seem paradoxical, but it really is not. The low ratio can be explained by the risk factors involved. A low P/E ratio suggests a great degree of uncertainty and risk about the ability of a company to earn money. In the period 1959–1962, several South American companies sold at extremely low P/E ratios of three, four, and five times earnings. American corporations at the same time were selling at from 10 to 50 times earnings. The risk of loss brought about by the instability of the foreign governments and the economic uncertainty about the future of the companies suggested a low P/E ratio. Possibly these were good companies, but the risks were too high for the investor to pay a high price for a dollar of future earnings. One need not go abroad to find companies selling at low price-earnings ratios. In 1962 Benguet Mines sold between 1 1/4 and 1 1/2 and had earned $.80 per share in 1961. Benguet Mines is a Philippine gold mining company that is traded on the New York Stock Exchange. It was trading on a 1.56 to 1 to a 1.87 to 1 P/E ratio because of the risks inherent in the company.

A company sells at an extremely high P/E ratio when present earnings are low or nonexistent and yet the future expected earnings justify a higher price. In this situation one would expect a high P/E ratio. This high ratio does not signify quality. It simply means that earnings currently are extremely low. Future earnings are expected to be higher but not excessively high. Many speculative companies with a poor record of earnings will have a high or infinite ratio. Thus, the speculative company might have either a high or a low P/E ratio.

EXPANDING GROWTH COMPANIES

The expanding growth-type company tends to sell at a higher P/E ratio than a company that is not growing rapidly. Railroads, historically at least, have sold at lower ratios than industrials. They are not considered in the growth class. In recent years public utility companies have done extremely well. The P/E ratio of the utility industry has approximated the ratios of the industrials. The public utility group has three distinct categories of utilities—growth, income, and those combining both. The growth utilities such as Pacific Gas & Electric, Florida Power, or Arizona Public Service sell at a higher P/E ratio than the income companies. They are comparable to such industrial companies as IBM, Litton Industries, and Xerox, which tend to sell at higher ratios than companies like Ford, General Motors, and Chrysler, which have growth potential but are more cyclically oriented. If we find the quality company that shows a great deal of growth potential, we must pay a higher price for this growth. Companies with outstanding growth possibilities tend to have higher P/E ratios.

DEBT VS. NO-DEBT COMPANIES

Companies in an industry class that have no debt tend to sell at higher P/E ratios than companies in the same class that have a great deal of debt. The theoretical discussion of this topic in Chapter 14 suggested that as a company increased the amount of debt in its capital structure the P/E ratio declined. The rationale for this behavior is found in the stability of earnings of the no-debt company. Other things being equal, the greater the debt the greater the instability of earnings. We investors want stability of earnings; therefore, we are not willing to pay a high price for unstable earnings. In addition, debt in the capital structure, particularly excessive debt, might lead to an earnings deficit or insolvency. The threat of insolvency would tend to dampen the eagerness with which we demand a particular company's stock.

DIVIDENDS AND THE PRICE-EARNINGS RATIO

A company that pays a higher dividend than its competitor will tend to sell at a higher P/E ratio. A company that pays out little or no dividends or a small dividend in relation to earnings will tend to sell at a lower P/E ratio, other things being equal. Two comparable companies with approximately the same earnings rate would sell at a different P/E ratio because one paid a greater dividend.

At this point we might ask about the company that does not pay a dividend but sells at a high P/E ratio. In this situation the company would be classified as a growth company. Even though it pays no dividend, the expectations about future earnings are so great that it sells at a very high P/E ratio. Companies that are classed as income investments tend to sell at lower ratios than growth companies. Even though a dollar of dividends today is better than a dollar tomorrow, the expectation is not very great for increased earnings. Therefore, an investor is not willing to pay a high price for the earnings. It is difficult to classify a company's P/E ratio by its dividend policy alone. Whether a company is a growth or an income company has a greater impact upon its P/E ratio than its dividend policy.

The Dangers of a Change in the Price-Earnings Ratio

The P/E ratio is reasonable only to the extent that the present expectations about earnings are fulfilled. This is particularly significant when securities are purchased for extremely high multiples of earnings. In order for the P/E ratio to remain high, the expected earnings must be maintained along with the quality of the company, if we consider the P/E ratio a measure of confidence. If the earnings of a company decline because of a drop in sales or an increase in expense, there will be an adverse effect upon investor confidence and the P/E ratio of the company. Not only will the price drop because of a decline in earnings, but the price will drop further because the company will begin to sell at a much lower P/E ratio.

Assume for the moment that a company is selling for $50 per share at a 50 to 1 P/E ratio because investors have a great deal of confidence in the ability of the company to increase its earnings in the near future and in the long run. The company earns $1 per share at present, and expectations about future earnings are optimistic. Many investors expect the company to earn $3 in two years. Therefore, the company is selling at 16 to 17 times its expected future earnings, which is not too high a price to pay for a good stock. Suddenly, the earnings outlook for the company changes. Almost overnight the expectations for the future earnings drop to $.50. We would expect the price to drop from 50 to 25. The current P/E ratio is 50/1, earnings now are $.50, and a price of 25 is justified. However, this is not the case. As the earnings decline we are no longer willing to pay 50 times earnings for a share of stock. Now we are willing to pay only 15 times earnings for a dollar of earnings. The price of the stock drops not from 50 to 25 but from 50 to 7 1/2. Thus the investor has lost on paper much more than the 50 percent indicated at first by the earnings decline. Xerox, late in 1968, was a good example of this phenomenon.

A change in the P/E ratio can result from a change in the confidence about the future earnings of a company. At one time IBM sold as high as 66 times earnings. In the market decline during the first half of 1962 it dropped to a level of approximately 40 times earnings. Earnings did not decline. A change simply occurred in thinking about the reasonableness of a 66 to 1 P/E ratio, and the price came down. This same condition existed for IBM in 1968.

The situations just described point out the danger in buying a stock with an extremely high P/E ratio. A change in earnings or a change in confidence about the future will produce some dramatic results in stock prices. Any method of selecting securities that considers a high P/E ratio a measure of confidence must follow very closely the trend of future earnings, the competitive position of the company, and the attitude of investors about a stock. Any detrimental change will have an important and downward impact on earnings and price. Without an accurate and continuous appraisal, one could lose a significant amount of funds. As long as earnings increase and there is confidence, we can safely hold onto the security. If earnings and confidence change, we must be prepared to sell it.

Some investors buy only low P/E ratio stocks. If earnings improve, so will the ratio, and they will have a double benefit.

The Price-Earnings Ratio as a Guide to Investment Decisions

How can we use the P/E ratio to aid us in making an investment decision? First, we can obtain some idea of what is a reasonable price to pay for a stock by comparing its present P/E ratio to its past levels of P/E. We can learn what is a high and low P/E ratio for the individual company. We can compare the P/E ratio to the market, giving us a relative measure of the height of the market. We can also use the average P/E ratio over time to help us judge the reasonableness of the present levels.

We realize that a high P/E ratio is 35 and above, an average P/E between 14 and 20, and a low P/E ratio 10 to 1 or below. A growth company will sell for a high P/E ratio, and an income stock at a lower one. All of this suggests that we attempt to purchase a stock close to what we judge to be a reasonable P/E ratio based upon the comparisons we have made. We must also realize that we must pay a higher price for a quality company with quality management and an attractive earnings potential.

The best application and use of the ratio comes when we attempt to estimate the future expected price of a company's stock. If we remember the valuation equation, we find we need several estimates before we can determine the expected yield of a common stock that includes both capital gains and dividend income. First, we need an estimate of future earnings. Second, we need an estimate of future dividends based upon these earnings. Third, we must know what is a reasonable P/E ratio for the stock, and fourth, we must estimate the stock price at the end of the forecast period, usually five or seven years, or before, if the risk is great. We multiply the P/E ratio that we can reasonably expect at that time by the estimated earnings in that final year. The fifth and final step is to use a discount rate that provides a present value of the future price and dividend income equal to the current market price of the stock. The rate that equates this income and capital stream to the present price represents the yield to estimated maturity. If the resulting rate is sufficiently high, we will consider the investment satisfactory consistent with the risks involved. If the rate is too low, we will reject it from our investment consideration. The method of valuation described briefly here was covered fully in the discussion of the theory of valuation in Chapter 7.

Market Price Action and Price-Earnings Ratio of Chas. Pfizer, G. D. Searle, and Smith Kline & French

Price Trend and Market Action

In Figure 11–4 we find that the drug stocks in general did not respond to the market direction from 1966 through 1968. All three of the drug companies we have been considering for investment have moved down, cyclically. Therefore, we consider these companies as having a weak market position. Pfizer demonstrated a better market price stability than either Searle or Smith Kline & French. When this analysis was made,

TABLE 16–3

Price range of Pfizer, Searle, and
Smith Kline & French, 1957–1968

YEAR	Chas. Pfizer		G. D. Searle		Smith Kline & French	
	HIGH	LOW	HIGH	LOW	HIGH	LOW
1968*	77 3/4	56 3/4	58 3/8	42 1/8	55 1/4	41
1967	93	68 1/8	61 1/4	37 1/2	65	47 1/8
1966	76 1/2	52 3/4	66	32 3/4	86 1/4	46
1965	75 1/2	49 1/4	70	50 1/4	86 3/4	70 1/4
1964	52 1/8	44 1/4	85	55 1/8	74	58 1/4
1963	55 1/2	44 3/4	64 1/4	30 3/8	69 3/4	59 1/4
1962	57 7/8	33 1/4	48 1/8	26	77 1/2	45 1/8
1961	53 7/8	30 5/8	49 5/8	21 3/4	77	46 1/8
1960	38 1/4	26 3/8	23 1/4	16 3/4	64 3/4	38 1/2
1959	45 1/4	30 1/2	19 1/4	15	61 7/8	32 5/8
1958	37	16 5/8	19 1/4	12 1/2	not available	
1957	21 7/8	14 1/4	18 1/4	11 1/2	not available	

* *New York Times*, August 9, 1968.
SOURCE: Standard & Poor's *Industry Surveys—Drugs, Cosmetics*, May 2, 1968, p. D27 and D28.

the companies were selling below their highs of 1965 through 1967. The prices of Searle and Smith Kline & French were low historically and Pfizer was not far from its historic price.

Price-Earnings Ratio

The price-earnings ratios of the three companies in Table 16–4 have consistently been above the P/E ratios of the Dow Jones Industrial Averages. G. D. Searle's P/E ratio had approached an extreme high in

TABLE 16–4

Price-earnings ratio of Pfizer, Searle, and
Smith Kline & French, 1957–1968

YEAR	Chas. Pfizer		G. D. Searle		Smith Kline & French	
	HIGH	LOW	HIGH	LOW	HIGH	LOW
1968	24.4	17.8	27.0	19.8	17.5	13.1
1967	32.3	23.6	32.1	19.6	22.4	16.2
1966	24.9	17.2	40.5	20.1	30.4	16.2
1965	28.0	18.2	40.7	29.2	30.1	24.4
1964	23.0	19.5	46.4	30.1	28.0	22.1
1963	26.8	21.6	45.9	21.7	29.9	25.4
1962	30.1	17.3	46.5	25.0	37.3	21.7
1961	31.1	17.7	over 50	29.1	41.6	24.9
1960	24.4	16.8	41.4	29.9	39.5	23.5
1959	30.0	20.2	35.2	27.3	35.9	19.0
1958	25.0	11.2	36.6	23.7	25.7	13.7
1957	15.5	10.1	34.8	22.0	16.6	12.6
Average 1957–1968	21.9		32.3		24.5	

SOURCE: Standard & Poor's *Industry Survey—Drugs, Cosmetics*, May 2, 1968, pp. D27 and D28.

1961 when there was great investor confidence in its future. Since 1961 the ratio has declined, yet greater investor confidence has been shown for Searle, as reflected by the P/E ratios in Table 16–4, than in Pfizer or Smith Kline & French. Searle's average and current P/E ratio is substantially above the other two companies. Because of competitive pressures in the industry, a slowing-down of product development, and increased government regulation, investigation, and control, it appears that the P/E ratios existing in 1968 were a better reflection of the risk character of the company than the twelve-year average ratio. If we had to pick a leader based upon P/E ratios it would be G. D. Searle.

Current Yield

The current yield of all three of the companies is low based upon the level of prices and dividends and compared with the current yield for the Dow Jones Industrial Averages. Smith Kline & French had the highest current yield of between 4.9 and 3.6 percent, as indicated in Table 16–5. Except for Smith Kline & French, the low yields suggest that we would be interested in these stocks for growth and not current income. Certainly anyone interested in current income would not find these securities attractive for investment.

Yield to Maturity

Since we are not interested in the current yield alone but in the future earnings as a percent of our investment, we must calculate the yield to

TABLE 16–5

Dividends, yields, and payout ratio for Pfizer,
Searle, and Smith Kline & French, 1957–1968

	Chas. Pfizer			G. D. Searle			Smith Kline & French		
	CURRENT YIELD %	DIVI-DEND $	% PAY-OUT	CURRENT YIELD %	DIVI-DEND $	% PAY-OUT	CURRENT YIELD %	DIVI-DEND $	% PAY-OUT
YEAR	H	L			H	L			H	L		
1968	2.6	1.9	1.45	35	3.1	2.2	1.30	56	4.9	3.6	2.00	56
1967	2.1	1.6	1.45	37	3.5	2.1	1.30	63	4.2	3.1	2.00	61
1966	2.7	1.9	1.45	36	4.0	2.0	1.30	71	4.3	2.3	2.00	63
1965	2.6	1.7	1.30	36	2.6	1.8	1.30	70	2.6	2.1	1.85	58
1964	2.6	2.2	1.15	37	1.8	1.2	1.00	52	2.7	2.1	1.55	54
1963	2.3	1.9	1.05	37	2.4	1.1	.72	48	2.5	2.2	1.50	59
1962	2.9	1.6	.95	35	1.7	0.9	.43	52	3.0	1.7	1.35	60
1961	2.8	1.6	.85	34	2.0	0.9	.43	53	2.7	1.6	1.25	61
1960	3.0	2.1	.80	39	2.4	1.7	.40	65	3.2	1.9	1.25	69
1959	2.6	1.8	.80	39	2.7	2.1	.40	67	3.7	1.9	1.20	64
1958	4.5	2.0	.75	43	3.2	2.1	.40	70	4.4	2.3	.87	54
1957	4.9	3.2	.70	40	3.0	1.9	.35	62	4.1	3.1	.73	47
Average 1957–1968				37				61				59

SOURCE: Standard & Poor's *Investment Survey—Drugs, Cosmetics,* May 2, 1968, pp. D26, D27 and D28; Figure 11–4.

an estimated maturity date sometime in the future. Table 16–6 provides estimates of the dividends we expected to receive from 1969 to 1975 based upon the previous forecast of earnings presented in Table 12–5. The estimates of future earnings were based upon the trend of past earnings averaged with the estimate of earnings based upon the relationship of earnings to sales method. The estimates were extended to 1975. The twelve-year average dividend payout ratio was then multiplied by the estimated earnings to establish the annual expected dividend through 1975. The payout ratio for each company was different, indicating a different management attitude toward dividends.

The yield to maturity for each of the companies was calculated, based upon forecasted dividends and the current P/E ratio and forecasted earnings through 1975. The current P/E ratios were used rather than the twelve-year P/E ratio, because they were thought to be a better indication of risk. The growth of earnings based upon past growth rates even with the low current P/E ratios provides substantial expected yield to maturity for Searle, Smith Kline & French, and Pfizer. The expected seven-year yield to maturity for Searle was 22 percent, 14 percent for Smith Kline & French, and 11 percent for Pfizer (see Table 16–7). On this basis of yield to maturity, as calculated, we would have to select Searle as our number one choice. The price, P/E ratio relationships, and yield to maturity are summarized in Table 16–8. The recent price action of Searle has not been as good as Pfizer or Smith Kline & French. While recent market action has not been favorable, Searle does offer the greatest prospect for profits based upon our estimates.

The estimates of yield we have used represent only one set of assumptions. Realistically we should ask, "Can these three drug companies maintain their past growth rate of earnings?" Even if the rates were cut in half, they would still be substantially higher than GNP. If the expected yield to maturity were cut in half for each company, it would result in compound yields of 5.5 percent for Pfizer, 11 percent

TABLE 16–6

*Estimated earnings[a] and dividends[b] of Pfizer,
Searle, and Smith Kline & French, 1969–1975*

	Chas. Pfizer		G. D. Searle		Smith Kline & French	
	Est. Earnings	Est. Div.	Est. Earnings	Est. Div.	Est. Earnings	Est. Div.
1975	5.91	2.20	6.92	4.20	5.95	3.50
1974	5.40	2.00	5.96	3.65	5.47	3.20
1973	4.92	1.80	5.11	3.10	5.04	2.90
1972	4.50	1.65	4.44	2.70	4.68	2.75
1971	4.10	1.50	3.79	2.30	4.30	2.50
1970	3.78	1.45	3.26	2.00	3.92	2.30
1969	3.45	1.45	2.80	1.70	3.59	2.10

[a] Based upon average of earnings estimate in Table 12–5.
[b] Based upon average payout and rounded to nearest $.05.

TABLE 16–7

Expected yield on investment for Pfizer,
Searle, and Smith Kline & French

Chas. Pfizer

YEAR	RETURN OF CAPITAL	EST. DIV.	TOTAL RETURN	PRESENT VALUE AT 10%		PRESENT VALUE AT 12%	
1975	$129.42ª	$2.20	$131.62	× .513 =	$67.52	× .452 =	$59.49
1974		2.00	2.00	× .564 =	1.13	× .507 =	1.01
1973		1.80	1.80	× .621 =	1.12	× .567 =	1.02
1972		1.65	1.65	× .683 =	1.13	× .636 =	1.05
1971		1.50	1.50	× .751 =	1.13	× .712 =	1.07
1970		1.45	1.45	× .826 =	1.20	× .797 =	1.16
1969		1.45	1.45	× .909 =	1.32	× .893 =	1.30
Total Present Value					$74.55		$66.10
Present Market Price 8/9/68						$70	
Yield to Maturity						11%	

G. D. Searle

YEAR	RETURN OF CAPITALᵇ	EST. DIV.	TOTAL RETURN	PRESENT VALUE AT 20%		PRESENT VALUE AT 22%	
1975	$138.40ᵇ	$4.20	$142.60	× .279 =	$39.78	× .249 =	$35.51
1974		3.65	3.65	× .335 =	1.22	× .303 =	1.10
1973		3.10	3.10	× .402 =	1.25	× .370 =	1.15
1972		2.70	2.70	× .482 =	1.30	× .451 =	1.22
1971		2.30	2.30	× .579 =	1.33	× .551 =	1.27
1970		2.00	2.00	× .694 =	1.39	× .672 =	1.34
1969		1.70	1.70	× .833 =	1.42	× .820 =	1.39
Total Present Value					$47.69		$42.98
Present Market Price 8/9/68						$42.88	
Yield to Maturity						22%	

Smith Kline & French

YEAR	RETURN OF CAPITAL	EST. DIV.	TOTAL RETURN	PRESENT VALUE AT 12%		PRESENT VALUE AT 14%	
1975	$ 92.23ᶜ	$3.50	$ 95.73	× .452 =	$43.27	× .400 =	$38.29
1974		3.20	3.20	× .507 =	1.62	× .456 =	1.46
1973		2.90	2.90	× .567 =	1.64	× .519 =	1.51
1972		2.75	2.75	× .636 =	1.75	× .592 =	1.63
1971		2.50	2.50	× .712 =	1.78	× .675 =	1.69
1970		2.30	2.30	× .797 =	1.83	× .769 =	1.77
1969		2.10	2.10	× .893 =	1.88	× .877 =	1.84
Total Present Value					$53.77		$48.19
Present Market Price 8/9/68						$48.88	
Yield to Maturity						14%	

ª Based upon 1975 earnings times a 12-year average P/E ratio of 21.9 and current P/E ratio of 21.9.

ᵇ Based upon a current P/E ratio of 20 to 1, times estimated earnings of $6.92 in 1975.

ᶜ Based upon current P/E ratio of 15.5 to 1, times estimated earnings of $5.95 in 1975.

for Searle, and 7 percent for Smith Kline & French. And even with these reduced rates of return, Searle would offer an expectation of yield above 10 percent—not a bad rate of return. But the rule of reason must apply. At this point, we must sit back and reflect on the facts and raise

TABLE 16–8

Relative rank of price, price-earnings, and yields

PRICE, PRICE-EARNINGS, AND YIELD:	CHAS. PFIZER	G. D. SEARLE	SMITH KLINE & FRENCH
Trend of price	1	2	3
Recent price stability (1968)	2	3	1
Highest P/E ratio	3	1	2
Dividend yield	2	3	1
Market action compared to market average	1	3	2
Yield to maturity (7 years estimated)	11%	22%	14%

the question, "What did we forget?" or "What can go wrong?" We must be able to accept our own conclusions based upon our own analysis. Remember Murphy's Law: If anything can go wrong, it will!

The Decision

After a long and tedious but thorough analysis we are ready to make our decision. In actual practice the whole process might not take very long if the data are available. A summary of the data upon which a valuation analysis is made is presented in Table 16–9. This is not the only way in which a valuation analysis is made, but it has been successful because it focuses upon investment fundamentals. The variables must be constantly checked and re-examined. The methodology employed is not a panacea for all investment decisions. In spite of any weaknesses in the valuation analysis or in our judgment, the data leads us to the conclusion that G. D. Searle would be a satisfactory investment.

In the previous edition, the same three companies were analyzed. Because the yields were so low, none was recommended for purchase. We suggested the investor wait for lower prices. This time our decision was in favor of investment because of the changed variables. We would be willing to accept all three companies because expected yield to maturity is satisfactory.

TABLE 16–9

Summary of earnings and price analysis of Pfizer, Searle, and Smith Kline & French

	CHAS. PFIZER	G. D. SEARLE	SMITH KLINE & FRENCH
Competitive position of company	3	1	2
Earnings and profitability	3	1	2
Operating characteristics and efficiency	3	1	2
Current financial position	3	1	2
Capital structure and debt position	3	1	2
Management	1	1	1
Price	3	1	2
Current yield	2	3	1
Yield to maturity (7 years estimated)	11%	22%	14%

Summary

The price we pay for a stock is as important as the factors of quality we want in an investment. Paying too much will result in heavy loss to the investor. We must, therefore, become familiar with the historical price of our stock and its market performance before we purchase. Perhaps we should consider price as a range rather than as a specific amount. We should attempt to buy at an attractive price.

An examination of the P/E ratio of our company will help us determine what is a fair price. The higher the P/E ratio of an investment-grade security, the greater the confidence investors have in the future growth of the company. Growth companies, companies with little debt, and companies that have a high degree of excellence tend to sell at a high P/E ratio. Companies that are purchased for income tend to sell on a lower P/E basis. Low-quality or high-risk companies tend to sell at extremely low or high ratios because of the risks involved or the lack of earnings.

As a general rule we are wise to seek quality and then try to buy it at a reasonable P/E ratio. We should try not to buy at too high a ratio for a company's stock because of the possibility of loss. The best bargains might be in quality companies that are selling at low P/E ratios relative to their past price and future earnings. As a norm, 10 times earnings is low; 15 to 1 seems to be a "normal" P/E ratio for most investment-grade companies. A P/E ratio above 25 to 1 and as high as 50 to 1 is high and indicates a growth company or a poor quality speculative company. The quality of the earnings and the overall quality of the company compared to the yield to maturity on the common stock will determine if an investment is satisfactory. If after careful analysis we think we will obtain a satisfactory yield on a quality investment commensurate with risk, then we should decide to invest. If the return is not satisfactory in spite of investment quality, we should decide not to invest.

Our estimates provide only one method and one set of data for making an investment decision. Our analysis of fundamentals is a successful way in which to make a decision about a specific common stock. It is not a panacea and the data and analysis are subject to sound judgment and reasoning.

Review Questions

1. (a) Why is the price paid for a common stock so important for investment success?
   (b) Can we pay too much for a quality company?
2. Why should we review the historical price and price range of a common stock?
3. What is meant by the term *market performance* or *market action* of a stock?

4. What is the P/E ratio, and how is it determined?
5. What is the significance of the P/E ratio, and how can it help us determine whether the current price of a stock is reasonable?
6. What has been the trend of the P/E ratios in the market over the past decade?
7. Is there a normal P/E ratio for a stock? Explain.
8. What is the relationship between the P/E ratio and risk?
9. Is there an absolute high or low P/E ratio?
10. (a) Would we expect the P/E ratio of a speculative company to be high, low, or both? Explain.
    (b) What would we expect from a growth company? Relate this to the discussion about the P/E ratio and valuation in Chapter 7.
    (c) What would we expect the P/E ratio to be for a company with a large amount of debt in its capital structure?
    (d) What would we expect the P/E ratio to be for a company with cyclical earnings?
    (e) Would we expect a high or low P/E ratio if the company had a stable dividend policy?
11. What are the dangers involved in purchasing a high P/E ratio stock?
12. The average P/E ratio allows us to forecast future price of the stock based upon future estimated earnings. Discuss.
13. Why is current yield inadequate to determine the investment expectation of a stock, particularly a growth stock? Comment.
14. Explain how we estimate yield to maturity based upon expected dividends over the next five years and expected price in five years. Can we rely on these estimates?
15. How is risk related to our final decision?

Problems

1. Examine the range of prices over the past 10 years of the common stock of the three companies under your analysis. Which appears to have the greatest growth and stability?
2. Examine the range of the P/E ratios for the three companies over the past 10 years.
3. Compare the market price and P/E ratio of the three companies with the Dow Jones Industrial Averages or the average that is comparable to your industry. Has the market action of the companies been better than the market as a whole? Comment.
4. Do the companies sell at a high or low P/E ratio in comparison to stocks in the industry and compared to the Dow Jones Industrial Average (or Rail or Utility if they apply)?
5. (a) What has been the amount of the dividend and dividend yield for the companies from 1957 to the present?
   (b) Estimate future dividends based upon the past payout ratio and future expected earnings.
6. (a) Based upon a reasonable or normal P/E ratio, what can we expect the price to be in five to seven years based upon earnings at that time?

(b) Based upon the current market price, what would be the yield through the next five to seven years? Use the discount table presented on page 84 to make the calculation.

7. (a) Which company offers the highest yield to maturity?
   (b) Is this yield a satisfactory compensation for the risks involved?
   (c) Are the yields satisfactory based upon our own risk/reward requirements?

8. Based upon the analysis of company earnings and the forecast of future earnings, based on the analysis of price and P/E ratios, and based upon yield, which of the companies, if any, would you select for investment?

Sources of Investment Information

Barron's
Clarke Dodge Investment Survey
Commercial and Financial Chronicle
Moody's manuals
Standard & Poor's *Investment Surveys*
Standard & Poor's *Stock Guide*
The Value Line Investment Survey

Selected Readings

Balog, James, "Forecasting Drug Earnings (A Review)," *Financial Analysts Journal* (July-August, 1966), p. 39.

Breen, William, "Low Price-Earnings Ratios," *Financial Analysts Journal* (July-August, 1968), p. 125.

Hammel, J. E. and D. A. Hodes, "Factors Influencing P/E Multiples," *Financial Analysts Journal* (January-February, 1967), p. 90.

McWilliams, James D., "Prices, Earnings and P-E Ratios," *Financial Analysts Journal* (May-June, 1966), p. 137.

Mayer, Robert W., "Price Earnings Ratios: A Prospect," *Financial Analysts Journal* (November-December, 1967), p. 109.

Miller, P. F., Jr., and T. E. Beach, "Price-Earnings Ratios: A Reply," *Financial Analysts Journal* (May-June, 1967), p. 109.

Molodovsky, Nicholas, "Recent Studies of P/E Ratios," *Financial Analysts Journal* (May-June, 1967), p. 101.

Murphy, J. E., Jr., and H. W. Stevenson, "P/E Ratios and Future Growth," *Financial Analysts Journal* (November-December, 1967), p. 111.

Murphy, Joseph E., Jr., "Return, Payout, and Growth," *Financial Analysts Journal* (May-June, 1967), p. 91.

Nicholson, S. Francis, "Price Ratios," *Financial Analysts Journal* (January-February, 1968), p. 105.

17

INVESTMENT ANALYSIS
Case Study of the Electronics and the
Electronic Products Industry

So that the method of analysis presented in the preceding chapters is fully understood, let us discuss another case. The method we used in making a comparative analysis of different companies provides a clearly organized path to follow. However, it does take a good deal of time to obtain the information and summarize the data.

In examining the electronics industry to bring together the content of analysis, we shall discuss each factor of analysis and reach a conclusion, with every effort made to indicate why the conclusion was reached. It is possible in making the final recommendation about the comparative superiority of a company that the company will not be successful. It is also possible that the qualitative and quantitative conditions will change, so that the original conditions of analysis no longer apply. We may make errors of judgment about the future, for no one can forecast future events with certainty. Obviously we must keep abreast of competitive conditions, and we must anticipate change.

One other point must be made about the possibility of poor judgment. We do not invest in only one company or one security. We invest in several companies to spread the risk. The act of diversification should minimize the possible loss from mistakes made in the selection or timing of the purchase of one security. We shall discuss this subject at greater length when we examine investment management principles.

The Growth of the Electronics Industry

The word electronics was not in our vocabulary in 1940.[1] It was not until the early 1950's that we had an industrial classification called the electronics industry. Professors Glover and Lagai,[2] in their book *The Development of American Industries*, had no such classification; their listing was "The Electrical Industry," and included in that listing were some of the devices that we now refer to as being within the electronics industry. The radio and the phonograph are examples. Perhaps Edison, Marconi, and DeForest could be considered the fathers of the electronics industry. The industry has changed and it has grown. In 1950 it had half a billion dollars in sales, thirty times as large as in 1940.

The growth of the electronics industry is further revealed in Table 17–1. The factory sales of the industry increased from an index of 100 in 1957–1959 to an estimated 278 for 1968, surpassing the growth

TABLE 17–1

Sales of electronics industry compared to national economy by index (1957–1959 = 100) and as a percent of Gross National Product

YEAR	INDEX OF INDUSTRY SALES	FEDERAL RESERVE BOARD INDEX OF INDUSTRIAL PRODUCTION	INDEX OF GNP	INDUSTRY SALES AS A PERCENT OF GNP
1968E[a]	278	164.0	181	2.98
1967	264	159.0	172	2.92
1966	262	156.3	162	3.08
1965	201	143.4	149	2.57
1964	182	132.3	138	2.51
1963	176	124.3	129	2.60
1962	149.1	118.2	121	2.37
1961	137.2	109.8	114	2.33
1960	122.5	108.7	110	2.15
1959				2.02
1958	100.0	100.0	100	1.90
1957				1.86

a E = estimated.

SOURCES: Standard & Poor's *Investment Survey—Electronics, Electrical*, July 18, 1963, p. E8; and December 21, 1967, p. E2.

1 Haworth F. Hoch, "Electrical and Electronics," *Financial Analysts Journal*, January-February, 1961, p. 95.
2 John C. Glover and Rudolph L. Lagai, *The Development of American Industries*, 4th ed. (New York: Simmons-Boardman Publishing Corporation, 1959).

of GNP and the real output of our society as measured by the Federal Reserve Board Index of Industrial Production. Electronics sales accounted for a larger share of GNP in 1968. Electronics sales in 1957 represented 1.86 percent of Gross National Product, and by 1968 the figure had reached 2.98 percent. This is truly a remarkable record of growth.

The growth of the industry by the major type of product is shown in Tables 17–2 and 17–3. Industrial electronic products increased output by over 400 percent from 1957 through estimated output in 1968. This segment of the industry has grown at a faster rate than the industry as a whole. The consumer products segment of the industry also grew rapidly between 1957 and 1968, experiencing a growth of over 300 percent. The least rapidly growing segment of the industry was the components group, and yet it grew 10 percent between 1957 and 1968; this was a slower growth rate than that of the national economy. The growth of industry can be seen in Table 17–3, where data is presented on a per capita basis. The electronics industry, in total, has been able to increase its per capita sales in every year from 1957 to 1968.

Much concern has been expressed over the future growth potential of the electronics industry. Estimates have been made that sales would reach almost $20 billion by 1970. One estimate suggested a sales volume of $18.1 billion by 1970. The assumption upon which this figure was based was of an average growth rate of 9 percent,[3] an average of the 7 percent growth rate predicted by the Electronics Industries Association

TABLE 17–2

Dollar sales for the electronics-electrical industry
by subindustry (millions of dollars)

Year	Consumer Products	Industrial Products	Military Aerospace	Replacement Components	Industry Total
1968E[a]	5,150	5,700	12,680	660	24,190
1967E[a]	4,800	5,300	12,220	650	22,970
1966	4,574	4,949	10,700	640	22,863
1965	3,658	4,265	8,969	630	17,522
1964	2,940	3,568	8,775	620	15,903
1963	2,604	3,325	8,841	590	15,360
1962*	2,407	2,450	8,348	620	13,825
1961	2,087	2,200	7,045	765	12,097
1960	2,101	1,850	6,124	730	10,805
1959	2,098	1,600	5,373	680	9,751
1958	1,647	1,380	4,750	585	8,362
1957	1,717	1,300	4,130	610	7,757

[a] E = estimated.
* Not strictly comparable with earlier data.
SOURCE: Standard & Poor's *Industry Survey—Electronics, Electrical,* July 18, 1963, p. E8, Table 1; and December 21, 1967, p. E2.

3 "Electronics—An Interview with George J. Pandapas and Herman Fialkov," *Financial Analysts Journal,* March-April, 1960, p. 35.

TABLE 17–3

Per capita dollar sales of the electronics-electrical industry by subindustry and industry total

YEAR	CONSUMER PRODUCTS	INDUSTRIAL COMMERCIAL	MILITARY AEROSPACE	COMPONENTS	INDUSTRY TOTAL	POPULA- TION
1968E[a]	$25.40	$28.00	$62.50	$3.24	$119.14	203.0
1967E[a]	24.10	26.60	61.50	3.26	115.46	199.1
1966	22.13	25.10	54.50	3.26	104.99	196.9
1965	18.75	21.93	46.10	3.23	90.01	194.6
1964	15.30	18.55	45.60	3.22	82.67	192.1
1963	13.76	17.54	46.55	3.11	80.96	189.4
1962	12.89	13.17	44.88	3.33	74.09	186.6
1961	11.36	11.98	38.35	4.16	65.85	183.7
1960	11.63	10.23	33.89	4.03	59.80	180.7
1959	11.85	9.03	30.34	3.84	55.06	177.1
1958	9.46	7.93	27.28	3.36	48.02	174.1
1957	10.08	7.63	24.25	3.58	45.55	170.3

[a] E = estimated.

SOURCE: Standard & Poor's *Industry Survey—Electronics, Electrical,* July 18, 1963, pp. E8 and E24; and December 21, 1967, p. E2.

and the 11 percent predicted by the Institute of Radio Engineers. This would be somewhat below the 20 to 25 percent compound rate of growth for the decade of the 1950's, but still very substantial. These forecasts were actually conservative, since the most optimistic forecast for 1970 was exceeded by $4.5 billion in 1968. If we can assume that the growth of a product-oriented industry follows the S-shaped pattern, then it is logical to assume that the growth rate will diminish for the industry as a whole in the decade of the 1960's and the first half of the 1970's. A sustained growth of between 5 and 10 percent is possible for the next decade, a higher rate than the growth of the national economy. The 10 percent growth rate is likely to come in the area of industrial electronics.

The Products of the Industry

Some of the products produced in the electronics industry are easy to envision and understand. We know what a radio is or a television set or an AC motor. Some of the other products are somewhat difficult to comprehend. What, for example, is a transistor, or a transducer, or a tunnel diode? These products form the basis for a multimillion-dollar industry, but relatively few people know their functions. Appearing below is a list of definitions of terms frequently used in the electronics industry. This might help to identify some of the products produced in the industry and their uses. The source of this data is Standard & Poor's *Industrial Survey—Electronics, Electrical,* December 14, 1967, p. E11.

CAPACITOR—A device consisting of two conductors carrying equal but opposite electric charges which are separated from each other by a non-conductor. The primary function of a capacitor is the storage of electrical energy.

DIODE—An electron tube or semiconductor material with two electrodes that is most commonly used to convert alternating current into direct current.

ELECTRON—The elementary unit of a negative electrical charge.

FUEL CELL—An electrochemical device that converts chemical energy directly into electrical energy.

HYBRID CIRCUIT—An assemblage of passive and active subminiature devices on an insulating substrate to perform a complete circuit function.

INFRARED—That portion of the frequency band that is above microwaves and below the lowest frequency (the color red) of visible light. Infrared radiates from and is absorbed by all materials.

INTEGRATED CIRCUIT—A complete functional circuit consisting of transistors, diodes, capacitors, and resistors all constructed within or on the surface of a monolithic chip of silicon.

LASER—A device for the amplification or generation of coherent light signals (Light Amplification by Stimulated Emission of Radiation).

MAGNETRON—A high-vacuum tube capable of producing high power output in the microwave region of the frequency spectrum.

MASER—A device for the amplification or generation of microwave signals (Microwave Amplification by Stimulated Emission of Radiation).

MICROWAVES—Very short electromagnetic waves lying between the television and infrared bands in the frequency spectrum. Microwaves are finding increasing usage in the communications field.

MONOLITHIC—A semiconductor integrated circuit which is complete on one chip or piece of substrate.

RECTIFIER—A device, either vacuum tube, semiconductor, gaseous or electrolytic, used primarily to convert alternating current into direct current. The basic method of operation of rectifiers and diodes is identical, with various types and sizes of one often overlapping the other. Generally, the main point of difference is that rectifiers usually have a larger current capacity than do diodes.

RELAY—An electrically operated switch, usually composed of an electromagnet, an armature, and one or more contact springs, used to open or close an electric circuit.

RESISTOR—An electrical component that restricts the flow of current into a circuit, thereby permitting control of the voltage across it.

SEMICONDUCTOR—A material whose ability to conduct a flow

of electrons is intermediate between that of a conductor (such as copper, which freely permits passage of an electric current when a difference of potential is applied to it) and that of an insulator (such as glass, which allows only a small amount of current to pass through it).

SOLAR CELL—A device used to convert electromagnetic radiation from the sun into electrical energy.

SOLID STATE DEVICES—Elements that can control current without moving parts, heated filaments or vacuum gaps. Semiconductors are the best known solid state devices.

SONAR—Apparatus or techniques that employ underwater sound waves to locate and track objects below the surface of the water.

TELEMETRY—That field of instrumentation dealing with the transmission of measurement data from a remote location to a more convenient location and the reproducing of this data in a form suitable for display, recording, or insertion into data-processing equipment.

THERMOELECTRICITY—The direct conversion of heat to electricity and the reciprocal use of electricity to create the effect of heat or cold.

TRANSDUCER—A device used to change one form of energy into another. For example, a loudspeaker is a transducer that changes electrical energy into acoustical energy.

TRANSFORMER—An electric device which, by electromagnetic induction, transforms electric energy from one or more circuits to one or more other circuits at the same frequency, usually with changed values of voltage and current.

TRANSISTOR—A semiconductor device with three or more electrodes, commonly used to amplify or switch electric current.

The electronics industry is divided into four basic categories: (1) military, (2) components, (3) industrial commercial, and (4) consumer or entertainment. All these groups can use the electronic products defined in the list. The classification by end use rather than by specific item or component is helpful in anticipating the present and future demand and sales level of a particular product.

Military Electronics

Missiles. The category of military electronics includes electronic equipment for missiles—for example, missile testing equipment, flight-control apparatus, and missile communication equipment. An impressive array of antimissile equipment is also being developed.[4]

Aircraft. The electronic content of manned aircraft has increased tremendously in recent years. Electronic equipment for the F-104 ac-

---

4 Standard & Poor's *Industry Survey—Electronics, Electrical*, June 21, 1962, p. E10, and December 14, 1967, pp. E9 to E27.

counts for 30 percent of its cost.[5] This equipment performs the functions of navigation, communications control, and identification. Manned aircraft is the biggest single item in the military budget. The F-111, F-4, A-7, and C-5A should generate billions in revenues in the years ahead.

Communication, Space Programs, Infrared, and Microwaves. The demands of the free world suggest a growing need for communications now and in future satellite projects. The space program uses today millions of dollars of electronic equipment, and with expansion, billions of additional dollars will be spent for this purpose. The space program was scheduled for reevaluation in the future before Apollo, which might have led to a reduction in expenditures in this area. But now it looks as though these expenditures will continue.

The infrared segment of the industry should experience remarkable growth. Expenditures for 1963 exceeded one-third of a billion dollars in 1962, a significant increase compared with $5 million, 10 years earlier.[6] More than a half billion was spent in 1968. All applications of infrared are based upon the principle that infrared—the frequency band that lies between the microwave and visible light bands—radiates from and is absorbed by all materials. Its uses include: (1) identification of substances by analysis of their frequency absorption spectrum, (2) determination of the temperature and location of objects by detection of their infrared radiation, and (3) provision of large quantities of radiation for heating, drying, and curing processes.

The work with infrared by the military is classified. Its application in the area of automatic detection of missiles holds a great deal of promise for its future and the expansion of the electronics industry. It shows promise for application in nonmilitary areas such as temperature measurement and control, analytical instrumentation, industrial photography, transportation, food processing, space heating, and cooking and baking.

Microwave transmission also offers a great deal of expansion possibilities. It costs less over long distance and rough terrain than the lower-frequency transmission.

Electronic Components

Electronic components are the building blocks used to construct the electronic devices produced for the government, industry, and the consumer. They represent a second major area of the electronics industry. The segment comprising passive components, those containing no energy source, represents about 57 percent of the market. The active component segment, which includes the conventional tube, semiconductors, and

5 *Ibid.*
6 *Ibid.,* p. E11.

transistors, makes up the remainder of this division. The most important developments in this area are in miniaturization and solid state physics. Almost every firm in the industry is engaged in research on one phase or another of miniaturization, and more than fifty firms have various contracts for research in the maser-laser area. The development of the maser brings a method of amplifying microwave signals by solid state techniques. The laser is a maser that works at optical frequencies and opens the optical spectrum for exploitation by all means currently used in the radio and microwave spectrums.

Industrial Electronics

Industrial electronics grew more rapidly than any other segment of the industry from 1957 through 1968, because of the automation of office equipment and increased use of computers. This area overlaps that of office equipment. The automation of all phases of industry offers great hopes for this segment of the electronics industry.

Consumer Electronic Products

We are most familiar with consumer electronics. It includes television—black and white and color—radio, hi-fi components, and FM and stereo. This segment of electronics was the first to gain industry stature. The growth of color television and the potential threat of foreign competition are the high and low spots of this category. Atomic energy, utility and industrial electrical equipment, and household appliances are other areas in the broad product-based electronics industry.

Competitive Position of the Leading Companies

The leading companies in the electronic products-electronic group are listed in Table 17–4. These companies were ranked according to their 1968 sales and growth in the lower portion of the table. International Telephone maintained the number one position in amount of sales between 1957 and 1968. The other companies were in the top positions in the industry with respect to size.[7] Litton was second in size followed by TRW, Raytheon, and Honeywell Incorporated. Litton maintained its growth rate leadership followed by Texas Instruments, International Telephone, TRW and Honeywell.

This is a growth industry, and we must use the criterion of growth rather than income to select our companies for investment consideration. This requires an examination of the growth of these leading companies over the 1957–1968 period.

7 Standard & Poor's *Industry Survey—Electronics, Electrical,* June 21, 1962, p. E10, and December 14, 1967, pp. E9 to E27.

TABLE 17–4

Sales index (1957–1959 = 100) for leading
electronics companies, 1957 to 1968

YEAR	AVCO	BECKMAN	IT&T	LITTON*	HONEY-WELL	RAYTHEON	TEXAS INST.	THOMPSON RAMO WOOLDRIDGE
1968 E	287	310	473	2,532	348	332	573	359
1967	260	310	396	2,215	303	294	486	277
1966	200	278	304	1,977	265	188	494	222
1965	147	246	254	1,486	203	130	371	171
1964	143	207	229	894	193	121	279	142
1963	170	193	203	701	188	130	235	124
1962	137	183	154	499	173	154	205	118
1961	107	168	130	317	136	150	199	105
1960	107	139	122	238	124	143	198	108
1959	102	110	109	159	111	131	164	107
1958	94	97	99	105	95	100	78	87
1957	104	93	92	36	94	69	57	106
1957–59 in millions	(301)	(142)	(698)	(79)	(345)	(376)	(117)	(376)
Company ranked by size of 1968 sales	6	8	1	2	5	4	7	3
(million $)	865	130	3,300	2,000	1,200	1,250	670	1,350
Growth rank based on est. 1968 sales	(8)	(7)	(3)	(1)	(5)	(6)	(2)	(4)

* Fiscal year ended June 30.
SOURCE: Standard & Poor's *Industry Survey—Electronics, Electrical,*
December 21, 1967, p. E30; and *The Value Line Industry Survey.*

Litton Industries demonstrated the greatest growth of the eight companies listed, a growth nothing short of astounding, even though this was due to acquisition and not internal growth, unlike the other companies. Sales increased by over twenty-five times between 1957 and 1968 (fiscal 1969). Texas Instruments did not grow as much as Litton, but it showed substantial growth in sales. Texas Instruments' sales increased almost six-fold over the period. The third ranking company based upon size and growth rate was International Telephone and Telegraph. Logically it would be the third candidate for investment consideration. Honeywell, included in the first edition of this book and retained for comparability, would be ranked in the middle, based upon growth rate and size. The company had substantial growth for the period, its sales increasing by almost 350 percent from 1957 to 1968.

Based on the premise that those companies that have achieved a position of dominance in the industry and have grown rapidly will offer an opportunity for successful investment, we shall examine Litton Industries and Texas Instruments as the potential investment candidates in the electronics-electronic products group, retaining Honeywell for comparative purposes. The companies' past growth of sales is shown in Table 17–5, and data about each company in Figure 17–1.

Litton Industries

Litton Industries has had an extremely rapid growth since its beginning in 1954. Based upon estimates of future sales, it appears that the growth will continue. As we see in Table 17–5, sales are estimated at $3,500 million for 1973, almost double 1968 sales. Litton is a large, well-diversified, electronics-based company conducting business in the military, industrial, commercial, and consumer markets. It has thirty divisions, each of which is run by a general manager who acts somewhat autonomously but is subject to policy decisions from top management. The company is represented in nine foreign countries and operates 1,500 branches in the United States and 790 abroad. In 1962 Litton operated 5.9 million square feet of manufacturing and research facilities and employed 35,000 persons, 5,000 of whom were scientific, engineering, and technical personnel.[8] In 1968 Litton employed almost 76,000 people.

TABLE 17–5

Dollar sales in millions and index of sales (1957–1959 = 100) of Litton Industries, Texas Instruments, and Honeywell, Incorporated

	Litton Industries			Texas Instruments			Honeywell, Inc.		
YEAR	SALES	INDEX	ANNUAL CHANGE IN %	SALES	INDEX	ANNUAL CHANGE IN %	SALES	INDEX	ANNUAL CHANGE IN %
1973 Eª	$3,500			$1,500			$1,875		
1968 Eª	2,000	2,502	14.3	670	573	17.9	1,200	348	14.9
1967	1,500	2,215	12.0	525	486	−1.6	1,000	303	14.3
1966	1,172	1,977	25.4	580	494	32.7	914	265	24.3
1965	934	1,486	32.2	437	371	33.2	735	203	10.1
1964	706	894	27.6	328	279	18.8	667	193	2.9
1963	553	701	40.7	276	235	15.0	648	188	8.9
1962	393	499	57.5	240	205	3.2	595	173	26.7
1961	250	317	31.2	233	198	.1	470	136	10.3
1960	187	238	49.8	232	199	20.4	426	124	11.7
1959	125	159	50.8	193	164	110.0	381	111	16.1
1958	83	105	197.1	92	78	36.7	328	95	1.1
1957	28	36		67	57		324	94	
Average 1957–59	$78.9			$117.5			$344.9		
Average Annual Rate of Growth 1957–1968		49.0%			26.0%				12.8%

ª E = estimated.

SOURCE: Standard & Poor's *Industry Survey—Electronics-Electrical*, July 18, 1962, p. E37; December 21, 1967, pp. E37 and 37; and Figure 17–1.

8 Litton Industries, Inc., *Special Company Studies* (Clark Dodge & Co.), August, 1962, pp. 1ff.

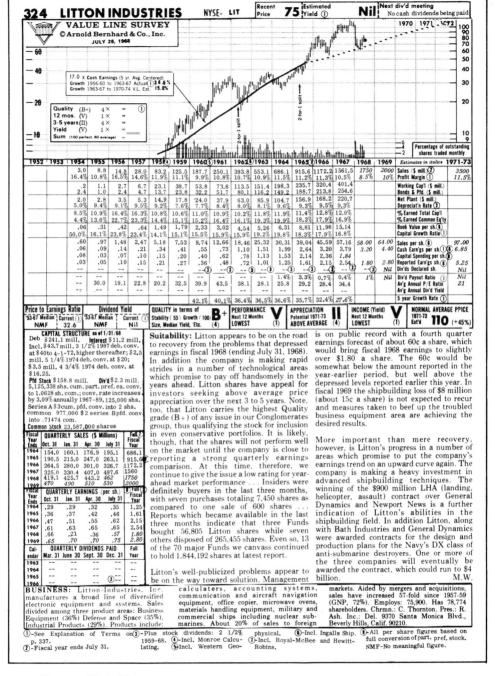

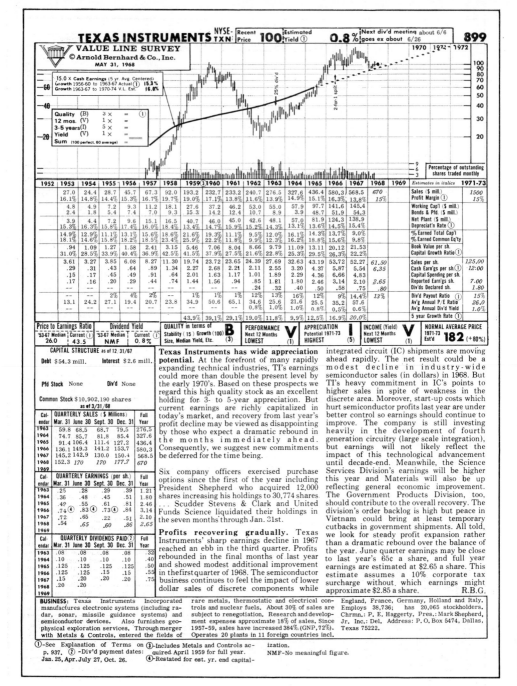

FIGURE 17–1 (b)

Value Line *information about Texas Instruments*

SOURCE *The Value Line Investment Survey,* Arnold Bernhard & Co., May 31, 1968

HONEYWELL NYSE- **HON** — Recent Price **126** — Estimated Yield① **0.9%** — Next div'd meeting about 8/20, goes ex about 8/26 — **857**

VALUE LINE SURVEY
© Arnold Bernhard & Co., Inc.
MAY 31, 1968

14.0 X Cash Earnings (5 yr. Avg Centered)
Growth 1956-60 to 1963-67 Actual ① 12.1%
Growth 1963-67 to 1970-74 V.L. Est'd 14.0%

Quality (B-) 2 × = ①
12 mos. (III) 3 × =
3-5 years (III) 3 × =
Yield (V) 1 × =
Sum (100 perfect, 60 average)

Percentage of outstanding shares traded monthly

	1952	1953	1954	1955	1956	1957	1958	1959	1960	1961	1962	1963	1964	1965	1966	1967	1968	1969	Estimates in italics 1971-73
Sales ($ mill.)	165.7	214.0	229.4	244.5	287.9	324.9	328.5	381.4	426.2	470.2	595.9	648.5	667.2	700.4	914.4	1044.9	1200		1875
Profit Margin ①	14.7%	15.9%	16.8%	19.6%	19.1%	17.0%	17.7%	19.5%	16.4%	14.9%	13.8%	15.3%	17.0%	15.6%	15.6%	14.2%	15%		17%
Working Cap'l ($ mill.)	76.9	77.1	82.4	86.1	111.4	131.9	135.4	149.3	137.4	171.2	167.8	208.9	188.6	215.1	237.2	298.5			
Bonds & Pfd. ($ mill.)	51.0	35.0	35.0	35.0	44.0	44.0	44.0	44.0	42.8	91.6	90.4	117.9	110.9	157.9	186.1	246.3			
Net Plant ($ mill.)	23.0	25.8	29.3	36.6	45.0	63.5	72.1	75.7	98.4	126.5	143.9	152.3	199.5	245.2	289.0	332.5			
Depreciat'n Rate ①	11.5%	11.0%	11.1%	11.2%	9.9%	8.3%	8.6%	9.3%	8.3%	8.6%	10.4%	10.5%	10.6%	10.9%	11.5%	12.1%			
% Earned Total Cap'l	9.9%	11.1%	14.3%	16.2%	14.8%	12.1%	11.8%	13.9%	12.3%	9.5%	10.0%	10.9%	12.2%	10.0%	11.1%	9.6%			
% Earned Common Eq'ty	16.7%	13.9%	19.3%	21.2%	19.0%	14.1%	13.8%	16.3%	13.7%	12.1%	12.2%	14.5%	15.6%	13.0%	13.8%	11.5%			
Book Value per sh.	4.53	5.63	6.46	7.23	9.02	11.30	12.18	13.38	14.28	15.00	15.87	17.29	19.17	20.07	22.80	24.71			
Capital Growth Ratio ①	11.8%	10.9%	15.1%	17.4%	14.9%	10.9%	11.5%	14.5%	12.1%	12.4%	15.2%	18.3%	21.3%	20.4%	23.2%	23.8%			
Sales per sh.	14.65	17.15	18.07	19.23	21.76	23.33	23.51	27.25	30.39	33.50	42.42	46.15	47.45	49.78	62.99	71.73	82.50		130
Cash Earn'gs per sh. ①	1.10	1.13	1.62	2.01	2.20	2.09	2.27	2.86	2.72	2.86	3.42	4.16	5.11	5.31	6.38	6.97	8.25		14.25
Capital Spending per sh.	.37	.57	.69	1.03	1.16	1.88	1.28	1.02	2.19	3.13	2.69	2.23	5.45	5.85	6.09	7.05			
Reported Earn'gs sh.	.75	.78	1.21	1.49	1.68	1.54	1.62	2.10	1.87	1.74	1.86	2.42	2.89	2.61	3.07	2.85	3.30		6.35
Div'ds Declared sh.	.56	.66	.65	.75	.88	.88	.93	1.00	1.00	1.00	1.00	1.00	1.03	1.10	1.10	1.10	1.10		2.40
Div'd Payout Ratio ①	54%	48%	40%	38%	39%	41%	38%	32%	37%	36%	30%	25%	21%	21%	18%	16%	14%		17%
Av'g Annual P/E Ratio	17.2	19.2	18.2	19.4	22.6	29.7	28.6	30.6	39.1	42.2	26.0	23.3	22.4	26.4	23.7	29.6			26.0
Av'g Annual Div'd Yield	4.3%	3.7%	3.0%	2.6%	2.3%	1.9%	1.9%	1.4%	1.4%	1.4%	2.1%	1.8%	1.6%	1.7%	1.5%	1.3%			1.5%
5 year Growth Rate							10.6%	11.3%	13.8%	13.4%	10.5%	7.7%	7.4%	9.7%	11.9%	13.2%	14.8%	15.5%	15.5%

Price to Earnings Ratio		Dividend Yield		QUALITY in terms of		PERFORMANCE Next 12 Months	APPRECIATION Potential 1971-73	INCOME (Yield) Next 12 Months	NORMAL AVERAGE PRICE
'53-67 Median	Current ①	'53-67 Median	Current ①	Stability (30) Growth (95) **B-**		**III**	**III**	**V**	1971-73 Est'd **165** (+30%)
25.5	37.6	1.8%	0.9%	Size, Median Yield, Etc. (2)		AVERAGE (3)	AVERAGE (3)	LOWEST (1)	

CAPITAL STRUCTURE as of 12/31/67
Debt $221.5 mill. Interest $9.2 mill.
Pfd Stock $24.8 mill. Div'd $.74 mill.
247,536 shs. 3% $100 par preference stock each conv. to 1.1 com. shs.
Common Stock 14,583,788 shares as of 3/31/68

	QUARTERLY SALES ($ Millions)				Full
Cal-endar	Mar. 31	June 30	Sept. 30	Dec. 31	Year
1963	147.6	162.4	160.0	178.5	648.5
1964	157.6	163.1	158.4	188.1	667.2
1965	154.1	171.2	170.8	204.3	700.4
1966	201.2	225.3	227.7	260.2	914.4
1967	228.7	260.1	259.1	297.0	1044.9
1968	286.4	298	290	325.6	1200
1969					

	QUARTERLY EARNINGS (per sh.)				Full
Cal-endar	Mar. 31	June 30	Sept. 30	Dec. 31	Year
1963	.42	.58	.65	.77	2.42
1964	.58	.64	.63	1.04	2.89
1965	.49	.69	.61	.82	2.61
1966	.60	.66	.67	1.14	3.07
1967	.41	.65	.64	1.15	2.85
1968	.61	.80	1.09		3.30
1969					

	QUARTERLY DIVIDENDS PAID⑦				Full
Cal-endar	Mar. 31	June 30	Sept. 30	Dec. 31	Year
1963	.25	.25	.25	.25	1.00
1964	.25	.25	.25	.275	1.025
1965	.25	.275	.275	.275	1.10
1966	.275	.275	.275	.275	1.10
1967	.275	.275	.275	.275	1.10
1968	.275				
1969					

Suitability: Honeywell offers participation in the fast-growing commuter industry. This quality issue has advanced some 30% in price during the past three months, and we expect it will perform at least on a par with the market averages in the months ahead. The stock's recent strength has discounted some of its 3- to 5-year appreciation potential, but Honeywell is still a worthwhile holding in this regard.

Major Funds are net buyers. Eaton & Howard Stock Fund and Putnam Investors Fund recently took initial positions of 30,000 and 50,000 shares, respectively. Three others have increased their commitments while the Madison Fund, in contrast, liquidated its 20,000 share position.

Computers turn the profit corner. Honeywell's massive investment in the computer industry has retarded its earnings growth during the past few years. But this investment has begun to pay off and should underwrite rapid profit expansion well into the 1970's. First quarter earnings were up almost 50% to 61c a share. This gain is more impressive in recalling that last year's net was boosted by 13c a share from a sale and leaseback program which was terminated at mid-1967. Honeywell's computer business has developed to the point of current profitability. An expanding line of mainframe and peripheral equipment backed by a strong service organization has firmly entrenched Honeywell in this dynamic industry. We look for the Computer and Communications Group to pace the company's progress for the next several years. Meanwhile, sales of controls for the residential and commercial building market have improved substantially from a year ago. While this trend will be influenced by the availability of mortgage funds over the balance of the year, we estimate the construction market will continue strong. Industrial process controls have been affected by the slowdown in capital spending this year and will not likely show a meaningful improvement by year-end. Finally, Honeywell's Aerospace and Defense business continues strong. Ordnance shipments would be reduced in the event of peace in Vietnam, but increasing Mark 46 contracts, unaffected by Vietnam, would make up part of this decline. On balance, we look for this year's earnings to reach $3.30 a share and perhaps higher even with a reduction of some 20c a share from the prospective surcharge on corporate taxes. R.B.G.

BUSINESS: Honeywell Incorporated is the leading manufacturer of temperature controls for residential and commercial applications, industrial controls such as flow meters, pressure gauges, pyrometers. Also makes photographic equipment, farm controls, medical recording and measuring systems. Military products (31% of sales) include flight controls for manned aircraft, missiles and launching systems, warheads and sonar. Expanding Electronic Data Processing Div. produces full range of computer sizes. Operates more than 40 plants in U.S. and abroad. Since 1957-59, sales have risen 203% (GNP, 72%). Wage costs: about 46% of sales. Employs 69,248. has 35,000 stockholders. Chrmn.: J.H. Binger, Pres.: S.F. Keating, Inc.: Delaware. Address: 2701 Fourth Ave., South Minneapolis, Minnesota 55408.

①-See Explanation of Terms on ①-Excl. $30 mill. subs. debt conv. to p. 937. ⑦-Div'd payment dates: common at $103.25 per share. Mar. 10, June 10, Sept. 10, Dec. 10.

FIGURE 17-1 (c)

Value Line *information about Honeywell Incorporated*

SOURCE *The Value Line Investment Survey*, Arnold Bernhard & Co., May 31, 1968

> [Litton Industries is] engaged in advanced research and develop-
> ment in electronic field and produce and market diversified elec-
> tronic and electromechanical products, including military equipment
> and systems, components, business machines and communicative
> equipment and systems. Major lines are electronic components, sys-
> tems and research for defense (inertial guidance systems, technical
> data processing systems, digital computers, underwater logging equip-
> ment, direction finding antenna systems, advanced· development
> laboratories); business machines (electronic computers, cash registers,
> calculating and adding machines, office equipment); communications
> equipment and systems (sound records, facsimile transmitters and
> receivers, single sideband radio systems, command consoles, airborne
> recorders); precision components (display tubes, magnetrons, klys-
> trons, transformers, direct writing cathode ray tubes, micro-wave
> power assemblies); seismic exploration instruments; and research
> evaluation centers.[9]

Litton manufactures its communication equipment through Wes-
trix, microwave equipment through Autron, recording equipment
through Ma and Svenska, and instrumentation through Western Geophysical. In 1962 it acquired Cole Steel Equipment Company, a manufacturer of office furniture. Ingalls Shipbuilding Corp., which builds
nuclear powered submarines and other craft, was also acquired in 1962.

Litton is not only in electronics but is moving toward automation
of office equipment through Monroe and Cole Calculating. It is represented in the atomic power field through Ingalls Shipbuilding. In
many respects it is not solely an electronics company but handles a
widely diversified line of products in both office and electronic equipment. The sales of the company are divided: 36 percent from business
equipment, 35 percent defense and space, and 29 percent industrial
products. It is truly a conglomerate, since its industrial products division
includes calculators, accounting systems, communication and aircraft
navigation equipment, office copiers, microwave ovens, commercial ships,
nuclear subs, and materials handling equipment.

Texas Instruments

Texas Instruments Incorporated is one of the leading producers of transistors in the United States. The company manufactures, in addition,
electronic systems including radar, sonar, and missile guidance systems,
and semi-conductor devices. It also furnishes geophysical exploration
services. Through a merger with Metals and Controls it entered the
fields of rare metals, thermostatic and electrical controls, and nuclear

9 *Moody's Industrial Manuals* (New York: Moody's Investors Service, Inc., 1963),
   p. 1109.

fuels. Approximately 16 percent of its sales are to the government.

Texas Instruments has seven divisions. The *Products Division* produces silicon and germanium transistors. The *Components Division* develops and makes diodes, rectifiers, capacitors, resistors, and solid-circuit semiconductor networks. The *Apparatus Division* produces and develops electronic and electromechanical components, assemblies, and systems for industrial application and for the United States government. Individual products include control devices, test equipment, recorders, and petroleum instrumentation. Items for the military, used in fields of undersea warfare, missiles, and surveillance, include electro-optical subsystems, radar, microwave equipment, and infrared devices.

The Metals and Controls Division is a wholly owned subsidiary having three product groups. The first is the metallurgical group, which produces composite clad metals, electrical controls, and thermostat metals. The controls group manufactures motor controls and protectors, thermostats, precision switches, and circuit breakers. The materials and energy group, the third product line of the division, manufactures nuclear fuel elements for both military and industrial application.

The fifth division of Texas Instruments, the *Science Services Division,* is composed of three parts: (1) a group of wholly owned geophysical companies, which are known collectively as the *GSI Division* and offer worldwide geophysical exploration services to the petroleum industry; (2) the geoscience department, which concentrates on military applications of geophysics; and (3) the data-processing department, which programs and processes scientific data.

The sixth division is the *Engineering Supply Company.* It distributes electronic industrial and geophysical supplies principally in the southwestern United States. The seventh division is the *International Division*, which handles all overseas sales. Texas Instruments operates in a highly competitive field and employed more than 38,000 people in 1968.

Honeywell Incorporated

Honeywell Incorporated is the leading manufacturer of temperature controls and systems for residential and commercial applications. It makes industrial controls such as pressure gauges and pyrometers, as well as other products such as photographic equipment, flow controls, and medical recording and measuring systems.[10] The company markets electronic data-processing systems, which should become more important to future growth, and has both medium- and large-scale computers. Honeywell has also developed systems for the automation of production lines, and since automation benefits industry, Honeywell should share

10 "Electronics," *The Value Line Investment Survey,* May 31, 1968, p. 957.

in industry's growth.[11] In short, it produces residential, commercial, and industrial controls, products for aircraft, spacecraft, and missiles, specialized ordinance systems, electronic data-processing systems, instrumentation for industry and science, semiconductor products, and photographic products. Honeywell operates more than 40 plants in the United States and abroad. The company employed over 69,000 men and women in 1968.

Summary of Position of the Three Companies

The relative competitive position of the companies is summarized in Table 17–16. Litton is the largest of the three companies that we are considering, and the table reflects its strong relative position in the market. Litton has demonstrated the most rapid growth of sales in the past, and it has also had the greatest stability of sales of the three. The acquisition program is most likely to continue, and based upon the expected growth of the industry and the past growth of Litton, we can expect a continued growth of Litton at a rate faster than that of Texas Instruments or Honeywell, both of which have demonstrated excellent market growth potential in recent months.

Obviously, the comments we make about the competitive position of a company are relative and apply only at a given time. We must constantly reexamine the competitive position of each company to be aware of change. A lessening in demand for military and industrial application of electronic equipment, automation devices, and data-processing systems because of changes in the missile or space programs or because of industrial changes would have a strong impact upon each of these companies. At that time we would be required to reassess the competitive position of each company. Litton had a serious setback in its earnings in 1967 and early 1968. The assumption made in the analysis was that Litton would resume its growth because of the high quality of management and information that solutions to its problems had been reached.

Earnings and Profitability

The growth of adjusted earnings and cash flow for Litton, Texas Instruments, and Honeywell has been substantial. Except for 1968, Litton had a consistent and stable growth rate of earnings and cash flow as seen in Table 17–6. Texas Instruments' earnings have increased but have been less stable. Both Honeywell and Texas Instruments have had erratic earnings. Texas Instruments reached a peak of earnings in 1960 and then declined, reached another peak in 1966, and declined again. The 1960 earnings decline was brought about by a severe drop in the price of transistors that resulted from increased foreign competi-

11 Standard & Poor's *Industry Surveys—Electronics, Electrical,* December 14, 1967, pp. E8 to E27.

TABLE 17–6

Adjusted earnings and cash flow per share in dollars for Litton Industries, Texas Instruments, and Honeywell Incorporated

	Litton		Texas Instruments		Honeywell Incorporated	
YEAR	ADJUSTED EARNINGS PER SHARE	CASH FLOW PER SHARE	ADJUSTED EARNINGS PER SHARE	CASH FLOW PER SHARE	ADJUSTED EARNINGS PER SHARE	CASH FLOW PER SHARE
1968 E	1.80	2.20	2.65	6.35	3.30	8.25
1967	2.54	3.79	2.10	5.54	2.85	6.97
1966	2.15	3.90	3.14	5.87	3.07	6.38
1965	1.61	2.64	2.46	4.37	2.61	5.31
1964	1.25	1.99	1.80	3.20	2.89	5.11
1963	1.01	1.51	1.21	2.55	2.42	4.16
1962	.72	1.10	.85	2.11	1.86	3.42
1961	.48	.73	.94	2.21	1.74	2.86
1960	.36	.55	1.56	2.68	1.87	2.72
1959	.27	.41	1.44	2.27	2.10	2.86
1958	.21	.34	.74	1.34	1.62	2.27
1957	.15	.21	.44	.89	1.54	2.09

SOURCE: Figure 17–1.

tion. Virtually overnight the price of transistors was cut in half. The volume of production has now increased, and with mass-production economies the earnings of Texas Instruments should improve. Honeywell experienced a similar drop in 1960 and 1961, but its earnings began to improve in 1962. The 1967 drop for both companies was due to a change in the market for products.

The total cash flow of Texas Instruments and Honeywell is substantially greater than that of Litton. However, Litton has experienced the greatest growth per share of cash flow as well as the greatest stability of cash flow and earnings per share, except for 1968. The sales growth of Litton and the stability of its profit margin has allowed the company to increase its earnings substantially. Based upon the amount of past profit margin, earning power, and net income as a percent of sales as presented in Table 17–7, we would have to rate Texas Instruments first, Honeywell second, and Litton third. Based upon stability alone, we would rank Litton first, Honeywell second, and Texas Instruments third. These relationships are summarized in Table 17–16 on p. 546.

Future Earnings

A forecast of earnings for each company is presented in Table 17–8. Two methods were used to estimate future earnings per share. First, the trend of earnings method was used, which simply extended the trend of earnings of each company based upon past performance. Chart

TABLE 17–7

Profit margin, earning power, and net income
as a percent of sales for Litton Industries, Texas
Instruments, and Honeywell Incorporated
(in percent)

	Profit Margin			Earning Power			Net Income as a Percent of Sales		
YEAR	LITTON	T. I.	HONEY-WELL	LITTON	T. I.	HONEY-WELL	LITTON	T. I.	HONEY-WELL
1968 E	8.5	15.0	15.0	—	—	—	2.4	4.3	3.3
1967	10.5	13.8	14.2	—	—	—	3.8	4.0	4.0
1966	11.3	16.3	15.6	14.9	17.2	12.6	4.8	5.8	5.0
1965	10.9	15.1	15.2	13.0	17.3	12.2	4.3	5.7	5.3
1964	11.4	14.9	17.0	14.9	19.2	16.6	4.4	5.5	6.2
1963	10.9	13.9	15.3	14.0	16.1	16.5	4.2	4.4	5.3
1962	10.7	11.6	13.8	12.7	11.7	15.0	4.1	3.6	4.5
1961	10.8	13.8	14.8	12.8	15.2	14.4	4.1	4.1	5.3
1960	10.6	17.1	16.4	14.1	24.6	17.8	4.0	6.7	6.2
1959	11.1	19.0	19.5	12.9	27.2	15.8	4.8	7.3	7.7
1958	11.9	19.8	17.7	12.1	24.0	13.4	4.4	6.5	6.9
1957	14.6	16.7	17.0	19.2	19.8	13.8	6.5	5.6	6.6

SOURCE: Standard & Poor's *Industry Survey—Electronics, Electrical,* December 21, 1967, pp. E30 and E31; Figure 17–1; and *Moody's Industrial Manual,* 1967, pp. 912, 2181, 3076.

17–1, which provided the estimates in Table 17–8, presents these relationships. The second method was the projection of the line of average relationship between company sales and earnings per share. These forecasts appear in Chart 17–2 and were then recorded in Table 17–8. These estimates were then averaged to provide an estimate of future earnings. Both estimates were then balanced against the profits that would result from the expected future sales of the company. It was assumed that Honeywell's sales would grow at 15 percent, Litton's at 14 percent, and Texas Instruments' at 12 percent, based upon a qualitative judgment of expectations of each company in a competitive industry. The estimate of growth of sales will vary according to the judgment of the analyst.

The forecasts of earnings indicated that Litton would have a substantial growth of earnings between 1968 and 1973 but not at as great a rate as in the past decade. From past performance we can expect greater stability of earnings from Litton than from the other two companies. Texas Instruments was expected to have an above-average increase in earnings between 1968 and 1973, and earnings were expected to be more stable in the future. The earnings of Honeywell were expected to be strong, and the rate of growth greater than Litton's or Texas Instruments'. The relative position of each company with respect to future earnings is presented in Table 17–16 on p. 546.

TABLE 17-8

Forecast of earnings of Litton Industries, Texas Instruments, and Honeywell Inc. (in dollars)

	Litton Industries				Texas Instruments				Honeywell Inc.			
YEAR	TREND OF EARNINGS METHOD[a]	SALES TO EARNINGS RELATIONSHIP[b]	AVERAGE EARNINGS	DIVIDENDS (IN STOCK)	TREND OF EARNINGS METHOD[a]	SALES TO EARNINGS RELATIONSHIP[b]	AVERAGE EARNINGS	DIVIDENDS[c]	TREND OF EARNINGS METHOD[a]	SALES TO EARNINGS RELATIONSHIP[b]	AVERAGE EARNINGS	DIVIDENDS[d]
1973	5.30	5.50	5.40	2 1/2%	6.50	6.05	6.27	1.60	4.80	6.50	5.75	1.90
1972	4.50	4.80	4.65	2 1/2%	5.50	5.20	5.35	1.35	4.50	5.75	5.12	1.70
1971	3.80	4.20	4.00	2 1/2%	4.70	4.60	4.65	1.15	4.10	5.10	4.60	1.50
1970	3.20	3.75	3.48	2 1/2%	4.10	4.15	4.12	1.00	3.80	4.50	4.15	1.35
1969	2.80	3.30	3.05	2 1/2%	3.40	3.70	3.55	.80	3.60	4.10	3.85	1.10

[a] See Chart 17-1.
[b] See Chart 17-2.
[c] Based upon a 25 percent payout expected for 1970 to 1973 and estimated 1969.
[d] Based upon a 33 percent payout.

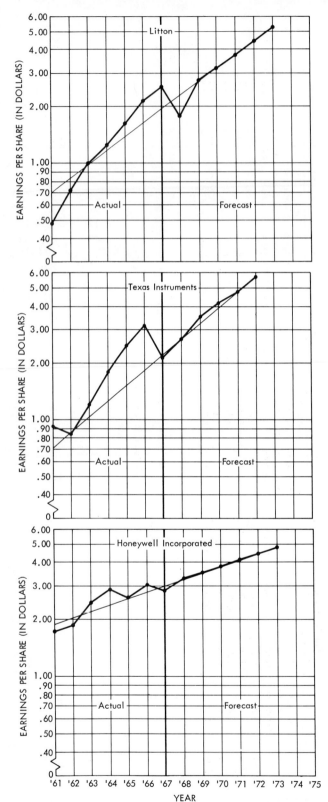

Chart 17–1

Forecast of earnings per share of
Litton, Texas Instruments, and
Honeywell, 1968–1973

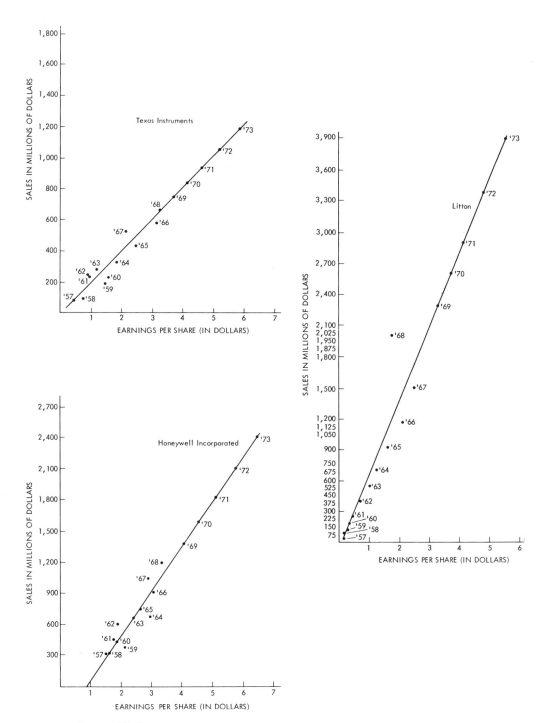

CHART 17–2

Line of average relationship between sales and earnings for Litton, Texas Instruments, and Honeywell

TABLE 17-9

*Operating ratio, sales and net income
per employee, sales and net income per
dollar of plant, and capital expenditure as
a percent of plant for Litton Industries, Texas
Instruments, and Honeywell, Incorporated*

COMPANY	OPERATING RATIO PERCENT			SALES PER EMPLOYEE $			EARNINGS PER EMPLOYEE $			SALES PER $ OF NET PLANT			EARNINGS PER $ OF NET PLANT			CAPITAL EXPENDITURE AS A PERCENT OF GROSS PLANT		
	'57	'61	'66	'57[a]	'61[a]	'66[b]	'57[a]	'61[a]	'66[b]	'57	'61	'66	'57	'61	'66	'57	'61	'66
Litton Industries	85	89	91	1217	10870	14450	79	481	734	5.96	6.60	6.99	.90	.29	.33	25	26	18
Texas Instruments	83	86	89	3860	13364	14950	216	535	876	4.46	5.18	4.67	.25	.21	.27	34	16	35
Honeywell, Inc.	83	85	90	6795	9795	14230	448	509	706	5.11	3.72	3.15	.34	.19	.16	28	24	21

[a] 1962 Employees
[b] 1966 Employees

SOURCES: Standard & Poor's *Investment Survey—Electronics, Electrical,* July 18, 1963, p. E30; December 14, 1967, p. E29; and *Moody's Industrial Manual,* Moody's Investors Service, New York, 1963, pp. 1108 and 1169; June, 1967, pp. 3075, 3076, 2180, 911, and 912.

Operating Capacity and Efficiency

Each of the three companies has experienced an increase in its operating ratios, which once again reflects a basic problem of not only the electronics industry but almost all industry—that of decreasing profit margins or increasing operating costs. Honeywell had experienced the biggest increase in its operating ratio. Sales and earnings per employee were better for Texas Instruments than the other two companies, whereas Litton had the greatest sales and earnings per dollar of plant investment. Texas Instruments had the highest capital expenditures per dollar of plant in 1966.

The evidence presented for these companies is somewhat conflicting. This, of course, makes it difficult to reach a decision. In terms of operating efficiency, Honeywell and Texas Instruments are superior to Litton Industries. In terms of employee productivity, we would list Texas Instruments first, Litton second, and then Honeywell, in 1966. When we consider earnings to plant, we would consider Litton as being in first place relative to the other companies. (The relationships are summarized in Table 17–16.) Texas Instruments is best on the basis of 1966 capital expenditures as a percentage of gross plant, followed by Honeywell and Litton.

The Financial Position of the Companies

The financial liquidity and current financial position of the three companies can be assessed by examining the data in Table 17–10. Litton, based on an analysis of its current assets and current ratio, is in the most liquid position. Both Texas Instruments and Honeywell are in a good current financial position but somewhat less liquid than Litton. The cash position of Litton is weak by comparison, and its DSO ratio is high. Texas Instruments had a lower DSO ratio and better net sales to inventory and sales to working capital ratios than either of the other two. In spite of the relative position of one company to the other, each was in a relatively good financial position. We would conclude that the overall liquidity of each company was adequate, that Litton's short-term current position had weakened between 1957 and 1962 but had improved slightly in 1966. Litton's decrease in DSO might be a reflection of a change in credit terms, or it might mirror a better collection of receivables; its current financial position is on the borderline of conventional accounting limits. It is obvious that this is a management policy designed to maximize utilization of cash.

Long-Term Financing

The long-term financial position of the three companies was adequate, based on the capital structure and debt analysis presented in Tables 17–11 and 17–12. Litton Industries had the greatest percentage of debt

TABLE 17–10

Current financial analysis of Litton Industries,
Texas Instruments, and Honeywell Incorporated

TYPE OF ANALYSIS	Litton Industries			Texas Instruments			Honeywell Incorporated		
	1957	1962	1966	1957	1962	1966	1957	1962	1966
Current ratio	2.7:1	2.4:1	2.3:1	2:1	2.4:1	2.3:1	3.3:1	2.8:1	2.1:1
Acid test ratio	1.3:1	1.4:1	1.5:1	1.7:1	1.5:1	8:1	1.5:1	1.4:1	1.3:1
Cash as a percent of current assets	11	6.4	7.	25.	31	34	8	6.	11
Receivables as a percent of current assets	36	51	47	55	40	38	40	44	41
Inventories as a percent of current assets	45	41	45	38	30	32	52	49	48
Other current assets as a percent of current assets	11	3	1	20	1		1	1	
Credit sales to days' sales outstanding (DSO)	51	83	73	66	51	60	73	70	74
Net sales to inventory	5.6:1	5.4:1	5:1	8:1	8:1	7:1	3.6:1	4.7:1	4.1:1
Net sales to working capital	4.2:1	3.5:1	3.7:1	6:1	4.5:1	4:1	2.7:1	3.6:1	3.9:1

SOURCE: Based upon data obtained from *Moody's Industrial Manual,* Moody's Investors Service, New York, 1963, pp. 1108tt, 516EE, and 1169tt; and June 1967, pp. 912, 913, 2179, 2180, 2181, 3075, and 3076.

TABLE 17–11

Capital structure composition of Litton Industries, Texas Instruments, and Honeywell Incorporated

	1957		1962		1966	
	DOLLARS IN THOUSANDS	PERCENT OF TOTAL	DOLLARS IN THOUSANDS	PERCENT OF TOTAL	DOLLARS IN THOUSANDS	PERCENT OF TOTAL
LITTON INDUSTRIES						
Long-term debt	$ 5,000	40.0	$ 60,239	37.0	$203,049	39.7
Preferred stock	75	0.1	1,200	0.5	9,973	1.9
Common stock	119	0.9	4,800	3.0	20,471	3.9
Capital surplus	4,200	33.0	47,367	29.3	153,059	30.0
Retained earnings	3,300	26.0	49,000	30.2	124,530	24.5
Total	$ 12,694	100.0	$162,606	100.0	$511,082	100.0
TEXAS INSTRUMENTS						
Long-term debt	$ 7,000	26.1	$ 7,400	7.3	$ 51,935	19.3
Preferred stock	–	–	3,217	3.2	–	–
Common stock	3,200	12.0	3,945	3.9	10,834	4.1
Capital surplus	6,200	23.3	9,400	9.3	64,578	23.9
Retained earnings	10,100	38.6	77,000	76.3	141,908	52.7
Total	$ 26,500	100.0	$100,962	100.0	$269,255	100.0
HONEYWELL INC.						
Long-term debt	$ 44,000	22.0	$ 65,400	20.9	$161,095	31.1
Preferred stock	–	–	25,000	8.0	25,000	4.8
Common stock	10,000	5.0	10,536	3.4	21,774	4.2
Capital surplus	72,000	36.0	76,605	24.4	75,180	14.5
Retained earnings	74,000	37.0	135,833	43.3	234,068	45.5
Total	$200,000	100.0	$313,374	100.0	$517,117	100.0

SOURCE: *Moody's Industrial Manual*, Moody's Investors Service, New York, 1963, pp. 1109, 517, and 1170 and June, 1967, pp. 912, 2181 and 3075.

TABLE 17–12

Long-term debt analysis and return on capital for
Litton Industries, Texas Instruments, and
Honeywell Incorporated

Debt Limits	Litton Industries			Texas Instruments			Honeywell Inc.		
	1957	1962	1966	1957	1962	1966	1957	1962	1966
Number of times fixed charges earned	9	6	11	13	14	23	10	8	9
Number of times fixed and contingent charges earned	9	5	8	9	12	23	10	6	8
Total debt to net worth %	117	136	129	92	10	75	50	63	107
Long-term debt to fixed assets %	89	78	121	46	17	42	70	98	46
Long-term debt to working capital %	70	53	63	63	14	37	33	37	56
Rate of return on equity %	23	16	12	19	10	16	14	12	14
Rate of return on capital %	16	10	13	16	10	14	12	10	11

SOURCE: *Moody's Industrial Manual*, Moody's Investors Service, New York, 1963, pp. 1109, 517, 1170; and June, 1967, pp. 912, 2180, and 3075.

in its capital structure, and debt to net worth and debt to fixed assets ratios were high. The large amount of debt gave it the advantage of a low-cost capital structure with a great deal of financial leverage. With a growth in sales, the leverage in Litton's capital structure should be beneficial; at the same time we must realize that the debt is convertible debt that has the effect of diluting future earnings per share. Texas Instruments had the best rate of return on equity and total capital. Honeywell was in second place with its 14 percent return on equity but had the lowest rate of return on total capital in 1966, as seen in Table 17–12. Litton was second in rate of return on total capital in 1966 but the rate of return has tended to decrease.

Texas Instruments has grown through equity funds and debt. The long-term debt in the capital structure represents a modest amount, but has fluctuated between 10 and 92 percent of debt to net worth. Texas Instruments' debt to net worth and working capital are reasonable. Honeywell does not have a great deal of debt in its capital structure, and the amount has been decreasing. The times charges earned ratios for all the companies were satisfactory, with Texas Instruments the best. Overall, Texas Instruments has the most conservative capital structure of the three companies for a firm engaged in a highly competitive and changing industry. Future financing for Litton will be obtained from equity funds or internal sources. Based upon Litton's cash position, the stock dividends will most likely continue in the future. The capital structure and debt relationship are summarized in Table 17–16.

The Management

The aggressive manner in which Litton Industries and Texas Instruments have grown suggests a competency of management. Litton, the company with the greatest growth in sales, began in 1954 and in less than a decade was an industrial giant with a well-diversified product mix in the electronic-atomic and office equipment industry, looking forward to $3.5 billion in sales by 1975. From its very beginning it was technically and scientifically oriented, from its engineers to its managers. Its sales growth and profits and its research and development expenditures reflect a quality of management. In 1961 Litton spent 20 percent of its sales on research and development. Texas Instruments spent 15 percent on research and development in the same year. This 15 to 20 percent of sales, a large expenditure for research, has continued as a company policy.

The strength of Litton's experienced management is in its ability to expand through judicious mergers and to put together an enterprise that is well diversified to meet competition in the industry. In 1967 and 1968 the company had difficulties in several divisions but appeared to have them under control by the fall of 1968, and management expected a resumption of earnings growth.

Litton's management has demonstrated its ability to grow internally and externally and to change to meet the changing demands placed upon its business. This management has been led by Charles "Tex" Thornton and Roy L. Ash. Thornton put the company together from scratch in 1954; by 1963 it was the 100th largest company in the United States. He was responsible for the management reorganization at Ford after World War II and helped build Hughes Aircraft from $112 to $200 million in sales. He uses scientific techniques and is considered by some to be the best corporate executive in the United States.

Roy L. Ash, 49, president of Litton, was educated at Harvard and graduated in 1947. In 1948 Ash was with the Bank of America, and from 1949 to 1953 he was chief financial officer of Hughes Aircraft Company. He helped Mr. Thornton establish Litton in 1954. From 1953 to 1958 he was a vice-president of Litton, became executive vice-president in 1958, and president in 1961. Both Thornton and Ash and the major managers of Litton have an exceptional talent for solving temporary setbacks and producing the right product at the right time.

Texas Instruments

Texas Instruments is managed under the leadership of P. E. Haggerty. Haggerty received his B.S. in electrical engineering from Marquette University in 1936, and holds several honorary law degrees from various universities, including Marquette. He was the assistant manager of the Badger Carton Company in Milwaukee from 1935 to 1942, and general manager of the Laboratory and Manufacturing Division of Texas Instruments from 1945 until 1950. In 1950 he became the executive vice-president of the company, and in 1958 the president and a director.

Texas Instruments has been a dynamically growing firm with an excellent management. It has undergone a complete reorganization of its divisional structure and has strengthened its competitive position. Much of the success of Texas Instruments depends upon the price structure and product development. The company spends about 15 percent on R&D, has outstanding capabilities in solid state technology, and has had excellent results in improving production and testing methods. New products have resulted from these expenditures. Several developments of new businesses were mentioned in the 1968 annual report.

> Among the 105 integrated circuits introduced by TI during 1968 were 29 in a new line of high-speed Emitter-Coupled Logic (ECL) digital circuits. They are particularly important because they are being designed into the ultra-fast, next-generation computers. Linear integrated circuits also grew in importance as sense amplifiers for computer applications.
>
> More than a dozen types of Metal Oxide Semiconductor (MOS) integrated circuits were produced on a pilot-line basis in 1968. Facilities to make them in large volume will be completed in the Houston plant in the first quarter of 1969. Although these circuits currently operate slower than bipolar types such as TTL, they are well-suited for such human-operated applications as microfilm readers and stock market displays.
>
> Because more MOS circuits can be built on a single silicon slice, with fewer process steps, the cost of each circuit is lower than bipolar circuits. Their lower cost and high circuit density make MOS circuits desirable for certain computer memory applications.
>
> A TI computer-aided design technique has reduced the normal design cycle for MOS circuits by 50%. This makes it feasible to provide custom designs faster and at less cost. . . .
>
> Control products gained a greater share of the U.S. electrical appliance and climate control markets in 1968 with established lines of thermostats, relays, and thermal overload protectors. In the international market, sales were especially strong in Holland, Italy, Canada, and Latin America.
>
> A new market opened up in the U.S. for thermal controls de-

signed to protect fluorescent lamp ballasts. New industry safety standards specify that ballasts now must be made with such devices pre-set to cut off the current if the unit overheats. TI has expanded capacity to produce millions of these protectors yearly.

TI in 1968 further penetrated a number of major markets for precision controls, including aerospace, telecommunications, data processing, and computer peripheral equipment. For instance, TI circuit breakers and other electrical controls are in all three new large "air bus" commercial aircraft. The Apollo 8 spacecraft contained more than 300 TI precision switches and numerous semiconductor components.

Manufacturing capabilities for control products were expanded during 1968, including the occupancy of a major portion of a new 185,000-sq. ft. building on the Attleboro site.[12]

The biggest question facing Texas Instruments is whether costs can be reduced in the face of declining prices to maintain earnings and future profitability. Up to 1968, management has appeared capable of doing this.

Honeywell Incorporated

James Binger is the president of Honeywell. He received his A.B. from Yale University in 1938 and his LL.D. from the University of Minnesota in 1941. Binger was also admitted to the bar in that year, and from 1941 until 1943 he practiced law. He joined Minneapolis-Honeywell in 1943. From 1945 to 1946 he was assistant secretary, in 1946 he became assistant vice-president, and in 1950 general manager and vice-president of the Valve Division. He was appointed a company vice-president in 1952, moved on to occupy a director's seat in 1959, and became president in 1961.

Honeywell had "taken off," said *Value Line*.[13] Sales and earnings advanced sharply, and Honeywell undertook a drive to continue the increase in sales and profit. Its depreciation charges have doubled in recent years, and it is reaching the profit point on several new products. The company entered the computer field in 1955 and is beginning to show signs of reaping the rewards. The success of the computer program is likely to help Honeywell.

Summary of Three Companies' Management

All the companies have been able to expand sales. None has any unusual labor problems. All except Honeywell have had good government relations. Honeywell had been indicted under the Sherman Anti-Trust Act for its position in the pneumatic temperature control industry, but

---

12 Texas Instruments, *Annual Report*, 1968, pp. 7 and 9.
13 *The Value Line Investment Survey*, September 6, 1961, p. 721.

the results of this action did not have a serious effect on the company's growth. Led by Litton and Texas Instruments, the companies employ scientific techniques. Each has demonstrated ability to develop new products, and to build employee, community, and stockholder goodwill. Each management has shown some ability to solve the cyclical and secular problems of change and growth. In this respect Litton and Texas Instruments appear slightly superior to Honeywell, but this could change with the modest difference between the companies. The relative position of the management of each company is summarized in Table 17–16.

Price, Price-Earnings Ratio, and Market Action

The qualities of the companies have been fairly well determined, and we know what earnings we can expect from each company in the future. In an attempt to obtain a satisfactory investment we have considered many qualitative factors. We examined the competitive position of the companies, the earnings and profitability ratios, the operating characteristics of each company, and their financial position, and we attempted to assess the abilities of management as indicated by their achievements and goals.

Now we must consider whether the price we must pay for the stock will provide us with a satisfactory investment, based upon the P/E ratio, the trend of the market price, and the current price level and market action. The price range and P/E ratios for the companies appear in Table 17–13. All the companies have sold at relatively high P/E ratios compared to the market as a whole. Texas Instruments had the highest current P/E ratio and the highest average P/E ratio. These high P/E ratios reflect a certain degree of confidence in the future earnings growth of these companies; they are not unrealistic. The price range of the companies has been wide, and the price basically unstable. Table 17–13 reflects this price fluctuation. The market price of stock in 1968 was selling at reasonable market levels compared to the past levels.

The long-term market action for Litton has been superior to the market and to Honeywell and Texas Instruments, as can be seen in Figure 17–2. The market action of Honeywell has been superior to Texas Instruments over the long term. The short-range market action has been much better for Honeywell, but the increased price has taken away yield based upon market prices. Texas Instruments' market action was weak and Litton appeared to be improving in August of 1968.

Table 17–14 provides the historic pattern of dividends and yields for the three companies. Litton has consistently paid a 2 1/2 percent stock dividend. Texas Instruments pays a small cash dividend of $.20

TABLE 17-13

Price range and price-earnings ratios for Litton Industries, Texas Instruments, Honeywell, Inc. (prices in dollars and eights)

	Litton Industries			Texas Instruments			Honeywell Incorporated		
YEAR	HIGH	LOW	AVERAGE P/E RATIO	HIGH	LOW	AVERAGE P/E RATIO	HIGH	LOW	AVERAGE P/E RATIO
1968	104.6	62.0	31.0	114.7	86.2	37.9	139.6	89.3	34.7
1967	120.3	79.4	27.0	144.6	99.4	42.0	117.7	63.4	33.0
1966	84.3	55.2	30.5	139.6	81.6	33.5	96.0	53.4	24.4
1965	73.5	35.3	33.3	98.4	46.5	29.5	79.7	58.2	26.5
1964	37.3	26.7	24.8	47.3	30.0	21.4	74.3	57.5	22.8
1963	39.3	26.0	31.5	38.7	22.6	25.6	75.1	42.2	24.3
1962	33.5	17.0	34.1	50.1	19.5	34.6	66.5	35.0	27.3
1961	35.6	18.4	43.5	82.5	38.0	66.1	85.3	61.7	42.4
1960	20.3	12.2	39.9	102.4	59.2	50.6	89.3	61.7	40.5
1959	15.7	9.5	34.5	77.3	24.4	34.9	75.0	55.6	31.1
1958	9.5	3.6	30.8	34.3	10.5	30.6	63.0	38.0	31.3
1957	5.5	3.0	28.4	12.5	6.2	21.3	65.4	36.6	33.3
Price August 9, 1968	70.5			92.2			117.5		
Current P/E ratio	39.2			34.8			35.6		
12-year average (1957–62)	32.5			35.9			31.0		

SOURCE: Standard & Poor's *Industry Survey—Electronics, Electrical, December* 14, 1967, pp. E34, 36, 37; and Standard & Poor's *Stock Guide, March,* 1968, p. 128, 106, 210.

per share per quarter. Honeywell has paid a cash dividend for many years and paid a $1.10 dividend in 1968. The yield on all these companies was low because they were basically growth companies. In consideration of the yield to maturity concept and capital gains, the

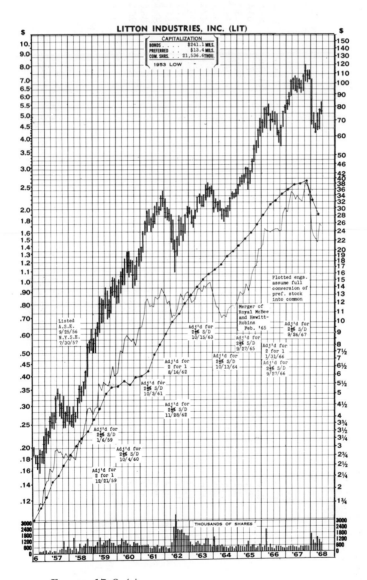

FIGURE 17–2 (a)

Long-term market action of Litton

SOURCE *3-Trend Cycli-Graphs,* Securities Research Co.

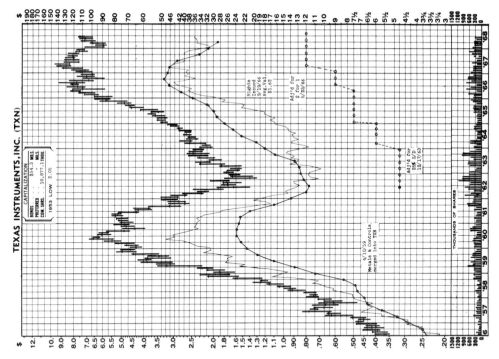

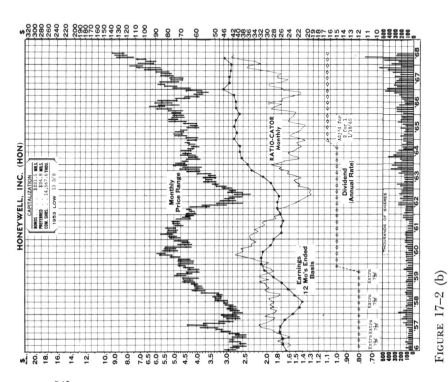

FIGURE 17–2 (b)

FIGURE 17–2 (c)

Long-term market action of Honeywell and Texas Instruments

SOURCE 3-Trend Cycli-Graphs, Securities Research Co.

TABLE 17–14

Dividends and current yields for Litton Industries,
Texas Instruments, Honeywell, Incorporated

YEAR	Litton Industries		Texas Instruments		Honeywell Incorporated	
	DIVIDEND	CURRENT YIELD	DIVIDEND	CURRENT YIELD	DIVIDEND	CURRENT YIELD
1968	2.5%	Stock	$.80	.9%	$1.10	1.0%
1967	2.5%	Stock	.75	.9%	1.10	1.2%
1966	2.5%	Stock	.55	.6%	1.10	1.6%
1965	2.5%	Stock	.50	.8%	1.10	1.6%
1964	2.5%	Stock	.40	1.1%	1.025	1.6%
1963	2.5%	Stock	.32	1.1%	1.00	1.8%
1962	2.5%	Stock	.24	.8%	1.00	2.1%
1961	2.5%	Stock	nil	—	1.00	1.4%
1960	2.5%	Stock	nil	—	1.00	1.4%
1959	2.5%	Stock	nil	—	.925	1.4%
1958	nil	—	nil	—	.875	1.9%
1957	nil	—	nil—	—	.875	1.9%

SOURCE: Standard & Poor's *Industry Survey—Electronics, Electrical*, December 14, 1967, pp. E35 and E36; and Standard & Poor's *Stock Guide*, March, 1968, p. 128, 106, 210.

possible rewards are impressive. Table 17–15 presents the calculations of the yields for the 5-year forecasted period. The conservative estimates of earnings provided in Table 17–8 and a conservative dividend payout ratio and P/E ratio were used to estimate yield to maturity. The discount rate was then applied to the expected future income stream and the present value was established. That rate that equalized the present value of the income stream with the current market price of the stock was the yield to maturity. The approximate yield was 23 percent for Litton, 21 percent for Texas Instruments, and 10 percent for Honeywell. These relationships are summarized in Table 17–16.

The Decision

Based upon this analysis at the time considered, we would decide to buy Texas Instruments, Litton, or Honeywell in that order. Each offered the expectation of a satisfactory yield, size, growth, and stability as well. Texas Instruments would be the author's first choice, followed by Litton, in view of the expectation that the excellent management of Litton would be able to continue the past growth even with a reduced rate of growth and some fundamental problems. What would you have decided?

A Recapitulation of a Previous Decision

In the first edition of this book, the decision was to buy Litton at 77 in October, 1963, since it offered the expectation of a yield of between 10 and 12 percent. In the five-year period since then, the stock split

2 for 1 and has paid a 2 1/2 percent stock dividend in each year; one share in 1963 is now equal to approximately 2.26 shares at a price of 70, as of August 9, 1968, and each $77 invested originally was worth approximately $158 on that date. The yield to maturity actually earned was between 15 and 16 percent. The original decision turned out quite well for the investor who followed the direction of the analysis

TABLE 17–15

Estimated yield to maturity for Litton Industries,
Texas Instruments, and Honeywell Incorporated,
based upon forecasted earnings, dividends,
and price, 1969–1973

Litton Industries

YEAR	RETURN OF CAPITAL	DIVIDENDS	TOTAL	PRESENT VALUE AT 22%	PRESENT VALUE AT 24%
1969		2½% Stk			
1970		2½% Stk			
1971		2½% Stk			
1972		2½% Stk			
1973	$198.32[a]	2½% Stk	$198.32	$ 73.39	$67.63
Total Present Value				$ 73.39	$67.63
Market Price 8/9/68				70.625	
Approximate Yield to Maturity				23%	

Texas Instruments

YEAR	RETURN OF CAPITAL	DIVIDENDS[b]	TOTAL	PRESENT VALUE AT 20%	PRESENT VALUE AT 22%
1969		$ .80	$ .80	$ .67	$ .66
1970		1.00	1.00	.69	.67
1971		1.15	1.15	.91	.63
1972		1.35	1.35	.65	.61
1973	$225.10[c]	1.60	226.70	$ 91.13	$83.88
Total Present Value				$ 94.05	$86.45
Purchase Price 8/9/68				$92.25	
Approximate Yield to Maturity				21%	

Honeywell Incorporated

YEAR	RETURN OF CAPITAL	DIVIDENDS[c]	TOTAL	PRESENT VALUE AT 10%
Total Present Value				$116.28
1969		$1.10	$1.10	$ 1.00
1970		1.35	1.35	1.12
1971		1.50	1.50	1.13
1972		1.70	1.70	1.16
1973	$178.25	1.90	1.90	$111.87
Total Present Value				$116.28
Purchase Price 8/9/68				$117.625
Approximate Yield to Maturity				10%

[a] Based upon a 12 year average P/E ratio of 32.5 and a 2½% compound dividend that results in 1.13 shares owned in 1973 and earnings of $5.40 per share.

[b] Table 17–8.

[c] Based upon a P/E ratio of 35.9 and estimated 1973 earnings of $6.27.

TABLE 17–16

Summary of relative rank of comparative investment analysis for Litton Industries, Texas Instruments, and Honeywell Inc.

	LITTON INDUSTRIES	TEXAS INSTRUMENTS	HONEYWELL INC.
Competitive Position of Company:			
Size in industry	1	3	2
Growth of sales	1	2	3
Stability of sales	1	3	2
Future growth of sales	1	3	2
Product diversification	1	3	2
Earnings and Profitability:			
Past earnings:			
Amount per share	3	2	1
Rate of growth	1	3	2
Stability	1	3	2
Profitability:			
Rate earned on common equity	3	1	2
Rate earned on total capital	2	1	3
Profit margin (1968)	3	1	2
Earning power (1968)	2	1	3
Net income to sales (1968)	3	1	2
Stability	1	3	2
Future earnings:			
Growth	2	3	1
Stability	1	3	2
Operating characteristics:			
Operating capacity	1	2	3
Operating rate	2	2	1
Growth of plant	1	2	3
Operating ratio (lowest)	3	1	2
Operating Efficiency:			
Sales per dollar of plant	1	2	3
Sales per employee	2	1	3
Earnings per employee	2	1	3
Earnings per dollar of plant	1	2	3
Capital Expenditures	3	1	2
Current Financial Analysis:			
Current ratio (highest)	1	1	1
Acid test ratio (highest)	1	3	2
Composition of current assets (greatest percent cash)	3	1	2
DSO (lowest ranked first)	2	1	3
Net sales to inventory (highest ranked first)	2	1	3
Net sales to working capital (highest ranked first)	3	1	2
Debt Limits:			
Time fixed charges earned	2	1	3
Times fixed & contingent charges earned	2	1	2
Total debt to net worth (smallest)	3	1	2
Long-term debt to fixed assets (lowest)	3	1	2
Long-term debt to working capital (lowest)	3	1	2
Management:			
Ability to maintain competitive position	2	1	3
Ability to expand	1	2	3

TABLE 17–16 *(continued)*

	LITTON INDUSTRIES	TEXAS INSTRUMENTS	HONEYWELL INC.
Ability to maintain profit margin	3	1	2
Ability to maintain efficient production	3	1	2
Ability to finance growth	1	2	3
Ability to meet secular and cyclical change	2	1	2
Stockholder, employee, and community relations	2	1	2
Expenditures on R&D	1	2	3
Product development	2	1	1
Overall capabilities	2	2	1
Price and Price/Earnings Ratio:			
Price range stability	2	3	1
P/E ratio	2	2	1
Market action	2	3	1
Current yield	2½% Stock	.9%	1.0
Yield to maturity	23%	21%	10%

and bought the stock. An investment of $83 dollars in Texas Instruments in 1963 would have been worth $231 five years later. The yield for the period was over 22 percent without dividends, substantially more than with Litton. In the original analysis, Texas Instruments was expected to earn between 14 and 16 percent, higher than that expected from Litton. An investment of $119 in Honeywell in 1963 was worth $236 per share in 1968, a yield of 14 percent.

The original analysis erred in the amount of the return, estimating 14 to 16 percent for Texas Instruments, 10 to 12 percent for Litton, and 4 to 6 percent for Honeywell, as compared with the actual yields as shown above. The companies were ranked properly and the investment decision was satisfactory, but the magnitudes were wrong. This is not bad, considering that nothing was changed in the analysis for the five-year period.

Conclusion

The comparative analysis allowed us to come to a logical conclusion and decision about which company to purchase. The analysis was imperfect, yet it was accomplished through a logical method from data relatively available. It raised important questions that must be answered before investment takes place. It is only a part, however, of a rational thought process. We must still add the experience and judgment of the mature investor when the final decision is made.

Review Questions

1. What has been the pattern of growth of the electronics industry compared to the national economy?

2. What are the basic devisions of the electronics industry? Indicate the products included in each division.

3. What are the leading companies in the industry? Why should Litton Industries, Texas Instruments, and Honeywell be chosen, based on the data presented as the leading three companies in the industry?

4. Explain specifically what Litton, Texas Instruments, and Honeywell produce.

5. Which of the three companies in the chapter appears to be best in respect to:
   (a) Competitive position
   (b) Present and future earnings
   (c) Operating capacity and efficiency
   (d) Current financial position
   (e) Capital structure
   (f) Management

6. Which company appears to be most reasonably priced in relation to its present price and P/E ratio?

7. Which company appears to offer the greatest growth of earnings and dividends?

8. What yield could one expect to earn over the next five years on the basis of the forecasts we made?

9. In terms of yield and risks, qualitative and nonqualitative factors, which company would we select for investment? (Do you agree?)

Problems

1. Bring the analysis of the electronics industry up to date. By use of the same analysis that was undertaken in the chapter, indicate whether you would consider the same three companies the dominant firms in the industry.

2. What companies should we select based on our analysis?

3. Study the industry and select the leading companies in the industry.

4. Based upon the following criteria, which company or companies should we now consider for investment?
   (a) Competitive position
   (b) Earnings and future earnings
   (c) Operating characteristics
   (d) Current financial analysis
   (e) Capital structure analysis
   (f) Management
   (g) Price and P/E ratios
   (h) Yield to maturity five years hence

5. If the conclusions reached in the analysis are different from those in the text, why did changes in the companies suggest a different decision?

Sources of Investment Information

Analysts' reports
1968 annual reports of Litton, Honeywell, and Texas Instruments
Clark Dodge Investment Survey
Department of Defense
Electronics Industries Association
Forbes
Interviews with management
Missiles and Rockets
Standard & Poor's *Investment Survey—Electronics, Electrical*
The Value Line Investment Survey—Electronics
Who's Who in Business

VII

STOCK MARKET ANALYSIS

Fundamental and Technical

18

STOCK MARKET ANALYSIS

Investment analysis requires an intensive and extensive study of economic and financial data of the national economy, the industry, and the company to arrive at the fundamental value of an investment security. The fundamentals we studied in the valuation process were the company's competitive position, its earnings and profitability with an emphasis upon future earnings, its operating characteristics, financial position, both long term and short term, and the management of the company. We studied the price patterns of the company's common stock and the P/E ratio to determine the reasonableness of the current price. Based upon estimated future earnings and price, we then estimated the yield we expected to receive. If the yield was satisfactory for the investor when the risk and reward were weighed, then we might decide to invest in the security. Before we make the final decision to invest, we must consider the general level of the stock market itself. This will be the area of inquiry in this chapter.

The Independence of the Stock Market

The stock market as a whole might not act rationally and consistently in terms of the fundamentals that we have studied. Often the market for a stock behaves contrarily to what the fundamental economic conditions suggest. The economic position of a company and the national economy might be strong, and yet the stock market might drop in price. This might be because of a change in expectations, but it is a drop, nevertheless, and the drop is inconsistent with the facts. By contrast, the fundamental position of the economy might be weak, and yet the stock market as a whole might be strong. When this happens, some writers suggest it is because the technical position of the market is weak. The technical weakness might be because the stock is in the hands of weak or small stockholders who are selling, and in the hands of market speculators who are selling because of a short-term swing in the market. Strength in a weak market might come about because only a small amount of stock was available to be purchased or because traders are covering their short sales in the market.[1] Whether the market is technically weak or strong, there is a hint in these comments that the stock market as a whole might behave differently from conclusions drawn from a fundamental investment analysis. We must, therefore, study the stock market itself to learn if its actions are consistent with our investment decisions.

The stock market has its likes and dislikes, which are somewhat different from the trend of the market or the national economy as a whole. We considered this when we talked about the market action of a stock. Investors and speculators tend to favor certain securities in certain industries. Several examples of this were given in previous chapters. Certain individual securities may move ahead or fall behind the general level of the market. This suggests that not only are market movements independent of fundamental economic forces but that certain stocks, perhaps a minority, cause changes that accentuate the movements of the market. This action is usually a short-term phenomenon. The psychology of the market might, however, allow investors or traders to become blinded to the economic realities of the trend of the stock market. Under conditions where sharp technical changes occur in the market, it is possible to pay too much for a security and it is possible to find bargains.

E. F. McDonald, a sales promotion firm, is an example of a company whose stock sustained an inordinate increase in price because of an overenthusiastic group of buyers who were influenced by the momentary market psychology. E. F. McDonald was bringing out a new trading stamp for A&P called Plaid Stamps. The company's earnings were slightly above a dollar a share, and investors or speculators had pushed the price up to over $100 a share in a short period of time. It sold at over 100 times annual earnings. The stock split 3 for 1, then later dropped to 11 in a declining stock market. At over 100, it had been selling far out of line with the market. Subsequently, the earnings of the company declined, and the price dropped to a lower level. The price movement

---

1 A short sale in essence is selling borrowed stock with the hope that the price will decline. When the price does decline, the trader buys back the stock and returns it to its owner. The transaction is facilitated by the stockbroker who arranged to buy the shares. When a person sells stock short, he is said to take a short position in the stock. We have assumed that investment purchases are long, that is, the investor buys the securities outright and owns them as an investment. The investment concept suggests a long-term period.

of the stock was somewhat independent of the market.

The market as a whole also acts independently of the realities of the business and economic world that we refer to as fundamentals. The trend of the market may follow economic conditions, but its cyclical movements react independently of fundamentals. They react to temporary technical, psychological, and emotional events that can be seen but might be unforeseen.

The strength of the cyclical activities of the securities market is apparent from the studies that have been made about the relationship between individual prices and the stock market as a whole. The studies conclude, and this is a professional opinion, that the movement of the market as a whole is responsible for the price movement of the better-quality common stocks. Probably two-thirds of the movement of the price of an individual stock is accounted for by the movement of the stock market as a whole. In the major movements, or under conditions where there is a strong upswing in the market, the movement of the market accounts for an even greater amount of stock price change. The market movements in the early part of January, 1963, are an example of the movement of the market as a whole. The quality issues moved up first. When the rise continued for a few weeks, the weaker issues began to move up. In the latter phase, most of the price increase in individual stocks was carried along by the general movement of the stock market. The market action was vigorous and the momentum of the market carried all stocks upward. In some cases, the strong bullishness or bearishness of the stock market explains 90 percent of the price movement of the individual stock.

Since the stock market does act independently of the fundamental economic or business outlook for an individual company, and since the stock market from a technical viewpoint has a life of its own, and since the individual common stocks that are traded are influenced strongly by general movement of the market, then it remains for the investor to analyze the market as a vital part of his investment function. He must determine, in view of fundamentals or technical considerations, where the market is and where it is going. This is simply an extension of one of the factors of investment analysis. Timing of the purchase of securities to put the investor in the best possible position for obtaining capital gains is an important part of portfolio management. Often timing makes the difference between a successful investor and an unsuccessful one. We assume that when the investor attempts to determine the level of the securities market and to forecast its actions, he will make some errors of judgment. But it is far better to make errors of judgment about the stock market than to make no estimate or forecast at all, or to ignore the condition of the market. Without placing a great deal of emphasis upon timing of purchases and the level of the stock market, there is no real portfolio management at all.

Measuring the Movement of the Market

When we discuss the subject of the general movement of the stock market, we are usually referring to a stock market average or index that is supposed to reflect the entire market. The average or index is a scientific collection of securities or a group of securities that have been in use for some time to reflect the level of the market. One such, based upon scientific principles of weighted index construction, is Standard & Poor's Index. The Dow Jones Averages are an example of securities that have been selected historically as being representative of the market as a whole. No attention has been given to weighting in the compilation of the Dow Jones Averages. Whether the average is scientifically constructed or a discretionary average, we assume that if the price index or average goes up, the market as a whole goes up. One could compute the total movement of the stock market by computing daily the total dollar value of all the shares traded and dividing into this figure the total number of shares. This would provide a weighted average price of the shares traded each day and would reflect the condition of the stock market. In some ways this method might have superiority over the averages and the indexes, but it would be difficult, expensive, and time-consuming to compute. It would also be inaccurate for comparison since the shares traded each day would differ, and there would be little uniformity in the average. Such a method would ignore the practical qualities and advantages of sampling theory in attempting to describe the average behavior of a time series or a market by using a small number of items rather than a large number. Many stock market averages or indexes have been constructed to indicate the movement of the stock market as a whole. We will examine the best known, which are the Dow Jones Averages, the New York Times Averages, Standard & Poor's Index of Stock Prices, and the New York Stock Exchange Indexes.

The Dow Jones Averages

The Dow Jones Averages are among the oldest and most familiar. They are published in the *Wall Street Journal,* and include the Dow Jones Industrial Average (DJIA), the Dow Jones Rail Average (DJRA), and the Dow Jones Public Utility Average (DJPUA). Since the *Wall Street Journal* is the leading daily financial newspaper and one of the best dailies in the United States, and since the Dow Jones Averages are quoted widely over radio and television, they are widely followed by investors. The Dow Jones Industrial Average consists of 30 stocks that cover a broad group of industries. The companies are considered to be market-tested companies in their respective industries and representative of their industrial class. The list of stocks in the DJIA includes the following companies:

Allied Chemical	General Electric	Sears Roebuck
Aluminum Co	General Foods	Std Oil of Calif
Amer Can	General Motors	Std Oil of NJ
Amer Tel & Tel	Goodyear	Swift & Co
Am Tobacco	Inter Harvester	Texaco
Anaconda	Inter Nickel	Union Carbide
Bethlehem Steel	Inter Paper	United Aircraft
Chrysler	Johns-Manville	US Steel
Du Pont	Owens-Illinois	Westinghouse El
Eastman Kodak	Procter & Gamble	Woolworth

The DJIA is computed by adding the prices of the securities included in the averages and dividing by an adjusted denominator. The denominator has been adjusted periodically to reflect the changes that have occurred in the securities, such as stock splits and stock dividends. In the case of a 2-for-1 stock split, for example, the average would drop if no adjustment were made, since one-half of the price of the security would be subtracted. In making the adjustment, we would either add in the stock twice or adjust the denominator to compensate for the split. The adjustment of the denominator is the method the DJIA has used in the past. On December 10, 1969, the divisor used in computing the DJIA was 1.894.

The securities in the DJIA are changed from time to time to reflect changes in the representative character of the averages. In 1950, American Smelting and Refining, Corn Products, Loews, National Distillers, and National Steel were included in the industrial averages. In 1963, these securities were replaced by Alcoa, Anaconda, International Paper, Owens Illinois, and Swift. The securities in the DJIA are selected and do not represent the range of stocks in the securities market or the New York Stock Exchange. They have been selected to reflect the market as a whole, but not by a scientific method of statistical sampling.

The DJRA[*] is made up of 20 railroad companies that geographically and commercially represent the leading railroads in the country. The rail average, like the industrial average, is an integral part of the Dow Theory, which will be explained later. The divisor on December 10, 1969, was 4.721. The railroads in the average were:

Atchison	Illinois Central	St Louis-San Fran
Canadian Pacific	Kansas City Sou	Seab Cst L RR
Ches & Ohio	Louisv & Nash	Southern Pacific
Chi Milw St P&P	Missouri Pac	Southern Railway
Den & Rio Gr W	Norfolk & West'n	Union Pacific
Great North Ry	Northwest Industries	Western Pacific
Gulf Mobile & Ohio	Penn Central	

*SPECIAL NOTE: The DJRA, in being since 1897, was changed in January, 1970, to the Transportation Average, or DJTA, owing to mergers, acquisitions, and diversification by the railroads. The 20 stocks in the index now include 11 railroads, 6 airlines, and 3 trucking companies: Canadian Pacific, Great Northern, Louisville & Nashville, Norfolk & Western, Penn Central, St. Louis-San Francisco, Santa Fe Industries, Seaboard Coast Line Industries, Southern Pacific, Southern Railway, and Union Pacific; American, Eastern, Northwest, Pan Am, TWA, and UAL, Inc.; and Consolidated Freightways, Pacific Intermountain Express, and U.S. Freight Co.

The Dow Jones Public Utility Average consists of 15 growth and income securities that encompass both gas and electric utilities and represent all parts of the United States. Again these companies tend to be representative of the leading companies within their classification. On December 10, 1969, the divisor was 3.912. The companies included in the list were:

Am Elec Power	Consol Nat Gas	Panhandle EPL
Cleveland E III	Detroit Edison	Peoples Gas
Colum Gas Sys	Houston Lt & Pw	Phila Elec
Comwlth Edison	Niag Mohawk P	Pub Serv E&G
Consol Edison	Pacific Gas & El	Sou Cal Edison

The fourth of the Dow Jones Averages is the 65 composite average made up of the 30 industrials, 20 rails, and 15 public utility companies in the other averages. The combined average provides an overall view of the direction of the market of the better-quality securities and does not reflect the action of securities traded on the over-the-counter market. We can keep up to date on the Dow Jones Averages easily by daily reference to the *Wall Street Journal,* the source of the sample in Figure 18–1, pp. 560–61. The divisor for 65 stocks on December 10, 1969, was 10.568.

The New York Times Average

Another stock market average familiar to the financial community is the New York Times Average, reported daily in *The New York Times* since 1911 and consisting of an average of 25 industrial companies, an average of 25 railroad stocks, and a 50-stock composite average. There are substitutions from time to time when the securities listed are no longer in existence or when a company is merged. The divisor is held constant in computing the New York Times Average. If changes occur that affect the total value of stock prices, the numerator is adjusted. If a stock split of 2 for 1 is recorded, for example, the price is multiplied by 2 after the split to provide consistency in the average and to avoid the depressing influence of the stock split. This method is just the reverse of that used in the Dow Jones Averages. The New York Times Average is an unweighted average of prices, like the Dow Jones Averages.

Standard & Poor's Stock Price Index

Standard & Poor's Index of Stock Prices is a base-weighted aggregate showing the relative changes in the stocks included in the index compared to a base year. In the case of the Standard & Poor's Average the base year is 1941–43 = 100.

> This method of computation has two distinct advantages over most index number series: (1) it has the flexibility to adjust for arbitrary

price changes caused by the issuance of rights, stock dividends, split-ups, etc., and (2) the resultant index numbers are accurate and have a relatively high degree of continuity which is especially important when long-term comparisons are to be made.[2]

Standard & Poor's Composite Average combines 500 stocks. Included are 425 companies from 85 industrial groupings, 25 railroad companies, and 5 utility groups totaling 50 companies. The index is broken down further into the various industry segments, facilitating comparison of the market action of individual companies. Standard & Poor's Index has the added advantages of being widely known, broad in scope and representativeness, and fairly sensitive to market change.

The New York Stock Exchange Common-Stock Index

In July, 1966, the New York Stock Exchange began the publication of its own common-stock index. This index measures the price trends of the 1,267 common stocks listed on the Big Board. In addition to the total, all-inclusive common-stock index, separate indexes are calculated for finance, transportation, utility, and industrials. *The Finance Index* includes 75 issues of closed-end investment companies, savings and loan holding and investment companies, and companies in commercial and installment finance, banking, insurance, and related fields. *The Transportation Index* is based on 76 issues representing railroads, airlines, shipping, motor transport, and other operating, leasing, and holding companies in the transportation field. *The Utility Index* includes 136 separate stocks of operating, holding, and transmission companies in gas, electric power, and communication. The biggest and broadest index is *The Industrial Index*, comprising 980 listed stocks on the **NYSE** not included in the other indexes.[3]

The indexes are computed by multiplying the price of each stock by the number of its listed shares. It is therefore a capitalization-weighted index. Companies with the largest capitalization such as **GM**, Standard Oil of N.J., AT&T, IBM, and du Pont will have the greatest impact on the index. Every half hour the change in average price is reported in dollars and cents and in index form with the number of points change from the previous day's close. On the hour, the same information is presented for all of the indexes plus the reported volume.[4]

December 31, 1965 is the base date and it was set at 50.00. The base

2 Standard & Poor's *Trade and Securities Statistics Security Price Index Record*, 1962, p. 2.

3 John Kirk, "N.Y. Stock Exchange Launches Its Market Indicator," *Banking*, August, 1966, p. 4.

4 *Ibid.*, p. 5.

market values are adjusted for stock splits and dividends, rights for the purchase of additional shares, rights to subscribe to other issues, and mergers or acquisitions that change the value of the base values. If the index moves up substantially due to a rise in market values, it will be readjusted or "split" by the NYSE. The method of computing

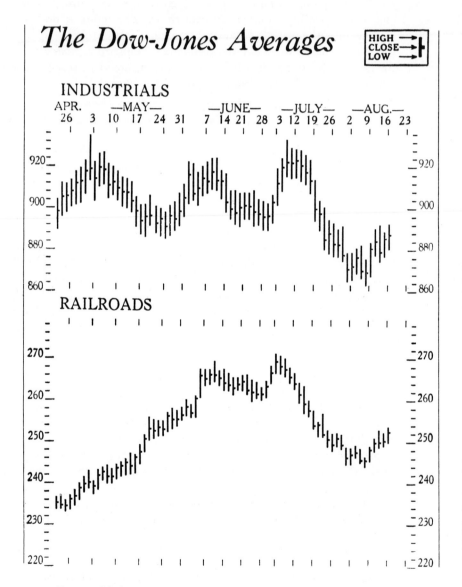

FIGURE 18–1

SOURCE *The Wall Street Journal*

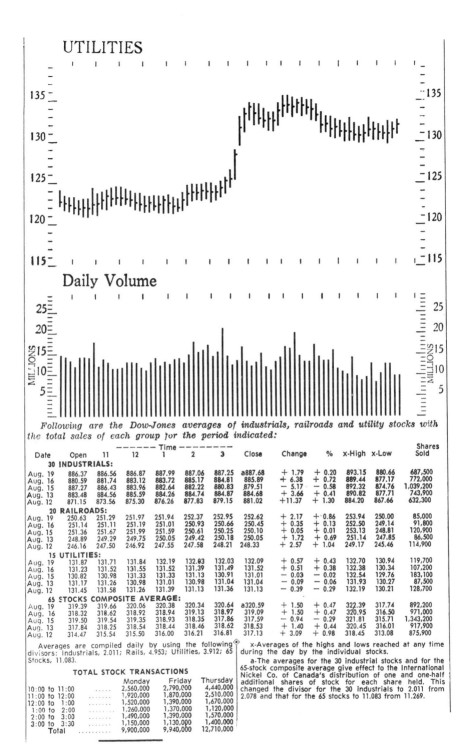

UTILITIES

135
130
125
120
115

Daily Volume

25
20
MILLIONS 15
10
5

25
20
MILLIONS 15
10
5

Following are the Dow-Jones averages of industrials, railroads and utility stocks with the total sales of each group for the period indicated:

Date	Open	11	12	1	2	3	Close	Change	%	x-High	x-Low	Shares Sold
30 INDUSTRIALS:												
Aug. 19	886.37	886.56	886.87	887.99	887.06	887.25	a887.68	+ 1.79	+ 0.20	893.15	880.66	687,500
Aug. 16	880.59	881.74	883.12	883.72	885.17	884.81	885.89	+ 6.38	+ 0.72	889.44	877.17	772,000
Aug. 15	887.27	886.43	883.96	882.64	882.22	880.83	879.51	− 5.17	− 0.58	892.32	874.76	1,039,200
Aug. 13	883.48	884.56	885.59	884.26	884.74	884.87	884.68	+ 3.66	+ 0.41	890.82	877.71	743,900
Aug. 12	871.15	873.56	875.30	876.26	877.83	879.15	881.02	+11.37	+ 1.30	884.20	867.66	632,300
20 RAILROADS:												
Aug. 19	250.63	251.29	251.97	251.94	252.37	252.95	252.62	+ 2.17	+·0.86	253.94	250.00	85,000
Aug. 16	251.14	251.11	251.19	251.01	250.93	250.66	250.45	+ 0.35	+ 0.13	252.50	249.14	91,800
Aug. 15	251.36	251.67	251.99	251.59	250.61	250.25	250.10	+ 0.05	+ 0.01	253.13	248.81	120,900
Aug. 13	248.89	249.29	249.75	250.05	249.42	250.18	250.05	+ 1.72	+ 0.69	251.14	247.85	86,500
Aug. 12	246.16	247.50	246.92	247.55	247.58	248.21	248.33	+ 2.57	+ 1.04	249.17	245.46	114,900
15 UTILITIES:												
Aug. 19	131.87	131.71	131.84	132.19	132.83	132.03	132.09	+ 0.57	+ 0.43	132.70	130.94	119,700
Aug. 16	131.23	131.52	131.55	131.52	131.39	131.49	131.52	+ 0.51	+ 0.38	132.38	130.34	107,200
Aug. 15	130.82	130.98	131.33	131.33	131.13	130.91	131.01	− 0.03	− 0.02	132.54	129.76	183,100
Aug. 13	131.17	131.26	130.98	131.01	130.98	131.04	131.04	− 0.09	− 0.06	131.93	130.27	87,500
Aug. 12	131.45	131.58	131.26	131.39	131.13	131.36	131.13	− 0.39	− 0.29	132.19	130.21	128,700
65 STOCKS COMPOSITE AVERAGE:												
Aug. 19	319.39	319.66	320.06	320.38	320.34	320.64	a320.59	+ 1.50	+ 0.47	322.39	317.74	892,200
Aug. 16	318.32	318.62	318.92	318.94	319.13	318.97	319.09	+ 1.50	+ 0.47	320.95	316.50	971,000
Aug. 15	319.50	319.54	319.35	318.93	318.35	317.86	317.59	− 0.94	− 0.29	321.81	315.71	1,343,200
Aug. 13	317.84	318.25	318.54	318.44	318.46	318.62	318.53	+ 1.40	+ 0.44	320.45	316.01	917,900
Aug. 12	314.47	315.54	315.50	316.00	316.21	316.81	317.13	+ 3.09	+ 0.98	318.45	313.08	875,900

Averages are compiled daily by using the following◊ divisors: Industrials, 2.011; Rails, 4.953; Utilities, 3.912; 65 Stocks, 11.083.

x-Averages of the highs and lows reached at any time during the day by the individual stocks.

a-The averages for the 30 industrial stocks and for the 65-stock composite average give effect to the International Nickel Co. of Canada's distribution of one and one-half additional shares of stock for each share held. This changed the divisor for the 30 industrials to 2.011 from 2.078 and that for the 65 stocks to 11.083 from 11.269.

TOTAL STOCK TRANSACTIONS

		Monday	Friday	Thursday
10:00 to 11:00	.....	2,560,000	2,790,000	4,440,000
11:00 to 12:00	.....	1,920,000	1,870,000	2,510,000
12:00 to 1:00	.....	1,520,000	1,390,000	1,670,000
1:00 to 2:00	.....	1,260,000	1,370,000	1,120,000
2:00 to 3:00	.....	1,490,000	1,390,000	1,570,000
3:00 to 3:30	.....	1,150,000	1,130,000	1,400,000
Total	.....	9,900,000	9,940,000	12,710,000

FIGURE 18-1 *(continued)*

changes appears in Figure 18–2. The NYSE Common Stock Index has been linked statistically to the weekly SEC Index of common stocks from 1939 to 1964. The NYSE Index has been computed on a daily basis since May 28, 1964, and the four industry group indexes since December 31, 1965.[5] An example appears in Figure 18–3.

The reaction to the NYSE Common Stock Index by the professional in Wall Street was critical. Many felt that it was another index that was too broad and wouldn't show a thing. However, "Seven months and one major market reversal later, Wall Street's technical analysts—whose main concern is the exegesis of charts—are looking on the Big Board's market yardsticks with all the respect of gypsies fondling a potent new deck of tarot cards."[6] The reason for this changed feeling was the "signal" of a bullish market given by the NYSE index in mid-November, 1966. The Dow Jones Industrial Averages didn't break out above the 820 barrier with a confirmation of the industrials index and the transportation index until the second week in January, 1967. The NYSE Indexes do not have "history" or "lore," but they are good indicators of market behavior. Students of investment would be wise to watch them with care.

Which Average Should Be Used?

The selection of the average to use for determining the direction of the market must rest on practical grounds rather than on what is, statistically, the best average. The best answer to this question is to use

---

NET CHANGE IN AVERAGE PRICE

THE net change in average price of NYSE shares (shown on the ticker tape as "MARKET") is derived from the net change in the NYSE Common Stock Index as follows:

FORMULA:

$$\text{Change in Average Price} = \frac{\text{Average Price of Shares Listed}}{\text{Index Value}} \times \text{Change in Index}$$

EXAMPLE: *If Index Value = 79.20, down from 80.00, and Average Price of Shares Listed = $50.00, Change in Index = 0.80*

and

$$\text{Change in Average Price} = \frac{50.00}{80.00} \times 0.80 = 50 \text{ cents } (Down)$$

As shown in the above example, a decline of 0.80 in the NYSE Common Stock Index would reflect a decline in the "market" of 50 cents. A proportionate decline in the Dow-Jones Industrial Average at mid-1966 levels would amount to about 9 points.

FIGURE 18–2

Method of computing changes in NYSE index

SOURCE *Banking*, August, 1966, p. 5.

---

5 *Ibid.*

6 "New indexes get there first," *Business Week*, February 25, 1967, p. 124.

the average that is most familiar and available. People who read the *Wall Street Journal* will find the Dow Jones Industrial Average the most convenient. Reference to Figure 18–4 will indicate that the averages tend to follow each other very closely in the timing of their peaks and troughs and in the magnitude of change. These averages reflect conditions in securities traded on a national, registered exchange. They do not reflect the changes in securities on the over-the-counter market. These are provided in the National Quotation Bureau Average, an index of

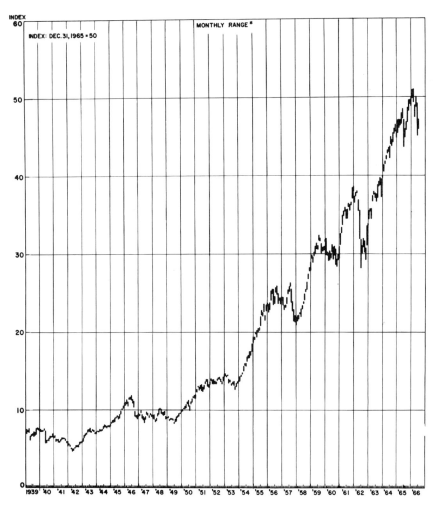

FIGURE 18–3

The New York Stock Exchange Common Stock Index

SOURCE *Banking*, August, 1966

over-the-counter market stocks. This also follows the pattern of the other averages satisfactorily, since the cyclical highs and lows of the averages tend to come at about the same time, as do the monthly highs and lows. The Dow Jones Averages tend to be a good indication of what is happening in the great industries, whereas Standard and Poor's Index will give an indication of change in a broader group of companies. All the averages are old enough to provide adequate historical data. The New York Times Average is more sensitive to change. Based upon availability alone, as was suggested, the Dow Jones Industrial, Rail, and Public Utility Averages would be the most desirable to follow, although it appears that the New York Stock Exchange Common Stock Index is an excellent indicator of the general level of the market, too, and better suited to determine changes in the market compared to the Dow Jones Industrial Averages.

The Economic, Money Market, and Technical Indicators of the Stock Market

Once we have established a reasonably accurate method of measuring the stock market, we must turn to the question of how we can hope to determine the relative height of the market and its direction. We are concerned with the position of the market as it affects our decision to buy or sell. We are interested in whether the market is high or low and if it is going up or down. Or in the stock market vernacular, is the market bullish or bearish? We concentrate our attention on the trend of the market and the cyclical swings, and we try to ignore day-to-day fluctuations. Investors, speculators, and market analysts have used many methods to determine the position of the stock market and its future course. These fall into many categories from the sublime to the ridiculous. Some forecasters, for example, use sunspots and the phases of the moon to forecast the market. These methods are less than satisfactory as tools of market analysis. However, a small element of truth exists in the basic premise underlying these attempts or theories to forecast or explain the market. Although they should be put aside as being an incomplete guide to market action, they cannot be ignored.

At this point we will consider several of the more conventional methods of market forecasting and the determination of the level of the market under three major classifications: (1) economic indicators of the market, (2) money market indicators, and (3) the technical indicators of the stock market. Each indicator might be helpful to the investor to determine the present and future position of the market, although none is considered the panacea for all problems of prediction. Each is considered an aid to market analysis, none as dogma.

Economic Indicators and the Stock Market

At one time, students of the stock market and professional analysts. and investors used pig iron production as a method of predicting stock market prices. The rationale was quite simple. If pig iron production were high and increasing and this trend were expected to continue, it was taken as a sign of a high level of economic activity. If economic activity were high, then the stock market would tend to rise or remain high. On the other hand, if pig iron production were expected to decline, the stock market would probably move to lower levels. The pig iron figures still have value, but they are no longer in use to the extent that they once were. Today, we have replaced pig iron production as an indicator of economic activity with broader and better aggregate economic indicators, such as the Federal Reserve Board Index of Industrial Production, and Gross National Product, National Income, and Disposable Income estimates. These measures were discussed earlier where we pointed out that a healthy economy was a prerequisite for a healthy and profitable industry or company. In addition to the aggregate measures, more specific indicators of economic activity are used to help forecast

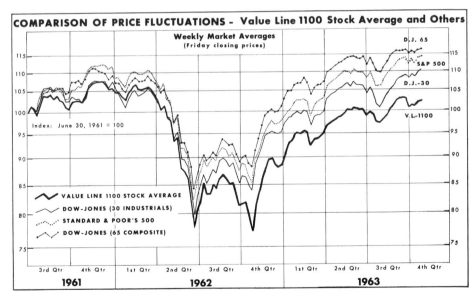

FIGURE 18–4
Comparative price movements of selected market averages

SOURCE *The Value Line Investment Survey,* November 1, 1963, p. 259

the stock market, such as auto production, steel production, and housing.

The economic indicators are used in much the same way as we used the estimates of pig iron production. Changes in the aggregate and specific indicators are used to predict changes in the stock market. The essential ingredient is an accurate forecast of the indicator, whether it is aggregate output or a specific indicator such as housing. With a forecast of economic activity, a person could, within reasonable limits, determine the present position of the market and make a reasonably accurate estimate of what could be expected in the future of the securities market. Some members of the financial community reverse the procedure and use the stock market as a forecaster of business activity. They reason that if the market goes down cyclically, then business will be poor. However, we consider economic activity the indicator of the stock market. Assuming a forecast of improved economic conditions and corporate profits, the stock market should be strong or improve. Given a condition of weakness in economic conditions, then the market should decline. Thus we should use the forecast of the Gross National Product, Federal Reserve Board Index of Industrial Production, National Income, corporate profits, and other indicators of economic activity as an indication of what we can expect to happen to the stock market. There is some indication (not conclusive proof) that expected economic activity six months to a year in the future tends to forecast the stock market. In January of a given year, for example, if business is expected to improve as we look six months ahead, the present level of the stock market should be high. If we forecast a decline in business activity six months from January, then the stock market should be low.

Early in 1968, the forecasts of business conditions, economic activity, and corporate profits suggested some strength in the national economy for all of 1968. The Gross National Product and the FRB Index were expected to improve somewhat above the 1967 levels. Auto production was expected to maintain the excellent 1967 level. The estimates for 1968 housing production were optimistic but steel production was "flat." The federal income tax surcharge of 10 percent in 1968 was expected to reduce corporate profits in the third and fourth quarters, but profits, it was felt, would continue strong for the entire year. The Vietnam conflict, inflation, and civil strife tended to dampen the economy in spite of a high level of economic activity. The net result was to be an improved economy in 1968. What should we have expected from the stock market as a result of the analysis of the estimates or forecasts of the economic indicators for mid-1968? Based on these estimates, we would conclude that the market should remain firm but no major upward movement would result. The expected strength in the market partially reflected the strength expected in the economy in 1969.

Once an estimate is made, it must not remain static. It must be revised against the reality of the expectation of the economy. Even though the full-year forecasts had been made in 1968 and suggested the economy would remain stable in 1969, forces were at work that could bring about a contraction of economic activity and lower stock market prices. For in spite of a higher expected GNP in 1968 and 1969, the possibility of a cessation of hostilities in Vietnam and a decline in demand for goods and services might have led to a decline in economic activity and a corresponding drop in the market. As it turned out, price inflation was substantial, interest rates rose sharply, and the stock market declined—but not because of peace and a lowered demand for goods and services. It dropped because of an expected recession in 1970.

Anyone working with economic forecasts as a basis for the expectation of market activity must realize the error involved in prediction. The estimates must be adjusted for the possibility of error and revised continuously for the best success. The investor using the economic indicators as a guide to market activity must consider them rough tools for trend and cyclical forecasting but not useful in forecasting the daily movements of the stock market. It is also assumed that as investors, we will not trade frequently but will buy or sell from our portfolios on the basis of fundamental and major swings, rather than temporary and transitory changes, in the stock market.

We can use the specific economic components of the GNP to support forecasts based on the overall condition of our economy expressed by the GNP estimates, and we can use the FRB Index of Industrial Production. In Figure 10–3, p. 297, various indexes were presented as indicators of economic activity. If we think that employment is stable, that industrial output is increasing, that freight-car loadings will be higher in the next year or next quarter, then we can assume that the stock market will be strong, since economic conditions exert a powerful influence upon the stock market as a whole. However, the conditions in these segments of the economy can change suddenly. If they are to be used as indicators of the stock market, they must be used with care and revised. Otherwise they are unreliable, particularly since we are dealing with rapidly changing economic conditions and changing expectations.

Bond Yields, Money Market Indicators, and the Stock Market

A close relationship exists between the money market, the bond market, and the stock market, although it is sometimes difficult to observe. The term "money market" usually refers to the market for short-term debt instruments of both private and government corporations or political units. The bond market is the market for long-term debt of private and government corporations or political entities. Many forces have an impact upon the bond market and the money market, including changes in the stock market. One effect, in its simplest form, is the movement of money between the markets. If, for example, stocks are sold, the funds used from the sale can be held in cash, used to purchase other stocks, or used to buy long- and short-term debt instruments. The purchase of debt securities would be most likely when common stocks were expected to drop in price or when the current returns on common stock were low. On the other hand, when funds were needed for the stock market, they could come from idle balances, sales of other stocks, or from the sales of long- and short-term debt securities. The effects of the shift of funds between the money market and the stock market are apparent. A sale of stock tends to result in an increase in the supply of securities, which tends to decrease price and increase yields. The effect on bonds is just the reverse. The purchase of debt securities tends to increase their price relative to common stocks and decrease the yields. A purchase of stock and a sale of bonds tends to improve the price of stocks and reduce the yield on stocks, and it decreases the price of bonds and increases bond yields. There are times, however, when relative demand results in lower stock and bond prices.

The relationship between yields on bonds and yields on common stock is the foundation for several indicators that help to forecast the future of the security markets. As we discuss several of these money market indicators of the stock market, keep in mind the mobility of funds between the money market and the stock market and the impact of the flow of funds upon yields. All these concepts assume that monetary and fiscal policy remain neutral and have little or no effect upon the flow of funds from one market to the other.

STOCK YIELDS AS A MARKET INDICATOR

One method of forecasting the stock market and determining if it is high or low is through the dividend yields on high-grade common stocks. Using stock yields as a guide to the height of the market is quite simple. If stock yields are low, the stock market is high, and if stock yields are high, the stock market is low. The premise upon which this concept is based relates to the price of the stock. As stock prices go higher, the yield moves lower. When yields are low, the investor earns much less on common stocks than he could earn from other securities. Common stocks become an unattractive investment. The investor sells common stocks to purchase other more attractive-yield securities. When yields on common stocks are high, on the other hand, the investor is enticed away from other investments that offer lower yields. Thus he is in a position to benefit from better yields on stocks and has the possibility of earning capital gains.

One problem we face is how to know what is high or low when

we talk about yields on common stock. What is high or low depends upon the relative condition of the money market and the level of the stock market. A study made by the Cowles Commission covering the period 1871–1937 concluded that stock prices were high when average yields were below 3 percent, and the market was low when yields were above 8 percent.[7] Only four times has the composite yield of Standard & Poor's Stock Price Index been above 8 percent: in 1931, the first quarter of 1938, the last quarter of 1941, and the first quarter of 1942. 1931 was a year of depression, as was 1938, and 1941–1942 was the beginning of World War II. Based upon the same composite average, the market was too high in 1961 when yields dropped below 3 percent. (See Table 18–1.) The market was also high, based on this thesis, in 1964, in 1965, and in June, 1968.

TABLE 18–1

	Yield on Corporate Bonds	Dividend Yield on Common Stocks	Differential Bond Yield —Common Stock
	%	%	%
1968 (June 1)	6.64	3.07	—3.57
1967	5.82	3.20	—2.62
1966	5.34	3.40	—1.94
1965	4.64	3.00	—1.64
1964	4.57	3.01	—1.56
1963	4.50	3.17	—1.33
1962	4.62	3.37	—1.25
1961	4.66	2.98	—1.68
1960	4.73	3.47	—1.26

SOURCE: *Federal Reserve Bulletin*, June, 1968, pp. A31 and A32.

The conclusion we can draw from the stock-yield concept is: Buy stock when the yields are relatively high and sell stock when yields are relatively low. Relatively high would be 5 percent, historically, and in a period such as 1968 when money was extremely tight; relatively low would be 3 percent. Even this hypothesis has serious limitations, since the investor would be required to move into and out of the market frequently. Based upon the composite yields of Standard & Poor's Averages, the investor would have purchased stocks from 1950 through 1958, sold in the fourth quarter of 1958, purchased again in 1960, and sold in 1961 when the yields dropped below 3 percent. He would have sold in 1964 and 1965, purchased in 1966 and 1967, and sold in 1968.

These comments are based upon the quarterly averages of yields

7 Cowles Commission for Research in Economics, "Common Stock Indexes, 1871–1937," Monograph No. 3, 2d ed. (Bloomington, Indiana: The Principia Press, Inc., 1939), p. 47.

of industrial common stocks in Standard & Poor's Index and the composite yield, which includes industrial, rail, and public utility securities. It is possible that several times since 1930 the yields on stock moved above or fell below the limits suggested by the Cowles Commission. On an average basis, however, there were few times when yields went below 3 percent or above 8 percent. Certainly, a current yield as high as 8 percent is an extreme case.

There is some merit in using stock yields as a guide to the level of the stock market. The widest range between the high and low point of the industrial averages came prior to the 1960's. The fluctuations in yields have been narrowing since 1930. A high average yield in the stock market of 1968 would have been close to 3 1/2 percent. A low average yield was close to 3 percent. As a guide to market activity, the investor might consider purchasing high-quality securities when the average yield is between these two levels. This assumes that the investor is following an investment policy that allows full management of funds and that some trading is allowed, consistent with the cyclical movements of the stock market.

STOCK YIELD–BOND YIELD DIFFERENTIAL AS A MARKET INDICATOR

Stock yields and bond yields are brought together to form an approach to stock market forecasting that bears a close resemblance to stock yields as a market indicator. The stock yield–bond yield differential concept is used to determine the position of the market and to some extent forecast the market level by examining the difference in yields. Usually bond yields are lower than stock yields. This has been the historic pattern, and the difference between the yields has been significant. However, at times the yield on common stock has fallen below the yield on bonds. This has been true for the period from 1960 through 1968 as indicated in Table 18–1. This leads us to the heart of the concept. When yields on stocks are higher than yield on bonds and the difference between them is large, then common stock should be purchased. When the yields on common stocks are equal to or lower than the yield on bonds or when the differential between them is slight, then common stocks should be sold.

In 1938, industrial common stocks in Standard & Poor's Daily Price Index yielded 8.86 percent, compared to 3.20 percent for AAA Bonds in the industrial, rail, and utility group of the Standard & Poor's series. The differential was large enough to suggest the purchase of common stocks. The industrial yields in 1936 and early 1937 were much lower; industrial securities had a yield between 3.10 percent in the first quarter of 1936 and 4.02 percent in the first quarter of 1937. The AAA bond yields in 1937 were 3.30 percent, resulting in a small differential between bond and stock yields. According to these figures, stock should have been sold in 1937 and not purchased again until the differential had improved, as the low differential would have forecast a market decline. In 1961, the yield on bonds stood at 4.66 percent, the average for the year, and common-stock yields were at 2.98 percent for a differential of −1.26 percent as seen in Table 18–1. Since that time the differential has increased persistently because of tight money-market conditions.

Bond yields were above stock yields, and this should have signaled a drop in the market. The market drop did come in 1962, again in 1966, and in early 1968, which does indicate some validity in this concept. However, it must be used with caution. Its greatest value would be to aid the investor in determining whether the market is relatively high or low for assistance in buying and selling common stock on major swings. It would be difficult to use in market trading for the inexperienced investor or speculator. It has not been successful in forecasting all movements of the stock market, and in earlier times it has been incorrect, especially after the crash of 1929 and during the depression years of the 1930's.

STOCK PRICES AND MONEY RATES

Three market indicators that relate directly to the movement of the stock market have had at one time some validity. All are based upon the relationship between the movement of the short-term money rates, the long-term money rates, and the yields on common stock. These indicators assume that the movement of money rates precedes the movement of stock prices.

Movement of Short-Term Rates. The first has to do directly with the movement of the short-term money rates. In prosperity, as more and more business borrowing takes place, an increase in money rates is likely to occur, particularly in the later phases of the market cycle. The sharp rise in money rates precedes a decline in stock prices. Professor Grodinsky stated: "The culmination of an upward move in the stock market and the beginning of a downward movement was invariably signaled by a sharp advance in money rates."[8] This relationship existed until the 1929 market crash. Sharp increases in money rates occurred in the fall of 1966 and in 1968. This would suggest the avoidance or sale of common stocks at those times.

Bond Prices and Stock Prices. A second indicator relates to bond and stock prices and is almost identical in logic to the relationship between short-term money rates and stock market prices. Under conditions of prosperity, the businessman borrows more and more heavily. The demand for long-term funds forces the cost of money higher. At such a time, common stock becomes more profitable and investors

8 Julius Grodinsky, *Investments* (New York: The Ronald Press Company, 1953), p. 410.

favor it. This adds to the supply of funds for common stock but takes funds away from the bond market. Thus in prosperous periods bond prices fall and stock prices tend to rise. Later in the prosperous periods, borrowing becomes less profitable for the businessman, borrowing stops, business becomes less profitable, common stocks are less attractive, and stock prices drop. All this activity begins with a decline in bond prices, which precedes the decline in stock prices.

Commercial Bank Loans. The third indicator relates to the investment practices of commercial banks. Commercial banks are in business to make loans to businesses, real estate borrowers, and consumers. When business and economic conditions are poor, the banks build up excess reserves. If they cannot make loans to business, they lend to the government by the purchase of government bonds. When business improves, the banks sell the government securities and make more loans to business. As the prosperity phase of the cycle continues, more and more demands are made for business loans. Less money is invested in government bonds. Therefore, as the bond accounts of the commercial banks decrease, this is an indication that the market is reaching a peak. If, on the other hand, the bond accounts of the commercial banks are increasing, it indicates that the market is relatively low. As a market indicator, this tells the investor to sell stock when bond accounts of commercial banks are small and buy stocks when they are large.

There is an element of truth in each of these market indicators. The premise upon which they rest, however, is that we enjoy an orderly and free money market and that complete freedom of movement of funds exists between the money market, the bond market, and the stock market. It further assumes that the movement in interest rates and stock yields is determined by funds moving from bonds into stocks, a sign of strength for stocks, and from stocks into bonds, a sign of weakness. However, this is only a part of the total money market. Since World War II, the central bank policy through the Federal Reserve System and fiscal policy through the Treasury have had a much greater impact upon the money market than has the movement of money from common stocks to bonds and vice versa. Before predicting the direction of the stock market based upon money market indicators, we would carefully analyze all of the forces operating in the money market. This would require particular attention to Federal Reserve and Treasury policy as it affects the money market conditions.

NEW OFFERINGS OF STOCK AS A STOCK MARKET INDICATOR

One aspect of the capital market that bears directly upon the stock market is the underwriting of new issues of common stock. When business is expanding and in need of additional capital, the new firms resort to the equity market for funds. In addition, when business is good and the stock market is high, corporate financial managers take the opportunity to raise capital. During the latter half of 1960, early 1961, and 1964, the market for new issues of common stock was extremely good, and many small companies resorted to the capital markets for funds. When the number of new issues is increasing and they are being taken off the market with support from investors, this is a sign of strength in the stock market. However, if the new issues decline in volume and are difficult to market, this is a sign of weakness. If, after a market rise, new stock issues are sold only at prices below their offering price, this is a sign that the market is too high and will probably decline.

Several times in financial history new issues have been sold only at lower prices. During 1961 and 1964 there were a great many new issues and the stock market was strong, as indicated in Table 18–2. A great deal of speculation also took place in new issues that were traded in the over-the-counter market. Late in 1961, interest in these issues began to diminish. In the subsequent market decline of 1962, scheduled sales of many new speculative issues were postponed. The speculative excess had stopped, and the investor turned to more traditional methods of valuation of securities and hence to a higher investment grade of security. The dollar volume of new issues declined in 1962 but increased sharply in 1964. In mid-1968, speculative interest in new issues was exorbitant. An investor using the change in volume of new security issues as a guide to market activity would have heeded the market warning and established a more defensive investment policy at this time. The volume of new issues served as a guide to the height of the market, indicating that the market was relatively high.

The Technical Indicators of the Market

As we said earlier in the chapter, the stock market has a life of its own independent of the fundamental attributes of investment value possessed by the individual companies that constitute the market. Collectively

TABLE 18–2

New issues of corporate common stock
(billions of dollars)

Year	Value	Year	Value
1954	$1,213	1961	$3,294
1955	2,185	1962	1,318
1956	2,301	1963	1,011
1957	2,516	1964	2,679
1958	1,334	1965	1,547
1959	2,027	1966	1,939
1960	1,664	1967	1,949

SOURCE: *Federal Reserve Bulletin*, December, 1963, p. 1695; and June, 1968, p. A44.

the market acts and reacts to news about business and government as does an individual stock. The technical position of the market is important, since a market can be too high or too low, overbought or oversold. There are technical indicators or theories that attempt to establish the relative height of the market through an examination of the technical aspects of the market rather than fundamentals. Most of the theories assume that the movement of the market tells all, or as the professional states it, "the market discounts everything." Some individuals, known as "tape readers," examine only the stock transactions in the market as reported by the stock ticker. Their decisions are made only on the basis of the price and volume figures they observe on the tape carrying the transactions of the New York Stock Exchange and the American Exchange. Others are "chartists," or point-and-figure experts, who interpret and forecast only by the use of price movements of the stock. The individuals who read tapes and charts for the most part speculate in the stock market. We, however, are interested in some of the better-known technical market indicators as an aid to learning where the market is and where it might go.

The Dow Theory is probably the most widely followed theory about the technical action of the stock market. Part of the reason for its popularity is the widespread use of the *Wall Street Journal* and *Barron's*, both of which are publications of Dow Jones & Company, founded in 1882. Part of the reason too is the success that has been attributed to the Dow Theory by the Dow theorists. Another reason is that it is one of the oldest theories of stock market activity in the United States. The Dow Theory was first presented by Charles H. Dow, who founded Dow Jones & Company and who later was the first editor of the *Wall Street Journal* and subsequently the publisher of *Barron's* magazine. Charles Dow never published a formal treatise on his theory of the stock market. Most of the Dow Theory comes to us from the students of the stock market who followed closely Dow's interpretation of the stock market in 1901 and 1902.

One student of the stock market and former editor of the *Wall Street Journal* wrote a column putting into print the theories of Charles Dow. He was W. P. Hamilton, at one time (1903–1929) the most prominent Dow theorist. Hamilton wrote a book on the Dow Theory called *The Stock Market Barometer*.[9] Another student of the market, Robert Rhea, wrote *The Dow Theory*[10] in 1932, and G. W. Bishop, Jr. wrote *Charles Dow and the Dow Theory* in 1960.[11] Rhea not only wrote about

---

9 W. P. Hamilton, *The Stock Market Barometer* (New York: Barron's, 1922).

10 Robert Rhea, *The Dow Theory* (New York: Barron's, 1932).

11 George W. Bishop, Jr., *Charles H. Dow and The Dow Theory* (New York: Appleton-Century-Crofts, 1960).

the Dow Theory, he put it into practice. The best-advertised modern practitioner of the Dow Theory is E. George Schaefer.[12]

Most of the modern practitioners and interpreters of the Dow Theory since Dow have not added a great deal to the theory except refinements, but they have eliminated some of the errors in it. Dow and his followers considered the stock market an excellent barometer of business but did not consider his theory a method of providing market tips.

THE MOVEMENT OF THE MARKET

The Dow Theory is based upon the movements of the DJIA and the DJRA. The movements of the market are divided into three major classifications: the primary movement, the secondary movement, and the daily fluctuations. The primary movement is the trend of the market, which lasts from one year to 28–33 months or longer. The trend of the market is either bullish (up) or bearish (down). The bear markets historically have lasted a shorter period of time than the bull markets. The determination of the primary movement or trend of the market is the basic objective of the Dow Theory.

The secondary movement of the market is shorter in duration than the primary movement, and it is opposite in direction. The secondary movement usually lasts from three weeks to three months and usually retraces one-third to two-thirds of the previous advance in a bull market or the previous decline in a bear market. Secondary movements frequently end in dullness in the stock market activity.

Day-to-day fluctuation is not a part of the Dow Theory interpretation of the stock market. Since the daily movements go to make up the longer movement in the market they must be carefully studied, however, along with the primary and secondary movements.

FORECASTS AND THE DOW THEORY

The forecasts of the Dow Theory are based upon the primary and secondary movements of the market. It is assumed that the movements of the market discount everything. All we must do is watch the averages. They will help to determine the direction of the market.

It is also assumed that the averages cannot be manipulated. Manipulation of the stock market was a grave problem prior to 1933. It was possible for "bear" pools to force a stock below its fair value, or for "bulls" to force a price higher and higher and then unload the stock to the public, causing a sharp drop in price. These manipulative practices have been curbed by the various Security Acts, so this part of the theory is somewhat meaningless in today's economy.

12 E. George Schaefer, "Hold Stocks for Final Market Upsurge," *Forbes,* December 1, 1962, pp. 38–49.

The Dow Theory's purpose is to determine where the market is, but it also indicates where the market is going, although not how far or high. The theory, in practice, states that if the cyclical swings of the stock market averages are successively higher and if the successive lows are higher, then the market trend is up and we are in a bull market. Contrarily, if the successive highs and successive lows in the stock market are lower, then the direction of the market is down and we are in a bear market.

In order for us to be certain that the primary trend is up or down, the industrial averages and the rail averages must confirm the same market action. Figure 18–5 provides an illustration of how we might use the Dow Theory. The trend of the market from P_1 to P_3 is bullish because P_2 is higher than P_1 and P_3 is higher than P_2, and also because T_2 is higher than T_1 and T_3 is higher than T_2. The railroad averages confirm the movements of the industrial averages. When the trend of the market changes, we notice that T_4 is lower than T_3 and P_4 is lower than P_3. When this information is coupled with the successively lower bottoms of the railroad averages, we find confirmation of a bear market with a primary trend downward.

One problem with the Dow Theory is that the confirmation of the market does not come until after a substantial rise or fall. In Figure 18–5 the points of confirmation of the bull market are A and A_R. Until these points are reached, the Dow theorist does not know if the market is in a primary trend upward or beginning a secondary movement downward. This is illustrated when the market reaches T_3. At this point the market could continue down, and by going below T_2 might indicate the beginning of a primary movement in a bear market. However, the bear market cannot be confirmed until the market moves to P_4, turns around, and goes to point X and below. At point X we have a bear market that must be confirmed by the movement of the rail average to point X_R. The investor would move out of the market at point X. He would miss the top of the market P_3, but he would prevent a further market loss. The upturn in a bear market would be similar to the movements traced for a bull market.

THE LINE MOVEMENT

In addition to the major movements of the market, the line movement is used as a part of the Dow Theory. A line movement in the stock market is a trading range where the Dow Jones Averages fluctuate within a narrow price range of about 5 percent of the amount of the averages. The line might last several weeks or longer and is looked upon as a period of accumulation or distribution of stock. If both the DJIA and the DJRA break out of the range on the upside, this is an indication that the market will move up. It is then assumed that the period was one of accumulation. If the averages move down and break through

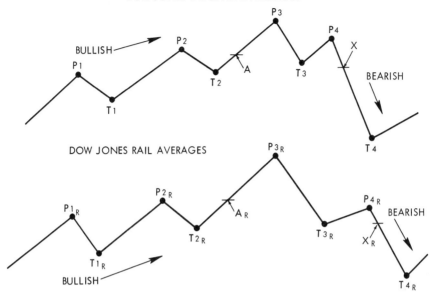

FIGURE 18–5

*Determining the direction of the
market using the Dow Theory and
the Dow Jones Averages*

the trading range, then it would be considered a period of distribution and would indicate a continued downward movement in the averages. If both the averages do not confirm the breakthrough of the line movement, then the direction the market will take is in doubt.

THE SUCCESS OF THE DOW THEORY

The Dow Theory was successful in showing the turn of the big bull market in October, 1929. The industrials gave the signal on October 22, and the rails confirmed on October 23:

> On the late Charles H. Dow's well-known method of reading the stock market movement from the Dow Jones Averages the twenty railroad stocks on Wednesday, October 23 confirmed a bearish indication by the industrials two days before. Together the averages gave a signal for a bear market in stocks after a major bull market with the unprecedented duration of almost six years.[13]

Again in 1933, the end of the big bear market was signaled by the DJIA on April 10 and the rails April 24. In 1949, the Dow Theory signaled the end of the 1946 bear market on August 1 for the industrials and October 10 for the rails. The Dow Theory has not always been

13 *Wall Street Journal,* October 25, 1929, p. 1.

correct, and the proponents of the theory do not consider it infallible. Most advocates claim that it will be right seven out of ten times, an excellent percentage of correct decisions. The Dow Theory is a helpful tool for determining the relative strength of the stock market. It has been successful too when used as a barometer of business. Some evidence suggests that the Dow Jones Averages move up six months ahead of a business upturn in the economy and tend to move down from three to six months ahead of a decline in business activity.

The movements of the stock market from 1959 through August, 1968, appear in Figure 18–6. The investor faced this market in 1968. The market was bearish because in 1966 a new high had been reached that had not been penetrated. The market moved down to the 740 level, established a new low, then went back to 950, failed to penetrate, and dropped back to 850. At this point the new low was higher than the previous low. The market would have to penetrate the 950 level before a bull market was confirmed. Late in 1968 some chartists considered the 820 level a resistance point and were bullish when the market went above this in January, 1968, an interpretation based upon the Dow Theory. The theory has been successful for many Dow theorists, but all experts warn that it is only an aid to intelligent investment.

Breadth Index

Some market traders and investors criticize the Dow Theory because it does not reflect the movement of all the stocks in the market, that

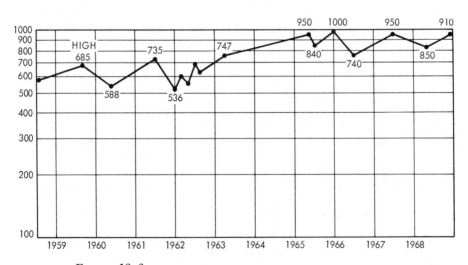

FIGURE 18–6

The actual direction of the market in 1968, indicated by the use of the Dow Jones Industrial Averages and the Dow Theory

the Dow Jones Averages are not representative of the market, since not all stocks move in the same direction at the same time as the Dow Jones Averages. Some chartists now consider the NYSE Index a better guide to the market. There is some validity in this criticism of the Dow Jones Averages. When one considers that there are over 1,100 companies whose shares are traded on an active day in the stock market, we realize that the averages might not reflect the entire movement of the market. In order to overcome this weakness, some market analysts use an index that covers all securities traded and hence is referred to as a breadth index.

The breadth index is computed by dividing the net advances or declines in the market by the number of issues traded. The information is obtained from the *Wall Street Journal* as shown in Figure 18–7. The number of companies whose shares were traded on Friday was 1,512. Of these, 632 securities increased in price, 654 decreased, and 226 remained unchanged. The net declines numbered 22, and the breadth index ratio on that day was minus 1.5 percent (−22/1512). The figures obtained are then combined in a moving average of 150 days, or they are used for comparison with a base year. Today the base year could be 1957 or a later date. The resulting figures are compared to the Dow Jones Averages. The breadth index either supports or is contrary to the movement of the Dow Jones Averages. If it does not support them, this is considered a sign of technical weakness in the market—a sign that the market will move in a direction opposite to the Dow Jones Averages. If, on the other

MARKET DIARY

	Mon	Fri	Thur	Tues	Mon	Fri
Issues traded	1,507	1,516	1,560	1,529	1,539	1,512
Advances	779	792	636	776	925	632
Declines	491	472	707	532	421	654
Unchanged	237	252	217	221	193	226
New highs, 1968	73	53	63	59	56	29
New lows, 1968	15	13	18	16	16	35

DOW-JONES CLOSING AVERAGES

	----MONDAY----			
	1968	—Changes—		1967
Industrials	887.68	+ 1.79	+0.20%	912.27
Railroads	252.62	+ 2.17	+0.86%	257.06
Utilities	132.09	+ 0.57	+0.43%	131.65
Composite	320.59	+ 1.50	+0.47%	326.86

Ex-dividend of International Paper Co., 33¾ cents, lowered the industrial average by 0.19.

Ex-dividend of Southern Pacific Co., 40 cents, lowered the rail average by 0.10.

The above ex-dividends lowered the composite average by 0.07.

OTHER MARKET INDICATORS

		1968	Change	1967
N.Y.S.E.	Composite	55.54	+ 0.19	52.32
	Industrial	58.10	+ 0.22	54.05
	Utility	44.45	+ 0.05	44.71
	Transportation	49.74	+ 0.19	55.87
	Financial	69.20	+ 0.45	51.36
Standard & Poor's Industrial		107.70	+ 0.32	101.86
American Exchange Price Index		$28.73	+$0.09	$21.14
N.Q.B. Over-Counter Industrial		404.60	+ 2.77	331.57

Volume of advancing stocks on N.Y.S.E., 5,920,000 shares; volume of declining stocks, 2,770,000. On American S.E., volume of advancing stocks, 2,920,000; volume of declining stocks, 1,800,000.

FIGURE 18–7

Statistics for the breadth index

SOURCE *The Wall Street Journal*

hand, the breadth index should confirm the movement of the Dow Jones Averages, then this is interpreted as a sign of technical strength. In other words, strength is indicated if the market moves up or down and the breadth index parallels this movement, weakness if the breadth index and Dow Jones Averages move in opposite directions. The breadth index is a valid addition to the Dow Theory and the movement of the Dow Jones Averages. It has been helpful in anticipating changes in the direction of the stock market.

Volume of Trading

The volume of shares traded in the market serves as another guide to the technical strength or weakness of the stock market. The volume-of-trading concept suggests that an upward or downward movement of the stock market accompanied by a large volume of trading is a sign of strength, a movement without volume a sign of technical weakness. The volume concept has a very short-term impact on the market. It is usually associated with a turn in the market. Assume that the stock market begins to move up after a period of decline; we are hopeful that the upward movement is an indication that the market has changed its course. However, we observe that the market rise was accompanied by a relatively small volume. This would indicate that the market is technically weak, and we should not expect a continued rise. If the upward movement were accompanied by a large volume of trading, then we could assume that the market was technically strong. There is no assurance, however, that the movement will continue upward. The volume concept is best used with another market indicator such as the Dow Theory.

The Odd-Lot Volume—Public Participation

Who is buying or selling is also a technical indicator of market strength or weakness. It is generally thought that the professional investor is the astute and informed or strong investor and that the public is the weak or emotional investor. If the professional investor dominates the stock market, then the market is technically strong. On the other hand, if the public is in the market, this is a sign of technical weakness. The weakness concept comes from the habit of public buying being concentrated at the top of the market cycle and public selling coming at the bottom of the market. The quantity of odd-lot purchases and sales are the indication of the extent of public participation in the market, because the assumption is made that small investors do not buy in round lots; so the greater the volume of odd lots, the greater the public participation. And if the odd-lot volume increases either in sales or purchases, this is interpreted as a sign of technical weakness. The data about odd-lots is readily found in the *Wall Street Journal*.

According to the public participation concept, one should be quite apprehensive about the rise in public participation and consider the market technically weak. In defense of the public, we might state that public participation cannot generally be used as an indication of market weakness. Several studies have indicated that the public in general does not move into the market at the peak and move out at the bottom. Often just the reverse is true, and we might conclude that the public is just as sophisticated about investment matters as is the professional investor.

Short Sales as a Market Indicator

The volume of short sales (short interest) in the stock market is also an indication of the technical strength or weakness of the market. A short sale involves the sale of borrowed stock. When a short sale is made, there is an increase in the supply of stock on the market, tending to reduce the price. When a short sale is completed, the purchase of the stocks tends to increase the price. Those who follow and use the volume of short sales as an index of strength of the market state that as short sales rise, strength is indicated, and when short sales decline, technical weakness is shown. A large short interest in a rising market is a particularly strong indication of strength: first, because the market has absorbed the additional supply of stock, and second, because if the market should begin to decline, the short interest will help to support the price of the stock. As the market drops, the speculators will buy at lower prices, make a profit, and support the market.

As a technical indication of stock market strength, the short-interest concept is excellent when used with a general theory of the market such as the Dow Theory. Figures on the volume of short interest in the market can be obtained from *Barron's* magazine or the *Wall Street Journal*.

An example of the use of the short-sale approach can be demonstrated by considering a time when the Dow Jones Averages were trying to break out of a trading range of 800 to 840 in October, 1969. The *Wall Street Journal* reported the level of short interest in the market as follows:

NEW YORK—Short interest on the New York and American Stock Exchanges fell sharply last month, following an upturn the previous month.

The Big Board said short interest, as of the close of business last Wednesday, dropped to 16,584,001 shares from 18,281,429 reported Sept. 15. It was the lowest level since July 15, when short interest totaled 16,393,757 shares, according to the exchange.

The 1,697,428 drop was the largest monthly decline on the Big Board since mid-July 1968, when a 1,818,325 decline in short interest was registered.

Short interest on the American exchange stood at 6,191,021 shares, down 510,707 from a revised 6,701,728 shares in mid-September.

The Big Board said a short position of 5,000 or more shares, or a change of 2,000 or more shares since the last report, existed in 582 of the 1,772 issues listed on the exchange. On the American exchange 216 of the 1,155 stocks and warrants showed a short position of 5,000 shares or more.

A short sale is the sale of borrowed stock. The seller generally expects a price decline that will enable him to repurchase an equal number of shares at a lower price. The short interest is the number of shares that haven't been repurchased for return to lenders.

Fluctuations in short-interest levels of some stocks may have been caused by arbitrage situations. Those stocks are marked by the symbol (t) in the following tables.

In one major method of securities arbitrage, a profit can be made in situations where a company's stock is to be exchanged for that of another, or for a new issue, as a result of a proposed merger. The profit opportunity arises when the various stocks are selling at disparate prices.

An arbitrageur can make a small profit on each share by buying the stock of one company and selling short the stock of the other concern involved in the prospective merger.[14]

The decline in short interest in the market would be a bearish indicator; however, the decline took place in an "up" market, which could be bullish.

Confidence Index

The confidence index is used by some market analysts as a guide to the technical strength of the market and as a method of trading or timing the purchase and sale of stock. It is used by some analysts as a forecasting device, to determine the turning points of the market. The confidence index may be found in *Barron's* and is computed by dividing the yield on the Dow Jones 40 Bonds into the yield on Barron's Ten High Grade Corporate Bonds. On a certain day, the Ten High Grade Bonds yield was 4.16 percent and the yield on the Dow Jones Bonds was 4.91 percent, providing a confidence index of 84.7 percent as quoted in *Barron's*, where these figures are published regularly. The rationale of the confidence index is that investors will buy lower-grade bonds if their confidence is high. This tends to increase the demand for lower-grade bonds and lowers the demand for high-grade bonds. The effect is to decrease the yields on the low-grade bonds and increase those on the high-grade bonds. This tends to increase the confidence index. Thus, if the confidence index moves up, the market is technically strong, and

14 *Wall Street Journal,* October 21, 1969, p. 20.

if the confidence index moves down, it is a sign of technical weakness. As long as the index is above 88, there is unusual confidence in the market. If it falls, or if it is around 70, this is a sign of depressed conditions and a severe lack of confidence in the market. This index is not perfect and will not forecast accurately, nor will it determine the duration of the strength of the market. However, it is a specific factor that helps the investor judge the timing of the relative height of the market when making an investment decision.

Point-and-Figure Charts

Point-and-figure charts are used by market technicians to "predict" the extent and direction of the movements of the stock market. The charts are drawn on ruled paper as seen in Figure 18–8. The numbers to the left represent the price of the stock at 2-point intervals. The interval of price change can be 1, 2, 5, or 10 points, where 1 point equals $1, depending upon the time period orientation of the investor. An investor would be interested in a 5- or 10-point unit and a trader in a 1-point unit. If the price of the stock is high, a 5- or 10-point unit may be used; a 1-point unit or less will be used on low-price stock. Only whole number prices are recognized. In Figure 18–8 the initial price of 33 was entered into Column A as an X. Only if and when the stock moves up to 35 will another X be placed in column A. As long as the price continues to move up, the X's are placed in the same vertical column, in this case, Column A. The stock price in Figure 18–8 moved up from 33 to 37. If and when the price declines to a lower box or level, the chartist records the change by recording the O in the next column. In Figure 18–8 the stock moved down to 35 and the O was placed on the box in Column B at 35. Fractions are ignored in the recording process. No time is indicated on the point-and-figure chart, since price is recorded on the vertical axis and direction on the horizontal axis.

The simple rules followed by the chartist are: Put an X on the

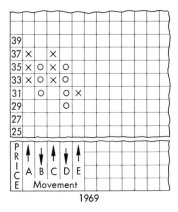

1969

FIGURE 18–8

An illustration of a part of a two-point point-and-figure chart

chart for a price rise to or through a whole number and an O if the price falls to or through a whole number; boxes are filled in only when price changes occur, and a new column is begun each time the direction of price is reversed.

The movements are then interpreted by the chartist. Figure 18–9 is an example of chart interpretation. As long as the market action is between points A and B, there is little indication of market action. As the price breaks out of the upper resistance point B, this is a bullish sign and a signal to buy. The price continues to move up; new highs are made on the chart by the price action, and the new lows are higher than the previous lows. The stock moves to a higher level and two new resistance points are made at C and D. The price finally moves through resistance point C, indicating that the stock should be sold, since there has been a breakout.

This is an oversimplification of the point-and-figure chartist's activities. The charts are helpful in interpreting the market price movement of a stock and should be consulted to improve the timing of an investment.

Investment Forecasting Services

Several investment services attempt to forecast the stock market using information similar to the material we have discussed in this chapter. The future outlook of the stock market is so important to so many institutions and individuals that these specialized forecasting advisory services were bound to develop. Townsend-Skinner and Harding have established indexes that help forecast the stock market based upon data obtained from the monetary system. *Buying Power vs. Selling Pressure*

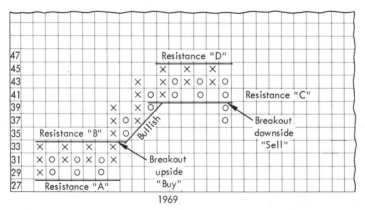

FIGURE 18–9

Example of use of point-and-figure chart for buying and selling

and *The Value Line Investment Survey* also provide a forecast of the stock market. In recent years a host of new services have been established and advertised regularly in the Sunday *New York Times*. The services offer the promise of nearly perfect market forecasts, with the implication that a subscription to the service will lead to instant riches. One source points out that it selects a group of stocks set for a turnaround. Another asks, "The Dow 30: Buy? Hold? Sell?" A third tells about five stocks in the public eye. One discusses the CATV industry; another provides a major reappraisal of 64 growth favorites; still another gives 35 items to analyze in predicting the stock market.

Market analysis is important to the investor; it is wise for investors to orient themselves to the stock market before they make investment commitments, and there are times when market analysis will indicate an obviously high position. However, the ads describing these forecasts or projections are designed to sell a service. Many of them are valuable and helpful to the investor, but point-and-figure charts, chart reading, and market analysis are not services. The practice of market forecasting will not always lead to success, and market analysis is not a panacea for investment decisions. An investor would be wise to sample the market letters of writers such as Dines and Granville, advertised in *The New York Times*, to understand the type of service offered. The services discussed below are older and more fundamental. They do not necessarily offer any great advantage to the investor, but are only examples of what is available.

Townsend-Skinner

Townsend-Skinner publishes a Major Trend Index, which is made up of three parts: (1) an activity of money ratio, computed by dividing commercial loans into the dollar volume of checks drawn against deposits, (2) the ratio of security loans and required reserves into net deposits and currency, indicating the availability of money, and (3) the inflation of money ratio, found by dividing gold reserves into deposits plus currency.

A base year is used for the Major Trend Index, and it is plotted and compared to the Dow Jones Industrial Averages. An upturn in the Major Trend Index should forecast an upturn in the Dow Jones Averages, and vice versa. This is a helpful time series based upon the banking system in operation, but no claim is made for its complete accuracy.

The Harding Index

The Harding Index computes a Stock Market Credit Indicator, using 1926 as a base year. It computes (1) bank debits to commercial loans, (2) bank loans to deposits, and (3) gold reserves to deposits. The average of the three ratios constitutes the Stock Market Credit Indicator. The movement of the indicator precedes the movement of the stock market. An upward turn indicates a rise in the market in the months ahead and a downturn predicts a declining market. It is claimed by the proponents of the index that the high and low points in the market can be determined within 10 percent.

Buying Power vs. Selling Pressure

A service that attempts to forecast the movement of the market based upon the volume of purchases and sales is *Buying Power vs. Selling Pressure*, published by Lowry's Reports, Inc. In contrast to the Harding Index and Townsend-Skinner Index, this is based upon stock market data and not upon monetary information from the banking system. In the Buying-Power Selling-Pressure system, buying power is defined as demand, and selling pressure as supply. Buying Power is determined by dividing the total number of shares traded in a day into the dollar value of the gains in those shares that have increased in price. Selling Pressure is found by dividing the total number of shares traded into the dollar value of the losses of those shares that decreased in price. Only round lots traded on the New York Stock Exchange are considered. If Buying Power moves up and Selling Pressure moves down, this is an indication of strength. If Buying Power moves down and Selling Pressure moves up, this is an indication of weakness. A sell signal is given when after a market rise there is an increase in Selling Pressure. This service does not attempt to predict the length or magnitude of the price trend. *Buying Power vs. Selling Pressure* is indicative of the technical strength of the market and helpful to the investor in timing the purchase of quality stocks.

The Value Line Investment Survey

The Value Line Investment Survey, basically an information service, provides stock market forecasts. It attempts to forecast both the prices of individual securities and the market trend. The forecasts of the market are usually short run and are based upon fundamentals rather than the technical position of the market.

On May 31, 1968, *The Value Line* made the following statement about the stock market:

> The Stock Market has been a mixed affair in recent weeks. Utility shares are moving sideways. Their earnings are rising as usual but long term interest rates are advancing and keeping these money stocks under pressure. Railroad securities have been strong. But the leadership in this group has been supplied by the holding companies that are turning into conglomerates. It is the possibility of escape from the railroad business that has captured the market's fancy. Industrials have given a relatively poor performance during May

after a spectacular upsurge in April. The basic situation of the market is essentially unchanged in recent weeks. Price/earnings multiples are high. The earnings improvement of the last four quarters seems about to reverse. If the 10% surtax is voted next month, a slippage in profits of corporations will begin to show as soon as the June quarter figures are released. If the tax fails to pass, earnings may continue to rise for a quarter or two more. But thereafter they will be extremely vulnerable to the effect of intensified monetary restraint almost certain to be applied if fiscal restraint is eschewed by Congress.[15]

The regular company reports of *The Value Line* attempt to be predictive and to anticipate changes in the market, but they do warn that not every stock will perform in accordance with its ratings.

Standard & Poor's *The Outlook*

The Outlook provides a forecast of the stock market for its subscribers. The forecast is based upon the technical condition of the market, but fundamentals are given major attention. A sample of its technique of commenting appeared in the June 23, 1969, *Outlook* when fears about a money squeeze were high:

> The probabilities are that better opportunities for broad-scale buying will be presented within the fairly near future, although it is as yet premature to depart from the cautious investment policy advocated in recent weeks. The stocks listed and appraised in this issue should do relatively well in the market now and are expected to be leaders during the next advance. The recommended issues fit the needs of almost any type of portfolio and plans can be made now on where to commit reserves once sound evidence appears that a bottom has been made.[16]

The forecasts are short run and must be written to cover a broad group of investors.

Summary

We should examine carefully the past, present, and future earnings of a company and the relationship between earnings, price, and the P/E ratio. Investment analysis stresses the economic and financial position of the company within an industry. The knowledge of investment fundamentals is important for investment success. However, a market analysis is important, too, particularly in the timing of purchases and sales. Securities generally follow the pattern of the stock market. In fact, 85 percent of the price movement of individual stocks is attributed to the market itself, whether the movement of the market is a result of

15 *The Value Line Investment Survey*, May 31, 1968, pp. 821 and 937.
16 Standard & Poor's *The Outlook*, June 23, 1969, p. 743.

economic fundamentals or the technical factors present in the market.

We must attempt to determine the market's current level, direction, and cyclical phase. As a first requirement, we must have an adequate measure of the stock market. Several indexes and averages attempt to measure the trend and direction of the market. The Dow Jones Averages, Standard & Poor's Index, the New York Times Averages, and the NYSE Stock Indexes are the most familiar averages.

Forecasting the stock market is difficult, but even if errors are made, the investor should attempt it. One way of forecasting the stock market is by the use of economic indicators. In this category we can use the GNP, the Federal Reserve Board Index, corporate profits, and other economic data. A second method of forecasting is through the use of bond yields and stock yields or the money market indicators. Included in the money market category are stock yields, stock yield–bond yield differentials, stock prices and money rates, and new offerings of stock. A third method of forecasting, particularly the short-range movements of the market, is by the use of technical indicators. These include the Dow Theory, the breadth index, volume of trading, odd-lot trading, short sales, and the confidence index. Point-and-figure charts are helpful in determining the technical position of the market. Investment services such as Townsend-Skinner, the Harding Index, and *Buying Power vs. Selling Pressure* may be used in making market forecasts. These are based upon the money market indicators or the volume of buying and selling in the market. Individual services, such as *The Value Line Investment Survey* and Standard and Poor's *The Outlook*, provide a forecast of the market in addition to providing factual information. Dines, Granville, and other point-and-figure chartists offer services that attempt to forecast the market. None of the methods of forecasting or determining the position of the market are infallible, nor do they guarantee results. They simply help the investor make a better market judgment.

Review Questions

1. The stock market acts rationally, and therefore it can be predicted with a little effort. Comment.
2. The stock market has a life of its own and acts independently from what basic economics or the so-called fundamentals might suggest. Comment.
3. What do we usually mean when we use the term *the stock market?*
4. What are the qualitative, quantitative, and technical differences between the Dow Jones Averages, the New York Times Average, Standard and Poor's Stock Price Index and the New York Stock Exchange indexes?
5. Is there one best average that can be used by the investor as an indicator of the market as a whole?

6. Discuss how we might use economic indicators to predict the stock market.

7. The money market indicators are sometimes used in an attempt to predict the stock market. How might stock yields, stock–bond yield differentials, money rates, and new offerings of stock be used as indicators of the height of the stock market?

8. What are the technical indicators of the stock market?

9. (a) Explain in detail the Dow Theory and how it might be used to determine the direction of the stock market.
   (b) Has the Dow Theory been successful?

10. Explain how the breadth index, volume of trading, odd-lot volume, short sales, and the confidence index may be used to determine the direction of the market.

11. Discuss how the interpretive forecasting services might help the investor to determine the direction of the stock market.

12. What is a point-and-figure chart and how is it used?

Problems

1. (a) What is the general level of the stock market, based upon the Dow Jones Averages or Standard & Poor's Index?
   (b) Is the market high or low, compared to its historic movement?
   (c) From comments in the financial press, is the market expected to go higher or lower?

2. Examine the following economic indicators and determine if they reveal whether the stock market will move up or down.
   (a) GNP
   (b) Federal Reserve Index
   (c) Corporate profits
   (d) Retail sales

3. Find current information about each of the following money market indicators, and determine which way they suggest the stock market will move.
   (a) Current yields on common stock
   (b) Stock–bond yields differential
   (c) Stock prices and money rates
       (1) Movement of short-term rates
       (2) Bond prices and stock prices
       (3) Commercial bank loans
   (d) New offerings of stock

4. Based upon the use of the following technical indicators, what is the present level of the stock market?
   (a) Dow Theory
   (b) Breadth index
   (c) Volume of trading
   (d) Odd-lot volume
   (e) Short sales
   (f) Confidence index

5. Indicate what these major forecasting services recommend will be the future direction of the stock market.
   (a) Townsend-Skinner
   (b) Harding Index
   (c) *Buying Power vs. Selling Pressure*
   (d) *The Value Line Investment Survey*
   (e) Standard and Poor's *The Outlook*

Sources of Investment Information

Banking
Barron's
Buying Power vs. Selling Pressure
Directory of Investment Publications
Federal Reserve Bulletin
Forbes
Standard and Poor's *The Outlook*
The Harding Index
The Value Line Investment Survey
Townsend-Skinner's *Trend Reports*
Wall Street Journal

Selected Readings

Cohen, Kalman J. and E. Eugene Carter, "Bias in the DJIA Caused by Stock Splits," *Financial Analysts Journal* (November-December, 1966), p. 90.

Drew, Garfield A., "A Clarification of the Odd Lot Theory," *Financial Analysts Journal* (September-October, 1967), p. 107.

Kewley, T. J. and R. A. Stevenson, "The Odd Lot Theory," *Financial Analysts Journal* (September-October, 1967), p. 103.

Levy, Robert A., "Conceptual Foundations of Technical Analysis," *Financial Analysts Journal* (July-August, 1966), p. 83.

Milne, Robert D., "The Dow-Jones Industrial Average Re-Examined," *Financial Analysts Journal* (November-December, 1966), p. 83.

Renshaw, Edward F., "Stock Market Instability," *Financial Analysts Journal* (July-August, 1967), p. 80.

Renshaw, Edward F., "The Stock Market and Prosperity," *Financial Analysts Journal* (January-February, 1967), p. 88.

"Smith, Adam," *The Money Game.* New York: Random House, 1968.

Stoffels, John D., "Stock Recommendations by Investment Advisory Services: Immediate Effects on Market Price," *Financial Analysts Journal* (March-April, 1966), p. 77.

VIII

PORTFOLIO MANAGEMENT

Theory and Practice

19

PORTFOLIO MANAGEMENT

Theory, Objectives, and the Individual Investor

Assuming now that we understand investment analysis and the process of security appraisal, as well as something about the psychology of the stock market, we are now ready to establish an investment portfolio to meet our needs and objectives. The securities we finally select and the results we actually achieve will depend a great deal upon our motives, our own personal needs, the amount of risk that we can assume, and our ability in judging the many variables intelligently in coming to the right conclusion. In this chapter we will discuss the concept of portfolio management theory and practice and some of the variables that must be considered. In succeeding chapters we shall examine more of the specifics of practical portfolio management.

Portfolio Management Theory

Before we enter the subject of portfolio management, we must discuss briefly what might be known as portfolio management theory. Porfolio management is the process of selecting a list of securities that will provide the investor with a maximum yield consistent with the risk he wishes to assume. According to theory, once an acceptable yield and risk level are established by the investor, the process of selection of securities attempts to balance risk and reward. The assumption is made in theory that we can measure yield as the result of income and capital appreciation received, and that we can measure risk as well. It also assumes that the investor will balance yield with risk and that the level of risk and reward in large measure must be defined by the individual.

It is inconceivable from a rational point of view that an investor would be willing to accept a smaller reward for the same degree of risk when the opportunity cost for a higher return is apparent. Very seldom will an investor accept maximum risk with the possibility of maximum reward. This process continues over time so that the investor, in the management of a portfolio, will follow the theoretical premise of the maximization of yield with a given level of risk or a minimum of risk by making adjustments in his portfolio that are consistent with his stated goals. Additional funds will be invested in securities that will continue to maximize yield and minimize risk, although money available for investment at any given moment of time may, in order to maximize yield and minimize risk, be withheld from the market until acceptable alternatives exist. In theory, security analysis provides us with a firm estimate of yield, and security and market analysis allow us to minimize risk.

But while it is important in theory to understand the objectives and principles of portfolio management, it is just as important to understand that in actual practice there will be a substantial amount of error in portfolio management. An investor should not expect 100 percent accuracy in making investment decisions. Price variations of at least 10 percent and as high as 20 percent from existing price levels can be expected. Performance must be measured over the entire investment period to get a true index. If an investor makes 55 percent of his decisions correctly and 45 percent wrong, he will still be successful in the long run.

Portfolio management theory reaffirms the concepts discussed in Chapter 1 where the relationship between risk and reward was discussed. In our discussion, risk was measured as the stability of yield in the past or the stability of price. The computer program presented in Chapter 7 used the stability of earnings growth rate and the deviation of earnings around this growth rate as a measure of risk. The results of the past proved an excellent measure of risk based upon the stability of earnings, yields, or price. Mr. Jack L. Trainor presents his ideas graphically in Chart 19–1[1] about the process of selecting portfolios based upon risk and reward relationships. Essentially the idea is to accept that combination of securities that optimizes the relationships between risk and reward. The curve farthest to the right would be the most desirable combination of securities to purchase for investment at a given moment of time; the arrow indicates the point of lowest risk and highest reward from a given combination of securities.

Essentially what we have on Mr. Trainor's graph is an indifference curve in which we are agreeable to any combination of risk and reward

---

1 Jack L. Trainor, "How to Rate Management of Investment Funds," *Harvard Business Review*, January-February, 1965.

along the curve, but the optimization of risk and reward is at the point on the curve indicated by the arrow. In Chart 19–2 we have two curves representing different portfolios balanced between risk and reward. In Curve AA we have risk relatively stable and varying yields obtainable from various portfolios. Obviously, this is a situation in which an investor is attempting to maximize yield with a given level of risk. Curve BB suggests that as yield increases, risk also increases. At this point we would have to go back to Mr. Trainor's example and select the portfolio that would optimize risk and reward. The percentage gradations of risk along the horizontal axis are arbitrary and must be defined by the individual investor. The measure of risk presented in Chapter 7 on the use of the investment computer program established a stability index equal to 100. A stability index of 30 would indicate much more risk than a stability index of 95 or 90, which is closer to what we might expect from the Dow Jones Industrial Averages. In Chart 19–2, Curve BB shows that increased yield is possible for increased risk up to a point, but that the relationship between risk and reward is not perfect and as risk increases we do not achieve a greater reward.

Dr. Harry Markowitz assumes that investors try to minimize risk by minimizing the deviations from the expected yield on the portfolio, and that they do this by diversifying the portfolio to achieve the desired results. Dr. Markowitz[2] has established a computer program

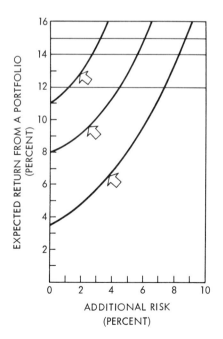

CHART 19–1

Investor's indifference curves

2 Harry M. Markowitz, "Portfolio Selection," *Journal of Finance*, March, 1952; and *Portfolio Selection* (New York: John Wiley & Sons, Inc., 1959).

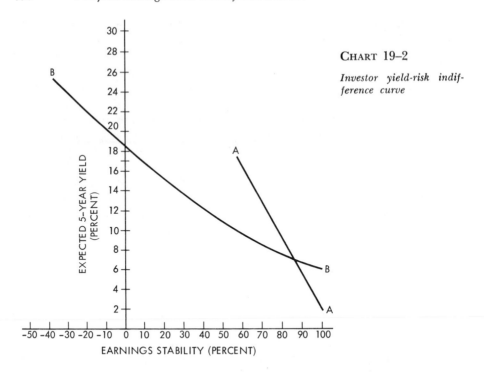

CHART 19–2

Investor yield-risk indifference curve

for selecting portfolios that attempts to give the most efficient diversification in terms of minimization of risk. Markowitz's program involves the complex mathematics of quadratic programming. Because this can be done only with the use of electronic computers, his theoretical ideas and their practical application are limited to the most sophisticated investors with a maximum of computer resources. Markowitz's basic theme is that the investor, being a risk averter, would rather have a 10 percent yield with a plus or minus 2 percent error variation than a portfolio that had a 10 percent yield with a 4 percent error variation, or a portfolio with 12 percent rate of return and a 3 percent error variation than one with a 14 percent return and 5 percentage points error variation. By judicious comparison of the expected rate of return, the standard deviation of estimates, and the lowest and highest expected range of returns at two standard deviations, the investor then selects various portfolios, one of which then can be chosen by the computer as the "most efficient" for the needs of the investor based upon risk and reward. In essence, the theoretical premise on which the Markowitz Model is based is simply that investors try to combine into one portfolio a list of securities that gives a maximization of yield and a minimization of risk where the risk is measured by the stability of the yield in terms of a standard statistical concept.

A great deal of work has been done on the application of the computer to the problems of risk, the valuation of common stock, and a selection of portfolios. One such model, by Richard S. Bower, is called "Risk and the Valuation of Common Stock," an unpublished paper completed at Dartmouth. In addition, students are referred to *Computer Applications and Investment Analysis* by Chace, Gifford, Bower and Williamson.[3] Another computer program is the one developed by Sharpe.[4] In addition, Buckford A. Wallingford has developed a program for portfolio selection.[5]

In actual practice the investor, with limited resources in terms of computer time and abilities, must put together a list of securities that offers an optimum combination of risk and yield. In theory the investor follows the type of practice suggested by Markowitz, but with a limited opportunity of putting theory into practice to achieve the same results as a computer model that scans the entire universe rather than just a small sample of stocks.

The Ingredients and Objectives of Portfolio Management in Practice

We select securities from a list of common stocks and bonds that generally meet our investment objectives. We do not need to analyze all securities, because a small number of the hundreds traded in the securities market have both quality and yield that would be attractive for most investors. It might be convenient to examine the investment services of Clark Dodge, Eastman Dillon, Union Securities & Co., Standard & Poor's, Merrill Lynch, or the Value Line Investment Service to obtain a list of securities from which we can make our selection. Many of these securities will meet our portfolio requirements. Both the ingredients and the objectives of portfolio management tend to focus on either averting risk or obtaining a proper yield.

The Ingredients of Portfolio Management

When we attempt to meet investment needs by selecting securities for a portfolio, we are engaging in portfolio management. Portfolio management, in total, includes the planning, supervision, timing, rationalism, and conservatism involved in the selection of securities to meet an investor's objectives. We will examine each phase and then look into

3 Richard H. Chace, Jr., William C. Gifford, Jr., Richard S. Bower, and J. Peter Williamson, *Computer Applications and Investment Analysis*, The Amos Tuck School of Business Administration, Dartmouth College, Hanover, New Hampshire, *Tuck Bulletin*, September 30, 1966.

4 William F. Sharpe, *Diagonal Portfolio Selection Model*, developed at Dartmouth.

5 Buckford A. Wallingford, III, *Portfolio Selection*, The Amos Tuck School, Dartmouth College, Hanover, New Hampshire, 1966.

the objectives an investor might establish in managing a portfolio. We assume that each individual investor has the education, experience, training, and time to provide the management for his own portfolio.

PLANNING

The first essential ingredient in portfolio management is planning. This means thought and preparation in establishing a list of securities to meet the needs of the investor. If an investor needs capital growth now and income in later years, the plan must reflect these needs. Very often investments are made without regard to any plan. Suddenly the investor finds he has a group of securities that make up his portfolio, but that might or might not meet his objectives. In investing this way, he could make errors that would lead to a financial loss. To handle the investment problem intelligently, we must have our objectives clearly defined and a plan established to meet these objectives.

We might be wise to write out our investment objectives and then originate a plan to meet them. Assume, for example, that we want an income portfolio. We know generally which securities will provide us with the greatest income. From among the income-type securities, we will select a group of stocks and bonds to meet our needs. As funds become available we plan to add to the various segments of our investment account. Nothing is haphazard; a well-defined course of action is determined in advance. This type of activity is essential to investment success. Planning, therefore, is a part of the risk aversion process.

TIMING

Another ingredient necessary for investment success is timing. This is also considered when the investment plan is being undertaken. The market fluctuates according to the economic and political climate. Individual stocks also vary in price, in time establishing a price range. In the process of analysis we must decide when a stock is high or low. We know we cannot always buy stocks at the low price and sell them at the high price, but we can tell within limits when a stock appears to be underpriced or overpriced. We should, therefore, try to purchase stock close to its low price, or at least at an attractive price consistent with its own price movement and future expectations.

An example of this might make our position clear about timing. In planning a portfolio for an individual, it was decided that Hertz Corporation, a leading company in the auto-leasing field, would be a desirable stock to have. It was overpriced in relation to its earnings. The price range for the stock was between 37 and 65 from 1958 to 1962. When the company was examined, it was selling at 52, a price thought to be high in relation to its future expected yield. Also, the stock market during 1962 showed signs of weakness, suggesting a decrease in stock prices. The conclusion was that Hertz would be an excellent buy at about 37, and an order was placed to acquire the stock at 37. The market did react downward, and the stock was acquired at that price. The price of 37 might not be the lowest for the stock, but it was much better than 52. In this case timing was very important in making an investment decision.

CONSERVATISM AND RATIONALISM

The investor should be conservative and act rationally when making investment decisions. The concept of conservatism is extremely important. One of the essential aspects of investment is to minimize risk. We wish to accept risk consistent with our gains, but not above our abilities. It is unnecessary to select something other than the best company to earn a profit. We should remember the statement, "Discretion is the better part of valor." It would be imprudent to accept risk beyond what is necessary. Risk and gain are correlated. We are wise to accept reasonable gain for reasonable risk rather than to accept undue risk with a strong possibility of loss.

A basic tenet of portfolio management is that rational decisions will be made. We cannot assume that all decisions will be correct, but they will be based on fact if we take a rational course of action rather than an emotional one. That is why planning is essential to success. Each time a stock is to be purchased we should know what place it has in the portfolio and what is expected of it. If, for example, Hertz were purchased at 37, we must know what to expect. If we establish the objective of long-term growth, then we expect to hold it for the long term. If another person bought Hertz at 37 for short-term gain in the hopes that it would rise to 55, then he should hold it for this period. If the objective is not reached, it should be sold and a new investment made. We buy on the basis of expectation, and decisions should be made rationally on this basis. In the process of being conservative and rational we are minimizing risk.

SUPERVISION

Portfolio management assumes periodic supervision of the securities in the portfolio. Some individuals advocate a buy-and-hold philosophy, where stocks are purchased and put away and forgotten. In our competitive society and in view of the fluctuation of the stock market, this is not a very prudent, conservative, or rational plan of action for sound portfolio management. A stock may be bought and held for a lifetime—but it should not be ignored. One should frequently analyze the company and the security to make certain that it meets the needs of the investor. The professional investment fund manager, for example, will examine each client's account once a month. If a change is suggested by research and analysis, the necessary action will be taken. Changes will be made if the fundamental position of the investment has changed.

If a stock appears overpriced in the market it might be sold. Supervision of this type prevents loss to the investor and should be considered as a vital part of portfolio management.

PERFORMANCE

It is important that we measure investment performance to make certain we are meeting our investment goals or the goals of our clients. In corporate financial circles we might refer to this as the recapitulation process. If we make an investment decision based upon the expectation of a 10 percent yield for a three- to five-year period, we should determine if we have met our objective or are in the process of doing so. This is particularly true if the investment has been sold. We want to know if it provided the expected yield, and if not, we should try to determine the reason. The variation in results and expectations is likely to be great, but the process should be undertaken. The investment community is becoming increasingly concerned about the performance of security analysts, investment advisors, and mutual fund managers. To date, half of the mutual fund managers have done better than the market and half have done worse. There is no clear-cut way in which we can always perform better than the market. Nonetheless we should measure our performance against our goals and objectives to make certain we do get the results we desire.[6] The constant measurement of performance tends to emphasize risk reduction and improvement of yield.

Objectives of Portfolio Management

The emphasis of portfolio management varies from investor to investor. Some want income, some capital gains, and some a combination of both. In spite of these variations, there are several objectives that we should consider as basic to a well-executed investment program. These might be more carefully defined as guiding principles in establishing an investment fund. They broaden the concept of rational and prudent action in making decisions.

SECURITY OF PRINCIPAL

The first consideration in establishing investment objectives is the security of principal. We should attempt to preserve the value of our investment account so that we will be able to obtain future income and growth. There are two groups of people to which this principle is extremely important. One is the investor with a small fund who

---

6 For those interested in the subject of performance, see Irwin Friend and Douglas Vickers, "Portfolio Selection and Investment Performance," *Journal of Finance*, September, 1965; Randolph W. McCandlish, Jr., "Some Methods for Measuring Performance of a Pension Fund," *Financial Analysts Journal*, November-December 1965; and W. Scott Bauman, "Evaluation of Prospective Investment Performance," *Journal of Finance*, May, 1968, p. 276.

says, "I'm interested in quick growth," and continues by saying: "It really doesn't make any difference if I lose my entire investment. I don't have too much to lose." This thinking can lead to unwise decisions and the acceptance of unnecessary risk. The result might be the inevitable: the investor might lose all of his capital.

The other investor is the wealthy man with the large investment account. His position is the same as the small investor's, but for a different reason. He rationalizes: "I'm wealthy; therefore, I can afford to lose some of my principal." This type of thinking might lead to undue risk resulting in a large capital loss that would be difficult to replace. Perhaps the wealthy individual can assume more risk with a portion of his investment fund. But this type of thought process should not govern his entire fund.

An investment fund is difficult to establish today from accumulated earnings. A few fortunate people inherit a fund already accumulated and intact. A person who can accumulate a fund over time, or a person who has inherited a fund, must protect his principal. He should not accept undue risk. The conservative investor, therefore, considers protection of principal an extremely important part of his investment management.

Security of principal means more than just maintaining the original fund. It means in addition that the purchasing power of the fund must be protected. We know that the purchasing-power risk is a very real risk assumed by investors. Inflation does make inroads in the purchasing power of the fund. We must take the necessary steps to maintain purchasing power by buying common stocks that are expected to increase in value if the purchasing power of the dollar declines. Common stocks are not a perfect hedge against inflation, but they are much better at the task than fixed-income securities such as bonds or preferred stocks. If we ignore the purchasing-power risk of our investment fund, we fail to recognize a real threat to our long-range investment objectives and our financial well-being.

STABILITY OF INCOME

In establishing an investment fund, an investor should attempt to achieve stability of income as a practical consideration. It allows him an opportunity to enjoy currently the benefits from his portfolio, in the form of income or a contingency fund available for reinvestment. And the income received in the form of dividends and interest is somewhat more valuable than a promise of future dividends and interest. Stability of revenues allows him to plan more accurately and logically what will be done with his funds, whether they are marked for reinvestment or consumption. Stability of revenue provides a more valuable fund than does sporadic, unstable, or uncertain income.

The investor must give recognition to the timing and amount of income that will be generated from his funds. This requires a detailed knowledge of the dividend policies of the companies: when they pay their dividend and in what amount. Usually companies pay dividends quarterly; but they pay at different times in the quarter. This is a technical point of portfolio management, but it is helpful to have a knowledge of the income pattern.

Not all investors will seek current income from their portfolios. Other considerations might dominate their investment decisions. This is true of the investor in a high income bracket or in a position where current income is not needed. For the majority of investors, however, income is necessary, and stability of income is a desirable feature of an investment portfolio.

CAPITAL GROWTH

As a general rule, growth of capital is a desirable objective of portfolio management. This does not mean that every investor must invest in growth stocks. This would be inconsistent with many investors' needs. A fund can be built up from reinvested income as well as through the purchase of growth shares. A larger fund, however, does provide more stability, more security, and eventually more income for the investor than does a smaller fund. Many investors have increased the capital value of their funds through reinvested dividends and interest income. Capital growth is necessary to improve the long-range position of the investor, to maintain purchasing power, and to offer flexibility of management. Capital growth focuses on yield and measures both risk and reward. The greater the assurance of capital growth, the greater the yield and the lower the risk.

MARKETABILITY

Another desirable objective of a sound investment portfolio is marketability. Marketability refers to the ability to buy or sell a security easily and quickly. It is a function of price and the size of the market for a given stock. The size of the market is determined in turn by the size of the company, the number of shareholders, and the general public interest in the stock. High-priced stocks, for example, are less marketable than low-priced. It is logical to expect that the marketability for a stock at the $400 level is less than for stock selling at $40.

The place where a stock is traded also has some impact on its marketability. Stocks listed on the New York or the American Stock Exchange have greater marketability and provide more information for the investor than those traded on local exchanges or in the over-the-counter market. However, the improvement in the OTC quotation system as a result of the Special Study has improved marketability, which makes where a stock is traded somewhat less important.

It is difficult to find price quotes on stocks that are traded infrequently. This can be disconcerting if the information is needed immediately.

Smaller companies tend to have less marketability than companies that are larger, simply because the larger companies have a greater number of shares outstanding. The increased number of shares traded allows a continuous market for stock. The concept of continuous marketability refers to the number of transactions and the close relationship in price between one sale and the previous sale. In the over-the-counter market, for example, a price range of 50 to 57 for a stock might persist. The price range for a listed stock might be 52 to 53. The narrower price range is a result of the continuous market and the large number of transactions. The over-the-counter market as a whole has been less continuous than the listed market, but this has improved with changes in quoting and reporting of price.

The size of the company influences marketability in another way. The larger companies tend to be more stable, and size and stability tend to make the company more marketable. Smaller companies often do not possess other investment characteristics as well, and therefore have less marketability.

The quality of the company also enters the picture. The market for investments is influenced a great deal by quality-oriented institutions. For this reason the quality companies tend to be more marketable.

LIQUIDITY

We stated before that one of the problems of the investor is to balance liquidity with profitability. Liquidity, or nearness to money, is desirable because it offers the investor an opportunity to take advantage of attractive investment opportunities. If liquidity is maintained in the portfolio, the investor will be able to take advantage of lower prices or special situations. Conservative portfolio management suggests that some liquidity be maintained, either by setting aside a portion of the investment fund for such purposes or by arranging to use interest and dividends to provide the liquidity to purchase new shares.

DIVERSIFICATION

An individual cannot select one security that will give him all that he wishes in an investment. There is no one panacea for investment needs. We cannot expect to obtain a high yield, for example, and assume little or no risk. Nor can we choose the company that will always perform better than other companies or the market as a whole. We might estimate that electronics is a growing industry and select the leading company for investment. However, concentration in one company's stock might lead to a substantial loss. It would be better to buy two companies that we think will be successful, and to buy in two or more growth industries, than to concentrate our investment in one stock. We do this simply to spread the risk of loss. The old saying, "Don't put all your eggs in one basket," is important. One company might fail, but it is not likely that all companies will fail. By buying stock in different companies we diversify the risk of loss.

We diversify too by the types of securities in which we invest. Some portion of every investment account should be in bonds. The amount of bonds in the portfolio will depend upon the height of the market and the needs of the investor. The remaining portion of the fund can be invested in a well-diversified list of common stocks. Whether the emphasis of the portfolio is income or growth, the investments should be diversified between fixed-income and capital-growth securities.

It is difficult to provide adequate diversification with a small fund. A fund of $100,000—not a large fund in investment circles—would have some bonds and from eight to twelve different common stocks in different industries. A larger fund of $5 million might be diversified widely between stocks and bonds and between industries and between as many as thirty different companies. The large portfolio encompasses almost every form of diversification: type of security, type of industry, type and geographical location of company, cyclical or growth company, and, where bonds are purchased, some maturity diversification will be achieved.

One can, however, overdiversify. One investment club, for example, had a fund of less than $10,000 invested in thirty different common stocks. Thirty companies are difficult to analyze and manage for a small group of people. A manageable amount of diversification for a $10,000 fund would be from three to six different common stocks. This number and balance could continue until the fund reached a much larger size. A $200,000 fund might have seven different industries represented and from fifteen to twenty different companies. The dangers of over-diversification are (1) the inability of one person to handle the job of portfolio management, and (2) less possibility of the fund's performing better than the market. Some funds are so large and so diversified that we can hope to obtain only average results from the portfolio. In the last analysis, the diversification of the fund is determined by the amount of the fund and the ability of the individual to handle the fund. It would probably be better to emphasize quality and restrict the number of investments than to expect overdiversification to solve all investment ills.

Diversification Principle. The principle to follow in diversification is to invest in a sufficient number of companies, based upon risk and yield, to assure that the investment performance desired will actually occur. If there are fifty companies at any given time that offer a yield expectation of 20 percent with a high stability of yield, then sufficient stocks from this group should be selected to insure that their average performance will give the investor a 20 percent yield with a minimum variation. Diversification, marketability, and liquidity are risk-reducing activities.

FAVORABLE TAX STATUS

One factor of importance in the management of investment portfolios is the tax position of the investor. Many financial decisions in
today's society are governed by federal income taxes. The problem is
how to keep as much of the income and capital gains as possible. With
progressive tax rates on ordinary income, it is difficult to keep a dollar
of income. The investor either invests in tax-free bonds or buys securities
that pay no dividend income but offer the promise of future rewards
in the form of capital gains. Long-term capital gains on the sale of a
capital asset are taxed at the maximum rate of 25 percent. A long-term
gain must be owned for six months or longer. Short-term capital gains are
taxed as ordinary income, at rates as high as 70 percent. (See Figure
19–1 for rates.) It is wise, therefore, for an individual in the 50 percent
or higher tax bracket to consider capital gains or to invest in tax-exempt
municipal bonds.

The high rate of federal income taxation has always been a concern, but increasingly, states are imposing income taxes on their residents
that make it vital to the wealthy investor to protect himself from
taxation and keep himself in a favorable tax position. In 1969, California income tax rates were as high as 10 percent and New York state
taxes went as high as 16 percent.

We learned in our discussion on municipal bonds that they are
free from federal income taxes on the interest received. A person in the
50 percent tax bracket who buys a 4 percent tax-exempt bond in effect
receives an 8 percent before-tax yield. An individual in the 71 percent
bracket receives a 13.8 percent yield when he purchases a 4 percent bond.
The method of arriving at the fully taxable equivalent rate of return
was presented in Chapter 3.

Often the tax position of the investor is ignored. One case occurred
recently which demonstrates the difficulties involved in considering the
tax factor in making decisions. An investor had established a portfolio
based upon a growth objective. He wanted future growth because he
did not wish to pay high income taxes; he was in the 71 percent tax
bracket. However, his investment portfolio had no tax-exempt bonds.
Several of the common stocks he owned were income rather than growth
stocks, with a high dividend rate. His portfolio policy did not reflect
his tax position. He should have attempted to maximize his investment
returns by minimizing his federal income-tax liability. Or consider the
wealthy industrialist in a top income-tax bracket who had invested
almost $200,000 in savings bonds over the years. He was keeping a
very small amount of the interest after taxes. The importance of obtaining a favorable tax status is particularly important when taxes increase
substantially as during a war or as was the case in 1968 when a long-
overdue 10 percent surtax on federal income taxes was levied by Congress.

The investor can minimize his tax liability by doing one or all of
the following:

Tax Tables for Persons With Incomes Under $5,000 ▶ WHO DO NOT ITEMIZE DEDUCTIONS ON THEIR RETURNS

If you checked as your filing status on page 1, Form 1040

Line 1a use ──▶ TAX TABLE A—For Single Persons
Line 1b, 1d, or 1e use ──▶ TAX TABLE B—For Married Persons Filing Joint Returns or Unmarried Heads of Household
Line 1c use ──▶ TAX TABLE C—For Married Persons Filing Separate Returns

Tables A and B reflect the lowest tax after considering both the 10 percent standard deduction and the minimum standard deduction. Table C shows the tax based on either the 10 percent or the minimum standard deduction.

1968 TAX TABLE A— For Single Persons

Read down the income columns below until you find the line covering the total income (page 1, line 9, Form 1040). Then read across to the appropriate column headed by the number corresponding to the number of your exemptions. This is your tax. Enter tax on line 12a. Also see page 10 for tax surcharge to be entered on line 12b.

If your total income is—		And the number of exemptions is—			If your total income is—		And the number of exemptions is—					
At least	But less than	1	2	3 — If 4 or more there is no tax	At least	But less than	1	2	3	4	5	6 — If 7 or more there is no tax
		Your tax (before surcharge) is—					Your tax (before surcharge) is—					
$0	$900	$0	$0	$0	$2,450	$2,475	$236	$124	$23	$0	$0	$0
900	925	2	0	0	2,475	2,500	240	128	26	0	0	0
925	950	5	0	0	2,500	2,525	244	132	30	0	0	0
950	975	9	0	0	2,525	2,550	248	136	33	0	0	0
975	1,000	12	0	0	2,550	2,575	253	139	37	0	0	0
1,000	1,025	16	0	0	2,575	2,600	257	143	40	0	0	0
1,025	1,050	19	0	0	2,600	2,625	261	147	44	0	0	0
1,050	1,075	23	0	0	2,625	2,650	265	151	47	0	0	0
1,075	1,100	26	0	0	2,650	2,675	270	155	51	0	0	0
1,100	1,125	30	0	0	2,675	2,700	274	159	54	0	0	0
1,125	1,150	33	0	0	2,700	2,725	278	163	58	0	0	0
1,150	1,175	37	0	0	2,725	2,750	282	167	61	0	0	0
1,175	1,200	40	0	0	2,750	2,775	287	171	65	0	0	0
1,200	1,225	44	0	0	2,775	2,800	291	175	68	0	0	0
1,225	1,250	47	0	0	2,800	2,825	295	179	72	0	0	0
1,250	1,275	51	0	0	2,825	2,850	299	183	76	0	0	0
1,275	1,300	54	0	0	2,850	2,875	304	187	79	0	0	0
1,300	1,325	58	0	0	2,875	2,900	308	191	83	0	0	0
1,325	1,350	61	0	0	2,900	2,925	312	195	87	0	0	0
1,350	1,375	65	0	0	2,925	2,950	317	199	91	0	0	0
1,375	1,400	68	0	0	2,950	2,975	322	203	94	0	0	0
1,400	1,425	72	0	0	2,975	3,000	327	207	98	0	0	0
1,425	1,450	76	0	0	3,000	3,050	333	213	104	4	0	0
1,450	1,475	79	0	0	3,050	3,100	342	221	111	11	0	0
1,475	1,500	83	0	0	3,100	3,150	350	229	119	18	0	0
1,500	1,525	87	0	0	3,150	3,200	359	238	126	25	0	0
1,525	1,550	91	0	0	3,200	3,250	367	246	134	32	0	0
1,550	1,575	94	0	0	3,250	3,300	376	255	141	39	0	0
1,575	1,600	98	0	0	3,300	3,350	385	263	149	46	0	0
1,600	1,625	102	2	0	3,350	3,400	393	272	157	53	0	0
1,625	1,650	106	5	0	3,400	3,450	402	280	165	60	0	0
1,650	1,675	109	9	0	3,450	3,500	410	289	173	67	0	0
1,675	1,700	113	12	0	3,500	3,550	419	297	181	74	0	0
1,700	1,725	117	16	0	3,550	3,600	427	306	189	81	0	0
1,725	1,750	121	19	0	3,600	3,650	436	315	197	89	0	0
1,750	1,775	124	23	0	3,650	3,700	444	324	205	96	0	0
1,775	1,800	128	26	0	3,700	3,750	453	334	213	104	4	0
1,800	1,825	132	30	0	3,750	3,800	462	343	221	111	11	0
1,825	1,850	136	33	0	3,800	3,850	470	353	229	119	18	0
1,850	1,875	139	37	0	3,850	3,900	479	362	238	126	25	0
1,875	1,900	143	40	0	3,900	3,950	487	372	246	134	32	0
1,900	1,925	147	44	0	3,950	4,000	496	381	255	141	39	0
1,925	1,950	151	47	0	4,000	4,050	504	390	263	149	46	0
1,950	1,975	155	51	0	4,050	4,100	513	399	272	157	53	0
1,975	2,000	159	54	0	4,100	4,150	521	407	280	165	60	0
2,000	2,025	163	58	0	4,150	4,200	530	416	289	173	67	0
2,025	2,050	167	61	0	4,200	4,250	538	424	297	181	74	0
2,050	2,075	171	65	0	4,250	4,300	547	433	306	189	81	0
2,075	2,100	175	68	0	4,300	4,350	556	442	315	197	89	0
2,100	2,125	179	72	0	4,350	4,400	564	450	324	205	96	0
2,125	2,150	183	76	0	4,400	4,450	573	459	334	213	104	4
2,150	2,175	187	79	0	4,450	4,500	581	467	343	221	111	11
2,175	2,200	191	83	0	4,500	4,550	590	476	353	229	119	18
2,200	2,225	195	87	0	4,550	4,600	598	484	362	238	126	25
2,225	2,250	199	91	0	4,600	4,650	607	493	372	246	134	32
2,250	2,275	203	94	0	4,650	4,700	615	501	381	255	141	39
2,275	2,300	207	98	0	4,700	4,750	624	510	391	263	149	46
2,300	2,325	211	102	2	4,750	4,800	633	519	400	272	157	53
2,325	2,350	215	106	5	4,800	4,850	641	527	410	280	165	60
2,350	2,375	219	109	9	4,850	4,900	650	536	419	289	173	67
2,375	2,400	223	113	12	4,900	4,950	658	544	429	297	181	74
2,400	2,425	227	117	16	4,950	5,000	667	553	438	306	189	81
2,425	2,450	231	121	19								

FIGURE 19–1 (a)

1968 Tax Rate Schedules

If you do not use one of the Tax Tables, then figure your tax on the amount on line 11d, page 1 of your return by using the appropriate Tax Rate Schedule on this page. Enter tax on line 12a. Also see page 10 for tax surcharge to be entered on line 12b.

Schedule I

Single Taxpayers not qualifying for rates in Schedules II and III, and Married Persons Filing Separate Returns

If the amount on line 11d, page 1, is: — Enter on line 12a, page 1:

Not over $500 ..... 14% of the amount on line 11d.

Over—	But not over—		of excess over—
$500	— $1,000	$70, plus 15%	— $500
$1,000	— $1,500	$145, plus 16%	— $1,000
$1,500	— $2,000	$225, plus 17%	— $1,500
$2,000	— $4,000	$310, plus 19%	— $2,000
$4,000	— $6,000	$690, plus 22%	— $4,000
$6,000	— $8,000	$1,130, plus 25%	— $6,000
$8,000	— $10,000	$1,630, plus 28%	— $8,000
$10,000	— $12,000	$2,190, plus 32%	— $10,000
$12,000	— $14,000	$2,830, plus 36%	— $12,000
$14,000	— $16,000	$3,550, plus 39%	— $14,000
$16,000	— $18,000	$4,330, plus 42%	— $16,000
$18,000	— $20,000	$5,170, plus 45%	— $18,000
$20,000	— $22,000	$6,070, plus 48%	— $20,000
$22,000	— $26,000	$7,030, plus 50%	— $22,000
$26,000	— $32,000	$9,030, plus 53%	— $26,000
$32,000	— $38,000	$12,210, plus 55%	— $32,000
$38,000	— $44,000	$15,510, plus 58%	— $38,000
$44,000	— $50,000	$18,990, plus 60%	— $44,000
$50,000	— $60,000	$22,590, plus 62%	— $50,000
$60,000	— $70,000	$28,790, plus 64%	— $60,000
$70,000	— $80,000	$35,190, plus 65%	— $70,000
$80,000	— $90,000	$41,790, plus 68%	— $80,000
$90,000	— $100,000	$48,590, plus 69%	— $90,000
$100,000		$55,490, plus 70%	— $100,000

Schedule II

Married Taxpayers Filing Joint Returns and Certain Widows and Widowers

If the amount on line 11d, page 1, is: — Enter on line 12a, page 1:

Not over $1,000 .... 14% of the amount on line 11d.

Over—	But not over—		of excess over—
$1,000	— $2,000	$140, plus 15%	— $1,000
$2,000	— $3,000	$290, plus 16%	— $2,000
$3,000	— $4,000	$450, plus 17%	— $3,000
$4,000	— $8,000	$620, plus 19%	— $4,000
$8,000	— $12,000	$1,380, plus 22%	— $8,000
$12,000	— $16,000	$2,260, plus 25%	— $12,000
$16,000	— $20,000	$3,260, plus 28%	— $16,000
$20,000	— $24,000	$4,380, plus 32%	— $20,000
$24,000	— $28,000	$5,660, plus 36%	— $24,000
$28,000	— $32,000	$7,100, plus 39%	— $28,000
$32,000	— $36,000	$8,660, plus 42%	— $32,000
$36,000	— $40,000	$10,340, plus 45%	— $36,000
$40,000	— $44,000	$12,140, plus 48%	— $40,000
$44,000	— $52,000	$14,060, plus 50%	— $44,000
$52,000	— $64,000	$18,060, plus 53%	— $52,000
$64,000	— $76,000	$24,420, plus 55%	— $64,000
$76,000	— $88,000	$31,020, plus 58%	— $76,000
$88,000	— $100,000	$37,980, plus 60%	— $88,000
$100,000	— $120,000	$45,180, plus 62%	— $100,000
$120,000	— $140,000	$57,580, plus 64%	— $120,000
$140,000	— $160,000	$70,380, plus 66%	— $140,000
$160,000	— $180,000	$83,580, plus 68%	— $160,000
$180,000	— $200,000	$97,180, plus 69%	— $180,000
$200,000		$110,980, plus 70%	— $200,000

Schedule III

Unmarried (or legally separated) Taxpayers Who Qualify as Heads of Household

(See page 3)

If the amount on line 11d, page 1, is: — Enter on line 12a, page 1:

Not over $1,000 ..... 14% of the amount on line 11d.

Over—	But not over—		of excess over—
$1,000	— $2,000	$140, plus 16%	— $1,000
$2,000	— $4,000	$300, plus 18%	— $2,000
$4,000	— $6,000	$660, plus 20%	— $4,000
$6,000	— $8,000	$1,060, plus 22%	— $6,000
$8,000	— $10,000	$1,500, plus 25%	— $8,000
$10,000	— $12,000	$2,000, plus 27%	— $10,000
$12,000	— $14,000	$2,540, plus 31%	— $12,000
$14,000	— $16,000	$3,160, plus 32%	— $14,000
$16,000	— $18,000	$3,800, plus 35%	— $16,000
$18,000	— $20,000	$4,500, plus 36%	— $18,000
$20,000	— $22,000	$5,220, plus 40%	— $20,000
$22,000	— $24,000	$6,020, plus 41%	— $22,000
$24,000	— $26,000	$6,840, plus 43%	— $24,000
$26,000	— $28,000	$7,700, plus 45%	— $26,000
$28,000	— $32,000	$8,600, plus 46%	— $28,000
$32,000	— $36,000	$10,440, plus 48%	— $32,000
$36,000	— $38,000	$12,360, plus 50%	— $36,000
$38,000	— $40,000	$13,360, plus 52%	— $38,000
$40,000	— $44,000	$14,400, plus 53%	— $40,000
$44,000	— $50,000	$16,520, plus 55%	— $44,000
$50,000	— $52,000	$19,820, plus 56%	— $50,000
$52,000	— $64,000	$20,940, plus 58%	— $52,000
$64,000	— $70,000	$27,900, plus 59%	— $64,000
$70,000	— $76,000	$31,440, plus 61%	— $70,000
$76,000	— $80,000	$35,100, plus 62%	— $76,000
$80,000	— $88,000	$37,580, plus 63%	— $80,000
$88,000	— $100,000	$42,620, plus 64%	— $88,000
$100,000	— $120,000	$50,300, plus 66%	— $100,000
$120,000	— $140,000	$63,500, plus 67%	— $120,000
$140,000	— $160,000	$76,900, plus 68%	— $140,000
$160,000	— $180,000	$90,500, plus 69%	— $160,000
$180,000		$104,300, plus 70%	— $180,000

11

FIGURE 19-1 (b)

607

a. Purchase tax-exempt bonds whose interest is free from federal income taxes.

b. Purchase bonds with a tax-free covenant. In this case the corporation agrees to pay the tax for the bondholder directly.

c. Purchase bonds with a tax-refund clause. In this case the bondholder pays the tax and is then reimbursed by the company.

d. Purchase securities that offer long-term capital gains taxed at a maximum of 25 percent of the gain. Actually, the investor has two alternative methods to calculate his tax liability for long-term gains. He can either pay a flat 25 percent of the gain or declare 50 percent of the gain and pay ordinary income taxes. If he is in the 50 percent bracket or above, it is wise for him to pay a flat 25 percent.

e. When purchasing and selling assets, look for a possibility of exchanging assets. This exchange is referred to as a *tax swap*. In this situation, the investor trades one investment, owned by him, for another productive asset owned by another investor. A doctor, for example, who owns an apartment house might wish to trade with an investor who has a list of diversified securities of equal value. No income taxes are paid on the transactions, and the tax base follows the asset that is exchanged. In this way a capital gains tax is postponed until the investor actually sells the asset.

f. Postpone income until retirement when current income is lower and taxed at a lower rate.

g. Maximize long-term gains and minimize short-term gains. Long-term gains are taxed at a maximum of 25 percent. Short-term gains are taxed as ordinary income. This would include writing off short-term losses against long-term gains.

h. Some states, such as Ohio, levy a personal property tax on securities. Productive assets, i.e., those paying dividends or interest, are taxed at a lower rate than unproductive assets. Therefore, where appropriate, invest in productive assets rather than unproductive assets because they are taxed at a lower rate.

i. Take advantage of tax-deductible annuities that allow income to be deferred until retirement.

j. Lastly, investors in the high tax brackets might consider companies whose dividends are taxed partially as a capital gain. Investment companies and some public utilities are in this category.

Portfolio Objectives and the Personal Characteristics of the Investor

In order to achieve the objectives that minimize risk and maximize reward, the investor must be certain that his personal qualifications will help him achieve these goals. Our financial position determines to a great extent our ability to assume risk and gain the perspective for investment success. In our discussion in Chapter 1, we found that a person must be in a sound financial position before he begins to invest, first, because money is needed for investment, and second, because of the risk involved. A strong financial position tends to minimize risk and maximize the opportunity for rewards in the future.

We will be influenced by our personal position in addition to our financial position. These will determine the type of investment activities we will engage in. The personal characteristics are age, marital status, family responsibilities, health, personal habits, willingness to accept risk, the money psychology of the investor, and his needs for profit. These will determine whether a person invests or does not invest in common stock. For example, some individuals could not possibly invest in equity securities because of their fear of loss. They might be able to bear the risk of loss financially, but not emotionally. Let us look more closely at personal characteristics to learn what impact they might have upon our investment needs.

The Age of the Investor

The age of the investor has a good deal to do with what happens with investable funds. It is difficult to make generalizations about this variable, but we can begin by saying that, generally, the younger we are the more interested we are in growth investments, and the older we are the more interested we are in income. Probably from 25 to 65 we are interested in growth, and from 65 on, retirement income would be our main concern. Possibly between 40 and 50 we would need income rather than growth because of the demand for educational funds for the children we might have in college. But there are always exceptions. A gentleman in his late 70's came to see a broker about buying stock. The broker suggested a well-diversified income portfolio. The elderly gentleman said in astonishment, "I don't want income stocks, I want something with growth potential." Obviously he was not investing to meet his own current needs.

Generally, younger investors tend to be less cautious than older ones. This might be because of willingness to accept risk, but it also might be because of lack of experience. We tend to accept speculative situations more readily when we are younger. Of course, there are also exceptions to this generality. Many young people, when given the responsibility of investing a fund, accept the challenge, invest with mature judgment, and are not willing to accept undue risk.

Marital Status and Family Responsibilities

The marital status of the individual has an impact upon his investment needs. A married man must provide for the physical and educational needs of his family. This tends to make him more conservative and less likely to speculate. The investment needs of a single individual are much simpler, usually because financial needs are less complex. The financial commitments of the married investor are much greater, other things being equal, than those of the single person. The cost of establishing a home often makes investment difficult for the family. If we are unmarried, we should be able to invest sooner because of our ability to accumulate an investment fund sooner.

The responsibilities of a family with one or more children have an impact upon investment needs. As the family increases in size, the need for both present and future income increases, and there are greater demands to provide food, clothing, shelter, and education. Assume for the moment a family with four children living on an income of $18,000. This seems to be a good salary, but providing for their physical needs requires a good deal of money. In fact this family could use additional current income. In addition their children will probably go to college. The cost of college averages $2,000 per year for a state-supported institution. A private college education costs $11,000 for the four-year period. When we multiply that by four, we have a whopping big $32,000 in the state institution or the state college and $44,000 for the private institution. Thus while the family needs a future fund to provide for education, it could also use more income to meet growing family requirements. If the young family has no investment fund, the only way it will be able to build one is by reducing the present level of consumption. In this case, even though income is required, the policy followed will be one of growth because this dominates the need of the family.

The responsibility for children is not the only family obligation that imposes conditions upon the investment of funds. Helping to care for aged parents or for sisters or brothers will have an important influence on investment policy. The increased financial demands require more immediate funds and suggest an income policy. A demand for funds in the future tends to suggest a growth policy or a reinvestment of income to build an estate.

The Health of the Investor

The health of the investor and his family also has an impact upon investment policies. An investor in poor health will be in a position in which his income will be in jeopardy, so his demands for current income will be great, precluding investment for growth. A healthy family allows investment decisions to be determined by more important investment criteria.

Personal Habits

The personal habits of an individual also influence his investment needs. A frugal individual will have no problem establishing a fund. His current and future needs will be minimal, suggesting a growth policy. Of course, the very frugal person will have less need for future income as well. At the other extreme is the spendthrift who needs more current income. The current demands might be so great that he is tempted to spend part of his capital in addition to income. Obviously, this investor must follow an investment program that maximizes current income. However, to insure the maintenance of the investment fund it might be wise to limit expenditures to income.

Most of us are neither extremely frugal persons nor spendthrifts. We will establish our investment program on the basis of normal expenditure habits. We will decide upon an income portfolio or a growth portfolio or a combination of both to meet our needs, depending upon family, age, health, present and future income, and the amount of our investment fund.

Willingness to Accept Risks of Investment

The emotional make-up of an individual will dictate his ability to assume the risks of investment. The risks are real; we must understand their nature and significance, we must be willing to accept them and provide against them. Individuals vary as to their willingness to assume purchasing-power risk, market risk, business risk, or the money rate risk. Some eagerly accept risk and are not alarmed if they actually lose large sums of money. These people are prepared financially and emotionally to invest. Others are so security-conscious that they could not risk the loss of a single penny. They are emotionally unable to accept the risk of loss, and should stay out of the stock market.

Although no normal person wants to lose money, we must be willing to accept the possibility of loss. However, in making investment selections we do so with the intent of minimizing losses and maximizing gains. Our emotional characteristics and our risk-taking ability are consistent with our investment aims. As normal investors, we carefully balance needs with what is attainable in the way of investment returns. Often we temper what we want with the return we are able to earn with safety, attempting to obtain a satisfactory return on our investment.

One of the important points to remember about investment is that while we can usually obtain results consistent with our objectives, there is no place for greed in the investment equation. If we are motivated by greed, we will often take unnecessary risks to achieve unrealistic goals unconnected with economic reality. The best policy is to know our investment requirements, the risks involved, and what returns can be anticipated. This knowledge will help establish a sound investment portfolio. Above all we should know ourselves, both emotionally and financially, to reach an intelligent solution to our investment problem.

THE MONEY PSYCHOLOGY OF THE INDIVIDUAL

The overriding question that we must ask is, "What is our psychological attitude about money?" Some people just can't bear the thought of parting with a dollar, even though many of these people have more money than they will ever need. Such people could not buy stocks. An example will demonstrate an extreme negative attitude toward loss of money. A college professor asked me for stock market advice. He asked if a mutual fund was a good and safe investment. Until this time, he had never owned a common stock. The mutual fund he mentioned was a good one and I recommended purchase. Two months later my friend approached me again. He said he would never again invest in the stock market because he had lost money. I had not watched the price action of the mutual fund so I inquired about the loss. He said he had "lost" $.51 a share during the months he had owned the stock and thought he had been cheated. Obviously this man is not psychologically attuned to the possible loss of money and should not own common stock.

By the same token, a person should not be so careless about money that he actually tries to lose to punish himself. Psychopathic gamblers, as an extreme case, are hell-bent for financial and personal destruction. Anyone with this psychological attitude toward stocks should stay away from the market. A person needs a sound psychological attitude toward money in order to make money. Few are outstandingly successful and shrewd when it comes to money matters. The book *Bulls, Bears and Dr. Freud*[7] will shed some light on this question of the psychological attitude of investors, as well as Adam Smith's *The Money Game*.[8] Before you or your clients begin an investment program, find out about your or their money I.Q.

The Investor's Needs

Whether we follow theory or practice, we must recognize that when we try to invest money for an individual, we must meet his needs. Some of the needs will be financial, some will be emotional and psychological. Certainly the primary motive for investment is profit. It might be for retirement, an education for Johnny, to improve one's standard of living, or to be benevolent and leave something for one's Alma Mater; nonetheless, the goal is profit.

A college professor at a university died some years ago and left his estate to the university. He had taught chemistry, and never earned more than $5,000 a year. His needs were modest. He lived close to the university; he married late in life and had no children; his wife preceded him in death. When we say his needs were modest, we overestimate his standard of living. He seemed as poor as a church mouse, and his students once took up a collection to buy him a new pair of shoes. Although his old shoes were held together with rubber bands, he refused such offers. He invested his funds. He had faith in the Chicago Furniture

7 Albert Haas, Jr., and Don D. Jackson, *Bulls, Bears and Dr. Freud* (Cleveland: The World Publishing Company, 1967).

8 "Adam Smith," *The Money Game* (New York: Random House, 1968).

Mart and bought this stock continuously. He never used the money himself, just reinvested it to let the fund grow. His life and his happiness were given to him by the university for which he worked. He asked only that he be allowed to work in the chemistry lab and teach. It is not strange for a professor to leave an estate to his university; the strange part is that he left over $1,000,000. His was an act of charity. He invested only for the benefit of others.

There are other motives that are equally strong for some people. Wealthy individuals want power, and they continue investing simply to maintain economic power and control over assets for their own benefit. Howard Hughes might be an example of a man who is investing for the power motive; certainly he has all the money he can use. Some invest for status so they can tell their friends that they own stock. Others have invested for educational reasons; colleges today have investment funds managed by investment classes. Baldwin Wallace College and the University of Toledo have student investment funds, the purpose of which is to educate the students in the art of investment analysis and management. The education motive is an extremely worthwhile objective if it is coupled with guidance and counsel that will lead to a better understanding of investment and investment decisions. More educational investment funds would provide a great deal of help to students in our educational institutions.

Portfolio Management Policies

Here we will discuss briefly some of the more common types of policies that might be followed in the management of an investment fund.

Aggressive-Defensive Policies

Aggressive Policy. An aggressive fund is one that is predominantly invested in common stocks. The assumption we make is that the market is strong and rising and that common stocks will be the best place for funds in a rising market. A fund with 80 to 90 percent or more common stock would be considered an aggressive fund.

Defensive Policy. A defensive policy is one that places emphasis upon securities that resist a decline in price. Bonds are a defensive-type security, as are preferred stock and cash. If we suspect that the market will decline, we should maintain a defensive market policy. Often, conservative investment management demands a defensive portfolio policy. A highly defensive portfolio would include 60 to 80 percent bonds.

Aggressive-Defensive Policy. An aggressive-defensive policy, often referred to as a balanced fund, is sometimes adopted by investors. The balanced-fund philosophy suggests a hedge against a rise or fall in the stock market. If the market goes up, the common stock will carry the fund up. If the market declines, the bond portion will prevent the fund from experiencing a complete loss of principal. Again, conservative financial management and difficult periods of recession often dictate a balanced-fund approach.

The Income and Growth Funds

The aggressive-defensive portfolio stresses the protection of capital. Another classification of portfolio policy stresses whether returns of the investor will be in the form of current income or capital gains.

Income Fund. The income fund places emphasis upon the maximization of current income. Capital gains and growth are given minimum significance in the income portfolio. The securities that provide income are the medium-grade bonds, preferred stocks, dividend-paying common stocks, and, for investors in the high tax bracket, tax-exempt securities.

Growth Portfolio. The growth portfolio emphasizes the capital growth of the investment fund. The purpose of the growth fund is to postpone current income so that the fund increases in value. The increased value will allow the investor to improve his income and growth position at a later date. Investors interested in growth would buy stocks that offer appreciation potential and do not pay cash dividends.

The Income-Growth Fund. This fund attempts to balance current income with some growth. The investor desires some current income, yet he wishes to build the value of his fund. The problem is whether to balance the securities in the fund between income securities and growth securities, or to choose a company that possesses both growth potential and income. These are sometimes referred to as straddle stocks. A good example would be the common stock of Cincinnati Gas and Electric. It has paid some dividends each year since 1853, and it has growth potential. A well-diversified list of comparable stocks would make an excellent combination income and growth portfolio.

Even though we stress theory in portfolio management, we must be practical and recognize the needs of individuals, their motives, their objectives, and their ability in managing investments. We must understand that individuals will react differently to market phenomena and the problems of portfolio management. To succeed in investments we cannot ignore individual variations; we must adapt them to the overall principles, practices, and theories that we espouse.

Summary

We face the investment problem of balancing the desire for liquidity and profitability with risk. Our needs are determined by our motives, our economic, social, and cultural heritage, and our willingness to assume risk. We are motivated strongly by profits. The need for profit varies. We desire profit for security, retirement, education, or to enhance our current standard of living. We have subsidiary motives for investing such as power, prestige, and benevolence. But profit is the common denominator of investment. The process of setting up an investment portfolio includes planning, supervision, conservatism, rationalism, and timing. The guiding objectives are to insure the principal of the fund in terms of purchasing power and amount and to obtain stability of income and capital growth. To achieve these goals we provide diversification, marketability, liquidity, and a favorable tax position. The policies of investors vary. From time to time we will be aggressive, defensive, or balanced between aggressive and defensive securities. We also might vary our investment needs between income and growth of capital. We must establish our own indifference curve between risk and reward, based upon portfolio management theory that allows us to optimize our investment results. Stability of earnings is looked at as a measure of risk, and yield for the period we consider for investment is the reward.

Review Questions

1. What is the fundamental investment problem? How is it related to risk and reward?
2. What are the investment motives an individual might have, and how do they affect investment needs?
3. How does an individual's financial position affect his investment needs? Discuss.
4. What effect do the personal characteristics of the investor have upon investment needs? Comment upon such specifics as:
   (a) Age
   (b) Marital status
   (c) Family responsibilities
   (d) Health
   (e) Personal habits
   (f) Willingness to accept risk
5. Explain what is meant by the terms *portfolio* and *portfolio management* in theory and practice.
6. What are the basic ingredients of portfolio management? Be sure to emphasize the significance of:
   (a) Planning
   (b) Timing
   (c) Conservatism and rationalism
   (d) Supervision
7. What are or should be the objectives of portfolio management? Discuss fully:
   (a) Security of principal
   (b) Stability of income
   (c) Capital growth
   (d) Marketability
   (e) Liquidity

(f) Diversification

(g) Favorable tax status

8. What portfolio policy might we follow to meet our needs? Under what conditions might we use each policy described in the text?

9. What would be your own indifference curve between yield and stability of earnings?

Problems

1. Examine carefully the motives that might govern investment needs.
   (a) If we were to establish our own investment program, what would be our governing motives?
   (b) What impact would our present and future level of income have upon our investment needs and our attitude toward risk and reward?

2. Analyze your personal habits and emotional characteristics and determine what effect this would have on your investment needs.

3. Establish a $100,000 portfolio to meet your investment needs. Before you begin, plan a management program carefully.

4. Explain how to go about meeting the objectives of good management.

5. Decide carefully which portfolio policy you will follow and why.

6. Demonstrate how you have maximized or optimized risk vs. reward.

Sources of Investment Information

Barron's

Clark Dodge Investment Survey

Portfolios of conservative investment funds as examples

Standard & Poor's *Investment Surveys*

The Value Line Investment Survey

Selected Readings

Aranyi, Janos, "Portfolio Diversification," *Financial Analysts Journal* (September-October, 1967), p. 133.

Babson, David L., "Performance or Speculation?" *Financial Analysts Journal* (September-October, 1967), p. 129.

Balog, J. and D. P. Moriarty, "Use of Scientific Knowledge," *Financial Analysts Journal* (July-August, 1967), p. 76.

Bauman, W. Scott, "Investment Management," *Financial Analysts Journal* (January-February, 1966), p. 88.

Baumol, William J., "Mathematical Analysis of Portfolio Selection," *Financial Analysts Journal* (September-October, 1966), p. 95.

Bingham, Albert Young, "Relative Performance—Nonsense," *Financial Analysts Journal* (July-August, 1966), p. 101.

Birmingham, John M., Jr., "The Quest for Performance" (Keynote Review), *Financial Analysts Journal* (September-October, 1966), p. 93.

Briggs, George C., "Performance and Portfolio Management," *Financial Analysts Journal* (September-October, 1967), p. 123.

Good, Walter R., "How to Avoid Over-Priced Stocks," *Financial Analysts Journal* (November-December, 1966), p. 79.

Hall, J. Parker, III, "Toward Effective Portfolio Management," *Financial Analysts Journal* (January-February, 1966), p. 91.

Lambert, E. W. and A. E. Hofflander, "Liquidity in Investing," *Financial Analysts Journal* (September-October, 1967), p. 141.

McCandlish, Randolph W., Jr., "Portfolio Evaluation," *Financial Analysts Journal* (November-December, 1967), p. 139.

Marks, Lawrence J., "In Defense of Performance," *Financial Analysts Journal* (November-December, 1967), p. 135.

Meyerholz, John C., "Competition and Investment Management," *Financial Analysts Journal* (January-February, 1966), p. 97.

Neil, Herbert E., Jr., "The Surtax," *Financial Analysts Journal* (November-December, 1967), p. 105.

Renshaw, Edward F., "Portfolio Theory," *Financial Analysts Journal* (March-April, 1968), p. 114.

Ricks, R. Bruce, "Tight Money and Investment Management," *Financial Analysts Journal* (January-February, 1967), p. 104.

Schutt, Leonard D., "Implementing Investment Policy," *Financial Analysts Journal* (March-April, 1966), p. 105.

Sherman, John C., "A Device to Measure Portfolio Performance," *Financial Analysts Journal* (January-February, 1966), p. 106.

Sieff, John A., "Measuring Investment Performance: The Unit Approach," *Financial Analysts Journal* (July-August, 1966), p. 93.

Smith, Keith V., "Needed: A Dynamic Approach," *Financial Analysts Journal* (May-June, 1967), p. 115.

Sosnoff, Martin T., "Hedge Fund Management—A New Respectability for Short Selling," *Financial Analysts Journal* (July-August, 1966), p. 105.

Wallich, Henry C., "Random Walk & Security Analysts," *Financial Analysts Journal* (March-April, 1968), p. 159.

Wendt, Paul F., "Determination of Investment Policy," *Financial Analysts Journal* (January-February, 1968), p. 91.

Woods, Donald H., "A New Perspective," *Financial Analysts Journal* (July-August, 1967), p. 73.

20

PROFESSIONAL ASSISTANCE
IN PORTFOLIO
MANAGEMENT

The previous discussion assumed that the investor would manage his
own portfolio. But management is a precise, time-consuming, and
difficult task, and good results cannot always be obtained even if he is
interested in the art of investment. For one reason or another he might
be unable to devote sufficient time to the management of his funds, or
have little or no inclination toward financial and investment matters.
In this chapter we will consider the personal requirements of portfolio
management. We will now assume that the individual cannot or does
not wish to manage his own portfolio; we will show how to shift the
burdens of portfolio management, what those burdens are, and the
alternative solutions.

The Portfolio Management Problem

The management of an investment portfolio requires knowledge, experience, timing, constant research, and the appraisal and reappraisal
of securities. We must be aware of the trends and developments of the
national economy, of the impact of political, social, and economic
change as it might affect an investment position, and of the activities
of the stock market. If we are to do a good job of management, we
must know the competitive position of the industry and, at the same
time, the changing competitive position of the companies within the
industry. Not only must we be familiar with those industries in which
we have invested, but also with the industries and companies in which

we do not invest. Other industries might in the future offer attractive outlets for our funds. If we are astute, we keep abreast of market developments and look for new and more profitable outlets for our funds. It is doubtful that many individual investors possess the training or experience required to carry out the investment program required for a substantial investment fund. Essentially the investor must be able to analyze securities intelligently, make a broad selection, and then decide how the money will be invested from among all securities available. The investor must combine the abilities of a portfolio manager and of a professional analyst to be successful in performing the investment function.

Individual Limitations

Many who invest do not have the training and experience to manage an investment account nor the time to become thoroughly informed about industries, companies, the national economy, and the securities market. Many have wandered into the investment arena with only a modest amount of knowledge. By absorbing and applying the concepts discussed here, an investor would have sufficient knowledge of investments to make his own decisions and manage his own funds. Nothing can guarantee complete success in the stock market, but a thorough understanding of principles gives an individual a greater chance to achieve it. Many investors, however, are limited even in their understanding of the information presented here. Let us take a closer look at these limitations.

EDUCATION

Often investors do not understand the basic workings of our economic system. They have never had formal training in accounting, economics, and investments, and many do not understand company balance sheets and operating statements. They understand the concept of earnings per share but find it difficult to relate to price and values as they exist in the marketplace. This group of investors is not quite sure what common stock is, what the function of the stock exchange is, and what a broker is supposed to do. In short, their investment and financial education is inadequate. Many investors have had a college education but no specific education in investment management.

However, professional analysts do have the necessary educational requirements. The educational levels in the analyst profession have been raised with the assistance of the Chartered Financial Analyst (CFA) program.

EXPERIENCE

Most investors also have limited experience in financial and investment matters—even those who own securities. They are usually aware of some investment media such as government bonds, savings bonds, possibly building and loan shares, and the investment aspects of life insurance. But few possess a complete knowledge of security analysis, and few have engaged in important financial transactions.

TIME

For most people, time is an extremely limited commodity. It is particularly limited for the successful lawyer, doctor, college professor, or businessman who has accumulated an investment fund. The successful professional man devotes most of his working hours to his own career and related activities. He does not have time to manage his investment account adequately. A man managing a business probably has little time for routine personal financial affairs, much less for the complicated problems associated with managing and analyzing an investment portfolio.

OBJECTIVITY

It becomes quite apparent that most people are not in a position to do justice to managing an investment portfolio; they need outside assistance. Paradoxically, even the financial analyst may be in this situation. He certainly has the time, training, and knowledge; but when he manages his own funds, he often loses a most important qualification —objectivity. He too may need assistance.

Investment Companies as an Alternative Solution

Investors who cannot supply management themselves have several alternatives for solving the management problem. Let us examine some of these alternatives.

Investment Companies

Investment companies offer a partial solution to portfolio management by providing expert research and professional management of funds over which they have control.

The growth of investment company assets (see Table 20–1) has been remarkable. In many respects investment companies are identical with industrial corporations or public utilities and railroads. Industrial companies invest their money in land, machinery, and buildings that are used to produce goods and services for other industries and the consumer. Investment companies invest funds contributed by investors in bonds, preferred stock, and common stock of other corporations.

The balance sheet of a typical investment company would list the securities owned on the asset side of the sheet. On the liability side would be the shares that had been sold to investors. The earning assets

TABLE 20–1

Growth of investment company assets
(millions of dollars)

As of December 31	Open-End Companies	Closed-End Companies	Total
1968	$52,677	$2,860	$55,553
1967	44,701	2,826	47,527
1966	34,829	2,418	37,247
1965	35,220	2,492	37,712
1964	29,116	2,289	31,405
1963	25,214	2,039	27,253
1962	21,271	1,777	23,047
1961	22,789	2,132	24,920
1960	17,026	1,775	18,800
1959	15,818	1,697	17,515
1958	13,242	1,633	14,875
1957	8,714	1,210	9,924

SOURCE: Standard & Poor's *Industry Surveys—Investment Companies,* September 11, 1969, p. 142.

of an investment company are the same as those of an individual investor who chooses to invest his money directly in securities. The earning assets produce income from two sources: from dividends and interest earned on the securities purchased; and from capital gains from securities purchased by the investment company.

Funds invested by investment companies are obtained in much the same way as capital is obtained by industrial corporations. The manufacturing company sells preferred stock and common stock and borrows money through the issuance of debt. Investment companies, as a group, can raise capital in much the same way, although the methods of individual companies will vary. If the company is a mutual fund, it sells only ownership shares. A closed-end company raises capital—both common and debt—exactly like an industrial company. In the final analysis, how an investment fund raises its capital depends upon the nature of the company and the policies established by its management. A simplified balance sheet of an investment company appears in Table 20–2. Note its similarities to and differences from the balance sheet of a typical industrial company.

TABLE 20–2

Balance sheet of a typical investment company

Assets		Liabilities	
Cash	$ 100,000	Bonds	$ 300,000
Short-term governments	200,000		
Bonds	300,000	Common stock	1,300,000
Preferred stock	100,000		
Common stock	1,000,000	Retained earnings	100,000
	$1,700,000		$1,700,000

There are two basic types of investment companies—*closed-end* and *open-end*. The closed-end investment company, sometimes referred to as an *investment trust*, operates in much the same way as any industrial company. It issues a fixed number of shares of common stock, which may be listed on an exchange and may be bought and sold just like any other corporation's stock. The stock of the Tri-Continental Company, a large closed-end investment company, is traded on the New York Stock Exchange, for example. When the stock of a closed-end investment company is purchased through a broker, the purchaser pays the broker a commission, computed in the same way as for any other listed security. The management of the closed-end investment company may from time to time issue additional common stock, but, for the most part, the number of shares of stock outstanding is constant. If management desires, it may raise capital by selling preferred stock or bonds. The majority of closed-end investment companies have bonds and preferred stock outstanding as a part of their capital structure.

LEVERAGE

The use of fixed-income securities to obtain capital for a closed-end company results in leverage for the common-stock owners of the fund, affecting both the assets and the net income of the investment company. The closed-end company that issues debt or preferred stock is said to have both *asset leverage* and *earnings leverage*, because preferred stock and bonds represent a fixed claim against the assets of the investment company. The interest on debt and the dividends on preferred also represent a fixed and contingent charge against the company's earnings. Since both income and asset claims are fixed, any increase in asset values, and any increase in earnings over the interest payments or dividend requirements, go to the common stockholders. As long as the closed-end investment company earns more on its assets than is necessary to pay the fixed claims and a similar amount to the common stockholder, then the owners will benefit. As earnings go beyond the point where bonds and preferred earn their guaranteed rate of return, the additional earnings are left to be paid to the common stockholders. As earnings increase, the rate of increase as a return to the common stockholders increases faster than the rate of increase of the return on the total assets. This leverage concept is similar to the subject of trading on the equity explained in Chapter 14.

Asset leverage occurs when the prices of the common stock owned by the investment company increase or decrease. If the value of the total assets increases, then there is a greater proportional increase in the value of the common stock of the investment company. Since the debt issued is a fixed claim against assets, any increase in assets goes to the

TABLE 20–3

Demonstration of asset leverage of a closed-end
investment company

Time Period 1:				Time Period 2:(20% increase in common stock)			
ASSETS		LIABILITIES		ASSETS		LIABILITIES	
Common Stock	$200	Debt	$100	Common Stock (+20%)	$240	Debt	$100
		Common (100 shares)	100			Common (+40%)	140
	$200		$200		$240		$240

common stockholders. Thus, as the value of the investments of an investment company increases, its common stock actually increases faster. Table 20–3 demonstrates asset leverage. In Time Period 1, the closed-end investment company had assets of $200, all invested in common stock. The capital was raised by the sale of $100 worth of bonds and $100 of common stock. In Time Period 2, after the value of the investments in common stock has increased 20 percent, the leverage is reflected in the change in the ownership account. The $40 increase in common-stock value results in a 40 percent increase in the common equity account. None of the increase goes to the bondholders because they have a fixed claim against the assets of the company. The result of the 20 percent increase in the assets of the closed-end company is a 40 percent increase in the value of its common stock. This is referred to as *asset leverage* and can be expressed as the following ratio: % Increase in Common Stock/% Increase in Asset Value. Thus, at a given volume of assets, a percentage increase in assets will be greater when it is related to the common equity account. As the assets increase in value without a corresponding increase in debt capital, the leverage effect is diminished. The asset leverage in the case given would diminish as the assets continued to increase in value.

The asset leverage effect of the closed-end investment company also operates when assets decline in value. Assume that the assets in Time Period 1 in Table 20–3 decrease by 20 percent instead of increasing in Time Period 2. The decrease would be magnified in the decline in the price of common stock of the company. In this case the decrease would be 40 percent. This is a disadvantage of the closed-end investment company that should be carefully taken into account when such a company is considered for investment.

Closed-end investment companies that raise a substantial portion of their capital with debt may be susceptible to wider fluctuation in value than investment companies with a relatively small amount of debt. If they invest the funds obtained from debt into common stocks, the result would be a more volatile market action. If the money were invested in debt securities, it would have little or no effect on market action of the shares of the fund.

The earnings leverage and the asset leverage of the closed-end investment company tend to accentuate the cyclical price movement of the stock. This can be an important advantage if the investor can anticipate changes in the market or if he is able to buy the stock at attractive prices for investment. On the other hand, a serious loss could result if the investor purchased shares in a heavily leveraged investment company at the wrong time. The leverage in closed-end companies suggests that the investor must exercise care in selecting and investing in this type of company to meet his objectives.

The Open-End Investment Company

In contrast to the closed-end company, the stock of the open-end investment company is not traded on an exchange; it is traded in the over-the-counter market by specific dealers who handle its purchase and sale. The open-end investment company is usually referred to as a *mutual fund*. The concept of mutuality is in the fact that there is only one class of owner, who shares the gains or losses of the fund with all the other owners. No leverage occurs in the open-end fund. The money that is obtained from the sale of shares is invested directly in the securities of other companies. Table 20–4 shows the balance sheet of a typical open-end investment company, or mutual fund. Owners of the fund in Part A contributed $2,400,000, or at least have a claim on this amount of assets, for the 240,000 shares of stock outstanding have a value of $10 per share. If we ignore the costs of selling the assets, this $10 figure is the net asset value per share of the fund. The mutual fund stands ready, through its agents or representatives, to buy or sell shares at this price, which is usually computed twice a day.

Reference to Table 20–4B will show the impact of a purchase of 100 mutual fund shares by an investor at a price of $10 per share, the net asset value at the time. The number of shares outstanding of the investment company increases by 100 and the immediate impact is to add $1,000 to the cash account. Eventually the $1,000 will be invested in bonds and common stock of other companies, in an attempt to meet the long-range objectives of the investor. If the market price of the investments owned by the mutual fund increases, then the mutual fund shares owned by the investor will increase by the same proportional amount. There is no leverage in this relationship. All owners mutually share the profits and losses of the fund.

The above illustration did not consider the cost of selling or purchasing open-end shares. There is a cost involved, however, since sales costs involved in distributing the mutual fund shares must be met. This charge, or commission, is usually referred to as the *loading charge*,

TABLE 20–4

Balance sheet of a small balanced mutual-fund
investment company

A

ASSETS		LIABILITIES & OWNERSHIP
Cash	$ 100,000	
Bonds	500,000	Shares outstanding 240,000
Preferred	600,000	Value $2,400,000
Common	1,200,000	
	$2,400,000	

B

ASSETS		LIABILITIES & OWNERSHIP
Cash	$ 101,000	
Bonds	500,000	Shares outstanding 240,100
Preferred	600,000	Value $2,401,000
Common	1,200,000	
	$2,401,000	

and it is paid only when shares are purchased. It is usually added to the net asset value per share and goes to the salesman or dealer and to the company handling the distribution of the fund. The commission varies from 5 to 9 1/2 percent of the net asset value.

The price for a mutual fund is usually quoted on a bid-and-asked basis. The bid price is the price that an investor would receive if he sold his shares; it is the same as the net asset value. The asked price represents the net asset value (bid price) plus the loading charge (the charge that covers the cost of selling). The price ranges for investment companies are quoted daily in the *Wall Street Journal*. The selling charge must be large enough to compensate the distributor adequately for his services; this encourages wider distribution of the fund.

Table 20–5 lists the fifty largest mutual funds in the United States, ranked by size of net assets.

The cost of purchasing mutual fund shares may be high. This has long been a criticism of mutual fund ownership. The commission, however, does cover both the cost of the purchase and the cost of the sale. Securities may be purchased on an exchange at a cost of less than 1 percent. If we consider the selling cost, then the round-trip commission would be 2 percent, which is closer to the cost of purchasing a mutual fund share. But in some cases, the cost of purchasing mutual funds is four times as great as in purchasing stock, even when we consider the commissions on a buy-and-sell transaction.

To invest small amounts of money on a regular basis, it is expensive not only to buy mutual funds but also to buy common stock listed on an exchange. On stock purchases of $200 or less, the round-trip commission might equal or exceed the cost of purchasing the same dollar amount of a mutual fund. Large dollar purchases of mutual funds do

TABLE 20–5

*Fifty largest mutual funds (as of
June 30, 1969)*

	NET ASSETS ($ MIL.)	POSITION
Investors Mutual	2,829.6	1
Dreyfus Fund	2,395.7	2
Massachusetts Investors Trust	2,259.1	3
Investors Stock Fund	2,214.6	4
Affiliated Fund	1,707.3	5
Wellington Fund	1,546.1	6
United Accumulative Fund	1,303.3	7
Fundamental Investors	1,260.0	8
Massachusetts Investors Growth Stk. Fund	1,193.6	9
Fidelity Trend Fund	1,135.5	10
Investors Variable Payment	1,052.7	11
Investment Company of America	1,030.8	12
Enterprise Fund	849.2	13
ISI Trust Fund	848.0	14
Fidelity Fund	821.1	15
United Income Fund	792.9	16
Puritan Fund	774.2	17
National Investors Corp.	762.5	18
Putnam Growth Fund	654.2	19
Hamilton Funds—Series H-DA	649.9	20
Technology Fund	629.5	21
Fidelity Capital Fund	621.4	22
Keystone Lower-Priced Common Stk. Fund (S-4)	569.8	23
Diversified Growth Stock Fund	540.4	24
T. Rowe Price Growth Stock Fund	525.5	25
Chemical Fund	521.4	26
Delaware Fund	457.0	27
United Science Fund	430.2	28
George Putnam Fund of Boston	427.4	29
State Street Investment	423.8	30
Broad Street Investing	402.7	31
American Mutual Fund	396.3	32
Dividend Shares	386.7	33
National Securities-Stock Series	361.7	34
Financial Industrial Fund	345.0	35
American Investors Fund	319.6	36
Channing Growth Fund	308.7	37
Keystone Growth Fund (K-2)	307.1	38
Group Securities-Common Stock Fund	303.0	39
Ivest Fund	295.1	40
Manhattan Fund	295.0	41
Value Line Special Situations	291.2	42
Putnam Investors Fund	288.4	43
One William Street Fund	280.8	44
Axe-Houghton Fund B	276.5	45
Oppenheimer	275.2	46
Boston Fund	273.6	47
Washington Mutual Investors Fund	269.2	48
National Securities—Growth Stock Series	259.2	49
Windsor Fund	257.5	50

SOURCE: Standard & Poor's, *Industry Survey—Investment Companies*,
September 11, 1969, p. 137.

have the disadvantage of high-cost commission. But small dollar purchases of mutual funds are comparable to small dollar purchases of common stock with respect to the commission paid.

The typical cost of buying a fund was 9 percent in 1969, with a range from 8 1/2 percent to 9 1/2 percent. The SEC has brought pressure on the funds to reduce these fees. Whether the SEC has the power to force rate reductions, and whether the reductions will go into effect at this time, are subject to debate.

Criticism of Mutual Funds—
The Wharton School Study and the SEC

Criticism has been leveled against mutual funds as a result of the Wharton Study and the Special Study by the SEC. Because the performance of no-load funds has been as good as that of load funds, we must look into these criticisms very carefully.

The Wharton Study, authorized by the SEC, made the following statements about the mutual fund industry:

1. The performance of mutual funds did not differ greatly from what would have been achieved by an unmanaged portfolio.
2. The turnover rate of the stock holdings of mutual funds was greater than the average turnover rate of all stocks on the New York Stock Exchange.
3. The growth of mutual funds has contributed significantly to the increase in stock prices in the last ten years.
4. The funds have little bargaining power in the creation of advisory-fee rates.
5. There may be a conflict of interest between management and shareholder in selling fund shares.
6. The sale of mutual fund shares is the determining factor in the allocation of buying and selling the funds' securities.
7. The structure of rates for large transactions is largely inflexible because of the "give-up."

The mutual fund industry answered the Wharton criticisms in the following manner:

1. While it is true that Standard & Poor's 500 outperformed the mutual funds, if similar indexes are selected for comparison with the average common-stock fund or balanced fund, the latter outperformed on a fractional basis.
2. While the funds had a higher (15.2 percent to 14.4 percent) turnover rate than the New York Stock Exchange, the exchange figure includes highly inactive preferred stocks and does not include "off-board" trading, so that conjecture about mutual funds increasing short-term market volatility is unfounded.
3. Furthermore, the share of the market controlled by funds is 4.5

percent (December, 1961), so that many other factors must have had a greater role in influencing the rise in stock prices. (This percentage has increased substantially by 1970.)

4. Since the Investment Company Act of 1940 does not mention fee rates for advisory services, the fees charged by the funds vary; the shareholder can decide on any of a number of funds to select and eventually must approve future management contracts.

5. There is no evidence that selling efforts by mutual funds dilute the performance of the management; additionally, shareholders benefit from fund growth via lower per-share operating costs and from "sliding scale" fee reductions.

6. Transactions are placed according to the best price and most efficient service; if these characteristics are similar, then it is natural for a fund to favor a broker who sells shares.

7. The "give-up" per se does not influence commissions on large or small orders. The rates charged by the brokers are set for them by the NYSE, which has not allowed for discounts for large volume transactions.[1]

Hugh A. Johnson, creator of Johnson's Charts, made the following statement in his analysis of the Wharton School report:

> "No one has spent more time with the Securities and Exchange Commission, examining the aspects and impact of performance comparisons of the investment records of mutual funds, than the writer. Therefore, no one can fully appreciate the eccentricities of the apples, peaches, and pears comparisons that have been perpetrated under the guise of investment analysis. But I hope that everyone can appreciate the sum and substance of the Wharton Report, which actually says that you cannot get diversification to compare with funds at a comparable cost; that the record of doubling the original investment in 5 3/4 years is excellent; that growth stock funds appreciate faster than the S & P Index in rising markets; that balanced funds are more stable than the market; that income funds produced more income in the last four years than a representative index of the market; that mutual funds faithfully dispatched their stated investment objectives; that their tremendous growth gives no evidence of affecting their performance; that, in short, they are doing exactly what they say they can do and doing it better than the individual investor can do it for himself."[2]

The SEC continued its study of the mutual fund industry and issued a surprisingly tough report in December, 1966.[3] The agency asked for legislation to curb the mutual fund industry in the following ways:

1 "Mutual Funds Look at Wharton Study," *Banking*, November, 1962, p. 8 ff.

2 Hugh A. Johnson, quoted in John A. Straley, *What About Mutual Funds* (New York: Harper and Row, Publishers, 1967), p. 76.

3 "SEC vs. Mutual Funds: Congress Will Decide," *Business Week*, December 10, 1966, p. 147.

1. Put a 5 percent ceiling on mutual fund sales charges that currently average 9.3 percent.
2. Enact a standard of "reasonableness" for management fees that currently average 1/2 of 1 percent of a fund's assets.
3. Ban "front-end load" plans. The front-end load contractual plan provides that half of the buyer's first-year payments go to the salesman.
4. Ban mutual-fund holding companies.
5. Prohibit "give-ups" of brokerage fees.
6. Grant volume discounts.
7. Police insider trading, so that fund managers do not take advantage of the fund's trades.
8. Take a more active interest in portfolio companies by prohibiting the sale of any company that manages a mutual fund if the ownership charge might burden the fund's shareholders or limit the fund's future action.[4]

The investment fund industry and the financial community in general have reacted against these proposals. Opposition has been strong and overt. One article suggested that "give-up" was preferable to the spreading around of trading activity, which would cause unnecessary fluctuations in the markets.[5] It was also stated that the 1/2 of 1 percent management fee was not excessive.[6] Another writer stated that the SEC was wrong in imposing a limit of 5 percent on commissions, banning the "front-end" contractual plans, and reducing the fees for managing funds.[7]

Any enactment of legislation will be up to Congress. At the present time, a major change in fee structure, however justifiable, seems unlikely, but other changes—minor ones—will be made.

Management of the Investment Company and the Mutual Fund

A major reason for purchasing open-end or closed-end shares is for the professional management that is provided. There is a slight difference in how the two types of companies are managed, but the net results of the excellence of management are approximately the same. Closed-end companies are usually managed by their officers, who are partners or officers in a brokerage or investment banking firm. Research for the closed-end company is done by analysts employed by the partners' firms.

---

4 *Ibid.*

5 "Some Reactions to the SEC Study," *Burrough Clearing House*, March, 1967, p. 10 ff.

6 *Ibid.*

7 R. Augenbluh, "SEC's Mutual Fund Proposals Strongly Opposed," *Commercial and Financial Journal*, May 4, 1967, pp. 1760–61.

The open-end investment company usually has a specialized investment management company managing the portfolios of the fund and compensated on a fee basis for services performed. The management of the open-end trust is then free to concentrate on the distribution of the shares of the fund to the public. The management of investment companies and mutual funds is considered to be professional. Its degree of excellence, of course, is not constant and varies with each company and fund.

Cost of Management

The cost of management of an investment company is indirectly paid by the owners of the shares outstanding. This cost is directly deducted as an expense from the income of the fund. Management expenses vary for each investment company. A typical ratio of expenses to revenues is 15 percent, but the Massachusetts Investors Trust, a growth, open-end investment company, has an operating expense ratio of 21 percent; while the Continental Financial Corporation, a closed-end company, has a ratio of 8.8 percent.

The cost of management services can be related to the total value of the investment company assets. This is a familiar way of expressing the cost of investment management services. Practically all investment trust and investment counseling activities are presented as a percent of the value of the investment fund. A typical fee charged by the investment manager for the management of an open-end investment company is 1/2 of 1 percent of the investment fund. Usually the open-end or mutual fund fee is based on the value of the fund, with the rate increasing with good performance and decreasing with poor performance compared to the performance of a market average. The expense–income ratio is used as a measure of management expense for the closed-end fund. Regardless of how the cost of management is measured, we must consider it when purchasing investment company shares, since we bear the burden of this cost.

Management Objectives

When management of an investment fund is undertaken, a basic portfolio policy is established. The first concept considered in shaping investment company policy is the concept of management itself. In most modern investment companies, the managers have complete discretionary powers to buy and sell securities for the fund based upon their judgment of the market and economic conditions.

Many investment companies established earlier in American financial history were not managed funds but fixed or semifixed companies. *Fixed* and *semifixed* refer to the securities that were purchased: once the basic list of securities was established, there was little or no change in the securities held. Even when economic and market conditions suggested that a change be made, no action could be taken by the originators or managers of the fixed fund. The fixed investment company in essence provided diversification, but little or no management. That is why investment companies today, both open-end and closed-end, are completely managed.

An important consideration in the management of an investment company is the type of securities that will be purchased and the portfolio policy that will be emphasized. Based upon the wishes of the managers, a specific type of fund will be established. Generally the classification of closed-end and open-end funds is broken down into eight distinct areas: (1) common-stock fund, (2) balanced fund, (3) bond fund, (4) preferred-stock fund, (5) specialty fund, (6) swap fund, (7) dual fund, and (8) performance fund.

COMMON STOCK FUND

The common-stock fund is made up of a diversified list of common stocks. This type of fund is the oldest and most numerous in closed-end and open-end investment companies, whose net assets account for about 60 percent of total mutual-fund assets. The management of the common-stock fund can be defensive or aggressive, depending on the condition of the stock market. Policy can also stress growth or income, again depending upon the discretion of management. A few examples of the various types of stock funds can be obtained from the *Wall Street Journal.* Massachusetts Investors Trust and Massachusetts Growth Stock Fund, Inc. are two examples of common-stock funds. The common-stock fund may be limited to a particular industry or group of industries. Group Securities, for example, is divided into aviation-electronic, capital growth, common stock, fully administered, general board, and petroleum shares. Managed Funds is divided into electric, general industries, metal-paper, petroleum, special, and transportation.

THE BALANCED FUND

The balanced fund is usually made up of bonds, preferred stocks, and common stocks in several different industries and companies. There are fewer balanced funds than common-stock funds. Balanced funds account for about 25 percent of total mutual fund assets. Some well-known balanced funds are the Boston Fund, Eaton & Howard Balanced Fund, the George Putnam Fund of Boston, the Scudders, Stevens & Clark Balanced Fund, and the Wellington Fund. Funds of this type take a conservative approach to the risks of investment—with a balance among bonds, preferred, and common stock. They offer the investor security of principal but not as much capital growth as the typical general common-stock fund.

THE BOND FUND AND THE PREFERRED-STOCK FUND

The bond fund and the preferred-stock fund are devoted to fixed-income types of securities. The Bond Fund of Boston, the Bond Investment Trust of America, several of the Keystone Custodian Funds, and the Manhattan Bond Fund are examples of the complete bond fund. Preferred-stock funds include National Securities—Preferred Stock Series and Investors Selective Fund, Inc. Bond and preferred-stock funds offer a high degree of security for the investor. They have not grown as fast in popularity as either common-stock or balanced funds; generally the safety of principal they offer has not been sufficient to offset the disadvantage of the decreased purchasing power of the dollar experienced in the last decade.

THE SPECIALTY FUND

The specialty fund is a classification of the investment companies that were discussed briefly under the general category of common-stock funds. Specialty funds most frequently invest in the common stocks of one industry, usually the stocks of the larger quality companies in the industry. The electronics industry has been the focus of several specialty funds. Some funds are considered specialty funds because they base the selection of securities upon special selection techniques or special investment situations. An example of a fund employing special selection techniques would be the Dow Theory Fund. Special situation funds grow out of reorganized, merged, or rejuvenated companies that offer the investor considerable opportunity for growth.

The Small Business Investment Company (SBIC) is an example of a specialized closed-end investment company. In 1958, the Small Business Investment Act authorized the formation of investment companies to invest solely in small business concerns; it also accorded them favorable tax treatment. Practically all these companies have as their objective long-range capital growth. The SBIC's have not been in existence long enough to judge their success. Some have done extremely well; others might be considered short-run failures.

SWAP FUNDS

A swap fund, or exchange fund, is a portfolio of securities deposited simultaneously by individuals who own sizable blocks of stock in which they have substantial and unrealized capital gains. Individuals, by making an exchange or "swap" of the securities they own for shares of the swap fund, obtain diversification, professional management, convenience, and a tax-free exchange. A sales charge is made just as with regular mutual funds. The minimum deposit is generally $25,000 and the minimum charge is 4 percent. The management fee is usually 1/2 of 1 percent.

Exchange funds do not make a continuous offering of shares. The offering period can be ninety days; sixty days is generally the regular period, with the possibility of a thirty-day extension. Capital gains taxes are paid when the shares are redeemed.[8] Some of the funds quoted in *Barron's* are Capital Exchange Fund, Empire Fund, and Ohio Capital. At the moment the Treasury Department has suspended the formation of new swap funds.

DUAL FUNDS

The dual fund was introduced to the stock market in 1967. This new type of investment company offers stock in two classes: income, for investors who want a minimum return of 4.7 to 6.4 percent, and capital, for those who seek growth. The income shareholders receive all the investment income from the portfolio, while the capital shareholders receive and enjoy the capital appreciation. In a sense you have two dollars working for each dollar invested; one investor gets the income and the other the appreciation. A leverage effect is at work, best understood by thinking of a convertible preferred stock with a variable dividend and a variable capital growth twelve to eighteen years hence.[9]

PERFORMANCE FUNDS

One criticism leveled against mutual funds has been their inability to do as well as the market. A new breed of investment fund manager has risen to the occasion to correct this, and now performance is emphasized. Performance funds do not follow the buy-and-hold, conservative practices of fund managers of the 1940's and 50's. They trade, they wheel and deal and emphasize timing and the short term so much that they have been referred to as "go-go" funds. Gerry Tsai and his Tsai Management and Research Corporation manage the Manhattan Fund, Inc., one of the best known of the performance funds. Tsai emphasizes growth; it has been said that his group wants 20 percent appreciation per year. Certainly the group does not object to "turning the fund over" to reach their objectives, since their turnover has been higher than 100 percent per year. The Manhattan Fund and the Mates Fund have done well for short periods of time, but the Manhattan Fund's performance was not good in 1968. Whether they will be as successful as more traditional funds over a longer period of time remains to be seen.

In considering the fund that will provide relief from our own management responsibility, we must tailor the fund to meet our special needs. Generally the needs of most investors would be met by a general

---

8 John A. Straley, *What About Mutual Funds?* (New York: Harper and Row, Publishers, 1967), p. 134.

9 Armon Glen, "Two Mints in One," *Barron's*, January 3, 1967, p. 5 ff. A later article points out the obvious advantages of dual funds: Armon Glen, "Double Trouble," *Barron's*, September 2, 1968, p. 3.

TABLE 20–6

Largest portfolio holdings of mutual funds (September, 1969)

Mutual Fund	Five Largest Industry Holdings	Ten Largest Common Stock Holdings	
INVESTORS MUTUAL	Oil & Gas	IBM	Kodak
	Utilities	AT&T	Standard Oil (N.J.)
	Business Equipment	Royal Dutch Petroleum	Texaco
	Electrical Equipment	Marathon Oil	Gulf Oil
	Retail Trade	GM	Goodyear Tire
DREYFUS FUND	Oil	Polaroid	Royal Dutch Petroleum
	Insurance	AT&T	Delta Air Lines
	Photographic Equipment	Anaconda	Norwich Pharmacal
	Retail Trade	Getty Oil	Penn Central
	Public Utilities	INA Corp.	Philip Morris
INVESTORS STOCK FUND	Oil & Gas	IBM	Gulf Oil
	Business Equipment	GM	Xerox
	Electrical Equipment	Minnesota Mining	Continental Oil
	Utilities	Kodak	GT&E
	Retail Trade	Royal Dutch Petroleum	Household Finance
MASSACHUSETTS INVESTORS TRUST	Oil	IBM	Amerada Petroleum
	Business Machines	Kodak	Gulf Oil
	Electric Utilities	Royal Dutch Petroleum	Xerox
	Drugs & Medical	Texaco	Polaroid
	Metals & Mining	GM	Southern Pacific
AFFILIATED FUND	Oil	IBM	Atlantic Richfield
	Paper & Pulp	International Paper	Royal Dutch Petroleum
	Chemical	Texaco	Schlumberger
	Steel	Standard Oil (Cal.)	Phillips Petroleum
	Electric Utilities	Crown Zellerbach	Union Carbide
WELLINGTON FUND	Utilities	IBM	Texaco
	Oil	Royal Dutch Petroleum	Procter & Gamble
	Food & Related Products	Standard Oil (N.J.)	FMC Corporation
	Office Equipment	Consolidated Foods	S. S. Kresge
	Chemical	General Foods	Westinghouse Electric
UNITED ACCUM.	Information Systems	IBM	Xerox
	Petroleum, Geology	Control Data	Teledyne
	Bldg. & Construct.	Raytheon	Atlantic Richfield
	Electronics	Philip Morris	Sperry Rand
	Diversified	Scientific Data Systems	Royal Dutch Petroleum
FUNDAMENTAL INVESTORS	Business Equipment	IBM	Sperry Rand
	Oil & Gas	Atlantic Richfield	Control Data
	Electrical & Electrs.	Burroughs	Uniroyal
	Paper & Container	IT&T	Celanese
	Construction	Continental Can	Avco

TABLE 20–6 (continued)

Mutual Fund	Five Largest Industry Holdings	Ten Largest Common Stock Holdings	
FIDELITY TREND FUND	Office Equipment	IBM	Chrysler
	Oil, Gas & Equipment	Texaco	Atlantic Richfield
	Diversified Companies	GM	Raytheon
	Electrical & Electrs.	Westinghouse Electric	Sperry Rand
	Financial	McDonnell Douglas	Xerox
MASS. INV. GROWTH STOCK	Business Machines	IBM	Amerada Petroleum
	Electrical & Electrs.	Xerox	Avon Products
	Drugs & Medical	Polaroid	Louisiana Land & Exploration
	Consumer Goods	Litton	Schering
	Photographic Products	Kerr-McGee	Merck

SOURCE: Standard & Poor's *Industry Surveys—Investment Companies*, September 11, 1969, p. 139.

common-stock fund emphasizing growth or income or both. Diversified common-stock investment companies invest in leading companies and industries; their funds should provide long-range growth comparable to the growth of the market and the national economy.

In the final analysis, the classification of an investment company is determined by the securities that have been selected by the company managers. The portfolios of two funds with the same stated objectives will emphasize different companies and different industries. Table 20–6 indicates the portfolio variations in ten mutual fund companies. For each, the five largest industry holdings and ten largest common-stock holdings are presented. Utilities and oils are leading industry classifications, and IBM is held by most of the companies. Some funds emphasize chemicals and some office equipment. A degree of likeness exists in the quality of each portfolio, but there are individual differences in the emphasis that each places upon a specific industry and company. The same type of analysis would reveal the similarities and differences in the portfolios of closed-end funds.

Investment Companies and Federal Income Taxes

Under the Internal Revenue Act of 1942, many investment companies enjoy tax privileges not shared by the typical industrial, public utility, or railroad company. The 1942 act provided that an investment company will not be taxed on its dividend or interest income or on any realized capital gains if it is a regulated investment company.

A *regulated investment company* is defined as a domestic corporation which at all times during the year is registered under the Investment Company Act of 1940 as a management company and satisfies the following prerequisites: (1) at least 90 percent of its gross income is derived from dividends, interest, and gains from the sale or other disposition of securities; (2) less than 30 percent of its gross income is derived from the sale of securities held less than three months; (3) its investments have the requisite diversification (among other things, at least 50 percent of assets must be in cash, government securities, or a diversified list of securities); (4) it distributes to its stockholders as taxable dividends at least 90 percent of its net investment income, exclusive of capital gains; and (5) it elects to be treated as a regulated investment company. Once the latter election is exercised, it is binding in all subsequent years. . . .

Under an amendment to the Internal Revenue Code that became effective on January 1, 1957, a regulated investment company may elect to retain long-term capital gains and pay a 25 percent tax on the same for the account of its stockholders. In that event, each shareholder must (1) include his share of the capital gain in his federal income tax return, (2) take credit for the 25 percent tax paid for his account by the company, and (3) add to the cost basis of his stock 75 percent of his share of the undistributed capital gain.[10]

By purchasing the shares of a regulated investment company, the investor retains his own tax position and does not suffer a tax placed upon both the investment company's income and his own. When purchasing investment company shares, the investor wants to know if the company is regulated or nonregulated as well as its composition of income. An investor in a high income tax bracket would look for a fund that concentrated on capital growth; one in the lower tax brackets would probably be indifferent to the capital-gain treatment of income from an investment company unless, for other reasons, he desired growth or income from his investment account. Almost all investment companies are regulated; they pay to investors the entire investment earnings and net capital gains and therefore pay no federal income taxes. The share owners must, however, pay taxes on the dividend and interest income and capital-gain income received.

Performance of Investment Companies

The current income from investment companies is nominal; emphasis is on the growth of the assets in the fund rather than current income. The ten-year performance of the leading mutual funds in Table 20–7 gives some indication of what would have happened to $10,000 invested in each of fifty mutual funds from December 31, 1958, to December 31, 1968. As the table shows, some funds did very well over the ten-year period.

The net asset comparison for the leading closed-end investment companies in Table 20–8 tells a similar story. Compared to the market

10 Standard & Poor's *Industry Survey—Investment Companies*, September 11, 1969, p. 142.

TABLE 20–7

*Ten-year performance of mutual funds; net
asset value on December 31, 1968, of a
$10,000 investment made December 31,
1958, assuming full reinvestment of all
capital gain distributions*

45 LARGE COMMON STOCK FUNDS

Fidelity Trend Fund	$82,691
Ivest Fund	79,890
Enterprise Fund	60,833
Value Line Special Situations Fund	55,005
American Investors Fund	48,484
Oppenheimer Fund	45,057
Fidelity Capital Fund	44,907
Putnam Growth Fund	36,387
Keystone Lower-Priced Common Stock Fund (S-4)	31,232
Dreyfus Fund	29,656
T. Rowe Price Growth Stock Fund	27,157
Diversified Growth Stock Fund	26,469
Windsor Fund	25,654
Keystone Growth Fund (K-2)	25,643
Delaware Fund	25,572
Investment Co. of America	25,490
Keystone Growth Common Stock Fund (S-3)	25,162
Chemical Fund	24,802
National Securities-Growth Stock Series	24,580
State Street Investment	24,241
National Investors Corp.	24,124
Channing Growth Fund	23,358
Technology Fund	22,691
Massachusetts Investors Growth Stock Fund	22,320
Fidelity Fund	21,370
United Science Fund	20,783
Washington Mutual Investors Fund	20,605
American Mutual Fund	20,145
Affiliated Fund	20,001
Investors Variable Payment Fund	19,802
United Income Fund	19,297
Financial Industrial Fund	18,998
Putnam Investors Fund	18,921
Colonial Fund	18,615
Eaton & Howard Stock Fund	18,001
One William Street Fund	17,933
Fundamental Investors	17,900
Founders Mutual Fund	17,396
United Accumulative Fund	17,323
National Securities-Stock Series	16,958
Dividend Shares	16,925
Broad Street Investing	16,095
Group Securities-Common Stock Fund	16,069
Massachusetts Investors Trust	15,913
Investors Stock Fund	15,098

5 LARGE BALANCED FUNDS

Puritan Fund	20,504
George Putnam Fund of Boston	16,519
Boston Fund	12,696
Investors Mutual	12,314
Wellington Fund	12,183

SOURCE: Standard & Poor's *Industry Survey—Investment Companies,*
September 11, 1969, p. 139.

TABLE 20–8

*Net asset performance of closed-end
investment companies*

	1966	1957–66
Adams Express	— 9%	+ 48%
American International	— 9	+ 46
Carriers and General	—15	+ 69
Consolidated Investment Trust	—12	+ 55
Dominick Fund	— 3	+ 85
Equity Corporation	— 7	+ 31
General American Investors	— 7	+ 76
General Public Service	— 7	+121
Lehman Corporation	— 4	+103
Madison Fund	— 8	+103
Niagara Shore	—10	+113
Tri-Continental	—10	+ 82
U.S. & Foreign Securities	— 9	+ 38
Standard 500 Stock Index	—13%	+ 72%

SOURCE: Standard & Poor's *Industry Survey—Investment Companies*, September 28, 1967, p. 143.

as a whole, as measured by Standard & Poor's 500 Index, the closed-end investment companies have followed closely the action of the market. Less than half of the closed-end investment companies presented exceeded the results obtained by the market as a whole over the period.

Studies of the performance of mutual funds are conflicting. Farrar's study[11] indicated that portfolios selected at random showed sharply lower expected returns than the funds and only moderately lower risk. Friend and Vickers[12] conclude that mutual funds as a whole clearly do no better than random portfolios in their common-stock industry selection. This is supported by the results in Table 20–9. If mutual funds do no better than random selections, then the fund managers are not using methods that would lead to results at least equal to the market. They should utilize random statistical techniques to assure owners that they will get "the market," rather than ignoring the concept of statistical randomness in stock selection. Certainly funds are large enough to offer this service to their investors.

Advantages and Disadvantages of Investment Companies

The major advantages of investment company shares for the investor revolve about management and diversification. Portfolio management

[11] Donald E. Farrar, *The Investment Decision Under Uncertainty* (Englewood Cliffs, N.J.: Prentice-Hall, Inc., 1962).

[12] Irwin Friend and Douglas Vickers, "Portfolio Selection and Investment Performance," *Journal of Finance*, September, 1965.

TABLE 20–9

*Cumulative mean performance relatives and
dispersion of performance relatives for 50
mutual funds and 50 uniformly distributed
random funds, for six holding periods,
1957 through 1963*

	HOLDING PERIOD 1957 THROUGH:					
	1958	1959	1960	1961	1962	1963
Cumulative Mean Performance						
Mutual Funds	145.9	159.8	158.9	202.6	184.3	223.4
Uniformly Distributed Random Funds	149.1	165.6	167.1	217.9	190.1	234.2
Standard Deviation*						
Mutual Funds	3.8	6.8	7.9	12.7	10.3	13.2
Uniformly Distributed Random Funds	1.8	3.4	4.0	6.6	5.0	7.2

* Adjusted for degree of freedom.
NOTE: Portfolios for mutual funds and random portfolios are assumed unchanged throughout the period.
SOURCE: Irwin Friend and Douglas Vickers, "Portfolio Selection and Investment Performance," *Journal of Finance*, September, 1965, Table 9.

is provided for the investor, as well as more diversification than could be obtained by a small common-stock investment account.

In addition, the investor has a wide choice of both closed-end and open-end funds to meet his objectives. He is likely to find leverage in some of the purchases of closed-end investment companies. And because leverage exists, the investor might buy the stock of closed-end investment companies below the market price of its shares. This offers the attractive possibility of price appreciation due to a temporary decline in the price of a closed-end investment company. The mutual funds do not offer leverage, but they offer diversification and management to the investor.

Investment in mutual fund shares creates in the mind of the investor a sense of security that allows him a long-run perspective. Without this attitude investment success would not be as great. The purchaser of a single stock often does not take the same position and will sell in the short run because he thinks he has made a mistake, when in the long run he would have done well if he had held.

The disadvantages of the purchase of investment company stock must be considered. First, the round-trip cost of buying or selling a mutual fund is usually greater than the commission cost of buying and selling common stock. (This is true for large purchases of mutual fund shares vs. large purchases of common stock. For very small purchases, commission costs of the mutual funds would probably be cheaper.) This disadvantage does not apply, however, to closed-end investment companies traded on a registered stock exchange.

A second disadvantage of investment company shares is the cost of management, which ranges between 1/2 of 1 percent and 1 percent of the net asset value of the fund, or about 15 percent of income. These figures will vary from company to company, some having relatively low cost of management.

A third disadvantage lies in the inability of the investor to ascertain the quality of the management of an investment company. Perhaps the best criteria would be performance and management cost. In spite of the difficulty of judging management accurately, the task must still be undertaken and a value decision made.

A fourth disadvantage is the emphasis upon selection and the general inability of investment companies to do as well as the market. Because of this, the problem of management is not completely solved by the purchase of investment company shares.

As much care must be exercised in selecting investment companies as in selecting common stocks. We must examine quality of management, portfolio policy, price, and cost of management. At best, investment company shares offer a partial solution to the problem of the complete management of an investment fund for an individual or institution.

The best way to select and analyze a mutual fund is by past performance. Wiesenberger's annual study of *Investment Companies* and *Johnson's Charts* might help the investor in this analysis.

The Trust Company and Commercial Bank as a Solution to Portfolio Management

The large, urban commercial bank offers, on a fee basis, several types of investment service that can partially or completely assume the responsibilities of portfolio management for the individual. The investment service performed by the trust or investment department of a commercial bank or trust company can be undertaken through (1) a trust agreement, (2) a common trust fund and short-term trusts, (3) an investment management account, or (4) a custody account. Not all of these services provide a complete management service, but each helps in the solution of the individual's management problem.

Trust Agreements

A complete investment management service can be offered under a trust agreement. In the usual trust, the person who has a sum of money to invest turns it over to a trustee. The trustee or trust manager manages the fund or properties for the investor's benefit, or for the benefit of his heirs or any other beneficiary. In the modern trust, the manager has complete discretion over the management of the fund, a discretion based upon conservative and prudent rules of investment management. The trust agreement for the management of an investment account is usually associated with the *testamentary trust,* in which the estate of an individual is turned over to the trustee at the time of death; in essence, the estate is left in trust for the heirs. The income from a typical trust goes to the beneficiary, and then the remainder of the trust goes to another named person when the beneficiary dies.

An example of this testamentary trust, which provides a life estate with a remainder to a group of beneficiaries, is as follows: Mr. Jones establishes a trust for the benefit of his wife and children. When Mr. Jones dies, the income from the trust goes to Mrs. Jones. When Mrs. Jones dies, the remaining portion of the estate is distributed to the children. Mrs. Jones has a life estate; the children have a remainder and are referred to as the remaindermen. Mrs. Jones pays income tax on the income from the fund, but she pays no estate or inheritance taxes. When the children receive the estate, they must pay the estate and inheritance taxes if the estate they receive is large enough to be subject to them.

THE TRUSTEE FUNCTION

In investing funds under a trust agreement, the trustee usually has complete discretionary powers of investment limited only by statute or general rules of law governing the trustee and the *prudent man rule* of investment, which requires that a trustee act in his investment matters as would a prudent man in similar circumstances.

Besides the testamentary trust, investment management can also be obtained through a *living trust.* Under the living trust, an individual places property and securities in the hands of a trustee who manages the assets for the benefit of the creator of the trust or for the benefit of an individual named in the trust agreement as the beneficiary. The investment manager under the living trust must exercise the same care, conservatism, and prudence that the investment manager would exercise under a testamentary trust. The management is the same under both types of trusts in spite of the legal difference; under both the investor receives competent investment management.

THE COST OF TRUSTEESHIP

The cost of management under the trust agreement must be considered by the investor. It is based on the size of the fund, as in the management of a mutual fund. An annual fee of 1/2 of 1 percent for a $500,000 fund is a common charge for establishing and maintaining the estate under a trust agreement. As the value of the fund increases, the percent cost of the trust diminishes. A minimum fee is established that precludes the small fund from management under a trust agreement. Small dollar funds in need of management can take part in the common trust funds that have been established through the investment and trust departments of commercial banks or trust companies.

The Common Trust Fund

The *common trust fund* is operated just like a mutual fund except that the units are somewhat larger. The Marine Midland Trust Company of New York started a Discretionary Common Trust Fund with a unit value of $100 for 16 accounts, June 6, 1944. On July 29, 1960, the unit value had reached $166.53 and 153 accounts were participating.[13]

The advantages of a discretionary common trust fund are the same as those of the mutual fund. It makes good investment management available to small accounts, and offers diversification and continuous management for the investor. The cost of the investment service, borne by the creator of the discretionary trust fund, varies among financial institutions. A typical schedule of annual fees for trust administration that would include investment management would be as follows:

$5 per thousand on the first $50,000 of principal;
$4 per thousand on the next $200,000 of principal;
$3 per thousand on the next $750,000 of principal;
$2 per thousand on all principals in excess of $1,000,000 principal including uninvested cash.

The minimum annual fee is $150.

If the trust is revoked during the life of the grantor, there is an additional charge of $200 plus money to cover the incidental expenses of the trustee. When the trust is distributed to the beneficiaries, a 1 percent charge is made on the value of securities and cash held in the trust. Based on these rates, the annual cost of trust administration of a $250,000 trust would be $1,050, or less than 1/2 of 1 percent. The annual cost of a $1,000,000 fund would be $3,300, or 1/3 of 1 percent, a modest cost for competent management.

Retirement funds set up under the Keough Plan and allowed by the federal tax code for self-employed persons may be kept at a commercial bank with the trustee. The funds may also be invested in stock of open-end regulated investment companies, in policies issued by an insurance company, in nontransferable securities or in special series of U.S. bonds authorized for this purpose. The cost of administering retirement plan trusts by a commercial bank is comparable to the cost of other trust work and allows the self-employed person an opportunity to gain a tax advantage and obtain professional management of his funds at the same time.[14]

Short-Term Trusts

Short-term trusts have become an important way to obtain professional investment management. They also provide certain tax benefits for the investor. If he is in the 50 percent tax bracket, for example, the income

---

13 *Sixteenth Annual Report, Discretionary Common Trust Fund* (New York: The Marine Midland Trust Company of New York, 1960).

14 *1968 Federal Tax Course* (Englewood Cliffs, N.J.: Prentice-Hall, Inc.), pp. 1836 and 1838.

from an investment would be taxed heavily. Establishing a short-term trust with his investment account provides such a high-tax payer one main advantage. The income from the trust assets is taxed at a lower rate than 50 percent, providing the income is not too large. In a sense the income from the trust is taxed as if it were an individual. Since the amount of income from a fund is usually not large enough to be taxed at a high rate, tax saving results. Assume, for example, that we are in the 50 percent tax bracket and have $40,000 of securities that provide an additional annual income of $1,600 before federal income taxes and $800 after. We have adequate income to meet the needs of our family, but the additional income is being taxed heavily. We can obtain relief from the heavy taxes by establishing a ten-year trust[15] for the benefit of our seven-year-old son. We transfer $40,000 of securities to the trust and direct that the trust income be accumulated for our son's benefit. The accumulation of income is taxable to the trust, which enjoys a $100 exemption, and the income tax is reduced to 20 percent, which is the rate on $1,500 of income ($1600—$100). Instead of paying $800 in taxes, we pay only $300, a saving of $500. At the end of ten years, the principal amount of the trust is returned to the creator.

We gain several advantages by the use of a short-term trust. First is the tax saving if we are in a high income-tax bracket. Second, the trust is a way of accumulating a fund for the education of our children or to support our parents or to provide charitable contributions. The third advantage is the professional management that we receive when the funds are put into trust. The responsibility of management and accounting are assumed by the fund managers. The cost involved for this management is comparable to the fees for a regular living or testamentary trust.

Investment Management Account

Most commercial banks, either directly or through their correspondent banks, offer to individuals and institutions a complete investment management service, usually including supervision and custody of securities as well as management. Additional services might include handling purchases and sales, the selling of rights, remittance of income, summary reports, and income tax service. The investor must usually approve the recommendation of the investment officer who handles the account. The investment officer will act either upon the written or oral instructions of the owner of the fund.

The management objective of the investment management account is established by the investor upon consultation with the investment officer of the bank. The officer exercises thorough care in establishing a portfolio to meet the needs and objectives of the investor. He must learn to know the investor personally and financially to arrive at

15 Minimum term for which a short-term trust can be established.

the best management. Whatever the specific objectives of each investor, the general overall policy of the institution is dictated by prudence, discretion, and conservatism.

The larger commercial banks and trust companies maintain research departments to support the investment management activities. The research activities provide the investment account managers with a list of common stocks and bonds that have been approved for investment. The list is maintained by the research department; through the research process new securities are added and old ones deleted. The account manager selects securities based on his market judgment. He maintains and supervises the account, and usually his decisions determine the individual securities that go into it.

The investment policy of each institution differs. A general policy statement as made by a trust company might include the following:

1. The basic investment policy will be one of careful selection of securities made after comprehensive study.
2. Emphasis will be placed on maximum investment return commensurate with safety.
3. The primary purpose will be protection of principal, but growth and income will also be emphasized.
4. Common-stock dollar averaging will be emphasized.
5. Long-term investment will be stressed.
6. Liquidity will be maintained by government securities, but funds will be fully invested.
7. The balance between growth and income will vary, depending upon the position of the market.
8. In carrying out these overall policy objectives, the managers must exercise individual care and initiative.

The cost of the investment management service of a commercial bank or trust company compares favorably with the cost of trust and mutual fund management. A typical schedule of rates would be:

1/2 of 1% per annum on the first $500,000;
1/4 of 1% per annum on the next $500,000;
1/8 of 1% per annum on all accounts in excess of $1,000,000.
The minimum fee is $500 per annum.

An individual with a $250,000 fund would pay $1,250 for management based on the above rates. A $1,000,000 portfolio would require a fee of $3,750. The cost of the services usually provided under a management contract is small in comparison to the investment management provided.

Weighing by objective standards the advantages or disadvantages of investment management accounts of commercial banks and trust companies is difficult. The investment managers vary widely in ability, judgment, and achievement. Little has been published about the success of management accounts because they are privileged and confidential information. The investor selecting a manager for his funds will have to rely on the reputation of the institution and the investment manager handling his account. This can only be judged from knowledgeable clients who have had success with a specific commercial bank or trust company.

Investment Counsel and Portfolio Management

The investment counselor offers the investor another alternative solution to his management problem. Service is offered to the individual investor and the financial institution, including mutual funds, on a fee basis. The majority of the investment counselors provide a complete investment management and research facility. They usually do not take custody of client's securities, nor do they act as a broker, banker, or underwriter. Their main forte is in providing impartial advice on a personal basis by trained managers. The investment counselor usually obtains all of his income from his clients for the investment service he renders. Some investment counseling firms have established their own mutual funds, and others have provided research and management for mutual funds.

Policy and Advice

The investment advice given is usually tailored to meet the needs of the individual seeking investment help. A summary of the objectives of one investment counsel will indicate the emphasis placed on individual needs:

> The objective of the work of this firm is the effective use of each client's capital to meet the client's individual needs. Since our clientele includes the most conservative type of institution, some of them exempt from taxation, as well as the active businessman willing to assume risks and paying exceedingly high taxes, the effective use of capital takes different forms.
>
> In all cases, however, conservation of capital as a working asset is implicit. Beyond that, the degree to which income or capital performance is emphasized is related to the individual needs of each client and to the degree of risk which it is reasonable for him to assume.
>
> We attempt to accomplish these objectives by the application of experienced and informed judgment after first obtaining from the client complete information regarding his investment needs. We then determine policy with respect to the distribution of capital between bonds and stocks, between short and long maturities of bonds, among government, municipal and corporate bonds and preferred stocks, and among the shares of companies in different industries.

The policies thus determined are sufficiently flexible to be varied in anticipation of changing conditions.[16]

Research and Management

The investment function of most investment counseling firms is divided into research, including analysis and evaluation of securities, and investment management. Research includes economic and political environment as well as the analysis of industries, common stocks, bonds, and preferred stock. The research group continually evaluates securities to learn of their ability to continue to produce income or earnings. The analysts also appraise the financial and operating characteristics of the company and maintain a close relationship with the companies in which these firms invest. Their work in research and analysis includes interviews with management, often considered one of the most important tools of the investment analyst.

Investment Decisions

The investment decisions for each investor's account are usually made by an investment committee. The committee brings balance and perspective to the investment decision-making process and is supported in this work by the investment research department. The investment committee continuously appraises industries, companies, and economic trends to insure the best service to its clients. An account manager, usually an officer in the firm, is responsible for each client's account. It is his responsibility to keep the investor up to date on his investment account and the securities in his portfolio. He maintains a continuous review of the account and from time to time makes suggestions and changes based upon the advice of the research department and the investment committee. The final decisions are made to meet the specific needs of an individual investor.

Cost of Service

The cost of the service provided by the investment counselor is not much different from the fees charged by trust companies and commercial banks for similar services. There is bound to be variation in the fee schedules among individual firms, but the usual annual fee is 1/2 of 1 percent of the market value of the principal amount of capital under supervision. The fee is reduced as the size of the fund increases, with an annual minimum charge of $500. One investment firm makes this statement about its fees:

> The fee for our services is based on the principal amount of capital under supervision. Our annual charge to individuals is 1/2 of 1

16 *Scudder, Stevens, and Clark Investment Counsel, Established 1919* (New York: Scudder, Stevens, and Clark, 1961), p. 8.

percent of the market value of the account, with a minimum fee as described in the separate fee schedule. Holdings of a personal nature are excluded from fee. On accounts of over $2,000,000 a reduced schedule goes into effect. The fee for supervision of investments producing taxable income is deductible for federal income tax purposes.

For most institutions our fees are calculated on a lower scale than for individuals. Size, purpose, investment restrictions, composition of the portfolio, and degree of responsibility are the determining factors.[17]

The advantages of employing an investment counseling firm are obvious. Competent management is provided at a relatively low cost. The individual and, to some extent, the institution employing the services of a counselor are relieved of the responsibility and demand imposed by the management of an investment account. The investment counseling services are not available for the small investor who has less than $50,000 or $100,000 to invest. This is also true for trust accounts and investment management accounts with a commercial bank or trust company. This is not a disadvantage of the investment counseling service, it is merely a limiting factor when we avail ourselves of the services of an investment counselor. The function performed is usually worth the fee, depending upon the counselor's ability.

Summary

The individual investor is faced with the problem of the management of his investment fund. Often the person with funds to invest does not have the training, experience, education, or knowledge to maintain his own investments. The investor might have the ability but not the time, or might have the time and possibly the ability but no interest in his financial and investment affairs. The professional analyst who is capable of managing his own account also needs independent counsel, to balance his own views of the market. All these investors need help in the solution of their management problems.

There are several alternatives if we need investment management help. We can invest in investment companies. Management is provided, and we are relieved of the responsibility of management. However, the cost of management and the cost of purchasing mutual funds is high, even though rates are somewhat reduced in the purchase of large amounts of mutual fund shares. Mutual funds provide a sense of relief from responsibility for the investor and emphasize the long-term perspective. The investor also has a better chance of achieving a yield equivalent to the market yield or a random yield than if he invested in one or two stocks. This combination makes mutual funds attractive for many

17 *Scudder, Stevens, and Clark Investment Counsel,* p. 8.

investors. Special funds, dual funds, and swap funds give the investor flexibility. The open-end investment companies provide the same service but offer the possibility of lower commission rates and of bargains because of financial leverage. The timing problem still remains with investment company shares. Investment companies have varied management objectives designed to meet the needs of different types of investors. The quality of management varies, and we must be aware of the qualities of the investment company before investment takes place.

The trust company and commercial bank offer investment service on a fee basis through living and short-term trusts and management accounts. The record of achievement is not completely known about this type of management service, so we must select an institution with a reputation for competent investment service. The management provided is usually well trained and conservative in its approach to the management function. The fund manager attempts to tailor the investment activities to our needs. The fees charged are modest for large funds but, again, prohibitive for funds under $50,000. The trust form may provide management of funds, but it is limited in general use for investment because of its relative inflexibility. There are some circumstances where it would meet our needs admirably. Many large banks have well-trained and adequate staffs to meet the needs of the investor. Common trust funds are available for the small investor.

The investment counselor offers another alternative to the management of our investment fund. Through impartial research of the national economy, industries, and companies, investment counsel offers competent management to meet our specific needs. Adequate research and management staffs are maintained to serve the client on a fee basis. The fee charged is modest for the services performed, but the minimum fee prohibits the small fund from being considered for management.

We must be aware that all the alternatives to investment management have some disadvantages; yet we are offered adequate solution to our investment management problems if we have sufficient funds.

Review Questions

1. (a) Discuss the problems of portfolio management.
   (b) What are the individual limitations that would prevent an investor from managing his own portfolio?
2. Explain the nature of investment companies, both open-end and closed-end, and comment upon how they might be used as a solution to the management problem.
3. What are the advantages and disadvantages of the closed-end investment company for the investor?

4. What are advantages and disadvantages of the open-end investment company as an outlet for investment?

5. (a) Who are the managers of investment companies, and how are they compensated?
   (b) Is the cost of management too high? Comment.

6. (a) Explain how the management objectives of investment companies differ.
   (b) What are some of the different types of funds that would be included in a list of investment companies?

7. What criticisms have been levied against mutual funds by the SEC and the Wharton School Study?

8. What are dual funds and swap funds?

9. Do investment companies enjoy any special federal income-tax benefits? Explain.

10. How have investment companies performed in the market in recent years? Comment.

11. Explain how an investor might solve his portfolio management problem through a trust department of a commercial bank or through a trust company.

12. If a mutual fund can achieve a yield equivalent to a random yield, then it has done its job. Comment.

13. (a) How might a trust, a common trust fund, or a short-term trust solve the portfolio management problem?
    (b) What is the cost of these trusts?

14. To what extent do commercial banks and trust companies provide investment management? What is the cost of this service?

15. Investment counsel is another way in which an investor might solve his portfolio management problem. What is the nature of such counsel, and what would such portfolio management cost?

Problems

1. Assume that we purchased $100,000 of Massachusetts Investors Trust —Growth Fund on January 2, 1957. All of the dividends received were reinvested, and we held the stock until December 31, 1968.
   (a) How many shares would we have purchased?
   (b) What would have been the price per share?
   (c) What would have been the value of our $100,000 at the end of each year?
   (d) What would have been the average yield?

2. Make the same comparison with $100,000 invested in the Dow Jones Averages and answer questions 1 (a) through 1 (d).

3. Based upon the comparison in 1 and 2, will we have benefited from management? Explain.

4. Compare the cost of portfolio management for the $100,000 invested

in mutual fund shares to $100,000 invested through a management
account with a commercial bank or an investment counselor for the
same period.
(a) Which would be most costly?
(b) What conclusion can be made from this comparison?

Sources of Investment Information

Barron's
Moody's Manuals—Finance and Banking
Standard & Poor's *Investment Surveys*
The Value Line Investment Survey
Wall Street Journal
Wiesenberger, *Investment Companies*

Selected Readings

Ellis, Charles D., "Performance Investing," *Financial Analysts Journal* (September-
October, 1968), p. 117.

Fox, Edward A., "Measuring Performance of Equities," *Financial Analysts
Journal* (September-October, 1968), p. 121.

Gentry, James A. and John R. Pike, "Dual Funds Revisited," *Financial Analysts
Journal* (March-April, 1968), p. 149.

Greeley, Robert E., "Mutual Fund Management Companies," *Financial Analysts
Journal* (September-October, 1967), p. 75.

Netter, Joseph, II, "Dual-Purpose Funds," *Financial Analysts Journal* (July-
August, 1967), p. 85.

Pratt, Eugene J., "Myths Associated with Closed-End Investment Company
Discounts," *Financial Analysts Journal* (July-August, 1966), p. 79.

Rinfret, Pierre A., "Investment Managers Are Needed," *Financial Analysts
Journal* (March-April, 1968), p. 163.

Shelton, John P., *et al.*, "Dual Funds: An Appraisal," *Financial Analysts Journal*
(May-June, 1967), p. 131.

Soldofsky, Robert M., "Yield-Risk Performance Measurements," *Financial
Analysts Journal* (September-October, 1968), p. 130.

21

PORTFOLIO MANAGEMENT AND TIMING

We have emphasized quality and the proper selection of securities through investment analysis. Timing of purchases was considered, but until now the prime goal was selectivity. However, some investors consider when to buy and sell even more important than what to buy and sell. In this chapter we will examine the problem of the timing of security purchases and methods that might serve as a solution to the timing problem.

The Timing Problem

The selection of investment securities must stress quality for the majority of individuals who invest. When quality companies are selected and finally purchased, we must recognize the importance of timing. When we examined the potential yield on a stock, we found that it might be of excellent quality but provide a yield that was unsatisfactory. The timing concept, very simply, gives recognition to the cyclical characteristics of the securities market. Many examples can be given to dramatize the importance of the timing of stock purchases of quality companies. International Business Machines (IBM) traded between 324 and 375 during the first eight months of 1968. General Electric traded between 80 1/4 and 100, du Pont ranged from 148 to 177 1/2, Procter & Gamble sold between 81 3/4 and 100 1/2. Any of these top quality companies could have been purchased for investment. If we had purchased these excellent companies at the wrong level, we might have lost a large portion of our investment fund.

Many long-term investors, however, invest on the assumption that it makes no difference what price you pay for a stock. In the long run, they reason, the good company will succeed, and the price of its stock will go up and will eventually be higher than the purchase price. Over long periods of time the stock market has risen and profits have been made in the securities market, particularly in the decade of the 1950's. However, some common stocks that were purchased in the 1920's failed completely in the 1930's; some, in fact, have not yet reached the price level that they attained in the 1920's. There are stocks that sold at all-time highs in 1967 and 1968 that may never reach these highs again. The point we must stress is that the proper timing of investment purchases can determine the success or failure of an investment program. Timing, therefore, should be considered as important as the qualitative factors of analysis.

The second point that must be emphasized is that investors—all shapes and sizes, learned and unlearned, intelligent and unintelligent, professional and nonprofessional—can and do make investment mistakes. No one has clairvoyance or the ability to determine exactly the highs and lows of the stock market. With thought, patience, and experience and without predicting the exact highs and lows of the market, we still can be successful investors.

Two additional items should be mentioned in regard to the problem of timing. The concept of timing suggests that not only should we purchase securities when they are relatively low but we should sell them when they are relatively high. The buy-and-hold investor would take exception to this statement. He would say that if you buy wisely— a quality company at a low price—then it is unnecessary to buy and sell the security. He would also say that buying and selling do not apply to all securities and that one cannot generalize about the securities market. But if the concept of timing has any validity, then the idea of selling a security if it appears to be too high is just as reasonable as saying that the stock is low in price and should be purchased.

The solution to the matter of proper timing of the sale rests upon expectations about the future. If, based on a reasonable and complete analysis, the present price is excessive compared to future yields from these earnings, then the security should be sold. On the other hand, if expectations about future earnings and yield result in a present value that is sufficiently higher than the present price, then we should consider the stock for purchase. The investor who suggests that we should buy and hold really is saying that it is difficult to determine whether the price is high or low, and will find it difficult to buy and sell a stock. Future yields should provide the clue of when to buy and sell. The buy-and-hold philosophy does, however, provide one solution to the timing problem, though not the best one, and we find many advocates of the buy-and-hold philosophy of investment management.

Another point that must be brought out in a discussion of timing is that there is often an urgency in investment decisions that is unwarranted. There is no such thing in the entire question of investment decision making as that an investor is required to buy a stock at a specific time. The *must invest* concept has no part in the intelligent process of investment analysis and management. We are always faced with other alternatives—for example, putting funds into bonds or fixed-income securities or simply holding cash and not making purchases of common stock. This is why investment "tips" are so incongruous with the investment decision-making process. The *tip* suggests the words "must" and "now" and detracts from the concept of proper timing along with the objective of quality of the investor. We should ignore tips in the investment process. We should never think that only one stock will solve our investment ills. There are always many alternatives for the investment of funds. Several solutions to the problem of timing will be considered.

The Bond Portfolio as a Solution

One solution to the timing problem would be to ignore stocks completely and invest only in bonds, which would be purchased and held to maturity. At maturity, the bonds would be reinvested in new bonds and again held until maturity. We would diversify the bonds by industry and maturity. This solution to the investment problem is simple and solves the problem completely. It even solves the problem for the investor in the high income-tax bracket. He can purchase tax-exempt municipal bonds and his timing, security, and tax problem are solved immediately. Or are they? Aside from the obvious point that the purchase of bonds has its own timing problem and that we must be just as selective about the timing of bond transactions as the timing of stock purchases, there are three other very serious limitations to the solution. First, bonds do not increase in price as the purchasing power of the dollar declines, as do common stocks, and so bond investment over long periods of time has not offered the investor relief from the purchasing-power risk. This was particularly true during the decade following World War II.

The second objection to a complete bond investment portfolio is that the return to the investor is lower than what might be earned from a common-stock portfolio. Over long periods of time when we consider dividend income and capital gain, the investor who stresses quality stocks and growth with some income should do better than the bond investor. Again, during the 1950's and even after the market decline and recovery in the 1962–1964 period, an investor in common stock would have earned a higher yield than the bond investor over the same period of time. Greater risk is involved in the purchase of common stocks than in the purchase of bonds, but the additional risk appears to be overshadowed by the potential gains.

The third objection is that in periods of rapidly rising interest rates such as we experienced in the period 1966 through 1969, bond prices fell. If we own bonds in such a period we could have a substantial capital loss unless we could hold to maturity. We would also suffer a loss equal to the difference between our original investment yield and the higher yield.

Bonds certainly have a place in an investment portfolio, but it would be unwise to solve the timing problem by investment in bonds only. The objections to a complete bond portfolio suggest that a better solution to the timing problem be found.

Patience, Price Setting, and Timing

One very good way to handle the problem of the timing of security purchases would be to establish price goals for each stock and try to buy the stock at the predetermined price. This process requires a great deal of patience and offers the danger that we might miss out on some potentially excellent investment securities. Assume, for example, that we decide to buy a stock at 45. The current market price is 60. The stock never goes down to 45, however, and continues up to 100. In this case we attempted to achieve a goal that was impossible or at least unlikely to occur. Or we might have been unrealistic in our appraisal of the company.

Another danger of waiting for a specific price to be reached is that a change may occur in the fundamental position of the company. An analysis conducted anew would reveal that the company was no longer desirable at the original price that was set. This again points up the need for continuous analysis of a company's stock.

An example might help to clarify the good features of the process of patience and price setting as a solution to the timing problem. Assume that an investor wishes to invest $100,000 he has inherited, most of which was the proceeds from life insurance and not previously invested. How should the investor begin his investment program, and what weight and consideration should he give to timing? The first step would be to place the funds in a liquid and marketable investment until his investment policy is established. Secondly, the investment objectives of the individual should be determined. Third, a portfolio should be constructed to meet his investment needs considering the risks that he can assume. Fourth, the securities to meet the portfolio requirements should be determined; and, fifth, the securities should be acquired over the next six months or longer at attractive prices when and if they occur, to meet the yield the investor desires. If the stock market is low, it would be possible to invest more quickly. This process emphasizes selection and timing, and it offers one solution to the timing problem.

An actual case will demonstrate how this method works in practice. Early in 1962, David Ganes inherited the tidy sum of $20,000. After considering the investment needs of Mr. Ganes, the investment counselor decided that he should have as his objective a combination of income and growth and that his portfolio should be defensive in character. The reason for the defensive position was brought about by the uncertainty in the stock market in 1962. The market had dropped sharply and had established somewhat of a resistance level around the 550–560 level of the DJIA. In order to achieve Mr. Ganes's objectives, it was decided that $10,000 of his funds should be put into a building and loan association to earn 4 percent. The remaining $10,000 was to be invested in a well-selected list of common stocks with both income and growth potential. Temporarily, all the money was kept in the bank for safekeeping while the portfolio was being established. The common-stock portion was to be invested in telephone companies, public utilities, and industrial stocks.

Between the counselor and Mr. Ganes, a tentative list of securities was considered for purchase. On June 21, 1962 two stocks were purchased, and three more on June 22. These purchases put 70 percent of the common-stock fund to work. Three additional companies were decided upon, but since it was thought that the current price was too high, a limited order was placed for them. The order for Hertz was entered at 35 and was exercised when the market moved downward in October, 1962, before the enactment of the Cuban quarantine. Subsequently in November and December of that year the other orders were exercised at favorable prices.

The portfolio was put together over a period of eight months. The prices paid for the securities were much more attractive than the prices that prevailed when the money was received by Mr. Ganes. The $10,000 in savings would be used as a protective fund and a portion used to acquire additional common stock at favorable prices. If Mr. Ganes and his counselor had acted in haste and invested the funds immediately, he would have suffered a loss. Patience and price setting can be an excellent way to provide one additional solution to the timing problem. Mr. Ganes is a fictitious name for our investor, but the results portrayed were authentic.

Stock Price Averaging Solution

Another way to solve the problem of the timing of portfolio purchases is to average the purchase price of the stock. The concept of averaging recognizes the inability of man to judge accurately when a stock is high or low. It assumes, basically, that we cannot judge the market and suggests that we should ignore any activities that would attempt to predict the highs and lows of a stock. Instead we are asked first to select quality stocks. Then we are asked, not to buy a security just once and put it away for safekeeping, but to buy it two or three times. If we do this, it is assumed that we will have a much more realistic price for the stocks we purchase. Since we are investing for the long run, it is assumed that we will be better off with averaging than we would be if we made only one purchase of a given stock for our portfolio.

A good example of averaging can be taken from a recent case. Mrs. Margaret Winslow purchased 20 shares of Procter & Gamble at 92. She realized that the company was excellent and would provide her with an excellent long-term investment. However, the stock had dropped to 64. She was concerned about the drop in the market value and wondered what should be done. She had an additional $1,000 that she wished to invest, thus adding to her problems. The solution according to averaging would be for Mrs. Winslow to purchase more of P & G at 64. The effects of the purchase would be to reduce the average cost of the shares she owned. With $1,000 Mrs. Winslow could buy an additional 15 shares of P & G. The effect of the purchase (ignoring commissions and taxes) would be as follows:

	SHARES	PRICE PER SHARE	VALUE
1st Purchase	20	$92	$1,840
2nd Purchase	15	64	960
Total	35	$80 (Averaged Price)	$2,800

Thus, Mrs. Winslow would now have 35 shares of Procter & Gamble at an average price of $80 per share. The average price of $80 is much better than a price of $92. It puts Mrs. Winslow in a much better position as a long-term investor. After she purchased P & G at 64, the price moved back up to 80 7/8, which was above the average price at which Mrs. Winslow had purchased P & G.

Mrs. Winslow would have been wise to buy Procter & Gamble for a third time to be consistent with averaging. Assume that the price of P & G drops to 52 1/2 and she buys an additional 20 shares of stock. She now owns 55 shares of P & G for a total cost of $3,850 and an average cost of $70. Mrs. Winslow is buying in a declining market, of course. She is, however, taking full advantage of the declining market to add a quality investment security at lower prices. The wisdom of Mrs. Winslow's purchases is apparent from the lower average price she has paid for her stock. The advantage and wisdom of her actions will become even more apparent when the price of the stock begins to move back up.[1] With an average cost of $70 per share, the stock need rise

---

1 The question often raised is what happens if the price of the stock continues to drop and the price finally drops to zero. In this case the investor loses all the money invested in the stock either by making only one initial purchase for the total investment or by dollar averaging. If it does happen, dollar averaging still has the advantage. The investor loses all his money, but he loses less per share!

only from 52 1/2 to 70 to eliminate the loss. This would be an increase of 33 percent. If all the stock had been purchased at 92 it would have had to increase 75 percent to eliminate the loss. Thus Mrs. Winslow buys several times, averages her purchases, and realizes a better price for a stock than she would have achieved by purchasing the stock at one price. One well-known investment counselor has recommended this system for purchasing stock. He suggested that the investor buy quality stocks—stocks that you would be willing to buy when they went down in price—and keep them in the portfolio as long-term investment. He also suggested that they be bought at lower prices to allow the investor a lower average price.[2]

The simple assumption upon which the averaging concept rests is much like the concept of price setting previously discussed. What is really being said is that we cannot predict the highs and lows and we do not know with complete assurance what is a fair price. Therefore, securities are purchased more than once and in this way an average price will result that will be more realistic than any single price. The low and the high price will not be achieved, but an average-of-the-market price would be better than buying the stock at the high of the market. General Motors, for example, sold as high as 58 and as low as 40 5/8 in 1961. If we had bought 100 shares of General Motors in 1961 and paid 58 for the stock, we would have invested $5,800 in the security. Now let us assume that we bought 25 shares of General Motors four times during the year instead of buying 100 shares at one time. Further, we will assume that we bought it at 58 twice and 40 5/8 twice. The average price for each share would be a little bit higher than 49 1/4. Thus by buying several times and dollar averaging we have an 8 3/4 point advantage over the single purchase at the high point of the market.

The astute reader will raise the question of what happens if you are able to buy the stock at the low of the market. You have actually paid more for the stock by averaging than by buying it at the low. This is true. However, we should be willing to trade the possible gains we might receive from being able to buy the stock at its low point for the losses we would sustain if we purchased the stock at the height of the price movement. In essence we are compromising our situation. We are willing to limit our gains and limit our losses brought about by the cyclical activities of the market, knowing that by doing this we will be assured of a better investment position in the long run, providing us with the growth trend of the market. And the act of averaging partially relieves us of our responsibility of attempting to pinpoint the timing of a purchase of common stock.

2 Ragnor D. Naess, partner in Naess & Thomas, New York, Speech to the Cincinnati Federation of Security Analysts, June, 1961.

Dollar averaging or dollar cost averaging is considered to be a better averaging technique because it helps to buy stock at a price lower than the average of the trend of the market, even though the market moves upward in a cyclical fashion. With dollar averaging, the investor buys the same dollar amount of stock at regular time periods. As the market price declines, he is able to buy more shares of stock with his fixed number of dollars. If the stock moves up in price, he will buy a smaller number of shares. The effect of these transactions is to lower his cost below the average of the market. Assume, for example, that a person buys $1,000 of stock at three different prices as follows:

		PRICE	NUMBER OF SHARES
(1)	$1,000	50	20
(2)	1,000	40	25
(3)	1,000	100	10
Totals	$3,000		55

The average price per share is $54.54 ($3,000/55). If he had purchased the same number of shares at the above prices, his average purchase price per share would have been $63.33. He would have the average of the market price under these conditions. Under dollar cost averaging he would have lower than the average of the market price. Dollar averaging is particularly attractive to smaller investors who are putting regular sums of money into the purchase of quality common stocks.

ADVANTAGES OF AVERAGING

The major advantage of averaging or dollar averaging is that it takes the pressure from the investor in timing stock purchases. The concept works with equal facility in a rising stock market or in a declining market. Ideally it works best when stock is acquired in a declining market. The dollar averaging or averaging down process reduces the average cost per share and improves the possibility of gain over the long term.

Another advantage of the averaging process is that it forces the investor to plan his investment program more thoroughly than if he were making a commitment at one time. A final advantage is that it provides for periodic and continuous review of the investor's portfolio and objectives. The process of averaging or dollar averaging tends to eliminate the cyclical characteristics of a stock but retains the trend of growth over time.

DISADVANTAGES OF AVERAGING

Several disadvantages of averaging might in some cases outweigh the advantages. The first disadvantage is the cost involved in purchasing the stock at several different times rather than at one time. This is particularly important for the investor with a modest fund who might be able to buy one round lot of stock but could not buy several round lots. The cost of buying does increase with more frequent purchases, although this should not be a major consideration in the purchase of common stock.

A second disadvantage is the inability or unwillingness of an individual investor to carry out an averaging program. It is very possible that the following situation might develop. Mr. Jones buys 25 shares of AT&T at 130. The stock begins to drop and finally reaches 103. Originally Mr. Jones was going to buy more stock, but when the stock reaches 103 he decides not to purchase it because he thinks the stock will go lower. On the other hand, assume Mr. Jones buys the stock at 103 and it moves to 130. He decides not to buy at 130 because he thinks the stock price is too high, and yet the stock moves to 165. The net result of all this is that he does not buy additional shares to either average or dollar average; he has ignored the timing problem completely and the advantages that might be achieved by an averaging program. Dollar averaging can take place by buying more than one security. Where one security is not attractive, another security can be purchased. The advantages of dollar averaging would continue.

A third disadvantage is that averaging emphasizes the timing of purchases and attempts to provide a solution to the problem, but it does not call attention to the problem of when to sell the securities that have been purchased. Dollar averaging simply assumes that stock once purchased will not be sold except infrequently and that the selling of the stock is only incidental to the entire investment process. There is an advantage in selecting quality companies for long-term investment and then holding the securities. The financial and economic affairs of a company do change. We should recognize when a company has changed its basic status in the industry, and once the change is recognized, we should act. Where the economic change is adverse to our interests, we should sell the stock of the company. If possible the investor should attempt to anticipate changes to protect his investment values as much as possible. Averaging or dollar averaging does not suggest a time when securities should be sold on an automatic basis. If we apply the technique of averaging, we must analyze and manage our portfolio the same way a completely managed portfolio would be managed.

Formula Planning Solution

By not telling the investor when to sell, dollar averaging or averaging does not emphasize sufficiently the fundamental problem of the investment management equation—bluntly stated as the *buy low–sell high* concept. If man were perfect in his judgment of the market and market conditions, he would buy low and sell high. This requires a great deal of patience and fortitude. It is full of pitfalls and errors in judgment. However, if we are to be successful we would essentially follow a path that would allow us to buy securities when they were cheap or low and sell them when they had risen in price. Many wealthy investors and financiers will trade in the market. That is, as the market goes down, they will take advantage of lower prices and buy, and when the market goes up, they will sell. This requires skill and precise timing, but it has been rewarding for many astute investors.

The buy low–sell high concept is excellent but difficult to employ, particularly for the small investor. A system is needed that will allow results comparable to what a skilled investor would achieve based upon good judgment on buying low and selling high, yet the system must be automatic so that once it is established, the person with only a modest skill in investment timing will be able to carry out the program successfully. Programs that provide an automatic timing device for guiding the buy-and-sell transactions of the investor on a prearranged plan to approximate good management are referred to as *formula plans*. The formula plan helps to tell us when to buy and when to sell, but it does not tell what to buy and what to sell.

Assumptions Upon Which a Formula Plan Is Based

The first assumption on which the formula plan is based is that a certain percentage of the investor's portfolio will be invested in fixed-income securities and a certain percentage in common stocks. The exact amount invested in each depends upon the height of the stock market at the time the investor begins the plan. It depends also on the temperament of the investor and how aggressive or defensive he wishes to be in his portfolio policy. It is not uncommon for an investor to follow a balanced-fund approach when the formula plan is established. The balanced-fund concept might require that initially 50 percent of the fund be invested in bonds and 50 percent in common stocks, or some other proportion. At the time the portfolio is established, an attempt should be made to determine the relative height of the stock market. If the market is relatively high, a greater percentage of the investment fund should be in fixed-income types of securities, perhaps a ratio of 70 percent bonds and 30 percent stock. If, on the other hand, the market is low, then one could reverse proportions. This requires a judgment about the height of the stock market and calls essentially for a timing decision. A balance of 50-50 between common stocks and bonds is the most advantageous ratio for a constant ratio plan.

The second assumption upon which the formula plan is based is that as the market moves higher the proportion of common stock in the portfolio either remains constant as a percent of the total or it declines. When the market declines, common stock becomes either an increasing percent of the total or it remains the same. One type of formula plan, for example, requires that as the stock market moves up, common stock is sold to keep the amount of common stock equal to the amount of debt. A second plan requires a decline in the amount of stock as a percent of the total portfolio when the market is high and an increase in the amount of stock as the market declines. More will be said about these formula plans later in the chapter. These changes simply recognize that a portfolio should be more aggressive when the market is low and more defensive when the market is high. It also assumes that as the common stock portion of the portfolio increases because of capital gains, some of the stock will be sold to realize the gains. In this way, an individual is guided in buying and selling his common stocks.

A third premise upon which a formula plan rests is that stock will be bought and sold when a significant change occurs in the price of the securities owned by the investor. A significant change in the level of the market as measured by a leading stock market index such as the Dow Jones Industrial Average, the Associated Press Average, or Standard & Poor's Average of 500 Industrial Stocks, might also signal a change. The time period between purchase and sale will depend upon the movement of the market or the securities owned. One way of making changes in an investment portfolio, for example, is to plan to sell the stock and buy bonds when the stock portion of the investment account increases 25 percent. Additional stock will be purchased if the securities owned or the stock market average drops 20 percent. The different percentages are established to make certain that the movements compensate each other. If stocks move from 100 to 125, for example, we would sell stock and buy bonds. If the market should decline 20 percent by moving back to 100, we would then sell bonds and buy stock. The amount of bonds that would be purchased or sold according to the prearranged plan of action would depend upon the degree of defensiveness or aggressiveness that was desired.

A fourth assumption is that the individual will adhere to the formula plan once it has been established. The investor will buy and sell based upon his prearranged plan, and he will not abandon his program once it has begun. This requires that we completely understand what the formula plan will accomplish. It requires patience too, for the investor must be patient with a formula plan if it is to be successful. If the investor begins to anticipate the market and makes changes accordingly, he is reverting to complete management and abandoning his plan. This would result in a loss of any advantage that is claimed by the proponents of the formula plan method of timing the purchase or sale of securities. In essence, we must have confidence in the formula plan and must understand the system before we begin.

A fifth requirement is that the investor select quality stocks that move with the stock market. These securities will be carefully selected to meet the standards of financial and investment analysis. Essentially a company will possess sound earnings, a good financial position and capital structure, a good management, a dominant position within the industry, and a relatively attractive price and price-earnings ratio. It is helpful if some dividends are paid on the stock. These securities are checked periodically for price and quality to make certain that they continue to meet the needs of the investor; the investor cannot ignore the securities once they have been purchased. The fundamental position of the company may change and the investor must be aware of these changes.

The last condition associated with formula plans is that they allow the investor to take advantage of the cyclical swings in the market, so that the benefits from the swings will accrue to the investor. The following example will demonstrate how we might be better off financially by using a formula plan. Assume that stock is sold when the value of the investment fund moves up 25 percent, and stock is bought when the market value moves down 20 percent. The value of the stock account will be kept at $1,000 and the total fund will be $2,000. When the fund moves up or down, the stock account will be adjusted to the $1,000 level. This is illustrated in Table 21–1 where we follow through two cycles of transactions. It moves up 25 percent and down 20 percent twice. In step (1) when the stock fund moves up 25 percent, the stock is sold and bonds are purchased. When the stock drops 20 percent, bonds are sold, and stock is purchased to bring the amount up to $1,000. The formula plan method allows a profit of $100, and we end up with a $2,100 fund. Without the formula plan we finish with the same amount with which we began—$2,000. Under the formula plan we are 5 percent better, under the assumptions provided. Even if we added on the cost of buying and

TABLE 21–1

Example of financial advantage
of formula plan

	Formula Plan			Buy and Hold Plan		
	VALUE OF STOCK	VALUE OF CASH OR BOND	TOTAL VALUE	VALUE OF STOCK	VALUE OF CASH OR BOND	TOTAL VALUE
Beginning position	$1,000	$1,000	$2,000	$1,000	$1,000	$2,000
(1) 25% increase	250	1,000	2,250	1,250	1,000	2,250
Sell stock Buy bonds	1,000	1,250	2,250	1,250	1,000	2,250
(2) 20% decrease	800	1,250	2,050	1,000	1,000	2,000
Buy stock	1,000	1,050	2,050	1,000	1,000	2,000
(3) 25% increase	1,250	1,050	2,300	1,250	1,000	2,000
Sell stock	1,000	1,300	2,300	1,250	1,000	2,250
(4) 20% decrease	800	1,300	2,100	1,000	1,000	2,000
Buy stock	1,000	1,100	2,100	1,000	1,000	2,000

selling the stock, we would be slightly better off with a formula plan than without.

TYPES OF FORMULA PLANS

No single formula plan is used by individual and institutional investors. Rather there are three basic formula plans that follow the pattern described above. The first is the *constant dollar stock plan*. The constant dollar stock plan begins with a fixed amount of money invested in stock and in cash or bonds. As trades are made, the amount invested in stock is kept at a fixed amount based on the original amount invested in common stock. The second basic plan is the *constant stock bond ratio plan*, which is based on a fixed relationship between bonds and stock. Once the ratio between bonds and stock is established, it is kept constant based upon the indicated changes in the market. If a 50/50 ratio between stocks and bonds had been established, then this ratio would be maintained as the market moved up or down by 25 percent. The third is the *variable stock-bond ratio plan*, which allows the investor to adjust his portfolio between stocks and bonds based upon the relative height of the stock market. When the market moves up, instead of maintaining a constant ratio between stocks and bonds, a ratio is adopted that decreases the emphasis upon common stock and increases the amount of bonds in the investment account. Adjustment is made for trend so that the ratio of stocks to debt depends on the range around a rising trend line rather than a horizontal trend line of the market.

Some Advantages of Formula Plans

The major advantage of the formula plan is its automatic character. Once the plan is established, we are freed from making emotional decisions based upon the current attitudes of investors in the stock market. We realize that we cannot possibly purchase stock at the lowest price and sell it at the highest price. We also know in using a formula plan that as the market moves up, we will sell some and take profits. When the market moves down, we will sell some bonds and buy stock. As prices move lower, the amount of stock that can be purchased increases, and we are then placed in a position where we will share in the market rise when it occurs. An emotional decision by the investor often is his undoing. Anything that allows the investor a modicum of success in the timing of purchases and sales and eliminates the error predicated upon incorrect reasoning in the market is desirable and beneficial.

The second advantage of the formula plan is related to timing the sale of stock. Most effort and discussion about timing is concerned with buying securities. The formula plan stresses both buying and selling. In essence it tells when to buy and when to sell even though it does not cover the problem of what to buy and sell. Selling a stock is often more difficult than buying. Assume, for example, that we buy a stock at 25 and it moves up to 35. Should we sell and take our profit, or should we continue to hold the stock? The buy-and-hold investor has a ready answer for this question. If the company is still fundamentally sound, and if earnings continue to promise a satisfactory yield, the stock should be held. But we are told that stock prices move in cycles, that at times a stock could be too high or too low. We would desire to take advantage of this situation in our investment program, yet we do not wish to be market traders. With a formula plan, when to sell becomes automatic. When the market moves up, stock is sold and bonds are purchased. When it is time to sell we must then examine our portfolio to determine which of the companies should be sold. At this point we either sell the weak securities and improve the quality of the fund should that be needed, or we sell those stocks on which we have a high capital gain. All of these activities force us to consider selling as a part of our investment program.

A third advantage of the formula plan method as a solution to timing is its versatility. It recognizes the defensive and aggressive characteristics of an investment portfolio. As the market moves up, the formula plan results in an increasingly defensive position. A greater portion of the portfolio is invested in debt securities and a lower percent in equity securities. When the market declines, the portfolio automatically becomes more aggressive. When the market is lower, common stocks are purchased, and this provides an opportunity to share in the future growth of the market. Thus the defensive and aggressive balance in the formula plan tends to make it attractive for the needs of most investors. The formula plan technique can be used with growth as well as income securities. Because both growth and income securities have cyclical characteristics, a problem of timing the purchase and sale of both types of securities arises. Income stocks can be purchased at a low and a high price just as growth stocks can. When an income stock increases in value, it would be desirable to sell it and buy it later at a lower price. The same is true for growth securities. A formula plan allows the investor to buy relatively low and sell relatively high whether the securities are income, growth, or a combination. Thus a formula plan as a timing technique is versatile in that it recognizes the aggressive and defensive characteristics of portfolio management and is applicable to all types of funds including the income and growth fund.

Some Disadvantages of Formula Plans

There are some disadvantages of the formula plan technique for timing the purchase and sale of securities. First, we must make a value judgment as to the relative height of the stock market for the variable ratio formula plans. We must establish a point where the fund will be balanced between bonds and stock. From this position of the market we will judge the final ratio between securities. For example, if the market is 20 percent above its average, then possibly 60 percent would be invested in bonds and 40 percent in stock. The portfolio would be somewhat defensive because of the height of the stock market. But we might make an error in judging the level of the market and set the average too low. If this should happen, we might find ourselves in the position of being fully invested in bonds with the market still rising. As the market continued to rise, we would not share in its growth. If we had begun a formula plan in 1948 we would have experienced this limitation. By 1956 we would have been completely out of common stock (at least with a variable stock-bond ratio plan), and we would have missed the great growth of the market from 1956 through 1966.

A second criticism of formula plans, related to the first, is that over a sustained market rise we would be better off in common stock rather than a combination of bonds and common. We recognize the fact that we might not be able to forecast a continued rise in stock prices. This takes some of the sting out of the second criticism. However, the astute investor or expert investment manager might argue that he could judge the market more accurately and then be more successful without a formula plan in a period such as the past decade where the market has moved steadily upward. If the market drops, however, we will have no market protection without bonds. A continued drop makes it difficult to recover our losses. If we have a continually rising stock market, this criticism is valid. If the market should decline periodically or change its direction, then a formula plan would offer advantages not possessed by a common-stock fund.

A third possible criticism is that we might choose securities that do not move with the market. We assume that quality companies will be purchased, and if and when the stocks are sold, good quality government securities or corporate bonds will be purchased, or even short-term government and municipal securities. We assume that such securities will follow market prices. As the market goes up, the securities we own will move up. This is important because the timing device for purchases and sales should coincide with securities we hold in the portfolio. Some securities do not follow the market movement. If securities do not rise in price when the market index moves up and the market average is used as an indication of when to buy or sell, then an unnecessary adjustment is made that further limits the ability of the investor to make a profit. Care, therefore, should be exercised in the selection of securities, to choose those that move with the market.

A fourth disadvantage of a formula plan is that it offers only modest opportunity for capital gains. A fully managed fund will offer a greater potential for gain even though we might not achieve this goal. This, of course, is also an advantage of a formula plan. It offers modest opportunity for capital gain, but it also provides security of principal in a fluctuating market.

In spite of the disadvantages of the various formula plan methods, they are used by a few investors in portfolio management and timing. Some institutional investors follow formula plans in their portfolio management work, even though the majority do not. Whether a plan is followed is not at issue. A good formula does help in the timing of portfolio transactions. Timing might be very poor if the principles involved in formula planning were not used.

Timing the Sale of Securities

Some investment managers and individuals think that the problem of timing and management cannot be solved by any formula plan. Their solution is complete management of the portfolio, which includes a recognition of economic trends and of the market cycle as a phenomenon of its own. They would suggest that we select and manage a portfolio with extreme care to take advantage of the changes in the market, stress the analytical process and the selection of quality companies, and direct our attention toward meeting our investment needs, following good principles of portfolio management, and attempting to select securities that would provide an adequate yield for the risk we were required to assume.

In our discussion of timing we emphasized the timing of purchases of securities and other solutions to the timing problem such as a bond portfolio, dollar averaging, or a formula plan. Now we will emphasize the management problems involved with when to sell securities. Here we assume that we will manage our portfolio completely; we will select quality issues and buy them at the proper price. Now we will consider when we should sell the securities we have purchased.

None of the suggestions about when to sell a stock should be considered as a panacea for the problem. A sale of a security or any other investment decision is usually a compromise of many variables. When and what to sell are in this classification. There is no precise way for the investor to know when to sell, but there are some guide lines that can be followed.

The first guide to follow in timing the sale of a security is to sell when the security no longer meets the original objectives that were established. Investment needs change, and this would call for a change in the type of security that should be held in the portfolio. Assume an investor, for example, has followed an income portfolio policy. Later his income needs are satisfied, and he no longer requires current income. His portfolio policy would shift to an emphasis on growth. This would require the sale of the income shares, and growth shares would be purchased. The same example could be given for the growth investor who now needs income and must sell his growth stocks.

A second reason that indicates a time to sell is when the stock market as a whole has moved up to a historical high and the stock itself is selling at an extremely high price. The investor must judge whether the market is high or low. When the market is high it would be wise for an investor who fully manages his portfolio to become defensive in his security holdings. This means he will shift out of common stock into more defensive bonds or high-grade preferred stocks. Such sales should be infrequent. There is also a potential loss in such transactions. A company's stock might, after reaching its high in the market, move into still higher ground because the future expectations are good. If an investor sold at this point, he might lose out on future growth. And yet, the judicious sale of securities might be extremely profitable.

A third guide in timing the sale of a stock relates to the expectations about the yield from the security. When a specific security no longer offers the investor the expectation of a satisfactory yield or yield to maturity, and there is a sharp difference between our own expectations and what can be reasonably obtained, then the stock should be sold. An investor who purchases a stock makes a value judgment based upon the future earnings potential of the company. Once the investor finds that a stock no longer provides an adequate yield on the current market price, then the stock should be sold. Evidence to support the decision will come from the price-earnings ratio, the projected earnings of the company, and the relative height of the price of the stock. A stock selling at an extremely high price, a high price-earnings ratio, or a high price to future earnings ratio, or that offers a low yield, should be a candidate for sale. A stock should be held only when future earnings justify the present price of the stock. The use of expected yield to maturity as a guide to buying and selling stock is fundamental to portfolio management. Litton in 1963 was an attractive investment at 79, offering more than a 10 percent yield; at above 120 in 1967 it offered an expected yield for the next five years well below 10 percent and should have been sold, tax position and other variables permitting. The computer program presented in Chapter 7 allows this type of decision to be made. Further refinements of the computer program and similar programs will have a great impact upon portfolio management in the future. Weston and Baranek's article on this subject indicates what might be done in the area of programming portfolio construction.[3] This is perhaps the most important guide in the management of a portfolio and is also consistent with investment theory.

3 J. Fred Weston and William Beranek, "Programming Investment Portfolio Construction," *Analysts Journal*, May, 1955, p. 51.

The fourth guide to selling under a completely managed portfolio is based upon competitive alternatives. The investor should consider selling the stocks that he now holds—after all factors are considered including risk, quality, and taxes—when a compelling alternative investment offers greater rewards comparable to risks. Simply stated, when an investor finds a security that offers greater expectations for financial reward in the form of yield, then his current investment should be sold and the new investment undertaken. This means that the investor should constantly review his own investments and other investment securities to determine if they would offer him greater profits in the future. There is nothing wrong with taking profit in the stock market and moving into a better investment security.

A fifth guide to the timing of the sale of securities relates to the tax position of the investor. No job of portfolio management can ignore taxes. Occasional selling of securities will realize capital gains or losses of the investor for tax purposes. This is referred to as *tax selling*. Tax switches would require, for example, that one stock be sold to establish a tax loss and a comparable security purchased to replace it in the investor's portfolio. This is really a technical trade to establish a loss or gain. The stock can be repurchased after 30 days and the long-term investment position maintained. (One must wait 30 days after a stock is sold before it can be repurchased to be able to declare the gain or loss. This is an IRS rule. If stock is repurchased before 30 days, it is considered a *wash sale*, and the IRS treats the transaction as if no sale were made. Under these circumstances, the gain or loss cannot be claimed for tax purposes.)

All of these are valid guides to an answer to the question of when securities should be sold. They offer no absolute solution. Only judgment over time will help the investor in making the decision of when to sell securities. Experience will dictate the best solution for each investor.

Summary

Investment timing is an important part of the investment decision-making process. The emphasis should be on quality securities, purchased at the best possible price. The management problem includes the timing of the purchase and sale of a security. A good manager considers timing when he sells. Several rules help him to make a decision about the proper time to sell. Stocks are sold (1) when they no longer meet the needs of the investor; (2) when the price for the market and the securities is at a historical high; (3) when the future expectations no longer support the price of the stocks or when yields fall below the satisfactory level; (4) when other alternatives are more attractive than the securities held; or (5) when there is a tax advantage in the sale of a security for the investor.

Many investors recognize that they cannot accurately time the purchase and sale of securities. One alternative to complete management is to invest entirely in bonds. This provides safety of principal and tends to make the timing problem less important, but it is not a profitable alternative. Another solution is to time the purchase of stocks so that they can be bought at the lowest price. This solution requires patience and sound judgment, but it ignores the problem of when to sell securities. Another solution is dollar averaging, in which the investor buys stock several times and eliminates the cyclical aspects of the price movement, hoping that the increasing trend of stock prices will eventually lead to investment success. This solution, however, does not consider when to sell. Another solution to the timing problem is some form of formula plan. The constant dollar fund, the constant stock-bond ratio plan, or the variable stock-bond ratio plan offer a solution to the problem of when to buy and when to sell. Each plan offers a partial solution to the investor and, if rigidly adhered to, should result in a modest profit and a good deal of security of principal for the investor. The best solution to the timing problem still remains in the hands of the experienced manager, who, with the aid of the above tools and with discretion, makes the decision of when and what to buy and sell. Individuals with proper education and experience can become competent in the aspects of timing in the management of investment accounts.

Expected yield to maturity can be and should be used as a guide to portfolio decisions. The computer program developed in Chapter 7 indicates the method of employing yield to maturity and the computer in making investment decisions.

Review Questions

1. What is meant by the timing problem in investment in securities?
2. (a) Explain how a portfolio invested solely in long-term bonds and held to maturity might solve the timing problem.
   (b) Would this be a satisfactory solution? Explain.
3. One solution to the timing problem is to establish a price we consider to be attractive and then wait until that price is reached. Comment about the advantages and disadvantages of this approach to timing.
4. (a) Explain the concept of dollar averaging and how it might be used in solving the problem of investment timing.
   (b) What are the basic advantages and disadvantages of dollar averaging?
5. (a) Explain how formula planning can be used as a tool to solve the timing problem.

    (b) What are the assumptions on which formula planning is based?
    (c) What are the three basic types of formula plans?
    (d) What are the advantages and disadvantages of formula planning?

6. (a) What are the solutions to the difficult problem of when to sell a security? Elaborate.
    (b) How does this relate to the fundamental problem of analysis?

7. Explain how expected yield to maturity and the computer may be used as a tool in making a decision of when to buy and when to sell.

Problems

1. Assume that we bought 100 shares of General Motors common stock, January 2, 1957, and sold it June 30, 1968.
    (a) What was the closing price of GM on the date of purchase?
    (b) What was the price when it was sold?
    (c) How many shares did we own on June 30, 1968, considering any stock splits or stock dividends? Please ignore cash dividends.
    (d) What was the total gain or loss in the value of the shares between date of purchase and sale?

2. Let us change our assumption and use simple averaging to solve our timing problems. Assume now that we bought 30 shares of GM on January 2, 1957, 30 shares June 1, 1957, and 30 shares December 29, 1957. Now assume we hold these shares until June 30, 1969.
    (a) What was the averaged price and total amount paid for the stock during 1957?
    (b) Compare this to the price and total value November 22, 1963.
    (c) What was the amount of the gain or loss in total?
    (d) How did this compare with the results under question 1(d)?
    (e) Explain the reason for the difference.
    (f) Redo the exercise but buy the same (dollar average) amount each time.

3. Now assume we bought 100 shares of GM at the low for the period between January 2, 1957, and June 30, 1969, and sold the shares at the high point.
    (a) What would have been our gain?
    (b) How does this compare with the results in 1 (d), 2 (c), and 2 (f)?

4. (a) What would have been the gain or loss if we set up a constant stock-bond ratio plan and invested in 50 shares of GM common on January 2, 1957, and invested the remainder in government bonds? Assume that this 50–50 relationship would continue and would be adjusted each time the market moved up 20 percent or down 20 percent.
    (b) Compare the gain in this case of 1 (d), 2 (c), 3 (a), and 2 (b).
    (c) Which method would have given us the greatest profit?
    (d) Should we use this method? Why or why not?
    (e) Would we be able to achieve comparable results? Explain.

5. What part would yield to maturity play in making your decisions?

Sources of Investment Information

Annual reports of General Motors
Barron's
Moody's manuals
Standard & Poor's *Investment Surveys*
Wall Street Journal

Selected Readings

Hayes, Douglas A., "The Undervalued Issue Strategy," *Financial Analysts Journal* (May-June, 1967), p. 121.

22

PORTFOLIO MANAGEMENT AND THE INCOME PORTFOLIO

The management of any investment fund assumes that the objectives of the investor will be clearly and correctly stated and that sound principles of management will be applied to the solution of the investment problem. Care will also be taken to provide continuous supervision of the portfolio to make certain that the portfolio meets the continuing and changing needs of the investor. Good management assumes further that there is a rational selection of companies from which the investments can be chosen. The emphasis is upon selection from a list of quality companies that have been analyzed in the past and will offer, from time to time, attractive yields. There are many satisfactory avenues for investments. We must limit our field of inquiry to only a few of the best companies. In this chapter the overall problem of selection will be considered along with some of the practical problems of portfolio management. The general problem of the income portfolio will be discussed and several cases given to illustrate the alternative solutions to various situations.

Security Selection—the Master List Concept

The establishment of an investment portfolio should be accomplished on the basis of rational choice. Ideally the selection of individual companies to meet portfolio requirements should be made from a list of companies that are considered to be of investment caliber after careful analysis. In the process of analysis described previously, the leading companies in the industry would be chosen for investment. The result would be a list of a minimum of 120 different companies of every industrial classification.

The task of keeping up to date on a list of between 120 and 500 companies would be formidable if not impossible for an individual. The largest institutional investors have a research staff of from 5 to 50 individuals trained in security analysis and investment management. Their job is to appraise and continually analyze the industries under their direction. They make recommendations to the management of their company as to the relative merits of the individual firms. Investment research organizations also divide the responsibility of research into the various industry categories. In this way they can provide up-to-date information on many companies. Investment firms and investment services such as Clark Dodge, Eastman Dillon, Merrill Lynch, Standard & Poor's, and Value Line provide the individual investor with investment information that allows him to manage his own portfolio.

Essentially the process of selection of companies follows the pattern of the diagram in Figure 22–1. The diagram portrays the selection process. It narrows from a list of over 4,000 companies in several hundred industries to a much smaller list of companies that appear to have superior investment characteristics. It is from among these companies that a list of securities suitable for income, growth, or a combination of both can be selected. The list of 4,000 companies represents only a few of the great number of corporate entities that exist today in the United States. There are perhaps a million and a half smaller corporations that are not large enough at present for sound investment characteristics but that will provide investment opportunities in the future.

Ideally, each security would be ranked according to its investment quality, to determine whether the expected yield was satisfactory. In terms of the discussion of this text, we would estimate expected yield to maturity five to seven years hence, which would provide the estimate of yield. The stability of earnings would serve as a guide to the risk associated with each investment. We could, of course, use the stability of past yield as a measure of investment risk. The security investments could then be ranked according to their risks and yields, and these in turn would determine whether the security would be used to satisfy income or growth needs. An income security would contribute over 75 percent of its yield to current income; a growth stock would contribute more than 75 percent of its yield in terms of growth of principal. A compromise security would offer the investor half of the yield in the form of current yield and half in capital growth. The securities would be ranked as shown in Table 22–1. Usually income securities provide virtually all the income in the form of current yield whether it is income from bond interest or dividend income from preferred or common stock. In addition, the income portfolio would attempt to minimize risk. Therefore, a high current income level associated with low risk would be the ideal income common stock. High yield preferreds and bonds would also fit the description of an income investment. In the computer program for valuation presented in Chapter 7 it was found that the DJIA stocks had an average stability of earnings of 88 percent.

The Income Portfolio

The main function of the income portfolio is to provide current income for the investor. The income obtained from the investment fund represents either a portion or all of the income of the individual. It acts

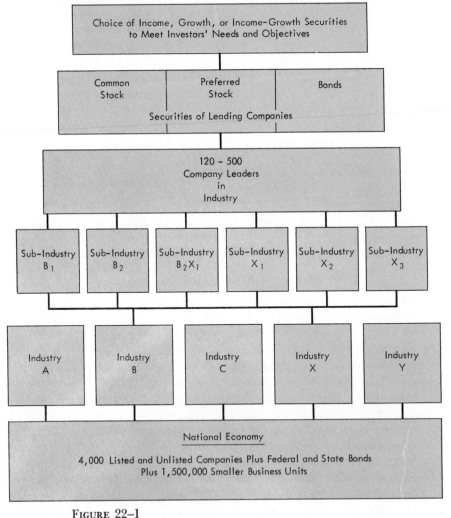

FIGURE 22–1

Selection of companies suitable for investment

TABLE 22–1

Income and growth securities ranked by yield

		RANK	PERCENT YIELD TO MATURITY	PERCENT OF YIELD CURRENT	STABILITY INDEX
Income Securities					
Security	A	1	6.1	90	88
Security	B	2	5.9	92	93
Security	X	3	5.8	100	85
Security	D	4	5.7	85	89
Security	F	5	5.0	87	95
Growth Securities					
Security	O	1	16.4	38	78
Security	P	2	12.1	25	89
Security	L	3	9.8	40	85
Security	Q	4	8.3	36	87
Security	E	5	8.3	48	89

either as a supplement to bolster a relatively low income, or it represents the only source of income that the investor possesses. But the income portfolio is not confined to the individual who has modest means and is attempting to improve his standard of living. Nor is it confined to the widow and orphan class. Possibly an individual with a large estate desires, as an investment objective, the maximization of current income. The income portfolio is dictated by the relative need of the individual investor and not his absolute needs. A wealthy individual with urgent current financial demands on his investment account and a strong desire to preserve his capital might attempt to maximize his current income, perhaps so that he or she might be able to give more charity currently and yet maintain the principal of the fund. In this case, the major portion of the current income of the portfolio will not be taxed since most of it will be given to philanthropic activities. Therefore, a maximization of current income is extremely important to this individual if he is to increase his giving power.

The variables involved in establishing an income portfolio are much the same as establishing any investment portfolio. The demand for income must be determined, the ability to assume risk must be established, and the general economic, physical, and social position of the investor must be ascertained.

There are two possible extremes in the management of the income portfolio. The first is the case in which an individual does not have a large enough investment fund to meet the current demands for income. Even if safety were ignored and speculative bonds and high yielding common stocks were purchased to provide more income, there would not be sufficient income to satisfy the investor. The solution to this problem must rest outside the portfolio; that is, additional help must come from family, friends, or the state. Or the fund itself must be given up. In this case either a portion of principal and income is returned to the investor until it is completely used up, or else the fund is used to purchase a fixed-income annuity, which might or might not be able to provide an adequate standard of living for the investor.

The other extreme in the management of the income portfolio is where the wealthy individual, with a large fund to invest, requires stability of income. The fund is managed with the object of maximizing the current income but, of necessity, giving proper consideration to the tax position of the individual. In this case there is no need to reduce the requirements of safety. The income from a $500,000 fund will, even at relatively low yields, provide a fairly substantial income. A $500,000 investment in 6 percent bonds would provide $30,000 of income before federal income taxes. Since the investor is in the $30,000 income tax bracket, his tax position has an important effect upon where the securities will be invested. An investor with $30,000 of security income would be in the 36 percent marginal tax bracket, assuming that the individual takes the standard deduction plus one $600 exemption. The taxable income would be $26,400, and the marginal rate above $24,000 based on 1968 rates was 36 percent, in the special tax category under joint returns. The investor could invest in tax-exempt bonds to yield 4 percent to maturity, in which case he would have a full $20,000 of income after taxes; under the fully taxable 6 percent bonds, the income after taxes would have been $23,290. The investor was in only a slightly poorer position with tax-exempt bonds yielding 50 percent less in current income.

Investors between the extremes make up the majority of income investors. This group is neither extremely wealthy nor desperately dependent upon the income from the fund to sustain themselves and their families. The preacher, the teacher, the lawyer, the housewife, and the businessman fall into the category of welcoming extra income and following an investment policy of attempting to provide maximum income consistent with risk. These investors follow the principles of sound portfolio management. They recognize the importance of safety of principal, diversification, and capital gains, but they stress income. They are concerned with planning, supervision, timing, and their tax position, but they want income to help them meet their current needs.

Securities That Meet the Needs of the Income Investor

The securities that meet the needs of the income investor stress safety of principal and current income. Securities that meet such needs are corporate bonds, Baa and above in rating, tax-exempt municipals, U.S. Government bonds, preferred stock, and common stocks that pay a high dividend and have stability of earnings. A prospect for continued or increased dividends from the common stock increases the attractiveness of this type of income security. Companies in this category change, of course, but in 1969 companies in this position were found in the non-growth public utilities, western railroads, the food industry, department stores, oil, chemicals, retail trade, soft drinks, and similar industries that had a stability of demand that reflected itself in the stability of earnings and dividends.

SPECIFIC SECURITIES TO MEET INCOME REQUIREMENTS

Securities that would provide the investor with a growing dividend appear in Table 22–2. The common stocks were traded on the New York Stock Exchange; they had a 10-year growth of dividends and were excellent growth companies as well. If we sought income common stocks, we would have looked at securities in Table 22–3 that would provide safety and income. Most of these appear in the master list of well-known investment services. Many of them are the leading companies in their industry. Obviously, these stocks will change, and their yield character-istics must be reexamined. Current yields on investment securities may be found in Standard & Poor's *Stock Guide*.

Stability and regularity of income must be stressed when the income portfolio is established. We must make certain that the income will be regular and certain in amount because the income investor must rely heavily on the income from his investments to meet his expenses of daily living. Care should be exercised to select securities that provide income at various times throughout the year. Ideally, we would want monthly income for the investor, but since most companies pay quarterly dividends, it is difficult to provide a stable monthly income. Diversifica-tion of securities with respect to the timing of dividend or interest payments remains important and desirable, and should be emphasized when and if possible.

The long-term securities of the United States government offered yields of approximately 4 percent in 1962 that might satisfy some of the income investors depicted in the cases later in the text. Corporate bonds of the individual companies that were of excellent quality could also be purchased on an attractive yield basis. Any investor interested in income would have a wide range of excellent companies from which to establish his portfolio. He could select from among these companies many secure bonds and preferred stock from which the income would be expected to vary between 4 and 5 percent. On a $100,000 portfolio, an investor in 1962 or at other times could expect a similar yield consis-tent with safety and with sound principles of portfolio management.

In early 1969 the yields on government and corporate bonds rose to above 7 percent. Actually long-term governments were above 6 per-

TABLE 22–2

Dividends doubled in ten years

*ISSUE	1968 DIVD. $	% Div. Incr. 1958–68	% Div. Incr. 1963–68	INDIC. CURRENT RATE $	APPROX. PRICE	YIELD %
AMP Corp.	0.40	378	200	0.48	44	1.1
Amer. Home Prod.	1.25	115	56	1.40	58	2.4
Amer. Hosp. Supp.	0.21½	252	123	0.22	34	0.6
Amer. Sterilizer	0.46	300	80	0.48	30	1.6
Avon Products	1.60	1,430	153	1.80	148	1.2
Baxter Labs	0.17	268	106	0.18	50	0.4
Bristol-Myers	1.10	503	144	1.20	63	1.9
Diebold, Inc.	0.42	180	64	a0.48	56	0.9
Dow Chemical	2.35	108	49	2.40	76	3.2
Eastman Kodak	1.09	206	71	1.16	77	1.5
ELTRA Corp.	1.05	1,763	118	1.20	36	3.3
Emerson Elec.	0.85½	389	110	1.00	54	1.9
Emery Air Freight	0.72½	559	190	0.80	59	1.4
FMC Corp.	0.82½	214	106	0.85	31	2.7
Federat. Dept. Str.	0.90	106	44	0.95	34	2.8
Genl. Tel. & Electr.	1.42	114	69	1.48	39	3.8
Genuine Parts	0.78¾	258	102	1.00	34	2.9
Georgia Pacific	1.00	116	73	a1.60	99	1.6
Gulf Oil	1.40	278	65	1.50	45	3.3
Hart Schaffner & Marx	0.73⅜	424	134	0.80	37	2.2
Heublein, Inc.	0.70	678	180	0.75	34	2.2
Hoover Ball & Bear.	1.30	829	172	1.40	40	3.5
Household Finance	1.05	100	48	1.10	43	2.6
Intl. Bus. Mach.	2.60	781	135	3.20	326	1.0
bInsilco Corp.	0.70	509	164	0.70	28	2.5
Lucky Stores	1.25	297	242	a1.40	53	2.6
Magnavox Co.	0.95	726	153	1.20	54	2.2
McDermott (J. Ray)	1.00	365	76	1.00	88	1.1
Minn. Min. & Mfg.	1.45	263	61	1.60	106	1.5
Overnite Transp.	0.97½	359	77	1.00	28	3.6
Parker-Hannifin	1.30	294	141	1.40	54	2.6
cPennwalt Corp.	1.30	110	44	1.30	46	2.8
Petrolane Inc.	0.80	176	48	0.80	46	1.7
Pittston Co.	1.20	173	60	a1.20	54	2.2
Plough, Inc.	0.55	238	80	0.60	69	0.9
Procter & Gamble	2.40	140	50	2.60	90	2.9
Purex Corp.	0.76	262	52	a0.80	30	2.7
Rohm & Haas	1.60	344	51	a1.60	100	1.6
Simplicity Pattern	0.66	214	110	a0.70	80	0.9
Standard Brands	1.42½	143	39	1.50	49	3.1
Standard Oil (Ind.)	2.10	147	66	2.30	62	3.7
Std. Pressed Steel	0.40	196	100	0.44	22	2.0
Sun Oil	1.00	127	77	a1.00	68	1.5
Warner-Lambert	1.02½	105	46	1.10	63	1.7
Winn-Dixie Stores	1.53	194	50	1.56	36	4.3
Witco Chem.	0.86	310	91	0.92	35	2.6
Xerox Corp.	1.45	3,650	500	1.80	268	0.7

* Listed on New York Stock Exchange.
a Plus Stock.
b Formerly International Silver.
c Formerly Pennsalt Chemicals.
SOURCE: Standard & Poor's *The Outlook*, May 12, 1969, p. 820.

TABLE 22–3

10 income stocks

*ISSUE	APPROX. PRICE	INDIC. DIVD. $	YIELD %	DIV. INCR. PAST 10 YRS.	EARN. $ PER SH. E1969
Brooklyn Union Gas	29	1.72	5.9	10	2.45
C.I.T. Financial	34	1.80	5.3	7	3.20
Consolidated Nat. Gas	28	1.76	6.3	6	2.60
Conwood Corp.	34	1.80	5.3	7	3.30
General Motors	78	E4.30ᵃ	5.5	5	5.70
General Pub. Utilities	27	1.60	5.9	10	2.20
Louisville & Nashville	78	5.00	6.4	0	10.00
National Fuel Gas	27	1.68	6.2	8	2.25
Reynolds (R. J.) Tob.	39	2.20	5.6	10	3.90
Union Electric	20	1.20	6.0	8	1.60

* Listed on New York Stock Exchange.
ᵃ E=Estimated.
SOURCE: Standard & Poor's *The Outlook*, June 23, 1969, p. 748.

cent. A person looking for an income investment in 1970 might find attractive outlets in this type of bond. They provide liquidity and stability of yield.

BALANCE IN THE PORTFOLIO

The balance between bonds (defensive securities) and stock (aggressive securities) will depend upon the outlook for the stock market and the political, economic, and cultural climate. In 1962, which was our point of departure in the first edition, the market had been testing new lows; the economy was moving along at a fairly good rate (FRB 119), but the prospects for 1963 were not outstanding. Cuba was a threat in the Western Hemisphere because of Castro's acceptance of military aid from the Russians. Berlin was the thorn in President Kennedy's side as Castro was the bone of contention in his throat. Ole Mississippi was a tragedy on the domestic scene. Integration was the issue, and no progress was made in Mississippi in the area of social rights. All of these conditions pointed to financial conservatism. New money being invested under these short-term influences would be placed in defensive securities. When prices moved down to more reasonable levels, they would be used to buy aggressive securities. The exact balance between aggressive and defensive securities would be determined by the individual. People needing income in 1962 would have been wise to stress safety and security. Bonds would have been an important part of the income portfolio at that time. As it turned out, the prospects for 1963 and 1964 improved considerably late in 1962, and an aggressive policy would have been indicated.

In 1968, however, the current yield on common stocks (DJIA) was close to 3 percent and yields on some industrial bonds was between 6 and 7 percent. Corporate bonds in 1968 would have been excellent for income portfolios.

Meeting the Needs of the Income Investor—Selected Cases

The following cases are presented to illustrate the problems and solutions involved in the establishment of an income investment portfolio and to demonstrate the fundamentals in the construction of any investment portfolio. Only a few cases are presented, but they are representative of the many and varied conditions under which individuals attempt to obtain current income from their investments. Obviously, the solution provided for each case and the criticism made about each special situation represent only one of the many alternatives that could have been chosen. The cases give a time perspective and a chance for management to take place over time.

THE CASE OF THE WORRIED WIDOW

Mrs. Elizabeth Eaton's husband died in August, 1962, leaving a modest estate of approximately $21,000 composed of common stock. The portfolio is presented in Table 22–4. Mr. Eaton had accumulated these securities throughout his life. For the most part, they were acquired in small amounts, with the goal in mind of leaving an estate for Mrs. Eaton. In addition, Mr. Eaton had a small insurance policy that covered funeral and legal expenses and provided a modest savings and checking account for his widow, thus adding to her total income. Mrs. Eaton herself had a $2,000 insurance policy, taken out when she was 30 years of age, which had a cash surrender value of approximately $1,400 at her present age of 62. Mrs. Eaton lived in her own house, which was valued at about $11,000 and completely paid for. She drove her own automobile, a 1960 Ford worth approximately $1,100. During the years 1962 through 1965, she would have an annual income of about $3,000 from the securities in the estate, the insurance policy, and income from part-time employment. When Mrs. Eaton reached 65, her income would remain about the same even though she would no longer be able to work and her life insurance income would stop, because social security benefits would begin. She also received a small railroad pension from her husband's estate. These changes would result in annual income of approximately $2,584 at age 65. The financial position of Mrs. Eaton is reflected in Table 22–5.

Mrs. Eaton was in only fair health and in her later years had spent an increasing amount of her income on medicine. She had two grown children, a boy and a girl, who had their own families and were independent and able to support themselves. Mrs. Eaton's children had assisted her in her needs and were able to help her maintain her home and possessions. They were not in a position, however, to con-

TABLE 22–4

Investment portfolio, Mrs. Elizabeth Eaton

Number of Shares	Company	Price[a] (August, 1962)	Dividends	Value	Total Dividends	Yield
655	**Building:** American Radiator & Standard Sanitary	13 1/8	$ .80	$ 8,597	$ 524.00	6.1%
7	**Containers:** Continental Can Company	42 5/8	1.80	298	12.60	4.2
5	**Automotive:** Cummins Engine Company	48 1/4B–51 5/8A	.55	250	2.75	1.1
6	**Insurance:** Hanover Insurance Company	48 1/2B–51 5/8A	2.05	300	6.30	4.1
150	**Paper:** Hammermill Paper	29 3/8	1.20	4,406	180.00	4.1
15	**Insurance:** Home Insurance	52 1/2B–53 3/4A	2.15	797	32.25	4.0
165	**Tobacco:** Scotten, Dillon Co.	21 3/4	1.40	3,589	231.00	6.9
27	**Insurance:** Security Insurance	84B–88 3/4A	1.60	2,332	43.20	1.8
11	**Insurance:** Westchester Fire Insurance Co.	34 1/4B–36 3/4A	1.40	385	15.40	3.9
				$20,954	$1,047.50	4.99%

[a] B = bid
A = ask

Portfolio Analysis by Industry

		Percent of Total
Automotive	$ 250	1.1
Building	8,597	41.0
Container	298	1.4
Insurance	3,814	18.3
Paper	4,406	21.1
Tobacco	3,589	17.1
	$20,954	100.0

TABLE 22–5

Balance sheet of Mrs. Elizabeth Eaton, August, 1962

Assets		Liabilities		$ 0
Cash	$ 400			
Insurance	1,400			
Savings bank	400			
Auto (Ford, 1960)	1,100	Ownership		35,254
Securities	20,954			
House	11,000			
	$35,254			$35,254

ESTIMATED INCOME OF MRS. ELIZABETH EATON IN 1962

Life insurance income benefits per year until age 65		$ 780[a]	
Social Security on Mrs. Eaton's income			
(assuming maximum)			$1,536[b]
Income from securities		1,048	1,048
Part-time work income		1,200	
Total income until age 65		$3,038	
Total income after age 65			$2,584

> [a] The proceeds of the life insurance are to be paid out until Mrs. Eaton reaches age 65.
>
> [b] Mrs. Eaton could have elected to receive social security benefits based upon her husband's income. This would begin at age 62 and would be based upon 75 percent of maximum monthly benefits of $128 times 85 percent. A reduction of 5 percent is made for each year that benefits are received before age 65. Since social security benefits are greater at age 65 on Mrs. Eaton's income, this benefit was accepted.

tribute much to her current living expenses. Each child had just enough income to care for the needs of a growing family. Mrs. Eaton was familiar with her husband's stock purchases and had no reluctance or fear of common-stock ownership.

What were Mrs. Eaton's needs and objectives? This is a good case because it allows the portfolio manager to react to conditions over time and to make changes. Obviously she was in need of income. The income she earned and the railroad pension and social security when she reached 65 were not enough to provide her with an exceptionally high standard of living. Mrs. Eaton wished to maintain her independence in her own home and did not want to rely upon her children for support. The possibility of illness was present, and in a few years she would lose the part-time employment income. Her income position was extreme. If she was to maintain her independence, she would have had to sacrifice some security to increase her income. She was also limited in the amount of risk she could assume.

Interestingly, the securities that Mr. Eaton acquired when he originally set up the portfolio were mostly purchased for income. The portfolio, Table 22–4, had an excellent overall yield of close to 5 percent. There were some weaknesses in the portfolio in this respect. Cummins

Engine Company, the leading company in the manufacture of diesel engines, was at the time an excellent investment, but it did not offer enough yield for Mrs. Eaton. Security Insurance also offered a low yield and could be eliminated from the portfolio. If these securities were sold, they would provide approximately $2,500 for reinvestment in some higher-yielding equity securities such as a high-yield preferred or common stock. Mrs. Eaton was not in a high income-tax bracket and need not consider tax-exempt securities. Fortunately she had sufficient savings, an adequate checking account balance, and no debts.

Some of the companies in the portfolio—Scotten, Dillon and the over-the-counter insurance companies—had limited marketability and would not be attractive or purchased by most individual investors. These companies, however, offered a favorable yield, and Mrs. Eaton was willing to give up some marketability to obtain the increased yields. The diversification of the portfolio was limited since the investment fund was small. It is difficult to obtain a great deal of diversification with a $21,000 fund. The bulk of the investments were in four industries, building, insurance, paper, and tobacco. One or two additional industries should be represented in the portfolio to improve diversification. This could be accomplished with funds generated from the sale of the two low-yielding securities.

Some debt securities or public utility securities would be a desirable change in the portfolio. Boston Edison, for example, yielded 4 percent, and General Motors was yielding something less than 5 percent in 1962.

Let us assume that two switches were made: first Cummins and Security Insurance sold, and 11 shares of Boston Edison and 30 shares of General Motors bought. What effect would this have on the portfolio? If commissions are ignored, this will use up the $2,582 obtained from the sale of the other securities. The income is increased about $42.25 per year; thus Mrs. Eaton's investment income will rise from $1,047.50 to $1,089.75. This is a modest increase, but the marginal income on the specific securities would be doubled. The total yield would increase from 4.99 to 5.21 percent. The diversification in the portfolio would be better and quality would be improved. One additional industry would be added and the funds distributed more evenly. The new portfolio would be as follows:

Industry	Dollars	Percent of Total
Automotive	$ 1,590	7.6
Building	8,597	41.0
Container	298	1.4
Insurance	1,485	7.1
Paper	4,406	21.1
Public Utility	990	4.7
Tobacco	3,589	17.1
	$20,955	100.0

Mrs. Eaton would not initially make any other changes. Her reasoning might express confidence in her husband's ability to select securities, which would preclude any buying or selling. The selling of the two stocks can be defended on a yield basis. Some investors might criticize the common-stock addition to the portfolio in 1962. Since the market was weak, it might have been wise to suggest bonds or preferred stock. This is a very defensible position to take. However, both investments purchased were excellent companies with a good dividend yield. The yield on preferred or bonds of comparable quality would have been slightly higher than the stocks chosen. Some quality preferreds, which are listed in Table 22–6, would have offered an attractive investment

TABLE 22–6

Income preferreds

COMPANY	APPROXIMATE YIELD
Allied Stores $4	4.7%
American Can $1.75	4.5
American Tobacco $6	4.6
Armstrong Cork $3.75	4.4
Brooklyn Union Gas $5.50	5.0
Cincinnati Gas & Electric $4	4.5
Commonwealth Edison $5.25	4.7
Consolidated Edison $5	4.8
Consumers Power $4.50	4.7
General Mills $5	4.4
General Motors $5	4.4
Macy, R. H. $4.25	4.8
Macy Department Stores $3.75	4.7
New York State Electric & Gas $3.75	4.6
National Distillers $4.25	4.8
Niagara Mohawk Power $3.60	4.6
Standard Brands $3.50	4.5

SOURCE: *Wall Street Journal,* New York Stock Exchange Transactions.

for Mrs. Eaton at the time. The common-stock purchase, however, could be defended on quality and on the possibility of greater future growth and income. Actually either preferred stock or a good-yield common stock could be defended for Mrs. Eaton.

As it turned out, the common-stock purchase would have been most desirable. The solution with preferred stock in the portfolio would have a stronger effect on current income. Income would have been increased from $1,047.50 to $1,127.95 if 23 shares of Brooklyn Union Gas had been purchased with the proceeds of the sale instead of GM and Boston Edison. The yield would be increased on the portfolio and the fund balanced as follows:

	DOLLARS	PERCENT OF TOTAL FUND
Cash	$ 52	.2
Common		
Building Industry	8,597	41.0
Container	298	1.4
Insurance	1,482	7.1
Paper	4,406	21.1
Tobacco	3,589	17.1
Preferred		
Brooklyn Union Gas	2,530	12.1
	$20,954	100.0

This portfolio promises better yield and better diversification. The yield would increase from 4.99 percent on the original portfolio and 5.21 percent on the all-common-stock portfolio to 5.30 percent with the purchase of the preferred stock.

Each solution would have improved the fund over what it had yielded originally with the additional merits of improving marketability, diversification, and safety of principal. The important question to raise, however, is whether the portfolio still meets the needs of Mrs. Eaton today. How would you answer this question?

In the future, Mrs. Eaton would be wise to adjust the portfolio consistent with her income needs. If the yields on any of her investments declined, it would be wise for her to find new investment alternatives that would offer a better yield consistent with safety. It is not likely that any additional funds would be added to her investment account. There is one possibility of adding an additional source of income to meet her needs. When Mrs. Eaton reaches age 65, the fully paid-up life insurance policy could be converted into a life income. This additional income would help to improve Mrs. Eaton's financial position and make life somewhat more comfortable for her.

THE CASE OF THE PROLIFIC PROFESSOR

Dr. James Cunningham taught English at a leading Eastern university. He was 36 years of age, married, and the father of five children. He and his family were in excellent health, and there was no history of chronic illness or insanity in the family. The children were 10 years old and younger and required constant supervision by Mrs. Cunningham. Jim loved his teaching and research activities at the university but found it difficult to provide for his family on a salary of $9,500. Fortunately for him a fund had been established for the education of his children by a wealthy aunt. The fund would provide for all of their education expenses, but little would remain for any other activities. Even with this major financial hurdle removed, it was difficult to supply the ever-increasing requirements of a growing family. Dr. Cunningham's job was secure, and he could look forward to annual raises.

When he reached the rank of professor, he could expect to earn between $16,000 and $18,000 per year. He had hoped to write a novel that would sell, but this could not be counted on in his financial planning. The Cunningham's financial balance sheet looked like this:

Assets		Liabilities	
Checking	$ 200	Auto loan	$ 400
Savings	200	Mortgage (4%)	15,000
Life insurance	1,000		
Auto	800		
House	18,000		
Retirement fund	3,250	Ownership	7,950
	$23,350		$23,350

When Dr. Cunningham retired, his teachers' retirement program would provide him with about 60 percent of his annual salary based on the average of the highest five years of income. His retirement salary would be close to $10,200 per year.

Dr. Cunningham had discussed his situation with his colleagues, some of whom were in much the same financial position. They recognized that it was difficult to raise a family on a modest salary and yet maintain an educated standard of living. Shortly after a rather lengthy discussion about this problem, Dr. and Mrs. Cunningham received word that Dr. Cunningham's grandfather had died and had left an estate of $40,000 after taxes. It was to be shared equally by Jim Cunningham and his wife. Both were saddened by the death of the grandfather but rejoiced in the good that they could achieve with the money he had bequeathed.

The problem that Dr. Cunningham faced was how to invest the $40,000. He recognized that it would be desirable to save the fund for retirement, yet his immediate needs were so great that he found it necessary to consider ways in which the money could be invested to improve his current standard of living. Dr. Cunningham concluded that he was interested in more income although he was not averse to some growth in his portfolio. He felt he could accept the risk of common-stock ownership, and yet he wanted some security of income. Dr. Cunningham was not in a position to worry very much about income taxes. With seven exemptions and the standard deduction, he was in the lowest tax bracket.

There were several alternatives to Professor Cunningham's problem, but we shall discuss only one. First, the good professor should have improved his checking account balance and his savings account. His checking account should have been increased to $500 and his savings account to $1,200. An additional $5,000 should have been invested either in long-term government bonds or possibly in a building and loan association where the yield might be close to 4 1/2 percent. Long-term government bonds would have yielded about 5 percent. This would have been looked upon as the emergency fund part of his investment, and at least this amount remained more or less permanently in fixed-type investments.

Some people might have suggested that Dr. Cunningham reduce the principal of the mortgage on his house. Actually, the mortgage was a very favorable VA mortgage with a 4 percent interest rate. Professor Cunningham would probably earn 5 to 6 percent on his investment, which was more profitable than paying off the mortgage. The property was more salable with a 4 percent mortgage particularly since the current rate of mortgage interest was 6 1/2 percent. This was important since the Cunninghams would be in need of a new house to provide more adequate facilities for their children. When they decided to buy a new house, the additional equity would come from the investment account, or the Cunninghams might borrow more money based upon Dr. Cunningham's larger income, if they could obtain the funds at a low cost. If they had to pay 6 1/2 percent for their money, it would probably have been better to take some money out of their investment account.

The cash surrender value of his life insurance policy indicates that Professor Cunningham did not have a great deal of insurance. It might have been desirable, now, to increase the amount of life insurance to meet the needs of his family. The insurance could be used not only to provide for risk of loss of family income but to add to Dr. Cunningham's savings when he retires. Once these adjustments were made, Dr. Cunningham would be in a position to establish his investment program.

The remaining amount of investable funds was $33,500. Since there was a great deal of uncertainty in the stock market in 1962, Dr. Cunningham would have been wise to provide himself with a balanced fund to be in a defensive position. Approximately 60 percent of his funds should have been invested in a well-diversified list of common stocks, and about 40 percent would have been invested in preferred stocks and bonds. The bonds and preferred stocks would have been purchased immediately, and the common stocks over a few months.

As a matter of conservative policy, it might have been wise to purchase each stock at two different times. If, for example, Dr. Cunningham decided to buy General Motors, he might have placed an order for 25 shares then and bought 25 more later. This would allow him to take advantage of dollar averaging and the change in market price.

The fund would be balanced at about $13,500 in bonds and preferred stock and $20,000 in common stock. The portfolio of Dr. Cunningham as it might have been established is presented in Table 22–7. Although a relatively modest amount that made wide diversification difficult, the portfolio is fairly well balanced and diversified between debt, preferred, and common stock. It is a defensive income portfolio.

TABLE 22–7

Suggested income portfolio for Dr. Cunningham

SECURITY	No. of Shares	Price ($)	Total ($) Amount	% of Total	Interest or Dividend	Current Income	Current Yield
Bonds			$ 9,900	29.5		$ 487.50	4.92
Pacific Gas 5s 91	5	105	5,250	15.6	5%	250.00	4.76
Auto Canteen 4 3/4s 81	5	93	4,650	13.9	4 3/4%	237.50	5.11
Preferred			3,910	11.6		185.00	4.73
Consolidated Edison	20	106	2,120	6.3	$5.00	100.00	4.71
Macy, R.H. 4. 25	20	89	1,790	5.3	$4.25	85.00	4.75
Common Stock							
American Telephone & Telegraph	50	105	5,250	15.6	$3.60	180.00	3.43
First National City Bank	50	49	2,450	7.3	$2.00	100.00	4.08
General Motors	100	53	5,300	15.8	$2.50	250.00	4.71
National Biscuit	50	38	1,900	5.7	$1.50	75.00	3.95
Philadelphia Electric	70	31	2,170	6.5	$1.20	84.00	3.87
Pittsburgh Plate Glass	50	54	2,700	8.0	$2.20	110.00	4.07
			19,770	58.9		799.00	4.04
Total			$33,580	100.0		$1,471.50	4.44

The common stock was diversified among the leading companies in six different industries. The yield on common affords some income from quality companies as well as the possibility of greater income in the future. There was some growth potential in the common stock. The overall current yield of the portfolio was very good for a market that was paying a high price for earnings. If a yield to maturity had been calculated, it would have been close to 8 percent.

The future management of the fund will focus attention on the purchase of common stock when it can be bought at attractive prices. It might also be possible to buy some stocks at lower prices, so it would not be wise to commit all of the funds at one time. The debt money could be used to buy additional common stock either in the companies selected or in additional companies that have good security of principal and safety of income at favorable prices. Dr. Cunningham's fund possesses flexibility, too. If he should decide to emphasize growth in the future, he could buy the growth-type stock with the preferred stocks and bonds instead of additional income securities. He also has some growth in his portfolio now.

This is only one possible solution to meet Dr. Cunningham's needs. It does meet the prerequisites of an income portfolio and the objectives and principles of good portfolio management.

THE CASE OF THE SERIOUS SCHOLAR

Professor Ganby was a professor of ancient history at a leading Midwestern university in 1962. He was married and the father of two grown children. He owned his own home, without a mortgage, close to the campus. His income as a full professor was close to $16,000 and his needs were modest. He and his wife entertained very little. They shared a quiet life on the campus, enjoying the cultural programs of the university. Professor Ganby's children were married and doing well financially. They needed no financial help themselves and were in a position to offer help to their parents if it was needed. Both Professor Ganby and his wife were in good health for people in their early sixties and were not in need of medical care.

During the previous 15 years, Professor Ganby had used his extra income to establish an investment account. He had adequate life insurance and savings. With his debt-free house and adequate income, he did not need extra income until he retired in about three years at the age of 65. He planned to get another teaching assignment at that time with a small college in the South near his boyhood home. His retirement income even without his investment income would adequately take care of his family needs, and with the additional teaching income, his income in retirement would be close to $12,000.

The income from his portfolio was really not needed currently, nor would it be needed when he retired. His investment position would suggest that he should establish more of a growth fund to leave to his wife. However, he had followed for the past decade a conservative policy of purchasing only income-producing public utility securities. Several investment counselors had suggested more diversification, but he ignored their advice and continued to hold his income utilities. His portfolio is presented in Table 22–8 A.

Professor Ganby probably refused to change his portfolio owing to his strong conviction in favor of public utilities stocks. The possibilities open to him should have been explored. Some critical comments can be made about the content of his portfolio. The obvious faults in the portfolio were the lack of diversification and the relatively low yield. All the public utilities Dr. Ganby owned were located in the Midwest. If he wished to confine his activities to public utilities, he could have selected a group of companies from some of the other growing states in the United States. He should have had some from the Southwest, Northwest, and Southeast, where electric utilities had grown at a very rapid rate. This would have allowed him to share in a wider range of electric utility growth.

The second weakness, the overall yield, was only 3.1 percent. This rate could have been improved by buying higher-yielding public utility shares or preferred stock or debt. One point that must be made

TABLE 22–8 A

Investment portfolio of Professor Ganby, 1962

COMPANY	NUMBER OF SHARES	PRICE	VALUE	DIVIDEND	TOTAL DIVIDEND INCOME	YIELD PERCENT
Cincinnati Gas & Electric	100	49	$ 4,900	$1.50	$150.00	3.1
Dayton Power & Light	100	28	2,800	.88	88.00	3.1
Ohio Edison	100	46	4,600	1.60	160.00	3.5
Central Illinois Public Service	100	69	6,900	2.28	228.00	3.3
Illinois Power	100	79	7,900	2.20	220.00	2.8
			$27,100		$846.00	3.1 av.

TABLE 22–8 B

Investment portfolio of Professor Ganby, August, 1968

COMPANY	NUMBER OF SHARES	PRICE, AUGUST 27, 1968	VALUE	DIVIDEND	TOTAL DIVIDEND INCOME	YIELD PERCENT
Cincinnati Gas & Electric	200	28 1/4	$ 5,650	$1.30	$ 260	4.6
Dayton Power & Light	100	30 7/8	3,087	1.52	152	4.9
Ohio Edison	200	28 1/4	5,650	1.42	284	5.1
Central Illinois Public Service	300	22 3/8	6,712	1.12	336	5.1
Illinois Power	200	36 3/4	7,350	1.80	360	5.0
			$28,449		$1,392	4.9av.

is that Professor Ganby's purchase price for all the companies was low. Any switch must consider the tax impact on the portfolio. The capital gains were long term, but a change might force the professor to pay a higher tax than he wished. However, he could have purchased higher-yielding public utility shares that might have put him in a better position for growth as well as income. In this respect, he might have considered the addition of Columbus and Southern Ohio Electric, Florida Power and Light, and Arizona Public Service. The income might not have been significantly higher, but the growth potential would have been greater.

The third point is a criticism of Professor Ganby's avowed policy of income. He should have emphasized growth since he really did not need additional current income to meet his modest needs. One or two well-chosen growth companies with a very low yield would have been extremely desirable. If he had passed away before he was able to retire, his wife would receive a comparatively modest income. A larger fund would help her obtain the necessary capital to increase income eventually. Also if Professor Ganby were ill and could not work, the growth fund could be converted to an income fund very readily.

These three criticisms suggest that Professor Ganby should have considered more carefully his investment goals and objectives; that his policy of being a secure, income-conscious public-utility investor might not be correct for his present and future needs. Regardless of what he decided to do, more attention should have been given to diversification and the tax aspects of the portfolio. As new capital was invested over the next few years, the funds should have been used for diversification and improvement of either the growth or income aspects of the portfolio, depending upon what Professor Ganby decided.

Table 22–8 B indicates what happened from 1962 until 1968. The value of Professor Ganby's fund improved only modestly but the income went up substantially. The professor would have been wise to heed our analysis. Unfortunately, he passed away shortly before retirement in 1965 and did not have time to enjoy the fruits of his modest investment program.

THE CASE OF THE INJURED INDUSTRIALIST

Gordon L. Jackson, 45, was the president and founder of a medium-sized manufacturing company, which he had built into one of the leading companies in the industry. In 1957, he sold out his controlling interest by selling his stock to the public. Shortly thereafter he retired from his demanding job to assume the duties of president of a private foundation. The sale of stock netted him approximately $700,000, and he promptly invested this fund in a selected list of growth companies. He did not need current income, since his foundation presidency provided him with an adequate income.

In late 1959 and middle 1960, two events changed his life completely. He was seriously injured in an auto accident in 1959 and was unable to continue in his position with the foundation. The stock market dropped sharply in the spring of 1960, and Mr. Jackson's $700,000 investment fund dropped to $500,000. This was a severe shock to Mr. Jackson. He needed income desperately to maintain his family and pay for medical expenses. He was disillusioned because of the drop in his portfolio and became disenchanted with growth securities. His wife had taken a job with a local publishing firm to help with the family expenses. Mr. Jackson did not wish to dip into capital now since this was to be his only source of income for the rest of his life. He needed money to help educate his children, Jeff, 19, Scott, 15, and Terry, 9. Fortunately his children would not be in college at the same time. It would be possible to provide for their college expenses out of current income if the boys helped with summer jobs.

Mr. Jackson decided that the best place for his funds was in secure investments that provided stability of revenue. Until the children finished school, he would need stable income to meet their expenses. He had lost his confidence in common stock because of the rise and fall of his investment account. He thought about corporate bonds in the Baa risk group that would yield about 5 percent. The $30,000 income he would receive would be taxed heavily ($25,000 of income would be from investment income and $5,000 from his wife's income). With three dependents and $2,000 a year deductible medical expenses, their joint after-tax income would be about $23,960, assuming a 10 percent deduction for donations and charitable gifts. In 1960 he found he could buy tax-exempt state and municipal obligations at a yield of 4.2 percent. If he put all of his investment funds into state and local bonds, he would have no taxes to pay on the $21,000 of income. His wife's $5,000 income would be essentially tax free since the $2,000 medical and the $3,000 of standard deductions would absorb all of her taxable income. With tax-exempt bonds as an income source, the Jacksons would have an income of $26,000, which would be $2,040 greater than their income when it was fully taxable. In 1960 he decided on this course of action and established a portfolio of well-balanced tax-exempt state and municipal bonds to meet his needs. It is unusual when only tax-exempt bonds are used in a portfolio. Based on the market condition, income tax, and the temperament of the investor, a portfolio of tax-exempt bonds was appropriate for Mr. Jackson.

The portfolio, as it finally evolved, was invested in public authority bonds because of their yield and their marketability. The portfolio appears in Table 22–9. It was assumed that Mr. Jackson bought the securities at par. The portfolio actually averaged out to a purchase at par, but the individual securities were bought at slightly varying prices. Even though the portfolio is concentrated in one type of security, there is geographic diversification and some diversification of maturity dates. The income provided from the portfolio will allow Mr. Jackson to support his family, educate his children, and generally provide an excellent standard of living for his loved ones. In the future, when the children are educated and safety of principal and income are not as important as

TABLE 22–9

Tax-exempt portfolio of Gordon Jackson

	RATE PERCENT	MATURITY	VALUE	INCOME
Chesapeake Bridge & Toll	5 3/4s	2000	$ 60,000	$ 3,450.00
Chicago O'Hare International Airport	4 3/4s	'99	60,000	2,850.00
Delaware Turnpike	4 1/8s	2022	60,000	2,475.00
Florida Turnpike	4 3/4s	2001	60,000	2,850.00
Mackinac Bridge	4s	'94	60,000	2,400.00
Maine Turnpike	4s	'89	60,000	2,400.00
New York State Power	420s	'06	60,000	2,520.00
Ohio Turnpike	3 1/4s	'92	60,000	1,950.00
Twin Valley	4 1/2s	'87	20,000	900.00
			$500,000	$21,795.00

they were to Mr. Jackson in 1959 and 1960, the portfolio can be better balanced in equities for growth.

Summary

The selection of securities for an income portfolio must emphasize the principles of good portfolio management even though current income is stressed. It must also stress safety of principal in the absolute and relative sense. The individual is wise to have available to him a list of common, preferred, and bonds from which he may select income securities to meet his needs. We must recognize that there are many ways to solve a particular problem of establishing an income portfolio, and many different types of investment problems relating to it. The individual with a modest income and a small fund will have a different problem from the wealthy person who wishes maximum income but is in a high income-tax bracket. The cases used were based on actual investors, using fictitious names.

The case of the worried widow was discussed to illustrate the problem of the modest fund trying to do a big job. Security of principal was relaxed and so was diversification because of the personal preferences of the investor. It also showed how changes could be made to improve the yield. The case of the prolific professor was the typical case for the income investor. A well-diversified portfolio was established to meet the needs of the professor with safety and some good features for future growth. The case of the serious scholar shows how individual conviction can dictate a portfolio's growth and how a lack of a clearly defined objective will affect a portfolio. Our injured industrialist was a wealthy man, yet he needed security of principal and income. Since he was in a relatively high tax bracket, a diversified list of marketable tax-exempt bonds seemed to be adequate to meet his needs. The solutions to these cases are illustrative only of many alternative methods of meeting the needs of different income investors. In the last analysis, in an income investment program, it is necessary to examine risks as indicated by stability of earnings or yield and yield that can be expected. In the case of the investors presented in the chapter, risk was low, stability high, and the yields expected and achieved were low.

Review Questions

1. What is the major objective of the income portfolio, and what types of securities would have the qualifications to meet these objectives?
2. What was the basic problem faced by Mrs. Eaton? Why was it difficult to meet her needs?
3. (a) What was Dr. Cunningham's basic investment problem?
   (b) Did he have more flexibility in solving his problem than did Mrs. Eaton? Explain.

4. (a) What was Professor Ganby's basic investment problem?
   (b) To what extent did Professor Ganby follow sound principles of portfolio management in meeting his investment needs?
   (c) How can we criticize what Professor Ganby did?

5. Mr. Jackson's case was unique. Was the solution to his problem the best solution? Why or why not?

6. Is it difficult in today's market to obtain a generous income from an investment portfolio without sacrificing quality? Explain.

7. Explain how risk and yield manifest themselves in the case of the income investor.

Problems

1. (a) Bring the portfolio of Dr. Cunningham up to date by providing new prices and current yield figures.
   (b) Analyze each security or company and estimate the yield to maturity from the investment for the next five years.
   (c) On the basis of your analysis, would you sell any of the bonds, preferred stock, or common stock?
   (d) Dr. Cunningham is now several years older (the case for our purpose was dated around mid-1962). How have his family or financial needs changed? In light of these changes would you require Dr. Cunningham to change his objectives?

2. Prepare an income investment portfolio for Professor Ganby that would have met his investment needs more adequately.

3. Recommend a better solution to Mr. Jackson's problem consistent with good principles of portfolio management and risk and reward.

Sources of Investment Information

Annual reports
Barron's
Clark Dodge Investment Surveys
Current analysis of companies previously completed
Moody's manuals
Standard & Poor's *Investment Surveys*
Standard & Poor's *The Outlook*
Standard & Poor's *Stock Guide*
The Value Line Investment Survey
Wall Street Journal

23

THE GROWTH PORTFOLIO

No word has been used more frequently in investment circles than "growth." This, for some investors, has been the magic formula, the panacea for all investment ills. At the turn of the decade in 1960, the following editorial appeared in the *Financial Analysts Journal* under the title, "Growth—The Hottest Word in Wall Street."

> There's no chatter on the Wall Streets of America where growth is not part of the conversation. There's no market letter which doesn't refer to growth at least once per issue. There's no book about the economic, business and investment aspects of our time without numerous mentions of growth; indeed, some books devote a chapter or more to growth. There's no modern-day speaker whose subject touches on finance and commerce who would dare to climb a podium and then omit the subject of growth. And certainly there's no respectable business and/or financial magazine (this one included) which fails to "sign up" an author who is conversant with growth.
>
> Truly, GROWTH, for all it implies in the money marts, has become a giant among words. On all financial ramparts, *growth* betokens a measure of magic.[1]

Since the sharp stock market decline of 1969, many investors have become disillusioned with growth stocks. At that time these stocks suffered a sharp drop in price. In spite of the decline in prices of many growth stocks and the accompanying disappointment in results, the concept of growth is still extremely important to a large group of

---

[1] *Financial Analysts Journal,* September-October, 1960, p. 3.

investors. The market decline of 1962 and 1969 simply demonstrated that an individual can pay too high a price even for a growth stock. As a portfolio policy, however, the growth concept is an intelligent and realistic solution to the problems of many investors.

The Concept of the Growth Company

No complete agreement exists as to the precise meaning of a growth company. Dr. Julian Buckley suggests that the characteristics of a growth company are:

> (1) Rapid sales increase over an extended period of time; (2) new product development and alert research department; (3) large capital expenditures; (4) high depreciation charges; (5) low dividend payments compared with earnings; (6) frequent stock dividends; and (7) above all, aggressive and able management.[2]

Dr. Philip Kotler holds that a "growth stock is the stock of a company which has shown for a number of years and/or is showing annual percentage increases in net earnings which substantially exceed the long run growth rate in the economy."[3] Leland Dake[4] suggests that a few of the characteristics a growth company possesses are rapidly growing sales and a climbing stock price. The methods of valuation discussed in Chapter 7 are essentially the ways in which growth stocks are valued. The literature referred to in Chapter 7 should be reviewed along with the discussion of growth stock P/E ratios and capitalization rates in that chapter.

These ingredients of a growth company can be put together in a workable way for the investor. The growth concept implies a growth in sales and in earnings greater than the rate at which the national economy and other industries have grown. Present in the concept of growth are the ideas that this rate will continue in the future and that the company will continue to grow at a greater rate than the national economy. There is also a high degree of certainty surrounding the expectation of increased sales and earnings. The corporation needs funds for the expansion of its facilities to provide for increased sales. These funds are generated from within through retained earnings and through depreciation allowances that retain funds within the business. Usually the depreciation allowances are high because the capital expenditures of the company are high. The growth rate of the company is so great that all or most of the earnings must be retained in the business.

2 Julian G. Buckley, "A Method of Evaluating Growth Stocks," *Financial Analysts Journal*, March-April, 1960, p. 19.

3 Philip Kotler, "Elements in a Theory of Growth Stock Valuation," *Financial Analysts Journal*, May-June 1962, p. 35.

4 Leland E. Dake, "Are Analysts' Techniques Adequate for Growth Stocks?" *Financial Analysts Journal*, November-December, 1960, p. 45.

To retain earnings, the company follows a policy of giving no cash dividends or of giving only stock dividends, which actually capitalizes the retained earnings of the company. The retention of earnings for reinvestment can be justified only on the assumption that the earnings, when reinvested, will continue to earn a higher rate of return than the rate of growth of the national economy, or a higher rate than the owner could receive if he invested his money elsewhere. We assume, of course, that the investment of earnings and funds retained by depreciation allowances will eventually lead to an increase in the market price of the common stock.

A time limit must be imposed on the concept of growth. The superior growth of a company cannot or will not continue indefinitely, but actually for a relatively short period of time. The change in the growth rate must be anticipated by the investor. This suggests that investment timing and management will be more important in the growth portfolio than in the income portfolio. If the earnings rate and subsequently the P/E ratio do decline, there will be a corresponding decrease in price, which if unanticipated, might lead to loss. It is possible therefore to err badly in the purchase of a stock that is selling at an extremely high price-earnings ratio. A stock might decline sharply because of the decline in growth rate and the lack of confidence in and decreased certainty about the future growth of the company's earnings, and the unwillingness on the part of the investor to pay the high price-earnings ratio for the current earnings of the company.

The investment quality, then, that a growth company possesses is a rapid growth in earnings that leads to a rapid growth in the price of the stock. The gain that the investor receives is reflected not only in current dividends but in the increased market value of the stock and increased dividend payments expected in the future. The basic theme of investment decision making established in this text still applies to growth stock. We still want a satisfactory yield consistent with risk. Risk is likely to be greater because price, earnings, and yields are less stable, and yields will be higher than from stock growing at a slower rate.

The Growth Investor

The growth investor, in contrast to the income investor, is not interested in current income. His present needs are satisfied from his current income level. Or he might have a need for more current income but is willing to sacrifice present consumption for the possibility of obtaining a greater income in the future. A man thirty years old might have a great need for current income, but as a matter of a conscious policy decides to save and invest in growth issues that provide no current income. The growth shares, he hopes, will increase in value and will offer an opportunity to purchase more goods and services in the future. Another type of growth investor is the individual who has no need for current income but will require in later years substantial amounts of income. Investment is made in such a way as to increase the future fund. It is expected that the companies in which investment is made will reinvest their earnings. A young doctor with a growing practice is interested not only in growth but in how he can keep some of his income that is subject to high tax rates. Certainly he is not interested in current income.

The growth investor expects a higher rate of return from a growth investment than from an income investment. When he states that he is investing for growth rather than income, there is an assumption made, realistically or unrealistically, that he will profit more from this type of investment. The reinvestment principle is at work too. The investor assumes not only that the growth rate will be greater but that by having the company reinvest his dividends he is sure to have a larger fund in the future. Unfortunately, the investor is not always successful in reaching his investment goal. Many have purchased growth stocks that did not provide the growth expected. In these cases the investor sustained substantial losses.

Another class of growth investor is one who is forced to invest his funds in such a way as to minimize the taxes he must pay. An individual in the 72 percent income tax bracket, for example, is paying the major portion of his marginal income to the government in taxes. If this investor can change his form of income so that it is taxed at a lower rate, he will be in a much better investment position. If, for example, his gains could be taxed as long-term capital gains rather than ordinary income taxes, he would be in an excellent tax position. Long-term capital gains are taxed at a maximum rate of 25 percent. To the extent that the investor can obtain long-term capital gains rather than pay a tax rate of 72 percent, his financial position is improved by an increase in after-tax income. The success of the wealthy growth investor depends upon his ability to select companies that will grow and provide a growth of principal in the future.

The Selection of Growth Stocks

The growth investor who is dependent upon long-term capital gains to meet his objectives should not be willing to sacrifice security of principal. Some investors assume that any company can be purchased at any time and at any price and if put away long enough, it will provide an adequate return. A great deal of speculation took place in the new issues of small growth companies that had made their public debuts in 1960 and 1961. Some have done well. Many more rose in price and then settled to new lows far below their issuance price. These were speculative securities and not growth investments. The growth in these companies never materialized. This was also the case for the "hot new issue" market of 1968. Many new issues were purchased in spite of what the prospectuses said. Some doubled in price hours after the initial offering. It was doubtful at the time the gains would continue. Eventually the speculative stocks would reach their level, most likely a lower level.

The growth investor must be extremely cautious in the growth portfolio that is put together. He should make certain that the company selected possesses not only growth but stability and quality as well. Here again the wise approach is to list those quality companies that possess sound investment characteristics as determined by the financial analysis of the company. We want these companies to have a satisfactory yield consisting mostly of capital gains and not current income. Often investment services provide a list of quality, investment-grade companies that are considered to be growth companies. Our own analysis will also lead to such a list.

A partial list of candidates for growth industries in the 1970's is presented in Table 23–1. These industries were expected to grow more rapidly than the national economy as of the late sixties. The list of growth industries is by no means stable. At one time, for example, aluminum, cement, building, container, and oils were the leading growth industries. However, the relative rate of growth of some of these industries has declined. Now some are expected to grow at the same rate as or more slowly than the national economy. Not all segments of these industries are growth industries. Some of the divisions of each are growing much more rapidly than the industry as a whole. It is in this area that we would find our growth companies.

The list of growth companies appearing on pp. 702–3 was presented in the first edition of this book as stocks that might fit the needs of the growth investor. The original table carried an earlier price and a price for January 2, 1964. In that edition, we provided only this information about the first five columns of the table:

The earnings of these companies, most of which are listed on the New York Stock Exchange, have grown rapidly in the past. Most of them have paid a very small dividend, a stock dividend, or a combination of

TABLE 23–1

A partial list of long-run growth industries for the 1970's

Aerospace	Leisure time
Banking	Office equipment
Building conglomerates	Oceanography precision instruments
Chemical	Publishing and education
Computers and computer leasing	Savings and loan holding companies
Drugs	Vending companies
Electronics	Utilities—electric & gas
Insurance, life	Telephone, independent

both, and have sold at high P/E ratios. Some are the leading companies in the industry. Since not all these companies are in the conservative growth investment class, they must be watched carefully to see if they continue to meet the criteria for growth investments. Some have done very well, some very poorly, demonstrating the difficulty in judging growth stocks. This is, of course, only a partial list of growth companies as a starting point for the growth investor.

In order to learn about our performance, we added the last five columns to Table 23–2. The prices were brought up to date and the gain or loss calculated for those companies that had not merged or for which data was not readily available. The average capital gain for the thirty-two companies brought up to date was 103 percent for a period of almost five years. The range in the percentage rates of capital gain for each stock was —33 percent to 333 percent. The average gain of 103 percent for the period resulted in an annual compound growth rate of approximately 15 percent. If we added the annual current dividend of approximately 2 1/2 percent, the equivalent yield to maturity would have been 17 1/2 percent.

The investor would have had to purchase all these stocks to achieve the results, or a randomly selected sample that would allow the results to be achieved. If only one or two stocks had been selected, the results might have been either delightful or disastrous. Hence, the need for diversification based upon sound statistical practice to assure results. The growth stocks in Table 23–2, however, actually did better than the income stocks we discussed in Chapter 22.

We can purchase other securities for growth in addition to common stock. Tax-exempt bonds might be an attractive investment for the growth investor. Municipal bonds were suggested in the previous chapter as a solution to the income needs of a wealthy individual. They offer stability of income, safety of principal, and, at the same time, a maximum of after-tax income. The case of the wealthy growth investor is much the same as that of the wealthy income investor. Where can an investor, for example, in the 72 percent bracket find a 14.3 percent before-tax return on his investment funds? Many growing corporations do not grow at that rate. However, a 4 percent tax-exempt municipal bond gives the 72 percent growth investor a rate of return that high.

A Representative Selection of Portfolios for the Growth Investor

The best way to demonstrate the principles involved in the growth portfolio is to consider several basic types of growth investors and attempt to satisfy their needs. The basic objectives of portfolio management must be met. We are interested in safety of principal, marketability, liquidity, and diversification. Current income will be undesirable and capital appreciation and a favorable tax position will be the important goals to be achieved. It would be best to accurately estimate the amount of expected future yield based upon sound principles of valuation, estimate the expected risks involved based upon the stability of earnings or yield, analyze the market for the stock based upon P/E relationships as a guide to whether the stock is realistically priced, then, based upon yield and risk, select a representative list of growth stocks to meet our needs. The first case is a hypothetical but practical case substantially removed from the excellent theory and practice suggested earlier. It appeared in *Medical Economics* some years ago. The income figures are low in terms of the level of income that a physician in Dr. Harris's place might receive today, and the other figures quoted are also more suited to the late forties than the early seventies. The case is quoted here at length because it reviews from a practical point of view the subject of financial analysis as well as of portfolio management. The case of Dr. Harris is one that illustrates some of the personal problems of the growth investor.

THE CASE OF THE PROSPEROUS PHYSICIAN

Paul Harris was troubled. At 47 he had a solid, $12,000-net medical practice, a nine-room house free and clear, and only a mild systolic murmur. His life was insured for $35,000, plus enough in endowment policies to put his two teen-age children through college. He had two cars in his garage and $10,000 of U.S. Savings bonds in his safety deposit box. What bothered him was his bank balance: $24,000.

The account, he knew, was top-heavy. A balance of $4,000, along with his government bonds, would be ample to meet ordinary contingencies. The remaining $20,000 was idle cash; and he was adding to it about $2,500 each year.

The doctor's financial life had reached the menopause. He needed some kind of investment program. The phrase sent a little shiver up his spine.

Not that he hadn't had the beginnings of such a program all along. His insurance policies, the bonds, the redemption of the mortgage on his house—all were aimed at building up some security for his family. Why not simply more bonds, more insurance?

He began inquiring around among his friends: some of the senior staff men at the hospital, a patient in the brokerage business, a golf partner who ran the trust department of the local bank. They came up with a number of ideas. Paul Harris holed up in his study one evening and sorted them out.

They shaped up like this:

Deposit the excess cash in mutual savings banks.
Buy more government bonds—U.S., state, or municipal.
Buy more insurance—paid-up life, endowment, or annuities.
Invest in corporate stocks and bonds.

TABLE 23–2

A selected list of rapidly growing companies

Company	Approximate Purchase Price, 1962	Dividend	Current Yield	P/E Ratio	Price January 2, 1964	Price August 28, 1968	Current Dividend	Merged or Split Action	Gain or (Loss) Per Share	Gain or (Loss) in Percent
American Hospital Supply	24	.25	1.0	30.0	22	30	.22		8	36
American Photo Company	26	.33	1.2	32.5	11 1/2	15	.06		(3 1/2)	(30)
Beckman Instruments	101	—		33.1	66 1/4	45 1/4	.50	2 for 1	24 1/4	37
Bobbie Brooks	37	.60	1.6	21.8	25 1/8	23 1/4			(1 7/8)	(7)
Bristol Myers Company	82	1.30	1.6	28.8	71	77 3/8	1.20	2 for 1	83 3/4	118
Brunswick Corporation	32	.60	1.9	11.6	10 1/2	17 1/2			7	67
Cenco Instruments	44	.50	1.1	26.7	53 1/2	42 1/2	.30	2 for 1	31 1/2	59
Chock Full o' Nuts Corporation	22	.40	1.8	31.4	13 1/8	19 1/8	.60		(6)	(31)
Control Data	37	—		92.5	90 1/4	124 7/8		1½ for 1	97 1/4	108
Drackett Company	26	.60	2.3	20.8	32 3/8	59		merged	49 1/2	127
Factor, Max	39	.60	1.5	26.9	39	67 3/8	.80	1½ for 1	67 1/8	198
Fairchild Camera & Inst.	46	.50	1.1	21.9	33 7/8	33 5/8	.50	1½ for 1	36 7/8	52
Financial Federation	92	—		15.9	70 1/2	38 1/4	1.24		2 1/8	6
First Charter Financial	43	5% stock		14.3	36 1/8	82 1/4			(6 1/4)	(7)
General Foods Corp.	82	1.80	2.2	28.3	88 1/2	37 1/8	2.40		10 5/8	40
Gibraltar Financial	38	5% stock		12.1	26 1/2					
Ginn & Company	24	.48	2.0	20.0	29 7/8			merged		
Great Western Financial	27	5% stock		10.8	16 1/8	27 7/8			11 3/4	73
Harcourt, Brace & World	31	.50	1.6	27.0	34 7/8	80	1.00		45 1/8	129
Hewlett-Packard Company	27	—		36.0	18 5/8	75	.20		56 3/8	304
Holt, Rinehart & Winston	34	.40	1.2	27.2	26 1/2			merged		
Hunt Foods & Industries	51	.50a	1.0	18.2	27 7/8			merged		
Int'l. Business Machines	449	3.00	.7	52.8	546	338	2.00	2 for 1	130	24

TABLE 23–2 (continued)

Company										
Jostens, Inc.	16	.30	1.9	26.7	15 1/8	32 3/4	.60	2 for 1	50 3/8	333
Korvette	46	—	—	30.7	32 1/2	—	—	merged	22 5/8	127
Lanvin–Charles of the Ritz	30	.32	1.0	26.1	17 7/8	39 3/4	.52	merged	—	—
Lehn & Fink Products	33	.80	2.4	18.9	30 1/4	—	—	merged	8	11
Litton Industries	117	2½% stock	—	33.4	132 3/4	70 3/8	2½% stock	2 for 1	10 1/4	21
Mattel	35	.28	.8	18.9	39 1/4	49 1/2	.40	—	40 1/2	62
Minn. Mining and Manufac.	63	.80	1.3	39.4	65 3/4	106 1/4	1.45	—	17 3/8	62
Monroe Auto Equipment	32	.50ᵇ	1.6	20.0	28	45 5/8	.60	—	54	174
Prentice-Hall, Inc.²	30	.40	1.3	33.7	31	42 1/2	.60	2 for 1	11 1/8	13
Procter & Gamble	78	1.50	1.9	29.4	82 1/2	93 5/8	2.40	—		
Random House²	24	—	—	21.8	9 1/8	—	—	merged		
Remco Industries	19	.29	1.5	15.8	8	17 1/8	1%	—		
Russ Togs	19	.60	3.2	15.8	19 3/8	44 1/4	—	1½ for 2	(9 1/8)	(114)
Ryan Aeronautical Company	20	.20	1.0	10.5	16 1/2	33 5/8	.20	—	(47)	(242)
San Diego Imperial	12	5% stock	—	10.9	10 3/8	—	—	merged	17 1/8	—
Swingline Inc.	33	1.00	3.0	15.3	37	25 7/8	40	4 for 1	66 1/2	180
Taft Broadcasting	17	.40ᶜ	2.4	12.6	25	33 3/8	60	2 for 1	47 3/4	191
Talcott (James) Inc.¹	43	1.00	2.3	21.5	24 3/4	26 1/8	1.00	—	1 3/8	6
Tampax, Inc.¹	66	1.10	1.7	36.7	75 3/4	182	2.60	—	116 1/4	153
Varian Associates	37	—	—	38.9	13 5/8	25 1/2	—	—	11 7/8	87
Winn-Dixie Stores	29	.84	2.9	21.5	31	32 1/4	1.56	—	1 1/4	4
Xerox Corporation	124	.40	.3	41.3	415	277 3/4	1.60	—	(137 1/4)	(33)
Zenith Radio Corporation	62	1.17	1.9	27.6	81 1/2	53 7/8	1.20ᵃ	2 for 1	26 1/4	32

All stocks listed on New York Stock Exchange except as noted:

1 Regional or over-the-counter.

2 American Stock Exchange

ᵃ Plus 5% stock.

ᵇ Plus 2% stock.

ᶜ Plus 2½% stock.

SOURCE: *Barron's*, January 27, 1964, pp. 28ff; *Wall Street Journal*; and Standard & Poor's *Stock Guide*, May, 1968.

During the next few weeks the doctor looked into each of these possibilities. Most mutual savings banks, he learned, are prohibited by law from accepting single deposits of more than $7,500. He could distribute his funds among several such banks, but decided it wasn't worthwhile. None paid more than 2 percent.

He ruled out buying more public bonds for the same reason. State and municipal obligations, his broker friend told him, were exempt from federal income taxes. This made them popular with upper-bracket taxpayers, whose bidding kept prices far above face value. As a result, the bonds were not a good buy for the ordinary investor. The tax-free feature did not offset the low yield unless the investor's taxes were above the 50 percent bracket.

As for U.S. Government bonds, the best of these for small investors were the "Series E" variety, like those Dr. Harris already had. They paid 2.9 percent if held to maturity. They could be cashed at any time and were the safest kind of investment. But the doctor felt that, for the time being, $10,000 worth was enough. He wanted a better return on his extra $20,000, plus something in the way of appreciation.

By now an insurance agent had picked up the Harris scent. The agent talked earnestly about how a family head "couldn't carry too much insurance" and how the right kind of policy "forces a man to save regularly." But he couldn't deny that, no matter how you slice it, no insurance policy today yields more than 2 1/2 percent.

At that, he almost put over a sale. The doctor's $20,000, the insurance man pointed out, would buy a life income of $151 per month, beginning at age 65. And by adding $2,400 a year until then, Dr. Harris could boost this retirement income to $460 a month.

He was much tempted to sign up. A number of his colleagues had gone for the annuity idea, and one of the older men he'd talked to at the hospital strongly recommended it.

But there was a catch. Paul Harris couldn't get over the way living costs had gone up since before the war. Maybe the price rise was over, maybe not. How would he feel if he socked out nearly all his life savings for a fixed income, then eventually found he couldn't live on that income?

The doctor decided that, though he might some day buy an annuity, he wasn't yet old enough to invest his money that way. He needed protection against possible long-term inflation.

So what it all boiled down to was stocks and bonds. He wasn't any too happy about that, either. The '29 crash had come during his last year as an interne. He remembered what it had done to his father. He remembered, too, that his father had been playing the market on margin, and had a weakness for little-known mining stocks. Paul Harris had other ideas.

The next Saturday afternoon he stopped by the town library and borrowed a book called *Investment for the Millions,* a publication of the Nonesuch Press. Whether the title referred to millions of investors or to millions of dollars, he wasn't quite sure. But he took the book home and read it. It turned out to be pretty sensible—up to a point.

The book spelled out a number of things that to Dr. Harris had been only hazy notions. Here's a capsuled version of what he got out of it:

Objectives. First decide what you're primarily after: safety, income, or prospect of capital gain. You can have some of all three. But the more you have of any one, the less you'll have of the others. In making up your mind, consider your age, health, earning power, family obligations. (Dr. Harris decided on a middle course: reasonable safety of principal, an income of around 5 percent, and a little play for his money.)

Diversification. Spread your funds among selected industries, companies, types of securities. Very generally speaking, bonds are safest; but they offer the lowest income and the least chance of appreciation. Common stocks are riskiest, but some offer attractive income or opportunity for capital gain. Preferred stocks rank in between.

Timing. The best investment program can go haywire if it's timed wrong. Theoretically, a business boom lifts stock prices, lowers bond prices; and vice versa in depression. But since the time of the New Deal, government and industrial bond prices have climbed steadily, without regard to the business cycle. Stock prices still fluctuate with business and profit prospects, but are more sensitive than ever to political and world events. To illustrate: Industrial profits are now far above the 1929 level, but stock prices are less than half their 1929 peak.

Timing Methods. Two principal kinds are in use: (1) Analytical. The investor weighs all known factors, economic and political, bearing on the future of business profits. He predicts the course of security prices accordingly. (2) Mechanical. The investor ignores business and political factors. He concentrates instead on security prices themselves. From their pattern in the recent past he predicts their future. Best known mechanical method is the Dow Theory. But there is no method, analytical or mechanical, that's infallible, even in the hands of an expert.

Industry Analysis. Most industries follow a life cycle, with four definite phases: (1) experimentation, with high infant mortality, as in television before the war; (2) vigorous growth with profits zooming, as in plastics and television today; (3) maturity, with steady profits, as in the chemical and automotive industries; (4) senility, with declining profits, as in the railroad and coal mining industries.

Then, too, some industries have sharper ups and downs between boom and depression than do others. Most volatile are producers of raw materials or of factory durable goods (copper, steel, heavy machinery).

Most stable are those producing goods for day-to-day consumption (foods, drugs). In between are producers of consumers' durable goods (autos, furniture). The investor should select his industries according to his primary objectives and the current phase of the business cycle.

Company Analysis. Most industries are dominated by a handful of top concerns. The wise investor sticks to these leaders, leaving lesser fry to speculators. He studies each outfit's background, management, products, markets, capital structure, current financial position, earnings, and dividend records. Much of this data is published in investment manuals, such as Moody's or Standard and Poor's.

Portfolio Management. Successful investment requires constant application. You can't just buy a security and forget it. A company doing well this year may be in trouble next year. The prudent investor follows the financial page of a big city newspaper, reads at least two investment journals regularly, studies all the literature his companies send him.

Paul Harris laid the book aside with a frown. What did the author take him for—a research institute? He couldn't keep up with his specialty journals, let alone the *Wall Street Journal, Barron's Financial Weekly,* the *Kiplinger Letter,* and similar publications.

For some moments he toyed with the idea of calling back the insurance agent. Then he remembered that somebody at the hospital had suggested he turn his problem over to an investment counsel. Next day the doctor dropped in at the bank to talk this over with his friend in the trust department.

Tactfully, the banker tried to kill the idea. Annual fees of investment counsel, he pointed out, start at one-half of one percent on the first two or three hundred thousand dollars, scaling downward on larger accounts. Few counsels accept accounts of less than $500,000. Some charge a minimum annual fee of $500.

But the banker had an alternative. Why not buy a share in the *bank's* common trust fund? This was a balanced portfolio—bonds and preferred and common stocks of numerous companies in many industries —designed for just such small investors as Dr. Harris. By pooling his kitty with others under the bank's management, he would have the whole problem off his hands. Besides, he'd be getting better diversification than he could get alone, even if he bought his stocks in only ten- or twenty-share lots.

The bank's trust fund paid around 4 1/2 percent. It was three years old, and in that time had fluctuated in value about as much as the stock market as a whole.

Paul Harris thanked his banker friend and told him he'd think it over. Next he called on his friend in the brokerage business, half expecting to be sold a bill of goods. But the broker agreed at once that $20,000 wasn't enough to set up a well-rounded portfolio. He suggested the doctor buy into several sound investment trusts.

These offered the same advantages as a common trust fund, plus several other good points. For example:

The investment trusts recommended by the broker were operated by large, well-established investment counsel or management firms. These firms had bigger, better-trained research staffs than had the local bank.

By buying into a number of good investment trusts, the doctor would obtain not only diversification of investments, but also diversification of the management of his investments. Thus he would be hedging against possible errors of judgment by any one investment counsel or management firm.

The recommended trusts paid an annual return of around 5 percent.

All these trusts had been in operation for ten years or longer. In that time the shares of each had gained more in value than had stocks and bonds generally.

The doctor heaved an inward sigh of relief. This was for him. He told the broker he'd take the matter under advisement and let him know in a few days. But he was pretty sure he'd found what he was looking for.

Driving to his office, he turned the whole thing over once more in his mind. Mutual savings banks? They paid too little, gave him no play for his money. Government bonds? Same trouble. Besides, his present $10,000 worth was more than enough, in relation to his total funds, for immediate security purposes. Insurance annuities? He was well insured already. And an annuity alone, offering no protection against long-range inflation, seemed too risky for a man still many years short of retirement age.

For Paul Harris's money, a stock-and-bond program was clearly the answer. And investment trusts were the medium through which to carry it out. His fund was too small for well-diversified direct investment. Anyhow, he had neither time nor training to manage properly an investment portfolio of his own.[5]

The solution of Dr. Harris's problem must be considered in terms of the securities market in 1949. The stock market was not high compared to today's market prices. Hindsight would tell us to invest everything we owned or could beg, borrow, or steal and put it in the securities market. However, in 1949, the market was at the 160–170 level measured by the Dow Jones Industrial Average. Many people thought that the stock market was high and feared a decline. The yield on long-term government bonds was around 3 to 3 1/2 percent. The savings bonds yield was 2.9 percent. The yield on tax-exempt municipals was low and would

5 This case was quoted from Lloyd E. Dewey and P. J. DeTuro, "Investing $20,000, A Case History," *Medical Economics*, April, 1949, p. 55.

not pay Dr. Harris a very high return. Some people thought we would have a post-World War II recession and were apprehensive about the general economic climate. Yield on the DJIA common stocks in 1949 was 7.1 percent, and stocks were selling at between eight and ten times earnings. In hindsight, prices were extremely low.

Dr. Harris decided upon a middle-of-the-road course of action and wanted income, growth, and "a little play for his money." Actually, he should have been interested in growth. He did not need the current income from his investment. He was adding $2,500 a year to his fund, and his relatively high tax bracket would not let him keep all of the fruits of his labors. He followed the right method, but he may be criticized for making the wrong decision as to what type of investor he should have been. In the case it is stated that "industrial profits are now far above the 1929 level, but stock prices are less than half their 1929 peak." This too would suggest common stock investment and growth.

The solution to Paul Harris's dilemma was not a combination of bonds and common stocks. Dr. Harris already had $10,000 in U.S. Savings bonds. The $20,000 should have been put into a list of well-diversified common stocks similar to the portfolio in Table 23–3. These were considered quality companies in 1949 although not each was considered a growth company. The suggested solution to Dr. Harris's problem offers safety of principal, some income, good diversification and marketability, and the potential for capital appreciation. The money that Dr. Harris had coming in each year might have gone to purchase a new car or a

TABLE 23–3

Suggested $20,000 portfolio for Dr. Paul Harris, 1949

COMPANY	No. OF SHARES	PURCHASE PRICE	TOTAL VALUE	% OF TOTAL	DIVI- DENDS PER SHARE 1949	TOTAL INCOME	CURRENT YIELD
General Motors	50	62 1/2	$ 3,125.00	15.7	8.00*	$ 200.00	12.80
General Electric	50	38 1/4	1,912.50	9.5	2.00	100.00	5.22
Phillips Petroleum Company	50	57 7/8	2,893.75	14.6	2.25	112.50	3.88
Socony-Vacuum Oil Company	100	15 3/4	1,575.00	7.9	1.10	110.00	6.98
National Dairy Products Corp.	50	33 1/4	1,662.50	8.4	2.20	110.00	6.61
Borden Company	50	44 5/8	2,231.25	11.2	2.70	135.00	6.05
Sears, Roebuck	50	39 1/2	1,975.00	9.9	2.25	112.50	5.70
General Foods	50	44	2,200.00	11.1	2.25	112.50	5.11
Houston Lighting & Power	50	45 5/8	2,281.25	11.5	2.20	110.00	4.82
			$19,856.25	100.0		$1,102.50	5.55

* Regular plus extra.

fur coat for Mrs. Harris. As a matter of being conservative about the ability to accumulate a $20,000 investment account, we suggest that Dr. Harris finance his car for one year rather than dip into his capital. It might be difficult for him to put the money back into his account. Actually, Dr. Harris should carefully estimate the after-tax cost of financing the auto. He might find the cost substantial, more than he could obtain in the stock market.

The solution really offers bold action at a time when the United States was emerging from a difficult post-World War II period. No one was certain about the future, and most investors were being conservative. The author remembers vividly a discussion with Dr. Henry Hawley at the University of Maine in 1949. The author told Dr. Hawley that he thought the market was too high and we were in for a downward adjustment. He agreed on that assumption. We were both wrong. It is possible, therefore, that the conservative investor would have put much more money into fixed-income securities, even tax-exempt bonds, rather than common stock as the sample portfolio suggests. This would have been consistent with the market situation at that time. Dowrie and Fuller aptly described the market attitude in 1949 by this statement:

> The collapse of the great stock price speculation culminating in 1929 and the persistence of the long depression of the 1930's greatly tempered the enthusiasm of advocates of the common-stock investment doctrine, and more favorable experience in the 1940's has only partially restored it.
>
> Rightly or not, the former assumption of perpetual growth appears unreal to the present-day investor, and the experience has demonstrated to him that the accumulated surpluses which were supposed to add permanently to the value of a stock could melt away almost overnight.[6]

Such action might have led Dr. Harris to a sound investment portfolio, but he would not have prospered if he purchased bonds. If he had selected the stocks in the recommended portfolio, he would be much better off financially today.

THE CASE OF THE INDIGNANT INSURANCE EXECUTIVE

George Morton, 55 years old in 1962, was married and the father of two children, a boy, 17, and a girl, 14. He was the owner of a large insurance agency in the East and had been extremely successful in his work. He was a hard-driving executive who had built up his insurance business by his own efforts. His income was large enough to put him in the 72 percent income-tax bracket. His current income was adequate to care for his needs well. Both Mr. and Mrs. Morton were in good

---

6 George W. Dowrie and Douglas R. Fuller, *Investment* (New York: John Wiley & Sons, Inc., 1950), p. 105.

health and kept physically fit through their activities at the country club to which they belonged. Their entertaining was modest, with most of their social activities centering around the country club.

Their older child would be going to college next year, and in a few years the daughter would be entering college. Once again there was no financial problem. Morton had a fund set aside for his children's education ($20,000) and also enough life insurance to provide additional funds for his family should he die. There was no question at all about his savings, life insurance, or the educational fund he had started. The home he now lived in was a modern ten-room house in a suburban community and fully paid for. The Mortons had two late-model autos and their son had an old convertible to take him to and from school. George Morton's son was a sensible, responsible, intelligent boy on the student honor role. He had paid for the auto from the money he earned doing odd jobs. Morton's financial position is summarized in Table 23–4.

Morton had done extremely well in his insurance business. He alone had decided upon his investment portfolio; he had sought outside counsel only upon occasion. He had been reluctant to have someone manage his portfolio for him. He thought it too costly, and that he really did not need expert advice or opinion. Morton was an individualist who wished to make his own decisions. He used several investment services and read the *Wall Street Journal* regularly. These activities kept him informed about investment matters. He had found, however, that since his investment account had grown in a short period of time, it had become increasingly difficult for him to devote time to his securities portfolio. His portfolio totaled over $88,000, and he had invested in 26 different companies in 24 different industries. The entire portfolio is presented in Table 23–5, pp. 712–13.

Morton had two principal considerations in setting up a growth portfolio to meet his investment needs. First, he was in a high income-tax bracket and did not need current income. This, of course, suggests a growth portfolio of investments that offer little in the way of current dividends. Second, Morton was getting on in years and hoped to retire by the time he reached age 65. The insurance business was becoming much more competitive. He had wondered how long he would be able

TABLE 23–4

Financial position of George Morton

ASSETS		LIABILITIES AND PROPRIETORSHIP	
Cash–checking	$ 3,000.00		
Bonds (College fund)	20,000.00		
Life insurance cash value	20,000.00		
Investment funds	86,312.50		
Autos	8,000.00		
House	40,000.00	Ownership	$177,312.50
Total assets	$177,312.50	Total	$177,312.50

to meet the competition and maintain his current standard of living. All of these add up to a growth portfolio for Morton for the next ten years. At that time, he would reappraise his investment needs and probably switch to an income portfolio.

The stock market had taken some violent turns since Morton put together his investment portfolio. The market began to decline in the fall of 1961 when it was in the 700–720 range of the Dow Jones Industrial Average and dropped to the 580–600 level in September, 1962. Morton's portfolio suffered a decline about equal to the overall decline in the market, as measured by the Dow Jones Industrial Average. In this case he had been extremely fortunate. Many growth stocks dropped as much as 50 percent. One of Morton's stocks reflected this change. Brunswick dropped from 60 to 17 3/4.

Mr. Morton had been an extremely able and effective insurance man and had attempted to bring his experience to the securities market. He had rejected outside counsel. The question that should be asked is whether his goal was correct for him and whether he selected the proper securities to meet his needs. Obviously, Morton was not in need of income, and the policy he established—growth—was best suited for his needs. He was attempting to time his income to meet retirement needs, which, at that time, would be much greater. Any capital gains that he might have then will be taxed at a very low rate since he will be in a lower ordinary income-tax bracket. His family needs will have been met and his standard of living will be modest. He should be in a good financial position at retirement with a growth portfolio policy. Morton also was a risk taker, and the purchase of growth stocks with their attendant risks would not be foreign to him. His high income-tax bracket made it imperative for Mr. Morton to adapt a growth portfolio to attempt to preserve his capital and provide for his retirement years.

Some of the securities that Morton had selected did not meet his needs. His portfolio was well diversified, and some of the securities were excellent companies with growth possibilities. But some of the weaker companies could have been eliminated. A few were really income securities rather than securities with growth potential. Socony Mobil, an excellent company for income, did not meet the portfolio requirements. The railroads in the portfolio were good for income but certainly not for growth. One or two railroads might possibly provide capital growth if earnings improved, but this was not a certainty. Almost all the utilities were in the income category except for Public Service of New Mexico. General Motors was an excellent company. Its yield was high enough to place it in the income category, but it did offer both growth and income potential. In addition its rate of growth was comparable to the national economy. Moore-Handley was a high-yielding company that did not really possess the characteristics Morton needed in an investment.

Some of the companies did not have the strength one would want

TABLE 23–5
Portfolio of George Morton

WHERE TRADED	INDUSTRY & COMPANY	1962 PURCH. PRICE $	NO. OF SHARES	TOTAL VALUE $	DIV. PER SHARE $	TOTAL DIV. $	CURRENT YIELD %	MKT. PRICE SEPT. 1962	GAIN OR (LOSS) OVER PURCH. PR. $	TOTAL GAIN OR (LOSS) OVER PURCH. PR. $	COMP. OF PTFOLIO %
	Autos										
NYSE	General Motors	49	100	$ 4,900.00	2.50 Incl. Extra	250.00	5.1	53	4	400.00	5.54
	Banks										
	First National Bank of										
OC	Cincinnati	53	100	5,300.00	2.00	200.00	3.8	56	3	300.00	6.00
	Building										
	Moore Handley										
OC	Incorporated	10	100	1,000.00	.60	60.00	6.0	10 1/4	1/4	25.00	1.13
	Chemicals										
NYSE	Monsanto	56	100	5,600.00	1.00	100.00	1.8	40 7/8	(15 7/8)	(15.40)	6.34
	Drugs										
	Drug & Food										
OC	Capital	10	100	1,000.00	—	—	—	8	(2)	(200.00)	1.13
	Electronics-Electrical										
OC	NuTone Inc.	20	100	2,000.00	3% stock	—	—	20 1/8	1/8	12.50	2.26
NYSE	Westinghouse Electric	43	100	4,300.00	1.20	120.00	2.8	25 3/4	(17 1/4)	(1,725.00)	4.86
OC	Electrolux	35	100	3,500.00	1.20	120.00	3.4	45	10	1,000.00	3.96
	Leisure Time-Amusement										
NYSE	Brunswick	60	100	6,000.00	.60	60.00	1.0	17 3/4	(42 1/4)	(4,225.00)	6.79
	Miscellaneous										
NYSE	Procter & Gamble	84	100	8,400.00	1.50	150.00	1.8	61 1/4	(22 3/4)	(2,275.00)	9.51
	Metals										
NYSE	Aluminum Ltd.	32	100	3,200.00	.60	60.00	1.9	19 1/2	(10 1/2)	(1,050.00)	3.62

TABLE 23–5 (continued)

			(100)							
	Oil									
NYSE	Socony Mobil	45	100	4,500.00	2.25	225.00	5.0	51 1/2	6 1/2	650.00	5.09
	Paper									
OC	Sorg	19	100	1,900.00	.70	70.00	3.7	14 5/8	(4 3/8)	(437.50)	2.15
	Railroads									
NYSE	Atchison Topeka & Santa Fe	25 1/2	100	2,550.00	1.45	145.00	5.7	21 3/8	(4 1/8)	(412.50)	2.88
NYSE	Southern Pacific	25	100	2,500.00	1.20	120.00	4.8	23 5/8	(1 3/8)	(137.50)	2.83
NYSE	Union Pacific	32 1/8	100	3,212.50	1.60	160.00	5.0	30 3/8	(1 3/4)	(175.00)	3.63
	Trucking									
OC	Consolidated Freightways	11 1/8	100	1,112.50	—	—	—	12 1/4	1 1/8	112.50	1.25
OC	Merchants Fast Motor Lines	31 5/8	100	3,162.50	.67	67.00	2.1	23	(8 5/8)	(862.50)	3.58
OC	Pacific Inner Mountain Express	12 1/4	100	1,225.00	.65	65.00	5.3	14 5/8	2 3/8	237.50	1.38
	Trucks									
NYSE	Mack Trucks Inc.	43	100	4,300.00	1.80	180.00	4.2	34	(7)	(700.00)	4.86
	Utilities-Electric & Gas									
OC	Central Maine Power	31 7/8	100	3,187.50	1.60	160.00	5.0	35 1/4	3 3/8	337.50	3.60
NYSE	Niagara Mohawk Power	43 3/4	100	4,375.00	1.80	180.00	4.1	43 3/4	—	—	4.95
OC	Public Service of NM	32 3/8	100	3,237.50	.68	68.00	2.1	33 1/2	1 1/8	112.50	3.66
NYSE	Rochester Gas & Elec.	26 5/8	100	2,662.50	1.80	180.00	6.7	24 7/8	(1 3/4)	(175.00)	3.01
NYSE	Columbia Gas System	26 1/2	100	2,650.00	1.10	110.00	4.2	24 3/4	(1 3/4)	(175.00)	3.00
	Water									
OC	General Waterworks	25 3/8	100	2,537.50	3%	stock	3.0	25 1/4	(1/8)	(12.50)	2.87
	Total			$88,312.50		$2,850.00	3.22%			$10,937.50	100.00%

for a long-term growth portfolio. Moore-Handley, Drug and Food Capital, and Sorg were good companies, but others in the same industry were stronger competitively than the three. Armstrong Cork in the building industry, Smith Kline & French in the drug industry, and Scott in the paper industry would have better suited Morton's needs. It is wise, even though growth is emphasized, to insist upon the best quality in the common stocks that are chosen. In a weak and indecisive stock market, strength in the securities selected is of the utmost importance. This was the type of market in which Morton was investing.

Morton also ignored his tax position. He was in the 72 percent income-tax bracket. His income from his fund was about $2,850. After taxes he would have $798 remaining from his investment account to add to his current income or to reinvest. This was not a part of his portfolio objective. He was receiving too much income from his portfolio and not enough growth. Again he should have spent time examining the possibility of low-yielding stocks that would provide growth, such as those companies listed in Table 23–2. Morton might have been wise too if he had considered tax-exempt securities for his portfolio needs. A portion of his fund could have been invested in municipal bonds that would offer a much higher after-tax income than he received. If the income was reinvested, he would have been in an excellent position to build up his estate. At the same time he would have put a more defensive characteristic in his investment portfolio to hedge his long-range position in the market.

Morton had a tax loss on his portfolio, as of September, 1962, which might have had an impact upon what he did with his investments. Since he had a net loss of over $10,000, it might have been wise for him to engage in some tax switching operations. That is, he could have sold some of the securities that were below the purchase price. This would establish a tax loss. Then he could have purchased securities in similar industries that would offer growth. He might have taken criticisms to heart and bought the securities that would help him to achieve his objectives. He should have compared the alternatives of the companies he owned with companies he might have purchased. The growth possibility of Florida Power and Light, for example, was better than the growth possibilities of the Santa Fe at the time. Taking a tax loss at the time would lower his personal tax without jeopardizing his long-term investment position.

In summarization, Mr. Morton should have improved the quality of his portfolio by selecting the larger, more competitive companies. He should have improved his growth position and tax position by switching out of income securities into capital growth securities and by investing in some tax-exempt municipals. His portfolio was well diversified, but not all of it was in growth securities. This case reflects, in a limited way, the problems encountered when the portfolio management is taken over by an experienced executive but an inexperienced investor.

THE CASE OF A WELL-ROUNDED, SPECULATIVE CAPITAL GAINS PORTFOLIO

The investor is often called upon to select a group of stocks with the characteristics that should lead to capital gains. The investment portfolio of Mr. Morton was criticized because it was not completely invested in growth stocks. What, we may ask, does a growth portfolio look like when it has sufficient securities that should lead to capital gains? Clark Dodge provided one solution to the more speculative capital gains portfolio for its clients in September of 1962. They said: "While this is an interesting portfolio for the particular purpose, it should not be construed as a general model. . . ."[7] The portfolio appears in Table 23–6.

The portfolio selects the growth industries such as utility, finance, insurance, office equipment, electronics, aerospace, and drugs and cosmetics. The oil and gas and miscellaneous would generally be considered speculative growth industries. The companies considered in these two categories are in a sense special situations designed to lead to capital gains. Clark Dodge explains its position with respect to two of the companies:

> The chief attraction of Western Natural Gas is its assumed candidacy for sellout, which last year resulted in the stock's selling 75% above the current market. The contention that Western will be sold is bolstered by two factors. (1) The company has sold its Venezuelan and Canadian properties representing much of its long term potential and (2) El Paso Natural Gas, which owns 20% of Western, will probably have to make substantial refunds next year when the FPC settles its rate cases and only will regard this holding as a source of cash.
>
> Sanders Associates, among the smaller electronics companies, has a well established reputation for high technical competence and has been a favorite of our electronics specialist. Sales and earnings for the year ended last July advanced 100% and for the current fiscal year the company predicts that sales will increase further by over 50% and will, therefore, exceed $60 million; the current order backlog is over $100 million. Earnings should rise over 30% to at least $1.70 per share, on the basis of which the stock, at 35, is selling at about 20 times estimated earnings. Listing on the New York Stock Exchange is under consideration.[8]

The speculative growth portfolio is more immediate for its attempts

7 *$200,000 for Capital Gains* (New York: Clark Dodge & Co., Inc., September 17, 1962), p. 1.

8 *$200,000 for Capital Gains*, p. 1.

to obtain capital gains. Yet stocks have been used that are basically growth stocks with an expectation of a market price increase. The speculative capital gain portfolio is much more market oriented than a more defensive, conservative growth portfolio.

TABLE 23–6

A speculative capital gains portfolio[a]

SHARES		1961–1962 RANGE	PRICE	DIV.	YIELD	COST	%	INCOME
	Utility							
400	Tampa Electric	51–29	37	$ .80	2.2%	$ 14,800	7	$ 320
	Finance							
350	James Talcott	62–29	43	1.00	2.3	15,000	7	350
	Insurance							
100	Travelers	174–92	144	1.60	1.1	14,400		160
175	Transamerica	52–27	40	.80[c]	2.0	7,000		140
	Total					$ 21,400	11	$ 300
	Oil & Gas							
500	Belco	25–12	13	.50	3.8	6,500		250
3,000	Medallion Petroleum	3–1.50[b]	2.25[b]	—	—	6,250		—
150	Texas Gulf Producing	53–28	42	.80	1.9	6,300		120
500	Western Natural Gas	21–11	12	.25	2.1	6,000		125
	Total					$ 25,050	12	$ 495
	Office Equipment							
50	IBM	607–300	384	3.00	0.8	19,200	10	150
	Electronics & Aerospace							
250	Litton Industries	76–38	62	1.50	2.5	15,500		—
200	Sanders Associates	54–20	35	0.80	0.2	7,000		16
250	United Aircraft	56–37	49	2.00	4.1	12,250		500
	Total					$ 34,750	17	$ 516
	Drug & Cosmetic							
150	Avon Products	107–58	80	1.20	1.5	12,000		180
200	Bristol-Myers	103–60	78	1.30	1.7	15,600		260
	Total					$ 27,600	14	$ 440
	Miscellaneous							
100	Chrysler	62–38	59	1.00	1.7	5,900		100
80	Corning Glass	195–105	173	2.00	1.2	13,800		160
300	Dymo Industries	38– 8	22	—	—	6,600		—
200	Paramount	62–63	31	1.00[c]	3.2	6,200		200
100	Singer Mfg.	129–63	110	3.00	2.7	11,000		300
	Total					$ 43,500	22	$ 760
						$201,200	100	$2,931

a While the statistics and statements contained herein have been obtained from sources we believe to be reliable, we do not guarantee them.
b Canadian funds.
c Stock dividend.

SOURCE: *$200,000 for Capital Gains* (New York: Clark Dodge & Co., Inc., September 17, 1962), p. 2.

The growth portfolio emphasizes safety of principal and quality and at the same time stresses capital gains, because of a tax problem or because of a desire on the part of the investor to preserve capital and to provide greater income in the future. The growth securities that the conservative investor would select are similar to those in the speculative portfolio that was discussed. However there would be better balance in the portfolio between industries, even though it would continue to stress common stock. The common stocks selected would follow a no-cash dividend policy, a stock dividend, a modest cash dividend, or a combination of both cash and stock. The securities selected would be leading companies in the industry and would have the qualities of growth discussed previously.

The growth portfolio in Table 23–7 could be used as a pattern for the growth investor. Certainly the individual issues could be changed,

TABLE 23–7

*Suggested portfolio for the conservative
growth investor*

INDUSTRY & COMPANY	1961–1962 PRICE RANGE	PRICE	DIVIDEND	YIELD	PERCENT OF THE PORTFOLIO
Utility-Electric					*18%*
Arizona Public Service	44–34	37	$ .80	2.2%	6
Florida Power & Light	87–59	75	1.12	1.5	6
Houston Lighting	128–87	119	1.60	1.3	6
Telephone					*18%*
American Tel. & Tel.	140–103	108	3.60	3.4	9
General Tel. & Electronics	33–24	26	.76	2.9	9
Industrial					*64%*
Aerospace					*8%*
Martin Marietta	31–22	26	1.00	3.8	8
Finance					*8%*
James Talcott	62–29	43	1.00	2.3	8
Drug & Cosmetic					*8%*
G. D. Searle	151–66	135	1.60	1.2	4
Smith Kline & French	77–46	71	1.25	1.8	4
Electronics					*8%*
Litton Industries	76–38	54	Stock	2.5	8
Insurance					*8%*
Hartford Fire Insurance	90–57	78	1.10	1.4	8
Leisure Time					*8%*
Hertz	69–39	39 1/2	1.20	3.0	8
Office Equipment					*8%*
IBM	607–300	384	3.00	.8	4
Xerox	172–94	145	.40	.3	4
Publishing					*8%*
Prentice-Hall, Inc.	50–28	28	.40	1.4	8

but the construction and emphasis would be similar. The size of the fund would have an impact upon the number of industries and the number of companies that would be included. The portfolio, as presented, would be desirable for a $100,000 to $300,000 fund. If the fund were larger, more diversification would be needed. If it were smaller than $100,000, the industrial diversification would be kept, but the number of companies would be reduced. The portfolio has flexibility in terms of its usefulness to the large or small investor.

The condition of the stock market and the continued success of the companies would determine if they would remain in the portfolio. The portfolio is not timeless; it must be considered in the light of the general market conditions. When this portfolio was suggested, the market had just had a severe downward adjustment. In late 1962, the economic forecasts suggested little or no improvement in the national economy in 1963. Any growth pattern that was established would be considered within this frame of reference. Some investors would suggest a more conservative approach—perhaps 25 to 50 percent of the account in fixed-income securities such as bonds or tax-exempt municipals. The criteria used in establishing the portfolio in Table 23–7 precluded debt. The assumption was made that over the long term we would see a continued use in the stock market.

The technical considerations involved in the selection of the portfolio revolved about security, diversification, and balance among the growth companies. The public utilities were chosen because of their excellent past record of growth and their future expected rate. Florida, Texas, and the Southwest have been the fastest growing segments of the country. The telephone industry was selected not only because of being a growth industry but because of its future in world and space communication. The various industries and companies were selected simply because they offered, at the time, the best expectation for growth of any of the industries in our economy. The expectation of yield to maturity for each company would be approximately 10 percent from 1962 to 1967. The balance in the portfolio was arbitrary. However, the 36 percent in electric public utilities and telephones was done as a defensive measure. The 64 percent in selected industrial companies was for aggressive action in a rising market. These were some of the leading companies in the United States. If such a portfolio had been put together at attractive prices in 1962, the investor would have had an excellent growth portfolio—or would he? How would the investor have done if he had purchased all the stocks and in the suggested amounts? The portfolio, if it had remained untouched, would have a value of 155 percent of the base year period. This provided a capital growth for the period of slightly less than 8 percent per annum. When current dividends are added to this figure, the yield was close to 11 percent.

The Conservative Growth Portfolio

The current yield on the basis of original cost was close to 3 percent. Eight of the companies lost amounts ranging from 5 to 39 percent of value. Seven gained substantially, in amounts ranging from 12 to 858 percent of original cost. The portfolio did meet the original expectations of 10 percent. Performance could have been improved over the period by elimination of stocks that performed poorly. The stockholder did well, but he could have done better with management.

THE CASE OF THE ANXIOUS ANALYST

Bob Martin, a 35-year-old New York investment analyst, was concerned about his finances and his investment portfolio. He had just suffered a loss in the stock market; and even though he was an experienced investment analyst, he was concerned about his next move.

At the time, Martin had an income of $14,000, and he lived in an attractive $37,000 home in the suburbs with his wife and three young boys, aged 9, 7, and 5.

His life insurance program amounted to approximately $50,000 of ordinary life and term insurance with a cash surrender value of approximately $1,400. He and his family were in good health, his job was secure, and eventually he would make $20,000 a year.

He could not expect any inheritance from his family nor from his wife's family, and he was dependent upon his own abilities to provide for his family's needs. He owned two automobiles, one to get him back and forth to the station and a second one, the family station wagon. It was a 1960 Ford and there was a bank loan on it.

His house had a $20,000 mortgage, and he was able to meet the payments of principal, interest, and taxes easily from his current income.

In the past two years he was able to put aside about $750 a year into the securities market. Unfortunately, he had made several loans to purchase additional stock, and owed the bank in his town $3,000.

His investment portfolio consisted of several rather speculative securities that he had bought when the market was high and held in the market decline of 1961–1962. In that decline, he had lost approximately 33 percent of the value of his investment funds, which brought the value of his shares down below the value of the loans in which they were secured. The bank, however, did not press for payment.

Martin maintained an adequate balance in his checking account and also had his current obligations under control. His balance sheet and portfolio appear in Table 23–8.

This was an unfortunate case of an investor buying growth securities that did not possess the qualities a conservative growth investor would want in a portfolio. Even though he was a professional analyst, he violated certain basic investment principles. In essence, he was an anxious investor who attempted to obtain quick profits in the market

TABLE 23–8

*Analyst Martin's speculative growth portfolio
and balance sheet*

SHARES	COMPANY	PURCHASE PRICE	PRICE OCTOBER 1962	VALUE OCTOBER 1962
27 1/2	American Automatic Vending	$10	$ 8	$ 220
13	American Financial	23	14	182
41	Arkansas Valley Industries	21	17	697
70	Hallicrafter	19 1/2	11	770
50	Rocket Power	7	3 1/2	175
				$2,044

*Balance Sheet of Bob Martin
(October, 1962)*

Cash	$ 300	Bank loan	$ 3,000
Retirement fund	4,100	Life insurance loan	800
Life insurance	1,400	Current bills	600
Stocks & bonds	2,044	Auto & furniture loan	1,600
Autos	1,800	Mortgage	20,000
Furniture & personal	9,000	Net worth	29,644
House	37,000		
Total assets	$55,644	Total liabilities	$55,644

rather than to emphasize the long-term, quality growth stocks. He was very anxious to build a fund to educate his young children, but in his eagerness to obtain an investment fund he became heavily indebted. His overzealous desire for gain actually put him in a position where he lost a great deal of money.

What can we recommend to our anxious investor? First, he would have been wise in spite of the loss to liquidate his investment account and improve his fundamental financial position. In other words, a reduction of debt was in order. Fortunately, the loss that he sustained can be written off against income taxes, which will soften the impact. Once he paid off the debt, he should have attempted to establish an investment program that was much more conservative. If he selected common stocks, they should have been quality stocks that sold at an attractive price-earnings ratio in relation to future expected earnings and offered an attractive yield to maturity. He should have added to the fixed-income portion of his portfolio before he attempted ownership securities. He was not in a tax bracket that suggested that the income tax was a burden. So as new funds were made available from his income, he would have used these to build up his portfolio and eventually provide the basis for a college education for his children, his basic objective.

Summary

The concept of growth is familiar to almost all investors. The growth company is one that is growing in sales and earnings faster than than the national economy. It is assumed that the rate of growth will continue in the future. Another characteristic of the growth company is its noncash dividend policy. Money is needed for reinvestment within the business to provide for the necessary expansion of facilities. The yields on such investments are usually better than yields that could be earned elsewhere. The investor who purchases growth shares is interested in future income and capital gains and not present returns. The investor in a high income-tax bracket or one who wishes to build an estate would be interested in a growth company. The valuation of growth shares was emphasized in Chapter 7. The problem is one of estimating future yields, and risk. Again, the stability of earnings or yield is the basic measure of risk. The examples of companies for potential growth presented in the first edition were found to be growth companies because of the substantial yield realized between 1963 and 1968.

Several cases were presented that demonstrated the position of various growth investors. The case of investing $20,000 for Dr. Harris demonstrated the whole investment process as well as some of the personal problems involved in investing. A solution was presented for Dr. Harris that would provide him with growth in the future. Mr. Morton's problem was somewhat more complex. He had put together a large fund with growth as his object. Yet some of the companies were not in the growth category. Morton could afford to be a growth investor, but he could have invested more wisely in growth stocks or even in tax-exempt municipal securities. The yield on his portfolio was too high for his tax bracket, and he could have improved the quality of his holdings. Mr. Martin was too speculative in his investment program.

The Clark Dodge speculative capital gains portfolio emphasized capital gains in the near term. It was not given as a general pattern to follow but only to illustrate one solution that was considered to be a good capital gains portfolio. Most of the securities used were from growth companies. The conservative growth portfolio presented a pattern for establishing a less speculative growth portfolio. The securities used in such a portfolio will vary, but the basic form and diversification of the portfolio serve as a basic guide for the growth investor. The conservative growth portfolio actually bettered the expected 10 percent yield with a 10 percent surplus. One half of the companies lost money, but the gains overshadowed the losses. The construction of the growth portfolio indicated that we must adhere to the principles of diversification to be successful.

Review Questions

1. What do we generally mean by the term *growth stock?*
2. Explain what a *growth investor* is.
3. What types of securities, companies, and industries are typically put into the growth category?
4. Review the case of Dr. Paul Harris. What was his basic investment problem? Do you agree with the solution?
5. Examine the case of George Morton and explain his investment needs and objectives. Comment upon his solution to his problem. What are the weaknesses of his position? What are the strengths?
6. What were Bob Martin's investment position and his needs? Did the securities he chose fit his objectives? What did he do wrong?
7. What is the difference between a speculative capital gains portfolio and a conservative growth portfolio?
8. What part does expected yield and stability of yield play in the valuation of growth stock and the establishment of a growth stock portfolio?

Problems

1. Bring the portfolio of George Morton up to date from the September, 1962, period.
   (a) How many shares of each security does he now have?
   (b) What is the total value of each security?
   (c) What is the gain or loss on the portfolio?
   (d) What is the total value of the fund and the total gain or loss?
   (e) What is the dividend yield of each company?
   (f) Indicate the amount of money that would be received each month.
   (g) What is the total yield from the portfolio?
   (h) What was the total yield on Mr. Morton's portfolio from September, 1962, until the present?
   (i) Indicate the securities, if any, that Mr. Morton should sell and tell why.
   (j) What new securities should Mr. Morton purchase, and why?
2. Bring the conservative growth portfolio in Table 23–7 up to date. Answer the questions in 1 (a) through 1 (j) above for this portfolio.
3. Establish a better portfolio to meet Mr. Morton's needs. Defend your position. Provide a complete set of data similar to the information required in questions 1 and 2.

Sources of Investment Information

>   Analyses previously completed
>   Annual reports
>   *Barron's*
>   *Business Week*
>   *Clark Dodge Investment Survey*
>   *Commercial and Financial Chronicle*
>   *Forbes*
>   *Fortune*
>   Moody's manuals
>   *Newsweek*
>   Standard & Poor's *Investment Surveys*
>   Standard & Poor's *The Outlook*
>   Standard & Poor's *Stock Guide*
>   *The Value Line Investment Survey*
>   *Time*
>   *Wall Street Journal*

Selected Readings

Jones, Charles H., Jr., "The Growth Rate Appraiser," *Financial Analysts Journal* (September-October, 1968), p. 109.

Molodovsky, Nicholas, "Growth Stocks: A Note," *Financial Analysts Journal* (September-October, 1968), p. 103.

24

INVESTMENT OBJECTIVES OF INSTITUTIONAL INVESTORS

We might be called upon to act in the capacity of investment analyst or adviser to an institutional investor. In our capacity as an individual acting for an institution we must be aware of the investment requirements that are to be met. We are investing other people's money and not our own. A great deal of similarity exists in the investment process of the institutional and the individual investor. The methodology and investment process should be the same even though investment policies of institutions differ markedly from the objectives of the individual. The life insurance investment manager is concerned with safety of principal and is limited by law almost completely to investment in high-quality government, municipal, and corporate bonds and real estate mortgages. Most individuals would not be as singular in their investment objectives and portfolio plans. A casualty company, on the other hand, will invest in common stock. Since there are bound to be differences among the institutional investors with regard to their investment policies and practices and since an individual must adapt himself to the management of institutional portfolios, we should spend a few brief moments in understanding institutional investment activities.

This area of investment is growing rapidly, particularly in its new emphasis on variable annuities, and the growth of mutual funds and of the life insurance-mutual fund company. This chapter serves only as a brief introduction to the subject. Students and investors who are interested may pursue it further with the selected readings that appear at the end of the chapter.

The institutional investor represents a powerful force in our industrial and financial community. In one sense, he dominates the investment and financial market. The investment managers of the institutional investment accounts, because of the funds they control, collectively possess a latent power over the management of the corporations owned. This is not, however, the objective of the investment manager of these funds. The objective is not power or control but earning a satisfactory return on the investment consistent with the stated objectives.

Life Insurance Companies

The Business of Life Insurance Companies and the Source of Funds

The business of the life insurance company is to protect the individual if a person should die. Protection is also provided, if the insured lives, by the buildup of the cash value of the policy. Life insurance offers two promises to the purchaser: an estate if the insured should die, and an estate if the insured should live. A premium in exchange for his protection is paid by the insured. Premiums represent the major source of income of the life insurance company. The premium income is used to pay for the expenses of the operation of the company. In the life insurance industry these expenses are referred to as loading charges and represent the first item of expense in establishing the premium.

A portion of the premium is used to pay death claims to the beneficiaries of the insured. The payment of death claims, the second item of expense, varies from year to year. Over a period of time, the number of people insured who die out of 100,000, or any larger number, can be determined accurately. The number of deaths per year and the amount of death claims paid is an important determinant of the amount of the premium an individual must pay. As a person becomes older, the life span is shortened and the possibility of death becomes greater. The premium for an older person must be larger to provide funds for the increased costs of paying these claims.

The third major item of expense that makes up the premium is the reserve. The reserve is a sum of money that accumulates each year for the benefit of the life insurance policy of the insured. The amount paid into the reserve from premiums each year plus the income earned from the investment of the reserve funds must be sufficient to provide the face value of the policy when the policy matures. Under an ordinary life policy, maturity would be at age 100, based upon the Commissioners Standard Ordinary Mortality Table. A 10-year, 20-year, 30-year, or fully paid-up life at age 65 would also mature at age 100, but is paid up at an earlier date. Enough money in each of these policies would be paid into the reserve so that the fund plus investment income would equal the face value of the policy at age 100. The endowment policy has a much higher premium because it usually endows or has a cash value equal to the face value much before age 100. Both ordinary life and endowment policies have a cash value. Term insurance has no reserve and no savings feature, so there is no investment aspect associated with this type of policy.

The reserve that is built up to allow the life insurance policy to endow at age 100 is invested at an assumed rate of return. The rate is guaranteed by the insurance company, but it does vary from time to time. Once the guaranteed rate is established, it does not change while the policy is in force. If the rate of return earned on the premium reserve exceeds the guaranteed rate, or if management expenses are lower than estimated, or if the mortality rate is lower than expected, the surplus funds will be used for the benefit of the policy owner or the stockholder. Usually the life insurance company builds up a contingency reserve fund to compensate for the variation in management expenses, death benefits, and earnings on the reserve fund. If the contingency reserve exceeds the amount determined by management as necessary to meet its contingencies, it may be paid to the owners of a stock company as a dividend. If it is a mutual company, the policy holders are the owners, and they will receive the dividend. In a stock company, the policy owners and the stockholders are separated. The owners receive the dividends, and the policy owners receive only the contractual, guaranteed rate of return on their invested reserves. This rate is usually stated in the contract. The dividends to the policy owner in the mutual company are usually quite substantial. The premiums paid to the mutual company, however, are somewhat larger than the premiums paid by the policy owner of a stock company.

Most life insurance companies offer accident and health insurance along with the various life insurance contracts. The accident and health policies provide for payment of income and medical fees while a person is disabled. The premiums must cover this risk. It is difficult actually to determine in advance the number of people who will become ill or disabled. Each company must establish its own experience in paying claims and establish premiums for this type of business. The funds obtained from the premiums are invested by the company to provide additional funds to meet the risks assumed. At the present time, the amount of premium income from accident and sickness and health insurance is a small portion of the revenues of most life insurance companies. The premium income from the sales of life insurance dominates as the major revenue source of the life insurance company.

INVESTMENT OBJECTIVES OF LIFE INSURANCE COMPANIES

The establishment of investment objectives of the life insurance company reflects the source of its funds. Investment objectives reflect also the commitment the company has made about the funds placed in the custody of the company by the policy owners. Since the policy agreement states that interest on reserves will be guaranteed, the life insurance company must invest in securities or investments that provide stable income equal to or higher than the guaranteed rate of interest on the reserves. The income must be stable since the guarantee given by the life insurance company remains in force for the life of the policy. Investments that provide fixed income for a long period of time, such as government and corporate bonds and mortgages, provide excellent outlets for funds of the life insurance company.

Liquidity. The need for liquidity as a major factor in life insurance company investment management is negligible. Liquidity is provided through the regularity of receipt of premium income. The premium usually covers management expenses and cash disbursements in the form of death benefits and other payments. The funds that remain go to increase the reserves of the company. Since this money need not be paid until a later date, the funds can be invested in securities that do not possess a great degree of liquidity. The insurance company, to remain fully invested, can and does invest a substantial amount of funds in real estate mortgages. Long-term bonds that will be held to maturity also provide an excellent investment for the insurance companies, as a group.

Time Period. The investment function as it exists in the life insurance company is long term rather than short term. The nature of reserves and the obligations of life companies necessitate a long-term investment policy. Only a small portion of life insurance company investments are short term, except for long-term securities that are approaching maturity. The average investment period for an insurance company is much longer than the average period for the individual investor. Because the life insurance company has a long-term investment program, it can purchase long-term bonds to hold to maturity. Life insurance companies can buy entire issues of bonds from small and medium-sized industrial corporations that are attempting to raise long-term capital. The life insurance company negotiates directly with the company seeking funds. Private placements, as they are called, provide relatively low-cost capital. These issues are exempt from registration with the Securities and Exchange Commission and one of the accompanying costs of obtaining capital is eliminated. The interest cost on these securities tends to be only slightly higher than the market rate of interest.

Regulation of Investment Objectives. The life insurance companies are limited in their investment activities by comprehensive state regulations designed to protect the policy owner. They are coordinated through the commissioners of insurance within each state. The regulation of life insurance investment activities is comparable to the regulation of trusts. Some states apply the prudent man rule of investment to life insurance investment. Other states provide a list of securities that can legally be owned for investment by life insurance companies and trust funds. Most states provide some control over investment policy. The usual restrictions govern the quality and type of investment the life insurance company can make. Investment is limited to the highest quality bonds in the first four ratings based upon the ratings of Moody's and Standard & Poor's services. Thus, bonds cannot be purchased below a Baa rating, must meet minimum standards of safety, and must not be speculative. Life insurance companies are permitted to invest in real estate mortgages; these and bonds make up the bulk of life insurance company investments. The amount invested in common stock is limited to a small percent of the total funds, expressed as a percent of investable funds or surplus, usually less than 5 percent of the total. State regulations strictly enforce the common-stock rule.

In recent years some states have allowed life insurance companies to sell variable annuity contracts for retirement programs through life insurance rather than the fixed-annuity contract under the usual insurance company retirement program. The fixed-income annuity provides a fixed income for life or for a certain number of years and is limited to investment in fixed-income securities. The funds under the variable annuity contract can be invested partially in common stocks; its major advantage is its ability to provide against the risk of inflation. The correlation between a rising price level and the rising stock market level is not perfect, however, and the variable annuity is not a perfect answer to inflation. The amount invested in common stock will be determined by the contract and the regulatory agency. Variable annuity contracts are not numerous.

Only a small proportion of the total assets of life insurance companies are invested in common stocks. The very nature of the life insurance contract and the instability of common stocks precludes such ownership for the majority of insurance companies. But the amount of common stock as a percentage of total investments owned by life insurance companies has steadily increased from 1957 to 1968. Table 24–1 reflects this growth. Common stock as a percentage of assets increased from 3.3 to 5.2 percent, reflecting the "aggressive" investment policy of life insurance companies in recent years and the liberalization of regulatory agencies. An interesting parallel is the growth of policy loans of life insurance companies from 1957 to 1968. They increased from 3.8 to 5.8 per cent of total assets. This reflects an increased demand for policy loans of all types. During the period, policy loan interest rates remained relatively low, although other interest rates rose. Many policy loans were made at that time so that the policy owner could invest the proceeds in the stock market.

Risk Taking. The life insurance company is not in a position to assume risk. Risk taking is forbidden by state regulation and is precluded by the need for stable income and principal values. The purchasing-power risk is shifted to the policy owner, as the company deals only in dollar claims.

The money rate risk is also a minor problem for the insurance company. Money rates do, of course, change from day to day. There are two ways in which management can compensate for changes in yields. First, the investments can be allowed to reach maturity, which will prevent a loss of principal even if a loss of interest income occurs. The life insurance policies sold tend to reflect the current level of interest rates. If, for example, the market rate of interest is 4 percent, a 2 1/4 percent rate is guaranteed on invested reserves of the life insurance company. Money invested at the time will earn 4 percent for a period of 20 to 25 years. The period is long enough to cover the guaranteed rate of interest and the bonds that are held to maturity. If in the next year the yields went to 6 percent and were expected to continue in effect, the insurance companies could increase the guaranteed rate to their policy owners to perhaps 2 1/2 percent. The new policies, therefore, would receive the higher yield and the old policies would continue to receive a guaranteed yield based upon the original contractual rate. The rate of interest in the market earned by the insurance company and the rate that is guaranteed to the policy owners are closely correlated. This condition of correlation between interest earned and interest received plus liquidity at maturity eliminates the problem of compensating for the changes in the money rate. A second way to compensate for money rate changes is to manage the bond portfolio carefully to take advantage of expected changes in yields. In this way the bond portfolio manager compensates for the money rate risk.

The fact that bond investment dominates the investment policy of life companies does not mean that risk is absent. Many investment managers play the pattern of rates aggressively and imaginatively. Some have had brilliant success in "playing" the bond market.

The business risk is not an important problem for most life insurance companies since they own few equity securities. The stability of income necessary to meet the life insurance commitment and the regulated aspect of the life insurance industry reduce to a minimum the business risk associated with ownership securities. The small amount of ownership securities held by most insurance companies is not sufficient to cause a catastrophic loss even if the total value of securities were wiped from the books.

The market risk is only a small problem for the insurance company since the bulk of the securities are not subject to the vicissitudes of the stock market. Again the nature of the life insurance contract and the regulation of investment policy provide a conservative policy of nonstock investment, which eliminates the problem of the stock market risk. In essence, the life insurance company is not prmitted to assume the stock market risk. This risk will become greater, however, as the amount of equity ownership in life insurance companies increases.

Taxation and Investment. Life insurance companies enjoy a partial exemption from federal income taxes, to prevent the investment income to the policy owner from being taxed twice. This assumes that all the income received by the company will eventually be paid to the policy owner. This is true of the mutual companies, but in the case of the stock companies all the money earned from investment above the liability reserve and the guaranteed dividend is paid to the stock owners. Since the earnings are paid to the stockholders, this removes them from the exempt category. There is some controversy over the income tax exemption of life insurance companies. The tendency, at present, is for taxes to be levied upon the income of insurance companies at increasingly higher rates. In the past, these companies gave little consideration to the impact of federal income taxes on their portfolio decisions because their earnings were almost completely tax exempt. The predominant asset owned by life insurance companies in 1957, 1963, and 1968, as can be seen in Table 24–1, was corporate bonds, with residential mortgages a close second. Municipal bonds, with their tax advantage, were only a a small portion of their investments. However, as the companies' income is taxed more heavily, we shall probably see more and more of their funds invested in tax-exempt municipals.

PORTFOLIO POLICY AND MANAGEMENT

The majority of life insurance companies follow a conservative, riskless, and defensive investment policy. High-quality bonds make up the bulk of their investments, and risk-type securities such as common

TABLE 24–1

Assets of life insurance companies, end of 1957,
1963, and 1968 (millions of dollars and
percent of total)

	1957		September, 1963		March, 1968	
	DOLLARS	PERCENT OF TOTAL	DOLLARS	PERCENT OF TOTAL	DOLLARS	PERCENT OF TOTAL
Government securities:						
United States	7,029	6.9	5,384	4.2	4,582	2.6
State and local	2,376	2.3	3,892	2.8	3,007	1.7
Foreign	1,285	1.3	2,713	2.0	2,973	1.7
Total	10,690	10.5	12,429	9.0	10,562	6.0
Business securities:						
Bonds	40,666	40.1	53,357	38.5	66,412	37.0
Stocks	3,391	3.3	5,562	4.0	9,348	5.2
Total	44,057	43.4	58,919	42.5	75,760	42.2
Mortgages	35,236	34.8	49,233	35.5	68,055	37.9
Real estate	3,119	3.1	4,339	3.1	5,263	2.9
Policy loans	3,869	3.8	6,585	4.7	10,362	5.8
Other assets	4,338	4.3	7,259	5.2	9,475	5.3
Total assets	101,309	100.0	138,764	100.0	179,477	100.0

SOURCE: *Federal Reserve Bulletin*, December, 1963, p. 1687; and June, 1968, p. A36.

stock are a small portion of total investment funds. Some life insurance companies in managing a portfolio will trade their securities to take advantage of changes in interest rates. Some will purchase bonds with lower bond ratings to improve their investment yield. The basic policy of life insurance company investment is buy and hold, even though some trading takes place. This policy is expressed in the mortgage investments of life insurance companies and in private placements. The bonds purchased are usually held to maturity. At the same time, a few life companies have become much more sophisticated in their investment practices. Some have adopted excellent computer techniques for the selection of common stocks. Travelers and Nationwide are two companies that have done excellent work in this area. In addition, life insurance companies are managing pension funds in increasing amounts, where performance and results are found more and more important than on the basic life insurance contract. The life insurance company must perform comparable results on pension trusts if they are to be competitive. Life insurance companies have become more aggressive in competing with other institutional investors, such as mutual funds, for the savings and investment dollar of the consumer. Many life insurance companies merged or acquired mutual fund companies in the late 1960's so that they could compete.

The investment function centers on the new money and maturing investment that comes in each day, that must be invested. Diversification of corporate bond investments is maintained by industry and company. Maturities of security investments are staggered to provide a diversification of timing of maturities related to bonds and mortgages. Since common stock investment is not a major part of life insurance companies' investments, liquidity is obtained from continuing revenues and from investment income and is not a major problem in portfolio management. Carrying out the investment policy and objectives of the life insurance company is the responsibility of the company investment officers and a staff of investment analysts. The quality of management must be judged on the basis of conservative and qualitative standards imposed by the regulatory and the contractual conditions imposed upon the insurance companies. The investment returns for life insurance companies, independent of underwriting profits, are largely dependent upon the trend in rates of long-term debt and mortgage securities.

Fire and Casualty Companies

Nature of the Business

Fire and casualty companies sell insurance to cover the risk of loss of property or injury to people. Most companies insure against the usual insurable risks, such as property insurance, which includes fire, windstorm, hail, explosion, riot, and civil commotion, and casualty insurance, which includes injury to people in fire, storms, riots, and the like and injury to workmen, property damage, and auto damage. The fire and casualty insurance coverage is commonly associated with real property —the home and personal property in the form of the automobile. However, an extremely wide range of other real and personal property is covered. Specialty companies have been formed to provide coverage for auto insurance and marine insurance. Real property is usually insured up to 80 percent of its value. Personal property is insured for the full amount with the actual claim determined by the value of the property at the time of loss.

Estimating the amount of loss that will be sustained each year because of fire, windstorm, and automobile accidents is difficult. The premium paid by the insured is usually for a short period lasting from one to three years. The amount of the premium must cover the losses during the period of insurance and provide for the management expenses of the company. During some years, the premiums will be more than enough to cover all insurance costs; at the end of the year an underwriting profit will be realized. In other years premium income will not be adequate to cover the losses, and an underwriting loss will be suffered. A reserve fund to cover the years of underwriting loss must be maintained. The fund comes from previously accumulated profits and from the funds contributed by the owners of the insurance company. The reserve fund is necessary to protect the policy owners of the company.

Source of Funds and Investment Policy

The source of funds for investment by fire and casualty companies is the premiums collected in advance (the unearned premium reserve) and funds contributed by the owners. The investment policy of the fire and casualty company is determined by the nature of the business and by the source of funds. Generally, if the equity in the fire or casualty company is high, a large proportion of funds is invested in common stock. If the owners' equity is small, preferred stock and high-quality bonds will dominate the investment portfolio. Other factors have an impact on the investment of these companies. First, fire and casualty companies can accept greater risk than insurance companies because they are investing their own money rather than the money of the policy owners. This specifically refers to the policy reserves of the life insurance company; there is no comparable policy reserve in the fire and casualty company. Second, stability of income is not as important to the fire and casualty company as it is to the life insurance company. Therefore, the casualty companies can invest more heavily in common stocks. But there is a wide range in the investment policies of the fire and casualty companies: about 35 percent of their security investments are in common stocks.

Third, marketability and liquidity are more important for the fire and casualty company than the life insurance company. Securities might and can be sold to meet underwriting costs and losses. This is true even though underwriting profits are kept within the business and income from investment is paid out to the stockholders. Fourth, one of the risks assumed by the fire and casualty company is the risk of inflation. Inflation has had an adverse effect upon underwriting costs and has placed the fire and casualty companies in a position where they must compensate for the risk through common-stock investments. Fifth, the state laws governing fire and casualty company investments require that they invest a minimum proportion of their investments in high-grade bonds. The bulk of the investments may be invested at the discretion of the company and its investment management group. There are no stringent rules that apply to the fire and casualty companies comparable to those imposed upon the life insurance companies. The freedom of management and the fact that management is not inhibited should lead to higher returns on investment.

TYPE OF INVESTMENT POLICY

The investment policy of the fire and casualty company is aggressive rather than defensive compared to the life insurance company. It might be considered a managed aggressive policy, since the fund managers have almost complete discretion over the investment of funds. The biggest portion of the investable funds are placed in common stocks and government bonds. The bonds act as a reserve to meet the liabilities of the company and to provide liquidity; that is the defensive portion of the investment fund. The common-stock part of the investment fund is the aggressive portion, needed because of the risks assumed by the companies in this category.

In examining the policy and objectives of the fire and casualty company investment program, we begin with the conservative portion of the fund. The major portion of the investable funds is invested in well-known, high-quality industrial common stocks, preferred stocks, and government and municipal bonds. Generally, corporate debt obligations represent a small part of the total portfolio. The greatest portion is invested in federal, state, and local municipal obligations. Particularly strong interest is shown in municipal bonds because the interest income is exempt from federal income taxes. Since the fire and casualty companies do not enjoy special exemption from these taxes, they are interested in tax-exempt securities. The smallest portion of the investment funds of casualty companies is invested in preferred stock. In 1966, 84.0 percent of all fire and casualty company assets were invested in securities and 16.0 percent in other assets. About 46 percent of the investments were in corporate bonds and government and municipal securities, 35.3 percent in common stock, and 2.7 percent in preferred stocks. Table 24–2 reveals the asset composition of fire and casualty companies in 1966.

TABLE 24–2 (A)

Grand totals of 792 stock fire & casualty companies

ADMITTED ASSETS

			%	Dec. 31, 1966
BONDS: U. S. Government	13.8	$4,284,761,484		
Other government	0.7	207,304,759		
State, municipal, etc.	11.5	3,568,289,441		
Special revenue, etc.	14.5	4,500,220,567		
Railroad	0.3	89,808,350		
Utility	1.9	592,675,042		
Miscellaneous	3.3	1,020,735,569		
Total bonds			46.0	$14,263,795,212
COMMON STOCKS: Railroad	0.3	$ 93,539,807		
Utility	6.6	2,047,509,648		
Bank	2.6	819,923,650		
Insurance	7.8	2,405,032,418		
Savings and loan	0.1	19,431,451		
Miscellaneous	17.9	5,567,071,346		
Total common stocks			35.3	10,952,508,320
PREFERRED STOCKS: Railroad	0.1	$ 36,930,236		
Utility	1.6	478,749,412		
Bank	....	5,367,652		
Insurance	....	11,081,429		
Miscellaneous	1.0	301,464,279		
Total preferred stocks			2.7	833,593,008
Mortgages			0.2	66,241,850
Real estate			1.4	421,041,153
Collateral loans			....	16,475,131
Cash			3.1	978,281,765
Premium balances			7.5	2,323,116,212
Other assets			3.8	1,179,725,424
TOTAL ADMITTED ASSETS (Statement)			100.0	$31,034,778,075

LIABILITIES

Losses—Adjustment expenses		$ 8,680,739,901
Commissions, taxes, etc.		458,837,349
Federal income taxes		117,009,002
Unearned premiums		8,361,176,163
Rate and retrospective returns		116,248,996
Perpetual deposits		2,779,163
War shipping administration		45,757
Additional reserve noncancellable accident & health		19,692,506
Dividends to stockholders		61,975,241
Dividends to policyholders		56,664,440
Reinsurance treaty funds		469,057,166
Borrowed money		8,309,686
Other liabilities		410,592,222
Unauthorized reinsurance		172,853,060
Special reserves		36,202,462
Excess statutory loss reserves		55,873,436
Total liabilities		$19,028,056,550
Capital paid-up	$1,320,088,161	
Net surplus	8,388,339,900	
Voluntary reserves	2,298,293,464	
Policyholders' surplus (Statement)		12,006,721,525
TOTAL		$31,034,778,075

734

TABLE 24-2 (B)

Grand totals of 336 mutual companies

ADMITTED ASSETS

	%	Dec. 31, 1966
BONDS: U. S. Government	18.4	$1,756,545,047
Other government	0.7	68,335,639
State, municipal, etc.	17.4	1,662,420,216
Special revenue, etc.	16.3	1,550,583,304
Railroad	1.7	161,875,810
Utility	6.4	613,074,629
Miscellaneous	6.6	623,630,815
Total bonds	67.5	$6,436,465,460
COMMON STOCKS: Railroad	0.1	$ 13,807,505
Utility	2.7	257,731,900
Bank	1.2	109,227,694
Insurance	3.3	313,631,505
Savings and loan	0.1	5,696,198
Miscellaneous	8.4	803,025,305
Total common stocks	15.8	1,503,120,107
PREFERRED STOCKS: Railroad	0.1	$ 4,259,908
Utility	2.0	189,609,952
Bank	....	2,440,553
Insurance	0.1	7,782,639
Miscellaneous	0.7	70,402,919
Total preferred stocks	2.9	274,495,971
Mortgages	1.0	93,191,667
Real estate	2.3	223,019,694
Collateral loans	....	1,519,205
Cash	3.0	284,145,486
Premium balances	4.8	459,932,077
Other assets	2.7	255,500,195
TOTAL ADMITTED ASSETS (Statement)	100.0	$9,531,389,862

LIABILITIES

Losses—Adjustment expenses		$3,437,844,324
Commissions, taxes, etc.		163,439,364
Federal income taxes		30,542,339
Unearned premiums		2,267,968,210
Rate and retrospective returns		36,040,477
Perpetual deposits		8,918
Additional reserve non-cancellable accident & health		2,232,165
Unabsorbed premium deposits		59,838
Dividends to policyholders		57,024,510
Reinsurance treaty funds		98,745,271
Borrowed money		1,325,000
Other liabilities		156,765,840
Unauthorized reinsurance		20,482,839
Special reserves		98,546,646
Excess statutory loss reserves		264,389,050
Total liabilities		$6,635,414,791
Guaranty funds	$ 81,686,273	
Net surplus	2,485,273,250	
Voluntary reserves	329,015,548	
Policyholders' surplus (Statement)		2,895,975,071
TOTAL		$9,531,389,862

SOURCE: Best's *Fire and Casualty Aggregates and Averages* (New York: Alfred M. Best Company, Inc., 1966), pp. 54 and 152.

INVESTMENT MANAGEMENT OF FIRE AND CASUALTY
COMPANY FUNDS

The investment managers carry out their investment function with a relatively small staff. One Philadelphia fire and casualty company managed a $100,000,000 investment portfolio with a three-man investment staff and a board of directors that made the final decisions. They employed only one analyst. The bulk of their information and research was obtained from analysts employed by brokerage firms. This service was provided by the broker free of charge. It was assumed that when shares were purchased as a result of the research supplied by the broker, the brokerage house would be given the commission. The majority of fire and casualty company investments are managed by a research staff and managers, much the same as those of a life insurance company. The size of the department will vary with the size of the casualty company. Usually the investment department makes recommendations to the board of directors and does not assume the final authority in making the investment decision.

The quality of investment management of fire and casualty companies is difficult to determine based upon the limited information presented periodically by the company. The profit position of the company cannot be used as a criterion for successful management because of the impact of underwriting profits or losses upon earnings. Many companies suffer annual underwriting losses and prosper only because of their investment income. Since the dividends of a fire and casualty company are determined by the investment income, an increase in dividends might reflect a better investment performance, but this can be used only as a relative indication of investment success. Generally, the management of fire and casualty funds is undertaken by intelligent, experienced, and capable individuals who do a competent job of investment management.

Thrift Institutions—Savings and Loan Associations and Mutual Savings Banks

Savings and loan associations and mutual savings banks grew substantially between 1957 and 1968. Their growth is reflected in the asset and liability position of these institutions in Tables 24–3 and 24–4. The "thrift" companies receive money from depositors or owners and invest the funds for their benefit. One distinction between the mutual savings banks and the savings and loan associations is the type of ownership. The mutual savings banks are owned by the depositors, making them truly mutual in character. The depositors share in the earnings of the bank after all expenses, reserves, and surplus contributions have been

TABLE 24–3

*Assets and liabilities of savings and loan
associations (millions of dollars)*

ASSETS	1957	1963	1968
Mortgages	$40,007	$81,247	$124,306
U.S. Government obligations	3,173	6,087	9,821
Cash	2,146	3,809	2,772
Other	2,770	5,399	9,330
Total	$48,138	$96,542	$146,229

LIABILITIES			
Savings capital	$41,912	$83,446	$125,694
Reserves and undivided profits	3,363	6,583	9,556
Borrowed money	1,379	2,605	4,808
Loans in process	1,484	2,108	2,463
Other		1,800	3,708
Total	$48,138	$96,542	$146,229

SOURCE: *Federal Reserve Bulletin*, June, 1963, p. 821; and June, 1968, p. A36.

TABLE 24–4

*Assets of mutual savings banks (millions of
dollars and percent of total)*

	1957		September, 1963		April, 1968	
ASSETS	$	% OF TOTAL	$	% OF TOTAL	$	% OF TOTAL
Loans:						
Mortgages	$20,971	59.6	$34,964	71.4	$51,199	75.1
Other	253	0.7	667	1.3	1,267	1.8
Total	$21,224	60.3	$35,631	72.7	$52,466	76.9
Securities:						
U. S. Government	7,583	21.5		12.4	4,303	6.3
State and local	685	2.0		.9	221	.3
Corporate and other	4,344	12.3		10.5	9,113	13.4
Total	$12,612	35.8	$11,700	23.8	$13,637	20.0
Cash	889	2.5	848	1.8	871	1.3
Other assets	490	1.4	775	1.7	1,190	1.7
Total assets	$35,215	100.0	$48,955	100.0	$68,164	100.0
LIABILITIES						
Deposits	$31,683	90.0	$43,712	89.3	$61,554	90.3
Other liabilities	427	1.2	1,124	2.3	1,553	2.3
Surplus accounts	3,105	8.8	4,118	8.4	5,058	7.4
Total liabilities	$35,215	100.0	$48,955	100.0	$68,164	100.0

SOURCE: *Federal Reserve Bulletin*, December, 1963, p. 1686; and June, 1968, p. A35.

made. The mutual savings banks have no capital stock, and, as in the case of life insurance companies, the owners and depositors are one and the same. The interest paid on the money in the mutual savings bank is not a guaranteed rate. Earnings are determined at the end of the interest period, and the board of trustees declares an interest payment on the depositors' accounts based on these earnings. Mutual savings banks operate under the laws of the state in which they are chartered. They are located primarily in the East, with more than half in New York and Massachusetts; there are a few in the Middle West.

Most savings and loan associations are also mutual corporations in which the members' savings are technically invested in ownership shares. However, some are formed as private corporations and issue stock to the owners. The depositors are not owners in the stock company as they are in the mutual savings and loan association. Savings and loan associations may be federally chartered, or they may be chartered by the state. The federally chartered institution has two regular investment programs: the savings share account plan, a passbook account, and the investment share account plan, evidenced by a share certificate with a $100 par. The same dividend rate is paid on the balance in each type of account.

The Function of Thrift Institutions

The principal function of both the savings and loan associations and the mutual savings bank is to accumulate the savings of many people and to lend these savings safely and conservatively to other people for the purpose of buying, building, or improving real estate. The loans are usually a first mortgage on the property. Sometimes the savings and loan associations are referred to as building and loan companies, which adequately describes the functions performed. These institutions thus provide investors and owners with safe outlets for their funds, and homeowners with an adequate source of long term funds for the purchase of a home. Tables 24–3 and 24–4 indicate the sources and uses of funds and the direction investment takes.

Investment Policy of the Thrift Institution

Mutual savings banks invest almost all their funds in residential mortgages. Because they are permitted to invest in mortgages in other states, they have a significant impact on the mortgage market. Savings and loan associations invest predominantly in real estate mortgages, with the lending policies determined by their boards of directors. The investment policies of both the mutual savings banks and the savings and loan associations are governed by state and/or federal law depending upon the origination of their charter. The state usually limits the securities that may be purchased; most of the institutions are limited to the prudent man rule or to a legal list of investment-grade securities defined by the state. New York State, for example, includes first mortgages on real estate; federal, state, and municipal securities; railroad and public utility bond issues; stocks of trust companies if they are determined eligible by the banking board; and stocks of housing corporations. In the case of federally chartered **savings and loan associations**, the funds can be invested only in first mortgages on improved real estate. Surplus funds may be invested only in obligations of the United States or the Federal Home Loan Bank. Most of the mutual savings banks and savings and loan associations invest their surplus funds in state and municipal obligations.

Increased competition between the commercial banks and savings institutions may lead eventually to a broadening of the lending activities of the mutual banks and savings and loan associations. Legislation in 1962 allowed commercial banks to raise the interest rate paid in savings deposits to a point competitive with the interest paid by the savings banks. At the same time, the interest rate was raised on savings accounts in the mutual savings banks and savings and loan associations. Interest rates on mortgage loans were raised and more profitable outlets for their funds were sought. Current practice suggests that savings associations in the future, where they are legally permitted, will make more consumer loans, home improvement loans, and possibly loans to businesses.

Savings Banks and Their Investment Policy

Mutual savings banks and savings and loan associations do not invest in ownership securities; since they are dealing in dollar claims, there is no need to accept that risk. Security investments are confined to high-grade, fixed-income securities. The income from investments is taxable, and these companies are interested in and purchase tax-free municipal securities to improve their after-tax earnings. Although withdrawals from share accounts can be held up, the policy is established to meet withdrawals promptly, and meeting withdrawals on demand requires a certain degree of liquidity. With the greatest percentage of their assets in mortgages, it is important to have that liquidity provided by the federal, state, and municipal securities owned.

The overall investment policy of the savings and loan associations and mutual savings banks can be termed conservative, defensive and riskless investment with limited diversification in fixed-income debt securities. Competitive conditions in the industry suggest that the investment and lending function will broaden and become more inclusive in the future.

Commercial Bank Investment Policy

The Business of Commercial Banks

The primary purpose of a commercial bank is to make loans to business. The loans have usually been short term and have been made to finance the purchase of inventory or to obtain money to finance customers' receivables. In recent years longer-term loans have become more important to commercial banks. Essentially, the short-term loans made to businesses are working capital loans. The short-term commercial loan has traditionally been profitable for the commercial bank, and at the same time it has offered the bank liquidity. The profitability and liquidity aspect of the commercial loan fits admirably into the earning requirements of the commercial bank, whose fundamental problem is to provide liquidity in the short run and yet to maintain long-run profitability. Table 24–5 indicates the importance of loans in the overall assets of the commercial banks. Over half the earning assets of commercial banks in 1958, 1963 and 1967 were in the business loan category, an amount that increased to almost 65 percent in 1968. This reflected both a larger demand for loans and the higher interest rates that made these loans more profitable for the bank.

Table 24–5 also indicates that many of the loans are not of the

TABLE 24–5

Loans and investments of commercial banks, 1958,
1963, and 1967 (millions of dollars)

	1958		1963		1967	
	$	% OF TOTAL	$	% OF TOTAL	$	% OF TOTAL
LOANS[a]						
Commercial loans	$ 40,425	20.5	$ 49,862	20.7	$ 88,443	24.5
Agricultural loans	4,973	2.5	7,541	3.1	9,270	2.6
Security loans	4,661	2.4	6,878	2.9	9,995	2.8
Loans to financial institutions	719	.4	19,583	4.4	14,437	4.0
Real estate loans	25,255	12.8	36,725	15.2	58,525	16.2
Other loans to individuals	20,698	10.5	32,661	13.6	51,585	14.3
Other loans	3,437	1.7	3,812	1.6	5,659	1.6
Total	$110,168	50.9	$145,049	60.2	$233,180	64.6
INVESTMENTS						
U. S. Government:						
Bills	6,294	3.2	9,128	3.8	na[b]	
Certificates	7,399	3.8	3,216	1.3	na	
Notes	13,396	6.8	23,821	9.9	na	
Bonds	39,287	19.9	27,378	11.4	na	
Total	66,376	33.7	63,543	26.4	62,473	17.3
State & municipal	16,505	8.4	27,817	11.5	50,006	13.8
Other securities	4,070	2.1	4,606	1.9	11,471	3.2
Total	$ 86,951	44.1	$ 95,966	39.8	$123,950	34.3
Total loans & investments	$197,119	100.0	$241,015	100.0	$361,186	100.0

[a] Beginning with June 30, 1948, figures for various loans are shown gross (i.e., before deduction of valuation reserves); they do not add to the total and are not entirely comparable with prior figures. Total loans continue to be shown net.

[b] na = not available.

SOURCES: *Federal Reserve Bulletin*, December, 1963, p. 1678; April, 1962, p. 430; and June, 1968, p. A24.

commercial variety. Collectively, loans to individuals and real estate loans are more important as an earning asset to the bank than the traditional commercial loan. The composition of earning assets reflects the change that has come about in modern commercial banking systems. At one time a commercial bank was thought of as a businessman's bank. Today, it is for all people, including the consumer, the stockholder, the mortgage holder, and other financial institutions. The commercial banks are really "department store banks" and not just for the businessman. The newer fields of endeavor have been undertaken by commercial banks to improve both their earnings and their competitive position within the industry.

The other major earning asset of the commercial banks is their investment in debt securities. The business of the bank is to be liquid as well as profitable. The short-term securities in the investment account provide the degree of liquidity that is needed. The government securities act as a secondary reserve for the demand deposits of commercial banks and provide liquidity at the same time. The essential purpose of liquidity is meeting the demands for withdrawals from the depositors. Longer-term securities are purchased when the commercial banks' needs for liquidity are met.

The Source of Investment Funds

The source of funds over which the bank management exercises control comprises primarily time and demand deposits and the total capital retained through earnings and the sale of stock. The ratio between nongovernment demand deposits and bank capital varies. The commercial banking system as a whole maintains a ratio of deposits to capital of 5 to 1. The ratio of nongovernment demand deposits to total capital accounts was a little less than 5 to 1 in 1968. The ratio of total deposits to total capital account at the same time was a little over 10 to 1. This deposit figure included government, nongovernment, time, demand, and interbank deposits. Demand deposits are the major source of investable and loanable funds for the commercial banks; next in importance are time deposits, and finally ownership capital. The greatest increase in bank deposits in recent years has been from the growth of time deposits and certificates of deposit.

The increase in time deposits relative to demand deposits reflects one change our banking system has undergone in recent years. The savings function has improved in our financial system, whereas demand deposits have declined in relative importance, because of the increased competition for funds. Corporations that at one time retained idle funds on deposit in the commercial bank now invest in government securities to improve earnings. Corporate treasurers have become much more sophisticated in the handling of corporate funds, keeping the demand deposits of their company at a minimum and investing instead in short-term debt securities such as Treasury bills and the short maturities of municipal obligations. Rising interest rates have made other outlets for funds more attractive, savers have put their funds to work in savings accounts, and these changes have taken their toll of demand deposit growth. The commercial banking system, therefore, has not increased as rapidly as other segments of the financial system.

Determinants of Investment Policy of Commercial Banks

The investment policy of commercial banks is determined both by regulation and by the nature of the banking business. The commercial banks are subject to state regulation through the state bank examiner and/or they are regulated by the Federal Depositors Insurance Corporation (FDIC) and/or the Federal Reserve System. The regulation provides for conservative supervision of both state and national banks through bank examinations. The federal regulations allow commercial banks to own all bonds of investment quality in the top four of Moody's and Standard & Poor's ratings. Banks cannot buy common stocks or speculative bonds. Another regulation provides for diversification of loans and investments. To insure the safety of depositors' funds and to prevent loss through poor judgment resulting from the lack of diversification, a commercial bank usually cannot loan or invest more than 10 percent of its unimpaired capital and surplus in one asset.

The second important factor influencing the investment policy of the commercial bank is the nature of the banking business and the source of funds. First, the commercial bank needs liquidity in its non-loan portfolio to protect the bank's loan position. Deposits are payable on demand, and funds to pay depositors should not come from the liquidation of commercial loans, or instability in our commercial banking system would result. Liquidity comes usually from the investment account rather than the loan account. Funds are invested in government bonds of short maturities to provide this liquidity. Each bank must maintain legal reserves in the form of deposits with its Federal Reserve Bank, with short-term investments in government securities as a secondary reserve providing funds in time of need in addition to legal reserves.

A system of diversification of maturities is used that provides liquidity at maturity for the major portion of the security investments. Each commercial bank staggers the maturities in its investment portfolio so that a regular portion of its funds come due at different times. The government bond portion of the investments of commercial banks, for example, was divided between short-term and long-term securities on June 29, 1963. Treasury bills and certificates accounted for 19.3 percent of the government securities, Treasury notes 37.4 percent, and Treasury bonds 43.3 percent. Over half of the short-term government securities had relatively short maturities. Comparable information for 1968 was not available.

A third determinant of investment policy of commercial banks is their limited ability to sustain loss. Banks are investing depositors' money, which leads to financial conservatism, and the reserve provided by ownership capital is small. The equity account of a bank, therefore, provides little protection for the depositors' funds. Care and conservatism must be exercised in the investment of bank funds. The limited ability to assume risk leads to other influences upon investment policy. The banks require stability of principal in their investment program. For this reason, they invest in quality bonds that are highly marketable. The banks need not be concerned with purchasing-power risk since they deal in dollar claims; they do not assume the business or market risk because they do not and cannot buy equity securities. They are, however, affected by the money rate risk. If a bank is heavily invested in long-term government bonds at a low interest rate, for example, and the interest rate rises, then the price of the bonds will fall. If the bank had to sell securities at a depressed price, it could suffer a substantial loss. The bond market tends to move as sharply and change almost as rapidly as the stock market. Losses can be sustained, therefore, even in a conservative bond portfolio.

Fortunately, commercial bank portfolio management provides diversification of maturities to achieve liquidity and security of principal by waiting until the bonds mature. Many diversify among the middle maturities. In addition, if the bonds must be sold and a loss sustained, it will not be as great as might be expected. The loss can be deducted as an expense, only a portion of the investment account is involved, and the money can be invested in higher-yielding bonds that will tend to reduce the effects of the loss.

The tax position of the commercial bank represents the fourth influence upon its investment policy. Commercial banks are not given special consideration under the federal income tax laws as are life insurance companies. They are subject to the full impact of federal income taxes. Most commercial banks are taxed at the top rate of 52 percent on their net income, and so they invest in income-tax-free state and municipal bonds. This is even more important under the present circumstances, when the federal 10 percent surtax on corporate income taxes is in effect.

A 4 percent municipal bond provides the commercial bank with an 8.33 percent fully taxable equivalent yield. Table 24–5 indicates the dollar amount invested in state and municipal securities. In 1968, they represented almost one-half of total commercial bank investments. This is a significant share of the overall bank investment portfolio and offers the commercial banks an attractive outlet for their funds.

Summary of Investment Position of Commercial Banks

The actual investment and loan policy of commercial banks will vary depending upon the demand for funds, the condition of the money market, Treasury and Federal Reserve policy, and the general level of the economy. During World War II, many banks had 90 percent of their earning assets in government securities. The loan and investment balance in Table 24–5 reflects the situation in banking attitudes in 1958 and 1967. Government securities are important, as are tax-exempt state and municipal obligations. The largest earning asset of the commercial banking system is loans, reflecting the traditional concept of the commercial bank. The loan concept has changed, however. The banking system as a whole has moved away from the traditional commercial banking theory of short-term business loans, to longer-term loans and to loans to individuals. The shift in emphasis of bank lending reflects the changing pattern of function and competition within the financial system.

The investment policy of commercial banks, in summary, is dominated by state and federal regulation, the demands for marketability and liquidity imposed by depositors and the nature of the commercial banking business, the demand for business loans, the need for security of principal, the inability to assume risk because of the thin equity position, the mobility of the claims of depositors, the competitive position of the individual bank in its local and regional environment, and the conservative attitude of bank portfolio managers. The management of a bank portfolio requires great skill and a mental capacity to understand the complex and changing character of the money market.

Pension Funds

The purpose of the pension fund is to provide income after a person has retired from gainful employment. Most American businesses provide some form of retirement program for their workers to safeguard their financial future in their old age. The asset values of pension funds have increased dramatically in the past decade, owing to the increase in the number of pension plans and in the number of workers covered by private pension funds. Most of the early pension plans were voluntarily adopted by companies to solve the problem of retirement of salaried employees on an annual contract. Today pensions are bargained for along with wages and working conditions by organized labor groups. The growth of pension plans must be attributed to both union and management and to the development of Social Security. The growth of old age and survivorship benefits has stimulated the growth of private pension plans. While both systems of retirement income have grown, there have been express advantages for the government Social Security program because it gives greater mobility to the worker and does not penalize the older worker who has no vested interest in the retirement program with the company in which he seeks employment or in which he was employed late in life.

Source of Pension Fund Money

The contributions to the corporate or business pension program are either contributory or noncontributory. Under the contributory plan, the employee makes a contribution to his pension fund through a deduction from his pay check. Under the noncontributory plan the entire cost of the retirement program is paid for by the employer. Either method results in an additional cost to the employer, but in the contributory plan there is a saving that goes to the employee if he should leave the company. Either plan results in a type of contractual saving for the benefit of the employee in his retirement years.

Types of Pension Plans

Regardless of how the money is contributed, there are two types of private pensions plans, insured and noninsured. The insured plan is guaranteed by an insurance company; reserves are built up and invested under a program that will provide a certain sum of income in the future for the employee, based on the amount contributed to the program and the length of time it is in force. There were 79,830 insured pension plans of all types in force in the United States at the end of 1966 under management by insurance companies, and 7.8 million Americans were covered under the plans.[1] The value of the reserves of these plans was $29.4 billion.[2] Two subtypes of plans dominated. Deposit administration group annuity plans covered 51 percent of those covered under all insured pension plans at the end of 1966. Under this plan a single fund is set up for all employees in the pension group, and as an employee retires, money is withdrawn to buy an annuity. The other insured plan was the deferred-annuity, group-annuities type, in which a paid-up annuity benefit is purchased each year for each employee. Upon retirement, an employee receives income from the total annuity benefits he has accumulated.

The noninsured pension plan places the burden of providing the retirement funds upon the employer. Usually the employer accumulates or attempts to accumulate reserves for the payment of pension liabilities. If this is done, the funds are considered to be funded. In addition, business corporations often employ commercial banks or trust companies to manage the funds, in which case they are referred to as trusteed plans.

---

1 *Life Insurance Fact Book* (New York: Institute of Life Insurance, 1967), p. 34.
2 *Ibid.*, p. 34.

The Institute of Life Insurance estimated that 22 million persons in the United States were covered by noninsured, private pension plans at the end of 1966. Assets of these funds totaled $35 billion on that date. The total funds under the management of both insured and noninsured pension plans were $94 billion, and the plans covered 30 million people. The most important type of fund in terms of assets and people at the end of 1966 was the noninsured fund.[3]

The Investment Policy of Pension Funds

The investment policies of the insured pension plan are much the same as the general investment policy of the life insurance companies. The noninsured investment funds are much less rigid and have a great deal of flexibility in establishing investment policies. Most noninsured pension funds are not fully funded, and pension liabilities are not formally stated. Therefore, the investments of the pension fund can be in securities that do not assure stability of principal or income. Since they have no fixed commitment, they can accept more risk by purchasing common stock. The pension funds are long run and do not need a significant degree of liquidity. They do not need a great deal of stability of income because of the lack of a fixed contractual arrangement. The investment policy of the pension funds as a group may be summarized somewhat as follows: they assume a conservative amount of market risk, are interested in long-term appreciation as a hedge against inflation, do not need liquidity of income, and are exempted from federal income taxes.

The composition of corporate pension funds reflects the conservative investment growth policy suggested by the nature of the pension fund commitment to the employee. The bulk of the security investments are in corporate bonds and common stock. Preferred stocks represent the smallest security investment. Holdings in bonds of all types accounted for slightly more than half of security investments, common stock slightly more than one-third and preferred stock was somewhat less than one-tenth. Because pension funds can assume more risk than life insurance companies and commercial banks, they invest more heavily in common stocks. They also engage in private placements and sale-and-leaseback arrangements to improve their earnings potential. Some private pension funds invest their money in the shares of the company for which the fund was established. Sears is one of the best known of this type: the Sears fund has an unusually large share invested in Sears stock. But the average private pension fund is more diversified than the Sears fund.

Public pension funds have not been discussed. They are larger in dollar amount and embrace a greater number of people than the private funds. In 1960, government funds had a book value of approximately 56.0 billion dollars, compared to 50.0 billion dollars for all private

3 *Ibid.*, p. 36.

pension funds. The investment policy of public or government pension funds is very conservative. The public pension fund invests predominantly in a diversified list of government securities.

College Endowment Funds

Colleges and universities in the United States are constantly seeking new revenue sources, public and private, to provide staff, buildings, and libraries to meet the needs of an exploding student population. For private colleges, this means active alumni fund-raising campaigns to build new buildings; for state-supported institutions, endless hours of discussion and reporting to state officers and state legislators to explain the needs of higher education for more and more dollars of public funds. The state legislators in turn are often concerned with how they will be able to meet the need for ever-increasing funds imposed by an expanding population requiring more and more services. No state institution, however, is supported solely by tax dollars. Most states impose tuition charges on the student to meet the operating cost of the college or university. The private institution needing operating income to raise faculty salaries, to increase research expenditures to promote scholarly activity, and to provide scholarships for the brilliant but needy students, looks to endowment funds in part to provide funds.

The Source and Management of College Endowment Funds

Most college endowment funds come from loyal alumni and private grants. The gifts might be in the form of cash, proceeds from life insurance, securities, or real estate. The majority of funds are administered by the trustees of the college or university, when the trustees are knowledgeable about investment matters. One Midwestern university uses a three-man committee of the board of trustees to manage the investment fund of the university and has appointed a three-man advisory board from the academic and administrative staff of the university to advise the trustee group. All the advisory members have had investment experience. Some college endowment funds use professional investment counsel.

Most of the funds are unrestrictive as to how the funds will be invested. Some funds limit the investment outlets. How the money will be invested is determined by the use to which the money will be put. A fund that provides annual scholarships must provide regular income to meet the conditions of the trust endowment. A fund that is to be used for future needs of the university can be invested without regard to current income, and it can be invested in growth shares to provide the greatest future benefits. The fund manager must consider restrictive covenants imposed by the donor in establishing investment objectives. In spite of the necessity of earmarking the proceeds of an investment fund, the manager of a university fund is usually unrestricted in his management activities. This means that there are no restrictions on common-stock ownership or on owning real property, if it is a satisfactory and productive investment.

The fund manager must act wisely and with prudence. He should have long-range investment objectives. There is little need for liquidity and marketability. Income taxes are not a problem, since educational and charitable funds are exempt from federal income taxes. The fund manager must employ the virtues of good portfolio management and consider security of principal, diversification of investments, and timing. He must plan his activities to obtain the full benefits from the investment account.

The College Endowment Funds in Practice

College endowment fund management has been somewhat conservative and defensive in character. The representative list of the endowment funds of colleges and universities bears this out. Collectively the funds are balanced between common stocks, fixed-income securities, and productive real estate. The advantages of a balanced fund are apparent. First, they allow a portion of the total fund to move freely with the economy and either prosper or decline. At the same time they have a stable base of fixed-income securities that will provide a guarantee of funds for the future. The balanced fund combines the advantages of equities and fixed-income obligations.

The variation of investment policy among the colleges and universities listed in Table 24–6 is pronounced. Toronto University (Canada) is the most conservative with 81.9 percent of its funds in bonds, cash, and preferred stocks and only 16.5 percent in common stocks, as of June 30, 1967. Ohio State University had 79.8 percent of its funds in common stocks and 5.4 percent in bonds, preferred, or cash, which by contrast to Toronto is quite liberal. One aspect of college endowment funds that is different from other institutional funds that have been examined is the amount of money invested in real estate and mortgages. Several colleges own rental apartments and housing tracts, and some even own complete businesses. Usually the real property would be managed separately from the security portion of the endowment fund. The actual investment policy of colleges has been aggressive, yet balanced between income needs and capital growth. As a matter of practice, no college endowment fund should be without a substantial portion of investment-quality equity securities.

An Example of a College Fund

Most college funds allow the investment manager wide discretion over the management of the account. The manager exercises his authority within the framework of conservatism and prudent management. Although this conservatism establishes the rules for investment, it does

TABLE 24–6

INSTITUTIONS	TOTAL[a]	Percent of Total (At Market Values 6/30/67)		
		COMMON STOCKS	BONDS, CASH AND PREFERRED STOCKS	REAL ESTATE, MORTGAGES, OTHER[b]
Amherst College	$ 98.5	47.5%	50.8%	1.7%
Bowdoin College	31.9	55.3	36.9	7.8
Brown University	76.4	67.3	23.3	9.4
California Institute of Technology	129.6	58.1	30.7	11.2
California, University of	259.4	60.1	24.7	15.2
Carnegie-Mellon University	77.1	56.8	24.4	18.8
Case Institute of Technology	37.2	48.8	40.0	11.2
Chicago, University of	287.3	55.1	24.2	20.7
Cincinnati, University of	42.5	61.2	36.1	2.7
Cornell University	211.1	62.6	36.7	.7
Dalhousie University (Canada)	33.2	34.3	61.4	4.3
Dartmouth College	123.6	61.7	27.8	10.5
Duke University	89.9	66.1	33.9	—
Emory University	111.8	71.5	15.5	13.0
Harvard University	1,038.1	57.1	37.9	5.0
Johns Hopkins University	160.4	56.9	30.5	12.6
Lafayette College	35.4	68.6	22.0	9.4
Lehigh University	40.0	60.1	30.8	9.1
Mass. Institute of Technology	396.4	46.8	47.8	5.4
McGill University (Canada)	99.2	58.5	29.0	12.5
Michigan, University of	60.4	54.8	32.7	12.5
Minnesota, University of	74.3	42.4	54.6	3.0
Mount Holyoke College	36.4	65.0	24.4	10.6
Northwestern University	236.4	59.1	15.5	25.4
Oberlin College	78.7	63.5	26.8	9.7
Ohio State University	38.5	79.8	5.4	14.8
Pennsylvania, University of	183.9	53.5	32.9	13.6
Pittsburgh, University of	77.9	52.0	34.5	13.5
Pomona College	38.9	46.5	19.4	34.1
Princeton University	350.9	76.2	22.3	1.5
Purdue University	25.9	51.4	24.4	24.2
William Marsh Rice University	126.3	61.3	9.8	28.9
Rochester Institute of Technology	48.7	76.6	23.4	—
Rutgers University	31.9	63.4	36.5	.1
Smith College	58.4	65.9	34.1	—
Stanford University	195.0	39.0	49.3	11.7
Swarthmore College	47.6	77.3	20.2	2.5
Toronto University (Canada)	26.9	16.5	81.9	1.6
Tulane University	56.8	40.3	26.1	33.6
Union Theological Seminary	29.0	59.0	40.8	.2
Vanderbilt University	97.7	45.7	25.9	28.4
Vassar College	63.9	58.5	41.3	.2
Washington University (St. Louis)	124.3	72.6	22.3	5.1
Wellesley College	104.3	55.9	43.5	.6
Williams College	57.7	58.8	38.6	2.6
Yale University	504.8	64.1	29.8	6.1
All 70 Endowment Funds	$6,592.0	57.8%	31.8%	10.4%

[a] In millions of dollars.
[b] Not including college plant as such.
SOURCE: *Brevits*, published by Vance Sanders & Company, Inc., Boston, March, 1968, Vol. Y, No. 3, p. 1.

not hamper flexibility. Many college endowment funds invest in a wide selection of common stocks, preferred stocks, bonds, and real estate to meet their investment needs. Managers of college funds must consider the objectives of the fund and the limitations imposed by specific donations and then select the types of securities that will meet the needs. A case based on the experience of a small fund of a Midwestern university will illustrate some of the considerations of the management of such a fund.

The university received a list of securities from the proceeds of two estates that established the first trustee-managed endowment fund of the university. The value of the fund was approximately $300,000 and consisted of the list of securities found in Table 24–7. The securities

TABLE 24–7

University trusteed endowment fund
before management

SHARES	SECURITY	SHARES	SECURITY
50	Allied Mills, Inc.	322	Massachusetts Investors Trust
95	American Can Company		
306	American Telephone & Telegraph Company	126	N. Y. State Electric & Gas
100	Baldwin-Lima-Hamilton	255	Owens-Corning Fiberglas
50	Burroughs Corporation	105	Parke, Davis & Company
48	Cincinnati Gas & Electric Company, Pfd.	100	Parker Rust Proof Company
306	Davidson Bros., Inc.	40	Pennsylvania Railroad Company
85	Detroit Edison Company		
515	Dividend Shares, Inc.	200	Procter & Gamble Company
50	E. I. duPont de Nemours & Company	12	Quaker Oats Company, Preferred
205	First National Bank of Chicago	34	Radio Corporation of America
90	General Electric Company	50	Republic Steel Corporation
315	General Motors Corporation	105	Rochester Gas & Electric Company
15	International Harvester, Preferred	111	Sears, Roebuck & Company
318	International Harvester	8	Standard Oil Company, New Jersey
9	International Paper Company	20	Sunshine Biscuits, Inc.
5	Kentucky Utilities Company, Preferred	54	Swift & Company
		319	Texaco, Inc.
90	S. S. Kresge Company	25	Texas Gulf Sulphur
		100	U.S. Steel Corporation

DOLLARS	
2,000	American Telephone & Telegraph Co., 4 3/8% Debentures
200	Burroughs Corporation 4 1/2% Conv. Debentures
1,070	James D. Lacey Timber Company Bond
5,000	U.S. Treasury Note, 4%, due 8–15–62

represented a portfolio of equity securities of varying quality. In addition to this equity fund, another fund amounting to $500,000 was owned by the university but was not managed. It was created by donations to the university for special purposes, such as scholarships, prizes, and awards to students. The $500,000 portion of the fund was invested in fixed-income securities that provided adequate and stable revenues for the purposes for which the fund was established. The two funds together, the $500,000 of fixed-income securities and the $300,000 of equity securities, constituted the total fund, from the point of view of management. Although the trustees did not manage the fixed-income fund, it was theirs to use and was considered the conservative portion of the fund for management decisions.

The managers had complete freedom to buy and sell securities without regard to income taxes. A six-man committee, three of whom were members of the board of trustees, established income growth as their objective. They wished to build up the fund, and yet they wanted some income for scholarships and research. One donor had imposed certain restrictions on the use of the money he contributed. First, the money was to be used to aid his nieces and nephews in financing their education if they needed financial assistance. The remaining money could be used at the discretion of the board of trustees for the scholarly activities of the university. There was little need for liquidity. Since more than half the funds were invested in fixed-income securities, it was decided that the $300,000 estate should be invested in common stock. The investment committee followed, in effect, a balanced-fund approach with more than half of their funds in debt securities and the remaining in equity securities. The committee thought they were in an excellent position to assume the risks inherent in the purchase of common stocks. It was decided that equity purchases would be confined to quality equity securities of companies that were leaders in their industry and were primarily domestic corporations. Essentially a buy-and-hold philosophy was established, and diversification among industries and companies was desired. Growth companies that provided some dividends were emphasized. Debt securities and preferred stocks were to be eliminated from the portfolio along with small amounts of stock in companies that were not to be emphasized.

The committee decided in the first months of operation to sell Allied Mills, Baldwin-Lima-Hamilton, Burroughs, Davidson Bros., Inc., Dividend Shares, International Harvester Pfd., International Paper, Kentucky Utilities Pfd., Kresge, Parker Rust Proof, Pennsylvania Railroad, Quaker Oats Pfd., Sunshine Biscuits, Swift and Company, and Texas Gulf Sulphur. The American Telephone and Telegraph debentures and the convertible debentures of Burroughs were sold. The committee decided to buy 15 common stock shares of American Telephone & Telegraph, 50 of du Pont, 100 of W. R. Grace, 100 of National Cash Register, 100 of RCA, and 100 shares of Standard Oil of New Jersey. This was done in the early months of 1961. The portfolio, as it was adjusted by the committee and reflecting some additions in shares, is shown in Table 24–8 as it was September 29, 1961. Additions to the fund would be invested in common stocks that yielded close to 3.5 percent, which was the yield on the fund. If the fixed-income portion fund was included, the balance between debt and equity would be approximately 41 percent equity and 59 percent debt. Contrary to the other college and university funds, no preferred stock or real estate was owned. The trustees did not intend to buy real estate for investment, nor did they anticipate the purchase of preferred stock. The majority of changes and the policies established strengthened the fund substantially except for the sale of Texas Gulf Sulphur, which experienced a price explosion in 1964 when a major new ore discovery was made in Canada.

TABLE 24–8

University trusteed fund after management

	MARKET VALUE (9–29–61)	PERCENT OF TOTAL
Banks & Finance		
Commercial Banks		
246 First National Bank of Chicago	$ 22,386.00	7.17
Open-End Investment Companies		
326 Massachusetts Investors Trust	4,971.50	1.59
Industrial		
Autos		
315 General Motors	15,631.88	5.00
Building		
255 Owens-Corning Fiberglas Corp.	19,507.50	6.25
Chemicals		
100 E. I. du Pont de Nemours & Co.	22,237.50	
102 W. R. Grace & Co.	7,293.00	
	29,530.50	9.45
Containers		
95 American Can Company	4,239.38	1.36
Drugs		
105 Parke, Davis & Co.	3,438.75	1.10
Electronic-Electrical		
90 General Electric	6,750.00	
50 Litton Industries	6,981.25	
135 Radio Corporation of America	7,374.38	
	21,105.63	6.76
Machinery-Agricultural		
318 International Harvester Co.	16,019.25	5.13
Office Equipment		
100 National Cash Register	10,900.00	3.49

TABLE 24–8 (continued)

	MARKET VALUE (9–29–61)	PERCENT OF TOTAL
Oils-International		
108 Standard Oil Co., New Jersey	4,657.50	
640 Texaco, Inc.	32,080.00	
	36,737.50	11.76
Retail Trade-Grocery Chains		
100 Kroger Co.	2,875.00	.92
Retail Trade-Department Stores & Mail Order		
111 Sears, Roebuck	7,867.12	2.52
Steel		
70 Armco Steel Corporation	5,040.00	
50 Republic Steel Corp.	2,918.75	
100 U. S. Steel Corporation	7,987.50	
	15,946.25	5.11
Miscellaneous-Soap		
406 Procter & Gamble	38,200.00	12.23
Public Utilities		
Electric & Gas		
100 Cincinnati Gas & Electric	4,450.00	
85 Detroit Edison Co.	4,760.00	
126 New York State Electric & Gas Corp.	4,630.00	
209 Rochester Gas & Electric Co.	6,185.75	
	20,025.75	6.40
Telephone		
321 American Telephone & Telegraph	38,600.25	12.33
Total Common Stock	307,098.76	98.37
Bonds		
1 James D. Lacey Timber Co. Bond	41.80	
5 U.S. Treasury Notes, due 8–15–62	5,046.88	
Total Bonds	5,088.68	1.63
Total Portfolio	$313,069.44	100.00

Summary

The investment principles governing the management of institutional investments are the same as those applied to the management of funds for an individual. The manager must be concerned with the objectives of security of principal, income, liquidity, marketability, and tax status. In his management work he must be conservative, patient, and rational, and he must plan carefully and consider timing when he purchases securities. In addition to the general principles, policy will be governed by legal contracts and the needs of the individuals using the services of the institutional investors. Life insurance companies must be ready at any time to meet the cash value of each life insurance policy in force. The life insurance company guarantees a fixed rate of interest. They are limited in their investments by state regulation to the best-quality fixed-income investments. Some of the insurance companies do invest in equities, but this is a small part of their total investment. The amount of common stocks held will probably increase in the future. Thus, legal restrictions, ability to assume risk, tax position, and the insurance contract dictate investment policy for these companies. The bond investment account, however, is managed aggressively by most insurance companies.

Fire and casualty companies have greater flexibility in the management of their funds. Since the money invested belongs to the owners of the company, they can accept more risk. They are interested, too, in tax-exempt securities because of their high tax bracket. The insurance contract that these companies issue is surrounded with uncertainty. They attempt to improve their capital gains to meet the uncertainty of their underwriting contract.

Savings and loan companies and mutual savings banks invest primarily in real estate mortgages and invest only incidentally in fixed-income obligations if and when they do invest. Competition in the future might draw them into a wider range of investment activities.

Commercial banks are interested in liquidity and are limited by law to investment in bonds. They make longer-term loans but are governed by liquidity and security of principal in making investments.

Pension funds invest in a wide range of securities and approach closely the investment function of the individual investor. This is also true of the college endowment fund. Both pension funds and college funds have freedom of choice to invest in a wide range of securities. College funds have the widest discretion, and many own some productive real estate as an investment. Both the endowment fund and pension fund tend to invest in quality securities.

The institutional investors vary in the results that they have achieved. However, they stress quality, planning, and conservatism in their approach and have a long-range outlook in their orientation to the securities market.

Review Questions

1. Distinguish between institutional investors and individual investors. In what way do their investment objectives differ?
2. (a) What are the business and sources of funds of a life insurance company?
   (b) What type of securities do life insurance companies purchase?
   (c) What governs their investment policy?
   (d) What risks can the life insurance company assume? Explain.
3. (a) What is the nature of the business of fire and casualty companies?
   (b) What types of securities do they purchase?
   (c) What risks can they assume and why?
   (d) How do they differ from the life insurance company?

4. (a) What is the nature of business of the savings and loan company?
   (b) What is the basic investment policy of the savings and loan companies, and how do they meet the investment risk?
   (c) Are there any indications that this investment policy will change?
5. Explain the investment function as it operates in the commercial bank.
6. (a) Define the investment objectives of the pension funds.
   (b) What securities do they purchase?
   (c) Have they been successful? Comment.
7. (a) Explain the investment function of a college endowment fund and how it operates.
   (b) What are the needs of a college fund?
   (c) What securities do they purchase to meet those needs?
   (d) Who manages the typical college endowment fund?

Problems

1. Bring the university investment fund in Table 24–8 up to date.
   (a) What is the value of each security?
   (b) What is the percentage gain or loss on each stock?
   (c) What is the total percentage gain or loss on the fund? What does this amount to on an annual compounded income basis?
   (d) What is the current income and yield?
   (e) What is the total percentage yield from the fund? Include capital gains and current income.
   (f) Should we recommend that the university sell any of its securities?
   (g) If a sale is recommended, what securities should be purchased in their place and why?

Sources of Investment Information

Analyses previously completed
Annual reports
Barron's
Business Week
Clark Dodge Investment Survey
Commercial and Financial Chronicle
Forbes
Fortune
Moody's manuals
Newsweek
Standard & Poor's *Investment Surveys*
Standard & Poor's *Stock Guide*
Standard & Poor's *The Outlook*
The Value Line Investment Survey
Time
Wall Street Journal

Selected Readings

Amos, William W., "New Holding Company Moves by Insurance Companies," *Financial Analysts Journal* (March-April, 1966), p. 133.

Bailey, E. Norman, "Real Estate Investment Trusts: An Appraisal," *Financial Analysts Journal* (May-June, 1966), p. 107.

Bower, R. S., and J. P. Williamson, "Measuring Pension Fund Performance: Another Comment," *Financial Analysts Journal* (May-June, 1966), p. 143.

Dietz, Peter O., "Pension Fund Investment Performance—What Method to Use When," *Financial Analysts Journal* (January-February, 1966), p. 83.

————, "Pension Funds Performance," *Financial Analysts Journal* (March-April, 1968), p. 133.

Fuss, Daniel J., "Investing for Small Life Insurance Companies," *Financial Analysts Journal* (March-April, 1966), p. 115.

Hicks, William C. S., "The Fire and Casualty Insurance Industry," *Financial Analysts Journal* (March-April, 1966), p. 120.

Hofflander, Alfred E., Jr., "Multiple Line Insurance Companies," *Financial Analysts Journal* (November-December, 1967), p. 151.

Hoffman, Leroy R., Jr., "Investment Considerations for Non-Life Insurance Companies," *Financial Analysts Journal* (March-April, 1966), p. 129.

Lorie, James H., "NABAC Study on Pension Funds," *Financial Analysts Journal* (March-April, 1968), p. 139.

Mennis, Edmund A., "Growing Pension Funds," *Financial Analysts Journal* (March-April, 1968), p. 122.

————, "Trends in Institutional Investing," *Financial Analysts Journal* (July-August, 1968), p. 133.

Miles, Joseph E., "Insurance Portfolio Strategies," *Financial Analysts Journal* (September-October, 1967), p. 147.

Polakoff, Murray E., "Public Pension Funds," *Financial Analysts Journal* (May-June, 1966), p. 75.

Ritter, Lucy E., "Common Stocks for Life Insurance Portfolios," *Financial Analysts Journal* (January-February, 1966), p. 109.

INDEX